Hearth
&
Home

NORMAN J. G. POUNDS

Hearth
& A HISTORY OF MATERIAL CULTURE
Home

INDIANA

UNIVERSITY *Bloomington and Indianapolis*

PRESS

First Midland Book Edition 1993

Manufactured in the United States of America

Library of Congress Cataloging-in-Publication Data
Pounds, Norman John Greville.
Hearth and home.

Bibliography: p.
Includes index.
1. Material culture—Europe.   2. Europe—Social life
and customs.   I. Title.
GT76.P67   1989   306'.094   87-46367
ISBN 0-253-32712-1
ISBN 0-253-20839-4 (pbk.)

2 3 4 5 6 99 98 97 96 95 94 93

To
HENRY MAURICE PORTER
in affection
and gratitude

Contents

PREFACE

Europe is but an excrescence on the western margin of Asia. It is a small landmass and was until late in human history largely uninhabitable. Its northern regions lay deep under a continental ice sheet, its more southerly endured intermittently the rigors of a subarctic climate. Yet it was Europe that during recent centuries achieved a dominant role in the world, the source of technical innovation and political example.

The human species, like those discoveries on which its cultural achievements have been based, had its origins outside Europe. *Homo sapiens* may have emerged in East Africa. Animals were first domesticated, seeds were sown, and crops harvested in the Middle East. The earliest cities were in the valleys of the Tigris-Euphrates, of the Indus and Ganges and on the plains of China.

When the earliest steps in human progress were made in Africa and Asia, Europe offered only an inhospitable environment. The Ice Age had not yet ended in northern Europe when the first crops were being sown in the Middle East. If there were to be innovations in technology and the art of living they were most unlikely to have been made within Europe. They had to originate where the climate was more propitious and the population denser, and from here they were diffused through Europe. There was throughout most of human history a cultural gradient that dropped from the Middle East and the Balkans toward central, western, and northern Europe. The diffusion of successive innovations along this route is one of the themes of this book.

Another theme is the varied resource pattern of the continent, which not only provided a fertile ground for the development of imported technologies and cultures but also encouraged their further interaction and growth. The ancient cultures of the Middle East and beyond reached relatively early a plateau above which there was little further development before modern times. Europe—or the greater part of it—has not ceased to advance materially. This advance became greatest in western Europe until a point was reached at which the cultural gradient sloped downward from west to east, and the flow of technical innovation was reversed.

A third theme is that advance in material culture is exponential. This condition is inevitable as developments in one field interact with those in another. The greater the number of separate innovations or discoveries, the greater is the possible number of linkages between them. This growing complexity of material culture in the nineteenth century makes its study on a continent-wide basis quite impossible, and for this reason a cutoff date has been chosen about the middle of the century.

This book is concerned with material culture. This is not to deny the significance of nonmaterial aspects of culture. Folk art and religious cults are as much a part of popular culture as village settlements and styles of house building. Indeed, the two are intimately linked. The relationship of material with nonmaterial culture is stressed in chapter one, but thereafter the emphasis is on the material aspects of daily life.

The writer is indebted to many friends in both Europe and America for the interest they have aroused and the stimulus they have provided. He would mention in particular the late Carl Sauer of California and Stith Thompson of Indiana, and Professor Estyn E. Evans of Belfast, as well as friends and colleagues at Indiana University. His travels in Eastern Europe, where folk culture comes closer to the surface of modern life than in the West, have served to deepen his interest. One of the most illuminating insights into the past was a visit to the Village Museum at Bucharest. But for errors in fact, observation, and judgment he is alone responsible.

PART ONE

Origins and

Dispersals

Chapter 1

PROLEGOMENON

And yit is wynter for hem worse, for wete-shodde thei gange,
A-fyrst sore and afyngred . . .
Now lorde, sende hem somer, and some manere joye
Piers Plowman, B Text, XIV, lines 161–62

*L*ife is compounded of physical needs and intellectual aspirations and fears. The former are easy to catalog and evaluate. They are food, shelter, and whatever bodily protection the climate renders necessary. These basic necessities have changed little in the course of human history, and bodily needs in the form of calories and proteins were much the same in Paleolithic times as they are today. Sometimes the requirements have been exceeded, inducing a sense of well-being; at other times the provision of fundamental necessities has fallen short, with danger to health and even to life. This book is, in the main, a history of the ways in which these basic needs have been satisfied.

But it is impossible to draw any clear line of separation between the satisfaction of the needs of the body and the development of intellectual, even of spiritual, concepts. The two are intertwined at every point, and in "primitive" thought they were one. The concept of popular culture embraces both, and if they are separated in studies of cultural history and folklife, it is usually only for the convenience of exposition.

We are concerned here primarily with preindustrial society, which inhabited most of Europe until the end of the eighteenth century and was to be found in some areas as late as the early twentieth. It was, as Robert Muchembled has so eloquently shown, a society dominated by insecurity and fear.[1] It was haunted by the specter of famine and disease, the latter striding along in the footsteps of the former. Famine arose from crop failure, and this, in the main, from the uncertainties of the weather. It took many forms; no two famines conformed to the same pattern. Differing crops were affected in different places. Sometimes murrain struck the animals, and the plowing oxen died; sometimes it was plague that reduced the human population. Whatever the cause, it lay beyond the mental comprehension of simple people. They lived in ignorance and dread of what blows a savage nature could deliver next. The poet of Piers the Plowman wrote in the late fourteenth century: "Ere five years be fulfilled such famine shall arise / Through floods and foul weather fruits shall fail."[2] He expected a crisis every few years. If it came more frequently, mortality and suffering increased. If longer periods intervened between successive crises, people had more time to recoup their losses and accumulate greater reserves against the next one.

One thinks of hunger and famine as recurring hardships before the industrial age. It is likely, however, that cold was no less important. Throughout much of Europe winters were severe. There is little point in citing statistics. They are averages, usually for a term of many years. They disguise the day-to-day fluctuations and ignore the fact that an average temperature of thirty degrees Fahrenheit in Saxony is consistent with many days when it might dip to zero and, at nighttime, a great deal lower. Against such cold people had little protection. Clothing for most was inadequate, and stout footwear entirely lacking. What proportion of deaths in winter was from hypothermia we have absolutely no means of knowing. There were no symptoms by which it could be readily recognized by contemporary people.

In addition to natural hazards there were the more artificial dangers from war and civil disturbance, from assault, robbery, and death on the highway and in the home. It was a violent age. Rarely did governments attempt to restrain its violence and even less frequently did they succeed. What security could the individual find? How could he or she gain protection from the four horsemen of St. John's apocalyptic vision: war, famine, disease, and death? They rode together, one or the other in the van, but always the horseman of death following behind and gathering where the others had sown. The only protection that most people ever knew was that afforded by their own kinship group and the community of their village or hamlet. The family, whether the nuclear family of parents and children or the extended family that included grandparents and, often enough, aunts, uncles, and cousins, was the foremost defense that society could offer against the hazards of life. The family was a group for the purposes of producing and preparing food, of creating a home, and of mutual protection. It had few romantic associations; violence was as frequent within the family as in the society beyond its limits. But it was a necessity, not only for procreation but also for living. There was a horror of living by oneself. The individual who lived alone was virtually an outcast, whom it was easy to blame for all the misfortunes of the community. Those who cast spells and were said to have made the animals sterile and stunted the crops were most often old people living alone with no one to witness their actions. One belonged to the community in virtue of being a member of a family or kinship group.

The community was only a kinship group writ large. It was made up of many family or extended family groups, each living in its own home and cultivating its own pieces of land. But overall the community could at most consist of a hundred or two people. In so small a group intermarriage was such that everyone was a cousin, however far removed, to everyone else. Such complex interrelationships, revealed, for example, in Le Roy Ladurie's intimate study of the Pyrenean village of Montaillou,[3] made little contribution to harmony within the community. Indeed, the effect was the opposite. Close relation-ships intensified the internal jealousies and feuds. There were always quarrels about dowries and inheritance, about the division and reapportionment of land, about plowing obligations and rights to common of grazing or woodland. Yet there had to be a limit to internal disputes and quarrels, a limit beyond which such divisions threatened what little security the community possessed. In the last resort its members *had* to cooperate in plowing their fields, in sowing and harvesting, in allocating among themselves their meadow, pasture, and wood. They *had* to assist one another in roof raising and maintaining the humble tracks that served as roads, and they *had* to assist and support one another in the observance of their customs, in resisting insofar as they were able the demands of their lord and their church, and in protecting themselves against their common enemies.

Each community viewed its neighboring community with ill-disguised suspicion. It did business with them, its members intermarried with them, but they remained at best "half foreign," to be watched with care and never taken to their hearts. Beyond the range of neighboring communities, a day's journey or more away, all was foreign; there could only be suspicion, even hostility, toward such "foreigners." One could not trust them, nor was there any need to do so. They lived beyond the horizon, out of sight and out of mind.

Preindustrial Europe was made up of such cells, hundreds of thousands of them. They existed in a state of near isolation, broken only by their relations with their territorial lord and with the church, and of near self-sufficiency. In time of crop failure and subsistence crisis, they had nowhere to turn for help. If their village was destroyed in war, those who survived wandered homeless out into a world that had no place for them. Each cell, by and large, ran its own affairs. It had a court that in a rough way settled local disputes. It had a reeve, *praepositus,* or headman who tried to hold the community together. By and large, it was a self-regulating society, neither needing nor wanting interference or supervision from without.

Such was the "world view" of the villager of preindustrial Europe. Townspeople, or at least some of them—for urban society was more structured than rural—had a broader vision, and their cultural and economic linkages extended over a much wider area. But urban society is something to which we shall return later. The emphasis here must be on rural society because, until new forms of social growth brought about by industrialization became apparent, up to 80 percent of the population lived in the countryside and worked on the land.

The Spirit World

The concept of an orderly world in which immutable laws governed the events of nature was entirely foreign to all except a very small minority of intellectuals in preindustrial Europe. Instead, nature was seen to be capricious and wanton, to be placated rather than understood. The total unreliability of the weather, the unpredictability of the harvest, the erratic progress of epidemic disease, and the random phenomena of mortality itself all confirmed such a view of the world. It was for the men of the Enlightenment to begin the task of reducing these haphazard events to a kind of order and to express them in terms of scientific laws and statistical probabilities. Earlier men and women could only people their world with spirits, unseen, unknown, and often enough unnamed. There were spirits in the forests and fields; they governed the weather and the ripening of the crops.

They cast their malign influence over the farm animals, bringing about abortion and disease. They brought death to the young and accident and illness to adults. The variety of the spells that they cast defied enumeration. Life was enveloped in a spirit world.

How far back in human history can we trace such a view of nature? The earliest peoples were illiterate, and their thought processes must always remain unknown, but many of their artifacts, at least from the Upper Paleolithic, can be regarded only as traces of sympathetic magic. Even the cave paintings of the Dordogne and of Spain, depicting the hunt for deer and other animals, can be understood as an enactment of the events of hunting, intended to insure success. Burial rites imply the existence of a spirit world to which the dead had recently been assimilated. As one moves into historical times, one finds that the existence of spirits is implicit in much of the folklore and legend. Only a fraction of the vast body of story has survived, much of it smoothed and softened, and the creatures of the spirit world translated into people and animals. Much of it was subsumed under the broad mantle of Christianity. Spirits became saints, and propitiatory rites were translated into the rituals of their name days. Instead of appeasing malevolent spirits, one enlisted the aid of good spirits, the saints. From this practice it was but a short step to the veneration of objects that could be regarded as part of them, and, if these did not readily come to hand, then a pilgrimage might be undertaken to places that had been hallowed by their presence.[4]

A medieval bishop in southwest England instructed his priests to record such stories as were current in their parishes—for the spirit world was very local, and different spirits inhabited neighboring parishes. Unhappily, such records as may have been compiled from the bishop's venture into the sphere of active folklore have long been lost. This is a pity, since the parish priest was close to the people; he was one of them and shared in their fears and anxieties. Indeed, the church saw it as one of its tasks "to break down the long de facto traditions of local loyalties and customs, and ensure that the local priest would see himself as an integral part of a larger church." This ambition was not achieved generally before the sixteenth century. No distinction was made between the sacred and the profane, and the priest's own ministrations within the church were a part of the universal magic whose purpose it was to appease or placate the spirits and enlist their support on behalf of their flock. Popular culture expressed itself in a "vision of the world which was superficially Christian but fundamentally animist."[5]

In this struggle against the evil or malign forces that surrounded them, people resorted to the dance, to celebratory feasts, to acting out certain rituals. These practices served a twofold purpose. On the one hand, by the strange logic of "primitive" peoples, these rites and ceremonies were held to influence the course of nature. Midsummer and midwinter had their appropriate rites, which differed from one place to another, but all had the same intent, to insure that the cycle of nature continued unchanged. Ceremonies accompanied the planting of the seed and the harvesting of the crop. To some extent these rites survive, though in few parts of Europe are they observed with the intensity and conviction that would have marked their enactment in the Middle Ages.

The author remembers, in the summer of 1939, riding his bicycle to a hilltop in West Cornwall, where, on the eve of the feast of St. John, a beacon fire was to be lighted at midnight. This was also the longest day of the year, and the propitiatory fire was intended at once to celebrate the feast of the saint, to measure the progress of the seasons, and, in a peculiar way, to insure that the cycle would be renewed. That summer the beacon was lighted and extinguished by the rain. The following summer it was the authorities, in the shape of an air-raid warden, who forbade the exercise for fear that it would instead beckon German bombers to the site.

The "fun and games" of earlier peoples had another and no less significant purpose. It was essential that the unity of the community be preserved, despite all the internal forces of greed, jealousy, and suspicion that would have torn it apart. To join in feasting, dancing, and ritual at set times of the year drew the members of the community together. There was social pressure to participate, for it was "peasant culture in action."[6] Folk customs survive in their present anemic condition because they are deeply rooted in the human consciousness. To most people in the urban and educated West, such practices as the spring rituals performed on the first of May may be a meaningless survival. But to the Communist world, which, after all, embraces a large part of peasant Europe, this day remains one of celebration. Communism has absorbed the rite of spring into its cult, just as Christianity did the more varied practices of the pagan world of animism a thousand or more years earlier. These occasions of feasting and games were an intense, crowded time when people could forget their misfortunes and fears and the malign forces that stalked the world, if only for the moment.[7]

In the last few pages reference has been made mainly to the Middle Ages. Records of medieval folklore and custom are few, and what has survived into modern times is only an expurgated version of what was known in medieval and earlier times. This is because, from the sixteenth century onward, church and state in unholy alliance tried to destroy the medieval world view, and in this they by and large succeeded. A feudally structured society, with its emphasis on the localized cells of which society was built, gave way to centralized government. The state played an increasingly dominant role. A French king in the seventeenth century could say *l'état, c'est moi,* "I am the state." Local affairs were dominated increasingly by central authority. The same trend was apparent within the church. The "protestant" revolt shook the medieval church to its foundations, and out of the conflict, as by a kind of dialectic, there emerged the post-Tridentine establishment, more centralized, more streamlined in its organization, more unified doctrinally, and more determined than ever it had been to root out those beliefs and practices that it could not reconcile with its newly found spiritual purity. The Counter-Reformation may have been sparked by the earlier Protestant Reformation, but something of the kind would have happened anyway. This centralizing, authoritarian trend was part of Europe's reaction to a crumbling feudalism. It was not, in religious terms, restricted to the church of Rome. Martin Luther, who started with "a plea for individual liberty and freedom of conscience," ended as an absolutist in matters of state as well as of church.[8] And Calvin, together with his successors in Scotland and New England, carried his authoritarian ideas of religious conformity almost as far as the Council of Trent and the Inquisition had managed to do.

This assertion of authority by both state and church penetrated right down to the local cells—manor, parish, community—of which society was built. Henceforward, they seemed to say, the security of all was insured by their own ministrations. The law was upheld by the one, and the spirits kept at bay by the other. Together, whether Catholic or Protestant, they imposed a uniformity of belief and practice on their subjects, controlling both their bodies and their minds. Swinburne wrote, "Thou has conquered, O pale Galilean; the world has grown grey from thy breath."[9] He was wrong, but only in ascribing this feat to the later years of the Roman Empire. It did not happen with the triumph of Christianity. It was achieved by Luther, Calvin, and the Council of Trent in the sixteenth and seventeenth centuries. This was when authority tried, with a not inconsiderable measure of success, to impose on society its own gray world of repression and dogma.

No one could say that the medieval world was not violent, brutal, and cruel, but with the triumph of authoritarianism, cruelty became institutionalized. There were, of course, pogroms and Crusades during the Middle Ages—against the Jews, the Cathari, the infidels—but at the humble level of the local community there was a degree of toleration. This ended with Reformation and Counter-Reformation.[10] In varying ways those rites associated with the passage of the seasons were discouraged or abolished, dissent was punished, and everything possible was done to root out the animism and magic that had endured and had been practiced from the earliest times until the sixteenth century. This campaign against all those primitive and traditional rituals which could not be related directly to the accepted doctrines of the church culminated in the late sixteenth and seventeenth centuries in a virulent and brutal attack on sorcery in general and witchcraft in particular. Sorcery of some kind had been practiced throughout the Middle Ages. Water taken from the baptismal fonts was used for superstitious purposes. Little attempt seems to have been made to restrain it, beyond denying access to the consecrated water by fastening a lid to the font. No doubt the priest himself sometimes participated, thus demonstrating that he was at one with his flock. This state of affairs changed with the Reformation. Both Catholic and Protestant strove to eliminate *popular* magic. The easiest victim was the witch, who seemed to symbolize all the occult forces that the churches were striving to suppress. She was usually elderly; she commonly lived alone; she was probably an awkward neighbor with a shrill and malicious tongue. She had few friends, and against irrational accusations there could be no rational defense. And so witches perished in the sixteenth, seventeenth, and early eighteenth centuries in most countries of Europe, both Catholic and Protestant, as well as in New England.[11]

The campaign against witchcraft ended in the eighteenth century, not because the churches had changed their stance on the matter, but because a new and vastly more powerful weapon began to be used against surviving elements of popular culture, namely, reason. The unfettered use of human reason was the new religion. Of course, it could not take over or supplant the established religious orthodoxies, but here and there it was able to spread doubt and almost everywhere to soften the rigors with which the fundamentalists imposed their views and awarded their penalties. The result might have been a revival of popular culture. In the long run there was such a movement, but it came too late, and smacked too much of antiquarianism to be taken very seriously. Among its manifestations were the creation of secret societies; a belief in druids; the revival of folk customs, such as the rites of spring, of midsummer, and of harvest; and the refinement of folk dances until they became an art form totally divorced from their popular roots.

Popular culture of the pre-Tridentine period, with its infinite shades of local color, was in the end replaced by a mass culture, broadly uniform over large areas. The role of the church tended to diminish; that of the state, to increase. The chief vehicle of mass culture that began to permeate rural society—it had for generations been present in urban—was the printed word.[12] Society did not suddenly become literate; there had long been a small minority that could read a simple text. Indeed the churches had encouraged literacy by making available catechisms, liturgical books, and even the Bible printed in the vernacular tongue. In the later years of the seventeenth century, there was an explosion in printing and publishing. The evidence of wills and deeds shows that an increasing proportion of the population in western and central Europe were able to sign their names and, presumably, to read. It is probable that books on theology predominated, but even these undermined the role of the priest and presbyter by making their ministrations less necessary. Of course, there were various forms of censorship, including the *Index librorum prohibitorum* of the Roman Catholic church. It is significant that the latter achieved approximately its modern form in the mid-eighteenth century, when the threat from the "Enlightenment" was greatest. But the presses also turned out little books on the useful arts, narratives of travel, broadsheets and chapbooks on every conceivable topic. Most of these never reached the populace, for whom, in any case, they were not intended, but their contents percolated slowly downward from the literate classes—the gentry, bourgeoisie and clergy—toward the masses.

At the same time travel became a normal activity, at least in western, central, and much of southern Europe. There was no conspicuous improvement in the quality of the roads, but the apparatus of travel—coaches in their infinite variety, changes of horses, inns—made movement about Europe faster, less uncomfortable, and, above all, safer. Of course, there were areas, some of them of vast extent, that were untouched by roads and unvisited by travelers. But wherever the traveling public went, new ideas were disseminated and a slow erosion of local custom and practice began. In short, a mass culture was very slowly diffused, in which there was little room either for the animism and localisms of earlier popular culture or for the hierarchical cultures of institutional religion.

These changes, from a popular culture whose roots were local and often pre-Christian, to a hierarchically organized culture whose aim was to impose conformity and uniformity, and, lastly, to a mass culture, were not abrupt or easily measured. Nor did they occur uniformly. They are best conceived as waves that spread from western Europe toward the north and the east, overflowing the more populous, urbanized and developed areas, but avoiding those more sparsely populated. In a telling passage, Thomas Hardy, after commenting on the springtime rites practiced by the villagers in the Vale of Blackmore, commented that "ancient superstitions linger longest on the clay." To him the clay lands, anciently forested and opened up only in relatively recent times, represented resistant areas, where popular culture was yielding only slowly to mass culture. The date would probably have been in the 1840s, so that the scene that Hardy witnessed would have been a genuine survival, and not a revival. But when Hardy's sophisticated travelers joined in the ritual celebrations, they can have had no concept of the significance of the latter. Theirs was only a patronizing interest in something "primitive," like that of many folklorists of the late nineteenth and early twentieth centuries. Chaunu has emphasized that the attitudes of mind that peopled the world with spirits and believed that by some "magic" they could be controlled lingered longer on the margins of the agricultural world, in the mountains and forests.[13] Superstition was to be found more among the shepherds than the agriculturalists, who had in some measure succumbed to spiritual authoritarianism. The modern pogroms against witches began in the mountains of Switzerland, Savoy, and the Pyrenees. Admittedly they spread to much of Germany and even to England, for everywhere there was a human substratum susceptible to such beliefs and vengeful enough to implement them in attacks on witches.

The "witch craze" ended late in the eighteenth century, and the last witch-burning in Europe was in Poland in 1793. The reason cannot be said to lie altogether with the spread of the ideas of the Enlightenment, though there was no lack of *éclairés* who denounced the practice with all the vehemence and logic they could muster. After all, Voltaire and Diderot were not read in the villages. It lay rather with the gradual replacement of popular culture by a mass culture. Popular culture had not itself brought about the persecution of witches, but it created a mental attitude that regarded spirits and sorcerers as normal denizens of the earth, who had to be guarded against. Of course, medieval people believed in witches as they did in the devil and in spirits of all kinds. But they did little about them. It was only when these primitive instincts were marshaled by the authority of church and state that the common people condoned the excesses that came to be practiced. The spread of mass culture sapped the strength of "primitive" belief in the spirit world, and the pogroms against witches slowly disappeared from the European scene.

Spain, it is sometimes said, displayed during these years a toleration that was absent from central Europe. Such a judgment is hard to support in a country where the Inquisition was more active than anywhere else. It appears that witches were not pursued as vigorously here as elsewhere, only because there were bigger fish to catch—Jews, Moors, and heretics. Why bother with a poor and crazed old woman when there were Jews, and sometimes rich ones, to be caught? This raises an important issue in the thought and culture of Europe: To what extent did the persecution of witches give way to pogroms against the Jews? This transition could, in the preindustrial age, happen only in eastern Europe and Russia, because the diaspora of modern times had not yet brought about the dispersal of Jews in significant numbers. In fact, the last witch-burnings and the first anti-Jewish pogroms came very close to one another in time.

This brief discussion of popular culture raises an important question: where, in a book that is concerned with material culture, to draw the line between it and the more intellectual or spiritual aspects of culture. Every aspect of material life had its accompanying rituals, its "magic" directed to securing a happy outcome. No doubt many of these rituals and observances had become stereotyped long before the end of the preindustrial age. They had been reduced merely to occasions for communal jollification. Others had been suppressed in the course of the "spiritual conquest of the countryside." Yet others, like May Day, harvest festivals, and Christmas, were absorbed into an all-pervasive mass culture.[14]

Nevertheless, a line must be drawn and, in the present context, it is taken to lie where ritual and custom are no longer seen to be an *essential* part of the process of cultivating the fields and building and maintaining a home. When the rites of spring, midsummer, and midwinter are observed in their own right and are no longer conceived as an integral part of a process of production, then they can without great loss be excluded from a study of material culture.

The Content of Material Culture

What then is there to study? At the beginning of this chapter *material* culture was loosely defined as the modes by which elementary human needs for food, shelter, and clothing have been satisfied. This definition may serve for the material culture of the simplest, most "primitive" peoples, but human needs tend to become more varied and more complex. That is the nature of progress. What was a rare luxury by way of food, housing, or household goods in one age became a necessity in the next. The simple categories of needs cease to be adequate. The satisfaction of one made it easier to supply other wants. Agriculture provided the materials for constructing houses and weaving cloth. The development of the metal crafts contributed to the success of agriculture as well as to the building and furnishing of homes. And with the growth of interlinked technologies, the ability of man increased both to satisfy his elementary needs and to reach beyond them. Every people in every age had its necessities and its luxuries. Always there were new satisfactions to be obtained, and in the last half century these have increased exponentially, and with them the techniques by which they can be achieved.

The theme of this book, briefly expressed, is that the initial stages in material progress originated outside Europe, most of them in the broad region of the Middle East. They were diffused very slowly westward and northwestward. They then assumed ever more sophisticated forms, which culminated in the eighteenth century in the application of mechanical power to production processes. The level of technological development achieved in Europe at that time so far transcended what was found in any other part of the world that Europe became an exporter of technology and culture, as it had once been the recipient.

Core and Periphery

A secondary theme is that only by technological innovation can an ever-broadening range of human needs and aspirations be satisfied. Innovation, as a general rule, is a localized phenomenon. One cannot exclude the possibility of parallel invention—history shows too many examples for this to be possible—but fundamental innovations can be attributed to specific regions, if not actually to particular places, from which they were diffused (fig. 1.1). The nature of innovation and diffusion is discussed in the next chapter. It is sufficient to note here that resulting progress had to be uneven across the face of Europe. There were, of necessity, precocious regions, and, on the other hand, there were regions where some innovations came slowly and late and others not at all. When the classical civilizations were flourishing in the Mediterranean basin, there were large areas of northern Europe that had not developed beyond the level of the Stone Age. Europe has always had its underdeveloped areas, where techniques were relatively backward and levels of welfare low. Now they are singled out by an egalitarian Economic Community and their development is stimulated by injections of capital. In the past either they were ignored or their weaknesses were exploited.

The speed of development has varied from one place to another. A series of "hearths" or "core areas" has emerged, flourished, and, in many instances, decayed. Southern Italy, once in the forefront of development, has now become the recipient of "foreign" aid. Northwest Europe, once on the remote periphery of the Roman Empire, had developed by the nineteenth century the greatest productivity and highest standards of living in Europe and in the world. Factors in such growth and decay are difficult to isolate, but fundamentally they concern physical endowment and the human use made of it. And the latter in turn hinges on receptivity to innovation and the cumulative results of millions of human decisions.

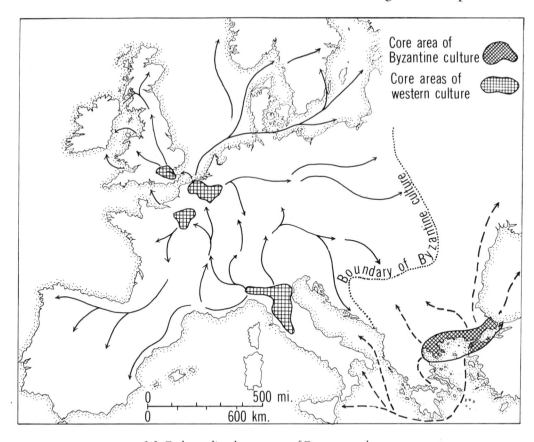

1.1. Early medieval core areas of European culture

The core areas where innovation was most likely to be adopted and material progress was most rapid and far-reaching were, without exception, lowland areas, with a good soil and relatively easy accessibility. Not all such areas, by any means, became the foci of cultural development, nor did such an area that emerged in prehistoric times necessarily retain its preeminence. The light, rich soils of loessial origin that occurred in south Germany and the Danubian basin were relatively densely settled in the Neolithic and became the foci of a very slow progress in material terms. With the rise of metal-using cultures, new core areas emerged; in the Balkans, Italy, and Spain. In its turn, classical civilization achieved a higher material culture than had previously been known in Europe. But its hearth was essentially the Mediterranean basin, beyond which, in Gaul, Britain, and the Balkans, it was to be found only in well-placed centers surrounded by backcountry, on which its cultural influence was at best limited.

During the Middle Ages, Italy—particularly the area from Rome northward—perpetuated the cultural and material standards of the classical world. Urban life, the crafts, rural settlement, and the practice of agriculture harked back in varying degrees to the practices of the Roman Empire. Elsewhere the legacy of Rome wore very thin, and in some areas, the interior of the Balkan peninsula for example, the slate was wiped almost clean. When, in the seventh century, the Slavs spread across this region, they can have encountered little that would have told them that the Romans had once been masters here. More survived in the west from the material world of the Romans. There was a degree of continuity in urban life and in rural settlements. Fields continued to be cultivated and crafts to be practiced.

When, some five hundred years after the eclipse of the Roman Empire in the west, progress in material culture again became apparent, it was in areas that had been marginal to the Roman world: the southern Low Countries, the Paris basin, and the middle Rhineland, or even beyond the former limits of the empire, in Westphalia, Saxony, Bohemia, and central Poland. The core area that embraced northern Italy thus came to be paralleled by another that spanned northern France, the southern Low Countries, and the lower Rhineland. It is not easy to define the advantages that this region possessed. It had been peripheral to the Roman Empire, its population density had been low, and there had been little urban development. From the eleventh century this region, which must be taken to include southeastern England, with which it was in frequent and regular contact, developed rapidly. It became a hearth from which urbanization, crafts, and trade spread eastward and southeastward across Europe.

Figure 1.1 shows in simplified fashion this core area of northwest Europe and, highly generalized, the spread of innovation and of higher material standards in later medieval and modern times. There has been, from the early Middle Ages to the nineteenth and even the present century, a cultural gradient, sometimes steep, sometimes gentle, but always dropping as one traverses Europe from its northwestern hearth toward the north, east, and southeast. In almost all material respects, northwest Europe was more advanced than central, just as central was ahead of eastern and southeastern. In the following chapters there will be frequent allusion to this eastward diffusion of the material advantages of western progress. At the beginning of the modern period, northwest Europe drew ahead of Italy in the measurable aspects of culture: population and urban growth, manufacturing production, and agricultural output. Modern manufacturing industry owed everything to developments that took place in northwest Europe. It was entirely fortuitous that this region was found to embrace the largest of Europe's resources in solid fuel. The coalfields merely reinforced and extended an advantage that this region already possessed.

The diffusion of material culture was not only spatial. It was also social. It was always a political and social elite that was the best-fed, best-clothed, and best-housed segment of society. It was able to adopt innovations before other people could do so, and it set standards for the imitation of others. Whatever aspect of material welfare one chooses, from glazed windows to the use of soap and wearing of underclothes, we find that progress was first significant among the upper classes, and that it spread slowly downward to the lower social orders. This twofold direction of diffusion, both spatially eastward and socially downward, has operated for almost fifteen centuries. This movement is represented graphically in figures 1.2 and 1.3. But diffusion of cultural traits is never uniformly outward, on a broad front that sweeps aside or overwhelms whatever obstacles and resistance lie in its path. Instead, it infiltrates around them, as if leaving them to be subdued or ingested at a later date. This pattern occurred in Europe. There were areas, like Thomas Hardy's Vale of Blackmore, that proved resistant to change and were bypassed. Europe is dotted with such areas, most of them mountainous with little

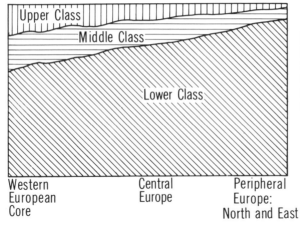

1.2. The cultural gradient between western and eastern Europe, showing schematically the diminishing proportion of the population with middle- and upper-class material culture.

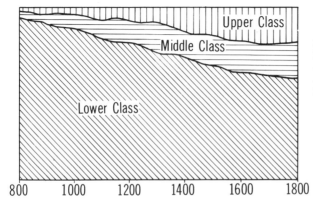

1.3. The cultural gradient in medieval and early modern Europe, showing schematically the increasing proportion of the population with middle- and upper-class material culture.

by way of resources to attract the pioneer, where ancient superstitions and customs, modes of building and managing the soil that have been abandoned in more progressive areas, and old forms of dialect and patterns of thought have lingered into modern times.

But if we project our viewpoint far enough into prehistory, we find no core areas, no cultural hearths. All Europe was backward and undeveloped. Across much of the continent north of the Alps lay tundra, slowly yielding to the advancing wave of coniferous forest. Yet farther to the north were the remains of the ice sheet that had once covered much of the continent. Emerging cultures were to be found in the Middle East and in South and Southeast Asia. It is here that one looks for the roots of the agricultural revolution, for the origins of metalworking, and the birth of permanent settlements and the earliest cities. It was here that the first great cultural innovations originated, and from here they were diffused westward and northward (fig. 1.4). Europe derived its inspiration from the Middle East. There was scarcely an innovation of fundamental importance for European man but had its origins in the plains of the Tigris and Euphrates or in the arc of mountains that encloses them. From here the developments were carried westward and northwestward, by land routes and by sea, to Anatolia, to Greece and the Balkan peninsula, and thence to Italy and the Danube basin. Peoples and their cultures

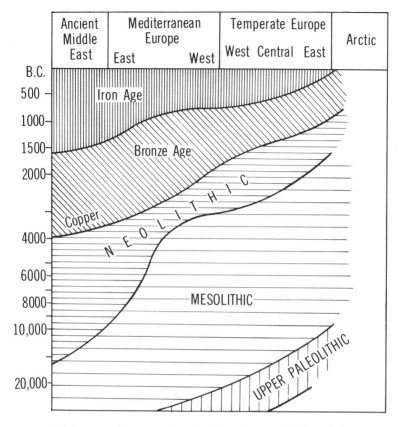

1.4. Diagram illustrating the diffusion of material culture in Europe
and its progression from the ancient Middle East to the
Mediterranean, and then to western and eastern Europe.

came in waves, or at least appear in retrospect to have done so, each wave being
technically a little more advanced than that which preceded it; each the bearer of some
innovation. Sometimes the newcomers passed it on to those whom they found already
there; sometimes the latter were resistant to change. But gradually material standards in
Europe were raised toward the level of those in the Middle East. When, one may ask, did
Europe reach the level achieved in the latter region, and then begin to exceed it? That
question is impossible to answer. Standards varied too much in both regions for such a
level of generalization to be possible. But it is apparent that at the time of the Roman
Empire, the Levant was ahead of most of the European provinces of the empire in terms
of arts and crafts, population, and urbanization. And, despite the attacks of Parthians and
Turks, this lead was retained through the early Middle Ages. It is possible that not until
the thirteenth century did the Christian West reach an equality with the now Islamic
East, and from that date, in material terms, Europe drew ahead. From that time onward,
Europe began to repay its debt to the non-European world.

Chapter 2

REVOLUTION AND DIFFUSION IN PREHISTORIC EUROPE

The raw material of prehistory is not men, but things.
——Stuart Piggott

Every culture, every era, exploits some few out of a great number
of possibilities. Changes may be very disquieting, and involve
great losses, but this is due to the difficulty of change itself, not to
the fact that our age and country has hit upon the one possible
motivation under which human life can be conducted.
——Ruth Benedict, *Patterns of Culture*

*F*or most of its long history the human race has lived under the shadow of
the Ice Age. Its earliest and most primitive members entered Europe
before the ice sheets of the last, or Quaternary, Ice Age had begun to spread. They came
from Africa or the Middle East, heavily built creatures with receding chin and forehead,
prominent brow ridges, and a small cranial capacity. Their skeletal fragments have
survived, as have some of the crudely shaped tools that they used. They retreated and
readvanced with each successive advance and retreat of the ice. Enforced adaptation to a
changing environment no doubt sharpened their mental processes, just as there must
have been some biological selection to meet the extreme conditions of the glacial period.

The Legacy of the Ice Age

The glaciers began to spread outward from both the Arctic and the Alpine regions more
than a million years ago. They vanished from northern Europe no more than ten or
twelve thousand years ago. During this long period of time there were at least four
advances and retreats of the ice, separated by the "interglacials," when the climate
became milder and plants and animals spread northward. With each advance and
subsequent retreat, the ice laid down a sheet of clay and stones, material that it had worn
from the rocks of mountain areas of the far north of Europe. As the ice melted after each
advance, the water rushed to the sea, carrying vast quantities of clay, sand, and gravel,
much of which it laid down in deposits that lie across Europe from Britain to Russia. And
after the ice had gone the deposits dried out, and the wind whipped up clouds of dust

that it dispersed far over Europe. This matter sank back to earth to form a fine porous deposit, which became the loess, a soil so light, fertile, and easy to cultivate that it became one of the first to be cultivated and remains today one of the richest.

As the climate grew colder with each advance of the ice, vegetation and animal life began to change. Broad-leaved trees gave place to conifers, and, closer to the margin of the ice, conifers yielded to the lichens and mosses of the tundra. And with changes in climate and vegetation came different animals. Warmth-loving animals disappeared, replaced by reindeer, elk, and wolf, until an improving climate brought back the species that had lived here before the ice came. Some species became extinct, unable either to adapt to the harsh conditions or to migrate to areas less severe.

The Ice Age had its human witnesses. They lived by hunting whatever prey there was and by collecting edible berries, fruits, and roots. Their lives must have been migratory because the animals on which they lived moved with the seasons. Short-lived summer settlements alternated with those used in the winter. They occupied caves wherever these structures were to be found, but over much of habitable Europe there was no such protection. Paleolithic man must have made do with insubstantial shelters, roughly made from branches and leaves. Not until late in prehistory does one encounter evidence for more permanent structures.

Little has survived to tell us how these Paleolithic peoples lived—what they ate and how they protected themselves from the cold. Nor do we know much of their social organization, nor how they communicated with one another. They left no monuments to guide us, and the discovery of an inhabited Paleolithic site is a matter of chance. Yet such a site was found about 1966 near the Mediterranean coast at Nice.[1] It had been used only in summer. Its inhabitants built huts, oval in plan and made of stakes, firmly planted in the ground and bent over to form a kind of ridge roof. They used their time to hunt, fish, gather edible seeds and plants, and to make stone tools and implements. Animal bones excavated at the site show that they preyed upon deer, wild oxen, and boar, and even the now-extinct elephant.

The settlement at Nice has been dated to some three hundred thousand or more years ago. It is not the oldest human settlement to have been found, but it is one of the earliest to contain evidence of huts. No human remains were discovered, but there were many stone tools. These had been cut from rounded pebbles of flint or of other material that lent itself to chipping or flaking. Most were of a kind that could be held in the palm of the hand and used for chopping meat and wood. A cutting edge was created by flaking *both* sides of the tool and might have been very sharp until worn down by use. The Nice site was probably occupied during the relatively mild interglacial that came between the second, or Mindel, glaciation and the third, or Riss.

There had been progress during the previous million years. Stone tools discovered at Nice show an advance on the earliest types known, but progress was immeasurably slow. During the last one hundred thousand years it began to accelerate, and, after the most recent, or Würm, glacial advance—about fifty thousand years ago—technological growth became more clearly marked. This period of development is associated with the arrival of a new people. Those of Middle Paleolithic Europe, including the inhabitants of the Nice settlement, were classed as Neanderthal. Henceforward, it is a less primitive, less heavily built type, known as Cro-Magnon, that predominates. Whether Neanderthal man evolved by a process of genetic selection into Cro-Magnon man, or whether the latter was in reality a newcomer, possessing a keener intelligence and equipped with better tools, we have at present no means of knowing. Far more precisely dated skeletal remains are needed before any conclusions can be reached. If the former was the case, genetic evolution must have been very rapid; if the latter, the Cro-Magnons' spread across Europe must have been accomplished in a short period of time. But, on balance, it seems that the ancestry of European peoples in the historical period is to be found among the Cro-Magnons; the man from Neanderthal was only a cousin.

The maximum extent of the Würm advance of the ice occurred between fifty and thirty thousand years before the present. Thereafter the climate grew milder, but not regularly and consistently. Instead there were fluctuations, with warmer and drier periods separated by a return to cooler and moister conditions. About twelve to ten thousand years before the present there occurred a short-lived warm phase known as the Alleröd. It was at about this time that the ice sheets finally vanished from northern Europe. This period was followed by a cool phase and, some two thousand years after the Alleröd, by another relatively warm period. This was in turn succeeded probably nine to ten thousand years ago, by a cooler and drier phase known as the Boreal. A warmer, moister phase, the Atlantic, followed and lasted from about eight thousand years before the present to 4,500, when there was a return to cooler and drier conditions.

The climatic succession has been reconstructed primarily by examining the types of vegetation, revealed by the analysis of the pollen grains that were scattered on the air and trapped and preserved in peat. The evidence of peat bogs reveals only local conditions, for pollen travels short distances on the wind, and discrepancies are found in the chronology of climatic change by investigators in different parts of Europe. But of the general trend there can be no question. The climate became progressively warmer, and with climatic change there came change in both the physical and the biological environment.

The melting of the last ice sheets returned vast quantities of water to the oceans. Their level rose; valleys near the coast became "drowned," forming deep and sinuous waterways penetrating the land; coastal plains were submerged, their forests killed, and tree stumps buried under silt and sand. In modern times such fossilized roots have occasionally been exposed, giving rise to countless legends of drowned lands and cities beneath the seas. The increase in the water surface must itself have influenced the climate of neighboring land areas, in all probability making them moister and reducing the extremes of temperature.

More important than the rise in sea level was the change in vegetation: the northward progression of warmth-loving species at the expense of those which had flourished in the cold of postglacial Europe. The northern tundra became restricted with the extension of the taiga, or coniferous forest, and broad-leaved trees followed, forming a belt of dense woodland all across Europe, from the Atlantic coast to the plains of Russia. This, in turn, brought about a change in wildlife. The reindeer and elk, which Paleolithic man had hunted and which, in some areas at least, seem to have provided much of his food, disappeared from most of the continent. Their place was taken by other animals, not only small rodents but larger creatures like boar and oxen, better suited to feeding in the forests. This development in turn must have led to changes in ways of hunting. No longer was it possible, except in the Arctic and perhaps on the grasslands of the east European steppe, to pursue large herds of animals. Hunting in a landscape of woodland and thicket was much less productive.

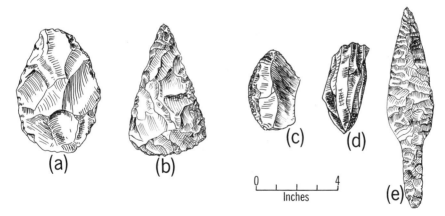

2.1. The progression of flint "core" tools: (*a*) hand axe (older Paleolithic); (*b*) hand axe (Middle Paleolithic); (*c*) scraper (late Paleolithic); (*d*) point (Mesolithic); (*e*) pressure-flaked dagger (Neolithic).

While the ice sheets were retreating from their Würm maximum, man continued to perfect his tools of stone and bone and to use them in the hunt and for cutting timber for fuel and building huts. The flaking of stone—mainly flint—became more refined and more specialized. Cores continued to be used as axes, scrapers, and "choppers," but the flakes struck from them were themselves shaped into points and arrow heads (fig. 2.1). Upper Paleolithic man developed the art of flaking and shaping flints to a level that has never been surpassed. Few stones, however, were capable of being flaked or chipped to produce sharp-edged tools. Foremost among them was flint. It occurred in river gravels, but the best for making tools was that freshly quarried from the chalk rock. Its occurrence was highly localized. It was to be found over much of southeast England, in Belgium and northern France, and in a few other restricted areas in western and central Europe. Paleolithic man must first have quarried the flints where they outcropped on the hillsides. Then he followed the "veins" in which they occurred into the hills, and lastly, when this was no longer practicable, he sank shafts onto the flint-bearing beds and quarried them underground.

Flint "mines," opened up by prehistoric man, have been explored at numerous sites in western Europe. Prominent among them are Grimes' Graves in eastern England and Spiennes in Belgium. Here even the methods of the "miner" can be reconstructed. He used the antlers of deer as picks to break up the soft chalk in which the nodules occurred. The flint was destined to make cutting and boring tools of all kinds and was distributed from the workings over large areas of western and central Europe. The earliest long-distance trade was in flint. But freshly dug flints are heavy, and most were cut or flaked to something near their final shape before they left the workings, which comprised, in modern terms, both mine and dressing floor.

Flint tools were sharp and effective. In the Upper Paleolithic they were in increasing demand both for hunting and for cutting the trees that were, in the gradually improving climate, beginning to spread across Europe. In many parts of Europe, where flint did not occur naturally, substitutes had to be found. Foremost among these was chert, chemically very similar to flint, but lacking the uniformity of texture that made flint so easy to manipulate. In some very restricted areas, obsidian, a fine-grained igneous rock, was used. But these materials did not suffice. Late Paleolithic man found that many stones of more common occurrence could be ground or polished by rubbing and would thus take and hold an edge, at least for a short time. Limestone, sandstone, and slate could be used in this way and were to be found almost everywhere.

The Neolithic Age was, in technical terms, marked by the use of polished stone tools. This development did not mean the end of flint mining and "knapping." Instead, flint tools of increasing sophistication continued to be used, for their razor-sharp edge could not be imitated in polished stone. At the same time, the use of stone tools permitted other materials to be employed. Hunting yielded vast quantities of antler and bone. Antler picks were not only used in mining flint but were chiseled and filed to the shape of harpoon and spear heads (fig. 2.2). As the Upper Paleolithic merged into the Neolithic—the so-called Mesolithic period—tools and weapons of bone became so common that they can be said to have typified the material culture of much of northwest and central Europe.

These advances in material culture were achieved against a changing but overall improving physical background. Climate was becoming warmer and the forest was advancing inexorably across the continent, the conifers first, and the broad-leaved trees, especially the oak, ash, elm, and beech, following. The new, postglacial environments offered greater scope for human initiative than those which had gone before. But they called also for better tools and improved technologies—the finely flaked flints, polished stone tools, and weapons of bone and antler. Above all, the new physical conditions permitted and encouraged the spread of agriculture, the formation of permanent settlements, and the accumulation of artifacts of all kinds. A better life became possible for more people with a smaller effort. Conditions allowed people to spare time from their round of hunting and food gathering for other pursuits that bore little relation to them. Pottery and modeling in clay and the painting, drawing, and scratching of hunting scenes upon the walls of caves and on pieces of bone may have been a form of sympathetic magic, but they also show that there was time and a desire for such pursuits.

Innovation and Diffusion

Material progress is made by a twofold process of innovation and diffusion. Each improvement in the method of fashioning flint tools or of making harpoons or spears was an innovation. We cannot say whether it originated at one or at several places at about the same time. There is good archeological or historical evidence for parallel innovation at widely separated places. After all, successful innovation is a way of meeting a challenge posed by the environment. If we claim that the human mental and physical endowment was much the same everywhere, it is impossible to exclude the probability that the same challenge met with the same response over wide areas and in many places. Looking back over the span of historical time, innovation can be seen to have occurred in two ways. It might have resulted from an accident, from something out of the ordinary run of things, and the recognition that something useful had taken place, or it might have been a consequence of a deliberate search for a better way of performing simple tasks. If a useful "accident" had occurred, then the problem was to repeat it under what can only be called "controlled" conditions. There is a Celtic legend about St. Piran, the

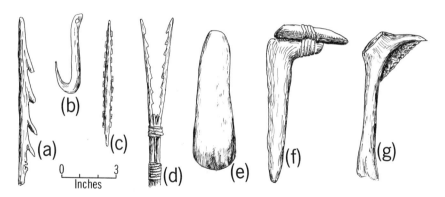

2.2. Mesolithic and Neolithic tools: (*a*) harpoon; (*b*) fishhook; (*c*) spear point; (*d*) fish harpoon: all these are of bone. (*e*) Polished axe; (*f*) hoe or adze, of stone mounted on wood; (*f*) flint blade mounted on antler.

patron of tin miners. After making the precarious voyage from Ireland to Cornwall, in some insubstantial craft, the saint was washed up on the Cornish coast. Wet and exhausted, he built a hearth, made a fire, and slept beside it. When he awoke he found a small stream of white metal emerging from the ashes on the hearth. His saintly intuition told him that this substance was tin, and he continued his journey, spreading both the Gospel and the rudiments of metallurgy. This is legend, a rationalization of something that had happened a long time previously, but one may fairly ask how many times late Paleolithic man must have built an unrecognized lump of metalliferous ore into his hearth, unknowingly raised the temperature, and awoke to find a piece of soft, partially smelted metal. Sooner or later someone *must* have smelted metal *and* found a use for it. In the long run, all discoveries must be made, though some have had to wait a very long time. The discovery of the qualities of the fungus penicillium was a very simple one, yet its recognition and repetition had to wait until the mid-twentieth century.

It was the separation of the essential from the nonessential elements that proved the most difficult. The smelting of a metal, or, for that matter, any other physical, chemical, or biological process, was not until modern times seen for what it is, something that can be defined in scientific terms, analyzed, and repeated. It was, rather, a kind of magic, enveloped in ritual, as the inventor strove to recollect and repeat what he had done and, perhaps at the same time, to guard the secrecy of the process. This mixture of science and magic is shown in the account by Theophilus, written in the twelfth century, of how to make a steel file (see p. 42). Not until modern times has this magical and ritualistic aura been stripped away from most scientific processes; in some respects it is with us still.

Most innovations, however great their subsequent usefulness, were not made in a blaze of publicity and eagerly welcomed by an expectant public. They crept in almost unnoticed. They may, indeed, have been far from welcome, violating local custom and upsetting vested interests. Even in nineteenth-century France, it is said, the scythe was resisted for harvesting grain because it deprived the gleaners of the ears of wheat left on the ground by the older process of reaping with the sickle.

Most innovations, however, probably resulted from a conscious search for improved tools and better ways of carrying out familiar processes. Refinements in the pressure flaking of flints must have originated in this way. The "inventor" could visualize the end product and, within limits, he could experiment with differing methods of achieving it. Such innovations were not tied to a particular place, and we must assume that parallel, if not identical, discoveries were made in different places. Processes that had been developed for one material—flint, for example—were adapted to others, like chert and obsidian. Most advances in material culture resulted from small increments in human skills. They cannot be dated and may have been adopted almost unconsciously. Yet in the aggregate they amount to the difference between barbarism and civilization. It is likely that truly significant innovations, like the introduction of agriculture or the smelting of metals, were the product of both accidental discovery and a continuous process of conscious refinement and adaptation to specific ends.

An innovation, once achieved and tested, had to be diffused or spread among those who might be expected to use or benefit from it. There were, before the eighteenth century, no media to disseminate information, no technical journals, no traveling salesmen to press their wares. Information in general and knowledge of a new process in particular could be spread in only two ways: by the physical migration of people and by the communication of ideas by some form of cultural contact or trade. Both processes were important in prehistoric times, but new technologies were most often borne by migrating peoples, and it is usually by means of the artifacts that they carried with them and then discarded that their migration routes can be traced. But no migration in prehistoric or historic times was of such magnitude that it totally supplanted or displaced earlier peoples and simpler technologies. New techniques were passed on by the newcomers. Sometimes they were accepted wholly or in part; sometimes rejected. It does not follow, because an innovation seems in retrospect to have been useful, that its value was at once recognized. The bearers of the metal-using cultures did not always find that their innovations were eagerly received by those among whom they had intruded. Many are the instances of the rejection of an innovation of significance. One cannot tell why; that would be to penetrate the minds of those who, deliberately or not, made the decisions. There were always vested interests in doing things in the old ways. Always someone stood to lose through change, whether in technology, or organization, or social structure. This, the inertia of human societies in the face of innovation and change, is one of the themes of this book.

There is an interesting anecdote regarding the Neolithic settlement of Jarlshof, in the north of Scotland. "The villagers lived simply but efficiently," wrote Jacquetta Hawkes,[2] "making the best use of whatever was to hand in a country so cold and exposed. . . . They kept herds of shorthorn cattle and two breeds of sheep, cultivated their fields, and also hunted seals and went fowling and fishing." They fashioned "their implements from bone and the local slate and quartz, and even [carved] domestic pots out of soft rocks." Then,

> an event occurred which must have caused great excitement among the simple villagers and served to link them with the outside world. A bronzesmith suddenly arrived in the hamlet, set up his workshop in one of the courtyards, and began to mould swords, knives and other articles that must have impressed the locals as . . . the height of luxury and scientific wonder.

We can suppose that the smith, on the contrary, felt himself wretchedly benighted, and often cursed an unjust fate which had deprived him of his more comfortable livelihood farther south. For he may well have been one of the victims of the blacksmiths [ironworkers] and their new metal, whose arrival in Britain threatened many of the bronze founders with unemployment.

The spectacle of structural unemployment in the Bronze Age brings this distant time closer to our own.

The diffusion of fresh techniques, new ways of making and doing ordinary things, like building homes, plowing, sowing, and reaping, making tools, and burying the dead, must always have been a complex and unpredictable process. A traveler or a migrant might bring such an innovation into an area. If accepted, as copper working appears to have been at Jarlshof, this area might become a new "hearth," from which the skill was spread to others. Thus, in *almost* random fashion, have innovations been diffused from the hearths where they originated. Yet their spread has not been wholly random. Their reception was dependent upon a physical environment able to receive them. Flint working without a natural supply of good flints, agriculture without good soil, potting without clay would have been impossible even if the idea of doing these things had been present.

There are two concepts in the history of material culture that must be rejected. The first is that new techniques and modes of organization necessarily advanced on a broad front, like the tide spreading slowly across a broad, sandy beach. It is easy to represent the diffusion of the metal cultures or the practice of agriculture in a series of maps, with lines showing the progress made by certain dates. These illustrations have a dynamic quality, suggesting overpowering movement that sweeps away all that is outdated and archaic. Such maps have, indeed, been used in this book in figures 2.3 and 2.13. What they ignore is the fact that at any one time there were enclaves of backwardness lying behind the advancing wave, and that, in front of it, there lay islands of the newer technology, like pioneers in the backcountry. The frontier between the old and the new, the more primitive and the more complex, was never simple. At best it was a zone within which technological advance was complicated by contrasts in culture, even in speech; by mutual hostility, by environmental differences, and, above all, by the randomness with which information and people traveled.

The second concept that must be dismissed is that early peoples had some idea of progress, of human betterment through the gradual evolution of technologies. They held no such view. They lacked that historical sense which would have allowed them to compare their present lot with that of their forebears. If there was any long-term change, they conceived of it as being in the opposite direction. The golden age was always in the past. Man had fallen from a state of bliss. He was not thought of as moving inexorably toward it. Not even the Greeks had clearly formulated any concept of progress, though they were well aware of the fact that many peoples were less advanced than themselves. Throughout the Middle Ages society and culture were conceived of as manifestations of a divine plan. Human progress as a result of human initiative was inconceivable. The idea of progress, though anticipated by Bacon and Descartes, was a product of the scientific revolution of the eighteenth and nineteenth centuries.[3] Only then were future developments in agriculture, metalworking, the organization of production, and the treatment of disease *seen* both to be possible and to lead to the betterment of the human condition. The idea of progress was born when people moved away from a fatalistic, religion-dominated pattern of thought and mode of behavior.

European Prehistory

The prehistory of Europe lasted an immensely long period, from the arrival of the first hominids to the emergence of the classical civilizations. More than a million years separated these events. Change within this period was immeasurably slow. There were no "revolutions," in the sense of sudden and dramatic shifts in the direction of change. Even the introduction of agriculture and the domestication of animals and plants, of the smelting of metals and the refining of iron to steel, were long, slow, and gradual processes. Each lifted mankind onto a higher plane of technical efficiency and material well-being, but the developments spread so slowly from the eastern Mediterranean, by way of the Balkans, to central and western Europe, that one might be excused for thinking that they were not welcomed. In many instances they were probably neither understood nor well received.

Nevertheless, innovations were made, gained acceptance, and spread, and they constitute the broad chronological framework of prehistory. It has, at least since the later nineteenth century, been the practice to divide the span of European history before the classical era into the ages of stone, bronze, and iron, according to what appeared to be the dominant material used for tools. The age of stone tools was divided into an Old Stone Age, or Paleolithic, and a New Stone Age, or Neolithic, with a Mesolithic period bridging the two. The Bronze Age was preceded by one, relatively short as prehistoric ages go, characterized by the use of native copper or of a copper-arsenic alloy. And iron was known, though little used, long before the end of the age of bronze. This time framework is necessarily imprecise and is based upon a single aspect—the use of tool-making materials—of material culture in a specific area. The "ages" of stone and metal are not absolute measures of time. Bronze was widely used in the Middle East, and iron was becoming known at a time when tools were of polished stone in much of Europe, and, in the north, flaked stone and carved bone were in general use. Each culture, each technical innovation, spread outward like the ripples from a stone thrown into a pond, the later innovations never quite overtaking the earlier. Figure 2.3 shows how the practice of agriculture spread outward from the earliest cultivation in the Middle East. In cultural terms, some five thousand years separate Greece from Scandinavia.[4]

We are invited by Thomas Hobbes to believe that "the life of man [was] solitary, poor, nasty, brutish and short," always lived on the edge of famine and catastrophe. This may not always have been so. The harsh fluctuations of the Ice Age brought about the extinction of many species, but man was not one of them. Unlike most other animals, the human species learned to adapt to changing physical conditions. It learned to build homes, make fire, wear clothing, and, above all, to diversify its diet. Mankind became omnivorous, or almost so, learning to eat almost everything that could be digested. The earliest societies that have been studied, like that which lived beside the sea at Nice, ate the flesh of many wild animals, as well as fish, shellfish, and the seeds and roots of wild plants. These foods must have yielded some kind of balanced diet, and in their variety lay an insurance against the failure of any one of them.

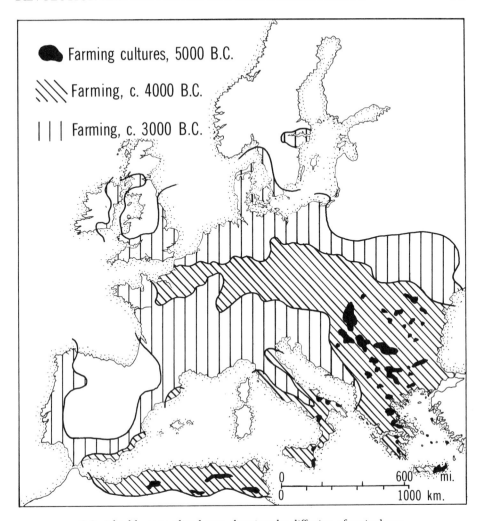

2.3. A highly generalized map showing the diffusion of agriculture

Life was marginal in the sense that a slight adverse shift in the supply of game or of edible plants could be fatal. The human species is seen as always pressing against a restricted food supply, a Malthusian situation that must at intervals have cut the population down to a size that resources could support. Yet there is evidence that some animal species have an innate means of regulating their numbers, a sense of imminent overpopulation and disaster that has led them to restrict their increase. It is sometimes held that the human species shared this ability with the lower animals; that it was able, by some mechanism that has unhappily been lost, to adjust its numbers to available resources. There appears, indeed, to have been a stable relationship between the human species and the environment, its numbers keeping a little below the maximum that could have been supported at the contemporary level of technology. This does not mean that there were no crises, no periods of scarcity when food was inadequate. Climatic fluctuations, both long-term and short, were always a risk that the human species had to face, and, indeed, still faces today. But the shortfall in food supply was usually small, and human losses could be repaired within a generation or two.

What then was the human population? There is no direct means of counting the heads of the people. That it was sparse compared with later, agricultural societies is apparent, and it is no less clear that it must have varied greatly with local conditions and resources. What we need to ask is this: Where were the nearest communities to the one that has left such scanty but nonetheless invaluable traces beside the shore at Nice? These people had no permanent settlement. Their lives were nomadic, but the study of comparable peoples today shows that their wanderings were not wholly unsystematic. Each group had its territory, which it probably guarded with the jealousy and tenacity of a robin fighting for its garden patch. Within there was a regular movement between more or less fixed points, for the human being is very much a creature of habit. Sooner or later we may chance upon these points and thus be enabled to reconstruct the territories and the progress of the community through the year. And by extrapolating from known territories, one might arrive at an estimate of the total population. But that time is not yet. One can only hazard the guess that total numbers must be reckoned in thousands rather than millions.

The First Farmers

The last years of the Paleolithic and the Mesolithic that followed were a time of rapid change. The graph of human progress, which had for a million years been almost flat, began to rise ever more steeply. The fundamental innovation was agriculture, but other and in some ways related changes took place around this time. Settled communities began to be established; weapons and tools were greatly improved; clay was burned to make pots; food supply became more varied and more assured, and *perhaps* language evolved into a more sophisticated and flexible mode of communication. Each incremental change made future change more likely. Human progress became, as it were, exponential.[5] What accident set off this chain reaction we cannot know, but it is more than possible that climate played a role. The span of human history up to this point had been lived under the shadow of the Ice Age, and its great fluctuations may have hindered progress by making it difficult to adapt to them. By contrast, those which accompanied and followed the last retreat of the ice were gentler undulations on the climatic graph, presenting, in Toynbeean terms, more of a challenge and less of a threat.

About the tenth or twelfth millennium before the present, the climate grew warmer, and, as we have seen, warmth-loving plants and animals spread northward. At the same time, northern Africa and parts of the Middle East became drier. The Sahara Desert began to form, squeezing people into the great river valleys, like those of the Nile, Tigris, and Euphrates, and northward toward Europe, where conditions were becoming easier for human habitation. Changing climate provided the conditions for the development and spread of agriculture. It did not determine where and why this happened. It has been claimed that population had grown beyond the capacity of a hunting and gathering economy to support. Agriculture without question made it possible for the land to support a denser population, but can it really be supposed that Mesolithic or Neolithic man consciously sought for a means to make a more intensive use of the soil? Almost certainly not. It is more probable that agricultural land use itself led to an increase in population by increasing the food supply, and that this in turn brought about a further expansion of agriculture.

The discovery of agriculture was not a sudden or revolutionary development. The transition from hunting animals to protecting, rearing, and using them, from gathering wild seeds and berries to cultivating the plants that bore them, was a very gradual process. It could have been accomplished in many places and at almost any time when environmental conditions were ripe. It took place independently at several places on the earth's surface and was concerned with the plants and animals appropriate to each.

In both the domestication of animals and the cultivation of crops, Europe received its inspiration from the Middle East. Agriculture was probably practiced earlier here than in China, Southeast Asia, and sub-Saharan Africa, and unquestionably earlier than in the New World, though each of these areas constituted a separate hearth from which the practice of agriculture was diffused.

Early man had long lived in a kind of symbiotic relationship with animals. He hunted and trapped them. The waste that accumulated around his campsite attracted animals that came to rely on him almost as much as he did on them. The dog was one of the earliest of such camp followers. Young animals, captured in the chase, might be kept, fattened, even bred. At the same time man learned to "manage" the wild herds, following their movements, attracting them to him, and slaughtering them as it became necessary. The Lapps of northern Scandinavia lived on and with the reindeer in this way into modern times, and yet the reindeer never became a fully domesticated animal. Its environment was so restricted, its food base in the mosses and lichens of the arctic so narrow, that it was better to leave it to fend for itself rather than to feed it in captivity.

Of true domestic animals, the goat and sheep are in all probability among the oldest.[6] The natural habitat of the wild species from which they derived lay mainly in the mountains of Anatolia and the Middle East. They were not to be found naturally in Europe and must have been brought in as already domesticated animals. The horse was probably tamed in the Eurasiatic steppe, and the donkey in the coastal regions of the Mediterranean. Of fully domesticated animals, only the pig and the ox are likely to have originated in Europe. They were creatures of the woodland, and woodland was scarce in the Middle East.

The domestication of wild animals is very difficult to date, since bones found at excavated sites are as likely to have resulted from the hunting of wild as from the slaughter of domestic animals. The dog had been domesticated by late Paleolithic or Mesolithic times and was probably used in hunting. The sheep and goat were not tamed in the Middle East much before the eighth millennium B.C., and were not taken to Europe until many centuries later. Domestic animals were kept for many purposes. Foremost was the provision of meat and milk. Their skins were important as clothing, and at a relatively early date in the Neolithic it was found that their droppings added to the fertility of the soil. Sheep, it might be supposed, would have been kept for their wool. But wooled sheep seem to have been the result of selective breeding, and it was not until several millennia after their first domestication that their wool began to be spun and woven.

Like the domestication of animals, the cultivation of crops originated in the Middle East, and Europe derived its inspiration from the Fertile Crescent and its bordering highlands.[7] Here the great rivers that developed as the ice sheets melted over the Caucasus and the mountains of Armenia laid down vast spreads of fertile silt, and spring floods continued to irrigate and fertilize them. In the moist and ameliorating climate of postglacial times, a rich vegetation spread across these lands. Here Abraham's ancestors must have watched as edible plants shed seeds that germinated in the fertile soil. To gather, transport, and *plant* these seeds was nothing revolutionary. Almost anyone could have done it, and what was important was the diffusion of the seeds rather than the knowledge of how to reproduce them.[8]

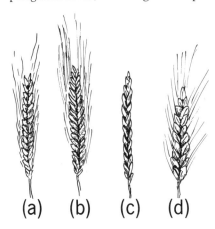

2.4. Early types of wheat: (*a*) Einkorn; (*b*) Emmer; (*c*) Spelt; (*d*) common wheat.

The earliest cultivated crops were primitive forms of wheat (fig. 2.4) and barley. These grew wild in the foothills that dropped down to the plains of the Tigris and Euphrates. Their seeds were gathered and stored; some were eaten; some were put aside to be planted later. In this process there was inevitably an element of selection. In general, the biggest and best were used as seed. The wild varieties had, in order to survive, to scatter their seeds as widely as possible, and for this reason had developed a brittle rachis, or seed-holding spike. The first farmers in all probability gathered their seed from those heads which had not scattered their grain into the soil.[9] In these ways, and without any knowledge of the scientific basis of their action, they gradually evolved a more heavily yielding and more easily harvested strain. By a similar process of genetic selection, the seeds of most cultivated grains gradually lost the hulls or glumes that enclosed them and hindered milling. Successive mutations gradually changed the character of cultivated plants, until they could scarcely be recognized as members of the wild species from which they derived. At the same time, however, some primitive species survived into modern times, like the variants of wheat that were still cultivated in the nineteenth century as spelt, Einkorn, and Emmer.

From the foothills, cultivation spread onto the plains of the Tigris and Euphrates. This appears to have been effected by small, settled communities, which used sickles made of flints mounted in a wooden haft for reaping. The earliest agriculturalists alternated between hunting and farming, returning to the chase while the crops were growing or after they had been harvested. Gradually more and more of the population became settled, and the fields that surrounded their villages, more intensively cultivated. The hunting and gathering components of their economy began to diminish, but never wholly disappeared. Even today hunting survives as a recreation for certain social classes that have long since ceased to depend on it for their living.

The crops that thus began to be cultivated had two important assets. Their food value was high, and most were capable of being stored for long periods. Although the human species is omnivorous, its diet requires certain constituents: protein, energy foods or carbohydrates, and sources of vitamins and trace elements. Some foods, including most green vegetables and fruits, are so low in protein and carbohydrates that it is not generally possible to consume enough of them. The only crop, or group of crops, that can be said to satisfy the human dietary requirements is cereals. "There is no other group of plants which combines high calorific and protein content with high productivity and adaptability; and therefore no other group of plants which could have supported the population increases that occurred."[10] The pulses—peas and beans—yield protein more richly but are, compared with cereals, much poorer in calorific value. Root crops, consisting largely of carbohydrates, have high energy values but are poor in protein, and fruit and green vegetables are low in both but contribute important vitamins.[11]

It is thus no accident that the agricultural revolution was based on cereals. Not only were they among the easiest plants to domesticate, but prehistoric man must have discovered early that they yielded the most satisfactory diet, especially if supplemented with animal fats, pulses, and vegetables. Such a combination has ever since remained the basic human diet.

A characteristic of cereals is that, unlike green vegetables and most animal products, they can be kept without deterioration for a long period of time. The ability to store food from one harvest to the next, and even longer, to transport it without loss over great distances, and thus to insure against localized scarcity, was of immense importance in the development of large settlements and a specialized, nonagricultural population. Of course, grain had to be protected against damp and rodents and other pests. Late in the prehistoric period, storage pits were sometimes dug and lined with grass or straw, and in more recent times barns have served this purpose.

It is not easy to date the beginning of agriculture in the Middle East, because it is almost impossible to separate cultivation from the collection of wild seeds. In the 1950s an intensive archeological study of prehistoric sites led to the location and dating of some of the early experiments. Excavations at Jarmo, in the Zagros mountains of eastern Iraq, revealed a community of perhaps 150 that grew wheat and barley, lived in mud-built houses, used tools of flaked flint, wove baskets, and made pots of baked clay.[12] Indeed, their way of life was little different from and probably not inferior to that of many of the peasants who inhabited this region in recent times. The Jarmo settlement was dated to about 7000 B.C.. But this community was a fully developed agricultural society. Excavations have pushed the origins of agriculture back by several thousand years. In some of the earliest finds, the grains of wheat and barley were of so primitive a form that it is impossible to say whether they derived from wild or cultivated plants. It takes many years—centuries perhaps—for the unconscious and unscientific form of plant breeding practiced by early peoples to show results in improved strains. These finds, dated to about 12,000 B.C., must mark the transition from the collection of wild to the cultivation of domesticated seed. This change took centuries, and its diffusion from its hearth in the Fertile Crescent was even slower.

The spread of agriculture is difficult to follow. In its early stages it left very little trace, and it is always hard to know whether the evidence of cereals belonged to wild or cultivated varieties. This evidence consists of carbonized grains recovered from hut sites, the imprints of seeds in the soft clay of pottery before it had been fired, the marks left by harvesting on flint tools, pollen found in peat deposits, and even undigested grains in fossilized human excreta. There must remain, hidden beneath the soil, a vast amount of evidence, but finding it is a matter of chance as much as of judgment.

The practice of agriculture was brought to Europe by way of Anatolia and the Balkan peninsula. The earliest cereal cultivation in Europe is thought to have been in Thessaly, a fertile plain in northeast Greece. It has been dated to about 6000 B.C. but was probably preceded by a long period when cultivation was not clearly distinguishable from collecting. During the next thousand years agriculture spread northward through the Balkans and over much of the Hungarian plain. It also appeared to the north of the great arc of the Carpathian mountains, brought there in all probability from the plains of the lower Danube (fig. 2.3).[13] From the middle Danube valley it was carried to central and western Europe during the fifth millennium B.C. This particularly rapid spread is to be related to the warm, moist conditions—the Atlantic phase—which after about 5000 B.C. spread across much of Europe. By about 3000 B.C. agriculturalists had reached the Atlantic coasts of France and the Spanish peninsula, had overspread northwest Germany and Denmark, and had reached southern Scandinavia and the British Isles.

At the same time farmers spread westward from Greece, along the shore of the Mediterranean, settling where the soil seemed suitable for cultivation. By 4000 B.C. Neolithic farmers had reached southern Italy and Sicily, and a thousand years later they were established on the coast of Provence and the plains of the Spanish peninsula. Settlers in Spain established contact by sea with those of western France and Britain. An Atlantic culture took shape, characterized by the building of great stone monuments, not only "henges," made up of standing stones, but also dolmens or tombs. It used to be assumed that these structures derived their inspiration from the chambered tombs and great stone monuments of Greece. But it is now known, through carbon-14 dating, that they are in fact older than the monuments found in the eastern Mediterranean and represent a local development in Atlantic Europe. It is also clear that they are Neolithic in date and thus contemporary with the earliest farmers. The building of great stone monuments was preceded by the raising of long barrows and the so-called causewayed camps. The former were burials; the latter, probably related to the ceremonies that surrounded the disposal of the dead. Both they and the henges that succeeded them represent an enormous expenditure of human labor. Silbury Hill, on the chalk of southern England, is said to have required eighteen million man-hours of work, and Stonehenge, with the transport of its stones—some of them from great distances—must have demanded a great deal more. These vast undertakings called for immense powers of organization. They imply a developed social structure, under someone in absolute control, and with perhaps a servile class that carried on much of the heavy work. They are also said to be linked with social changes that were taking place in the Neolithic. That they represented ways of disposing of the dead is obvious, but, like churches at a later date, they were also instruments of a kind of social cohesion, symbols of the community that labored to create them. At a time when population was increasing and perhaps exerting pressure on available agricultural resources, they were a visible assertion of the community's claim to the land that it used.[14] These great monuments, lastly, are evidence of the surplus, disposable capital that had been accumulated within an agricultural society. They could not have been created by the preagricultural peoples of the Paleolithic and Mesolithic. The social organization of the latter was probably too loose, and the time that they could spare from their hunting and gathering activities was certainly too limited. Agriculture was both the basis and the precondition of more developed conditions of material welfare.

But why, we may ask, had it taken three thousand years for agriculture to spread from

2.5. The Døstrup plow from Denmark

Greece to the British Isles? By what means had it been diffused? Was it brought by immigrants, or were earlier hunters and collectors converted to the superior merits of tilling the soil? There is no answer. It is clear that when the growing of crops began in the Middle East, the postglacial climate of central and northern Europe remained severe, and that hunting reindeer herds, fishing, and collecting the summer growth of berries was the only practible way of life. It is no less clear that the population was very sparse and that large areas were uninhabited. Farmers must have intruded into this Upper Paleolithic and Mesolithic environment, first in Greece, where physical conditions were more welcoming; then, as the climate grew warmer, into the Balkans and central Europe. But why did they come? They can hardly have been tempted by the prospect of colonizing climatically marginal land in central Europe. More likely they were driven forward by some force that they could neither understand nor control.

This force is likely to have been population growth. It is assumed that the practice of agriculture and the formation of permanent settlements was followed by a growth—perhaps rapid—in the size of the population. Expectation of life was short in a hunting and collecting society. With an improved diet and, perhaps, freedom from the hazards of the chase, life expectancy, and thus the size of the completed family, increased. But Neolithic man was restricted in the soils that he could till with his simple tools, and the extent of suitable soils was limited. As population grew so, he advanced inexorably toward and beyond his frontier of settlement. This would explain why the advance was so slow. It also shows why earlier cultures survived in areas ill suited to cultivation by reason of poor soil or harsh climate. It has even been suggested that by the third or even fourth millennium B.C., population had begun to pile up along the coastal regions of Atlantic Europe, unable to advance farther in their search for good soil.

The first farmers had a keen eye for the quality of the soil. They broke it up with a digging stick, but in time they learned to use a light plow such as that found in a Danish bog (fig. 2.5). In consequence, they looked for light soils that could be stirred most easily with such tools. The best was the loess, which, as mentioned earlier, had been deposited by the wind at certain stages of the Ice Age. It was fertile, could be cultivated easily, and, though far from unwooded, was normally free of dense vegetation. Wide expanses of loess were to be found in the Danube valley, over the plains of south Germany, and along the margin of the northern plain (fig. 2.6), and it is in these areas that evidence for Neolithic farming is most abundant. Indeed, there is very little such evidence except on these light and easy soils.[15] Figure 2.7 shows convincingly the correspondence between loess soils and Neolithic settlement in central Europe. These soils have continued to be used from that day to this, so that cultivation has obliterated much of the evidence for

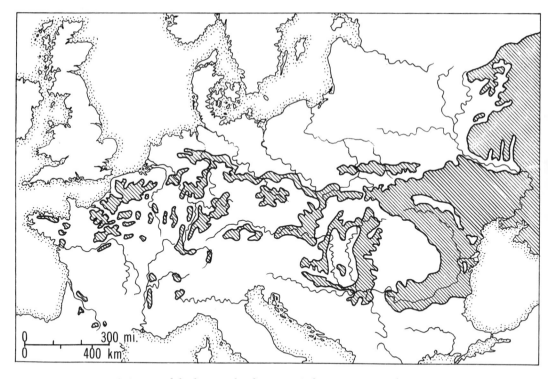

2.6. Map of the loess soils of Europe. (After A. Garnet, "The Loess Regions of Europe in Prehistoric Times," *G.J.* 106 (1945): 132–43.)

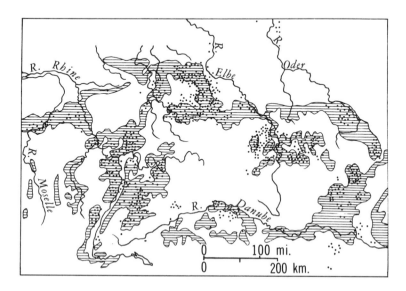

2.7. Neolithic settlement in Europe in relation to the loess. (After J. G. D. Clark, *Prehistoric Europe,* 96.)

Neolithic farming. Its density must have been much greater than is apparent from the map.

Land, once cleared of trees, would be likely to remain under cultivation for several years. The farmers would create a village, which may indeed have been rebuilt many times as the wood of the huts decayed and had to be replaced. Household waste accumulated; potsherds, small votive objects, articles of personal adornment were lost or thrown away and, excavated five thousand or more years later, are being used to reconstruct the lives and the economy of these people. Gradually, however, fertility would decline and crop yields diminish, and there was no alternative but for the community to move, make a "break" on virgin soil, and begin the whole cycle again. But pressure of numbers was restricting the extent of available land, and some farming communities would have been forced to seek land along their expanding frontier. But perhaps not all. We do not know the extent to which a community was able to claim successfully a larger area than it needed or was able at any one time to cultivate. If it was able to do this, we may perhaps presume that in the course of time it returned to its original fields and settlement, cleared away the growth of decades, and again cultivated land that had regained its fertility. Such a shifting agriculture continues to be practiced today in remote areas where space is still available for it.

Despite the general mobility of Neolithic peoples, most communities continued to inhabit the same sites for prolonged periods, long enough to construct homes that could be described as permanent and to acquire a store of household goods. Among these would have been querns and pots, used for preparing and storing grain. The making of pots of burned clay was one of the more significant consequences of a settled mode of life.[16] These utensils were not easily transported and were almost unknown to the hunting and gathering peoples. Even the earliest cultivators in the Middle East had no pottery, only bowls and querns cut from soft stone. Nevertheless, the practice of making pots and other less functional objects of clay, and of "firing" them on a hearth, developed early in the Neolithic and was diffused along with the art of husbandry.

Although there is evidence that pots were being made in Denmark before the end of the Mesolithic, the beginnings of pottery belong to the Neolithic. "Pottery had no single origin";[17] its raw material was to be found almost everywhere, and the temperature necessary to fire the clay was relatively low, commonly less than five hundred degrees centigrade. At about this temperature the body of the ware became hard enough to use, though superior pottery was later obtained by using higher temperatures.

Pottery is of great importance for the study of material culture (fig. 2.8). Pots may be broken, but sherds are almost indestructible and are in countless instances the only surviving artifacts of these early societies. There are so many ways to mix clay and to shape and decorate a pot or other clay object that communities and even individual potters developed styles of their own that have since served to distinguish their products from those of other peoples. When the same *type* of pot or other artifact is found over a limited area, it is customary to define it as a "culture." There were doubtless cultures in Paleolithic Europe, though they could not have been defined by their pottery. But during the Neolithic, thanks in large measure to pottery remains, these cultures are more clearly recognizable, and their territorial limits can be roughly defined.

There is unlikely to have been much long-distance trade in a commodity that could be made almost anywhere. For this reason local pottery styles have become particularly

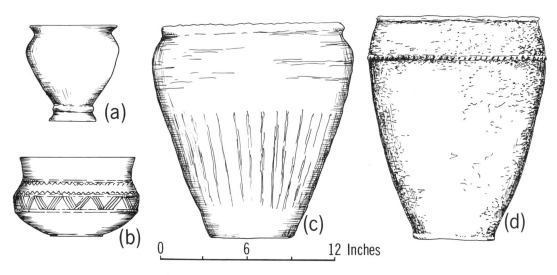

2.8. Prehistoric pottery types, ranging from Early to Late Iron Age

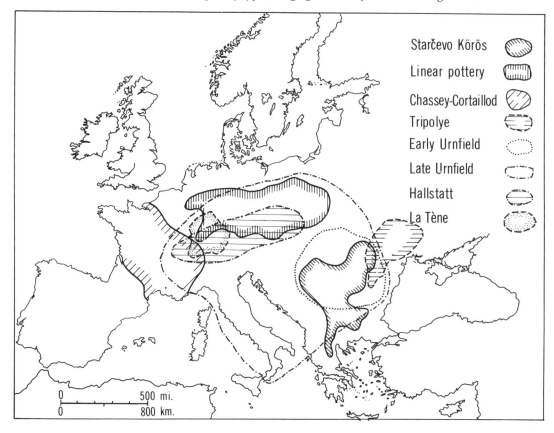

2.9. Culture areas, as defined by pottery and other "finds." The cultures represented were by no means contemporary, and range from c. 5000 B.C. (Starčevo-Körös) to the first century B.C. (La Tène).

important in defining cultural areas. Figure 2.9 shows the distribution of certain Neolithic pottery styles between the sixth and the third millennia B.C. The oldest occur in southeastern Europe, where the development of the Starčevo-Körös culture accompanied the spread of the first cultivators. This culture merged, at least spatially, into the Linear Pottery area, which extended through central Europe. To the northeast, and reaching into the Russian steppe, was the Tripolye cultural area, and beyond the Linear Pottery area, bordering the Baltic Sea, the TRB cultures. Along the Mediterranean shores of Italy and Spain, and clearly transmitted by sea, was the Impressed Pottery culture. Other, more localized cultures can be recognized in western Europe and the British Isles.

How valid, one may ask, is pottery in delimiting cultural areas in the Neolithic period, and have these areas any social or ethnic significance? The making and shaping of pots is only one aspect of material culture. There were many others, including the mode of constructing homes, of shaping tools, and cultivating crops. Far less can be known of these aspects of culture because the objects themselves have largely disappeared. It is impossible to say whether the people who, for example, made Linear Pottery shared other cultural traits, whether they had any social cohesion and communicated in some mutually intelligible language. Probably they did. We cannot otherwise understand the immense cooperative effort involved in building the great henges, alignments, and barrows of Atlantic Europe. We may perhaps recognize the beginnings of a social system, which, for lack of a better word, has been called tribal.

Excavation is revealing a growing body of evidence for the ways in which Neolithic farmers laid out their settlements and built their homes. In the Middle East primitive houses had been built of sun-dried mud bricks. This was the most readily available building material in a land where good timber was scarce. In time such structures crumbled, were flattened, and were replaced by new buildings constructed in the same way on top of them. The result was a mound or "tell," in which each generation built upon the ruins of that which went before. Tells are numerous in the Middle East, and from here this method of construction was carried both northward to central Asia and westward into Europe. The Troy that Schliemann identified as the "city" of Priam was, in the conventional chronology, the sixth of nine "cities" whose remains lay superimposed in the hill of Hissarlik. Immigrants from Asia brought with them their traditional modes of construction, and tells of great height have been found and excavated in the eastern Balkans. At Karanovo, near Stara Zagora in Bulgaria, a tell rises forty feet and was found to contain seven distinct occupation levels. But in this cooler and wetter land, trees grew bigger and more abundantly. Rainfall led to the disintegration of mud bricks, and the cultural legacy of the Middle East gave way to a new tradition of building in wood, using timber uprights to support a roof. Conflagrations were, in all probability, not infrequent, and, perhaps for this reason, houses ceased to be contiguous. Within any one community they might be scattered irregularly, arranged along a primitive street or even, as at a Tripolye culture settlement in the Ukraine, in a circle enclosing a primitive corral. This plan is, in fact, an anticipation of the later *Rundling,* or round village, of central and eastern Europe today.[18]

The Starčevo and Tripolye people built clusters of rather elongated, rectangular houses, whose size suggests that each may have been inhabited by a large or "extended" family. Sometimes these clusters occupied naturally defended sites, and the plans of some of the settlements suggest that all was not peaceful and quiet on the steppe and in

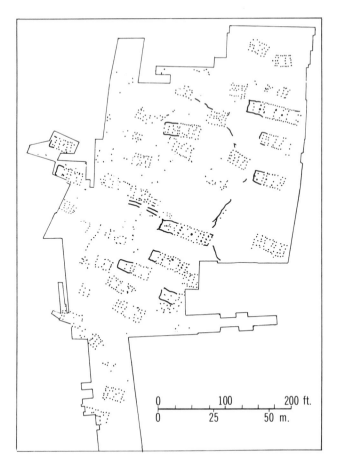

2.10. A Neolithic village settlement in the fifth millennium B.C. at Sittard, Netherlands. (After Stuart Piggott, *Ancient Europe,* 53.)

the Balkans as early as the fifth and fourth millennia B.C. Farther to the northwest, the Danubian or Linear Pottery people built even longer houses. At a village excavated near Cologne, there were houses twenty-five meters (eighty-two feet) in length and only about seven meters (twenty-three feet) wide. At Sittard, in the Netherlands, a village of such houses has been excavated. The houses were built wholly of wood and clay and were probably thatched. Although only post holes remain today, it seems that these homes were divided by cross-walls into rooms. Almost forty are represented in figure 2.10, but it is very improbable that all existed and were inhabited at the same time. The "long" houses (fig. 2.11) represent a building tradition that lasted many thousands of years, and their plan may still be encountered in some rural areas today.[19]

2.11. Neolithic longhouse, near Cologne, lower Rhineland. (After V. G. Childe, *P.P.S.* 14 [1948]: 177–95.)

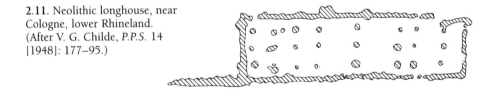

The Age of Metals

By the middle of the third millennium B.C., Neolithic cultures, practicing agriculture and using tools of carefully worked and polished stone, had spread across most of Europe. Not all of them were based principally or even partly on agriculture. Hunting and fishing remained predominant in the subarctic regions of the north, and there were collecting economies in restricted areas even within agricultural Europe. Then came an innovation of fundamental importance for human culture, the most far-reaching in its consequences of any, with the exception only of the development of agriculture: the discovery of metals. The material culture of modern times, even of classical and medieval, is based upon the use of metals—not only the precious metals but also iron, copper, lead, and tin. Most metals used in prehistory and antiquity occur in nature as ores in which the metal is chemically combined with other elements to form a wide range of minerals. Only copper and gold occur naturally in "native" form, uncombined with other substances. It is possible that primitive man might have found an almost pure iron in the form of meterorites that had fallen to earth. These occurrences were, however, rare—quite inadequate to have been a regular source of metal—and early man could not possibly have related them to the variegated rocks of the earth's crust.

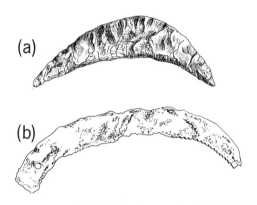

2.12. Sickles for reaping: (*a*) of flaked flint; (*b*) of iron. Both would have been mounted in wooden handles, and the iron blade shows a hole for fixing it.

The discovery of metals differed radically from the introduction and development of agriculture. Primitive man could observe in nature the processes of germination, growth, and ripening. He had only to control and hasten natural processes that were taking place before his eyes. The smelting of metals differed in that he could not possibly have visualized the end product. This result could be achieved only by smelting, and, as discussed earlier, for this he had to await an "accident" and to recognize its significance when it happened.

The art of smelting metals must have been discovered where their ores occurred close to the surface of the earth. Until their usefulness had been demonstrated, there would have been no point in conveying them far. The anecdote of St. Piran and the smelting of tin is wholly apocryphal, but it illustrates the way in which the smelting of copper must have been discovered. Copper ore, mainly in the form of the sulfide chalcopyrite, is not a common mineral. It is, however, found in the mountains of eastern Anatolia and Iran, as well as in Cyprus, Transylvania, central Europe, and the Iberian peninsula. Copper ore smelts at a lower temperature than most other metals, and at about one thousand degrees centigrade a pool of fluid metal forms in the furnace. Such a temperature could have been reached in a fire kindled for warmth or for preparing

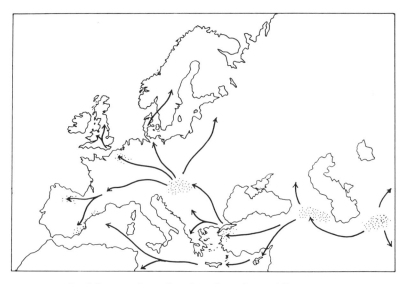

2.13. The diffusion of metalworking from the Middle East to Europe.
(Based on R. J. Forbes, *Studies in Ancient Technology,* 8:21.)

food, but smelting was contingent both upon incorporating a piece of the ore into the hearth and on a very strong draft to raise the temperature. Sooner or later both these contingencies might be expected to occur.

The ore of one metal is sometimes found in intimate association with that of another—lead ore with silver, arsenic with copper—and the smelting of both was effected at the same time, so that one metal became dissolved in the other. The effect of a small percentage of arsenic was to make the copper hard, a form of bronze, in fact. Doubtless, early metallurgists must have wondered why some copper articles were soft and others not, and probably thought that they had made a mistake in their "magic." This arsenic alloy became very fluid when heated and could be poured into molds. Before the end of the third millennium B.C., delicate copper castings were being made in Anatolia and the Middle East. The method known as *cire perdue* (lost wax) appears to have been used. A model was first made in wax; this was then wrapped in clay, and the whole heated until the wax had run out. This hollow mold (fig. 2.14) was then filled with molten copper, and the clay was stripped away after the metal had cooled.

But arsenic-bearing copper ores were not abundant or widespread, and arsenic-copper gave way in the course of the third millennium B.C. to bronze proper, an alloy of copper and tin. It is very difficult indeed to visualize the conditions under which it was found that copper with the addition of about 10 percent of tin yielded a tough and hard metal. The two minerals rarely occur naturally at the same site, except in Cornwall, and the regular manufacture of bronze necessitated the transport of cassiterite, the ore of tin, over great distances from where it was found.

There were many places in the Old World where the smelting of copper *might* have been discovered. In fact, the innovation appears to have been first made in the mountains bordering the Fertile Crescent, where agriculture also had its origins some five or

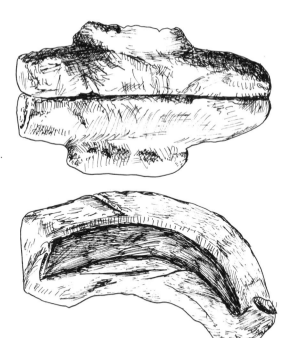

2.14. Clay mold for casting a bronze sickle; Danish. (After A. Steensberg, *Ancient Harvesting Implements* [Copenhagen, 1943].)

six millennia earlier. Stuart Piggot has drawn a distinction between what he calls innovating and conserving societies, the latter content to accept any stable relationship with the environment, the former willing to experiment and innovate. The people of this region of the Middle East clearly belonged among the innovators. Bronze working spread at an early date into Anatolia and Egypt, in both of which there were deposits of the necessary ores. Copper smelting and the fabrication of bronze were adopted in the Aegean region in the third millennium B.C. Bronze was found in the first settlement at Troy, and the Early Helladic culture of Greece made extensive use of metal. From here bronze working spread in two directions, northward into the Balkans, where copper ores occurred widely and tin was obtainable from Bohemia, and westward through the Mediterranean basin. Spain, where both copper and tin were obtainable, became a bronze-making region, and it has even been claimed that eastern Mediterranean peoples settled along the Spanish coast for the purpose of working the metals found in the mountainous hinterland. From the Spanish peninsula a bronze culture was carried northward to Brittany and the British Isles. Late in the Bronze Age metalworking grew to be of major importance in central Europe on the basis of the vast copper deposits of upper Austria as well as of Bohemia and Slovakia. Much of the bronze was cast to make axes and other cutting tools, but it was also hammered into a wide variety of decorative goods. The diffusion of metalworking followed routes similar to those taken by the spread of agriculture. The reason must lie in the physical build of the continent, in the orientation of mountain ranges and coastlines, and the direction of valleys that guided migrants.

The use of copper and bronze spread across Europe more quickly than the practice of agriculture had done. But the growing variety of articles of metal must not be allowed to hide the fact that chipped and polished flint and stone continued to be used, just as hunting and gathering long outlasted the advent of cultivation. Abundant though it had become, metal remained costly, and for most people's everyday needs, traditional tools continued to be used.

In the course of the Bronze Age man developed considerable skill in locating and exploiting minerals.[20] Flint had long been mined, using picks made from antlers. The ores of copper and tin were less easy to recognize than beds of flint, and the simple tools of the Neolithic miners were ineffective against the harder rocks in which they occurred. It is to be supposed that the first metalliferous miners located the metal-bearing lodes and then followed them into the ground. Undoubtedly they used bronze tools, and they also devised the method of "fire setting," which continued to be used in Scandinavia until the nineteenth century. A drift was opened in the direction of the mineral-bearing lode. Rock was broken up by building a fire against it and then removed by hand when the fire had subsided. In this way, elaborate gallery systems were developed in important copper-bearing regions. But much of the tin that was used to make bronze came from alluvial deposits. Cassiterite is a heavy and inert mineral. It had, during glacial times, been washed into the valleys, where it accumulated amid the sands and gravels of the stream beds. Prehistoric man, like his modern successors, probably panned these sands and so extracted the grains of tin ore. The tin used by prehistoric bronze workers was almost certainly alluvial.

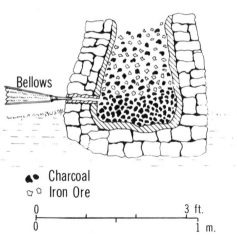

2.15. A section through a primitive iron furnace. It was roughly built of stone without mortar and would have been taken to pieces to recover the bloom of metal.

Smelting took place close to the pits from which the ore had been taken. The furnaces were low, stone-built shafts, lined with clay, like those later used for smelting iron (fig. 2.15). They were blown with primitive bellows, and the molten copper accumulated on the clay floor of the furnace. Most of the copper, alloyed with such arsenic or tin as might occur naturally in the ore, was cast in molds of stone. Most castings were axes. They were hard and could be hardened yet more by hammering; they could take a sharp edge, and they were capable of being used for felling a large tree, with important consequences for the environment.

Bronze was in general use in Europe by about 2000 B.C. About a thousand years later, iron began to be used and within the space of a few centuries had largely displaced bronze. Why, we may ask, did materials as easy to smelt and manipulate as copper and bronze give way to a substance as intractable as iron? The answer is most likely to lie in the localized occurrence of copper and the scarcity of tin. Bronze working was dependent on trade, sometimes over great distances, and always liable to interruption. Early in

2.16. An iron plowshare, one of the first fruits of metallurgy.

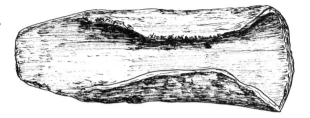

the second millennium there was such a period of disturbance, characterized, in Egypt at least, by the inroads of the "people of the sea." It is possible that the trade in copper and tin was so severely interrupted that people turned to iron.

The speed with which iron replaced bronze in the manufacture of weapons and tools suggests that some knowledge of ironworking had been gained long before the end of the Bronze Age. In contrast with the very restricted occurrence of copper, iron ore of some kind could be found almost everywhere. It occurred as veins in some of the oldest rocks, as beds in the younger, and as nodules in the marshes. There was no need, as there was with copper, to dig deep in search of it. Workable ores often lay close to the surface, and could be reached by shallow bell-pits. The ores of iron differed greatly in chemical composition and in the trace elements, like manganese, sulfur, and phosphorus, that they contained. But this was unknown to the Iron Age smiths, who could only judge empirically which ores were best suited to their needs. A substance as widespread as iron ore would sooner or later have found its way into a copper furnace and, even at the low temperatures achieved, would be likely to yield a lump of impure, soft iron. We may be sure, however, that as copper became scarcer the smiths turned their attention to this less attractive substance.[21]

They faced one serious problem. Whereas copper melts at a temperature of about 1080 degrees centigrade, which could be achieved in the small furnaces used at this time, iron melts at 1537 degrees centigrade, a level far beyond their range. At lower temperatures, however, the nonmetallic substances with which the iron was combined became viscous and, by repeated hammering, could largely be expelled from the metal. It was in this way, at a temperature of about 1200 degrees centigrade, that a bloom of soft iron was produced. It had no obvious uses, except to hammer into small decorative goods. It could not be cast like copper; if used in weapons or tools it bent upon impact; and if a fine edge had been given to it by hammering, this was quickly lost. Soft iron, from that day to this, has had little direct use except for making decorative ironwork. For most purposes it was far inferior to bronze.

But soft iron could be improved immeasurably in various ways. It could be hardened by a small admixture of carbon. The incorporation of about 4 percent carbon lowered its melting point and made it so fluid that it could be poured into a mold. This was cast iron, very hard but also very brittle. Prehistoric smiths never achieved a temperature high enough for so great an absorption of carbon to have been possible, but they could, by manipulating a bloom or bar of iron on the hearth, induce a very shallow penetration of the metal by carbon. Today we call this process "steeling" or case hardening. Steel consists chemically of iron with an admixture of 0.5 to 2.0 percent carbon. This process consisted in creating a thin skin of steel around a soft-iron core. Steel is harder than bronze and can take and retain a sharp edge very much longer. Without steel there could have been no tools for sculpture and woodworking. The fine masonry of the classical period would have been impossible; the dense woodland of northern Europe could not have been cleared; even the heavy plow, which alone could till the clay lands, could not have been made. Well might Rickard claim that the discovery of a way of "steeling" or carburizing soft iron was "the most portentous event in the development of human industry."[22] It is not difficult to visualize the early smith, manipulating a bar of soft iron on his hearth and, by "accident," carburizing it. This must have happened countless times. Sooner or later the qualities of the carburized metal would be recognized, the experiment would be repeated, and the process, doubtless surrounded by an aura of magic, would pass into the common use of smiths. Almost three thousand years later, when Theophilus wrote a kind of glossary, he described how to make a *steel* file: "Burn the horn of an ox in the fire, and scrape it, and mix with it a third part salt, and grind it strongly. Then put the file in the fire, and when it glows sprinkle this preparation over it everywhere, and, some hot coals being applied, you will blow quickly upon the whole, yet so that the tempering may not fall off . . . extinguish it in water."[23] Not until late in the eighteenth century was there any *essential* change in the process of making steel.

At the end of his prescription for making steel, Theophilus asked for the metal to be quenched in water. The effect of sudden cooling was to change the microstructure of the metal and to make it harder, though at the expense of becoming rather more brittle. It is not difficult to envisage how this innovation could occur. Nothing would be more natural than for the smith to hasten the cooling of a metal article in this way, and sooner or later the physical consequences would become apparent. It is not known when or where the process of quenching carburized iron came into general use. It is most likely to have occurred in Anatolia or the Middle East, but the date when it took place is very difficult to determine. Microscopic examination can show whether fresh metal has been "steeled" and quenched, but in iron found on archeological sites the surface layers in which the evidence would occur have usually rusted away. In a passage in the *Odyssey* Homer compared the way in which his hero put out the eyes of the Cyclops with burning coals with the noise of quenching iron: "I was reminded of the loud hiss that comes from a great axe or adze when a smith plunges it into cold water—to temper it and give strength to the iron."[24] The process would appear to have been common knowledge in the ninth or tenth century B.C.

The word "tempering," despite its use in this translation of the *Odyssey,* is normally given to a separate and distinct process, whereby the steel is heated to a temperature not greater than 727 degrees centigrade and then allowed to cool slowly. The effect is to bring about a further change in the crystal structure of the metal. A well-tempered steel lacks the brittleness that results from quenching and is strong, hard, and flexible. It is doubtful whether the prehistoric smith, or even the smith of the classical era ever *consciously* practiced the tempering of steel, though he may well have achieved this result without ever knowing that he had done so. Nevertheless, by the end of the Iron Age, ironworking skills had reached a very high order, especially around the eastern Mediterranean. Some of the tools excavated show a level of sophistication not improved upon until modern times. A smith in what is now northern Israel, for example, was able to create an adze by welding together steel for the cutting edge and soft iron to prevent brittleness.

Iron appears to have been first smelted and forged in the Middle East or Anatolia, and it was probably in this general region that the further innovations described were made. From here they spread to the Aegean. But iron was slow in displacing copper. It was first used to make ornaments, while weapons continued to be made of bronze. Homeric heroes in the *Iliad* wore helmets and breastplates of beaten copper or bronze, but their swords were increasingly of steel. The balance was tipped in favor of iron only very slowly as the superiority of steeled iron came to be demonstrated. By the beginning of the last millennium B.C. iron-using cultures were beginning to establish themselves in central Europe and to expand westward. The Hallstatt culture, which takes its name from a site in Upper Austria, was notable for its ironworking and for other crafts that the use of iron tools made possible. From south Germany the expanding Hallstatt culture and its Celtic-speaking bearers spread westward to the Atlantic.

At the same time iron-using cultures of the Middle East, notably the Phoenician, spread westward through the Mediterranean, playing a kind of strategic game with the Greeks and founding colonies as far west as Tartessos and the Pillars of Hercules (or Gibraltar). The iron-bearing cultures were diffused by migration and conquest. This was a period of great unrest, even of recurring warfare, to which the more formidable weapons of steel must have contributed. Long iron swords and shields began to be used. The horse was adopted for rapid movement. Four-wheeled wagons came into use and two-wheeled chariots began to be used in warfare. In all these developments which characterized the Hallstatt and the succeeding La Tène cultures, the use of iron both for weapons and for the tools by which the instruments of war were created was essential.

Among the technical innovations made possible by the age of metals was woodworking on a far more sophisticated scale than had been possible in the Neolithic. This skill was demonstrated not only in the building of more elaborate homes, which in design and execution anticipated the vernacular architecture of the Middle Ages, but also in the construction of wagons, chariots, and a host of what, in more recent times, we have learned to call durable consumer goods.

The wheeled wagon or cart (fig. 2.17) probably originated in the plains of the Middle East, perhaps as early as the beginning of the third millennium B.C. It had solid, wooden wheels and was probably pulled by the ox or onager. From here it spread northward to the Russian steppe, where the small and now

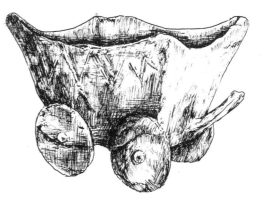

2.17. A model in clay of a Neolithic wagon of the third millennium B.C.

extinct Przewalski's horse had already been domesticated and was used to draw it. The four-wheeled wagon spread westward. It was a complex piece of joinery, and in the late Hallstatt and La Tène cultures, spoked wheels with curved felloes, or wooden rims, onto which metal tires had been shrunk, came into use. At the same time a two-wheeled chariot, lighter and faster than the wagon, was introduced and became the principal war machine of the Celts. A great deal is known about the wagon, in part because from the

Bronze Age onward small models of them were sometimes included in burials; in part because the chariot became as much a status symbol as it was a war machine and, as such, was placed in the burial chambers of its aristocratic owners. The wagons that we know from burials in central Europe during the second millennium bear a broad resemblance to those shown in medieval manuscript drawings and also to those met with on the roads of eastern Europe today.

How, one may ask, were these early wagons used? The two-wheeled chariots were symbols of princely power and machines of war, and it is unlikely that they had any other purpose. The four-wheeled wagons must have been among the tools of rural society, used to bring home the harvest, timber, and perhaps stone for construction purposes, and such has been their principal use from that day to this. Indicative of their importance in the Iron Age was the construction of roads of split logs, the so-called corduroy roads. They have been found only on land that would naturally have been wet, such as that around the Lake Villages in Somerset. The streets of the "town" of Biskupin, in Poland, founded in the sixth or fifth century B.C., were paved with such logs. Timber roads must have greatly facilitated the movement of wagons, and they, together with the massive fortifications that were beginning to be constructed at this time, represented an enormous consumption of timber, possibly more in the aggregate than was used in building houses. This development in turn necessitated ever longer hauls from the retreating margin of the forest.

Villages and Homes

In the fluctuating climate of postglacial times, protection from the elements was almost as necessary as food itself. Shelter in Paleolithic and Mesolithic times had been simple in the extreme, consisting only of huts, like those excavated at Nice (fig. 2.18), made of light branches and crudely thatched. Evidence for Paleolithic housing is slight; such insubstantial buildings have left little trace. The remains of Neolithic construction are more abundant and show a gradual evolution of the techniques developed during the Paleolithic. The fact that society was less mobile meant that homes were inhabited for longer periods. They were more solidly built, and around them accumulated the debris generated by human living. Furthermore, social groups became larger as dependence on hunting and collecting grew less, and we can see the beginnings of what can only be called villages.

The constraints on domestic building throughout prehistory were, on the one hand, the nature of available materials and, on the other, the needs and concepts of the builders. The settlement itself called for a dry site, but usually one in close proximity to the fields that were cultivated or the lakes that supplied fish. Caves were used for human habitation, as they had been since the early Paleolithic and continued to be into modern times. But they were not as common as is supposed and were a regular feature only of limestone country. Pit dwellings or *Grubenhäuser,* shallow holes in the ground, roughly roofed with branches and leaves, were also used where timber was scarce and have, indeed, remained significant in grassland areas such as the Russian steppe. Elsewhere construction was largely in timber, supplemented wherever necessary or desired by clay, mud brick, and stone.

A masonry tradition developed in southern Europe. Construction timber was far from abundant, but good stone was readily available, and, in a climate where fierce and

2.18. A reconstruction of the hut excavated near Nice. It was of Upper Paleolithic date. (*Sci. Am.*, May 1967.)

2.19. The rough shelter constructed today by shepherds in the Balkans. It cannot have differed greatly from much prehistoric "housing."

prolonged rainfall was rare, sun-dried mud bricks provided an effective and durable building material. Indeed, the mounds on which many settlements lay were created by the decay of mud-built houses. The only other region of Europe where stone construction was normal was in northwest Britain and in parts of Scandinavia. Here also timber was scarce and rough stone abundant. The primitive Neolithic settlement of Skara Brae in the Orkney Islands consisted of a group of rounded structures with immensely thick walls built of rubble masonry, laid without mortar. In most stone and mud-brick construction the roof—often flat—had to be of wood, though there was a tradition, deriving from southern Europe, of constructing corbeled roofs.[25] This feature gave rise to the dome, first exemplified on the grand scale in the Pantheon in Rome and the great churches of Constantinople.

Elsewhere construction was largely of wood. Most often posts, now represented only by "post holes," were set vertically and linked together by a rail. Commonly the gaps or spaces between the uprights were filled with osiers and daubed with clay. These materials were structurally weak but served to exclude the wind and rain. Sometimes the walls were made of closely spaced logs, split with their curved sides to the exterior. Sometimes a "log-cabin" construction was employed. The logs were laid horizontally and notched at the corners, as in American log cabins of recent date. Sometimes, as at Biskupin in Poland, the logs were tapered at their extremities and fitted into grooved uprights. In any case, clay was generally used to stuff the cracks between the logs.

In temperate Europe the frequent and sometimes heavy rainfall made it necessary to build a pitched roof, often supported by internal posts. The rafters of rough wood were usually covered with a thatch. The limited evidence suggests that such houses had gables at their ends, and that, at least in the Bronze and Iron Ages, these were being carved into elaborate forms—a device that has continued in peasant architecture until the present.

The floors of such houses were most often of beaten earth. They tended to rise with the accumulation of household waste and the occasional addition of a fresh layer of earth to cover the debris. There are instances, notably in the excavated sites at Aichbühl in Württemberg[26] and Biskupin in Poland,[27] of flooring with split logs. But these were low-level sites, only a short distance above the water table, and the floors may have been used to protect their inhabitants from the damp. One does not find such comforts in huts built on dry sites. A central fire served both to keep the hut warm and dry and for cooking. There was no chimney, and smoke escaped where it could. Fires are likely to have been of frequent occurrence, as the difficulty of starting a fire meant that it was kept burning at all times. There was little change in the materials in general use for home construction, but the advent of metal tools allowed timber to be prepared with greater care and precision, and most of the fine jointing of timbers belongs to the Iron Age.

The plan of the house was related in only the most general way to the materials used in construction. It was in most of Europe square or rectangular. The corners, as shown by post holes, were often rounded at first but became more regular with the development of techniques for jointing the timbers. A contrary tradition led to the development of round houses. Apart from a few early examples of square or rectangular

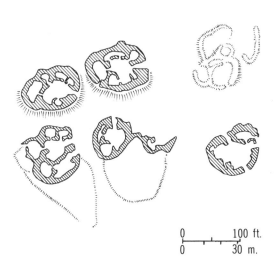

0 ———————— 100 ft.
0 ——+——— 30 m.

2.20. Rounded, stone-built huts at Chysauster, West Cornwall houses, those built in Britain were almost invariably round or oval in plan, with a central post or posts supporting a conical roof. Round construction was also practiced in parts of the Mediterranean basin. In Sardinia, round houses of the Bronze Age clustered around tall round towers known as *nuraghi*. In Greece there was a tradition of building round "beehive" tombs with corbeled roofs. It is noteworthy that these rounded structures were of rough masonry, and it may be that the absence of corners was due to the difficulty of constructing them without squared stone. This argument would also apply to western and northern Britain, where rounded huts were built of coarse stone from the cliffs and beach. At Chysauster in West Cornwall, a number of small rounded huts opened off a central courtyard, the whole enclosed by roughly built granite walls of great thickness (fig. 2.20).[28] In Britain and perhaps elsewhere the tradition of building in the round was carried over to timber construction. The post holes have been uncovered of numerous huts, more or less circular in plan, with wooden walls supporting a conical roof. This roof, especially if it was of a good size, was usually given additional support by a ring of posts within the hut. The round house that has been excavated at Little Woodbury on Salisbury Plain was a very large structure indeed, some fifty feet in diameter and capable

of accommodating an extended family and perhaps also some of their farm animals (fig. 2.21).[29] A feature of such large houses is that they often stood in isolation, sometimes surrounded by a ditch and palisade, whose purpose was more likely to be to restrain animals than to give protection. Within the boundaries, apart from the house itself, were pits for storing grain, in addition to small rectangular buildings, supported on posts, which may have served the same purpose.

With these exceptions, the European tradition was to build homes of square or rectangular plan. South of the Alps, where stone and mud brick were the commonest building materials, a house plan of *megaron* type developed in Anatolia and spread to the Aegean. It consisted of a rectangle with a porch added to one—usually the narrower—side. Within the classical world this was to evolve into the Greek "hall" or "temple" plan.

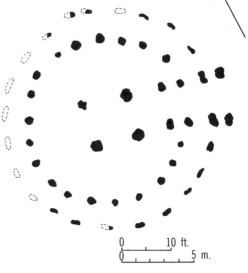

2.21. A round house of Iron Age date, excavated at Little Woodbury, near Salisbury, southern England. The plan shows only post holes. Four centrally placed posts supported a conical roof. To the right is evidence of a porch or entrance tunnel. (After G. Bersu.)

In the villages and incipient towns of the Iron Age, homes were closely juxtaposed, butting against one another or separated only by narrow alleys. The result was a warren of small rooms such as has been revealed by the excavation of many classical and preclassical sites. Such close spacing was

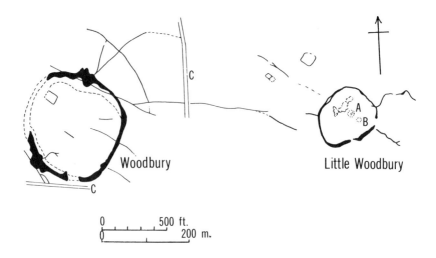

2.22. Woodbury and Little Woodbury. Houses such as that illustrated
in fig. 2.21 were isolated or only loosely clustered. They were
surrounded by a fence, and the sinuous lines reaching out from the
enclosures probably derive from fences used in corralling animals. *A*
and *B* are hut sites; *C,* modern roads. (After G. Bersu.)

characteristic of fortified sites but would have been impracticable, owing to the fire
hazard, where structures were mainly of wood.

In Europe north of the Alps the tendency in the Neolithic was for the house to
become elongated. The resulting "long" house became and for very long remained a
feature of temperate Europe. It was intended to house both a peasant family and its
animals, the latter living at one end—usually the downhill end of the house. The walls
might be of wooden posts or of stone, and the ridge roof was sometimes supported by
one or two rows of internal posts. The longhouse became less conspicuous in the later
Neolithic but nevertheless survived and continued to be inhabited throughout the
prehistoric period. Traces of longhouses are particularly numerous in Scandinavia and in
western Britain, chiefly because their walls were, at least in part, made of stone and thus
more likely to survive. Some are known to have been considerably more than a hundred
feet long, and rarely more than twenty feet wide. The longhouse has remained part of the
building tradition of temperate regions until the recent past. In its medieval form it was
divided by a crosswalk between the part intended for human and that for animal
habitation. In all instances it was possible to pass from one area to the other without
going out of the house.

Remains have survived of far too few prehistoric houses for it to be possible to
present a picture of their regional variations. No doubt local styles were as prominent in
houses as in pottery, but, unlike potsherds, timber rots. Nor is it much easier to explore
the plan and size of settlements themselves. All too often excavations have been of
individual houses, not of groups. Paleolithic settlements were almost certainly small,
because the economy they represented was incapable of supporting a dense population.
Agricultural settlements were larger, though it is far from certain whether they should be
called villages or hamlets. One of the most intensively studied of Neolithic settlements is

2.23. Plan of the village of Aichbühl, built on the shore of the Federsee, Württemberg. (Simplified from R. R. Schmidt, *Jungsteinzeit-Siedlungen in Federseemoor.*)

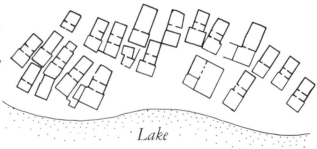

Aichbühl, in Württemberg (figs. 2.23, 2.24).[30] It occupied a lakeside site and consisted of more than twenty rectangular huts, each built of wood, with a ridge roof supported by posts. Each was divided into an inner and an outer room by a partition. Their orientation was uniform, the doorway facing southeast toward a lake. Before the entrance to each was a kind of "verandah," floored with split timber. The houses themselves were in general about thirty feet long, and up to twenty feet wide. Aichbühl may have had a population of more than a hundred, but this figure must be regarded as large for the Neolithic. Most other settlements of which there is any knowledge were appreciably smaller.

One must not look for a steady progression in the size and sophistication of settlements. There was, in fact, little change in either through the Bronze and Iron Ages. Many settlements, abandoned at the time of the Roman conquest, showed no outward sign of advance over those of the Neolithic. Change lay rather in the ways in which communities organized the space that they controlled, in their manipulative techniques, and in the amount of consumer goods that they possessed.

2.24. Reconstruction of Aichbühl. (Adapted from R. R. Schmidt.)

Toward the First Cities

Neolithic settlements had been marked by their open character. With very few exceptions, they had no defenses and little protection except for their stock. But the late

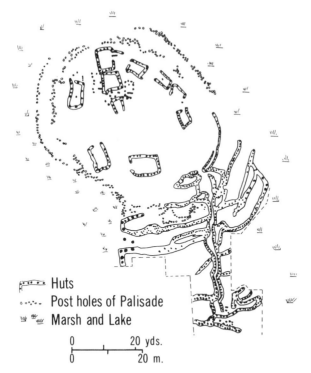

2.25. An Iron Age village at Starżykowe Małe in central Poland. Note the small cluster of rectangular huts, the enclosing palisade, and the complex and well-protected entrance. The settlement was almost surrounded by marsh. (After M. Gimbutas, *The Balts* [London, 1963], 81.)

Huts
Post holes of Palisade
Marsh and Lake

0   20 yds.
0   20 m.

Bronze Age and the Iron Age that followed were periods of unrest. In eastern Europe the danger was mainly from Scythian horsemen raiding westward from the Russian steppe. Settlements in Poland were established on naturally defensive sites, protected by lake or marsh (fig. 2.25). A large number of such fortified settlements have been found, of which that at Biskupin, near Bydgoszcz, is one of the largest and best known (fig. 2.26). It appears to have been established in the fifth century B.C. It was oval in plan, covered about five acres, and was strongly protected both by the water of the lake on which it lay and by a strong rampart of earth and timber. Within were over a hundred huts, arranged in thirteen straight rows, separated by roads of split timber. It was a tight, congested settlement, and there can have been very little room for animals, which must have been kept in enclosures elsewhere. But Biskupin, like most other settlements in the plain of eastern Europe, was permanently inhabited; it was not merely a place of refuge to be used in emergency.

Among Celtic societies farther west, warfare was endemic. The Celts developed the most potent military machine devised hitherto, the horse-drawn, two-wheeled chariot. Peoples were set in motion by the threat of war and, either as invaders or as refugees, moved westward toward the Atlantic, south to Italy and the Spanish peninsula, and across the seas to Britain. It was probably this turmoil which interrupted the trade in tin and greatly reduced the supply of bronze. Under these circumstances there was a move toward the construction of forts, both to protect existing settlements and to form refuges for the population. This trend showed itself late in the second millennium B.C., and was intensified during the following centuries. Forts became more numerous and more strongly defended and can today be recognized in their hundreds in western and central Europe. They were usually built on hilltops and took whatever advantage they could from the terrain. Along the Atlantic coast they were sometimes built on promontories or against the cliffs.[31]

Most such forts or "camps" of the late Bronze or Iron Age survive today as grass-covered banks and ditches. But their gentle contours belie their military strength. Multiple banks sometimes gave them a defense in depth. An important weapon in both defense and attack was the sling. Stocks of sling stones have been uncovered in some of the forts and it was imperative for the defenders to keep slingers from approaching too close to the fortified perimeter by constructing multiple banks and ditches. The banks themselves were more than loosely piled heaps of earth and stone. Many had been built over a skeleton or reinforcement of timber, which prevented the soil from being washed by the rain and permitted a bank to be built more steeply than would have been possible with the natural earth. From the timber-laced bank there developed the practice of constructing a vertical wall of timber, revetting the bank. Such defenses were inordinately extravagant of timber, and it was the needs of defense and building construction, not the spread of agriculture, that did most to reduce the extent of prehistoric woodland.

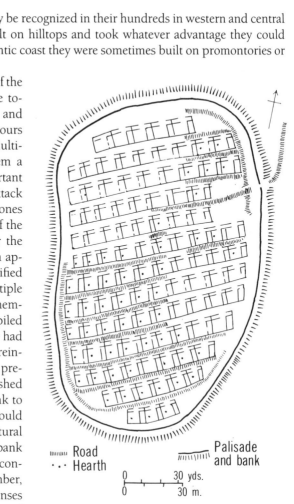

Road
··· Hearth

Palisade and bank

0 — 30 yds.
0 — 30 m.

2.26. The "town" of Biskupin in central Poland, of the fifth century B.C. Note the alignment of the rows of houses and the "corduroy" roads separating them.

The timber-laced fort appears to have derived from Middle Eastern or Anatolian examples. One of the early "cities" at Troy had such defenses, and the tradition survived in timber-laced walls of houses. But there were other ways of building the walls of such forts. At Heuneburg, close to the Danube River in south Germany, a fort was built by people of late Hallstatt culture on a hilltop. Its defenses, in part at least, consisted of masonry foundations on which were raised walls of sun-dried bricks. Furthermore, square towers were made to project from the walls. Both the plan and method of construction appear to have followed the example of the Greeks, however unsuited mud brick was to this wetter environment. The Celtic people, particularly those of the La Tène culture, were continuously at war with themselves and with their neighbors, and for this reason developed forts of exceptional strength. Their fortified hilltops were numerous in central and western Europe, and some were able to resist the might of the army of Julius Caesar. It became part of the Roman policy of conquest to destroy these hill forts and to transfer their population to lower and less defensible sites, where they could develop a form of urbanism more in tune with classical tradition.

That the Celtic hilltop forts were built for defense is apparent. What is not so clear is whether they were permanently inhabited by a large population or served only as refuges in time of invasion and war. The practice evidently varied. Many of the great hilltop forts in southern England covered so vast an area and contain so little evidence of human habitation that they must have served mainly as places of refuge. On the other hand, there were others, such as those in Gaul (France) besieged by Julius Caesar, which were almost as tightly packed with huts as Biskupin had been. Some such forts, Entremont, near Aix-en-Provence, and Ensérune, above Narbonne, both in southern France, had streets of stone-built houses. They were as much cities as were many of those in the Greek world at this time.

There is growing evidence that hilltop forts, with their multiple ramparts of earth and their cleverly planned entrances, were each the focus of a large number of villages, hamlets, and isolated farmsteads.[32] They were built by the labor of those who lived in these scattered settlements, and in emergency provided a refuge for them. They may have contained a store of food and weapons; they certainly had space for flocks and herds. Crafts may have been carried on there. They may also have held political and religious significance. They were centers of a kind of clan structure and may have been home to petty clan leaders. Tribal leaders may have been buried within them, or, at the least, their bodies may, after death, have been exposed there before the bones were disposed of. It is even possible to recognize on the ground today not only the fort but also traces of the settlements where clan members lived and of the fields that they cultivated (fig. 2.27).

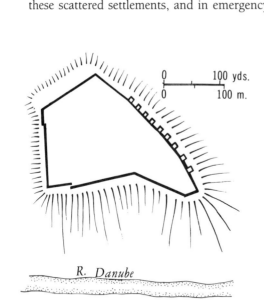

2.27. The Heuneburg, a hill fort in central Europe. (After John Collis, *Oppida: Earliest Towns North of the Alps,* 42.)

In the marshlands of northwestern Europe another type of settlement evolved in response to the prevailing dampness of the environment. A small cluster of houses was located on a low platform built of turf and mud and continuously heightened to keep the settlement clear of the slowly rising water level. These mounds or *terpen* were similar to the tells of the Balkans, though quite different in origin.

From Neolithic times onward, the primitive self-sufficiency of the local community began slowly to break down. The use of stone tools of ever-increasing refinement made it necessary for many settlements to draw on distant sources for flint, obsidian, and other kinds of stone. The age of metals called for a far more intensive trade. Copper ores were far from common, those of tin were rare, and long-distance trade in these commodities was essential. But the materials had also to be paid for, either by means of foodstuffs, the products of craft industries, or by commodities such as salt, jet, or amber. As early as the Neolithic, specialized craftsmen had appeared, knapping flints, carving bone, and polishing stone. The number of such specialists and the range of their products increased during the Bronze and Iron Ages. The metalworking crafts, for example, could never have been carried on successfully within the framework of the self-sufficing family. The experiments that led to the making of bronze or of steel tools could only have been carried on by men who devoted most of their time to the craft. Slagheaps sometimes show where prehistoric craftsmen were employed and, by their size, demonstrate the scale of their industry. The copper ores of Mühlbach, in Upper Austria, were exploited on a lavish scale, and must have supplied metal to much of central Europe.[33] Salt from the nearby Hallstatt deposits was worked by a large number of miners and was widely distributed. The Holy Cross Mountains of southern Poland were the scene of intensive iron smelting, and there were other ironworking centers of major importance in the lower Rhineland, southern England, and eastern France.

Little is known of the organization of these early metalworking centers. It is probable that the same men both extracted and smelted the ores, but it seems that the fabrication of the metal into weapons, tools, ornaments, and other objects was generally left to others. An Iron Age site at Gussage All Saints in southern Britain yielded a vast hoard of molds in which bronze objects had been cast. There was, however, no evidence of smelting, and the metal itself must have been imported, perhaps from Cornwall. There was a large and growing trade in copper, bronze, and iron between the smelting centers and the countless smiths who worked the metals into finished goods. The hilltop forts of the Celts may have had their resident bronze- and ironworkers.

Metals may have been the most important goods entering into long-distance trade, but there were many others. There is evidence at some Bronze and Iron Age sites for the manufacture of cloth on a more intensive scale than seems necessary for local use. Spindle whorls, loom weights, and weavers' combs have frequently been found, as have leather goods. There is evidence from south Germany of a surplus production of meat—perhaps dried or salted—as well as of grain and cheese. The existence of specialized craftsmen implies a trade in foodstuffs, if only over short distances. Other and less functional goods were found in the settlements of the last millennium B.C. Glass beads could not possibly have been made at some of the places where they have been found. Graphite, also from distant sources, was used to decorate pottery, and countless brooches, pins, and other articles of personal adornment entered into trade. And there is evidence that in the Late Iron Age peoples of northern Europe were acquiring a taste for wine, which could only have been obtained from beyond the Alps.

Within the hill forts that had permanent populations, some quarters were given over to metalworkers and other craftsmen, and at the opposite extreme were courtyard homes for the rich, and perhaps even public buildings that remotely resembled those of Greece. There can be little doubt that these "towns," or *oppida*, as the classical writers called them, were centers of specialized crafts and commerce, that they carried on trade with distant areas, including the Mediterranean cities, and that they were the "central places" of extensive areas.[34] To what extent they derived from Greek example, to what extent they arose from local developments north of the Alps, is far from clear. That they were a response to a developing specialization in manufacturing and trade is obvious. It is no less likely, as the case of Heuneburg, several centuries earlier, had demonstrated, that they owed something in layout and in the detail of their construction to the example of the Greeks. But their vast defenses were far more extensive than those of Greek cities, and it is difficult to resist the conclusion that they served as refuges for the surrounding population with all their farm animals.

The "urban revolution" was an inevitable consequence of the rise of specialized technologies, like those of the metalworkers. The latter required secure places in which to work and an assured supply of their essential raw materials and food. The city eventually became the focus of manufacturing and trade. It grew in size beyond the limits of the self-sufficing village community and came to depend on a supply of food from distant sources over which it may have had little or no control. Urban living began in the riverine civilizations of the Middle East and spread to Anatolia, the Aegean, Italy, and central Europe.[35] It was not a technical innovation, like sowing and reaping crops and smelting metals. It was, rather, a social process, made possible, even inevitable, by the surplus production generated by the new technologies. The details of urban planning and fortification, of home construction and public buildings may have been due to innovation and its conscious imitation. But the idea of specialized craftsmen and traders living together, enjoying the mutual protection that they afforded one another and perhaps collaborating to develop, even to exploit, potential markets, could emerge wherever there were enough specialized producers to make it possible.[36]

Such was the stage reached in Late Iron Age Europe. Meanwhile, urban development had made greater progress in the Mediterranean basin. Here, superimposed upon the specialized commercial and craft functions of the city, its original *raison d'être,* was another: the city became the center for gracious living. The surplus that arose from an improving agriculture, together with the profits from trade, made it possible to develop a concept of urbanism that went far beyond the creation of a scene for the practice of trade and the crafts. It converted the city into a center of culture in a broader sense. From being little more than an industrialized village, the city became the focus of artistic and architectural development, of educational and political development. In this sense urbanism in Europe was the creation of the classical civilizations. It originated in Greece, was taken to Italy, and was borne northward and westward by the soldiers and administrators of the Roman Empire. In any technological sense the classical civilizations contributed little to the skills possessed by Late Iron Age man. Their achievement was to infuse a new spirit into old forms, to rationalize and organize and to divert into creative activities a larger proportion of the surplus generated by agriculture, manufacturing, and trade.

This chapter has reviewed briefly the diffusion of those innovations which distinguished civilized from primitive living. Most, however modified in the process, derived from that broad geographical region which extends from the Black Sea and Turkestan to the Arabian and Saharan deserts and is loosely termed the Middle East. The reason for this pattern is probably to be found in the fact of the Ice Age. For by far the greater part of human history, much of Europe was either covered by ice or subject to the influence of the ice sheets. The period of time during which Europe, at least Europe north of the Alps, was capable of providing a home for man, in which he could experiment and innovate, has been very short. It must always be remembered that when the first seeds were conciously planted and allowed to grow in the hills that bordered the Fertile Crescent, the Ice Age had not ended in northern Europe, and when the first metals were smelted in the Middle East, agriculture had barely begun in Atlantic Europe. Not only did the Middle Eastern region possess immense environmental advantages in its climate, in the floodwaters of its great rivers, and in reserves of easily worked metalliferous ores; it also had a very much longer period of time in which innovation could take place. On any reasonable calculation of probabilities, the Middle East might well appear to be the most likely cradle of that civilization which ultimately spread across Europe.

Chapter 3

THE CLASSICAL FOUNDATIONS
OF WESTERN CULTURE

. . . the qualities of both gentleness and civility have come to the
Turditanians, and to the Celtic peoples too. . . . The Turditanians
have completely changed over to the Roman mode of life, not even
remembering their own language any more.

—Strabo, *Geography*, III, 2, 15

*T*he civilizations of Greece and Rome were rooted in the cultures of Late
Iron Age Europe. Their technologies were those developed and diffused
during the previous two or three thousand years. They were themselves not conspicuously innovative, and it is difficult to name any technical innovation for which the
classical people were in large measure responsible. This paradox—high civilization
without a commensurate level of invention—is difficult to resolve. It was implicit in the
previous chapter that advance in material cultures moved in a series of giant steps, of
quantum jumps. The adoption and diffusion of agriculture and the use of metals each
marked such a transition from a lower to a higher plane. Each increased the efficiency of
human labor, intensified the volume of production, and, as a consequence, improved the
quality of life. Each such advance removed people yet further from the interminable task
of seeking food. There should, by this argument, have been some technical innovation,
some mechanical or procedural discovery, that lifted the classical civilizations, in material terms, above the level of Iron Age cultivators. Yet there were no such innovations or
discoveries. The skills—if not the vision—of the Greeks of the age of Pericles were
scarcely different from those of the La Tène Celts, who also built and fortified their
oppida, forged and tempered weapons, and cast the most exquisite bronzes. The Greeks,
in fact, possessed only one skill denied to their Iron Age contemporaries: they were
literate, able to communicate by means of the written word and to preserve their
thoughts for posterity to read.

The City-State

There was, however, one particular institution that distinguished the cultures of the classical peoples of Greece and Rome from their Bronze and Iron Age contemporaries. This was the city, or *polis* (πόλις). Underlying the spread of classical civilizations was the diffusion of the city as an institution and a way of life. The classical writers had no doubt of its importance. "Let the wild beasts," wrote Cassiodorus, "live in fields and woods; men ought to draw together into cities."[1] Mankind, wrote Aristotle, is a "political" creature, one suited by nature to living in a *polis*,[2] and the noblest service that Greeks or Romans could provide for their "barbarian" neighbors and contemporaries was, they thought, to create cities for them to inhabit. Four centuries after Aristotle, Strabo remarked on the "qualities of mildness and civil life" that had developed among the inhabitants of southern Spain and attributed this to the fact that they had "changed to the Roman [that is, urban] mode of life." The Celts, by contrast, showed no such qualities, "for they mostly live in villages."[3]

The city almost defies definition. That it was a nucleated, or clustered, form of settlement is clear. In the popular imagination it was larger, generally considerably larger, than a village, and it had a broader range of functions. Agriculture is not normally practiced in the modern city. But this cannot be said of those of classical or even medieval Europe. These centers were intimately bound up with the life of the rural areas that surrounded them, and their inhabitants regularly made the journey to the fields. Furthermore, most *poleis* were very small, numbering their population in hundreds rather than in thousands. What distinguished the classical city from the village was not so much size and economic functions, for in these respects the two clearly overlapped, but the different qualities of life that they offered.

If we could piece together a composite picture of a Greek *polis,* we should represent it as a walled enclosure, set on rising ground and dominated by some kind of fortress or acropolis (ἀκρόπολις = "high town"), a survival from the earlier age of "despots." Within the walls there would have been narrow streets lined with small houses, simply built of mud bricks and wood with only a sparing use of stone. Somewhere amid the closely built houses would be a public place, or *agora* (ἀγορα), perhaps bordered by a pillared *stoa* and overlooked by a temple. On the edge of the built-up area, or even outside the walls, there might be a semicircular theater, with its seats rising in tiers above the *proscenium* (fig. 3.1). There might also be a gymnasium where the young could exercise and the old could sit by and watch. In some *poleis,* water was piped to a public fountain, even though the hydraulic engineering of the Greeks never attained the level later reached by the Romans.

These were the features that distinguished a Greek city from a village. They were essentially nonproductive, part of the city's social overheads. They brought people together for business and pleasure. There they might sit and argue. It is no accident that the Stoics derived their name from the *Stoa Poikile,* a public building in Athens, where Zeno used to debate the philosophical issues of his day. Private housing was simple, even squalid, but public buildings, by contrast, were lavish, even extravagant. Pausanias wrote of the *polis* of Panopus, in Phocis, "if city it may be called that has no government offices, no gymnasium, no theatre, no market-place, no water conducted to a fountain." But Pseudo-Dicaearchus, an obscure writer of the fourth century B.C., had no doubt of

3.1. The theater at Epidaurus in
southern Greece.

the status of Anthedon, because "the agora is all planted with trees and flanked by Colonnades."[4]

Pausanias, who in the second century A.D. wrote a topographical guide to Greece, seems to have had a kind of checklist: agora, temple, theater, and so on, by which he rated the *poleis* that he visited.[5] The same criteria were used by classical writers to evaluate cities outside Europe. Libanius's encomium of the city of Antioch stressed its public buildings and shady stoas rather than any economic activity that might have been carried on there.[6]

The Greeks rationalized the creation of the *polis* that focused their loyalties. It was formed, they said, by the fusion—*synoecism*—of small, rural settlements. "When several villages are united in a single community," wrote Aristotle, "large enough to be nearly or quite self-sufficing, the polis comes into existence."[7] An act of synoecism can only be presumed in most instances. It took place, if indeed it occurred at all, well before the beginning of recorded history. But there are instances in the fourth century B.C. of the physical creation of a city by the forced migration of the inhabitants of several villages to a common site. The cities of Megalopolis, Mantinea, Messene, and Tegea, all of them in southern Greece, were created in this way. The foundation of Megalopolis is, indeed, well documented. It was established about 370 B.C. by Epaminondas of Thebes for the purpose of restricting the military operations of Sparta.[8] According to Pausanias, no fewer than forty villages were depleted in order to populate the city. It was planned on a monumental scale. Its walls were nearly six miles in circumference. Within were an agora, a theater, and a stoa, all of which, as excavation has shown, were of exceptional size and elaboration. As a city, however, Megalopolis was a failure. Its population drifted back to the villages, and when it had ceased to fulfill its military function in the wars between the city leagues of Greece, it slowly decayed. The "Great City," wrote Strabo, "had become a great desert,"[9] and Pausanias found it "mostly in ruins, shorn of all its beauty and ancient prosperity."[10]

The story of Megalopolis illustrates the problem of the Greek *polis*. With very few exceptions it failed to establish a permanent economic base capable of sustaining it over the long term. Again, with certain exceptions, it remained predominantly agricultural. Its crafts were small-scale and unspecialized. "In small towns," wrote Xenophon, "the same workman makes chairs and doors and plows and tables, and often this same artisan builds houses, and even so he is thankful if he can only find employment to support him."[11] Long-distance commerce was almost nonexistent. A fundamental question, then, is how, without any advance in technology, a simple agricultural society could maintain so sophisticated a way of life and create unproductive monuments of lasting beauty. There is no simple answer. One is tempted to argue that this achievement was made possible by the exploitation of a servile class. Slavery, of course, existed throughout the classical world, and was no doubt important as a source of labor in cities such as Athens. Here, in the late fifth and fourth centuries, slaves may have made up a fifth of the total male population.[12] But it cannot be assumed that slaves were numerous or even that they played a significant economic role in the small *poleis* of the Aegean. The Athenians—again an exception—were accused of diverting the treasure of the Athenian League, accumulated for its defense against the Persians, to the adornment of their city. But no other *polis* had such an opportunity to misappropriate funds placed in its charge.

The quality both of life and of architecture found in the Greek *polis* must have arisen from the carefully planned use of resources, material and human. Building plans called for few materials that could not have been found nearby and few skills that could not have been developed locally. Furthermore, the agricultural year was marked by short periods of intense activity, when fields were plowed and the harvest gathered, alternating with spells when farming made few demands. Other societies have used such periods of enforced idleness in very different and less constructive ways. In the Greek *poleis* it became acceptable to use the surplus wealth generated by society to beautify cities, just as, in the later Middle Ages, wealthy merchants invested in church architecture. The decay, or at least the twilight, of the *polis* came when, for economic or political reasons, it ceased to be the accepted norm to devote time and energy to such works. The emergence of this urban culture within the Mediterranean basin was without doubt assisted by environmental factors. The Greek homeland was endowed with some of the finest building stone to be found in Europe. The climate encouraged an outdoor way of life, and the agricultural calendar provided periods of leisure from fieldwork.

Most *poleis* were the product of a long period of slow growth during the Archaic period. They were without regular plan. Their houses were built of adobe, perhaps on stone footings, flat-roofed and almost windowless, clustered into a warren of narrow streets. Demosthenes claimed that the Athenians were "in private life . . . severe and simple,"[13] and Pseudo-Dicaearchus described the streets as "nothing but miserable old lanes, the houses mean."[14] But there were some cities that contained the elements of a planned layout. They were, to use terms that will be employed later, "planted" rather than "organic" cities. Megalopolis was a "planted" city, though there is no clear evidence that its streets conformed to any regular plan. But there is evidence at Smyrna and

Miletus, in Anatolia, for aligning streets on a gridiron pattern well before the classical period of Greece, and when the Athenians established the port city of Piraeus, the planner Hippodamus of Miletus was called in to lay it out in regular blocks. A few years later a similar plan was used at the Athenian colony of Thourioi in southern Italy.

Thus, it might seem, the practice of city planning spread from Asia Minor to Greece, and thence to Italy. Reality, however, may have been more complex. In northern Italy, close to the mouth of the river Po, a similar plan has been discovered at the Etruscan sites of Marzabotto and Spina. These were founded about 500 B.C., long before Hippodamus began work at Piraeus. The innovation may well have originated at more than one place. A kind of planning has already been noted at Biskupin, in northern Poland, where the streets must have been laid out and the huts built perhaps a century before even those of Marzabotto. Rectilinear planning makes such effective use of restricted space that it would be surprising if it did not originate at many centers. The Romans adopted such a plan in their military camps and then in the cities that they founded. In many of the latter the Roman plan has survived with little alteration into modern times. Its use was revived during the Middle Ages, and it became the basis of urban planning throughout the United States.

Such was the *polis* of the Greeks, a restricted area of land with an urban central place, the two intimately linked politically, economically, and socially. The *polis* had its own government, though its independence was often qualified by membership in a league or confederation of *poleis*. It is almost impossible to enumerate the *poleis* of Greece in the fifth and fourth centuries B.C. They lay around the Aegean "like frogs around a pond." In all, about 340 *poleis* were at one time or another members of the Athenian League, but the total is far larger than this, since few lying at any great distance from the sea were ever brought within the alliance. In all, there may have been 200 in the Greek peninsula and perhaps 700 over the whole Aegean region.

Their range in size was wide. Athens itself, unquestionably the largest, may have had a population of about 300,000 at the height of its prosperity. But this size was exceptional. Xenophon regarded a city of 5000 as large,[15] and this was for the *polis* as a whole, including such of the population as continued to live in the countryside. The rural population of Attica remained large, perhaps as great as that of its central place, and when, in the face of Spartan invasion, it sought refuge within the city's walls, it caused appalling congestion and suffering.

The idea of the *polis* spread northward into continental Europe and westward around the shores of the Mediterranean (fig. 3.2). In the main it was carried by the Greeks themselves, who sailed westward to Italy and beyond to found colonies. Their purpose was in some instances commercial, but more often colonies were founded because population had grown too large in the mother city. The colony was as much like its parent city as was practicble, and in turn it too became a center of urbane living. The Greeks were discriminating in their choice of sites. They looked for a climate similar to that of the Aegean, for their open-air, face-to-face way of life could be lived only where the climate was sunny and warm. They settled the coastal lowlands of eastern Sicily and southern Italy, but their physical presence, if not their cultural influence, extended little beyond Naples or Epirus. In the western Mediterranean they founded settlements at Massilia, the modern Marseilles, which became the basis for their commercial and cultural intercourse with the Celts of Gaul and Spain.

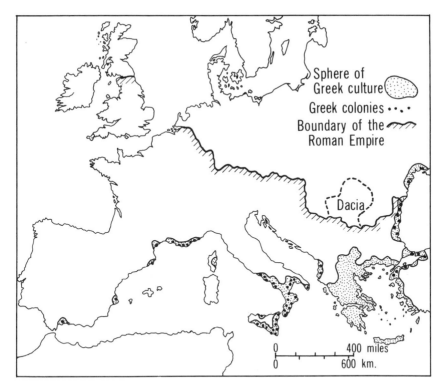

3.2. The frontiers of classical civilization, showing the expansion of
the Romans beyond the world of the Greeks.

The military campaigns and conquests of Alexander the Great, between 334 and his
death in 323 B.C., were followed by the foundation of some twenty Greek-style cities
between Anatolia in the west and the river Indus in the east. But this was sterile ground
for so fragile a growth as the Greek *polis*. Their purpose was military, and, though some
acquired the trappings of a city, they never became the scenes of political life as the
Greeks understood it. Indeed, only a few of them, including Alexandria in Egypt, have
survived as cities.

The institution of the *polis* was adopted by the Etruscans and Latins in Italy and,
somewhat modified, was passed to the Celts of western and central Europe. The
Etruscan cities of central Italy were only a little younger than the *poleis* of the Aegean, and
it is debatable whether their inspiration derived from the Greeks in southern Italy or
whether they developed locally from Iron Age antecedents. They formed a large group
that was spread northward from Rome to the Po valley. They tended to occupy sites well
protected by nature, and some—Veii, Caere, Perugia, and Orvieto, for example—
covered large areas and were protected by massive walls and gates.

Another urban, colonizing people at this time were the Phoenicians. They made
Carthage in Tunisia their chief base in the western Mediterranean, and from here
established colonies in Sicily and Spain. Phoenician cities were more narrowly based
than Greek. Their purpose was primarily commercial. Agriculture was of little impor-

tance, and no attempt was made to occupy the surrounding territory. There was no evidence for the symbiotic relationship of rural territory and central place represented in the *polis*. Furthermore, the cities were always coastally located, and their preferred site was an offshore island that gave them access to the sea and protection from the often hostile peoples of the nearby land.

The *oppida* of Late Iron Age Europe had affinities with the city-states of the Mediterranean region. They, too, were the central places for a tribal area; they had a resident, socially structured population that practiced crafts and carried on trade. They were strongly fortified and served as places of refuge for the people of their region. But the late La Tène Celts, who built the *oppida*, had not really begun to beautify their cities, to construct temples and stoas, and to create systems of water supply and the means of entertainment.

From City-State to Empire

Of all the city-states of Italy, that of Rome was to become by far the most important. It originated as a group of huts, no different from those of any other Iron Age settlement, located on the flattened summit of the Palatine Hill. Other villages were established on neighboring hills. About 575 B.C. this archaic Rome merged into early classical Rome. There must have been some kind of synoecism, whereby these villages were brought within a single city, and the whole was enclosed by the Servian wall. At the same time the city began to be dignified, in true Hellenic style, with temples and other public buildings, and to take on the aspect of a *polis*.

There was nothing in the siting or development of early Rome to suggest that it was within five centuries to become the capital of a vast empire. No Greek city ever established a lasting hegemony within the Greek world. The so-called Athenian Empire was in fact merely a league of city-states bound together to resist any renewed attack from the Persians. It was short-lived and broke up in confusion during the Peloponnesian War. The empire of Alexander lay mainly in Asia and disintegrated into the Hellenistic states soon after the death of its founder. The history of Roman expansion was very different. It developed more slowly; it progressed into areas less, not more, civilized than itself; and its direction of growth was, by and large, toward the north and northwest, into regions with a climate very different from that of the Mediterranean and with cultures immeasurably poorer. The Romans were led on from one conquest to the next by the ever-present danger from neighboring barbarian peoples, until in the first century A.D. they reached the line of the Rhine and the Danube. Here, with only minor changes, their boundary was to remain for four centuries.

The tasks that the Romans set themselves within the boundaries of their empire were very different from those envisioned by the Greeks. The latter expanded their culture area by exporting part of themselves. But their numbers were few, and thus the territory that they brought within their orbit was very small. By contrast, the Romans assumed a civilizing mission within a vast empire that they had conquered by force of arms. The Greeks made little impact on the barbarians among whom they settled. The Romans, by contrast, were conscious of a civilizing mission, to be achieved by the destruction of tribal loyalties and the foundation of cities. Their boundary against the barbarian world was carefully defined, as if to say to the tribes beyond, "thus far and no farther may you come." But this boundary did not, in material terms, mark an abrupt transition from a high cultural level within the empire to a lower "barbarian" level without. Even when the empire ended in the west in A.D. 476, it had not everywhere been brought up to a uniformly high level. "There were always barbarians within the Roman Empire," wrote Ramsey MacMullen, "left to themselves in remote mountains and deserts, or recently incorporated by conquest."[16] Many of these people were Roman citizens, and, after A.D. 212, all of them. Yet the culture of Rome had little impact on some of them, and its most valuable contribution to their welfare was the peace that it ensured for them to pursue their traditional ways of life. Such "barbarians" may have been few within Italy, but they were numerous in most parts of Spain except Andalusia and the Mediterranean coastlands. Rome had little impact on the Celtic peoples of western Gaul and western Britain and, perhaps, even less on the descendents of the Illyrians and the Thracians in the Balkan peninsula. Latin never became the universal language of the empire. There were islands of *latinitas* around the towns that the Romans had founded, but Celtic dialects and east European languages like Thracian continued to be spoken in rural districts. We have it on the authority of St. Jerome that a Celtic tongue continued in the fifth century to be spoken by the *Treveri* not far from the large Roman administrative center of Trier.[17]

But the survival of pre-Latin languages and personal names by no means implies that in material terms the native peoples had not gained by contact with the Romans. The archeological evidence, from Britain to the Balkans, shows a rural population living in just the same way, except more peacefully, as in the pre-Roman Iron Age. In southwestern Britain, an area in which the Romans showed some interest on account of its tin, there were people living in hut circles, roughly built of local "moorstone" or granite, and "throughout the Roman occupation the natives of southern Britain lived very much the same life as before."[18] At the other end of Europe the situation was similar. Neither the civilization of Greece nor that of Rome ever had much influence on the tribes of the Balkan peninsula. But, however primitive such peoples may have been, they cannot have been wholly uninfluenced by the culture of Rome. Their huts, settlement patterns, and modes of agriculture may have been those of the pre-Roman Iron Age, but they must at some time have experienced the passage through their territory of a Roman cohort or a Greek trader; they must have acquired the odd weapon or piece of pottery from the romanized settlers. They must, like remote African peoples at the end of the nineteenth century, have wondered suspiciously at the strange works of civilization in the distant town or trading post, but treasured nonetheless the odd trinket or tool that came from there.

If there were islands of pre-Roman barbarism within the empire, there was evidence also for the impact of Roman culture beyond its borders. Despite recurring conflict, the frontier was a zone of intercourse, where Roman and barbarian met and traded, where people from beyond the imperial limits were recruited for service in the Roman army. Our guide to the peoples of central Europe must be Tacitus, whose *Germania* portrays a fluid tribal organization, settled agriculture, and frequent conflict. It was a structured society, in which chiefs lived in a kind of barbaric splendor, happy to obtain by commerce or raiding some of the appurtenances of sophisticated Roman living. Roman artifacts, not only pottery and wine bottles but also drinking vessels and bronze statuary, have been found deep within "barbarian" Europe.[19]

Within the empire the city was the principal instrument of romanization. In Italy and other parts of the Mediterranean littoral, urban development was as old as Rome itself. It derived from Greek, Phoenician, or Etruscan tradition. Italy, before the creation of the empire, was made up of small city-states, less independent than those of the Greek world, but in their social organization and economic base not wholly dissimilar. But as the Romans spread into areas that had not been hellenized, they found that they had to create their own urban structure. This they did in three ways.

In the first place, the Romans founded colonies—*coloniae*—which partook in some measure of the character of Greek colonies. This practice had begun in Italy as early as the fourth century B.C. In the second century B.C. the first colonies outside the limits of Italy were established. Their motivation was more political than demographic. Their primary purpose was to secure conquered territory, and their earliest citizens were veterans of the Roman legions. Colonies continued to be founded until the second century A.D. At the same time the serving soldier also established settlements—large forts for garrisons, smaller ones to serve as marching camps. These, like the *coloniae,* were carefully planned. They were rectangular and were surrounded by bank, ditch, and palisade. Within the ramparts were two principal roads, joining the middle points of each opposite pair of sides. These, known as the *cardo* and *decumatus,* were the axes about which were organized the buildings of the settlement. This regular and uniform plan was probably adopted first in the legionary forts and was taken over in at least the later *coloniae,* founded for time-expired legionaries. The forts cannot themselves be regarded as towns; their function was military, but they attracted a civil population to their vicinity. This group, made up of craftsmen and servants, inhabited a *canaba,* an irregular settlement close to the fort itself.

But most cities of the Roman Empire derived from the defended settlements that already existed at the time of the Roman Conquest. Largest and most important of these were the *oppida,* which have already been described. Some, rebuilt and extended, continued under Roman rule to be the central places of local districts, *civitates,* which had replaced the tribal areas of the Celts. Others were moved a short distance. The Romans were rightly suspicious of the strongly fortified, hilltop *oppida* of the Celts and were determined to remove this threat to their authority. The *oppida* that had offered such strenuous resistance to Julius Caesar, such as Alesia, Bibracte, and Gergovia, were forcibly abandoned in favor of open cities newly planted on the plain below. The same happened in Britain and other parts of the empire. In Britain, Bagendon camp was replaced by Corinium (Cirencester), two miles away; Maiden Castle by Durnovaria (Dorchester), and Prae Wood by Verulamium, replaced in its turn by St. Albans.

The style of urbanism imposed by Rome upon the European provinces of the empire differed in some respects from the ideal of the Greek *polis.* The latter was a small, self-governing territory with an elaborately developed central place. The Roman town with its encompassing territory was a unit in an imperial system of administration. Towns were of varying status, according to who settled them and their degree of self-govern-ment. But Roman towns differed from Greek in other respects. They were not, at least in the first instance, intended to be defensible places. Legionary forts were, of course, enclosed by wall, bank, and ditch, but the ordinary civil settlement was open and undefended. To have allowed its citizens to fortify themselves would have been contrary to Rome's policy of maintaining peace so profound that warfare would be unknown. Aelius Aristeides, apostrophizing the empire in the second century, even claimed that warfare had disappeared from human memory. Such a claim was exaggerated; the peace of the empire was not unbroken. There was always conflict along its frontiers, and within there were sporadic revolts as the patience or the tolerance of one people after another was stretched to the breaking point by Rome's disregard for its practices and traditions.

But the greatest danger came from beyond the empire's boundaries. Before the end of the third century, Germanic tribes had broken across the line of the Rhine and Danube and had raided deep into imperial territory. Cities were quickly fortified against them, and many of these late Roman defenses survive today, showing all the evidence of hasty construction.

It is difficult to form any estimate of the population of cities of the Roman Empire. Their area can in many instances be measured. Some were very large, covering 250 acres or more, and Nîmes, Vienne, and Autun were each little less than a square mile in extent. Their population may, however, not have been as large as these remains suggest. Many, especially those in the provinces of the empire, were not closely settled, and their houses were often built on an atrium plan, with rooms opening off a central court. There were also large gardens and numerous open spaces. That many towns had only a low housing density is apparent from the sharp reduction that could be made in their area when it became necessary to cast a wall around them. In one case, Autun, the walled area was reduced from about 500 acres to 25, which suggests a very small urban population at this time. The great majority of Roman town sites continue to be inhabited, and whatever evidence there may be for their size and plan lies deeply buried beneath the accretion of almost two thousand years. But a few have been abandoned and can today be excavated and studied. Among them are the Italian cities of Pompeii and Herculaneum (Pompei and Ercolano in modern Italian), overwhelmed by the eruption of Vesuvius in A.D. 79; the British towns of Silchester, Wroxeter, Caistor-by-Norwich, and Caerwent; Ostia near the mouth of the Tiber; and, close to the imperial frontier in central Europe, Augst and Petronell.

Both Pompeii and Herculaneum were closely built up, with rows of houses and shops (figs. 3.3, 3.4). They had a density of perhaps seventy-five people to the acre. Silchester, by contrast, was a garden city, with, in all probability, fewer than five to the acre. This figure compares favorably with the housing density in most medieval towns, and very favorably indeed with that of industrial towns of the nineteenth century. To all this, however, the city of Rome was an exception. It was both large and densely built and was as far removed as was possible from the garden city of Silchester. "Old Athens and old Rome," wrote Boethius, "were both shapeless and irregular."[20] So also were most of the Italic cities of central Italy, but, unlike the latter, Rome continued to grow and became the largest city of antiquity, and probably the biggest to be seen in Europe before the nineteenth century. During the early years of the empire it spread far beyond its walls, and when the Aurelian Wall was built in A.D. 271–75, the city covered almost seven square miles, and its population may have reached half a million. At least 40 percent of this vast area was occupied by public buildings. Toward its periphery were the spacious villas of the rich, but much of the central area was horribly congested as well as badly built. The city authorities controlled the location and construction of public buildings, but there was little oversight of private development. The height of apartment blocks was restricted, and, after the fire of A.D. 64 the materials of which they were built were regulated, but no attempt was made to check the spread of the city.

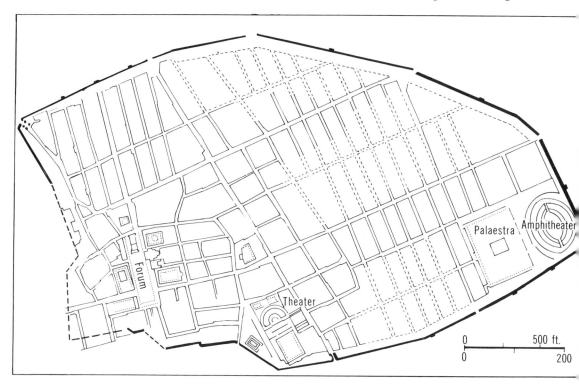

Palaestra · Amphitheater

Forum

Theater

0   500 ft.
0   200

3.3. The street plan of a Roman city: Pompeii. An area of slightly
irregular streets surrounds the Forum, but the rest of the city has
been developed on a very regular plan. Note the theater,
amphitheater, and "palaestra," or place for games and wrestling.

Building—Public and Private

Dwellings were of two types. There were rows of *tabernae,* shops with habitable rooms
behind and above (fig. 3.5). The demand for space led their owners to add a third and
even a fourth floor to the buildings whose mud-brick walls were incapable of supporting
safely even a second. What inhabitant of Praeneste or Tivoli, asked Juvenal, "was ever
afraid of his house tumbling down? . . . here we inhabit a city supported for the most
part by slender props; for that is how the bailiff holds up the tottering house, patches up
gaping cracks in the old wall, bidding the inmates sleep at ease under a roof ready to
tumble about their ears."[21] Cicero had been the owner of such property and wrote to his
friend Atticus that "two of my *tabernae* have fallen down and the rest are cracking: so not
only the tenants, but even the mice have migrated."[22] How contemporary it all seems.
This was the Rome that burned in the great fire of A.D. 64. It was rebuilt of masonry, with
travertine, tufa, or kiln-fired brick replacing sun-dried mud. This improvement may
have reduced the risks but did nothing to diminish the squalor, congestion, and
discomfort. Much of the rebuilding took the form of tenement blocks. Many rose to six
stories. Some were built around very small courts that served to light the interior rooms,
and most were constructed of stone, brick, or cement. How many such *insulae* there may

3.4. A street in Pompeii, destroyed in A.D. 79 by an eruption of Vesuvius, seen in the distance. Note the paved street, the sidewalks, and the stepping stones for crossing the road. The spaces between the stones were adjusted to the wheels of the carts that used the street.

3.5. A street in Ostia, showing one of the city blocks, with *tabernae,* or shops. A third floor has been destroyed. The structure is entirely of thin bricks.

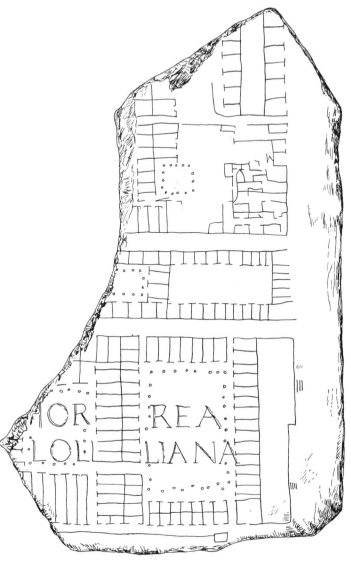

3.6. A fragment of the Roman city plan, known as the *Forma Urbis*. It shows, above, city housing, and below, the granary called *Horrea Lolliana.*

have been is not known. Suetonius spoke of the *immensus numerus insularum,* and the fragmentary plan of the city known as the *Forma Urbis* shows the ground plan of some of them (fig. 3.6).[23] These *insulae* were the result of Rome's peculiar problems of over-crowding. They were to be found also at Ostia, but there is little evidence for the building of apartment blocks, at least on this scale, elsewhere in the empire. Conditions of life within them must have been horrific: dark, overcrowded, and insanitary. Many continued to be inhabited by the diminished population of the early Middle Ages, and, under greatly altered circumstances, they appeared again to house the industrial pro-letariat of nineteenth-century cities. There was, however, some compensation. The urban masses of Rome were dangerous and pampered, and the emperors vied to provide

3.7. Rome: a row of shops near the Forum.

them with a minimal food supply and with baths and entertainment that took them away from their squalid quarters. Some of their places of entertainment—the Coliseum and the Baths of Caracalla and of Diocletian—are among the largest if not also the most attractive of the surviving monuments of classical Rome.

Other Italic cities, as well as many in Spain and Greece, must have been small-scale replicas of Rome, congested and overcrowded. But in the provinces, where the towns were founded and planned by the Romans on virgin sites, they were spacious and regular. Streets were straighter and wider; houses were larger and many were built around a courtyard, or atrium. No doubt there was an urban proletariat in such cities as Lyons, Nîmes, and even London, living in cramped quarters and perhaps in tenement blocks like those of Rome, but much of the housing was low density, and there were numerous open spaces.

A considerable area in all Roman towns was given over to the forum, which corresponded to the Greek *agora,* to baths, and to temples. To this extent the Roman *civitas* inherited the traditions of the Greek *polis.* Beyond its walls there might have been a theater or a stadium, for these took up a great deal of space and attracted large crowds. This is why a number of stadia have survived, while the forum, lying near the city center, has been built over.

Little has survived of the domestic buildings in most provincial cities of the empire; the standing structures at Ostia, Pompeii, and Herculaneum are quite exceptional and allow us to examine the plan of Roman urban housing. Ostia became, late in the republican period, the chief port of Rome, from which grain, imported from Africa, was sent up to the city by barge. It was thus more nearly a working-class city than the others, though it was not without its spacious villas. It was a "miniature Rome," and, since many of its buildings have survived, it is possible to see clearly what those of Rome must have looked like. The tenement blocks that are so conspicuous at Ostia are almost absent from Pompeii, a middle-class town of shopkeepers and craftsmen. Herculaneum, only partially excavated, was in part a town of elegant villas, built on the gentle slopes rising from the Bay of Naples; in part, of humble dwellings of ordinary people, fishermen and workers of all kinds. The Roman towns that have been excavated in Britain show nothing of the congestion of the Italic city. There were few *tabernae,* and much of the housing consisted of large, villa-like residences, which must have been the homes of well-to-do rentiers and rural landowners. But London was different. It was in all probability closer to Pompeii or Ostia in its plan and development, but such evidence of London's Roman housing as survives is buried beneath medieval and modern urban growth.

Building materials differed greatly. Traditional materials like wood, mud bricks, wattle, and clay continued to be used in towns but were supplemented increasingly with masonry construction and, above all, with bricks. Augustus, it was said, "found Rome a city of mud-bricks and left it a city of marble." This is exaggerated. Much of the city was still of unburned brick at the time of Nero's fire. Only after this tragedy were the huge *insulae* rebuilt with kiln-fired bricks and concrete. Rome had an abundance of good building stones. Foremost among them were travertine, a soft, attractive and easily worked limestone, quarried from the hills to the east of the city, and tufa, consisting essentially of compacted volcanic dust. No marble was to be found in the vicinity of Rome. The nearest came from Carrara, two hundred miles to the northwest, and much of that which was used in public buildings had been imported from Greece.

One of the more commonly used materials was *pozzolana* cement. This consisted mainly of volcanic dust, which had accumulated in thick deposits in the Alban Hills, to the southeast of the city. Mixed with lime, it provided a cement that set hard, even under water, and was much used in the monumental architecture of the empire. The practice—one can hardly call it the secret—of using cement disappeared from the later empire, and its reintroduction into European building in the nineteenth century revolutionized the construction industry. The most significant Roman innovation, however, was the use of bricks of kiln-fired clay. Roman bricks varied in size but were in general thinner and larger overall than those used in late medieval and modern times. The Romans became extremely skilled in brick construction. Brick was used as facing for large buildings, such as tenement blocks, as lacing or reinforcement in walls of rubble masonry, and, set on edge, as relieving arches over doorways and windows and in the massive barrel vaults with which the Romans learned to roof their vast buildings.

The Romans, like the Greeks, adapted their architecture to the materials at hand. The latter, with an abundance of hard, strong marble, tended toward a trabeate style, with beams and lintels to bridge open spaces. The Romans lacked this physical advantage but used brick and cement in the only way practicable, to build arched vaults and semicircular door and window openings.

A further contrast between Greek and Roman building styles stemmed from divergent attitudes toward public buildings. To the Greeks these structures were intended to be viewed from *outside*. Theirs was an outdoor world. They showed little concern for decorating interiors. No doubt the sunny climate and the clean air intensified this tendency to emphasize the landscape aspect of their buildings. Their neglect of interiors extended to private homes, which appear, in general, to have been small, simple, and unadorned. The aim of the Roman, by contrast, "was above all to create and adorn *interiors,* larger and more magnificent interiors to match imperial pride and the growing self-consciousness and importance of the individual."[24] The monumental architecture of Rome was built to be viewed from inside, and, seen from outside, was often poorly, even crudely, designed. The Pantheon, sometimes regarded as the supreme architectural expression of the Roman genius, is hardly an appealing structure when viewed from the piazza in front. The same would have been true of the great basilicas and bathhouses built across the city of Rome and in almost every city of the provinces. They were intended to be used, not looked at, and this tradition of plain exteriors and decorated interiors lasted well into the Middle Ages.

The practice of elaborating the interiors of buildings extended to private homes. Greek housing had been austere and simple. Roman housing was at first similar but became increasingly complex and elaborate in the later republican period. By the second century B.C. houses were being built with both atrium and peristyle, the former being a small and partially covered court around which were disposed the principal living rooms; the latter, a larger courtyard with a garden, open to the sky and surrounded usually by a colonnade and a covered walk. The house of the Vettii at Pompeii (fig. 3.8) is typical of such houses—spacious, comfortable, inward-looking, and very private. This dwelling appears to have been the home of a well-to-do merchant before its destruction.

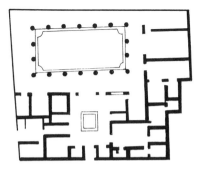

3.8. The House of the Vettii, Pompeii.

The *triclinium,* or principal living room, was richly decorated, and in most of the *cubiculae,* or bedrooms, there were wall paintings of Greek myths. Even humbler homes than that of the Vettii were built around an atrium, producing a courtyard house of a kind that was to remain part of the European tradition until modern times. The atrium house of Pompeii, Herculaneum (fig. 3.9), or Ostia foreshadows the Renaissance palaces of Italy, with their forbidding exteriors, narrow entrances, and light and airy courts within.

It is an open question how far down the social scale one finds homes of this pattern. It is unlikely that the ordinary people would have enjoyed the comfort and privacy of the

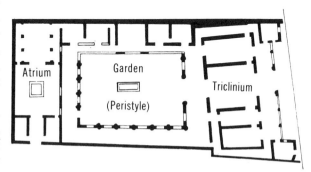

3.9. The House with the Mosaic Atrium, Herculaneum.

traditional Italic house. The excavation of Herculaneum has revealed a very wide range in the quality of domestic architecture. Each block of the town appears to have been "occupied by two or three rich and spacious houses, whilst the rest is taken up by more modest dwellings, huddled in narrow spaces and obliged to add upper storeys in order to gain sufficient floor-space."[25] Such dwellings commonly incorporated a shop, its wide-arched front opening onto the street, and, behind and above it, the dwelling apartments of its owner. Such combined shops and houses can still be seen close to Trajan's Forum in Rome, at Herculaneum, and, above all, at Ostia.[26] Such buildings ran to three or even four floors, and culminated in the *insulae,* which have already been described. Privacy, one of the dominant features of the atrium house, was lost in these humbler dwellings.

The evidence from Silchester shows conclusively that the earliest urban housing in the provinces was of wood and clay, not significantly different from that found at contemporary Iron Age sites.[27] Then, probably early in the second century, the rectilinear road pattern was laid out, and new homes, built partly or largely of masonry, were aligned along it. These dwellings differed fundamentally from those to be met with in Italy. Most consisted essentially of rectangular houses, with wings projecting from their extremities to enclose, in part at least, a courtyard. A covered portico was commonly built along at least one side of the court, giving a superficial resemblance to the classic peristyle. It is apparent, however, that the house to be found at Silchester derives more from the rural villa than from the Italic atrium house.

The Romans gave much attention to other less visible though no less important aspects of urbanism: piped water-supply, toilets, and the means of sewage disposal. In these respects Roman cities marked a considerable advance over Greek. The Romans were noteworthy for their hydraulic engineering. In some instances a supply of pure water was available close at hand. In others it had to be brought by conduit and aqueduct from a considerable distance. Rome itself was supplied by a complex system of canals from the Apennine foothills thirty miles away. The labor involved in their construction was immense. Even today, the shattered fragments of the Claudian aqueduct appear to dominate the Campagna to the southeast of Rome (fig. 3.10). Frontinus, who had been appointed *curator aquarum* in A.D. 97, left a treatise on the city's water supply.[28] He took an immense pride in the works that he supervised: "with such an array of indispensable structures," he wrote, "compare, if you will, the idle pyramids or the useless, though famous, works of the Greeks." The waterworks of Rome in scale and sophistication outdid those of every other city of the empire. Indeed, they had to in order to supply a city of more than half a million people. But every Roman city had its assured supply. Water was conducted over hill and vale. Shallow valleys were bridged, waterproof conduits were built across those too deep to cross in any other way, and siphons—a peculiarly Roman invention—were used to carry water across hills. Even today, the *Pont du Gard,* near Nîmes, the aqueduct that once supplied the hilltop city of Segovia, in Spain, or the stumps that are all that remain of the systems at Merida and Lyons, are impressive reminders both of the skill of the Roman engineers and the scale of their work. Not until the late nineteenth century were comparable works again erected in Europe.

No less necessary were the means of disposing of human and domestic waste. At Ostia is a domestic toilet with a pierced seat, no different from what one would find in a Western home at the beginning of the present century. But such private latrines do not appear to have been common. Most people relied on public toilets, each consisting of a

3.10. The Claudian aqueduct as it crosses the Campagna southeast of Rome. It brought water from springs in the Apennines, nearly forty miles away.

row of seats and totally lacking in privacy. Most towns had such "sociable latrines," and in the North African town of Lepcis Magna, there still remains a bank of over twenty toilet seats. This concentration of facilities was probably made desirable by the difficulty of clearing the excrement. The Romans do not appear to have used flowing water to clear their latrines—that was a somewhat unexpected development of the later Middle Ages. At Silchester a pit was dug in the garden adjoining each house and continued to be used, in all probability, until it had to be filled in and replaced with another. Blocks that made up more densely built cities were "honeycombed" with sewage pits, such as have been excavated in many medieval towns. One must never forget, when looking at the ruins of an urban site, that before the later nineteenth century, the stench of sewage was an ever-present evil. How contemporaries accustomed themselves to it, we cannot know.

Despite the not inconsiderable differences between Roman and Greek urbanism, both were the means whereby relatively large communities were enabled to live more rewarding lives than would otherwise have been possible. It was a very sociable way of life that characterized the classical city. The development of drama and philosophical dialogue was not inevitable, but without a "face-to-face" society, neither one would have been imaginable. Classical urbanism, without making any significant innovation—merely by refining and integrating elements that had existed in the earlier Iron Age cultures—made a fundamental and lasting contribution to the material culture of Western man.

The town, in the first place, consolidated its role as the central place of a distinct territory, for which it offered market facilities and a wide range of social, political, and administrative services. This arrangement had in some respects been anticipated in the

3.11. A horse-drawn, four-wheeled wagon, from a Gallic bas-relief. (After Esperandieu, *Recueil des bas reliefs, statues et bustes de la Gaule romaine* [Paris, 1907–15], 1:458.)

oppida and tribal capitals of Iron Age Europe, but the classical city institutionalized these relationships and made them permanent. A symbiotic relationship between the town and its surrounding country developed and dominated crafts, commerce, and cultural life until the emergence in the nineteenth century of the specialized industrial city. The country supplied grain and other foodstuffs to the town. The town reciprocated by providing the products of its crafts and, above all, its cultural amenities.

Despite the open character of its society, the classical city encouraged the concept of privacy. There was little privacy in the life of the Greek *polis,* but the town house of the well-to-do Roman was designed to cut the household off from the bustle of street and forum. The peristyle was, in effect, a very private garden, and from it developed the cloister, the architectural expression of retreat from the world. Thus the two contrary ideals, the creative stimulus of discussion and debate, of drama and public ceremony on the one hand, and contemplation and study on the other, both derive from the physical conditions of the classical city.

Lastly, the Roman city, if not also the Greek, established patterns of urban planning and of housing that are with us still. The concept of the rectilinear town plan ran through medieval urban development and underlies much of modern city growth. The regular arrangement of houses along a rudimentary street had been known in preclassical Iron Age settlements, but the system of rows of contiguous, masonry-built houses, with upper floors reached by an internal staircase, is Roman. So also is the ground-floor shop, opening onto the street, and also the *insula,* or apartment block of several stories. All these urban features, except the last, which did not make its unwelcome reappearance until modern times, continued to characterize the medieval and modern city. And if the Middle Ages failed to live up to Roman ideals in the matter of water supply and sanitation, the latter nevertheless continued to serve as models.

The historian Michael Rostovtseff once described the Roman Empire as "a vast federation of city-states." The *civitas,* heir to the *polis,* was the unit of which it was built. It is a mistake to translate both of these terms as "city." They denoted something broader than an urban settlement. They embraced both the urban central-place and a surrounding area, more or less large, of rural territory. Citizenship was not restricted to those who lived within the city itself; it extended to rural dwellers, some of whom might never have visited the urban central-place. In this, Rome only developed and extended a Greek concept. One cannot say how many of the inhabitants of the *polis* or *civitas* lived within or near its urban central-place and could enjoy its amenities. Their number must have varied greatly from one *polis,* one *civitas,* to another. A considerable part of the population of the *polis* of Athens lived outside the city, in villages and on farms. Indeed, if we are to believe Aristophanes, many an urbanite looked:

> . . . fondly countrywards, longing for peace,
> Loathing the town, sick for my village-home,
> Which never cried, "Come, buy my charcoal,
> My vinegar, my oil, my anything,"
> But freely gave us all.[29]

This is the city dweller's romantic view of the distant countryside. Nevertheless, life in one of the larger cities, with its noise and smells, its shortages and overcrowding, must have led many to question why they had ever left their rural homes. In Mediterranean Europe it is likely that a high proportion of the total population, whether or not it was engaged in agriculture, lived in townlike agglomerations from which it made its daily journey to the sometimes distant fields. This tradition has lasted till the present in southern Europe. In northern, on the other hand, towns absorbed only a small proportion of the population. In Roman Britain, for example, twenty to twenty-five places might have qualified as urban. The largest was London, but its population could not have been more than 36,000. On the other hand, Silchester, in many ways a typical provincial city, had no more than 4,000. The urban population of Roman Britain is unlikely, even in the second century when it was at its greatest, to have been much more than 100,000. This figure, in a total population of over two million, does not suggest that the country was highly urbanized. And many parts of the empire, notably the Danubian and Balkan provinces, had fewer and smaller cities than Britain.[30]

Rural Living

The great majority of the population of the Roman Empire lived in villages and hamlets and on isolated farms. We cannot know to what extent this rural majority shared in the life of the urban central-place. Of course, many drove their animals or carried their produce to the urban market and may have stayed on to gape, like country dwellers in every period, at urban sophistication. But this was possible only for those who lived within a short day's journey of the city. To most inhabitants of a *civitas* the city itself was a distant and almost foreign place. They were *pagani*—country folk. That the term later acquired a religious connotation is due to the fact that Christianity was itself spread from the cities and came last to the pagans who lived in remote country areas.

The villa was an intermediary in the slow process of Romanizing the countryside. It

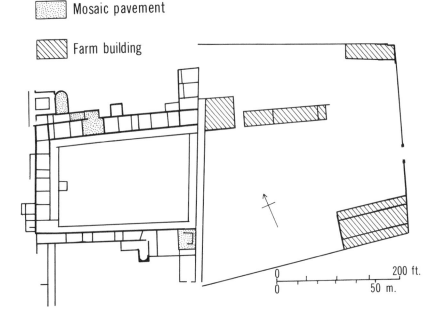

3.12. A fully developed villa at Bignor in southern England. The farm buildings occupied the forecourt to the east.

was the focus of a rural estate. In Italy the term was used for the elegant homes of the rich, such as were to be found along the shore, near Ostia, where the younger Pliny had his rural home, or at Tivoli, where the emperor Hadrian built his exquisite retreat. But throughout the provinces the villa was in most instances a working farm, owned by a rich provincial or, in a few rare cases, by a Roman who had settled there and had acquired land (fig. 3.12). Villas varied greatly in size, style, and degree of sophistication. Some, like Fishbourne in Sussex, England, were more palaces than homes. Others, like manor houses of a later age, allowed their owners to live comfortably if not elegantly. Some contained workshops and were, in effect, the centers of almost self-sufficing estates.

The villa consisted typically of a residential range, with colonnaded porch along its principal—usually south-facing—aspect. From it, wings protruded, partially enclosing a courtyard. The wings contained quarters for the servants or slaves and also workshops and farm buildings. Their plan and construction depended on local conditions. Most were built as much of timber as of masonry, and roofed with thatch as well as tile. Some had tessellated, or mosaic, pavements in the principal rooms, made from small colored stones laid in pictorial designs. There was sometimes a hypocaust, or underground fireplace, which heated the saunalike bathhouse; tile-built pillars supported the floor, while the smoke circulated between them. In many respects the villa replicated the luxurious urban house. It also served as a focus of Romanization. Some of its values and artifacts were doubtless adopted in the huts of the local peasantry, but the urban culture of Rome faded rapidly through the encompassing zone of villas and was barely perceptible out on the fringes of the *civitas*.

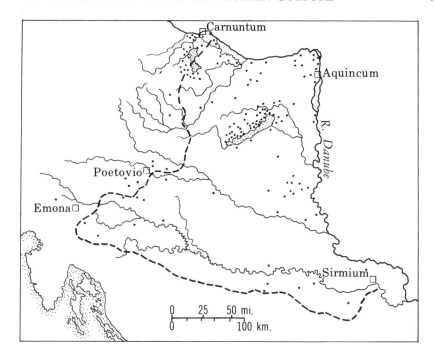

3.13. Distribution of villas in Pannonia. They cluster around the few towns but are particularly numerous on the south-facing slopes above Lake Balaton.

Figures 3.13 and 3.14 represent the villas that have been located in the province of Pannonia—essentially trans-Danubian Hungary—together with the location of inscriptions that have so far been discovered. The villas represent the first phase in the Romanization of the countryside; the inscriptions, the second. Beyond the latter, the impact of Rome must have been minimal, and popular culture was that of the Late Iron Age, as it had been before the Romans came to this Danubian province.

The rural population lived mostly in villages. Their houses were built of wood and differed in no significant respect from those of pre-Roman inhabitants. Some would have been sunk below ground level, so that their low walls supported only rough rafters and a thatch. Their inhabitants were engaged mainly in small-scale subsistence farming. Despite the writings of the Roman agronomists from Varro to Columella, very little is known about the practical aspects of farming. The experts wrote for the instruction of wealthy landowners and were concerned more with the management of an estate and the cultivation of exotic plants than with plowing the land. We are left with a considerable knowledge of how to graft a fruit tree but in total ignorance of how the fields were organized or of the kind of plow used.

All the evidence suggests that little advance was made in the practice of agricultue. In the Greek *polis,* land was mostly farmed in small peasant units. There is some slight evidence for estates, but these were very much the exception. In early Italy, also, small farms prevailed, at least until the time of the Hannibalic wars of the late third century

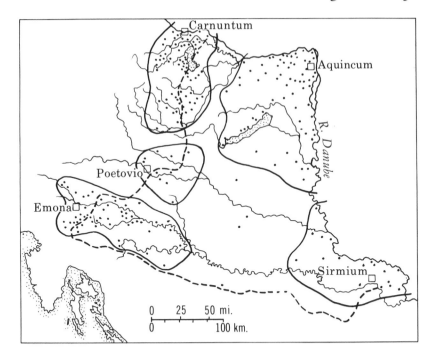

3.14. Distribution of Latin inscriptions in the Roman province of
Pannonia (eastern Austria and Trans-Danubian Hungary). The solid
lines delimit what may be taken as "city regions."

B.C.[31] Thereafter, and perhaps in consequence of the devastation of these years, the small
farm gave way to the large—the *latifundium*—whose broad acres were cultivated by
slave labor. Roman writers lamented the loss of the class of small, independent farmers,
as moralists have always done; *latifundia perdidere Italiam,* wrote the elder Pliny—"great
estates have been the ruin of Italy"—but it was these estates which supported the villas
of the provinces and the elegant life-style of the provincial elite.

It is doubtful, however, whether the organization of the land made much difference
to the actual practice of agriculture. Whether carried on by free peasants or servile
dependents, farming employed the same methods and tools and produced similar crops,
and these showed little advance on those of the pre-Roman Iron Age. The size and shape
of fields have always been dictated by conditions of plowing. Classical peoples, like
Bronze and Iron Age cultivators, used a light wooden plow, or *aratrum.* It consisted
essentially of a *sole,* which cut through the soil, a handle by which it was held into the
ground, and a beam to harness it to the ox. There were many ways to construct such a
plow. The most common, on the evidence of vase painting, was that shown in figure 3.15. The three components were fashioned separately and mortised together. This
light plow stirred the soil without turning it over and burying the weeds. Fields were
sometimes—perhaps regularly—plowed twice, once in each direction. The plow could
be carried to the fields and turned easily at the end of the furrow. There was no premium
on large fields, and the scanty evidence suggests that classical fields were, like the
"Celtic" ones before them, small and roughly square. There is no reason to suppose that

3.15. Decoration on a Greek bowl showing plowing and sowing. Light plows are shown, each drawn by two oxen.

in these respects agrarian conditions changed under the Roman Empire, and it seems unlikely that the practice of tilling the soil on large estates was any different from that on a humble peasant farm. There were in this respect no economies of scale.

A new type of plow, which was many centuries later to revolutionize agriculture, did, however, make its appearance

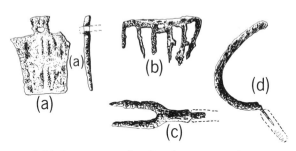

3.16. Roman agricultural tools: (*a*) mattock; (*b*) rake; (*c*) light fork; (*d*) sickle.

before the end of the Roman Empire. It was a heavy plow—*caruca*—in contrast with the light *aratrum*. It was equipped with a colter, which made a vertical cut through the soil, and a share, which was so shaped that the soil rode up over it and was turned. It was far more efficient than the light plow at breaking up the soil and burying the weeds, but against these advantages had to be set the facts that it was clumsy and heavy, could be turned only with difficulty at the end of a furrow, and required a team of draft animals to pull it. It was ill suited to the Mediterranean region, where land was hilly and the lack of feed made it difficult to keep much farm stock. Vergil gives an ambiguous account of such a plow,[32] but the elder Pliny has left a clearer and more precise description.[33] He claimed—probably correctly—that it originated in southern Germany and added significantly that it required to be supported by a pair of wheels. It appears, however, never to have come into widespread use in classical times and was not adopted at all in southern Europe. No example of a heavy plow has survived, and we know that it was used in northern Europe only from the chance find of the iron colters with which it was equipped. Several colters have, for example, been found in Britain. Even so, we cannot discount the possibility that the light plow may occasionally have been fitted with a colter. It seems probable that the heavy plow, insofar as it was used, was confined to villa estates, which alone could have provided an adequate team. So clumsy an instrument was ill suited to small fields and was probably used in large fields, where it would have been turned less frequently. In later centuries, a system of long, narrow strips, adapted to the requirements of the heavy plow, came to be adopted (see chap. 5), but there is no conclusive evidence for such fields in the Roman period.

The cultivation of cereals remained the mainstay of classical agriculture. In Attica, better known than any other part of the Greek world, barley was the principal crop and was grown on much of the flat land as well as on terraces cut into the hillsides. The Eleusis tribute list, a taxation of 329–28 B.C., suggests that more than three-quarters of the cropland was under barley, and that much of the rest was sown with wheat. The strain of barley grown appears to have been the common six-rowed barley (*Hordeum vulgare*).[34] It was better suited to the dry, alkaline soil than other cereals, but it yielded a very poor bread and was generally eaten as a kind of porridge, flavored with stronger-tasting seeds, such as those of flax and coriander.[35] The wheat grown was largely, if not entirely, the Emmer strain. It was a "naked" wheat, separating readily from its husk and easily milled. It was less suited to the soils of Greece than barley, and probably cropped less heavily. On the other hand, its gluten content helped to make a light bread, and it was always the preferred cereal. The poor, it might be generalized, ate barley; the rich, wheat—and so it has always been, with rye or oats sometimes substituting for barley.

Italy, with its more northerly latitude and slightly wetter climate, was better suited to wheat, and here Emmer was by far the most important bread grain. It was with good wheat that the Roman populace was bribed to keep the peace and to refrain from civil disobedience. North of the Alps, the dominant wheat was spelt (*Triticum spelta*), a hulled variety, separable only with difficulty from its husk, and from this the common wheats of today have mostly derived.[36] It continued to be cultivated in central Europe until modern times, but difficulties in threshing it have led to its gradual abandonment in favor of more tractable varieties (fig. 2.4).

Other cereals were only of small importance. Rye, widely grown to the north of the Alps, was carried by invaders into northern Italy but never established itself in the Mediterranean basin in competition with the more palatable wheat. It remained the crop of the cool climates and acid soils of northern Europe. Oats were known to the Romans but were of no importance except on the poorest soils of central and northern Europe, where they did better than most other cereals. Oats could not be used for bread making and were usually eaten as a kind of gruel or porridge, such as became traditional in Scotland, or baked into oaten cake or "flatbread," so called because the lack of gluten prevented it from rising. Oats were destined to become the chief feed for horses, but these were few in classical times. Millet, otherwise known as "panic," was grown in Italy, but the Mediterranean region in general was too dry for it, and northern Europe, too cool.

Within the classical world the practice developed of cultivating each field every other year and leaving it fallow during the intervening period. There was a grave shortage of manure, though many farmers learned to make good use of the little that was available. Regular fallowing was thus the only means of keeping the land in good condition. Even so, there is some evidence for overcultivation and for the resulting deterioration of the soil. Beyond the imperial frontier, where population was less dense, the problem was solved by a system of shifting cultivation, allowing the land to lie idle as soon as its natural fertility began to decline.

Animal rearing in southern Europe was severely restricted by the climate and the lack of feed during the hot, dry summer. Sheep and goats, which were best adapted to these conditions, were by far

3.17. A donkey mill, from a bas-relief in the Vatican Museum. The bases of such mills have been excavated at Pompeii.

the most numerous of domesticated animals. Much of the region was marginal in terms of animal husbandry and could be used only seasonally. For this reason a system of transhumance, of regular, seasonal migration, had developed. It probably owed its origin to a time when society itself was still nomadic, following a more or less regular pattern of movement according to the availability of fruit or game. In the pattern of transhumance as it developed in the Mediterranean region, the animals passed the winter in the lowlands but in the summer migrated to the hills, where the fierce heat was tempered by altitude and grass continued to grow. Greek literature contains many references to shepherds tending their flocks in the mountains.[37] The Roman evidence is more specific. The *Lex Agraria* of 111 B.C. provided for the maintenance, free from obstacles or encroachment, of *tratturi,* or migration paths, between lowland and highland in Italy, and the writer Silius Italicus described how a shepherd, high up in Monte Gargano, looked out over the Apulian plain and saw smoke rising as the dry vegetation was burned off to improve grazing in the following winter.[38] It was, however, in the Alps, where there were strong environmental contrasts within a short distance, that transhumance came to be and remained most important.

Diet throughout the classical world consisted largely of carbohydrates in the form of cereals. These were, whenever possible, cooked as a form of bread but were otherwise eaten as gruel. The grains were supplemented, as indeed they had to be for dietary reasons, with green vegetables, fruit, and olive oil, a source of protein. Fish was an important item of diet near the sea. Milk, mainly from the goat, was consumed, some of it preserved as cheese, but meat was little eaten by ordinary people. Few farm animals were reared, and most were kept as draft animals or to supply wool. If we are to believe writers like Martial and Athenaeus, the ancients sometimes indulged in gargantuan banquets at which meat delicacies of the most exotic kind were consumed. These feasts must have been infrequent, and in any case were restricted to the wealthy classes.

Pulses and flaxseed were a source of protein, but vegetable fat largely came from the olive. The plant was native to the eastern Mediterranean but spread, probably in preclassical times, around the whole Mediterranean littoral. It was exacting in its climatic demands and could not tolerate cold winters. Even in Greece and Italy, it was never found in the mountainous interiors. It was slow growing, and it was commonly said that a young tree took twenty years to bear fruit. An olive grove thus represented a heavy capital investment, and its destruction in war represented a far more severe loss than the mere burning of crops. The olive was eaten fresh, it was preserved in brine, and both flesh and seed were crushed for oil. Olive presses have been found of Minoan date, and they are numerous in the ruins of Pompeii. Production of and trade in olive oil were of considerable importance in the Roman period. It is doubtful whether any food product, even wine, entered more importantly into trade, and the thousands of amphorae that have been found were used primarily to store and transport it (fig. 3.18). It was a peasant crop. Aristophanes' countryman hoped to have:

> First a row of vinelets . . .
> Next the little fig-tree shoots beside them growing,
> Thirdly, the domestic vine . . . [but]
> Round them all shall olives grow to form a pleasant boundary.[39]

There was probably little commercial oil production in Greece, but in the Roman period groves were important on estates or *villae rusticae*. They are shown in some of the wall paintings found in southern Italian villas. The Roman agronomists, always attentive to

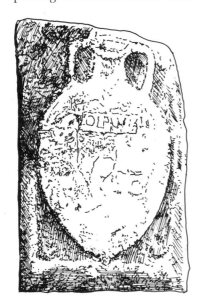

the needs of their wealthy patrons, gave much space to olive cultivation, which must have been a major source of income to villa owners.

The third pillar of Mediterranean agriculture, after cereals and the olive, was the grapevine. It too reached Europe by way of the Middle East. Its cultivation is represented in Greek tradition as having been brought by Dionysius from Anatolia. From Greece it was taken to Italy and thence was spread by the Romans to most of their European provinces. Wine, like olive oil, varied greatly in quality. No doubt, a coarse *vin ordinaire* was most commonly produced, but the Romans also developed superior wines, like Horace's Falernian from the plains of Campania, which were sold to the rich and consumed, if Martial is to be believed, in immense quantities at banquets. At the same time, large quantities of a tolerable wine were imported into Italy from many parts of the western Mediterranean, and the broken amphorae in which it traveled were piled up in the Monte Testaccio beside the Tiber

3.18. An amphora for storing olive oil, from Narbonne in southern Gaul.

on the southern edge of the city of Rome. Inspired by the mounting demand for wine, the cultivation of the vine spread through much of the Spanish peninsula, and in Gaul it

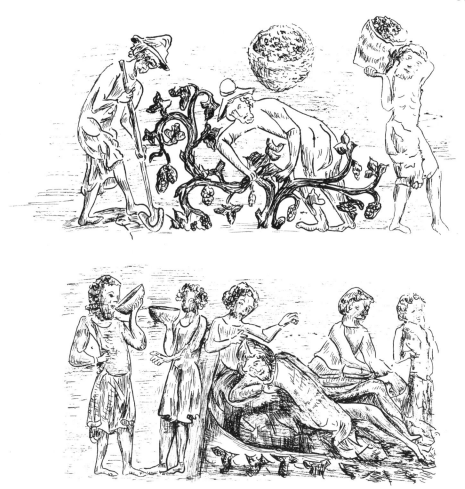

3.19. Viticulture and wine making permeate the art and iconography of classical and medieval Europe. The story of Noah's drunkenness was very popular. These drawings from the fourteenth-century Velislav Bible, now in Prague, show contemporary vine dressing and Noah sleeping off the consequences of his drinking.

had reached from the Mediterranean coast as far north as Paris before the imperial period came to an end.

Beyond the limits of the empire, agriculture was not greatly influenced either by the writings of agronomists or by commercial demands for food. The Germanic peoples appear to have cultivated small fields with light plows. According to Tacitus, they "changed their plowlands yearly, and still there is land to spare."[40] This can only be taken to indicate a system of shifting cultivation, in which a tract of land was tilled for a short time and then abandoned and another piece brought under the plow. This system, known to the Germans as *Feldgraswirtschaft,* continued to be practiced in some areas into modern times. Most cereal crops were grown, but rye was of increasing importance, an adaptation, it must be supposed, to soil and climate.

Diet among the Germanic tribes contained more meat and animal products than was usual within the empire. Physical conditions were better suited to stock rearing, and Tacitus tells us explicitly that Germany was "rich in flocks." Cattle were kept for the plow, and sheep for their wool. There are abundant remains of pigs, which must have run half-wild in the woods until rounded up for slaughter. No doubt hunting also played a more significant role in the provision of food than within the empire, and toward the northern frontier of settlement it was increasingly important. In his account of these northern peoples, Tacitus was obliged to rely on such reports, often exaggerated and misleading, as had reached him. Beyond the Germanic peoples, whom he identified as "settled," lived the Fenni of the Baltic region, "astonishingly wild and horribly poor. They have no arms, no horses, no homes. They eat grass, dress in skins, and sleep on the ground. Their only hope is their arrows, which, for lack of iron, they tip with bone." These were pre-Neolithic hunter-gatherers who had survived into the Late Iron Age. Yet the cynical Tacitus was not without admiration for the "noble savage," of whose way of life he had had no experience; "they count their lot happier than that of others who . . . hazard their own or other men's fortunes in the wild lottery of hope and fear."[41]

Arts and Crafts

The classical world showed little technical advance on methods practiced in Iron Age Europe. Of course, *forms* were more developed and aesthetically more appealing. A Greek vase or bowl may have been decorated more skillfully and its shape may have been more pleasing than that produced by Hallstatt or La Tène Celts or even by Minoan or Mycenean craftsmen, but there were no essential differences between the ways in which they were made.

The crafts by which the level of material culture was sustained can, for convenience, be divided into four groups. First was metalworking, with which must be associated the mining and smelting of ores; next, the spinning of thread and weaving of cloth. The third is the making of pottery and other ceramic goods, including glass, brick, and tile; and the last consists of woodworking. Least is known of cloth making and woodworking, since their products have largely perished; most about pottery, as ceramic goods are almost indestructible.

THE USE OF METALS

The metals in regular use were, as they had been for the last thousand years, iron, lead, bronze, and, in very small amounts, the precious metals. The Greeks developed a considerable skill in metalliferous mining. They reached the mineral-bearing lodes by means of shallow pits and drifts. They used iron picks for extracting the ore, which was broken into small particles by hammering. It was then washed and smelted. The only significant contribution of the Romans to technology as practiced by the Greeks was the drainage of mines by means of lifting devices actuated by a waterwheel. There was to be no further improvement in mining methods before the seventeenth century. Mining appears to have been carried on mainly by slave labor under conditions of almost military discipline. Work in the mines was appallingly hard, and the life expectancy of slaves consigned to them was short.[42]

Gold was obtained in its native, or almost pure, state by washing the sands and gravels of streambeds in ore-bearing regions. Tin was obtained in southwest Britain in the same way, but, as it was a sulfide, it had to be smelted before it could be used. The ores of iron, copper, lead, and silver were dug from the rock. Most were smelted with wood or charcoal fuel in low-shaft furnaces. The remains of many such furnaces, sometimes with slag on the floor, have been found in many parts of Europe, and, to clear up any doubt about how they operated, we have the pictures of them painted on Greek vases in the fifth century B.C.

Most famous of all classical mining sites was Laurion, near the southeastern tip of Attica. It yielded silver with some lead. Exploitation began in the preclassical period but reached its most productive level in the fifth century B.C. It was operated by the Athenian state and worked with slave labor, and its very considerable output paid in part for Athens's cultural achievements at this time. Gold was always less important than silver, because European reserves of the former were smaller. It is likely that the gold found in Mycenaean tombs of the Bronze Age was brought from Anatolia. The legend of Jason and the golden fleece, which relates to this area, is strongly suggestive of alluvial gold working. But gold ornaments and gold-encrusted furniture have also been found in Etruscan burial sites, and it is apparent that some gold was mined in Europe from quite early times. Most probably came from Spain and, under the empire, from various mines in the Balkan peninsula. The precious metals were, of course, used for currency, but much was invested in artwork and decoration. The statue of Pallas Athena which stood in the Parthenon, was covered with plates of silver made from the tribute of the Athenian League, an asset that could at any time be melted down and used.

Other metals were of greater significance in the context of material culture and human welfare. Lead was mined at first in conjunction with silver, but later for its own sake. Some was used in building construction, for roofing large buildings, and for holding the dowels in masonry. Most of the very considerable output under the Roman Empire was used for water pipes and water containers. A vast amount of lead went into the system of aqueducts and pipes that supplied the city of Rome, and provincial cities each had their smaller hydraulic systems. So much leaden pipework survives that it has even been suggested that lead poisoning was a factor in the economic decline and social change that occurred in the closing years of the empire. Such an idea will not bear close examination. The amount of lead used and the volume of water passing through it was only a fraction of that which entered into the domestic supply systems in the late nineteenth century.

Copper and tin were the other nonferrous metals in general use. Copper came at first from Cyprus, which gave its name to the metal. Then reserves were opened up in Italy, central Europe, and, above all, Spain. The relief carving of miners shown in figure 3.20 was found at Linares, in the Spanish copper belt. The only important use for tin was to alloy it with copper to make bronze, and bronze casting continued to be important throughout the classical period. But bronzework was almost entirely decorative or ornamental. For the manufacture of tools and weapons, bronze had been totally replaced by iron, steeled by the addition of carbon.

Iron ore occurred very widely in Europe and many deposits lay close to the surface and were easily worked. Smelting and ironworking were carried on in most parts of the classical world, as well as beyond its borders. There was, however, some trade in goods

3.20. Fragment of a carved slab showing miners on their way to work; from Linares in southern Spain.

of iron and steel because certain places acquired a particular reputation for the quality of their products. This was due, as a general rule, to the characteristics of the ores used. Among areas famous for their ironworking were Etruria, from which the Romans at first derived much of their iron, and the eastern Alps, where the industry has remained important until recent times. From the chief iron-mining and smelting areas blooms and bars of iron were carried to other parts of the classical world, where smiths worked them up into tools and weapons.[43]

The low-shaft furnaces in general use were incapable of producing more than a bloom of rather impure, soft iron. Blooms were then worked into bars and sheets for the fabrication of weapons and armor, nails and tools. These were often "steeled" in the manner described in chapter two. The question has often been raised whether the classical peoples were also able to make castings of iron. Cast iron has not been found at excavated sites. To make a casting the metal has to absorb a high percentage—generally over 4 percent—of carbon, in order to make it fluid. This process necessitates a higher furnace temperature than could be achieved under normal circumstances on a hearth or in a low-shaft furnace. On the other hand, Pausanias wrote in the second century that "Theodorus of Samos was the first to discover how to melt iron and make statues of it."[44] If Theodorus did, indeed, make cast-iron statues, it must have been by raising the furnace temperature either by increasing its height or by strengthening the blast—or both. If so, this must have been an innovation whose secret was lost. It was not until the end of the fifteenth century, with the introduction of the blast furnace, that fluid iron was again produced.

The smith became one of the most important of craftsmen in the classical world. In the Middle East he tended to be nomadic, traveling from one community to another, fabricating and repairing weapons and tools. Smiths were people apart, possessing exceptional skills and both respected and feared by the people they served. In biblical folklore, an aura of mystery surrounds the smith.

In the Greek world smithing appears to have been both a part-time peasant craft and the full-time occupation of men who employed slaves for the heavy manual work.[45] Rome relied at first on specialized Tuscan ironworkers and smiths, who used ore from Elba. In Rome, as in all large cities, there were smiths who bought their raw material as blooms or bars of soft iron from rural smelters. The demand for their skills was clearly increasing. A legion of six thousand men, it is said, required the services of two hundred smiths.[46] There were smiths in every legionary fort and marching camp. They were numerous in part because their work was labor intensive. They used no form of mechanical power, not even a waterwheel, to operate their bellows and hammers. All was done by the manual strength of the smiths themselves and of their slaves. It is probable that a large villa also had its smith, whose duty it was to forge woodworking tools, nails, and the colters that were fitted to the plows.

When Homer wrote, iron was still a fairly scarce commodity. By the time of the Roman Empire, "steeled" iron had almost wholly replaced bronze and copper in tools and weapons. There must have been an immense increase in the volume of iron production and its price must have fallen, bringing it within the range of ordinary people. They used it for felling trees, carving wood and stone, and for thousands of petty jobs in the household and on the farm, which had previously been performed with bronze or stone. The widespread use of iron must have reduced the drudgery in much of everyday life as well as making labor more effective and efficient. The variety of cutting tools available is illustrated in a stele showing a cutler's shop (fig. 3.21).

WEAVING AND CLOTHWORKING

The classical peoples inherited the techniques of spinning and weaving from their Iron Age predecessors. The materials used were almost exclusively flax, wool, and hair. Cotton had long been used for textiles in South Asia, and its cultivation spread to Egypt. Herodotus had heard of it, but no attempt appears to have been made before the Middle Ages to grow it in Europe, though it was probably imported and used there.

Although wool and flax were both produced in many parts of Europe, the best was held to be that from southern Italy, Spain, and Greece, while the coarsest came from Gaul. In southern Europe the flax plant was grown more for its oil-bearing seeds than for its fiber. In northern Europe, partly for climatic reasons, the fiber was more important. There was little trade in either wool or flax in the Greek period, but under the Roman Empire a demand arose among the rich for cloth woven from the best materials, like Cannusian wool from Apulia. But coarse wool and even goat's hair were used in weaving rugs.

Whatever the material used, the fabrication of textiles involved three separate processes: spinning, weaving, and finishing. Flax, furthermore, had to be retted, or soaked in water to loosen the fibers from the pulp, and scutched, an arduous process by which the fibers were themselves split into threads for spinning. Spinning was by distaff and spindle and was invariably women's work. It was an activity that occupied almost

3.21. A cutlery merchant's tombstone, first century A.D. This bas-relief shows the variety of knives available.

every minute of the woman's life when she was not engaged in domestic or field work. The bundle of fiber was placed on the distaff and drawn out in a continuous thread by the fingers of one hand while the other gave it a twist and wound it onto the spindle. A whorl, usually a pierced stone, was fitted to the latter to assist its spinning motion. Spindle whorls in their thousands are about all that has survived from the spinner's craft.

Weaving in classical times was on an upright loom. The vertical thread, or warp, was wound on the upper beam and kept taut by loom weights (fig. 3.22). Loom weights tended later to be replaced by a lower beam, and in the more sophisticated forms of loom the warp was wound from the upper onto the lower beam as weaving progressed. The weaver stood or sat in front of the loom and drew the weft between the threads of the warp, pressing each against the previous one by means of a comb. He was, in fact, assisted by a simple shed mechanism that parted the threads and allowed a shut-

3.22. A warp-weighted loom; fifth century B.C.; from a *skyphos* found in Boeotia.

tle to be passed between them. The loom was narrow, to fit the confined spaces of the houses in which it was used, and produced only a small piece of cloth. Weaving was a domestic occupation, probably carried on main-ly in winter, and much of the cloth made was probably worn by the family that produced it. Nevertheless, there were in Rome and doubtless also in other cities those who used superior qualities of wool to make more refined cloth for the market. The practice of wearing clothing of wool or linen spread throughout the empire. Julius Caesar expressed his surprise at seeing the native Gauls clad only in skins. But within a century, urban dwellers at least were wearing the flowing toga of the Romans.

No fabric was complete when taken from the loom, though it is doubtful whether peasants gave much attention to the finishing of cloth for their own use. Linen was commonly beaten to make it softer and, of course, it was bleached by exposure to the sun. Woolen cloth required more elaborate finishing. It was dyed, unless the thread had already been colored before weaving, and it was fulled, cropped, and stretched. Full-ing consisted of thickening or felting the cloth in water, with, usually, the addition of some such substance as fuller's earth, a detergent clay. The surface was then cropped with shears, and the cloth, which had shrunk in the process, was stretched. There are several illustrations in bas-relief of the finishing processes (fig. 3.23), and at the villa at Chedworth, in England, vats have survived in which fulling is said to have taken place. In time the loom became larger, the pieces of cloth longer and wider, and the weave more even. Refinements were introduced into the pat-tern as well as into finishing and dyeing, but the tools and methods of cloth production under-went no fundamental change before modern

3.23. Shearing and fulling cloth; from a Roman bas-relief of the third century A.D.

times. The limits of efficiency possible within the constraints of a peasant society were reached at an early date. The next stage was mechanization, and mechanical spinning and weaving did not come until the eighteenth century.

The classical civilizations also inherited the art of tanning leather and of using it to make footwear, bags, saddles, and other articles. The Greeks used leather to support the small pieces of metal that made up their helmets and armor. They commonly wore leather sandals, and a painted vase, probably of the sixth century B.C., shows a customer being measured by a cobbler for such footwear. Under the Romans the consumption of leather greatly increased, and "factories," or large workshops, were established to produce leather goods for the legions.

One may gain an exaggerated view of the importance of pottery in the ancient world because of the vast quantities that have survived. Shards are almost indestructible; every excavation site yields them in abundance, and the problem of disposing of food and drink containers would appear to have been almost as great under the Roman Empire as it is today. Greek and Roman pottery was, as a general rule, made from a well-levigated clay and turned on a wheel, worked usually by the foot. Urban and villa excavations have yielded refined or "polite" pottery, made in workshops, which can sometimes be identified by the style of the vessel and the character of its decoration. The tendency was, especially under the Roman Empire, for this better-quality pottery to displace the coarse peasant product, though the latter never ceased to be made.

To some extent the quality of the pot depended on the nature of the clay available, and for this reason, as means of transport developed, pottery tended to concentrate in a relatively small number of centers. The clay available in Attica was very plastic and held a high iron content that gave the pottery its familiar red color. In fact, the Greeks developed considerable skill in manipulating their clays and the temperatures of their kilns in order to achieve artistic color effects. They also used a colored slip to paint onto their pots the decoration that is sometimes so valuable a guide to their technology.

Similar skills were developed by the Etruscans in central Italy. The Romans were heirs to the ceramic traditions of both the Greeks and the Etruscans. In their hands the forms no longer show the spontaneity and beauty that characterized the Greek, but the abundance of their output is staggering. Serviceable, even artistic, pottery was mass-produced. Embossed designs were impressed on the vessels by means of wooden molds with such regularity that they lost their character and individuality. On the other hand, the numbers who could afford to use and enjoy them far exceeded the few who possessed hand-painted Attic vases. Most abundant was the *terra sigillata,* the so-called Samian ware, though it does not appear to have had any connection with Samos. It originated in the eastern Mediterranean, and for almost five hundred years pottery of this kind dominated the mass market. Its manufacture at Arretium (Arezzo) in Tuscany began in the first century B.C., and the earliest potters are said to bear Middle Eastern names. From here it was sold over the western Mediterranean. Then, in order to reduce problems of transport, "arretine" ware began to be made in Gaul, the Rhineland, and Britain. Nothing shows more clearly than the manufacture and use of arretine-type pottery the spread of improved standards of material well-being under the empire.

The manufacture of glass was first developed in the Middle East and spread to Greece. Early glass objects were wholly decorative and were a monopoly of the rich. Then the invention of glassblowing, probably in the Levant, cheapened production and increased its volume. Glass objects like bottles and vases became abundant, and their sale, like that of arretine ware, moved increasingly down-market.

Wood was used throughout the classical world both to construct homes and ships (fig. 3.24) and also to make furniture. The woodworker's craft was assisted by the

3.24. Shipping on the Danube, from a bas-relief on Trajan's Column in Rome. The scene shows masonry houses, similar to those in Italy. On the Danube they would have been of wood.

introduction of nails made of soft iron and of cutting tools with steel edges. Indeed, a carpenter's toolbag during the Roman Empire bore a close resemblance to one in the nineteenth century.[47] In addition to simple hammers, adzes, and axes, he would have had chisels, a plane, a claw hammer for lifting nails, and even a drill turned by a bowstring. In fact, the only important omissions from his tool kit were a screwdriver and metal screws. With better tools, woodworking became more sophisticated, timber-frame construction more elaborate, and the jointing of woodwork stronger. And these improvements, we must suppose, were passed on from the villas of the rich, where they were first employed, to the homes of the masses.

The manufacture of household furniture was introduced into Greece from Egypt and the Middle East and was passed from there to the Etruscans and Romans. Craftsmen made tables, chairs, and couches, the last consisting usually of a wooden frame, over which a cord mattress would have been stretched, together with a headrest. The Etruscans introduced a kind of armchair, which looks the height of comfort, and the Romans, a cupboard with shelves and hinged doors. Such a piece of furniture is illustrated in a fresco at Pompeii. Joints were carefully mortised, and the best items of furniture were strong and workmanlike. Although scarcely any furnishings have survived, there are many illustrations in decorated pottery and frescoes, as well as in the form of models. An important development in furniture making was the use of a primitive lathe to turn the legs of pieces of furniture. It may have originated in the Levant, but its adoption in the classical world led to an overrefinement of some aspects of woodworking. Rotary motion, produced in many cases by the cord of a bow, came into general use under the Roman Empire. It was also used in the potter's wheel and the waterpowered mill.

Woodworkers learned to choose the most suitable of available wood for their work. Forests were more extensive and varied in classical times than they subsequently became. Simple woods like holm oak, cypress, and cedar were used. Nevertheless, there was an import of exotic timber, and Cicero paid a million sesterces for a table of citron wood from Africa. This is indicative of the quality and price of the best furniture. All the pieces that we know, either directly or through illustration, were luxury products. Some were inlaid with metal and ivory. Much was carved into animal forms and claw feet, as intricate as any produced by Victorian craftsmen.[48]

Less is known of woodworking north of the Alps and among the poorer classes everywhere. One assumes that furniture was simpler and coarser, even though excellent timber was to be had in the northern forests. It is doubtful whether the peasant enjoyed the comfort of a couch for sleeping or the luxury of table and chairs. The homes of the greater part of the population within the empire and of almost all beyond its boundaries were virtually unfurnished apart from a few pots and maybe an iron trivet beside the hearth. Nevertheless, material standards were everywhere improving in classical Europe. Homes were better built; a rudimentary furniture was spreading down the social scale; pottery vessels were more numerous and of better quality; iron goods and tools were more widely used. Yet there was no technological breakthrough; the changes and developments that characterized the classical period lay rather in the sphere of organization and management.

The period of the Roman Empire was, by and large, one of peace. It did not, in general, have to contend with the destruction and social disturbance of warfare. Social and commercial intercourse were encouraged and led to a marked leveling up of standards. The overall production of goods was increased not only by the greater availability of materials but also by a growing specialization among producers. An exchange economy was developed; metal currency came into widespread use, as is shown by the coin hoards that have been found. The role of the classical civilizations, in particular that of Rome, was to integrate the advances that had been made in material culture, so that advance in one field contributed to development in others. The quality of Roman furniture would have been inconceivable without improvements in the quality of woodworking tools and thus development in steel metallurgy. Mass-production methods, notably in ceramics, allowed a vast number of people to be supplied with simple consumer goods. It was the breakdown of this system of specialization and exchange, with the consequent lowering of the quality of goods and reduction in their volume, that characterized the end of the classical civilizations.

PART TWO

Preindustrial

Europe

INTRODUCTION

Too often we allow ourselves to suppose that, could we but get
back to the beginning, we should find that all was intelligible and
should be able to watch the process whereby simple ideas were
smothered under subtleties and technicalities. But it is not so. Simplicity is the outcome of technical subtlety; it is the goal not the
starting point. As we go backwards the familiar outlines become
blurred; the ideas become fluid, and instead of the simple we find
the indefinite.

—Frederic William Maitland,
Domesday Book and Beyond

      The capture of Rome by the Goths in 410 and the abdication of the last
western emperor in 476 marked the end of the Roman Empire in the west. The Eastern
Empire continued to attract the allegiance of a diminishing area until 1453. The decline
of the Western Empire was accompanied by the invasion of peoples whom posterity has
termed barbarian. This may be to underrate their cultural achievement. They were not
savages. Many of them had lived for centuries in the shadow of Rome. They had
imported Roman artifacts, and their menfolk had served with the legions. When they
broke across the boundaries of the empire, it was not to destroy it but to enjoy the fruits
of its higher cultural achievement. But destruction there was. From the Rhineland to
Spain and throughout the Balkans, invading peoples lived off the land and ravaged the
cities. Trade, which had supported urban life, declined to a trickle. Each local area was
thrown back upon itself, and a level of self-sufficiency was reached similar to that of the
pre-Roman Iron Age. Material standards declined. Skills that the Romans had developed,
especially in building construction, surveying, and the plastic and graphic arts, were
neglected and forgotten. There was fear and insecurity everywhere.

    But not all was lost. The Roman cultural legacy—or elements of it—was preserved in
local areas, in Byzantium, in parts of Italy, and, above all, within the Catholic church,
whose head, the bishop of Rome, began to assume in some respects the mantle of the
vanished emperors. From these centers the culture of Rome, transmuted and abridged,
was diffused to western Europe, then to central, and lastly to the peripheral regions of
the east and north. It is with this spread of higher standards of material culture that the
next six chapters are concerned. The change was slow, almost imperceptible from one

generation to the next, but the cumulative effect of countless innovations and improvements—in building homes, in weaving cloth, and working metals—meant more goods, better tools, greater food supply, and more comfort and convenience. There was progress on such a scale that material life was transformed between the fifteenth century and the eighteenth.

Nowhere, however, were the benefits of this advance spread evenly. Society was structured—far more so than during the classical period. There were extremes of wealth and privilege. For much of this period, a large part of the population was unfree, but there were, in Frederic William Maitland's phrase, "degrees of unfreedom," ranging from the obligatory performance of certain tasks to complete servitude. But the improvement in material conditions was accompanied by a rise in personal status. Slavery disappeared, followed in most of Europe by the condition of near slavery known as serfdom. But elements of "unfreedom" remained, in some areas until the mid-nineteenth century: labor on the lord's demesne, unpaid work at harvest time, petty obligations to fetch and carry, limitations on the right to marry or to leave the lord's estate. These restraints and obligations were eroded slowly, first in Italy and northwest Europe, later in central and northern, and last in eastern Europe and the Balkans. The progression of "freedom" followed a path similar to that taken by material culture itself. The peasant in Poland or Romania was the last to be freed from onerous personal obligations, as he was also the last to benefit from the conveniences and decencies of modern life.

The reasons for this inequality lie in the slow diffusion of ideas, innovations, and institutions. If there is any historical justification for a class-structured society, it is this: a privileged class is the one most likely to make changes and to adopt innovations, which could then be improved upon or imitated by the humbler classes. And this, especially if we regard the insitutions of the church as part of the privileged stratum of society, is the path that most innovations and improvements in material culture have taken.

It is important, lastly, to distinguish between what may be termed the *necessities* of life and life's *niceties*. There are certain categorical imperatives—food, clothing, shelter—but they can be satisfied in many ways. Each generation elaborates and improves on previous standards, and what was acceptable in one age might not be tolerated in another. The provision of pure water, of sanitary conveniences, of an oven for preparing food, each passed from being the luxuries of the few to becoming necessities of the many. On the other hand, the external decoration of houses, pictures on the walls, table forks and napkins, glazed windows, and door locks, cannot be treated as necessities, however much they may add to the amenities of life. They are among its niceties, transmitted from the upper classes to the lower all the more readily because they became a kind of status symbol. Life became filled with gestures and symbols, denoting status, education, wealth, local allegiance, and group affiliation, none of which could be described as necessary, but all contributing to what was deemed a desirable standard of well-being.

Chapter 4

THE COMMUNITY OF THE VILLAGE

Tous les jours au milieu d'un champ
Par la chaleur par la froidure
L'on voit le pauvre paysan
Travailler tant que l'année dure
Pour amasser par son labeur
De quoy payer le collecteur
　—Nicolas Guérard, 1648–1719

*T*he essential conditions of human life are food and shelter. The supply of
the former was precarious and inadequate for most people throughout
the preindustrial age. The latter condition was, on the whole, more easily satisfied.
People lived mostly in small communities for mutual help and protection, and within
each such group they used whatever materials were locally available to create homes.
Within the walls of their own houses they could achieve some degree of privacy, and here
they could develop family life and store such goods as they had accumulated. The village
and, within it, the home together constituted the physical environment of rural life.

It is impossible to divorce the study of settlement from those of the economy and of
the environment. The three were intertwined at all points. The size of the settlement was
related to the extent of the fields and the methods of cultivation. Crop farming was, as a
general rule, accompanied by large village settlements; pastoral, by small or even by
isolated farmsteads. Agriculture was related no less to soil and climate, and the form of
settlement to conditions of water supply and the availability of a dry site for its homes.
Yet the relationship between environment, economy, and settlement was never simple or
direct and was, furthermore, continuously changing. There were always other factors—
social and political—to complicate the relationship. The need for protection might
dictate settlements far larger than local resources could easily support. In the Hungarian
plain, for example, where a small community was vulnerable to raids first by Tartars and
later by Turks, the village grew into a settlement of urban proportions, without ever
losing its rural character or acquiring in any significant degree the functions of a city. The
journey from the settlement to the more remote fields became so great that the peasants

could no longer make it every day and had, during the busiest parts of the farming year, to camp among their crops. The vast, sprawling *Agrarstädte* of Hungary were paralleled by those of southern Italy, Sicily, parts of Spain, and the Mediterranean islands. Here too the farming requirements of the community conflicted with the need for protection not only from human enemies but also from the malarial mosquito that lived and bred near the cultivated land. The village lay high on a mountain spur, protected by the steepness of the ascent, while the fields lay in the valley or on the plains, hundreds of feet below.

These extreme conditions, as if by a kind of dialectic, brought about their own destruction. As soon as social, political, or even technical conditions made it possible, large settlements disintegrated and broke up into smaller clusters situated amid the fields. The pattern of human settlement has always been in a process of change, as constraints were relaxed or intensified. But adaptation to changed circumstances was slow because alteration of one facet of rural life always brought with it disruption in others.

The only factors that were even approximately constant in the history of a settlement were those implicit in the environment itself, but even this element was susceptible to change through human agency. A settlement had to be close to, or within walking distance of, the fields that its inhabitants cultivated. There had to be a source of water, not difficult in much of Europe, but springs and wells were infrequent in many limestone areas, where they contributed to the formation of large and tightly clustered villages. The "spring-line" village remains a significant feature of parts of southern England, northern France, and the north German plain. The quality of the site itself was always important. Settlers sought a dry site, a very important consideration when the timber framing of a cottage was set directly in the soil and floors were only of beaten earth. They usually avoided the floodplains of valleys, and when settlements were sited on clay land, as indeed they had to be in much of the northern plain of Europe, the founders usually sought the protection of some elevation or of a patch of dry sand or gravel, left by the floods of earlier geological times. In parts of the Netherlands, where such small hillocks were rare, it was not uncommon to create an artificial mound, or *terp,* on which to build the farmstead. More than a hundred such *terpen* have been counted in the marshy regions of the Low Countries.[1] Where marshes have been reclaimed, and rivers constrained by levees, as they have been in many coastal regions of northern Europe, long, sinuous villages have been built along the crest of the winding levee: such was the need to escape the damp ground and the risk of flooding.

In hilly and mountainous areas there was a different kind of constraint on settlement. Villages and farmsteads were built on the south-facing slopes, leaving the north-facing almost devoid of human settlement. In the Alps specific terms were used to describe the sunny and the shady sides of a valley, respectively *adret* and *ubac, Sonnenseite* and *Schattenseite* (fig. 4.1). It often happens in a mountain valley that the sun never lights upon large areas during the winter months.[2] Only in southern Europe, where shade rather than sunshine was desired during much of the year, is this situation reversed. In much of Europe the home was built so as to receive as much sunshine as possible, or to reduce exposure to wind. Even the architecture itself was adapted in some degree to rainfall or snow or, at the opposite extreme, to the fierce, hot sunshine. Environmental factors were constant or changed very slowly. They might be and sometimes were ignored at a cost to the settlers. Sometimes expensive compromises were made. What

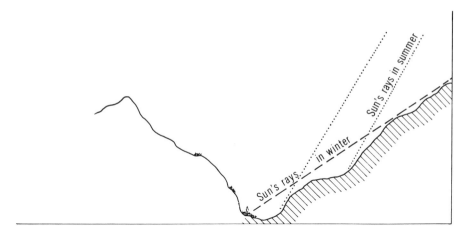

4.1. Diagram illustrating the *adret* and *ubac*
(*Sonnenseite/Schattenseite*) in a mountain valley. Settlements
would be more numerous on the sunnier northern slopes.

was a *terp* but a very costly—in terms of labor—attempt to modify a hostile environment?

The form and siting of settlements were also influenced by cultural, economic, and political factors. It has even been claimed that the shape of a settlement was due to the *ethnic* origins of those who made it. A century ago August Meitzen sought to explain the morphology of settlement in terms of the racial origins of the first settlers.[3] The pattern of hamlets and isolated farmsteads, characteristic, for example, of parts of France and western Britain, was held to be the mark of Celtic settlement; the large, clustered village was the work of the sociable and cooperative Germans, and a round or "ring-fence" village denoted the pastoral activities of the Slavs. Such a simplistic explanation of profound differences in the siting and shape of rural settlement has long been discredited. There are too many exceptions, too many examples of actual change in settlement plan, for such reasoning to be acceptable.

It is impossible to ascribe a socially conditioned action, like founding a village or building a home, to any form of inherited propensity. This, however, does not by any means exclude the possibility—even probability—that a migrating people will carry with them the concepts and practices to which they have become accustomed, even though these no longer accord with conditions in their new homes. The "Saxons" who in the Middle Ages migrated to Transylvania planned villages and built homes as similar as was practible to those which they had left in Germany. Even today there is a strong visual contrast between the "German" and the Romanian villages in this beautiful region. In the late nineteenth century, Cornish tin miners settled in southwestern Wisconsin to work the local lead deposits. They built homes as similar as possible in design and structure to those they had known in their native Cornwall. The latter were adjusted to the local building materials—granite, shale, and a severe shortage of timber. In Wisconsin, timber was abundant, and the local stone was a soft limestone. The "Cornishness" of the resulting buildings was a cultural trait that soon vanished. But other such imported characteristics, like "Dutch" gables in eastern England, less at variance with local conditions, have survived and figure prominently in village architecture. A settlement is always, in plan and style, a compromise between traditional ideas and current constraints.

But social and economic influences on the forms assumed by human settlement have always been preponderant. Over much of Europe the exploitation of the soil and the nature of control over the land both contributed to the formation of large villages. The cultivation of open fields called for the mutuality and collaboration of a large and compact settlement and would have been difficult without it. And it was just this mutuality which obstructed the enclosure of the open fields. In some parts of Europe in the eighteenth and nineteenth centuries, the enclosure of the open fields was in fact followed by the breakup of the village, as family farmers one by one built homes on their own compact and enclosed holdings.[4] A lower intensity of land use, with animal grazing partially or wholly replacing arable farming, necessarily dictated smaller settlements and, in some extreme cases, the isolated farmstead. It was the economy, not ethnic origins or even the physical environment, that in the last resort dictated the broad form of settlement.

Village, Hamlet, and Farmstead

One thinks of the village as the typical form of rural settlement throughout most of Europe. Indeed it has been over the great plain that reaches from the shores of the Atlantic Ocean to the Russian steppe, and also on the small and scattered lowlands of Mediterranean Europe. The tight cluster of houses with yards and ancillary farm buildings was, until the nineteenth century, home to the majority of Europe's population. Not surprisingly, the village and village life have etched themselves deep in the thought and feelings of European peoples. They are commemorated, eulogized, criticized in literature. Thomas Hardy's *Weatherbury*, Władisław Reymont's *Lipka*, Émile Zola's *Rognes*, each in its different way, penetrated the life and thought of villagers and exposed their economic and social relationships. For the settings of these novels were not fictitious. They were real places seen through the eyes of deeply perceptive people who lived in them and understood every facet of their life.

So dominant did the village become in rural life that one might be excused for thinking that it goes back far into European prehistory. In all probability it does not. The pattern of rural settlement in the provinces of the Roman Empire and, indeed, throughout Late Iron Age Europe consisted largely of small clusters of houses—hamlets or *vici*. They were distinguishable from the later villages of medieval Europe not only by their smaller size but also by the greater simplicity of their social and economic structure. The village of medieval and later times was a community, often several hundreds strong, with, on the one hand, a social cohesiveness that was institutionalized in manorial courts, parochial meetings, and common agricultural pursuits, and, on the other hand, a complex social structure with mutually dependent groups or classes.

One cannot say how big a village was. It might be as small as a dozen or twenty households, or as large as a hundred. It might include essential craftsmen like the miller, the tanner, or the smith. It would probably have contained a church, an open space or common, a pound for stray animals, and other elements of its local infrastructure.

But how did the village emerge from a loose pattern of hamlets and scattered homesteads? Was it by the consolidation of the latter, and, if so, was this a consequence of external danger, or was it imposed by a "lord" who had rights over the land and thought this the best mode of exploiting them? Or was the village organization brought, as some of the Germanists would have us believe, by an incoming or invading people who imposed their customs and institutions? There is no simple answer, and the range and complexity of rural institutions in the later Middle Ages and early modern times surely implies highly varied antecedents during the dark centuries that followed the collapse of the Roman Empire in the west.

The evolution of the village settlement can best be understood by examining the influences—political, social, economic—that were brought to bear on it. First, there was military necessity, the need for protection in an insecure age. The Roman Empire had been characterized by a degree of peace and security, not absolute, but at least greater than had been known in Europe before this time or was to be experienced again for many centuries. And the rest of Europe during the late Roman Iron Age appears to have been less disturbed than it had been when the La Tène–age *oppida* were built. Relative peace and security would thus appear to have allowed a more open pattern of settlement. This state ended with the great invasions of the late Roman period. The evidence for a change in the pattern of human settlement throughout much of Europe during the centuries that followed is fragmentary in the extreme. Literary sources are almost silent on the subject, and the archeological evidence is scanty and restricted to the few areas where an intensive search has been made for it. Among these is Etruria. Here the abandonment of isolated settlements began well before the end of the Western Empire and continued for many centuries afterwards.[5] Villas and *vici* gave place to clustered villages, some of them of very considerable size and most located on rising ground or at least defensible sites.

The reconstruction of the geography of earlier settlement is easier in Mediterranean Europe than elsewhere because masonry figured prominently in domestic construction. The effort of tearing out stone foundations was greater than was justified by the rewards. But north of the Alps most construction was in wood, which left no trace on the surface of the ground and but little beneath it. The study of place-names can often throw light on the history of forest clearance and settlement, but this evidence is sometimes deceptive. One cannot always be certain that a village was created when it received the name by which we know it. A settlement with a Germanic name may have had pre-Germanic antecedents. Nevertheless, the evidence is strong over much of Europe for the abandonment of small settlements and isolated farmsteads in favor of larger and more easily protected villages.

But protection from Dark Age marauders might be seen to lie not in large, protected villages but rather in centrally located places of refuge. Procopius described how Justinian ordered such fortified places to be built in the Balkans, and listed over two hundred of them, most of which can no longer be identified.[6] In Anglo-Saxon England *burhs* were established by the kings of Wessex and others. They had little or no economic function and must have served primarily as protection for the inhabitants of their local regions. Indeed, an Anglo-Saxon document of about 900 lists about thirty such *burhs* and suggests the area served by each. Even more to the point is a passage in the *Slavic Chronicle* of Helmold. Its author, writing of Holstein in the twelfth century, described how the people "came out of the strongholds in which they were keeping themselves shut up for fear of the wars. And they returned, each one to his own village."[7]

Evidence for village defenses is more difficult to find. An early medieval village might

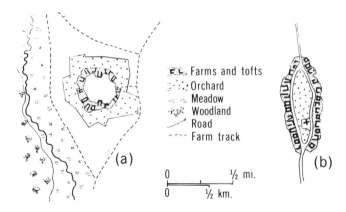

Farms and tofts
Orchard
Meadow
Woodland
Road
Farm track

(a)   (b)

0 _____ ½ mi.
0 ___ ½ km.

4.2. Types of village: (*a*) *Runddorf, Rundling,* or ring-fence village; (*b*) *Angerdorf,* or spindle-shaped village.

expect to be able to protect itself from the casual raider, intent only on stealing cattle, for there was little else to take. There was no defense against an invading horde. Many a village had a ditch, bank, and palisade; several examples have been excavated in eastern Germany and Poland, and many others in the west. The *Rundling,* or ring-fence village, in which the huts were set in a circle, enclosing a central open space, can be looked at as a means of protecting the animals at night and in time of danger (fig. 4.2). From the eleventh century the outermost courtyards of castles served this purpose, and there are instances of villages actually being set within their encompassing walls or palisades.

The vast majority of villages in Europe had no castle or strong point that could give protection and serve as a refuge, but they did possess a church. From the Dark Ages most churches, including rural churches, were built of masonry and were at least as capable as a palisade and ditch of giving shelter and protection to the villagers. It is difficult to know the extent to which churches were conceived as local fortresses; that they were used as such is apparent. In England there is a close similarity between some church towers of the twelfth century and the contemporary tower keeps of castles. But whether this likeness arises from an intended use of churches for defense or from the employment of the same master masons and workmen, one cannot know. In northern Britain there can be no question but that church towers in the later Middle Ages were built on the model of defensive towers, and one, at Salkeld, in Cumbria, was even built with grooves for a portcullis. There might have been an element of security in living within the sound of the church bells, but it must be said that in almost every instance the village can be shown to be earlier in origin than the church and its tower. Nevertheless, there are parts of Europe, notably Burgundy and Transylvania,[8] where the fortification of either the church or its churchyard was a common occurrence (fig. 4.3). The French chronicler Jean de Venette described how in the fourteenth century, "the peasants dwelling in open villages made fortresses of their churches by surrounding them with good ditches, protecting the towers and belfries with planks as one does castles, and stocking them with stones and crossbows. . . . At night the peasants . . . slept in these strongholds in comparative safety. By day they kept lookout on top of the church towers."[9]

More significant in the shaping of the village were questions of land tenure and church organization, of the development of feudalism and the parish. Slavery was institutionalized in the Roman Empire and barbarian Europe, but land appears, by and

4.3. A fortified church at Draas, Romania. Here the churchyard was fortified with wall and towers. Sometimes the church was developed into a kind of castle.

large, to have been held and cultivated by free farmers. They may have owned slaves but were not themselves organized into larger estate units. Villas, particularly the *villae rusticae,* which were, in effect, big working farms, must have had a large structured population. But villas were not villages and do not appear as a general rule to have given rise to villages. In fact, a new structure of land ownership and occupation was imposed on much of Europe during the centuries that followed the eclipse of the empire in the west. The land—or much of it—passed into the possession of lords, who held it in return for service that was due, in the last resort, to the king.

From the ninth or tenth century onwards, the system of dependence and obligation known as feudalism began to spread through western Europe, but it was several centuries before it became fully developed in eastern. Its dominant feature was landholding in return for service. The peasant held his land from a lord, to whom he owed service or a money payment in lieu of it. Where services were demanded, and that in the early stages of feudalism was almost everywhere, these could be exacted most conveniently from a large village. Indeed, it was almost impossible to perform such services on behalf of small and widely scattered settlements. Services commonly took the form of labor duties: plowing, sowing, reaping, carting, and other forms of manual work.

So arose the bipartite manor, a community living in a village, its surrounding fields divided into those which it held and cultivated itself and those—the demesne—on which it provided services for its lord. It was in the interest of the lord to develop a large settlement and to prevent its disintegration into small, disparate elements. A degree of discipline was necessary. A manorial court met at frequent and regular intervals—in England most often "from three weeks to three weeks"—to enforce local custom and to protect the lord's rights. The large, bipartite manor was thus institutionalized, and as long as the lord continued to cultivate his demesne and exact labor dues, there was little scope for change in the clustered village settlement. In England the constraint exercised by manorial control was gradually relaxed as lords abandoned direct control of their demesne, most often leasing it to well-to-do peasants. A similar process in eastern Europe was interrupted from the sixteenth century, as the lords found profit in regaining control over their demesne lands and reimposing and even extending the obligations of their peasants. This was the so-called second serfdom, when the lords returned in some measure to large-scale grain production to satisfy a growing and highly profitable market in the west.

There was thus a close, even intimate connection between the large village, the system of open-field cultivation, and the division of the cultivated land between peasant holdings and demesne. The intermingling of peasant strips, coupled with the common obligation of the peasants themselves to work the demesne of their lord, served to hold the community together. It was as difficult to escape from the village as it was from the manor itself. Furthermore, the peasants, or at least most of them, held rights in the local common, meadow, and woodland. Their domestic economy was dependent upon their exercise of these rights. If they absconded, they sacrificed them, and the peasants' "stint" in the common or the meadow passed to others. The system of land tenure—even the techniques of cultivation—that evolved during the early Middle Ages was a cement holding the community together in its tightly clustered settlement. Not until this cement had become rotten with age or had been corroded by the coming of a money economy or picked away by the judgments of lawyers, did the village community begin to disintegrate and its settlement to decay.

There was a practical limit, even in its heyday, to the size to which the village community could be allowed to grow. This was set by the available cropland and the distance that peasants could be expected to travel to reach their most distant fields. The point was reached—indeed it might have been reached on more than one occasion—when it became desirable to hive off a group of villagers and to found a secondary settlement at a distance from the original village. Such a settlement might occupy a clearing in the neighboring woods, or it might be at a distance of many miles. It might remain no more than a small hamlet, or it might grow into an open-field village like that from which it had sprung. As a general rule, however, such secondary settlements lacked the cement that had held the village community together. They were small and isolated. They had no demesne on which the peasants worked for their lord. Instead, land was usually held at a money rent. The land was not—indeed, could not easily be—organized in strips in an open field. Rather, the peasants cultivated small, enclosed fields. They followed no common cropping system and were free to depart from established custom—not that the medieval peasant was ever much of an innovator.

The village community began to decline when the mutual constraints and profits that held its members together began to decay. A typical chronology of events might be, first, the commutation of labor services for a money payment; then the lease of the demesne to one or more "farmers" who cultivated it at a rent and with hired labor. This stage might be followed by an agreement, not often arrived at unanimously, to consolidate the scattered parcels of land that made up each peasant holding. This arrangement might lead, again not without acrimony, to a partition of the totality of common rights in grazing and woodland. A final stage would be reached when the peasant abandoned the village and built a cottage on his own land. Of course, there might be legal as well as institutional and customary objections to taking the village apart in this way. In eastern Europe, as we have seen, the initial process of commuting peasant labor services was in fact reversed. In much of Europe, the end of labor dues was not followed by a reordering of the field system, chiefly because a matrix of vested interests prevented it. But where, as in England, the Low Countries, and much of Scandinavia, open fields were enclosed and parceled into holdings for individual peasant farmers, the way was opened toward the gradual disintegration of the village.

Even so, there were other restraints on change. The village has been thought of here as engaged almost exclusively in agriculture. Farming was its dominant occupation, but there were others. From late in the Middle Ages, craft industries became increasingly important in the countryside. Urban restrictions, associated chiefly with excessive regulation by the gilds, led weavers to move more and more to the villages, which, almost by definition, had no such corporate character. Spinning had always been a largely rural pursuit, and tanning and working in leather, wood, and metal were increasingly important. Such crafts benefited from concentration in a village. They employed the wives and younger sons of the peasants and were increasingly important as part-time occupations for those whose holdings were too small to demand continuous or full-time labor. Until late in the nineteenth century in some parts of Europe, part-time or seasonal village labor contributed a significant part of total industrial output. J. E. Tennent, for example, advised English travelers to visit the linen markets of the Low Countries in winter, for that was when rural workers had most to sell.[10]

Cottage industries decayed slowly during the nineteenth century, and their decline coincided approximately with the even more gradual abandonment of open-field farming. Together these two processes led to a decline in the village community, rapid in some parts of Europe but generally very slow. This was part of a general depopulation of the countryside, most marked in western Europe, but apparent almost everywhere. It was accompanied by a dispersal of rural population from agglomerated villages to scattered farmsteads, a reversal of the process that had probably taken place during the earlier Middle Ages.

A third factor in the medieval nucleation of settlement was the church and its parochial institutions. It would be an exaggeration to say that every village was the focus of a parish and contained its church, but in general terms there was a rough conformity between village community and parish. Christianity was disseminated from its urban foci into surrounding rural areas, and the process continued more actively after the period of the great invasions. The process consisted, broadly speaking, in the foundation of missionary churches, called in England "ministers," from which to proselytize the surrounding areas. Priests must have visited rural communities, where they preached at first from "preaching crosses" and later from rudimentary churches. The relationship at this early date between village, manor, and church is obscure. Each institution was at an early and evolutionary stage. They were to grow together so that in many instances and in much of Europe each was an aspect of the other two. But perfect conformity, in which manor fitted neatly into parish and had at its center village, manor house, and parish church, was perhaps the exception rather than the general rule.

It is in almost all instances unclear who established the earliest local churches. They might have been built by the community or established by the lord. However it originated, the church quickly assumed great importance in the lives of those who used it. The early churches emphasized the sacraments of baptism and burial, the rites of passage marking the beginning and end of human existence. These could not be performed everywhere. They had their places, the font and the cemetery, and these two were focal to the development of the parish. Their possession was a mark of parochial status. Private chapels, however exalted their patronage, however splendid they might be, lacked them, and their inferior status was thus apparent to all.

In areas where human settlement tended to be nucleated, the rudimentary church was, as a general rule, centrally placed. Its location, like that of the huts of the village, may have been fluid at first, but the construction of a masonry church had the effect of fixing its position for all time. Many a church that outwardly seems to be of late medieval or even eighteenth-century origin is found to hide the foundations of a Dark Age church. Surrounding the church was its cemetery, where all the people of the village lay buried or expected in their turn to lie. Graves were unmarked, their position quickly forgotten, and new burials were made on top of the old. The cemetery embraced the community's past, from which the present was loath to distance itself. The desire to be near the graves of one's ancestors went far back into prehistoric times and deep into human sub-consciousness. It was yet another bond between the members of the village community. Indeed, the baptismal font was itself a tangible expression of this chain of human existence and was often retained even when all else in the church had been rebuilt or renewed. Even the symbolism sometimes carved into the font, such as the "tree of life" (fig. 4.4), stressed the continuity of existence from one generation to the next.

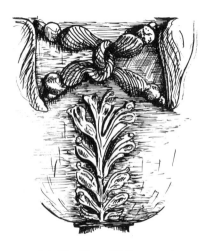

4.4. The Tree of Life, carved symbolically on the bowl of a baptismal font.

To live at a distance from the church was itself no small inconvenience. Those whose cottages lay in secondary or peripheral settlements complained bitterly of the difficulties of the journey to church or cemetery with unburied bodies and unbaptized children. Such complaints were most common in the late Middle Ages and were most often made in justification of a request for baptismal or burial rights nearer home; in short, for a kind of parochial status for one's own small community. This was, in fact, a step in the breakup of the large village. The church, furthermore, served as a storage place for some of the more prized possessions of the villagers and even as a place of refuge when times were disturbed.

Whether a new parish was or was not created in such circumstances depended largely on the wealth of the community that was making the request. More often than not, the bishop did not regard the new parish as viable, and rights were refused. For a parish was a unit of land that, notionally at least, was capable of maintaining a church and supporting a priest and his ministration. The wealth of a parish was expressed in the amount of tithe that it could contribute. The practice of contributing a tenth of nature's bounty for religious purposes long antedates the rise of Christianity.[11] It was enjoined by the law of Moses and was in some way practiced in the ancient Middle East and in Greece and Rome. The practice was taken over by the Christian church and supported by lay authority. Charlemagne enacted that tithe should be paid for the support of the church, and Anglo-Saxon rulers enacted similar legislation at about the same time.

The actual practice of tithing, the inclusion or exclusion of garden crops, of timber cut in the woodlands, and of the products of the fisheries, varied from one area to another, but, however assessed, tithe was a burdensome and regressive tax. As the system evolved during the Middle Ages, the clergy themselves gathered the tithe from the fields or had it delivered to the church. They became ruthless in collecting it, as indeed, they had to be, since it was the most important source of income for the church at the local level. Chaucer wrote of his parish priest that: "full loath were him to cursen for his tithes." But doubtless he "cursed" as vehemently as any, and with the backing of the courts, whenever his income was at risk. The levy of parochial tithes called for precise boundaries between parishes. Indeed, the parish is essentially a unit for the payment of tithe. As cultivation was pushed outward from the center, tithe began to be demanded by its priest. There must have been settlements out on the periphery that could claim—perhaps honestly—that they did not know where their tithe obligations lay. The bishop was called to adjudicate. A parochial boundary was delimited and thereafter, in many instances, ceremonially promenaded to impress it on the minds of parishioners. Decisions of this kind were influenced, no doubt strongly, by the wishes of the lord of the manor. It was doubtless convenient if parochial and manorial boundaries could be made to coincide. It simplified the payment of tithes and removed a cause of friction between parishes.

Traditionally, tithes were used for the support of the priest, the maintenance of the fabric of the church, and the relief of the poor. As a general rule they were adequate for these purposes but had to be supplemented by the gifts of parishioners if any particularly sumptuous building was undertaken. In fact, it became customary for the priest to be responsible only for the chancel or choir of the church. The nave was the sphere of the laity, who rebuilt and embellished it according to their resources and their inclinations.

In many, perhaps most, parishes the original church had been built and even endowed with a few fields, the glebe, by a lay lord, who continued to exercise some patronage, if not control, over it. It was *his* church, his *Eigenkirche,* and he exercised his rights of patronage with care and consideration, but there were inevitably instances of abuse, when unsuitable priests were presented and the priestly office was reduced to an appendage of the manor. In the course of the reform movements of the eleventh century, the church firmly set its face against such abuses. Its remedy was to induce the patron to surrender his rights over the church, including that of "presenting" a rector or priest, to the bishop or to a monastery. The efforts of the church met with considerable success. In England a third of the parishes passed in this way into the possession of monastic houses. The abbot or prior of the monastery assumed the rights and obligations of parish priest, but appointed a "vicar" who discharged the duties vicariously. The monastery, which received the tithe, usually made a handsome profit on the transaction, since the vicar received only a small stipend. The monastery also inherited the obligation to maintain the priest's part of the church, a duty that was discharged with varying degrees of zeal and efficiency. There are instances of the monastery passing on decorative features, like stained glass and paving tiles, to its dependent churches. There are, on the other hand, cases of utter neglect. *The Vision of Piers the Plowman* of the late fourteenth century is emphatic on the question of monastic neglect of parish churches: "even though it rains on their altars."

In most of Europe the system of tithe payment continued little altered into modern times. In those countries, notably Britain, which became Protestant at the Reformation, monasteries were dissolved, and the payment of tithe either lapsed or passed into lay hands. Everywhere the tendency was to commute it for a fixed monetary payment.

The role of the church in the community of the village was a great deal broader than the administration of the sacraments and the collection of tithe. It was the focus of social life, meeting place, safe storage, and, in emergency, place of refuge. Associations, fraternities, and gilds of villagers, as also of townsfolk, centered in the church. Here they met and, if they were affluent enough, built a chapel annexed to some part of its structure. Here they had masses sung for the souls of their departed members. From the church also was administered the parish stock, that store of implements and animals and even of money which the parishioners had accumulated against any misfortune that might befall them. Those parishioners who were wealthy enough to do so often left money and goods to the parish. The money was used in part to maintain and extend the church. But a bequest of animals, farming tools, or seed can only have been added to the parochial stock. Here too, they chose their wardens, who attended to most aspects of parochial life that did not fall within the purview of the manor court and its officials. Here the parishioners discussed the building, or rebuilding, of that part of the church— the nave, with its aisles, the porch, and the tower—which they thought of as belonging to themselves.

It must not be assumed that the community of the village always reached its decisions without friction or dispute. The fact that most of the members were interrelated, however distantly, in the "cousinhood" of the village and that the cultivation of their fields was dependent on mutual cooperation did not prevent their society from being torn by feuds. Most arose from disputed inheritances or trespasses in the open fields. The peasant was always land hungry and acquisitive, and the possession of land and yet more land was the height of his ambition. One reads of feuds pursued with such intensity that one family would refuse to be present in church if the other were there.

Rural society is generally supposed to have been made up of nuclear families, each consisting of parents and children. This view tends to be supported by the fact that in many parts of Europe taxes were levied on the "hearth" or household. But the nuclear family was not universal. It was found interspersed with "extended" families, in which grandparents and married sons and daughters may have also been present. Travelers in the Balkans commented frequently on the prevalence of a form of the extended family known as the *zadruga*. This has been regarded as a peculiarly Slavic institution, explicable in terms of the need to clear land and secure protection. The extended family was at one time a widespread institution but survived longer in the Balkans than elsewhere. A sketch made in the 1870s by the archeologist Sir Arthur Evans represented the *zadruga* as a large, enclosed farming unit, with a very large house (fig. 4.5). In fact, the *zadruga* represented a process whereby children remained in the parental home after marriage and eventually succeeded to the family holding.[12] The presence of married brothers within a household demonstrated only that they were joint heirs to their father. A prevailingly low age at marriage meant that the generation overlap was all the greater. But there must always have been the possibility that death would take its toll and the extended family would be reduced to the nuclear.

The Typology of the Village

These then were the centripetal and the centrifugal forces that brought the villagers together, held them in a small, closed society, and ultimately broke them asunder,

4.5. A *zadruga*, as sketched by Sir Arthur Evans in 1877. (From A. J. Evans, *Through Bosnia and Herzogovina on Foot* [London, 1877], 57.)

dispersing them to the ends of the parish. It follows that the village itself was fluid and changing. It was made up of cells, each the toft of a peasant, with cottage and outbuildings. These changed from one generation to the next. The huts themselves decayed, were destroyed, and were rebuilt. Tofts might divide to accommodate joint heirs and merge again as death took its toll. A hut or an annex might be built for elderly dependents, only to decay when it ceased to be needed. A village might be half-emptied by epidemic disease, only to fill again as the young, inheriting land at an earlier age than they might have expected, married younger and begat a larger family. The village community was like a pulsating organism, autonomous, self-sufficing, yet touched by external influences that ranged from war and pestilence to the exactions of church and state. Nevertheless, we can recognize in the shifting pattern of village settlements a number of separate and distinct types, each responding in some way to particular social and economic forces. The nucleated and the isolated settlements are only the extremes in a broad spectrum that ranges from the very large village of almost urban proportions, through loosely clustered and street and ring-fence villages, to small and isolated homesteads. But these categories are far from exclusive. They merged into one another. None was stable. They pulsated, growing and contracting with changes in their population. Large settlements and small have always existed together, and each at any particular time was the product of environmental constraints and pressures.

The plan of human settlements—the relationship of homes to one another, to their barns and other farm buildings, and to their fields—was subject to an immense variation from totally random to completely regular. The site of a settlement may reflect environmental constraints, but its internal plan responds only to social and economic pressures. The earliest village sites that have been excavated showed as a general rule an almost random placement of houses in relation to one another (fig. 4.6).[13] Buildings were, in any case, roughly constructed and probably short-lived. The wood of which they were built rotted quickly, or the cottage succumbed to fire and had to be rebuilt. With each rebuilding, as countless excavations have shown, the site was shifted, if only a short distance. An important stage in the development of any clustered settlement was the emergence of property lines, boundaries separating the plot of one cottage from that of its neighbors. One can still find settlements, especially in southeastern Europe, where there is no recognizable boundary between lots, and children and small animals wander indiscriminately between the houses. But in much of Europe boundaries were established early and the enclosed toft became a garden capable at the least of supplying vegetables. This became the normal pattern, with the toft even today playing an important role in the domestic economy. The boundaries of the toft set limits to the "migration" of the house, but, as long as its foundations were perishable, one could not prevent its ground plan from shifting and changing.

Another and probably contemporary development was that of roads or streets. One cannot be sure in many instances which came first, the streets or the houses. In so simple an example as that shown in figure 4.6 there were no roads as such, though customary use would have marked out tracks between the houses and from the houses to the surrounding fields. But once roads had become established, houses would tend to align themselves along them in whatever way proved convenient for the movement of animals and farm products. It is probably no exaggeration to say that the course of most village streets was dictated by the meanderings of farm animals, but such unplanned villages have since remained fairly stable features of the rural landscape.[14]

In contrast with these irregularly nucleated or agglomerated villages were those of more regular plan (figs. 4.2b and 4.7). The latter were dependent on a road or street system that constituted a prior feature of the landscape. In most instances these were "planted" villages. A *locator,* employed by whoever owned or controlled the land, traced their plan on the ground, marked the limits of the plots and of their accompanying fields, and allocated them to the settlers.[15] In its simplest form the planned village consisted of two rows of cottages, one on each side of a road. Behind each cottage was its cultivated land, a strip stretching away to the limit of the occupied area. The "street" or "forest" village thus came to be a sinuous line of cottages, sometimes of immense length. It was known in Britain and western Europe but was most highly developed on the plains of east-central Europe, where *locatores* were particularly active in the Middle Ages. A high proportion of the villages of eastern Germany, Poland, and the lower Danube valley were of this plan, which is readily apparent in the landscape today (fig. 4.8).

In a variant of the street plan, the double row of cottages withdrew to enclose an elongated, spindle-shaped "green." This green served many functions. It was common land where cattle might be grazed and geese allowed to wander. It was surrounded by fenced tofts of the villagers, so that animals could safely be left here. There might be a pond and most likely a well. Sometimes a church and cemetery stood within or at the

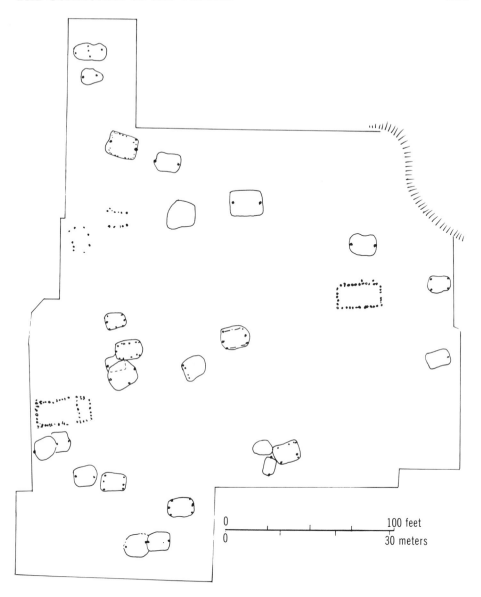

4.6. A Dark Age village, West Stow in Suffolk. This scheme illustrates the almost random placement of the huts. (Based on S. E. West, "The Anglo-Saxon Village of West Stow.")

edge of the green, and if the community had the right to hold a market, its stalls would have spread across it. The green did not have to be spindle shaped. It might be square, rounded, or even triangular in plan. Indeed, as noted earlier, the ring-fence village was so common a feature of some parts of eastern Europe that Meitzen regarded it as a specifically Slavic development. This, however, it was not. It was one of the many ways in which a settled community sought to enclose and protect itself and its animals.

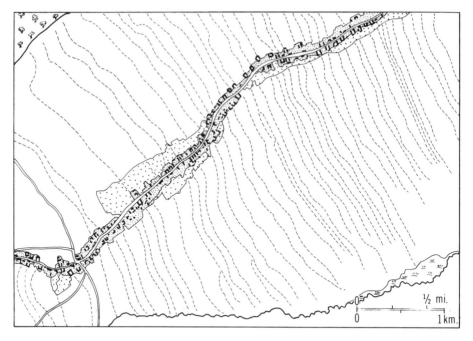

4.7. A street or "forest" village in eastern Germany. The settlement was open-ended, and could be extended in either direction as new settlers arrived.

4.8. A "street" village today, in the Voivodina district of northern Yugoslavia.

In some areas of Europe, notably the plains of the lower Danube valley, "planted" villages were often laid out on a rectangular or gridiron plan. As a general rule, these came later than the "street" villages and implied a larger body of settlers and a greater degree of administrative control. The village paths had clearly to be planned in advance of the arrival of the first settlers. Such villages became common when the Hungarian plain was recolonized after the expulsion of the Turks in the eighteenth century.[16]

Strongly nucleated or compact settlements occur mainly in two belts. The first lies across Europe from the Paris basin to the Russian steppe; the second is met with around the shores of the Mediterranean Sea. The largest rural settlements to be found anywhere lie here, involving even today arduous journeys from the villages to the fields. The Mediterranean village cannot be explained, like the nucleated village of northern Europe, in terms of manorial control and the constraints of cultivating the open fields. These institutions were rare in southern Europe. People tended to live in large, clustered villages for other reasons.[17] Among these was the classical tradition of urban living; a great many of these large settlements would in classical times have been regarded as *poleis*. Then, too, the need for security was greater, and a village perched high on the crags overlooking a coastal plain was almost impregnable to raiders by sea or land. It is also argued that malaria, which became endemic in some of the Mediterranean lowlands, forced people to find refuge above the flight of the mosquito. The situation in the interior of the Spanish peninsula was not unlike that to be seen in the Hungarian plain. Warfare had devastated the area, and as the Moors were driven back by the Christian armies of the north, the vast, empty plains of the Meseta were resettled by colonists brought in by their new masters, the religious, military orders. For both convenience and protection, the settlers were established in large villages, which the pattern of mutual obligation and help has served to perpetuate.

Throughout the Mediterranean world the tendency in more recent and less disturbed times has been for these strongly nucleated settlements to break up and, despite the cooperative nature of peasant society, for villagers to build homes isolated amid their fields. The traveler who today climbs to one of the hilltop villages of southern Italy or Spain finds them half-deserted and the shuttered houses crumbling to ruin.

A special case of the southern village is the *čiflik,* to be found in areas formerly under Ottoman rule.[18] Each was the focus of a feudal estate, owned by a Turkish "bey" and worked by half-free Christian "rayas." The latter commonly lived not in nucleated villages, as in the west, but in barracklike quarters surrounding an open courtyard and dominated by the home of the bey or his steward (fig. 4.9). Conditions of life must have been as bad as anywhere in Europe. The social system that supported such settlements was created after the Ottoman conquest in the later Middle Ages and lapsed with the expulsion of the Turks in the nineteenth century, but the physical structures of the *čiflik* village are still present and, in many cases, still inhabited.[19]

At the opposite end of the spectrum from large, compact settlements were hamlets and isolated farmsteads. Such a settlement pattern might have originated in many ways. It might have been an original feature of the landscape, established during the earliest phases of human settlement and enduring little altered until the recent past. In western Britain isolated farmsteads often bear names that speak of great antiquity. Alternatively they might derive in more recent times from the division of land between heirs or from the settlement of recently reclaimed marshland, as in the Low Countries. Around many

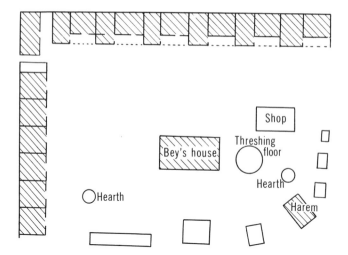

4.9. A *čiflik* in Macedonia. (After Jovan Cvijič.)

clustered villages there lay a circle of small and isolated settlements. Most such settlements were secondary, established by migrants from a village that had grown too large. Some were short-lived, founded when population was increasing, abandoned when it contracted. During recent centuries the large, nucleated village has tended to empty itself of people. The reason lay in the breakdown of the bonds of mutuality that had held the community together. The strongest cement of rural society had been the collaborative use of the open fields. When, under one pretext or another, these fields were enclosed and cultivated "in several," the compulsion to live together in a village community was reduced. At the same time the need to seek security in numbers became less pressing, and many a village family moved to a new home amid its fields. This happened as much in the overblown villages of Spain, Italy, and Greece as in central and northern Europe. Conditions of land tenure contributed to the process. The leasing of the lands of estates either for rent or on a sharecropping basis merely increased the number of more or less compact farm holdings, and on each there was the temptation to settle and build a home. Figure 4.10, based on the work of the late Harry Thorpe, shows how the Danish landscape was transformed within the span of less than a century from one of large, compact villages to smaller clusters ringed by separate farmsteads. This process has now run its course in much of Scandinavia and northwestern Europe. The village has been reduced to an irreducible minimum made up of church, school, essential craftsmen, a shop or two, and a small resident population. Where this process has not occurred, it is only because the cohesiveness of the village community, the interdependence of its members, has remained institutionalized in a common use of the land, of threshing floor and baking oven, and of the rest of the village infrastructure.

These constraints have remained powerful on the Meseta of Spain. Here a kind of feudal control has been perpetuated in the ownership of estates, and at the village level constraints on the peasantry have changed little since the end of the Middle Ages.[20] The peasant held his plot precariously on a short-term lease, which would have prevented him, even if he had had the capital, from breaking with common tradition or leaving his bleak, brown village of mud-built huts.

4.10. From open field to enclosed in a Danish village. The maps relate respectively to (*a*) 1769; (*b*) 1805; (*c*) 1893. (After Harry Thorpe, "The Influence of Inclosure on the Form and Pattern of Rural Settlement," *Tr. I.B.G.* 17 [1951]: 111–29.)

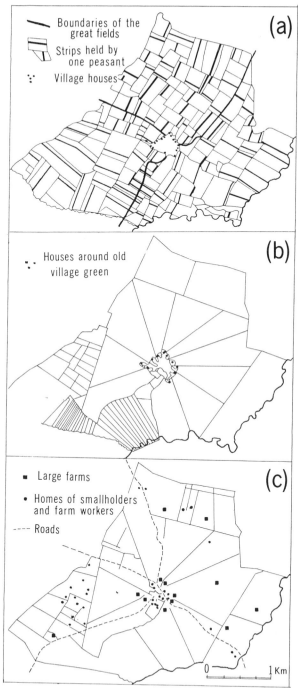

Boundaries of the great fields

Strips held by one peasant

Village houses

(a)

Houses around old village green

(b)

■ Large farms

• Homes of smallholders and farm workers

---- Roads

(c)

0 1 Km

4.11. An isolated farmstead in the Hungarian plain, a product of the eighteenth- and nineteenth-century dispersion of settlement.

In the Hungarian plain the danger of invasion and war had restricted human settlement to large, sprawling villages of urban proportions. Here animals were kept when they were not grazing the distant fields.[21] The peasants set out each morning in a fleet of wagons and carts, and here they returned at the end of the day. In this instance the loosening of the bonds of the community can be traced with some precision. Peasants first began to spend the nights amid their fields in tented shelters, or *tanyak,* during the busiest times of the agricultural year, returning to the villages with their animals in winter. As peace became more assured in the *puszta,* they stayed even longer in the fields, replacing their temporary shelters with more permanent homes. Gradually the balance was tipped. The dwelling amid the fields became a permanent home (fig. 4.11); that in the village was reduced to a residence for the winter months and, for the rest, was given over to elderly relatives and dependents. The pattern of settlement had been reversed without any change of revolutionary significance in modes of cultivation or land tenure.

It is possible to generalize and to regard specific settlement types as typical of particular areas. It does not follow, however, that one form prevails to the exclusion of all others; only that it is the most common type and the one that gives character to the region. Figure 4.12 illustrates this point, with "street" or "forest" villages predominant in the east and clustered villages in the west.

The nature of a settlement had important consequences for social and cultural life. The village was a community of mutually dependent families. They shared in various ways the labor of the fields. They used by agreement among themselves the common grazing, the meadow, and the woodland; they shared the well, baking oven, and threshing floor; and they joined together to erect a house and to maintain roads and

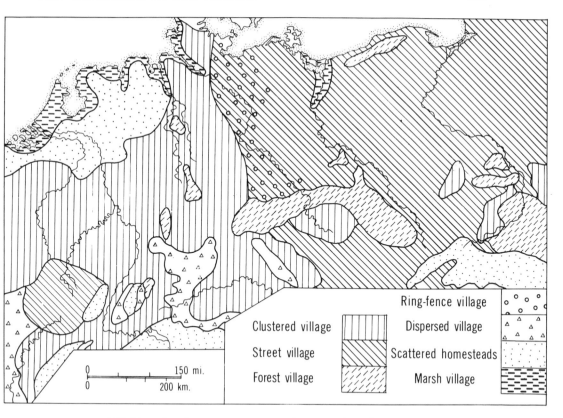

4.12. Map of settlement types in central Europe. (Based on R. E. Dickinson, *Germany* [New York, 1953], 144–48; J. M. Houston, *A Social Geography of Europe* [London, 1953], 103.)

bridges. Together they shared their simple pleasures, the feasting and dancing at harvest time and weddings, folk customs that marked the passage of the year, and the elaborate and traditional decoration of both their houses and themselves. But village society was far from egalitarian. It was, in fact, highly structured, and status was as significant in a peasant society as in any other. During much of the preindustrial period the village in much of Europe was subject to some form of manorial organization. It was a unit within an estate, whose lord received rents and services from the peasants who occupied and cultivated it. The peasants differed greatly in the extent of their holdings and in the services that they owed. In much of Europe many of them were unfree until the liberation of the serfs, which took place between the French Revolution of 1789 and the more general revolutionary movements of 1848. There were rich peasants whose holdings were more than enough to support a family and, at the opposite end of the rural spectrum, there were cottagers and landless peasants who could only live if employed as day laborers, working on the land of their richer neighbors. Peasant status changed during the period. In general there was a leveling up. The rigors of serfdom were softened in western and central Europe, and when at last it was abolished, there were comparatively few serfs remaining. At the same time, however, serfdom was intensified in eastern Europe, where it lasted in some form until 1848; in Russia, until 1861, and in Romania, even longer.[22]

Despite its social divisions, the rivalry—even hostility—of rich peasant and poor, and the deep feuds that always seemed to divide its people, the village had a real sense of community. Its customs and traditions were deeply rooted, and it resented interference from outside and every attempt to restrict its customs and liberties.[23]

The situation was different in small and dispersed settlements. There was little sense of community. The group was often no more than an extended family. The mutuality and also the conflict within the village were lacking. Plowing, harvesting, house and barn raising were individual, not communal activities. If such family groups stood apart from many of the activities of the village community, they were also free from its social and hierarchical structure. Material conditions of life were different in hamlets and isolated settlements from those in clustered villages. The former were less accessible to church and market, and, in more recent times, to shops and schools. They had of necessity to be more self-sufficing. It was often impossible to raise a large team, and the heavy plow was rare if not unknown; a light plow, even a caschrom, continued to be used until the nineteenth century. Homes and farm buildings were simpler in style and decoration, designed and built within the family, making little demand on the cooperative effort of the community. Society in an area of small and scattered settlements was based on kinship; in the clustered village, on community.

The village community was engaged in agriculture, but this did not absorb all its activities. There were craftsmen: a miller, a smith, a tanner. But many of the goods in common use were made by the peasants themselves. Most of their clothes were homespun. They did their own rough carpentry and with one another's help they built, repaired, and extended their cottages and barns.

Village and Church

Few villages were without a church, and there were no settlements, whatever their size, that did not belong to an ecclesiastical parish. The church in the physical sense changed and developed and became a dominant feature of both the rural and the urban landscape. It represented certain ethical and spiritual values, though the local peasantry who built and frequented it probably had little knowledge or understanding of them. To the peasants the church was the focus of their traditions and culture. Their feasts and fetes turned on the church's calendar, just as this reflected the rhythm of the seasons and of life on the land.

Within the church, in the stained glass of its windows and the paintings and frescoes on its walls, the biblical story unrolled in a giant strip cartoon, interspersed with moral injunctions couched in pictorial form: warnings to those who had blasphemed, spread rumor, and profaned the Sabbath, and, full in the face of the congregation as it stood or knelt, was the great doom itself, the last judgment, with the spirits of the elect on one side being welcomed into heaven and, on the other, the damned disappearing, head first, into the leaping flames of hell. It was very lurid and dramatic, but whether all who stood and wondered really thought that such things happened, or were greatly influenced by them if they did, we cannot know.

Among the expressions of pious sentiment was much popular superstition and plain,

4.13. Gossip and slander were, as countless cases before manorial and other courts show, the bane of village life. A motif often painted on the interior walls of a church depicted two women in animated conversation while the devil hovered above their heads, inspiring their words. This Finnish painting of the fifteenth century shows one of the women using a butter churn.

coarse fun. Many of the craftsmen who carved the corbels, wooden seats and bench-ends, and other decoration were local men, and much of their work must have been crude portraiture or realistic portrayals of events and scenes around them. The biblical story was always interpreted in contemporary terms.

It is impossible to say how many parishes there may have been in Europe at, say the end of the Middle Ages, when the "seamless web" of Christendom was torn asunder by the Protestant Reformation. There were about ten thousand in England and Wales, and some forty thousand in France. Add those in Germany and eastern and southern Europe, and the total could not have been much less than a quarter of a million. Each had its church and priest, supported by tithe and glebe and the donations of the faithful, and built with what elegance and splendor the local community could afford. Much as people might have distrusted the church as an institution and the priests as individuals, the fabric of the church continued into the nineteenth century to focus their loyalties and their hopes. Its feasts brightened their dull lives, and its services brought them together, as indeed they still do in parts of Europe, for purposes that were often far from spiritual. The people who built these churches and worshiped and carried on their daily business in them could rarely read and write. We have little record of their attitude toward life beyond what is implicit in the artifacts that they have left. By and large, it is only their material culture that we can study; what, if anything, lay deeper we can only guess.

A window into this peasant world of the past is, however, opened by a novel written toward the end of the nineteenth century by one of its number. Władisław Reymont lived for much of his life in the village of Lipce, in central Poland, and worked on the nearby railway. His most famous novel, *Chłopi,* or *The Peasants,* is concerned with the events of one year in this small, closed community. The area was at this time part of the Russian Empire, and the Polish Rising of 1863 was a distant memory. Lipce was a preindustrial village community, closely observed and described in intimate detail by one who had the deepest knowledge and understanding of every facet of its life. In Reymont's picture the influence of the church pervaded the village just as its rather plain brick structure still dominates the physical scene. The church was the common, the only meeting place, where the whole community gathered on Sunday. The priest was everyone's counselor and confidant, trying to distance himself from the eternal peasant disputes, which, whatever their nature, always turned upon the possession of land.

There is a pious legend that the end of the world was anticipated in the year 1000, and when this date passed without any untoward event, people turned with relief to everyday matters. In the words of the eleventh-century chronicler Ranulf Glaber, Europe began to put on its "white robe of churches." In fact, however, the rebuilding activity that characterized the eleventh and later centuries is likely to have been related more to the cessation of barbarian inroads than to any postponement of the day of judgment. In the Mediterranean region, most early churches were masonry built and of basilican plan. Elsewhere they were generally of wood and of simpler design. They commonly consisted of just two compartments, one in which the priest performed his "magic," the other for his flock. In the course of time masonry construction replaced timber. Although the two "cells"—chancel and nave—remained dominant, other elements came to be added: chapels along the sides of the church and a tower either where the two cells met or at the west end. The church became a barometer of rising population and increasing wealth. It underwent a piecemeal rebuilding and extension, and if any fragment of the original church survived, it was commonly embedded in masonry of a different age. Of course some, through poverty or misfortune, failed to grow, and survive today little different from what they were a thousand years ago. Others were transformed into vast temples of glass and stone. Many were razed in war; they burned or fell down through faulty workmanship and had to be rebuilt. Some were abandoned with the decline of the settlement that they served, fell to ruin, and crumbled into the soil. Most churches, like the villages around them, were in a process of constant change and renewal, reflecting the size and wealth and also the spirituality of the local population.

Throughout central and much of southern Europe there was a great rebuilding of churches in the seventeenth and eighteenth centuries. In part this was due to the destruction of war, especially of the Thirty Years War; in part, to the changed attitudes to church doctrine and discipline that sprang from the Counter-Reformation. It is the baroque church, with its strong visual elements of classicism, that dominates the countryside of south Germany, Bohemia, Austria, and even parts of Poland. In south-eastern Europe a different ecclesiastical organization, emanating from Constantinople rather than Rome, contributed to a different building tradition. This influence is apparent in much of the Balkans. Here the church dominated the lives of the people no less than in the west, but its role as a social focus was less apparent, and the Orthodox church did not become the meeting place of the communities that supported it.[24]

Most parish churches were built of materials that occurred locally, within the parish. The most common was timber. In some parts of Europe, notably Scandinavia and the great plain of eastern Europe, timber has remained an important material for church building. But timber structures decay readily, and most churches have been rebuilt with stone or brick. Even in Anglo-Saxon England, a time when domestic building was entirely in wood, many churches were built of stone. The builders adapted their style to the materials that were available. Sometimes they built with coarse stone, such as could be found in the boulder clay; sometimes with fine free-cutting stone taken straight from the quarry; sometimes with burned brick; sometimes even from the damaged masonry retrieved from a long abandoned Roman site. Much depended on local resources and on how much the community was prepared to invest in its church and all that it stood for. Sometimes a high-quality stone was imported at great cost from distant quarries and was used for the tracery of windows, the coins of buildings, the sculpture of capitals. But not infrequently we came across the work of the untutored local craftsman roughly executed in local materials, however unsuited these may have been for his purpose.

The style of churches became more elaborate, more highly decorated in the later Middle Ages. This development necessitated the use of stone of higher quality and the employment of skilled masons and sculptors, practices that were made possible by the greater wealth of the community and the more rapid communication of ideas. Architectural styles and motifs spread across major areas of the continent, carried by itinerant masons, each with a little collection of drawings and templates and a headful of ideas. Regional styles emerged, thus defining a kind of mental horizon for the people of a particular locale. There is no confusing a church built in the Paris basin with one in England or Italy, but their differences are only variations on a common theme. Despite differences in scale, in adaptation to liturgical demands, and in degrees of embellishment, most conformed to a common plan. They remained basically of two cells or compartments, nave and chancel, corresponding with the spheres of people and of priest.

The "white robe of churches" was for all practical purposes complete by the sixteenth century, when the Protestant Reformation split Europe into two hostile camps. In the regions that became Protestant, the medieval churches, stripped of much of their decoration and liturgical significance, continued in use. By contrast, in "Catholic" Europe there was a new spirit in architecture. A classical style replaced the Gothic, which had reached the peak of its development in the later Middle Ages. Repair and renovation were in the new style, but always adjusted, as in the Middle Ages, to the financial resources of the parish. A classical style somewhat more austere than in Italy or central Europe even overflowed the limits of Catholic Europe and gave the world the elegance of the "Wren" churches of London.

The Structures of the Village

For the rest, the village was made up of homes and farm buildings. These varied in scale and style no less than the church that they surrounded. They were built almost entirely of local materials, and most frequently of wood. In size they corresponded with the wealth and aspirations of those who built them, and in style and decoration they reflected both tradition and the constraints of climate and local resources. The essential element in a peasant hut was a living room with a place to sleep and a place to cook and prepare food. Even in Iron Age Europe these requirements had been met in a variety of ways. Tacitus described the rounded pit dwellings, sunk a few feet below the surface of

4.14. A nucleated village in the loess region of Lower Saxony.

the ground and roofed with branches. Such "dwellings" continued to be used for many centuries, and even in recent times homes were excavated in the soft loess soil of Romania and Bulgaria. Modern excavation has shown how extensive were these *Grubenhäuser* (fig. 4.15), especially on light and well-drained soil.[25] Many a Dark Age settlement consisted of little more than pit dwellings. They were quickly constructed, could be roofed with light timbers, and were admirably suited to the needs of a people that was still far from sedentary. In the course of time they came to be paneled with wood or woven osier and even divided by partitions into rooms.

Most houses in medieval Europe, however, were built above ground-level, of either wood or stone. Broadly speaking, timber construction was most common north of the Alps, and masonry or mud brick to the south. But there were many exceptions to such a generalization. Wood-built houses consisted generally of a frame or skeleton of stout timbers, infilled with woven osiers and daubed with clay or covered with roughly cut boards, just as in much of prehistoric Europe. Later, brick was sometimes used to fill the spaces between the studding of timber-framed buildings. Often, especially in eastern Europe, a hut was built of logs, laid horizontally and notched at the corners. But this was practicable only where there was an abundance of straight, round timbers. Wattle and daub, which gave rise to the attractive "black-and-white" construction so familiar in Germany and England, was probably a response to the growing shortage of good timber in the later Middle Ages and early modern times.

The upright timbers in early homes were generally planted directly in the soil, and their post holes are all we are likely to find of them. Then the practice developed, especially important on clay soils, of resting the structure on a sill plate of wood or a foundation or plinth of stone. This reduced the tendency for the timbers to rot, but wooden cottages had nevertheless only a short life. The answer to this problem was, of course, to build in brick or stone. At the village level this technique was practicable where suitable raw materials occurred locally, and this happened only in restricted areas. Mud brick was used but was unimportant north of the Alps, since it crumbled readily in damp conditions. In Mediterranean Europe its use has continued into modern times. In a dry climate it formed a durable building material and made a well-insulated home. In northern Europe the practice developed in some areas of using a well-puddled clay,

4.15. *Grubenhäuser,* or sunken dwellings. This drawing was made early in the nineteenth century in the Hungarian plain, but such dwellings go back to prehistoric times and can be seen today in the Village Museum in Bucharest. (From J. Paget, *Hungary and Transylvania* [London, 1839].)

mixed with pebbles and straw. In Britain this mixture was known as "cob." If protected from rain by, for example, a plaster rendering, it would often last as long as timber construction.

Masonry, if it is to be really durable, requires a lime mortar. Lime was, until modern times, expensive, and in many areas, where limestone did not occur naturally, it was unobtainable. Mud, laced with straw, was sometimes used as a substitute, especially in rubble masonry, but it had to be laid on thick and was best if protected from the weather.

North of the Alps, vernacular, or popular, architecture was before the nineteenth century mainly in timber, and wood construction has continued to be important in eastern Europe and Scandinavia until the recent past. Vernacular architecture in stone was significant only in the "stone belts," but elsewhere the peasant was often driven by necessity to use whatever stone the local environment offered. In fact, there were few areas, apart from the clay-covered plains, that did not yield stone of some kind, but much of it was too hard to be cut, or too fissile and soft to keep its shape. Such stone was used when nothing better offered, but it was often cheaper and easier to build in wood. The increase in the use of masonry for home construction at the humblest level is but one of the many indicators of rising material standards of living.

Masonry construction had other advantages than its greater durability. Stone-built homes were less susceptible to fire, which was one of the greatest hazards of living in any tight community. Some cities in the late Middle Ages and early modern times attempted to restrict the use of timber for this reason, but such regulation was never attempted in villages. Here fires were not infrequent among the wood-built houses and barns filled with hay and straw. In regions floored with clay, where one would look in vain for an adequate building stone, brick construction came into its own. The Romans had made great use of brick as well as of clay tile, but the art of making them appears to have lapsed at the end of the empire and was not revived until the eleventh century. The chief area of brick construction was the stoneless area of the northern Low Countries and the north German plain. From here the art of making and building with bricks spread to eastern England. But bricks were expensive: they were used first in churches and in urban construction. Only a sparing use of them was made in vernacular architecture before the eighteenth century, chiefly in fireplaces, chimneys, and baking ovens. Another advantage of masonry over wood was that it was less likely to afford refuge for rodents and vermin. The black rat, which played so important a role in the spread of the bubonic plague, could nest and breed very comfortably, and insects could make their homes amid the rotting timbers of a frame house. One of several factors in the disappearance of the plague from western Europe was without question the improvements made in the quality of building construction.

Whether a building was of stone, brick, or timber, there was always a problem in spreading a roof over it. Although corbeled ceilings of stone were known in classical times, and the Romans learned to construct massive vaults of masonry, the peasant always had recourse to timber. At its simplest, a roof—flat or pitched—consisted of branches roughly covered with grass and leaves. If the span was wide, a wooden support was used to hold it up. From this it was only a short step to constructing a ridge roof, held up by a line of posts, with rafters resting against it. The post holes in some of the larger Iron Age houses suggest two such lines of posts, as in figure 4.16d. The tendency, strongly marked from the Neolithic until modern times, to build houses that were very long in relation to their width was attributable in part to this difficulty in roofing a wide space.

Early roofs were almost certainly built of roughly trimmed branches. Later, heartwood, most often oak or elm, was used. The timbers were thicker and could be scarfed or jointed to make a strong and rigid roof. At the same time techniques were developed, mainly in the twelfth and later centuries, of constructing trusses to support the roof. Such techniques were first used in the great churches. Many roof structures of this age have survived and demonstrate the high level of skill achieved by the joiner and carpenter (fig. 4.17). But the peasant's cottage called for no such massive timbers, nor for such levels of technical skill. Only when large manorial halls began to be built did such refined building techniques pass from churches to secular buildings. The roof trusses to be found in a peasant cottage were simple in the extreme.

The timber roof, made up of trusses, rafters, and purlins, was only a support for the actual roofing material, which served to keep the weather out. This layer might be of thatch or wooden shingles, of slate or stone, of clay tiles, or even, in the cases of churches and some "grand" buildings, of lead. Thatch was without question the oldest and most widespread of these roofing materials. Its raw material—straw—was a by-product of agriculture. It cost nothing to produce, though the thatcher came to prefer the straw of one cereal over that of another. Wheat straw was thought to be more durable than that of other cereals, and oaten straw was too soft. The method of thatching, practiced since prehistoric times, was to take the straw in bunches and to secure it with string to laths fixed to the rafters. A well-thatched roof was waterproof, a good insulation, and durable, sometimes outlasting the laths to which it was attached. Shingles were thin slices of wood—most often of fir or pine, because these split easily—nailed to the laths. They were, and have remained, important in mountainous areas, where straw is scanty and timber abundant.

Other roofing materials were usually obtainable with greater difficulty, but often provided a more durable covering. Slate and stone—particularly limestone—which could be split thinly, provided an excellent cover, but were heavy and called for stronger

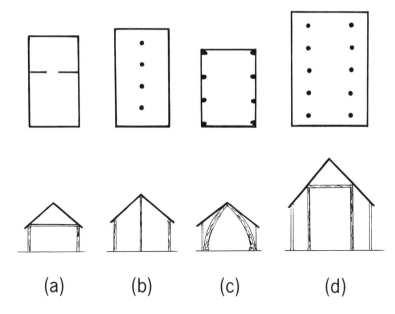

4.16. Plan and cross-sections through types of domestic buildings to show the development of truss construction: (*a*) simple tie beam; (*b*) center post; (*c*) cruck; (*d*) aisled hall.

4.17. A cruck building, probably late medieval, in use today in Herefordshire, England.

rafters than were necessary to support shingle or thatch. But suitable slate and stone had only a very narrow distribution and were not widely used until modern transportation made their movement practicable. Even today they are found chiefly in the mountainous areas of northwestern and central Europe. True slate can be split very thin, and, in addition to its use as a roofing material, was nailed to the timber framing of a house to protect its walls from damp. "Hung" slate, as this was called, became common during the eighteenth century in those areas where good-quality slate was abundant.

Artificial roofing materials have become increasingly important in modern times. In the more distant past they were restricted to clay tiles shaped and burned in a kiln, like bricks. These tiles could be made in shapes that joined and overlapped to make a waterproof cover, and, like slate, they could be hung on the walls of homes. Roofing tiles in the classical period had a curved or S-shaped section and were set so that each tile overlapped those on either side as well as above and below. The term "pantile" is usually given to such tiles. They were characteristic of the Mediterranean region. Their loose fit permitted air to circulate through the roof space, and their corrugations allowed the sometimes heavy rain to discharge freely. They came, however, to be used over a wide area in eastern France, where it cannot be said that they were particularly well suited to climatic conditions. This adoption must be regarded as a cultural borrowing of uncertain date, quite unrelated to local environmental factors. The Romans brought the use of the pantile to Britain, but here it failed to survive the barbarian invasions that brought the empire to an end.

In much of Europe the plan of a house derived from prehistoric prototypes. It was, as a general rule, rectangular, with a length considerably in excess of its width. The entrance, which might be at one end, or in the middle of a long side, led directly into the principal room. As houses became larger, they were divided into two rooms by a partition or cross-wall. The larger one became the living room, euphemistically called the "hall," and the other, the sleeping room or bower. The only source of heat was for many centuries an open fire set in the middle of the floor of the hall. There was no chimney. Smoke escaped where it could, and meat was even hung to cure amid the blackened rafters. In Poland, even in modern times, peasants distinguish between the "black room" (*czarna izba*) and the "white room" (*biała izba*) in their cottages.

The construction of a fireplace or oven came later and was always dependent on the use of masonry or, at the least, nonflammable clay. The Roman use of subterranean flues (the hypocaust) was not revived in medieval Europe. Instead, masonry hearths and chimneys were contrived in a corner or in a side wall of the main room. They had to serve for cooking as well as heating and were in the course of time graced with an assemblage of andirons, trivets, and spits of wrought or cast iron. In monasteries and great houses it became the practice to build a separate kitchen, sometimes detached from the rest of the building, in order to reduce the risk of fire, sometimes attached to the lower end of the hall. Great kitchens survive as large detached buildings as far apart as Glastonbury in England and the Rila monastery in the mountains of Bulgaria. Such buildings were often square in plan with hearths and chimneys in each corner. But separate kitchens were found only where there was a large community to be fed. The vernacular kitchen, when at last it made its appearance—not before the end of the Middle Ages—was an altogether humbler structure. It was small and equipped at most with an oven of masonry or clay. Sometimes, for reasons of safety, the oven stood in the yard, away from the house.

The floor of a house or cottage was only a degree less important for the safety and comfort of its occupants than the roof. The Romans had constructed floors of brick, even of mosaic made up of small *tesserae* set in cement. But such sophistication did not spread downward to the humbler citizen of the empire. The floors of their cottages were of beaten earth or clay, strewn at intervals with sand, straw, or rushes. They were likely to be damp at all times, but how damp depended on the ease with which the subsoil drained—hence the desire for a site on a patch of sand or gravel.

The refined floor construction displayed in Roman villas disappeared after the end of the empire, and little attempt was made to revive it until late in the Middle Ages. It is likely that stone slabs were again used first in churches, then in great houses. The *Terriers,* or surveys of church property, compiled in England in the seventeenth and eighteenth centuries show that many of the priests' houses still had floors of clay, but that stone and even wood were becoming more common. But not until the nineteenth and even the twentieth century in some parts of Europe did such materials begin to appear on the cottage floors of the rural poor.

The two-roomed plan became general throughout Europe north of the Alps. It provided the basic human requirements; it was relatively easy to construct and was versatile and capable of being extended as more accommodation came to be required. Of the home of Chaucer's "poor widow," the poet wrote: "Full sooty was hire bour and eek hir halle / In which she eet ful many a sklendre meel." From this two-cell house developed one with three rooms, the third being a service area at the lower end of the hall. From

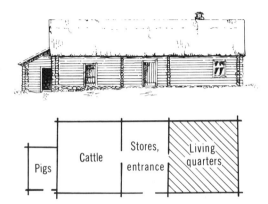

4.18. A longhouse in the East Baltic region, built of logs, notched at the corners. (After *Eth. Slav.* 8–9 [1976–77]: 45–60.)

the simple house there also grew the longhouse, in which an extension served to harbor the animals (fig. 4.18). Built on a grander scale, the two- or three-celled house became the manor, and, translated into masonry, the great hall of princely castles and palaces. From Ireland to Poland one can still recognize the basic plan, despite the accretions and extensions of modern times. A second story was added (fig. 4.19), first above the bower, then over the hall; a porch might be built, and an "outshut" or "linhay" constructed against the back wall of the house to serve as a kitchen, pantry, brewhouse, or store. Building materials, varying from one region to another, set their own constraints. Cottages became more highly decorated, as peasants lavished their skills on carving and coloring their homes to make them more personal and more individual. But beneath all these accretions there remained the Iron Age and early medieval two-cell home.

This simple plan evolved with the increase in wealth and technical skill. The first stage, after the development of kitchen and bower, was in some parts of Europe to add farm buildings at one or both ends of the hall block. These might take the form of projecting wings, partially enclosing a court or yard. Sometimes other ancillary buildings were built, forming a group of free-standing structures. Each homestead thus grew into an open cluster of discrete buildings. On the other hand, the group of buildings that lay around the yard might be drawn closer together until a point was reached at which a single roof could be made to span the whole. Such was the plan of the great farmhouses of central Europe. A home of more or less traditional plan occupied only a small part of its space. A central area, reached by farm wagons through a large gate, gave access to barn and stables as well as to the house itself. Such farms were almost invariably built of wood on a masonry foundation. They were one or two stories, with upper rooms in the living quarters and perhaps a hayloft above the stables.

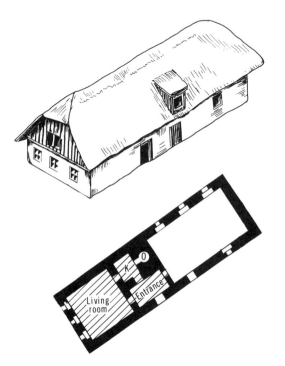

4.19. A longhouse with an upper floor over the living quarters, in Upper Austria. (After *Eth. Slav.* 2 [1970]: 43.)

In southern Europe the practice grew of building a second and even a third story in both the living and farm quarters (fig. 4.20). This was encouraged by the greater availability of stone, and the first floor at least was usually of masonry. But the tradition of large timber-framed buildings was preserved in the "chalet" construction of south Germany and the Alps. But how far back can one trace these types of construction? When did the massive farmhouses found today in many parts of central Europe begin to evolve from the simpler, early medieval house? The failure of earlier examples to survive makes it difficult both to date and to trace this development. It is doubtful whether it antedates the fifteenth century, when the peasantry in much of Europe began to enjoy a period of relative prosperity. Certainly, little of this extravagant development of domestic and farm building is apparent in late medieval illustrations, but in woodcuts and engravings, which became more numerous in the sixteenth and seventeenth centuries, the evidence for such structures becomes more abundant. It is likely, however, that most owed their origin to the greater freedom and prosperity of the rural population in much of Europe in the eighteenth century.

In all these developments the familiar constraints of climate and economy shaped the efforts of the peasant as he built and adapted his home. A fundamental reason for the large farmhouse was climatic. Long, severe winters with deep snow made it difficult to move about the farm. It was far more convenient to have direct access to the animals and even to the threshing floor without going outdoors, though this was a luxury which only

4.20. A "Turkish" house in Trnovo, Bulgaria. This example combines the Mediterranean tradition of building two or more stories and the Islamic tradition of having very few windows or other openings at ground-floor level and jettied upper floors.

4.21. The evolution of a farmstead at Gomeldon, Wiltshire, showing the abandonment of a longhouse plan and the adoption of separate house and byre. (After M. W. Beresford and J. G. Hurst, *Deserted Medieval Villages* [London, 1971], 111.)

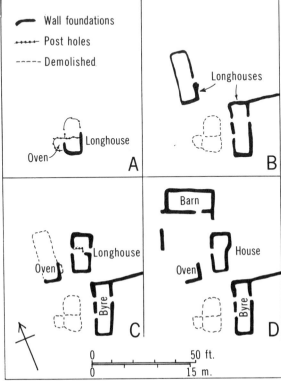

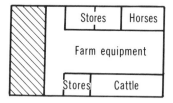

4.22. Westphalian house, with a miniature "yard," reached through large double doors, under the same roof as the house.

the better-off of the peasantry could afford. As a general rule, the *separate* barn, stable, and farmhouse (fig. 4.21) were to be found where the rigors of winter and the hardship of working outdoors were least. And that, by and large, meant the Atlantic fringes of Europe. The depth of snow and the violence of storms also influenced style and construction: steeply pitched roofs to shed the snow; large, overhanging eaves to keep rainwater away from walls and foundations; hipped gables and asymmetrical roofs to offer as little resistance as possible to the wind. The orientation of the cottage was often planned in order to catch as much of the sun's warmth as possible. Walls were built as thick as practicable, at least in central and eastern Europe, to provide insulation, and, as if this were not enough, the Polish peasant heaped straw and earth against the outside walls in winter. The roof was weighted down with stones in many Alpine areas, and in western Britain strips of granite were cemented to the roofing slates to hold them fast in gales.

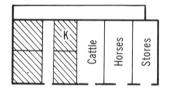

4.23. Swabian house, differing from the Westphalian in detail but with a broadly similar plan.

The heat of summer posed problems as well as offering opportunities. Thick walls and shuttered windows helped to keep the inside temperature low. Balconies, cantilevered out from the upper floors, provided space for drying corn, tobacco, and other plants, as well as a cool place for sleeping. Below the roofs, the intense heat that built up in attics was ventilated by means of louvered openings. Nowhere was the influence of summer temperatures more marked than in the Mediterranean region. Wherever stone was available, and that was almost everywhere, houses were likely to be of masonry construction. Roofs were of gentle pitch and often covered with pantiles, which fitted loosely and allowed the air to flow freely between them (fig. 4.24). Walls were thick against the summer heat and often painted white with limewash. Houses often ran

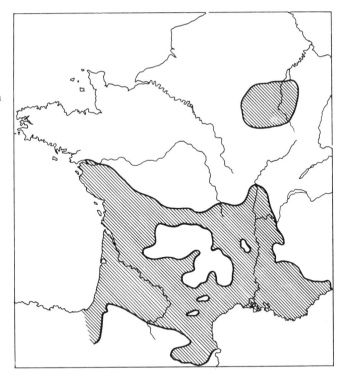

4.24. The distribution in France of low-pitched roofs with pantiles (*tuiles creuses*). Apart from their occurrence in Champagne, they are found throughout the south except in the wetter and more mountainous districts.

to two or three stories, facilitated by the abundance of building stone and encouraged by the close spacing of homes in the tightly nucleated villages. This suited the predominant economy, based, as it was, on breadgrains, the olive, and the vine. The ground floor served to press the grapes and olives and to store the wine and oil. The family commonly lived above, and a third floor, where the air could circulate through its unshuttered openings, was used for storing grain and other foodstuffs. Sometimes the ground floor may also have been used for stalling the cattle.

The basically outdoor pattern of life in southern Europe has led to other points of contrast in the plan and structure of homes. Although the living quarters were sometimes built *over* the cow byre, it was no less common to scatter the domestic and farm buildings around a court, a practice that derived from classical times. Even the stairs leading to the upper floors were frequently external, and the threshing floor, usually within a barn in northern Europe, was constructed in the open.

It would be a mistake to assume that the plan and structure of the peasant or rural house were automatic responses to climate and farm economy. That these influences were powerful goes without saying, but it was the peasants themselves who decided where and how to build, and they were also influenced by other factors than climatic considerations. Migration brought new turns and twists of style. Innovations and adaptations were made for reasons that at this distance in time we cannot penetrate. Some developments seem quite irrational, and for this reason generalization is difficult. Every region and district had its prevailing styles. One way of building a home or of laying out the structures of a farmyard merges into another: there were no firm boundaries between the different ways in which people in the past carried out the ordinary business of living and working. In this respect, as in so many others, Europe presents a kaleidoscope of changing styles that are impossible to describe in detail. Each represents the way in which a family or a community chose to respond to the particular circumstances in which it found itself. One trend is, however, apparent. Innovation always started in the homes of the elite, and gradually progressed downward toward those of the humblest members of society. The novelty in the manor house is likely, a century or two later, to become the commonplace of the peasant.

The study of the domestic buildings of the peasantry—vernacular architecture—has become a rich and rewarding field. Among countries where the subject has been pursued with the greatest vigor are Poland and, at the opposite end of Europe, the British Isles. The following pages are given over to an exposition of the styles met with in these contrasted environments. Between them they exemplify both the most primitive and the most developed forms of rural architecture to be found in Europe before the recent past.

The peasant cottage in most parts of Poland conformed to the simple traditional plan described on page 126. It consisted basically of living room with hearth for cooking and bedroom. It is possible to distinguish a southeastern region, where the tendency was to build a longhouse, from the northwest, where a more compact plan was general.[26] Traditional building was everywhere of wood, resting usually on a roughly made foundation of stone. Until the nineteenth century floors were of beaten clay, occasionally covered with sawn boards. Types of construction varied. Many cottages continued to be built, even in the nineteenth century, of round logs, notched at the corners, with the interstices rammed with clay and straw.[27] Such building was extravagant of wood and tended to be replaced with walls of sawn timber. Cottages were usually roofed with thatch or wooden shingles, supported by simple rafters, purlins, and laths. There was a considerable variation in the construction of gables. Sometimes they were built of planks laid in geometrical patterns; sometimes there were partial gables rising above a shingled apron; sometimes the roof was fully hipped (fig. 4.25). In some instances the entrance was at the narrow end of the building, protected by an overhanging roof supported on wooden columns. In others it was placed in the middle of the long side, as in the "hall house" in the west.

Existing cottages almost invariably have a stone-built fireplace and chimney, replacing the earlier hearth in the middle of the floor, where the cooking was done. The peasant Jan Słomka described how in the 1860s cast-iron wood-burning stoves came into use. But by no means did they displace the stone-built hearth. Cottages rarely had an upper floor, though there was often a storage space, reached by a ladder, above the bedroom. Color and decoration were according to regional styles. In the Kraków area it was common to plaster the stone footings and paint them blue; in central Poland the brown walls were sometimes painted in white with crude floral designs, and in many areas elaborately carved finials crowned the gables—a device that may have been of north German origin.[28]

It was not often that accommodation for the animals was to be found beneath the same roof as the living quarters of the peasant family, and the longhouse was rare. When it did occur it was probably introduced by German settlers, and the example shown in figure 4.25 was found, significantly, in the village of Kępa Niemiecka (German Kępa),

4.25. Two east European peasant huts: (*a*) a hut in the Carpathian Mountains that uses heavy log construction and wooden shingles in this forested region; (*b*) a hut in eastern Poland, using lighter timber, clay daubing, and thatch.

(a)

(b)

near Płock. Barns and stables, invariably small on peasant holdings, were freestanding structures, closely similar in design and construction to the houses themselves.

The gentry (*szlachta*) of Poland were very numerous and most were very poor—they were sometimes called the "barefoot" *szlachta*—and their manor houses in many instances differed from the peasant's cottage only in being somewhat larger and more pretentious. In construction and decoration they differed little from the humbler structures.

A thousand miles separate Wales from central Poland, but there is a fundamental similarity in their vernacular architecture. The oldest identifiable houses were rounded in plan, with a conical roof, and were built of rough timber. Such structures, of stone with a corbeled roof, have remained in use until recently for keeping pigs. The next stage in the development of the peasant cottage was represented by the single-room cottage. It was built of rough stone set in mud or clay. It was of a single story and was roofed with rafters and covered with thatch or slate. The floor was of beaten earth, windows were few and small, and a fire was maintained on a hearth at one end of the building, with the smoke escaping by a crudely constructed chimney in the gable. In no surviving example was there a masonry stove. This type of cottage has survived in the "black houses" of northwest Scotland.[29]

The simple one-roomed cottage underwent a slow evolution. The first step was to divide it internally, first by a temporary screen and then by a fixed partition, into a living room and a bedroom. The emergence of a desire for privacy and, with it, the creation of a separate bedroom or bedrooms is a mark of the slowly developing standards of material life. It is noteworthy that an independent bedroom seems everywhere to have come before a separate kitchen. The process was continued with the construction of further sleeping accommodation. There was no space within the four walls of the cottage for another room. Instead, a loft, commonly called a "cockloft," was built *over* the bedroom and was reached by a movable ladder. Space in the loft was narrow, and it was probably occupied by children. Few examples of this simple structure have survived, and many of them are in ruins. They have either been abandoned with the decline of hill farming during the past century, or have been replaced by more spacious and hygienic homes in recent years. Nevertheless, they represent a kind of housing that was once widespread in Europe but has now vanished from most parts. They have survived in the hills of western and northern Britain and in Ireland largely because these areas were little touched by the rural prosperity enjoyed by the rest of Europe.

The longhouse can be regarded as an outgrowth of the simple cottage, though when it evolved is far from clear. Its essential feature is the presence of home, barn, and stables set end-to-end under a single roof. The home was more sophisticated than the one-roomed cottage. It was larger; the bedroom was separated by a wall from the living room, and fixed stairs might lead to an upper floor above the bedroom and sometimes over the living room as well. The fire burned not on the floor but in a fireplace or stove built of masonry, against the end wall or projecting from the side of the house. The difference between the cottage and the longhouse lay more in the wealth and status of its owner than in any concept of how a home should be built.

The cow byre usually lay at a slightly lower level than the house, probably in order to prevent drainage into the latter. It was, of course, entered from outside, but there was always direct access from the living room of the house so that there was no need in bad weather to go out of doors for milking or feeding the animals. A dairy was sometimes constructed as a lean-to against the cow byre, and hay was commonly stored above the animal stalls. The longhouse formerly occurred widely in western and northern Europe. It was well suited to a peasant society in which animal rearing played an important role but was rarely found where arable farming prevailed.

Vernacular styles in England showed a greater range of plan, style, and building materials than was to be found in any comparable area in Europe. This variation was due in large measure to the abrupt changes in environment and resource. Nowhere else is it possible to find so close a relationship between buildings and local materials. The evolution of roof design from the simplest truss to the hammer beam can be illustrated in countless cottages and halls throughout the land. Wall construction, in masonry, cob, pisé, and timber framing in all its richness can be demonstrated from the later Middle Ages to the nineteenth century.

The typical home was, as almost everywhere else, the two-celled "hall and bower," with a tendency for a service room to appear at the lower end of the hall. A common feature was a cross-passage between the two cells. In elite and grand buildings this element developed into the "screens passage" that separated the great hall from the kitchen and service area. In such cases the bower, reached from the upper end of the hall, developed into a set of private apartments. Countless examples have survived. The plan is obvious in the great houses of the later Middle Ages, as well as in the colleges of Oxford and Cambridge. At a humbler level, the hall and cross-passage, modified and distorted in various ways, have survived in rural homes until today. These developments had their social consequences. Life in a great house had once centered in the hall, where all ate and many slept. The expansion of the bower into a set of private rooms encouraged the lord to withdraw from the rough and turbulent life of the hall to the quiet of the private rooms.

A feature of the cottage in England, distinguishing it from those of Poland, was the almost universal adoption of an upper floor. In the Polish *chalupa* this level rarely progressed beyond the stage of a kind of platform, or cockloft, contrived above the chamber and reached by a ladder. In England the greater wealth to be found among the rural classes permitted significant developments from the later Middle Ages onward. These changes were pioneered in the homes of the rich, and some of the refinements developed there may never have reached the cottages of the poor. The most common and aesthetically the most appealing was the practice of allowing the joists of the upper floor to protrude beyond the walls of the lower, so that the former overhung. There were many advantages to this mode of construction: the area of the upper floor was increased, the footings of the wall were protected, but, above all, the outside wall of the upper floor served as a kind of counterpoise, offsetting the tendency of the floor to sag. The jettied upper floor became almost universal in the course of the seventeenth and eighteenth centuries in those areas where timber framing was a common mode of construction. This jettied structure was often carried up for three or even four floors in grand and urban houses, but it became comparatively common in vernacular building as well.

A highly satisfying way of using the jettied upper floor is demonstrated in the so-called Wealden house, found in many parts of southeast England. It consisted of a basic, three-celled hall house, with bower at one end and service area at the other. In the original form of the Wealden house the hall rose to the rafters, but a jettied upper floor was added to both the bower and service ends, leaving the hall embayed between them. But the Wealden house was at the upper end of the vernacular range. It was a yeoman's house, too large and sophisticated to be regarded as peasant architecture.

England is fortunate to retain so much of its vernacular architecture from the eighteenth and earlier centuries. But much of what survives is from the upper end of the social scale. It represents the homes of yeoman, squire, and merchant, not of the peasant. The latter had probably changed little since the Middle Ages. They were insubstantially built, they decayed readily, and in more recent times they have been swept away in the interests of health and hygiene.

Conclusion

The drop in material standards that accompanied and followed the end of the Western Empire was catastrophic, even in Italy, which was one of the least exposed provinces of the empire. Villas were abandoned; roads and bridges fell to ruin; trade diminished. Life continued on a lower plane of comfort and material well-being. No one would dare to claim that, even at the height of imperial prosperity, all homes, with their furnishings and fittings, were of the standard demonstrated in the *villae rusticae*. They were not. Excavation has revealed *vici* in which the material level was little different from that of Late Iron Age Europe. Nevertheless, the great houses of the Roman world were an example that the humbler could in some way try to emulate. They created a demand for agricultural and manufactured goods of all kinds, with inevitably a spinoff for many of the humbler citizens of the empire. This process is abundantly shown not only in the diffusion of superior types of building but also in the use of pottery and metal goods, of cloth and household furnishings, among an increasingly diverse population.

After the period of the invasions and the tribal kingdoms that followed, Europe had the task of rebuilding its material fabric, of reestablishing standards in building and of recreating the facilities and conveniences of life. In the classical world standards had been set by the senatorial class, by landowners and provincial officials. It was they who built villas, led comfortable and cultivated lives, and were followed by those of humbler or poorer status. When Europe began slowly to rebuild, it was the church that took their place. Perhaps churchmen had longer memories, or at least easier access to the remains of classical civilization. There were few innovations or revivals that did not originate within the walls of church or cloister. The debt that the West owes to the church in fields as far apart as building construction, sanitation, and water supply has not often been fully recognized.

Innovation and change moved in two directions: socially, from the elite—the upper and ecclesiastical classes—to the peasantry, and geographically, from the south and west toward the north and east, from Italy and the Paris basin to central and eastern Europe and Scandinavia. That is why standards of housing in Poland and Russia in the nineteenth century can throw so much light on those in western Europe five centuries earlier. This slow but general improvement in material conditions is clouded by the emergence of localisms in all aspects of life. Some were spontaneous adaptations to environmental conditions; others reflect the migrations of peoples who took with them accustomed ways of doing things as part of their intellectual endowment. Yet others were idiosyncratic, chance happenings that took a hold on people's minds for no other reason, perhaps, than that they were different and heralded a change in the dull routine of their lives.

Chapter 5

FIELDS, FARMS, AND FOOD SUPPLY

To pass from hunger to subsistence and from subsistence to a degree of sufficiency is to make the transition from the ancient to the
modern world.

—Eugen Weber

The foundations of human welfare are rooted in the soil. It supplies almost the whole food supply. Until the recent past it provided the raw material of clothing, and from the products of the land, housing was built and tools were made. All other aspects of material culture are predicated on the use and misuse of the soil. Agriculture provides the continuum, the ground base, which continues little changed from generation to generation. Civilizations rise and decline and empires come and go, but the farmer continues at his slow pace to till the soil, almost immune to change.

The Roman Empire in the west collapsed during the fifth century. Its administrative structure decayed to the point where it could no longer resist the onslaughts of barbarian peoples who invaded its borders. Yet these events had little influence on agriculture. People continued to plow, sow, and harvest. The same crops continued to be cultivated in, as far as we can say, the same ways and with the same tools, subject to the same hazards of weather, insect pests, and plant disease. At this grassroots level, life was little altered when the Western Empire ended and the barbarian kingdoms took its place. Population declined; demand for foodstuffs contracted. Cities became smaller and fewer, but they continued to be supplied from their rural areas, and Rome continued to receive grain by sea, as it had done for centuries. Only the scale of trade was diminished. There may in some areas have been less wine and less olive oil in the local markets. Exotic foods and salted fish may have disappeared from the tables of the rich, but the bulk of the population in all parts of Europe continued to be nourished, as before, by gruel or flatbread made from poorly ground barley or rye, with a few vegetables and pulses for protein, herbs to give flavor, and milk, meat, and fish as occasion offered.

We are concerned here with the organization and efficiency of agriculture; with field systems and farm tools, with crops and their yields, and with the ways in which people stored, preserved, and consumed them from the eclipse of the empire in the west to the eighteenth or nineteenth century. In none of these respects was there ever any sudden or revolutionary change. Rather, there were small and gradual improvements in the layout of fields, in methods of draining and tilling the soil, storing and harvesting the crop. Progress was by very small increments, so small indeed that one is continually surprised at their cumulative effect.

Demand for foodstuffs was conditioned by two factors: size of the population and individual preferences in food. Both changed during the period. Population increased from a low following the end of the Western Empire to a high in the early fourteenth century. The total then fell abruptly and, from the late fifteenth or early sixteenth century, began a slow and far from regular growth, which has continued until today. Over the long term there was an improvement in the quality of the diet. Wheat very slowly replaced the coarse grains as the staple foodstuff. The consumption of meat and other animal products increased. Vegetables, pulses, and fruit became more important. This shift in diet first showed itself among the wealthier classes but gradually spread downward in modern times to the humbler.

But such improvements were neither regular nor uninterrupted. There were periods, many of them short-lived, when the trend was in the opposite direction. Rising population sometimes strained agricultural resources. There were periods of famine due to crop failure or the destruction of war. The Flemish chronicler Galbert of Bruges recorded that during a famine early in the twelfth century, the Count of Flanders ordered that the oats, normally used for malting and brewing, should be made available for bread making.[1] Oats, it might be said, were already a human food in rural areas, and the Count's ordinance was probably aimed at the better-fed townspeople. During a period of disastrous harvest in the 1690s, chestnuts, roasted and grated, served as human food, and there are countless records of the consumption of acorns and of the bark of trees during similar emergencies. In much of northern Europe buckwheat or *sarrasin* served as a standby when more palatable crops had failed.

The supply of food was itself conditioned by the extent of cultivable land, its fertility and management, and by the year-to-year fluctuations of weather. Early peoples were shrewd if unscientific judges of the quality of soil. They first occupied the land best suited to their tools and methods of cultivation, and only when this site was fully occupied did they spread onto land of lower productivity. When in the later Middle Ages both population and demand contracted, it was the marginal land that was abandoned and allowed to return to waste. But we must always remember that the excellence of a soil was a function not only of its inherent fertility. It depended also on its suitability to the tools and techniques that were available to cultivate it. Heavy, clay soils were intrinsically among the most fertile, but if the light plow was all that was available, they were not likely to be cultivated. Or, again, marshy soils are often rich in plant food, but cultivating them is dependent on land-drainage projects that were beyond the scope, both technically and economically, of early peoples. The history of agriculture in Europe is that of gradual improvements in the techniques of using the land, making it possible during the Middle Ages to cultivate land that held no value to farmers of the prehistoric or even the classical age. Without such improvements there could have been neither an increase in population nor any improvement in the quality of diet.

In the opportunities that it offered for agriculture, Europe north of the Alps differed fundamentally from the region that lay around the Mediterranean Sea. Mediterranean lands were more hilly than northern, and large areas were covered only by drought-resistant scrub, which at best provided coarse feed for goats and sheep. Low-lying, flat, and fertile land was of very restricted extent. It occurred in small patches between the mountains and the sea. The classical civilizations had developed on these areas of moderately good soil, and although efforts were made to use marginal lands by summer grazing in the mountains and terracing hill slopes for cultivation, nature set a limit to the size of the population that they could support. If demand for food increased in any one of these regions of cultivated lowland beyond a certain point, part of the population had to migrate. Migration and the foundation of colonies thus became an established feature of life in the classical Mediterranean world.

North of the Alps, by contrast, the potentialities of the land were far greater. Upland areas, many of them built of limestone, alternated with clay-floored lowlands and broad alluvial plains. Such lands may have been more difficult to subdue and harness to human needs, but the rewards that they held out were far greater. The climate beyond the Alps was more responsive. Summers were warm and wet, without the searing heat of the Mediterranean. Winters were short and rarely severe enough to inhibit plant growth for more than a brief period. In particular, the climatic regime of northern Europe permitted, even encouraged, an alternation of fall- and spring-sown crops. In the Mediterranean, a spring-sown crop was effectively ruled out because it did not have time to grow and mature before the onset of the dry heat of summer.

The Mediterranean has always attracted people to it. The blue skies, the bright sunshine, the clear air, and the beauty of its flowers and trees have been a constant lure to peoples of the cool, cloudy, and humid north. D. H. Lawrence speaks for countless generations who have been drawn as by a magnet to the Mediterranean. Yet this beauty, like the lushness of the tropical forest, was an illusion. The resources had no depth. The Mediterranean offered a stony soil for the seeds of civilization to root in. They germinated and grew quickly and then wilted. By contrast, the soils north of the Alps provided a deeper, richer, and more enduring, though at first more difficult, soil. In the long run it was northern and northwestern Europe that were able to sustain a stronger and more vigorous growth because they contained the means whereby population could increase with, at the same time, an improving level of well-being.

The Conquest of the Land

The spread of human settlements north of the Alps into areas that had previously been woodland and waste was the great creative achievement of the Middle Ages. Most of this advance was at the expense of the forest. Of course there had been forest clearance during the Bronze and Iron Ages, but the process gained momentum during the eighth or ninth century. Not without reason did the Anglo-Saxon riddle call the peasant *Har holtes fēond,* the "enemy of the hore wood." The life of a Celtic saint, Brioc, written about the eleventh century but relating to a period some five centuries earlier, tells how the saint and his followers reached a wooded valley in southwestern Britain. Here, "all girded themselves to work; they cut down trees, rooted up bushes, tore up brambles and tangled thorns, and soon converted a dense wood into an open clearing." While some built houses, others "turned up the sod with plows. Then the soil was worked carefully

5.1. Land reclamation and settlement, as depicted in the *Sachsenspiegel,* a record of village customs in central Europe.

with light plows, and being plowed with very small furrows, its produce was placed in due time on the threshing floor."[2] A drawing in the *Sachsenspiegel,* an account of rural customs and practices in Saxony, shows new settlers felling trees and building houses (fig. 5.1).[3]

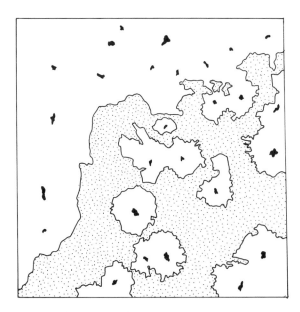

5.2. The process of land clearance in southern Germany, as shown on an early nineteenth-century map. Settlements are shown in black. The stippled area was still forest.

Everywhere in Europe north of the Alps, the work of land clearance and colonization went ahead. It was, as a general rule, a disciplined movement. It was not a question of the peasant venturing into the wilderness, staking out his claim, and making a home. There was, in theory at least, no land without its lord, whose permission and encouragement had to be sought. The lord was usually only too eager to have settlers on land that was his, for it had no value unless used, and he stood to gain from the rent. Suger, the abbot and administrator of the Parisian monastery of Saint-Denis, recorded in the twelfth century that "at Vaucresson we have laid out a township, constructed a church and houses and caused land which was uncultivated to be brought under the plough. . . . There are already there about 60 tenants. . . . The place before had more than two [square?] miles of barren land, and was of no profit at all to the church."[4] In this instance the settlement was planned and settlers were recruited by the monastery. A charter of the early thirteenth century, granted by the lord of Cornwood in South Devon to Benedict son of Edric Siward, records the creation of a settlement of a different kind. It grants "all my land of Cholwich in free, pure and perpetual socage, namely from the ford in the paved road . . . along the paved highway above Tolchmoor Gate and so westwards as far as the water of Tory [Brook] . . . [the bounds fallow]" at the substantial rent of four shillings a year. Benedict also received right of common over the neighboring moor, as well as permission "to take there hay, turves [peat], coal [charcoal], furze, and all other necessary commodities."[5] This was a simple grant of permission to "homestead," to create a farm on the edge of the vast waste of Dartmoor. The initiative probably came from Benedict, and the settlement consisted then, as it still does today, of a single homestead.

A last example of such a settlement is the scene that Pol de Limbourg and Jean Colombe painted in a book of hours for the Duke of Berry.[6] It illustrates the month of February. In the distance, beyond the snow-covered fields, is a village, with the spire of its church rising above the clustered roofs of the huts. In the foreground, on the very edge of a woodland, is an isolated farmstead. A cutaway shows the interior of the peasant's house, with three members of the household warming themselves before a fire. Outside are a sheep pen, a dovecote, and a row of beehives, the whole surrounded by a low fence of woven osiers. It is a perfect illustration of an isolated settlement, established at a distance from the village on which it depended.

These examples illustrate the penetration of the forest and waste by human settlement. They could be multiplied many hundreds of times. Before the Middle Ages, settlements had been merely islands of houses and fields, set amid the endless expanse of waste. Now they were spreading, sending out fingers of cultivated land to link up with one another. Woodland was pared away at the margin and honeycombed with clearings. Dry, infertile heathland was broken up and cultivated in France, the Low Countries, and northern Germany, and marsh-

5.3. Breaking up new land was generally done with a spade and was a particularly arduous task. Hence the appeal of the legend of Adam and Eve, with Adam usually represented with a wooden spade tipped with iron.

land that bordered the coast and lined the lower courses of rivers was diked, drained and protected from flooding, and used for grazing animals if it was not actually cultivated. Much of the work was supervised by monasteries, which tended, more than lay lords, to take the long view of investment in their estates. But the hard work—felling trees, digging, the cutting of drainage ditches, and the building of dikes—was performed by the peasant with the simplest and crudest of tools (fig. 5.3).

What we need is a map showing the spread of medieval settlement into the forest and waste. Such a map can be compiled only for small and restricted areas, for which the documentary sources—surveys, charters, rent rolls—can be supplemented by place- and field-names and the archeological evidence of former settlements and cultivated fields. In recent years much progress has been made in this integrated study, but its achievement for Europe as a whole remains tantalizingly incomplete.

In addition to this movement of colonization *within* Europe, there was also an outward movement along the frontiers of European civilization. The chief directions of this expansion were northward into Scandinavia and eastward into the vast marchland that stretched into the plains of Russia. Advance into the forested regions of northern Europe was slowed by the poverty of the soil and the harshness of the climate, and where settlements were made they were concerned as much with the mineral resources as with the agricultural. But eastern Europe was different. The great European plain broadened eastward to the Russian steppe. It was a gulf into which people had raided from the east from time immemorial. Invasion and war had inhibited population growth and cultural and political development. Vast areas were devoid of settlers, and political authority was too weak to offer any resistance. Authority over this wilderness was claimed by lords from central Europe. These then proceeded to bring in colonists, to establish villages, and to develop it. The *Slavic Chronicle* records that Count Adolf of Holstein developed his lands close to the Baltic Sea: "As the land was without inhabitants, he sent messengers into all parts, namely to Flanders and Holland, to Utrecht, Westphalia and Frisia, proclaiming that whosoever were in straits for lack of fields should come with their families and receive a very good land. . . . An innumerable multitude of different people rose up at this call and they came with their families and their goods into the land of Wagria [eastern Holstein]."[7]

This eastward movement of German settlers was largely, though not entirely, into lands previously occupied by Slavic peoples. German historians have commonly represented this as a *Drang nach Osten,* a drive toward the east, by the bearers of a superior civilization, before which the Slavs fell back in retreat. Looked at on a highly generalized map, with lines drawn to mark stages of the advance, this may well appear to have been the case. But the movement was not coordinated. The Slavs were not rolled back along a broad front. On the contrary, they continued to live alongside the Germans, some of them slowly assimilated to German culture. The eastward movement of Germans was organized by middlemen, who recruited settlers, arranged for their transport, and established them in their new homes. These *locatores* were intermediaries between the lord who claimed jurisdiction over the land and the land-hungry peasants who came in their thousands to settle there. The way in which these newcomers were established on the land is apparent in the long streetlike villages that they created, and in the narrow strips that stretched back from their cottages to the boundary of their land.

The increase in population and the resulting spread of settlements took the peasant from the good soils to less good; from lowland and valley to hillslope and plateau. The area of cultivated land continued to increase until early in the fourteenth century. Europe was then struck by the bubonic plague, known to posterity as the Black Death. Population contracted and marginal fields were abandoned. Villages in the least prosperous areas became smaller and some were "lost." They ceased to be inhabited and are visible today only as ridges and depressions beneath the grass, marking the sites of cottages and garden plots.

The advance of settlement was conditioned by two factors, the one technical, the other environmental. The light plow (fig. 5.4), known and used in prehistoric and classical Europe, was good only in friable soils, and even here did little more than stir the surface. Only with the greatest difficulty could it be forced through the heavy soils that were coming under cultivation. A stronger and heavier plow was needed. Such a plow was known in the late classical world but was

5.4. Forms of light plow in use in medieval Europe. They were without colter, moldboard, or wheels. They were superseded in much of western Europe by the heavy plow but survive in the east European *socha.*

little used. But during the centuries that followed the end of the empire, its use spread through western and central Europe. It made little progress in the Mediterranean realm, where there was less need for it and few possessed a team big enough to pull it.

As fully developed, the heavy plow consisted of a beam with a blade, or colter, set to make a vertical cut through the soil. Behind it were the share and moldboard, the former cutting horizontally at a preset depth below the surface. The sod, thus loosened, was made to slide back over the curved moldboard and was laid upside down on the soil already turned, thus burying the weeds. The beam of the plow was supported, as a general rule, by two large wheels, and the name of the heavy plow, *carruca,* was, in fact, derived from that for a small wheeled cart. Medieval art is strewn with drawings of the heavy plow, and we are left in no doubt whatever of what it looked like and how it operated (fig. 5.5). But these illustrations tell us nothing of where it originated. We may, however, be sure of one thing: it was not invented at some place at a particular moment. It developed slowly, as earlier plow types were adapted to new conditions, and what we see in late medieval drawings is the end product of a millennium of development.

The elder Pliny referred to a plow in use probably in northern Italy, which was drawn by eight oxen. This clearly was not the simple *ard* of Mediterranean lands.[8] Pliny also mentioned a plow, mounted on two wheels, which was in use in the Alps. Such plows

5.5. A heavy plow, with wheels, moldboard and colter, from the Jenstejn Codex, Prague.

were called *plaumorati*. This nonclassical word has been interpreted as *plovum Raeti,* "plow of the Rhaeti," and if this explanation is correct, the heavy plow may have originated in Switzerland and south Germany.

If we can conflate the two passages in Pliny, we may have an instrument that approximated the later heavy plow. The discovery of metal colters at many Roman sites to the north of the Alps has been taken by some to indicate a widespread use of the heavy plow. Perhaps so, but we also know that the *ard* was itself sometimes fitted with a colter and was thus used by the Romans. It was even possible, by tilting the *ard* to one side or the other, to turn the sod, as if with a moldboard. A further development was the replacement of the blunt tip of the wooden *ard* with a spadelike piece of metal that cut more deeply into the soil. Such a plow, known as the *socha,* remained in use in eastern Europe until recent times. If this "spade" share were twisted to one side, a rudimentary moldboard would result.

Clearly, these elements—colter, spade, moldboard, wheels—may have originated in different places and have been brought together, perhaps during the later Roman Empire, possibly during later centuries, and it seems likely that this innovation was made by peasants in central Europe and diffused thus through western and northern. It spread into the Slavic lands and may have been in use in France in the sixth century. Gregory of Tours noted with some surprise that the fields around Dijon were sown after a single plowing instead of being cross-plowed, thus implying that a form of heavy plow had replaced the *ard.* It used to be assumed that the heavy plow was brought to Britain by the Anglo-Saxons, along with much other Germanic impedimenta. This was almost certainly not the case. It had in all probability not even reached their homelands near the North Sea at the time of the invasions. On the other hand, the Caedmon Manuscript of the tenth century clearly delineates a heavy wheeled plow, and a very similar implement is shown in the Bayeux Tapestry. So the heavy plow was most likely introduced into lowland Britain between the sixth century and the tenth.

Henceforward the heavy plow dominated agricultural practice in much of western and central Europe and profoundly influenced the structure of rural life until the nineteenth century. Later medieval representations of the plow show it almost invariably

5.6. A swing plow, as illustrated in the Luttrell Psalter of the
fourteenth century. It has moldboard and colter but lacks wheels. It
was lighter and more manageable than the wheeled plow but made it
difficult to control the depth to which the share cut.

as a heavy, four-sided implement, with colter, moldboard and wheels. Yet it never, in fact,
completely displaced other types. The *socha* was common in eastern Europe. The Luttrell
Psalter shows a swing, or wheelless, plow, but similar in other respects to the heavy plow,
in use in England in the fourteenth century (fig. 5.6). It would have been easier to turn at
the end of the furrow than the heavy plow, but the lack of wheels made it difficult to
control the depth to which the share penetrated the soil. In areas of scattered settlement,
such as highland Britain, and many hilly areas in central Europe, it is highly improbable
that the heavy plow was much
used. It was difficult to manipulate on rough ground, and the
isolated farmstead would have
been most unlikely to have an
adequate team. Some form of
light plow continued in use, and
in Scotland and probably elsewhere, the caschrom, or foot-
plow, has continued to be used
until recently (fig. 5.7).

The adoption of the heavy
plow had important social consequences. Apart from its ability to
undercut the soil and bury the
weeds, it had two other characteristics. It was so heavy that it
called for a team of animals to
pull it, and it was difficult to turn
it and its team at the end of a
furrow. On the other hand, with
sufficient draft animals, it could
be forced through the heaviest

5.7. A caschrom, or foot-plow, in use in
western Scotland, early twentieth century.

soils. Pliny mentioned a plow team of eight oxen, but the size of the team must have

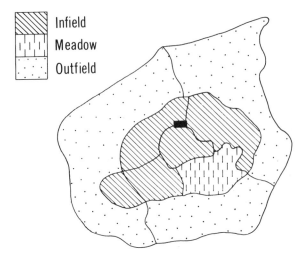

5.8. An infield/outfield settlement, from a seventeenth-century estate map. The shaded area would have been cultivated permanently; the stippled area only intermittently.

varied with local conditions and the availability of animals. No medieval drawing shows more than four beasts harnessed to the plow, and even a team of this size was beyond the means of most peasants. Collaboration was necessary if the heavy plow was to be used. The English Domesday Book of 1085–86 consistently shows a ratio of about 3.5 peasants to each plow team. The heavy moldboard plow was clearly adapted to the needs and provision of the village community, not those of the hamlet or scattered homesteads. Elsewhere a lighter, wheelless plow was used, similar to the classical plow of the Mediterranean.

The Fields

There is much uncertainty regarding the fields that these plows were intended to cultivate. The general shape of fields in the Late Iron Age is known from the balks and terraces that have survived through the simple accident that they have not since been plowed out and erased. Elsewhere they are revealed in the crop marks that show up on aerial photographs. It is unlikely that these early field systems were deliberately enclosed by fence or wall; more likely that stones that rose to the surface were deposited on the edge of the field and that soil creep tended to produce shallow terraces on sloping ground. Such fields could not have been cultivated continuously. Soil nutrients would quickly have been lost, especially on the lighter soils, which were most cultivated. A system of fallowing and perhaps some kind of crop rotation must have been used. The practice developed of cultivating intensively only the land close to the farmstead—the "infield"—and less regularly the "outfield" that lay beyond it (fig. 5.8).

This system of small enclosed fields was displaced over large areas of western and central Europe by one of large open fields, each made up of bundles of long narrow strips. An intermediate phase between enclosed and open fields may have been marked by open fields that were divided into small, irregular "quillets" and "stitches" (fig. 5.9). The length of each open-field strip represented the distance that the plow could be expected to travel before turning; its width, the amount of plowing that could be accomplished in a day. Of course, time blurred this simple plan, as strips were thrown together or divided between heirs. The strips and the bundles, or *virgates,* in which they were grouped, had no boundaries. The peasant knew instinctively the limits of his land. In fact he was helped by the way in which the plowman guided his plow. The sod was turned toward the middle of the strip, which thus formed a "ridge," separated by a "furrow" from the next. This "ridge-and-furrow" served a useful function. At a time when land was not drained artificially, the furrows served to carry away surface water from the fields. At the same time, in a very wet season, when water lay in the furrows, it might still be pos-

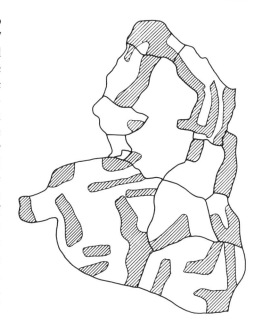

5.9. Quillets and stitches: small, unenclosed parcels of land within small open fields. Their irregular shape suggests that they were cultivated with very primitive plows. From a seventeenth-century estate map.

sible to snatch a crop from the ridge. "Cause the land to be well ridged up when you sow in marshy or watery land," wrote Walter of Henley in the thirteenth century, "so that the land may be delivered of the water."9

At the end of its furrow the plow had to turn—by no means an easy task with a large team. Here was a small area, the "headland," where the plow could be lifted out of the soil, perhaps cleaned of mud, and the oxen rested for a short time before the plow was again set into the soil. How often must the calm of the village community have been disturbed when one man's team trespassed onto a strip belonging to another. It required skill to handle an unruly team, but sometimes encroachment on another man's land was less than accidental. "If I went plowing," said Avarice in the *Vision of Piers the Plowman,* "I would skirt my neighbor's strip so closely, that I filched a foot or a furrow's breadth of his land." Such were the petty crimes of which the peasant was guilty, and for which he was arraigned before the lord's steward in the manor court.

The virgates, each of a dozen or so strips, were organized in open or "great" fields. The community would have several such fields, and each peasant possessed strips—how many depended on his wealth and status—in each of them. The great fields reflected the cropping system. This cycle consisted, in brief, of a simple rotation: (1) fall-sown grain, (2) spring-sown grain, (3) fallow. The principal fall-sown crops were wheat and rye, sown in October and harvested in mid-summer. The same great field would be sown with barley or oats or peas in the following March—there was no requirement that all should grow the same—and these would be ready for harvest soon after the wheat and rye were in. During the third year the great field was rested. The community's farm stock was turned into it to pick up what the harvesters had left and, most important, to make their own contribution to the soil's fertility in readiness for the next sowing of wheat or rye.

This system proved to be remarkably rigid and lasting. In many parts of Europe it survived into the nineteenth century (figs. 5.10, 5.11). It was made up of interlocking parts—plow team, strip, great field, fallowing, fallow grazing—none of which could be changed without bringing down the system of which it was part. Its concentration on cereal crops greatly restricted human diet and limited the farm stock that could be kept. It called for discipline and control within the farming community. It served to perpetuate the manorial system, in which the lord or his steward presided over a court that met regularly to enforce local custom and punish petty misdemeanors. Well might the historian speak of the tyranny of the open field. Over much of Europe where the open-field system prevailed, the peasant was not completely free until the eighteenth or nineteenth century. His rights in land were limited and he was subject to many petty and annoying restrictions. The heaviest of his burdens was to work on the land of his lord for a certain period—commonly two or three days—each week.

By contrast, those who lived in hamlets and isolated settlements were subject to little or no communal control. The manorial court did not pry into their methods of tillage. They owed a rent rather than labor services, because there was no place at hand where services could be rendered. There was a difference also in the landscape, between the "champaign," without balk or barrier, where the sinuous strips reached to the horizon, and the region of enclosed fields, where the hedgerows sprouted trees and gave the whole landscape a wooded aspect. The French called the latter *bocage*. The twelfth-century romancer Wace caught the differences in landscape and society when he contrasted "Li paisan et li villain, / Cil des bocages et cil des plains" (The peasant and the villein, the one from the bocage, the other from the open country).

The contrast between open-field Europe and enclosed, between the Europe of large, clustered villages, and that of farmsteads and hamlets, was never as clear-cut and precise as this description suggests. It is the role of theory to generalize, to ignore local accidents, to define a standard against which to measure reality. So, in the contrasted field systems of preindustrial Europe there were exceptions and compromises that reflected the many factors that were brought to bear on the evolution of agriculture and settlement. There were areas within the hilly regions where a rudimentary open-field system was evolving, with large, enclosed fields divided into quillets and stitches. Conversely, in eastern and southeastern England the movement toward the formation of communally cultivated fields was arrested, and the area remained predominantly one of enclosed fields. Similarly, in continental Europe, there were islands of "several" amid the open fields, and patches of open-field agriculture in areas that were largely enclosed.

What, then, were the numerous and diverse factors that determined the development of fields? The role of the plow has already been seen, and its importance cannot be overestimated. But the use of the heavy plow was itself dependent on the existence of a community large enough to possess a team. And this consideration in turn goes back, on the one hand, to the question of social organization—to kinship group or clan—and, on the other, to the capacity of the soil itself for the sort of intensive cultivation represented

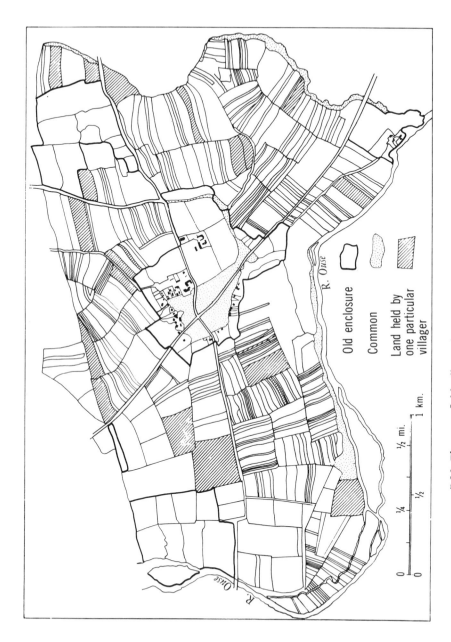

5.10. The open-field village of Goldington, Bedfordshire, at the beginning of the nineteenth century. (After F. G. Emmison, *Some Types of Common Field Parish* [London, 1965], 12–13.)

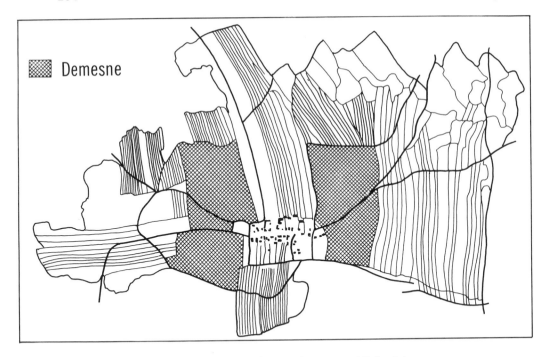

5.11. The open-field village of Owieczki in central Poland, late
eighteenth century. Note the basic similarity of this and the village of
Goldington (fig. 5.10), some six hundred miles away.

by the open fields. Many parts of Europe were intrinsically better suited for pastoralism
with subsidiary tillage than for regular cropping, and here small fields close to the
homestead were almost a necessity. We recall that "race" has been cited as a determining
factor in the ways in which villages were established and laid out. This, of course, is
nonsense. Race as such had nothing to do with the ways in which different peoples
managed these matters. In a sense, however, there is some truth in this claim. When
people migrate they take with them not only material goods but also a stock of ideas
about how things should be done. These notions may in time fade away and be lost,
replaced by those of the indigenous people, but some are likely to survive. William
Hardy McNeill, for example, described how in the thirteenth century, "pioneers from
western Europe who settled in Transylvania . . . brought the moldboard plow into the
region. But," he added, "the long acres and open-fields of the Saxon towns of Transylvania remained exceptional."[10] The Anglo-Norman barons who overran South Wales
in the twelfth century also took with them the practice of cultivating open fields, but it
appears that when, a century or two later, their firm hand was relaxed, the local people
reverted to their earlier practice of cultivating small, enclosed fields. Last, there is the
question of human decision, of how a community decides how and where to plow;
whether to extend an old field or to make a new; whether to consolidate and enclose the
strips in an open field or to throw down the boundaries and cultivate previously
enclosed fields in common. There is a passage in the novel of peasant life *Terre,* by Émile
Zola, which describes how such a decision was made in the mid-nineteenth century. It

has a ring of truth, and Zola in fact lived in the Beauce region of France, where the novel is set, observing the customs and practices of the peasantry. The matter in hand was the division of the fields and strips of Old Fouan, who was no longer able to work them, between his heirs. The wrangling was, by and large, between "progressives," who wanted no more subdivision of strips that were already narrow and uneconomic, and "conservatives," who wished to divide each parcel of land into as many pieces as there were claimants. In the end, after bitter wrangling, the division was made, with each parcener "certain that no one could have something that the other two hadn't got." Decisions must have been made in some such way over the previous thousand years. A field system is the resultant of all these factors. It is the way in which a conservative but practical people viewed their environment and balanced advantage against disadvantage, private profit against communal loss. Millions of separate decisions have resulted in thousands of different compromises between the extremes of complete enclosure and the boundless open fields.

This complex system of interrelationships represented by the open fields was extraordinarily difficult to dismember. That they were horribly wasteful is apparent to us, and was perhaps also to those who cultivated them. A century ago Frederic Seebohm described the system as "absurdly uneconomical," and condemned "the waste of time in getting about from one part of a farm to another, the uselessness of one owner attempting to clean his own land when it could be sown with thistles . . . from the neighboring strips of a less carefull and thrifty owner; the quarrelling about headlands and rights of way or paths without right, the constant encroachments of unscrupulous or overbearing holders. . . ."[11] Thomas Tusser in the sixteenth century denounced the "mingle-mangle" of intermixed strips,[12] and Arthur Young in the eighteenth century became almost apoplectic at the mere mention of open fields. "The open arable fields" of northern France, he wrote, "are cursed with all the mischievous circumstances known in similar cases in England, such as rights of common pasturage, . . . as well as that miserable phantastical division of property which seems to have been conceived, for giving an occupier as much trouble and expence as possible in the culture of his scraps of fields."[13]

And yet the system developed, survived for up to a thousand years, and was uncommonly difficult to change. Why? There are many explanations of the several aspects of the open fields. The practice of fallowing and of folding animals on the fallow and on cropland after harvest may have been rooted in the need to restore the fertility of the soil, but the peasant came to rely on the right to graze his animals on the stubble of the wheatfield. And so fallow grazing continued long after the droppings of the animals had ceased to be necessary for next year's crop. The scattering of the strips of each cultivator in the open fields has no such ready explanation. It has been attributed to a primitive sense of fairness, allowing each peasant to share in the good soil and the poor; "economy and efficiency," in Maitland's words, "sacrificed . . . at the shrine of equality."[14] Zola's peasants in this respect showed a scrupulous regard for equality. The practice has also been ascribed with a greater degree of probability to the division of land between heirs, to the land market that developed in peasant societies, and to a crude attempt to spread the risk of flood and frost.[15] There is no simple explanation, and as we push the record back through the Middle Ages to the dark centuries that followed the end of the Western Empire, the evidence becomes more complex and more obscure. The system survived because it represented so many vested interests that only a higher authority could break it apart. In the last resort this body was the state. In Britain, Parliament sorted out the confusion in cases where the local population would not, or could not, accomplish the task. In Sweden the government came down strongly in favor of the progressive peasant, but in much of eastern Europe the intermixed strips survived until they were submerged in collective farms under the Communist order. The fragmentation and scattering of his land was one of the most restrictive of all the burdens placed on the European peasant, and it was one from which escape proved most difficult.

In Mediterranean Europe little attempt was ever made to adopt the heavy plow, and the narrow cultivation strips of northern Europe were never part of the landscape. Fields were more compact, with the exception of the cultivation terraces that were cut into the hillsides. The small, square fields of southern Europe sometimes resemble those of the "enclosed" regions farther north. There was, however, one important difference. The southern fields bore crops of wheat and barley only in alternate years. This practice followed the dictates of climate; it was a kind of "dry farming." On the enclosed lands of the north, however, a wider range of crops was being grown. The farmer was free of communal restraints; however little he may have been disposed to experiment, he was nonetheless able to try new crops, to grow fodder, and blend animal husbandry with arable. Arthur Young, late in the eighteenth century, was lavish in his praise of enclosed cropland, not so much for the progress that it demonstrated as for the opportunities that it offered.

Crops and Cropping Systems

The plants known to the Iron Age peasant continued to dominate European agriculture until the nineteenth century. They were field crops, grown to provide breadgrains, the material for malting and brewing, and feed for horses, and they must have been grown on two-thirds to three-quarters of all cropland. They were rye and wheat, barley and oats. In some parts of Europe these crops were supplemented with buckwheat, which, despite its name, is not a cereal, and oil-bearing seeds like flax. From some time in the sixteenth century corn (maize) became an important alternative to the traditional breadgrains, and somewhat later potatoes, also an import from the New World, began to be grown, first in garden plots, then on land that might otherwise have been left fallow.

The four main cereals differed in their climatic and soil requirements and tolerances, and also in their bread-making qualities. Wheat and rye contain gluten, a nitrogenous substance that serves to enclose small bubbles of air when bread is baked, giving it a lighter texture. Barley, oats, and corn are all lacking in gluten, so that they can be used only to make a flatbread or a porridge. The light bread made from wheat or rye does, however, require the addition of leaven, which causes fermentation or yields a gas when heated. The use of leaven was well known in classical and medieval times. For this reason wheat and rye were always the preferred cereals, even if they cropped less heavily than others. Wheat and rye, furthermore, required a longer growing season. They were usually sown in the fall—most often in October—and were reaped in July or August. Wheat is the most demanding of cereals. It does not readily tolerate a severe winter or damp and acid soils. It does best on clay loam, like the loess of northern Europe. Rye, on the other hand, can withstand a severe winter and grows well on soils that are too acid for wheat.

Barley and oats grow more quickly and, north of the Alps, were usually sown in

March—hence their common name of "three-month" grains—and were reaped after the wheat and rye had been harvested. The fact that they need not be sown until spring made them important in northern latitudes. They were sown after the hazards of winter were over. Barley does best on an alkaline soil, and for this reason was much grown in the Mediterranean region. Oats can tolerate cool, moist conditions and can be grown successfully on the poor, acid soils that cover parts of northern Europe.

In southern Europe, where summers are long, hot, and dry, a spring planting left little time for growth before crops were withered by the heat. Cereals *had* to be fall-sown if they were to mature before the end of the growing season. Wheat and barley were indigenous to the eastern Mediterranean and did well in these conditions. They were the dominant and in most areas the only breadgrains in classical times, and remained so through the preindustrial period. Rye was rarely grown south of the Alps, and then only in mountainous areas, and oats scarcely at all. As a general rule wheat or barley alternated with fallow.

North of the Alps a more diverse system developed. In the later Middle Ages the practice most generally adopted was to grow winter grain, followed by a spring-sown grain and then fallow.[16] This three-course rotation must have evolved by a process of trial and error. It was once assumed that it grew from a two-course system, with alternating crop and fallow, as in the Mediterranean region. Such a system did, indeed, survive until recent times in remote areas of eastern Europe, and in the middle Rhineland, where there was a heavy urban demand for wheat and rye and very little for oats and barley, there was in fact a reversion from the three- to a two-field system.

In much of Europe the routine of plowing was adjusted to this rotation. The open fields were each cultivated and fallowed in their turn. Each open field may not have been tilled with the same crop, but each virgate, or bundle of strips, had to be cultivated in the same way. One cannot say for certain when this cropping system was fully evolved, but it had probably developed by the fourteenth century in most of open-field Europe, and it lingered on with little fundamental change over most of it until the eighteenth or even the nineteenth.

There must have been some substitution from year to year among the cereal crops. Sometimes rye or oats increased relative to wheat and barley; sometimes they declined. Occasionally, if autumn and winter weather was unusually bad, a spring-sown crop was substituted for the one usually planted in October. But, by and large, it was an inflexible system. It was adjusted to field systems and plowing routine, and left little to the discretion or judgment of the peasant. The plowing and cropping routine became yet another of the elements in the complex of interlocking factors that kept the open fields in being. It was a feature of this three-course system that there was a rough equality between the volume of winter- and spring-sown grains. Countless instances illustrate this joint production. In the fourteenth century the areas cultivated at the Cistercian grange of Veulerent, near Paris, were:

Wheat	365.5	arpents
Mixed spring-sown grain	333	arpents 10 perches
Fallow	323	arpents 9 perches[17]

The arpent was a variable measure of about an acre. The volume of the coarser grains— oats and barley—was such that much of it had to enter the human diet. Wheat and after it rye may have been the favored breadgrains, but much of Europe's population, especially north of the Alps, had of necessity to eat oats and barley. The consumption of breadgrains was a matter of status. The monastery of St. Pantaleon at Cologne received a quantity of oats, which were fed to the abbot's horses and any poor travelers who appeared. The lord abbot himself probably ate wheaten bread.[18]

Cereals were everywhere supplemented, as they had to be to insure a balanced diet, by several other crops. Most of these were grown in the enclosed tofts that surrounded the cottages. Here the peasant applied whatever manure he could gather and grew what crops he pleased. Foremost among these garden crops were peas and beans. There were many varieties that had been developed by unconscious selective breeding from the wild species of Neolithic Europe.[19] They were prominent in diet at least from classical times, both cooked with other vegetables and, dried and pulverized, baked together with flour as bread. Their dietary importance cannot be exaggerated; a meal of pork and beans was the highest luxury known to the peasant.[20]

Scarcely less important were garden vegetables grown for the pot. Every family that was able to do so cultivated a garden. Great houses and monasteries had large gardens, often enclosed by a wall. At the opposite extreme, the cottager cultivated his patch, enclosed by a hedge, no less assiduously. The vegetables were numerous and varied. Charlemagne prescribed a long list of those which he wished to see grown on his villas,[21] but the most important were without question the many varieties of brassica or cabbage, roots like carrot, turnip, beet, and onion, and many herbs and seasonings. Others were brought from the Middle East or North Africa by crusaders and merchants. Careful cultivation in garden plots led to the evolution of superior species, and by the sixteenth century the variety of vegetables available was not much less than that of today—with one significant exception. The potato did not make its appearance in Europe until about 1600. It was native to the Andean plateaus of South America, where the Spanish *conquistadores* found and described it. It was a very long time before the potato was adopted in Europe as a staple food.[22] It was a different and less appetizing vegetable than the smooth, white tuber grown today, which is, by and large, the product of selective breeding in the nineteenth century. But this lower quality does not wholly explain the reluctance to accept it as a human food. Peasants did not understand how to prepare and cook a plant so different from those which they were accustomed to. It was grown in garden plots, where it was regarded, like buckwheat, as a food to be used only in an emergency. Sometimes it was fed to animals and used for distilling, but it did not become a significant human food until the second half of the eighteenth century. The reason does not lie wholly with peasant reluctance to change but rather in the structure of farming, which so often made change difficult if not impossible. When the cultivation of the potato did at last begin to spread, it was in response not only to the rising population and the high price of cereals but also to the slow breakdown of traditional field and rotation systems.

Corn or maize received a warmer welcome than the potato. The accepted view is that the Spanish conquerors found many varieties of corn in the American lands that they had conquered and introduced them to Spain. Corn requires a hot, moist summer, and in much of Spain it grew quickly and yielded more abundantly than any of the traditional cereals. Within a century the cultivation of corn had spread to southern France and soon afterwards to Italy, the Danube valley, and the Balkans. On the other hand, the name by which it is known in much of eastern Europe is of Turkish origin, and it was also known as "Turkish corn." It is likely that from Spain corn was passed to the eastern Mediterranean and diffused by the Turks through the Balkans.

Why, one may ask, was corn cultivation adopted so quickly, whereas it took two centuries for potatoes to gain even a modest acceptance? Corn was climatically suited to many of the areas where fields were in the main enclosed and the peasant was able within limits to determine his own pattern of cultivation. On the other hand, corn never achieved any importance in the hidebound farming of open-field Europe. It is doubtful whether any crop newly introduced from America could have made much progress north of the Alps until the tyranny of the open fields had been ended.

There were other crops of localized importance. Millet, or panic, was grown in southern Europe and was used to make a coarse bread. Rice was known in Sicily and southern Spain, where it had been introduced by the Arabs. Buckwheat came into use in the later Middle Ages. It was the fruit of an herbaceous plant and resembled beech mast—hence its German name *Buchweizen*. It was once thought that it had been introduced from North Africa or the Middle East, and it is still known in France as *blé sarrasin*. It was, in fact, known in prehistoric Europe but appears not to have become a cultivated crop before the late Middle Ages. Thereafter, its cultivation became widespread in northern Europe. Its seed had a bitter taste and little food value, but the plant could tolerate a wet climate and poor soil. It was widely grown on sandy soils and was sometimes sown in late spring if winter crops had failed. But it was a poor substitute for cereals, and one to which the poor resorted only when everything else had failed.

Vegetable oil continued to be obtained in southern Europe from the olive. In northern, nuts were gathered and pressed in a simple mill. In the later Middle Ages certain plants began to be grown, especially in the Low Countries, specifically for the oil contained in their seeds. Among them was rape- or coleseed, a species of brassica. It was crushed in a mill and its oil used in preparing food and as fuel for oil-burning lamps. This remained an important use for rapeseed oil until, in the nineteenth century, it was displaced by whale oil and then mineral oil.

Not all crops had food value; some were grown because they provided the raw materials of craft industries. Prominent among them were flax and hemp. Both had been known and used since Neolithic times, but in classical times and later they were widely grown for the bast or tough fiber that occurs in their stems. This has continued until modern times to be their chief asset, though flaxseed, which contains a small amount of oil, was used as a human food. The narcotic powers of hemp (*cannabis*) appear to have been known and used from prehistoric times, but hemp was usually grown as a garden crop to provide the material for rope and cordage. It was especially important in coastal regions, such as Brittany, where the demand for ships' rigging was greatest. Flax was more useful. It yielded a finer thread, easily spun and woven, and from it was made from earliest times a very serviceable cloth. Linen had, in fact, been woven in Europe before woolen cloth was first made, and for making lightweight fabrics flax was unrivaled until the large-scale use of cotton began in the eighteenth century.

Both flax and hemp grew best in a damp, rich soil. Their cultivation called for intensive labor and quickly exhausted the soil. They were usually grown on small plots close to the villages. The preparation of both crops was arduous. As in classical times, they were first retted, or soaked in water, to separate the threads from the rest of the plant matter, and then scutched to break up the coarse fiber into finer thread for spinning. This was usually done by tearing it on a board studded with protruding wires or nails (see chap. 9). The preparation of flax and hemp was both physically exhausting and environmentally damaging. Retting the fibers in a river made its water undrinkable and was said to kill the fish. In medieval Normandy it was forbidden to soak the plants in running streams, and it seems that separate ponds were sometimes dug for the purpose. Flax and hemp were grown in all parts of Europe except the far north but were not of great importance in the Mediterranean region, where the climate was too dry. The most intensive cultivation of both crops was in a belt that extended across northern Europe from northwestern France into Poland. Here flax in particular became increasingly important from the fourteenth century. Linen clothing was worn more and more, with significant consequences for human health because it could be laundered more easily than woolen cloth and animal skins. By the eighteenth century the local cultivation of flax had come to support important linen-weaving industries in northern France, the Low Countries, and across Germany to Silesia.

Cloth, whether of wool or flax, was usually dyed. The range of colors was severely limited. People loved bright colors, but these were extraordinarily difficult to achieve. The dyes available before the nineteenth century were mostly of vegetable origin. Although a number of plants yielded coloring matter, three became preeminent: weld, which produced a yellow; woad or pastel, which gave blue; and madder, a source of red dyes. These were not the crops of every village, nor did the humble cottager who wove a piece of cloth resort to these dyestuffs in order to color it. Most dyes required careful preparation before they could be used, and the making of dyestuffs was restricted to relatively few areas and was carried on by professionals. Though woad was grown fairly widely, the others were really important only in areas such as northern France and Flanders, where clothworking was important. The rough homespun of the peasant was undyed and was generally drab in color. In the later Middle Ages other sources of dyestuffs became available. First was kermes, a dye obtained from parasitical creatures found in galls that formed on certain trees. The name is of Arabic origin (*Qirmiz*), and the dye was introduced from the Middle East in the fifteenth century. It yielded a bright scarlet and was very popular among the few who could afford its high price. Scarlet cloth was produced in Italy, and in 1467 Pope Paul II adopted it for the robes of the cardinals of the Roman curia, who have not ceased to wear it.

The opening up of the new world of America and Africa brought new dyestuffs to Europe. Wood like brazil, plants like indigo, and insects like cochineal added to the range of colors available to the cloth dyer and began to displace traditional dyes for those who could afford their high cost. Such were the coloring materials that continued to brighten the lives of some people until the discovery of aniline dyes in the nineteenth century.

Other industrial crops gained importance after the sixteenth century. Among them were tobacco, hops, and sugar beets. Tobacco smoking was introduced into Europe during the sixteenth century. At first, tobacco was imported from North America, and attempts to grow it in Europe were discouraged by governments and were generally unsuccessful. Not until the eighteenth century did tobacco growing become significant, chiefly in the Low Countries and the Rhineland.

The hop plant was native to northern Europe. It was mentioned in land surveys of the ninth century, but at this date its fruit was probably eaten as a vegetable. It was not until late in the Middle Ages that the dried fruit was added to ale both to flavor it and to help preserve it. The use of the hop for this purpose spread through northern Europe, and it was grown in most communities where beer was brewed. Not until the nineteenth century did hop growing begin to concentrate in a few areas where brewing on a large, factory scale had been developed.

The source of sweetening had since prehistoric times been honey. Sugar began to be imported into Europe in the later Middle Ages, at first in small quantities from the Levant, and then in increasing amounts from the West Indies. Indeed, the exploitation of these islands was shaped by Europe's demand for sugar. It had long been known that the white beet contained sugar, but it was not until the mid-eighteenth century that sugar was first extracted from it. Even so, it was an expensive process and did not become important until the period of the Napoleonic Wars, when import of sugar from the West Indies was cut off. Cultivation of beet was not practicable on a small scale. It was not a crop for the garden or small enclosure, and its adoption had to await the breakdown of the three-course, open-field cultivation. In fact, it proved to be ideally suited as a catch-crop, grown on fields that had previously been left fallow.

The *Capitulare de villis,* in which Charlemagne gave a long list of vegetables that he required to be grown on his estates, also named the fruit trees to be planted. These included, in addition to the apple, pear, plum, and cherry, some exotic fruits that could not have been expected to flourish on Charlemagne's northern lands: fig, almond, mulberry, apricot, and peach. Doubtless the list was taken from a perhaps classical source with little regard for the climatic realities of the lower Rhineland. Nevertheless, it suggests the range of fruit trees known in the early Middle Ages. These trees continued to be grown where the climate was suitable, but mostly in the gardens belonging to monasteries and rich laymen. The peasant would have had at most one or two of the more hardy trees growing on his toft.

Two tree crops were of particular importance, the olive and the grapevine. Olive oil had continued to be an essential element in diet in southern Europe. The tree was highly sensitive to frost and could be grown only close to the Mediterranean coast. It matured very slowly, and an olive grove represented a long-term investment, beyond the means of the peasant. There was a tendency not to replant groves damaged by frost or destroyed in warfare, and their extent was probably less during the Middle Ages than in classical times. It probably diminished yet more as animal fats became increasingly available in modern times.

Of the continued spread of the grapevine, on the other hand, there can be no question. Viticulture increased through much of the Middle Ages and did not contract significantly before the nineteenth century. There were many reasons for the popularity of the vine. It was a hardy and adaptable plant. It could withstand both cold winters and hot summers. It could tolerate poor soils, and, until the later years of the nineteenth century, was not particularly susceptible to plant diseases. The cultivation of the vine furthermore had theological sanction and encouragement, and every church required wine every day for sacramental purposes. This demand encouraged its cultivation in the most unlikely places, and physical conditions had to be adverse indeed to prevent a monastery from at least attempting to produce wine. Wine, lastly, was good to drink. Its consumption was a mark of status, and those who could afford to do so made sure of an

5.12. Pressing grapes; from the Holkham Bible, fourteenth century.

adequate supply. Wines varied greatly in character and quality, which seemed to bear little relationship to climate and soil. The great vintages are, it has been claimed,[23] a response to the slow development of soil and technique. By the end of the Middle Ages some countries and regions had established an unassailable reputation for their wines and were thus able to export them over half the continent. The wine trade was, in terms of bulk, probably the most important in the Middle Ages. And as the trade developed, so marginal vineyards, like those in southern Britain and the Low Countries, were abandoned. This change, it should be emphasized, was a consequence of the competition of the better and cheaper Bordeaux wines, not of any fluctuation in climate.

The peasant in southern Europe, where the vine grew most easily, may have had a few vines on his holding and have made a poor wine for his own use, but most of the "great" vineyards were, and have since remained, part of the demesnes of the landed aristocracy, and their vintages, then as now, were consumed only by the rich.

The Tools of Cultivation

The tools and methods used by the peasant to cultivate his land scarcely changed between the end of the Roman period and the eighteenth century. Only the plow showed any significant development and adaptation to new conditions. The equipment of the peasant is familiar through surviving illustrations. Many are marginal drawings in Bibles and psalters; some occur in woodcarvings and stained glass. They are used to illustrate the biblical narrative—for example, drawings of Adam digging and Eve beside him spinning (fig. 5.3). Many show the labors traditionally associated with each of the months: plowing, sowing, haymaking, harvesting the grain, and the miscellaneous activities of the winter months.[24]

Most famous of all such series is that painted in the early years of the fifteenth century by Pol de Limbourg and Jean Colombe for their patron, the Duke of Berry.[25] The pictures accompany a book of hours, or meditations. Each shows one of the castles or princely

5.13. The sower, as depicted in the Luttrell Psalter. Here a dog is employed to scare away the birds until the seed can be covered.

residences of central France, with, in the foreground, appropriate scenes of rural activity. The farming activities associated with each month vary somewhat, as might be expected, and the greatest variety is found in the winter months, when there was no dominant activity.

The plow was closely followed by the sower, who walked behind it, a bag of seed at his waist, scattering handfuls to right and left in turn (fig. 5.13). Behind the sower came the harrow, which broke up the clods of earth and covered the seed. It was a wooden frame with crossbars, into which were fastened spikes of wood or iron. It was always drawn by a horse, far more speedy than an ox, for the seed had to be covered quickly. The harrow was sometimes weighted with a stone to press its teeth into the soil. Drawings often show birds circling around the sower and harrow, and an appreciable amount of seed must always have been devoured before it could be buried (fig. 5.14). An eighteenth-century Cornish record shows payments to children for "scaring bards."

There was little work on the land during the next few months. Pigs were fattened for slaughter, and the labors of the month of November commonly show the peasants shaking acorns and beech mast from the trees for the hogs rooting below. Woodcutting,

5.14. The horse-drawn harrow was used to break up the earth and bury the seed. Here a sling is being used to drive off the birds. (After the Luttrell Psalter.)

5.15. Cutting hay, as depicted in a misericord at Boos, France. Note the use of a long-handled scythe.

5.16. Making hay beside the River Seine. After Pol de Limbourg, *Les Très Riches Heures*.

hunting, and just keeping warm occupied the winter months. Spring saw a return to work in the fields: spring plowing and sowing, followed in some areas by pruning the vines and loosening the soil of the vineyards.

June, sometimes July, was the month for making hay in northern Europe and was followed by the beginning of the grain harvest. Scythes, which had long handles and cut close to the ground, were used for hay, which was allowed to dry off before being raked and heaped into ricks (figs. 5.15, 5.16). Cereals were cut with short-handled sickles, which left much of the straw to be plowed into the ground. It seems generally to have been women's work. But if the straw was needed for thatching, it was cut closer to the ground (fig. 5.17). The grain was then tied into sheaves and carted to the barn. Threshing began almost at once, for few communities had

5.17. Cereals were generally harvested with a short sickle, so that the left hand was free to grasp the stalks. In this way less of the grain was scattered and lost. (From a Bohemian Breviary of about 1400.)

much of last year's harvest left in their store when the next harvest time came round. Threshing was by means of a jointed flail, which was, after the plow, the most familiar of agricultural tools. It consisted of two strong rods, about four feet long, attached at their extremities by a leather thong (fig. 5.18). The peasant held the end of one rod and swung it so that the other rod struck the threshing floor with its whole length. The flail could be a formidable weapon and figured prominently in peasants' risings. It was often their only weapon. The task of threshing was continued intermittently through autumn and winter. Sometimes it took place in the open air, but, as the weather deteriorated, it moved more and more to the barns. The grain was then tossed into the air, using winnowing vans of wickerwork, until the wind had separated the chaff from the grain (fig. 5.19). The storage of grain was always a problem. It had to be protected from damp and from rodents and other vermin. On large estates there were often masonry-built barns where grain could be stored in relative security. On the peasant holding there was no such convenience. At most there might be a wooden granary, supported on stone staddles or "mushrooms" to prevent rodents from climbing into it. One cannot know what fraction of the grain was lost to birds when it was being sown or to fungoid disease and vermin when in store. During the famine-stricken days before the next harvest, the peasant was often reduced to eating contaminated grain. Indeed, the common disease ergotism was induced by eating diseased rye. This condition, in extreme cases, included gangrene and psychotic disorders. It is claimed that symptoms of ergotism can be seen in some figures in Brueghel's paintings.[26]

The grain harvest lasted through August and was followed by gathering the fruit. This task was traditionally women's work, but in the wine-growing areas all hands were needed to bring in the grapes. The grape harvest was associated with September, but varied with the amount of sunshine during the summer months. Its date, in fact, can be used as a measure of the warmth of the preceding weeks.

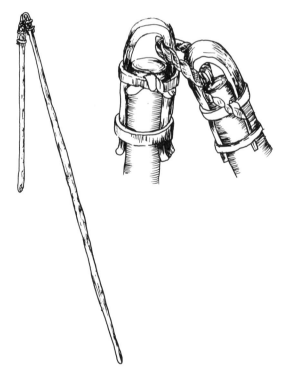

5.18. The jointing of a flail, as used in Poland in the nineteenth century. (After K. Moszyński, *Kultura Ludowa Slowiań* [Kraków, 1929]).

The year's routine described here is essentially that illustrated in the art of central and western Europe. It would have been different in southern Europe, and different again in the Alps and other mountainous areas. In Mediterranean Europe there was no spring sowing, and the greater warmth led to an earlier harvest in summer. Haymaking was of negligible importance, but the fruit harvest, especially that of the grape and olive, loomed larger and was followed by the crushing of the grapes and wine making.

The tools of the farmer underwent no significant changes until the nineteenth century, when the use of iron and steel became more abundant in plow and harrow, leading to significant changes in design. Hand tools played an important role, especially in the cultivation of garden plots and the management of tree crops. Most important without question was a spade of recognizably modern shape, but made of wood with a cutting edge of steel. It was the tool that the peasant used to cultivate his toft, and Adam's lot must have struck a chord with every villager. A mattock was used to break up fresh ground, and an axe, similar in shape to that used today, to fell trees. Only for weeding was an unfamiliar instrument used. Many drawings show the use of a forked stick to hold down the weed while another with a hook at the end pulled the root from the ground. A heavy curved knife was used for pruning, and shears with pointed blades and a rounded steel spring for sheepshearing.

A feature of most agricultural tools was the sparing use made of metal. Only the essential parts of the plow were of iron or steel; the harrow was often wholly of wood, and even the spade was only tipped with iron. Inventories mention harrows with iron "teeth" as if they were exceptional. Iron was indeed a scarce commodity, and steel was too expensive for most peasants to use. This situation began to change in early modern times. Metal tools became cheaper and more abundant, and their quality improved. Not only were harrows made of iron, but—the most significant change of all—an iron plow, lighter and more maneuverable, began to replace the clumsy, wooden instrument. Teams became smaller, the plow could be turned more easily at the end of its furrow, and the compulsion to organize cultivated land into long and narrow strips ceased.

5.19. Threshing with flails and winnowing with an elongated basket, used to pick up the grain and toss it into the air to remove the chaff and dirt. (From *A Book of Old Testament Illustrations of the Middle of the Thirteenth Century,* ed. S. C. Cockerell [Roxburghe Club, 1927].)

Both peasant and landlord needed some means to transport the produce of their lands: grain harvest to the barns, grapes to the presses, timber to the village for building or the hearth. The medieval cart derived from that used in Roman times. A four-wheeled wagon seems to have been used most often for long-distance transport and also for passenger travel. On the farm, however, it was a two-wheeled cart, more easily turned and requiring fewer draft animals than the wagon, that was most often used (fig. 5.21). It was roughly built, versatile, and functional. It had vertical sides, a tailboard that dropped to give added space, and shafts for harnessing a horse. Wheels, at least on carts shown in medieval manuscripts, were built of felloes and spokes and seem to have had metal tires, though there is every reason to believe that solid wheels continued to be used.

The farm cart has remained almost unchanged until today, serving its multitudinous functions. In some parts of Europe, notably central and western, a four-wheeled wagon came into general use. Its construction was similar, and it appears to have had two fixed axles, so that it could not make sharp turns. Its capacity, however, was much larger. The wagon seen in peasant markets in Poland today differs from that shown in sixteenth-century manuscripts only in having a front axle that swivels and can be used for turning, and in sporting discarded automobile tires on its wheels.[27]

Carts and wagons were of less importance in southern Europe. They were unsuited to the rough terrain that made up much of the region, and, in any case, draft animals

5.20. A painting prepared to illustrate Vergil's *Georgics*. It shows many aspects of the rural scene, including a heavy plow, a triangular harrow, sowing, and the cutting of branches to make a fence. (From *Manuscript Illustrations in the Library of the Earl of Leicester at Holkham,* ed. W. O. Hassell [Roxburghe Club, 1970].)

5.21. The type of farm cart used to bring in the harvest and to take goods to market. (After the Luttrell Psalter.)

were few. The transport of farm goods was most often accomplished by those universal beasts of burden, the donkey and its offspring, the mule, both able to tolerate the heat of summer and the slender nourishment.

Pastoral Farming

In no part of Europe was arable farming ever divorced from the rearing of animals, though it is convenient, for purposes of discussion, to separate the two. They were, in fact, complementary and neither could have been practiced without the other. But there was a gradation from economies in which pastoralism was dominant to those in which it was of only supplementary or minor importance; from cattle herders of the Norwegian fjords to crop farmers of the Paris basin and fruit growers of the Mediterranean. In each, a complex interdependence evolved between stock rearing and arable farming. In many instances the relationship had been established by the early Middle Ages and continued into the nineteenth century.

Most domesticated animals were multipurpose, providing milk, meat, and manure, as well as pulling the plow and the cart. The Germanic and barbarian invaders of western and southern Europe moved with their flocks and herds. Animals probably accompanied the Anglo-Saxon invaders of Britain, and, in the Bayeux Tapestry, horses are shown standing in the ships that brought the Normans to British shores. The most important domesticated animals, apart from the dog, were horses, cattle, sheep, and pigs and, chiefly in southern Europe, goats, donkeys, and mules. The number and variety of farm animals depended upon their role in the overall economy of each community.

5.22. A sled for transporting timber. It was used over grass as well as over snow. (After Gösta Berg, *Sledges and Wheeled Vehicles* [Stockholm, 1935], 78.)

Cattle breeding was almost universal except in southern Europe, and the ox was the most widely used of draft animals. Without cattle the fields could not be plowed, for the horse was never adept at drawing the heavy plow. Cattle also provided milk, though this was rarely, before the nineteenth century, the principal reason for rearing them. They yielded manure, but this was a bonus that only the more careful farmers were able to use to the full. Their carcasses provided meat, though cattle bred mainly for beef were unknown before the eighteenth century, as well as hides for tanning. Leather from oxhide was in most of Europe the material of footwear, harness, and even bottles and jugs. But the essential role of cattle was to pull the plow and the cart. Cattle were slow moving, but strong. They were undemanding in their food; meadow grass and hay sufficed, with sometimes a ration of oats at plowing time, when most was required of them.

Sheep were scarcely less a multiple-purpose animal than cattle. They yielded the wool of which much of the clothing was made. Sheepshearing was frequently represented in illustrations, always with pointed shears that differ in no way from those still used in some parts of Europe. If providing fleece was long the most important function of sheep, man nevertheless learned to use them in other ways. They were milked and cheese was made, and, folded on the stubble or the fallow, they contributed most of the manure that the land received. Lastly they yielded meat, and there was a greater readiness to slaughter sheep for this purpose than cattle, but most sheep were not eaten until their useful life was over.

The pig was kept only for the sake of its meat. It had no agricultural use, which helps to explain the cavalier attitude taken toward it. It was by nature a scavenger, picking up what food it could around the village and in the woods. Beech and oak woodland served best to fatten hogs, and a common measure of the extent of woodland was to say how many of the animals it could support. In describing woodland, a distinction was frequently made between that which could support hogs and that which could not. Among the labors of the months, at least in northern Europe, was the task of shaking down the acorns and beech mast from the trees to fatten the hogs before the onset of winter. Relatively few hogs could be kept through the winter months, when their natural food was scarce. It was customary to slaughter all that could not be fed and to salt the "sides of bacon." Salted bacon and pork were the only meat that many peasants were likely to eat, and even in the homes of the well-to-do, pigmeat in some form or other was an important source of animal protein. On the *villae* of the emperor Charlemagne about the year 800, there were reported to be 1025 hogs loose in the woods and 645 carcasses (*baccones*) freshly salted down. The importance of pigmeat in human diet remained considerable as long as there were woods to supply the basic food of the half-wild hog. With the depletion of the woodlands, which began in western Europe in the later Middle Ages, the hog became less a creature of the wild and more a denizen of the domestic sty, fed on household and farmyard waste. This was its chief role in much of Europe by the eighteenth century; only in the east did it continue to range the woods in significant numbers. In southern Europe the hog never achieved importance, because it could not derive a living from the dry woodland, and in the Middle East the taboo on pigmeat probably derives from the almost total lack of woodland.

The goat was to be found over much of Europe, but chiefly in the south. Its virtue was that it was almost omnivorous. It could browse even on the dry growth of a Mediterranean summer. On the other hand, it could climb and strip a tree, and its "poisoned tooth" was blamed for the devastation of many a hillside in the Mediterranean. Nevertheless, it was an important, sometimes the only, source of milk in those areas where it was kept, and cheese made from goat's milk has always been a source of protein.

Horse, donkey, and mule were kept almost exclusively as draft animals, and there was a widespread prejudice against using their flesh as human food. Throughout Europe the horse was the chief riding animal. The knight fought on horseback and in medieval art was rarely represented without his horse. The traveler rode on horseback, the only practicable alternative to walking, the horse pulled the wagons in which the families of the rich traveled, and the merchant often transported his wares piled on the backs of horses. As long-distance travel came to be organized, relay stations were set up along the more important highways, where horses might be hired or exchanged. Yet the horse was a costly animal to keep; more care was given to its breeding than to that of other animals, and its diet was more restricted. If it was to perform heavy work, it required an abundant diet of coarse grains, oats, and barley. To this extent the horse fitted into the three-course rotation of the open fields. On the other hand, it moved more quickly than the ox and was less suited to that most essential of farm duties, pulling the plow. Nevertheless, the horse was occasionally used for this purpose, and in some areas—central Poland, for example—became the most common draft animal. Doubtless there were reasons for harnessing the horse instead of the ox to the plow, but it is difficult at this distance in time to establish their logic. It is one of the countless inexplicable localisms that characterize the material culture of Europe.

The number of farm animals was restricted by the amount of food available. North of the Alps the problem was the length and severity of winter. In southern Europe it was rather the drought of summer that shriveled most green things. Man could not overcome these obstacles, but he could adapt to them. In northern Europe a partial solution was to conserve what fodder was possible and to cut down the size of flocks and herds each autumn to what the local resources could support. The annual slaughter of pigs in November or December was part of this routine. Cattle, which served so many purposes more important than supplying meat, were too valuable to be sacrificed in this way. When grazing ceased to suffice, they had to be given hay that had been cut and dried during the previous summer. Hence the importance of haymaking in the labors of the months. But meadowland, which was flooded and fertilized in winter and grew a lush grass in spring and summer, was always one of the least extensive of a community's lands. It usually fetched a far higher price than good arable, because, without it, the arable could not be tilled.

This problem was solved eventually by the cultivation of the so-called artificial grasses, plants that had the capacity to sustain the cattle and could at the same time be grown in rotation with breadgrains. The ideal solution was to grow fodder crops on the fallow, but this involved a change of almost revolutionary proportions. Artificial grasses, like clover and lucerne, were first grown on a significant scale in Flanders and elsewhere in the Low Countries in the later Middle Ages. This was a region where the system of three-course open-field cultivation was breached at an early date, if, indeed, it had ever been fully practiced. There was a looseness and flexibility in the farming structure that made it easy to innovate and cultivate new crops. The growing of crops specifically for animals to eat spread to England, but its diffusion into France and Germany was very slow. Over much of Europe, even in the later nineteenth century, the peasant knew nothing of fodder crops, and his cattle continued to be restricted by the limited winter feed available for them. Where fodder crops were adopted on a significant scale, they very quickly came to support a growing number of dairy cattle. Production of milk, butter, and cheese increased sharply, with a significant rise in the quality of human diet and improvement in health.

Sheep presented a lesser problem, because they could live on coarse grazing land for much if not all of the year. But they were also kept in considerable numbers in areas of high, arable farming, for here one-third of the land was always fallow, capable of providing a poor living for the sheep, which returned the compliment with their droppings.

Scarcity of fodder compelled the maximum use of marginal land. Near the limits of permanent settlement and cultivation there were always areas that for climatic reasons could be used for only part of the year. Such areas lay along the northern edge of human settlement in Scandinavia, on the Meseta of the Spanish peninsula, and in mountainous areas in other parts of Europe. The use of such areas was dependent on seasonal movements of people and animals from their winter homes in lower and more sheltered areas to summer homes on the margin of settlement. This movement assumed many patterns, but was everywhere of social and ritual significance for the community.

It is difficult to say how old is this practice of transhumance. There is some evidence that it was known in Iron Age Europe. That it was significant in the classical civilizations is apparent from ancient writers. In the Greek world the seasonal movement was restricted, and in some parts prohibited by the political boundaries between the *poleis*. On the other hand, the unification of Italy under Roman rule removed obstacles to the long-distance movement of flocks and herds, and regular paths (*calles*) were established between the winter grazing—*saltus hiberni*—in the coastal lowlands and the summer pastures—*saltus aestivi*—high in the Apennines. Its effect was to make use of mountain grazing, which was open only in summer, when the lowlands were burned brown by the heat. In the extreme north of Europe the practice of transhumance was broadly similar. In Scandinavia the population appears to have been increasing, and there was growing pressure on the restricted area of cultivable land. Hay was made in the valleys while the animals grazed the scanty pastures of the high *fjeld* during the short summer. In the words of *Egil's Saga:* "When Skallagrim's livestock was much increased, then went the cattle all up into the fells in the summer. He found there great odds in this, that those beasts became better and fatter which went on the heaths. . . ."[28] He even found that sheep could be left without loss on some of the higher pasture through the winter— sheep are always more hardy than cattle—and he therefore set up a small hill settlement on this high ground.

It was in the Alpine system, from the Pyrenees to the Balkans, that transhumance became most developed and most complex. Here the horizontal distance between valley settlements and the "alps," or highland pastures, was short. The snow limit retreated slowly up the mountainside in spring, revealing first the grazing land at intermediate heights, and then the highest of all. The animals followed the retreating snow and then returned in autumn as the increasing snow drove them to lower levels. In the meantime, a crop of hay had been taken from the valley pastures, sufficient to tide the animals over the winter.

The animals were driven to the highland grazing not merely to keep them alive through the summer. While there, they yielded milk and gave birth to young. The milk could not easily be brought back to the main settlement in the lowlands. It had to be preserved by converting it to the more manageable form of cheese. Cheeses in vast quantities were the chief material gain from the mountain grazing, and surveys of the Austrian monasteries show them receiving rents for these lands in the form of cheese.[29]

Transhumance of this kind was practiced wherever marginal environments lay close to centers of population. In Scotland, the *shieling* and in Wales the *havod* provided summer grazing and rough shelter for the shepherd or cowherd. Even in southwestern England, where the vertical distance between lowland and upland was rarely more than a thousand feet, there is evidence of a transhumance movement. Even at such low elevations there are place-names indicative of seasonal occupation, among them one that signifies a milking shed on the moorlands. A doggerel poem of the later seventeenth century, preserved in a commonplace book, tells succintly the role of transhumance in the local economy:

> Our best neighbour—and he's choice and good—
> Is the wild moor; there's the best neighbourhood.
> It keeps vast herds of cattle, I profess,
> And flocks of sheep even almost numberless.
> Thus we our stock do summer on the Down,
> And keep our homer grass till winter come. . . . [30]

The examples of transhumance have all been over relatively short distances, a couple of days' journey for slow-moving herds at most.[31] In every instance the permanent settlements were in the valley or the coastal lowlands, and only a few, generally unmarried, members of the community made the summer journey to the upland pastures. There were however, instances of transhumant journeys that covered hundreds of miles, and also of inverse transhumance, when the permanent home was at a higher level and part of the community moved *down* to the lowlands in winter. In the case of long-distance transhumance, the contrasted environments lay at a great distance from one another, and the actual migratory processes might occupy two or more months. In such instances the transhumant animals were left not in the care of a few junior members of the community but in that of professional shepherds and herders who stayed with them throughout the year. In such cases the link between the transhumant flocks and particular communities was broken; they ceased to be part of a localized, agricultural regime. Such a migratory pattern developed in Spain, with summer grazing on the plains of Old Castile, and winter in Andalusia.[32]

A body of folklore and ritual has gathered around the practice of transhumance. The departure of man and animals for the mountains in late spring and their return in autumn were major events in the peasant calendar, celebrated with a mixture of sorrow and rejoicing. So important was this use of marginal resources in a peasant community living close to the edge of subsistence, so integrated was it with other aspects of peasant life, that the system has proved remarkably durable. Sheep still migrate in Spain; in the Alps herds still climb to the high meadows in summer; in northern Greece one still sees the winter tents of the herdsmen before they return to their austere villages high in the Pindus Mountains for the summer;[33] and on farms in western Britain some of the stock is still moved the short distance to higher ground for the summer months. Yet transhumance no longer plays its former role. With the cultivation of artificial grasses and fodder crops, it is no longer essential to use the marginal resources of hill and mountain grazing.

Domesticated plants slowly evolved under the influence of selective breeding. The fact that selective breeding was unconscious did not make it less effective. The peasant had the wit, in general, to hold back for future sowing the best, not the worst, of his seed. Procreation among animals was more difficult to control. They grazed together, and not before the eighteenth century was any attempt made to mate animals with outstanding qualities.[34] There are instances of the import of cattle and horses for breeding purposes as early as the seventeenth century, but only the landowning aristocracy had the wealth to do this and the stabling to control the animals. The peasant had no conception of selective breeding and was happy enough to secure the services of a bull at the lowest possible price. As for sheep, they mated how and where they wished.

Serious attention was first given to stock breeding in England in the eighteenth century. One reason for this development was that ideas of what was wanted from animals were changing. In the past the edible qualities of the animal had not been very important. If their fleeces fetched a good price or they were strong at the plow, little else mattered. Then, with rising standards of living, more meat of better quality came to be demanded, and there was an increase in the consumption of milk products. In the hands of cattle- and sheep breeders—all of them landowners of some wealth—the desirable qualities in farm stock were gradually exaggerated, so that by the nineteenth century distinctive breeds of cattle, sheep, and even pigs began to appear. The merits of selective breeding probably became apparent to the peasant classes long before the opportunity presented itself of practicing it. The problem goes back to the open field and the common, where the advantages of the grazing to the peasant were offset by the promiscuity enjoyed by their animals.

Food Preparation and Diet

From early in the Neolithic, diet became increasingly farinaceous, as the cultivated cereals gradually replaced the fruits of hunting and gathering. Throughout the medieval period and also the modern until late in the nineteenth century, cereals continued to dominate but were almost everywhere supplemented with pulses, vegetables, and fruit and variable but generally small amounts of animal protein. It would probably be true to say that 90 percent of the foodstuffs made available were consumed within, say, ten miles of where they were produced. Given such a high level of self-sufficiency, there had to be considerable variations in diet throughout the continent, and each community had to set aside grain and other foodstuffs to last it through winter and spring, up to the next harvest. There was always scarcity in the weeks before the peasants went into the fields to reap the first fields of rye and wheat. Archbishop Eudes Rigaud of Rouen, in the thirteenth century, recorded conditions in the monasteries of his diocese.[35] They reported with a gruesome unanimity that they had only a few weeks' supply left and could barely endure until the next harvest. People were inured before the nineteenth century to hardship; scarcity was normal, famine frequent. The romantic view of the Middle Ages and subsequent centuries as an age of "coarse plenty" is very far from the truth. Some did indeed live well, even if their diet was severely unbalanced. A few did enjoy gargantuan banquets, but the care with which they were described is perhaps a measure of their infrequency.[36] The most abundant season for most people marked the onset of winter, now marked by the *feast* of Christmas. Its coincidence with the winter solstice suggests a very ancient origin, but it is likely that feasting was closely associated with the slaughter of farm stock that could not be held through the winter.

The fact that most sources of food became available seasonally and that most plants matured in late summer made storage and preservation absolute necessities. Broadly speaking, only three methods of preserving foods were available before the scientific revolution of the nineteenth century: drying, salting, and fermenting, and of these, by and large, drying was the easiest and most important. Some foods, cereals and nuts, for example, are already dry when harvested and with care can be kept for very long periods without putrefaction, but it was necessary to dry the grain artificially after harvest if the season had been wet. Grain-drying kilns were not infrequent at Roman and medieval sites in northwestern Europe. The consequences of eating putrefying grain have already been mentioned. Drying was also used to preserve certain soft fruits, notably grapes (raisins) and figs, and also, though on a very limited scale, fish and meat. And, of course, the principal animal feed, hay, was preserved by being sun dried.

Smoking is a particular form of drying and was used particularly for meat and fish. It was not, however, practiced as much in preindustrial Europe as might have been expected, largely, perhaps, because of the heavy demand for fuel and the need to build a masonry smokehouse. Sides of bacon were, however, suspended above cottage fires and were cured, perhaps imperfectly, in the wood smoke. Facilities for smoke-curing meat became more frequent in the great houses of country estates from the eighteenth century.

Salting is also a form of desiccation. Its use to preserve fish and meat was discovered very early in human history but could be practiced only where salt was available in quantity, and this, in effect, meant the Mediterranean basin, where the summer sun was strong enough to evaporate brine. Salt became one of the most important exports from southern Europe to northern, and the most northerly limit of commercial salt-making was effectively the Bay, that is, the Bay of Bourgneuf on the west coast of France near Nantes.[37]

The last method of food preservation in general use was fermenting. Fermented liquor preserved part of the substance, whether honey, grape juice, or malt, from which it was made and thus had a not inconsiderable food value. Beer, it is claimed, contributed about a seventh of the caloric intake of a Polish peasant in early modern times, and an even larger proportion of that of the gentry.[38] Fermentation also played a role in the preservation of some vegetables and is used today in making silage.

Storage presented no less a problem than the processes of preservation themselves. Prehistoric peoples used storage pits for cereals, but there was almost certainly a considerable wastage. In classical and later times, barns, usually timber built with floors of tile or rammed earth, were used. The problem was to keep the foodstuff dry and to exclude vermin and thieves. In none of these respects was there ever complete success, and every peasant was faced with deterioration and loss of part of his small store of food during the year.

The diet of most people for most of the time was narrowly restricted and monotonous, and when one item was substituted for another, as had to be the case in times of scarcity, the change was always for the worst. The consumption of coarse grains instead of breadgrains, or of buckwheat or chestnuts in place of either, marked a severe decline in standards, to be rectified as soon as harvest conditions permitted. There were times— subsistence crises—when such substitutions had to be made on so extensive a scale that even coarse substitute foods proved inadequate. There were numerous such crises in the later Middle Ages, and it cannot be said that they ceased to be a recurring factor in material welfare until the mid-nineteenth century.

All cereals consist of a farinaceous kernel or endosperm, surrounded by a hard coating, or pericarp. These, in turn, are enclosed by glumes or bracts, which have survived from the flower stage of the plant. In many early varieties of the breadgrains, these bracts were so firmly attached to the seed that they did not separate in the course of threshing and winnowing. In the course of unconscious selective breeding from which all cultivated plants have benefited, species of "naked" cereals, which fall away from their bracts, have been evolved. But hulled variants are still to be met with and are almost impossible to mill by traditional methods.

The milling process breaks up the pericarp, which it reduces to small pieces of husk, and thus liberates the white "flour" that makes up the endosperm. Unmilled grain is difficult to chew and digest, and it is probable that even the seeds of wild grasses were bruised and broken up between stones long before cereals began to be consciously cultivated. Such rubbing stones have been found from the Upper Palaeozoic. With the cultivation of cereals in the Neolithic, improved methods were devised of grinding them.[39] The saddle quern came into use. It consisted of a flat or slightly concave stone, upon which the moving stone was rubbed in a to-and-fro motion. Milling was normally a domestic occupation, left to the women. Exodus refers to "the maid servant that is *behind* the mill," a phrase strongly suggestive of a saddle quern (fig. 5.23). Grain was added to the quern by hand, and the ground flour and bran traveled away from the miller to the edge of the stone.

5.23. The "maid that is behind the mill"; an Egyptian terra-cotta showing the use of a rubbing stone and saddle quern.

Grinding on the saddle quern was a slow and laborious task, and in a large household it must have called for almost continuous employment. The invention of the rotary quern did something to reduce the labor, if only because rotary motion is less demanding than reciprocal.[40] In it the upper stone, or "runner," was pivoted above the lower, and, if well balanced, could be made to turn easily by means of a handle. The lower stone was shaped like a flattened cone, so that the grain traveled toward its outer edge, where it was collected. An early innovation was the creation of a hole in the runner, through which the grain could be introduced. The date when the rotary quern first appeared is obscure. It was known in Late Iron Age Europe and was used in classical Greece. Some form of rotary quern appears to have been widely used in the Roman Empire; Roman soldiers carried small rotary querns with them in order to make their own bread. "The role of armies," wrote Childe, "in the diffusion of rotary querns can hardly be overestimated."[41]

The burden imposed by the daily task of grinding cereals was in time erased by the use, first, of animal power and, later, that of water and of wind. Amid the ruins of Pompeii can be seen examples of donkey mills. They were, in fact, rotary querns of markedly conical shape, and the runner was carried upward to form a hopper into which the grain was poured (fig. 5.24).[42] A wooden shaft was passed through the latter and was harnessed to a donkey. This mill was larger than was needed in the home, and its presence at Pompeii probably suggests that there were professional bakers, at least in the cities.

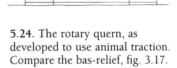

5.24. The rotary quern, as developed to use animal traction. Compare the bas-relief, fig. 3.17.

The next stage in the development of milling was the use of mechanical power to turn the upper millstone. The energy generated by flowing water may first have been used in the hills of the Middle East; the earliest clear references to water mills are from the first century B.C. They refer to a simple device by which the blades of a small paddle wheel, set horizontally, were placed in the water of a gently flowing stream and turned slowly by its current (fig. 5.25). The paddle wheel was linked directly, through a hole in the center of the lower stone, to the runner. This type of mill was small and ground very slowly. It nevertheless became common in much of Europe. It is probable that most of the mills recorded in the English Domesday Book of 1085–86 were of this type, and it continued in use in parts of northern and eastern Europe until recent times.[43]

It was not long, however, before this simple direct-drive mill was replaced by a more complex and effective device, consisting of a larger wheel, set vertically and linked by gears to the millstone. It is sometimes called a Vitruvian mill because it was described by the Roman architect in the first century B.C. The paddle wheel, which

5.25. A horizontal waterwheel; east European, nineteenth century. (After K. Moszyński.)

was usually very much larger than the horizontally set wheel, dipped into the water. It often turned more quickly, and the wooden gears by which it was linked to the mill permitted the stone to run much faster. The mill itself no longer had to be constructed directly above the mill wheel; it could be built on the firm ground of a river's bank, with

5.26. An overshot watermill. (After the Luttrell Psalter.)

the wheel thrust out into the water. The use of the Vitruvian mill effectively removed milling from the home and transferred it to a separate building, erected at considerable expense and operated by a professional miller.

This, in its essentials, is the kind of mill that spread through Europe in medieval and early modern times. Changes in design improved its efficiency, but its basic principle was unaltered. The Vitruvian mill was undershot; it used the energy inherent in *flowing* water. An improvement, apparently made at an early date, was to allow water to *fall* onto the wheel, either partway up—the breast wheel—or at the top of its turn—the overshot wheel (fig. 5.26). The use of the kinetic energy of falling water greatly increased the efficiency of the wheel, allowing it to turn stones of increasing size and, eventually, to be used in mining and metalworking. But the breast and overshot wheels required more careful engineering than the earlier undershot. The task of bringing water to the wheel at the requisite height usually called for careful surveying and the construction of a mill leat, which conveyed the water along the contours of a hillside from a perhaps distant stream. Provision also had to be made for the return of the water to the river after it had performed its task.

The social consequences of the adoption of the breast and overshot wheels were considerable. In the first place their cost of construction was high, far beyond the means of the peasant. They could only be built by the lord of the manor, and the manorial mill remained a significant institution into the nineteenth century. The costs of construction could be recouped only if the tenants were compelled to use their lord's mill—and to pay for the service. "Suit of mill" thus became one of the many obligations from which the peasant extricated himself only in modern times. The lord most often "farmed" the mill to someone who paid a fixed rent for the privilege of maintaining and operating it, and who charged the peasants a "toll"—as large as the traffic would bear—for his services. The miller acquired, and has retained, a reputation for dishonesty, for subtracting more of the peasant's grain than was just. Even Chaucer's miller "Well koude he stelen corn and tollen thries." Mills, second, were an encumbrance, an obstacle in the way of rural life. They partially blocked streams and obstructed navigation, especially those undershot mills which were constructed on boats moored in midstream. They drew off water from the rivers, and mill leats often had to be laid across peasants' land, where necessary repairs caused endless disputes.

In the course of the Middle Ages, the water mill came to be supplemented by the windmill. The latter was unknown to the classical civilizations and was first recorded in Iran in post-Roman times. There is no record of a windmill anywhere in Europe before the late twelfth century. Thereafter windmills became increasingly common. They had great advantages over the water mill. Neither frost nor drought hindered their operation. It was not necessary to engineer a mill leat across other people's land. All they called for was a site exposed to the free flow of the wind. In cities, where the demand for milling facilities was far greater than elsewhere, windmills were not infrequently mounted on the towers and walls. In southern Europe, where watercourses were likely to dry up in summer, windmills assumed particular importance, standing in rows upon hilltops, their numbers making up for their small individual capacities.[44]

In the earliest windmills there were four vanes, mounted on a shaft that was directly linked by gears to the upper millstone. The whole was fitted into a small wooden house that was made to rotate on a stout wooden post and could thus be turned to face into the wind at any time (fig. 5.27). But this mode of construction set a limit to the size of the mill itself, and toward the end of the Middle Ages the mechanism was placed in a tower built of wood or even of masonry. The shaft bearing the vanes was mounted in the rounded cap of the mill, which was made to rotate on wheels or bearings in order to face into the wind. The solid construction of the tower mill was a great improvement over the less substantial post mill and permitted a more heavily built mechanism to be used. It became more common, though the post mill never wholly disappeared.

5.27. A windmill of the post mill type. The beam to the left was used for turning the whole mill so that the sails faced into the wind. (After the Luttrell Psalter.)

There was always a temptation to use the hand quern to avoid payments to the miller, though this practice was strenuously discouraged by the lord and his servants, as well as by the miller. Querns, nevertheless, gradually disappeared from most of Europe, and in modern times were significant only in remote and sparsely populated areas where no mill was available. The grinding of cereals thus ceased to be a regular household task in much of Europe, and with it bread making began to desert the domestic hearth for the professional bakery. This was a fact of no little social significance, even though its progress is difficult, if not impossible, to follow. It marked a general improvement in the quality of bread, as well as removing much labor and inconvenience from the home.

Mills powered by wind or water accounted for most of the milling carried on in Europe until the middle years of the nineteenth century. A growing dependence then showed itself on imported cereals, mainly from the New World. Reliance on the older methods of milling was no longer practicable, and a search began for means of faster and more regular grinding. At the same time demand was increasing for a whiter bread, with a smaller admixture of bran, than could be made from flour milled in a traditional fashion. It had been the practice to sieve or *bolt* the ground flour through a cloth to extract the bran. Even though the sieves had come to be worked mechanically, bolting remained a laborious and uncertain process, and most bread was far from white. The roller mills, powered by steam engines, which made their appearance in the 1840s, not only hastened the process but also permitted the extraction rate—the percentage of bran included in the flour—to be varied.[45] This step in turn prepared the way for the variety of breads to be met with today.

The traditional mill, whether driven by wind or water, was built by local craftsmen of local materials; wood and wattle, stone and brick. But only rarely did a material suitable for millstones occur locally. They had to be hard, uniform in texture, and yet have and retain a rough surface. The Romans had used tufa, a slightly porous volcanic rock, found in central Italy. Iron Age peoples in northern Europe had learned the value of andesite from near Mayen in western Germany. This material continued throughout the Middle Ages to be shipped from Andernach, on the Rhine. In England it was known as "cullin" stone, from its supposed origin in the city of Cologne. In France "burr" stone from near Paris was widely used and was even exported to North America. In western Britain granite millstones were common. Everywhere there was a considerable commerce in heavy millstones that could grind effectively and yet not break or splinter in the process. Only the use of steel rolls in steam mills ended this reliance on a very limited supply of stone.

Despite its predominantly farinaceous character, diet was nonetheless a reflection of social status. The rich lived abundantly, if not well from a nutritional point of view. The poor had a frugal and nutritionally poor diet. Most people in most of Europe ate twice a day, with their heaviest meal after the day's work had ended. The consumption of a heavy meal around midday does not appear to have become common before the sixteenth century, and then only among the rich. The poorer classes were too busy in their fields for such luxury. The meal consisted mainly of breadgrains. Methods of preparation depended on the cereal. It can be assumed that wheat always and rye commonly were baked with some form of leaven in an oven. Alternative grains, barley and oats, were either boiled into a form of gruel, of which the Scottish porridge is a modern survival, or cooked as flatbread or cakes. According to the fourteenth-century chronicler Ranulf Higden, the Welsh ate "Brode cakes rounde and thynne / Of barly and of ote" but also "They have gruell to potage."[46] And such a diet was not restricted to the Welsh; it was common throughout Europe north of the Alps.[47] It was unappetizing and nutritionally inadequate but was seasoned with whatever vegetables and herbs were available. This assortment depended on the season, though peas and beans could usually be kept through the winter and were a valuable source of protein. Garlic, onions, and various herbs were added, all the more readily because many of these could be dried and stored. John Gardener, about 1440, prescribed what the peasant and his betters should grow on their garden plot:

> How he schall hys sedys sowe
> Of every moneth he moste knowe
> Both of wortys and of leke
> Ownyns and of garleke
> Percely, clarey and eke sage
> And all other herbage.[48]

5.28. The breadgrains in general use in England and Wales in the eighteenth century. The symbols show the composition of the average basket of breadgrains in the regions indicated. (Based on statistics in Sir William Ashley, *The Bread of our Forefathers.*)

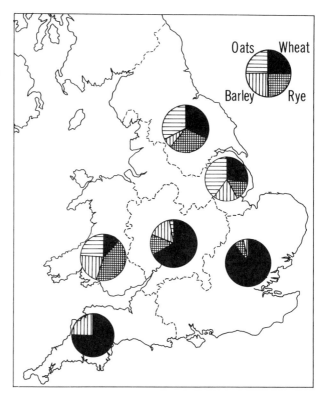

Add to these parsnips, turnips, carrots, and beets, and one has the ingredients of an appetizing, if not wholly nutritional, stew.

Diet almost everywhere was short of animal fats. Fish was available near the coast, where it played a significant role, and, dried and salted, was transported inland. Meat was scarce. Pigmeat was the most abundant, but other meats were eaten even by the poor at their rare feasts and more frequently by the rich.

There were great regional variations in diet, imposed in the main by local agricultural conditions. Most variable were the breadgrains. Even within England and Wales there were strong contrasts between south and north, east and west. Figure 5.28 shows the basket of cereals consumed in six major regions of Britain in the eighteenth century.[49] Wheat had assumed the dominant role in the south and east, but this shift had occurred only in recent years. A century earlier, rye was the dominant breadgrain in most areas and had been ousted only because in England there was capital enough to improve the soil by manuring and draining. At the end of the sixteenth century William Harrison was quite explicit on the matter:

> The bread throughout the land is made of such grain as the soil yieldeth; nevertheless, the gentility commonly provide themselves sufficiently of wheat for their own tables, whilst their household and poor neighbors in some shires are enforced to content themselves with rye or barley, yea, and in time of dearth, many with bread made of beans, peason, or oats, or of all together and some acorns among, of which scourge the poorest do soonest taste, sith they are least able to provide themselves of better. I will not say that this extremity is oft so well to be seen in time of plenty as of dearth. . . . [50]

At the other end of Europe and at about the same time, the average diet of both peasant and gentry was overwhelmingly of breadgrains, including millet and buckwheat. The difference between the two diets lay chiefly in the far greater volume consumed by the latter. In Poland the breadgrains and beer, itself brewed from malt, contributed respectively 81.6 and 76 percent of their caloric intake. Meat, fish, and animal fats formed 9 and 13 percent. In terms of volume, the gentry consumed per head considerably more than twice as much as the peasantry (Table 1).[51] There is little evidence that this diet had changed substantially in rural Poland before the late nineteenth century. It is wholly consistent with the details given by Władisław Reymont in his novel *Chłopi*.

Table 1. Diet in Poland about 1600 in Calories per Day

	Peasantry		Gentry	
Breadgrains, as				
bread and gruel	2354 }	81.6%	2985 }	76%
Beer, from malt	504 }		1092 }	
Vegetables	160	4.6%	318	6%
Meat and animal fats	315	9%	696	13%
Others	167	4.8%	255	5%
	3500		5346	

The human diet requires the presence of four elements in order to sustain normal life: a sufficient caloric intake to provide bodily energy; protein, from which tissues are formed; accessory substances, commonly known as vitamins; and, lastly, certain trace elements such as iron, phosphorus, calcium, and fluorine. It is doubtful whether the human diet has in these respects ever been wholly adequate. The presence of trace elements is due basically to local geology, and their absence contributes to certain ailments. Goiter, for example, can be correlated with a local deficiency in iodine. The role of trace elements is a discovery of the last century, and their presence or absence could not possibly have been known to earlier peoples. On the other hand, they learned the value of certain foodstuffs that we now know to have contained essential elements of a satisfactory diet. Instinctively they aimed at an adequate if not perfectly balanced diet, but very rarely indeed did they achieve it.

With so large a consumption of breadgrains, the caloric intake of all classes was adequate much of the time. Problems arose only in times of crop failure, when most of society, and particularly the poor, found their consumption gravely reduced or replaced by less adequate and often quite unpalatable substances. The amount of protein in the diet varied with wealth and social class. The rich were great meat eaters, and their intake was more than adequate. The poor, however, consumed little meat, and relied for protein chiefly on that contained in cereals and pulses. The "white meats"—milk, cheese, eggs— also supplied protein but were consumed perhaps less than they could have been. A widespread prejudice against milk and milk products, quite inexplicable in nutritional terms, led to a smaller consumption than could have been possible and also postponed the breeding of good dairy cattle. But conditions varied greatly from one region to another. Dairy products were of little importance in areas of open-field farming, but were relatively significant in, for example, the Alps and Scandinavia.

It was in the field of vitamins that the inadequacies of diets were most conspicuous. The abundant source of vitamin A in liver and fish oil was denied to much of the population, and the alternative source in green vegetables, butter, and eggs, was seasonal and little eaten. Very little vitamin A could be absorbed in winter, and by spring there was often a widespread deficiency, leading to night blindness and a weakening of the defenses against infection and skin diseases. Vitamin C is chiefly available in fresh fruit and certain vegetables. Their absence from the diet, inevitable for much of the year, led to scurvy, a condition of general listlessness when wounds failed to heal and old lesions reopened. Vitamin D is necessary to prevent that malformation of bones known as rickets. It is formed naturally in the body under the influence of bright sunshine, and deficiency is rare in southern Europe. In northern Europe it has to be supplied in the diet. The most abundant sources are fish and fish oils, eggs, and milk products, and these played only a small role in the diet.

The B group of vitamins is also contained in meat, especially liver and kidney, and in vegetables. Vitamin B_1 (thiamine) occurs in the outer layers of certain cereals and is lost if the bran is totally separated from the flour. This happens in modern milling techniques, but in earlier times much of the bran, with its vitamin B_1, passed into the flour and was eaten. Vitamin B_1 deficiency was probably rare, but there was a serious shortage of some other members of the group, particularly B_7, lack of which causes pellagra.

It cannot be doubted that the diet of most people before the late nineteenth century was seriously deficient in protein and in certain vitamins. The peasantry was not so much underfed, in the sense of having too small a volume of food to fill their stomachs, as poorly fed, with too much hydrocarbon and too little protein and vitamin-rich food. The rich fared better, if not as well as they could have done. All suffered through ignorance of dietary needs, and most consumed too few milk products, largely as a result of their prejudice against them. The poor were more likely to be stunted in their growth, to have malformed bones, to suffer from skin complaints, and to be more liable to infection because their diet lacked the essential vitamins. But the well-to-do, for whom these foods were available, nevertheless sometimes ignored them through a mixture of ignorance and prejudice, and in the end fared little better.

In addition to the contrast in diet between rich and poor, there was also a marked difference between that of the rural and of the urban population. The saving grace of the peasant was that he could grow vegetables on his toft. The town population in general had no such facility. There was little movement of green vegetables to the towns, probably because of their perishable nature, and even fewer milk and dairy products were consumed than in the countryside. Not until the revolution in both agriculture and food habits that took place in the middle and later years of the nineteenth century, was this situation changed.

A number of new foodstuffs became available in the seventeenth and later centuries. Some, like tea, coffee, and cacao, had little food value but contributed to the niceties of life, while others, including the potato and corn (maize), had an immense significance. Coffee had originated in southern Arabia. It had a mixed reception among Moslems, because the Prophet never quite made up his mind whether it was a stimulant or a sedative. Nevertheless, it was carried by the Ottoman Turks, always less dogmatic than the Arabs on the finer points of Islamic belief and practice, into the Balkans. The practice of drinking coffee was spread, probably by the Dutch, to western and central Europe. It became a social drink, leading to the popularity in the eighteenth century of coffee-houses, where small groups of people assembled to conduct business and discuss public and literary matters. That these small gatherings contributed significantly to intellectual life has been attributed to the fact that it was only a stimulant, and not alcohol, that was consumed. But coffee remained an expensive drink until after its cultivation had spread to southeastern Asia and to most countries of Latin America. It never became cheap but went a long way to displace beer. Its great merit from a dietary point of view was that the water used in making it had to be boiled and was thus sterilized.

Tea originated in China, and its name is a Dutch corruption of the Chinese. Its cultivation was carried by the Dutch to the East Indies but did not develop on a significant scale in India and Ceylon until the nineteenth century. In the meantime, the practice of drinking tea had spread overland to Russia and by sea to western Europe. The Dutch, who at first monopolized the trade, were the first to adopt the habit, but before long they were selling tea in Britain, France, and the rest of western Europe. Tea drinking had been anticipated by coffee by a few years, and tea was at first dispensed in coffeehouses. Tea, unless milk and sugar were added, was a mild stimulant, but other-wise it had no food value, and taking tea, like coffee, became a social practice. In the meanwhile, by the eighteenth century, control of the tea trade had passed from the Dutch to the English, and London became the chief tea market. Although tea was reexported from England to the Americas, as the Boston Tea Party demonstrates, and to other parts of Europe, tea drinking remained a localized practice. It was relatively expensive. Its consumption in Britain became general among the well-to-do, whose account books sometimes show a considerable expenditure on "bohea" or "cha." It became in the eighteenth century the focus of a light afternoon meal, which has since borne the name of "tea." This was a social occasion because there was really no need for a meal between "dinner" in the early afternoon and the evening's "supper." Until late in the nineteenth century, tea tended to be drunk by those classes which were already more than ade-quately fed. The working classes preferred beer or ale, which at least had some caloric value. In Britain, tea displaced coffee as the social drink par excellence, largely because Britain had come to dominate the tea trade but had little influence over that in coffee. In most of Europe, with the exception of the Netherlands, coffee has continued to rule supreme in this respect.

The third drink in this trilogy was cocoa, derived from the fruit of the cacao tree, which was native to tropical America. The drink made from the ground fruit had little food value. Although chocolate houses were established, the drink never achieved the popularity of tea and coffee. It was more difficult to prepare, but a major reason was that the Spanish Empire, in which it was grown, never showed a commercial acumen comparable with that of the Dutch and English. It became a popular drink only in northwestern Europe, and even there tended to be identified with the humbler classes, reflecting perhaps its lower price. On the other hand, the manufacture of a food from the cocoa bean—chocolate—began in the late eighteenth century, and by the mid-nine-teenth, "chocolates" in their many guises had become popular among the wealthier classes of much of Europe.

Tea, coffee, and even cocoa and chocolate may be classed among the "decencies" of life rather than as its necessities. The other new crops, corn (maize) and the potato, established themselves as necessities, essential for the well-being of a large part of Europe's population. The cultivation of corn was restricted by its climatic requirements.

There were marginal areas—central Spain, southwest France, northern Italy, and the Danube basin—where corn did well. It was welcomed because it was reliable and cropped heavily, but not all approved of it as human food. This attitude and the difficulty of adapting it to the field systems in use slowed its progress. John Locke, in the course of his travels in France in 1675–79, found that it "serves poore people for bred," but added that "the blade and green about the stalk [were] good nourishment for their cattle."[52] But in the next century Duhamel de Monceau found the bread made from it "heavy and hard to be digested."[53] Nevertheless the cultivation and consumption of corn spread with the increase in population in the later eighteenth and nineteenth centuries. Corn became the staple food, however inadequate from a dietary point of view, in many parts of Europe. In Bosnia, de Laveleye in the 1880s found "always maize," and near Tsaribrod on the borders of Bulgaria, a family "lived . . . on the produce of two acres planted with maize."[54] Nineteenth-century travelers commented on the extent of corn cultivation in Romania and the Hungarian plain, where it formed the chief food of the peasant who was obliged to sell his wheat into the market.

In Europe north of the Alps a similar role was played by the potato.[55] The tuber was introduced into Spain in the sixteenth century and became known in western and central Europe during the next century, but, as we noted earlier, it was not until late in the eighteenth century that it began to be widely cultivated. Eventually, it became the "bread of the poor," and cultivation spread rapidly throughout northwest and central Europe, and above all in Ireland. In 1819 the Comte du Chaptal could report that the conservative French peasant had at last accepted the potato as a regular part of his diet. Indeed there were areas where an overdependence on the potato developed. It allowed a family to be supported on a smaller holding than had been possible when breadgrains were the staple crop. Farms were divided and subdivided and still yielded, at least in terms of bulk, an adequate food supply. Among the areas which thus gave hostages to fortune were Flanders, parts of Scandinavia, and, above all, Ireland.[56] How the process would have ended, if the potato famine had not intervened, we cannot know. In that event, a fungoid disease spread through the potato crop in much of northwest Europe in 1845–46, gravely reducing the potato harvest and leading to severe famine and high mortality. But, despite this setback, the importance of the potato in human diet continued to increase, and its cultivation was intensified in central and eastern Europe.

The Social Aspects of Food

Eating has always been in some degree a social activity. To eat alone or in silence was sometimes necessary. It was required of members of many religious orders, but it was always regarded as a form of asceticism. Most people were accustomed to eating with the family or in small groups. Mealtimes were often the only occasion when the members of the family were brought together and conversation was possible between them. Communal eating became one of the decencies of life. But it went further than this. It became the symbol of a common bond between those who had participated. The strength and significance of this bond varied from time to time and from one society to another, but has never wholly disappeared. "Breaking bread together" remains a symbol of friendship and loyalty, and the formal dinner has become an essential function of many social groups.

Eating is thus performed at two levels. On the one hand, it is a necessary bodily function, performed at least twice a day and often hurried so that the day's work can be resumed. On the other hand, a banquet may consist of many courses—far more than is necessary biologically—spread over several hours and accompanied by speeches and music. For those who took part in such formal meals, the association of good company and good food was etched indelibly on the memory. Such feastings have been described, sometimes with a wealth of culinary detail, from Homeric times till the present. Athenaeus has left an account of such a banquet that lasted several days and was accompanied by a discussion of prearranged themes. The Athenaean banquet grew out of the Socratic symposium of some six centuries earlier. The only difference lay in the greater intellectual content of the latter and its more austere menu.

The idea of formalizing memorable occasions by a great banquet lasted through the Middle Ages. The coronations of monarchs, weddings of members of their families, and the enthronements of bishops were commemorated in this way, and in some instances the volume and variety of the food consumed were recorded.[57] There were commonly three immense but not clearly differentiated courses. Henry IV's coronation feast at Westminster included in its first course various meats as well as pheasant, heron, capon, and "Lambard pie." The second course included venison cooked in frumenty, "porcelle farce enforce," or stuffed pig, peacock, crane, and again pastry in the form of "graunt tartez." The banquet ended with a vast array of birds, including curlew, quail, and "smal byrdys," as well as rabbit and sugared quince. Such a meal must have lasted many hours. It was very high in protein and fat and had considerable nutritional value. But the human constitution could not have taken such meals except on infrequent occasions. Such records do, however, contribute to the illusion that medieval people were always lavishly fed, but enough has been said to show that this was not the case.

Few could aspire to banquets of this order, but at a humbler level most people of the time could hope to participate in periodic feasts, in the fall when the fruits of harvest had been gathered in—now institutionalized in Thanksgiving—or, in the midwinter, at Christmas. And at a yet simpler level they might enjoy a somewhat more abundant and leisurely meal once a week. There has thus always been a gradation between the infrequent formal banquet and the simplest of meals, taken hurriedly in the intervals between work.

Eating was not only a social activity; it was in some degree public. The great halls of a medieval home were intended to be the focus of life within a large household, the only distinction being made between the lord and his family, who ate at one end, and the humblest retainer and dependent at the other. In the later Middle Ages life tended to become less public, at least for those who could afford the luxury of privacy. Piers Plowman complained bitterly of this break with custom:

> Elyng is the halle   uche daye in the wyke,
> There the lord ne the lady   liketh noughte to sytte.
> Now hath uche riche a reule   to eten bi hym-selve
> in a pryve parloure   for pore mennes sake,
> Or in a chambre with a chymneye   and leve the chief halle
> That was made for meles   men to eten inne.[58]

(Deserted is the hall every day of the week, when the lord and lady do not choose to sit there. Now the rich have a practice to eat by themselves in a private parlor because of the poor people or in a chamber with a fireplace and abandon the great hall which was made for men to eat their meals in.)

For the lord and his family to eat in private was to breach the community of the household, to emphasize a class distinction that had been blurred in the rough and tumble of the communal hall. But it was this demand for privacy, this desire to be cut off, if only for a short period of the day, from the confusion and noise of the community, that increased and intensified in modern times. The social consequences were incalculable, from the strengthening of family bonds to the decoration of the home, hygiene, and the accumulation of private and personal belongings.

Chapter 6

THE PRIVACY OF THE HOME

Make the hall under such a fasshyon, that the parler be anexed to
the heade of the hall. And the buttery and pantry be at the lower
ende of the hall, the seller under the pantry, sette somwhat abase;
the kychen set somwhat abase from the buttery and pantry, the
pastry-howse & the larder-howse anexed to the kychen.

—Andrew Boorde, *A Compendyous Regyment or*
A Dietary of Helth, 1547

*I*t is not difficult to reconstruct the villages and houses of past generations;
enough of them have survived or have been revealed by excavation. It is a
great deal more difficult to penetrate these homes and settlements and to examine the
ways in which life was lived in them. Not that their inhabitants were private or secretive
people. On the contrary, their lives were lived under the eyes of their neighbors. They
could have had few secrets, and their homes lay open for all to see what was within. The
literate bourgeoisie, from the later Middle Ages onward, have left a multitude of diaries
and account books, wills and inventories, which serve to enlighten for us the dark
interiors of their homes. Not so the mass of the rural population. They were an
inarticulate people. Right down to the nineteenth century a majority, even in the most
developed areas of the west, were illiterate, and their thoughts and secrets died with
them. Not until late in the century does one gain a view, more or less complete, of the
way of life of the humbler members of the rural classes. And even then this understanding becomes possible only because they began to accumulate sufficient chattels to
bequeath by will and to inventory for probate purposes.

Wills and inventories became numerous in many parts of Europe toward the end of
the Middle Ages, and during the following centuries they increased both in number and
in the detail with which they recorded the possessions of the deceased. These documents
present the most intimate picture we have of the life and possessions of preindustrial
peoples.

Security

The rural cottage had a door—sometimes two—that was incapable of being securely
fastened, and windows that were at best closed with shutters. It was easy to gain entry,

and theft was common. Barbara Hanawalt has shown that in medieval England about a quarter of the crimes that came to trial were burglaries.[1] The value of goods stolen was generally small, for in most cottages there was little to steal. Burglary and housebreaking were most likely to occur during the late autumn and winter months. At this time of year there was not only a greater likelihood that cottages would contain a store of grain, which was one of the commodities most frequently stolen, but also a longer period of darkness to cover the actions of the burglar.

Most people were protected by the fact that they had little worth stealing and by the continuous watchfulness of ever-prying neighbors. Locks and heavy wrought-iron hinges were commonly fitted to the doors of great houses, which could also offer protection against forcible entry in other ways. Those who had small articles of value kept them, as a general rule, in wooden chests, bound with iron and fitted with one or more locks. Many such chests of late medieval and early modern times have survived, spacious enough to take a considerable volume of the household's heirlooms and too heavy to be transported easily. The peasant, who enjoyed no such advantage, sometimes entrusted his few valuables to the security of the parish chest, which was kept in the church. The English Patent Rolls record a pardon granted to a cleric who, in the church of Ticehurst (Sussex), broke "a locked common chest of the parishioners . . . and [took] out of it eight pound of wax and other goods to the value of 20 shillings."[2] This suggests the variety of ordinary goods that were committed to the uncertain safety of the parish chest.

The medieval burglar showed little skill, and most would have been incapable of picking a lock. But there were exceptions. The rogue in the medieval German epic of Meier Helmbrecht was:

> . . . a man of skill.
> Without a key he bursts at will
> The neatest-fastened iron box.
> Within one year I've seen the locks
> Of safes, at least a hundred such
> Spring wide ajar without a touch
> At his approach. . . . [3]

But the rogue Wolfstrüssel was evidently a professional.

Doors had been closed since very early times by means of a simple bolt, which could be pushed into a slot made to receive it. The problem was to devise a bolt that could be moved from *outside* the door.[4] This was a lock. The first locks, used in ancient and classical times, consisted of little more than a bent wire that could be inserted through a small hole and thus used to lift or move the bolt (fig. 6.1). Homer tells us how Penelope, when taking the bow of Ulysses from the locked closet, "passed the key through the hole, and with a well-aimed thrust shot back the bolt."[5] By Roman times iron locks were being used, fitted with keys, usually of bronze. The Romans first used wards, or obstacles within the lock, intended to prevent the wrong key from being used. And the Roman-style lock, with wards of ever-increasing complexity, continued to be used till modern

(a)   (b)

6.1. Medieval keys: (*a*) a hook for lifting a latch; (*b*) a key with wards. (After exhibits in the London Museum.)

times.[6] However complex the system of wards, there were always men like Wolfstrüssel with the skill to pick them. And so, from the eighteenth century, the "tumbler" lock, secured by pins that dropped into holes made to receive them, came gradually into use. But throughout the preindustrial period the lock and key with wards remained in general use. Such was the key that secured admission to the kingdom of heaven and was shown on the papal insignia and countless ecclesiastical coats of arms (fig. 6.2). Chests in which valuables were stored and the doors of great houses were secured in this way, and "ward" locks, little different from those of the Middle Ages, remain in use throughout Europe.

The padlock was a particular form of lock that could be used to fasten bags. Its name is thought to derive from "pad," or path, since it was used to secure the baggage of merchants and travelers. It was in use during the later Middle Ages and continues to be used today.

The risk of burglary was perhaps small beside the danger of fire. In both town and country this hazard was always present. In towns it was possible to keep a watchman permanently on duty to look out for the plume of smoke that rose when the domestic fire got out of hand. In villages this measure was not practicable, and the only safeguard lay in the fact that the houses were, as a general rule, too widely spaced for the fire to spread. Nevertheless, primitive fire-fighting tools were commonly kept in that universal depository, the church. One may still, on rare occasions, see a primitive pump as well as a row of large leather buckets (fig. 6.3) and long hooked spikes for tearing the burning thatch from the roofs of cottages.

Villages might have a protective fence and their inhabitants might develop the church and churchyard as a communal refuge, but it was far from common for the peasant house to be strengthened against intrusion or attack. Yet there were exceptions. Manor houses sometimes had a tower added to their hall, incapable of prolonged defense but adequate for protection against a casual raid. In some parts of Europe, where raids were somewhat more than casual, homes might almost be said to have been fortified. Their defenses usually took the form of a ground floor built of masonry, without window openings, and sometimes reached by a ladder from above (fig. 6.4). The upper floor, where the household lived, might be reached by an external stair and could be held against a lightly armed band. Such was the *kula,* still widespread

6.2. St. Peter, bearer of the great key, after a wall painting of the fifteenth century in Puhtaa church, Finland.

6.3. A row of leather buckets
for fire-fighting in a church in
Suffolk; probably of the
eighteenth century.

in that land of vendetta and feud, Albania and the western Balkans. But it is also to be
found in Romania and elsewhere in southeastern Europe (fig. 6.5).

Air and Water

Pollution has been a problem to human societies from very early times, though only in
recent years has it attracted worldwide attention. Indeed, it might be said that it was in
some respects more serious in early times than it is today. Preindustrial societies may not
have been vexed with smog and acid rain, but clean air and pure water have always been
scarce commodities. The wind may have blown across the countryside, but within the
cottage people all too often breathed air that was heavy with smoke and fouled with
smells that would not be tolerated today. And the water in which they occasionally
cleaned themselves and cooked their food, and which occasionally they drank, may have
been taken from a river polluted by the drainage from stables and domestic soil pits. The
great importance of the consumption of alcohol in all of its many forms was not that it
tasted good and made people happy but that ale and beer, wine and spirits were less
likely to be infected than the water that came from a well or river.

In much of Europe people suffered severely from the cold during at least part of the
year. Their ill-built houses were drafty, the windows unglazed, and the door ill fitting.
Their remedy was to close all openings and to fill the cracks with moss or clay, thereby
creating within their huts and cottages an atmosphere that was thick with smoke and the
smell of sweat. The alternatives offered them were to shiver or to choke.

It is difficult, at this distance in time and in an age that has very much more stringent
standards of cleanliness, to comprehend how fetid and offensive must have been the air
about most cottages and homes. Not only were there the smells that came from the
cottage floors of beaten earth, in or beneath which it was not uncommon to dispose of
waste food, but also the pervading smell of sewage. Beside these, the woodsmoke that
got into the throat and made the eyes run must almost have been welcomed because it
helped disguise the rest.

Great houses and religious foundations had toilets, even though they discharged all
too often directly into the river from which others drew their water. How often do we see
the toilets in a castle or great house merely projecting from its walls and discharging
directly onto the surrounding ditch? Many religious houses displayed great skill in
contriving their "reredorter"—so called because it lay behind the dormitory—over a
stream that carried its effluent downstream. Only in towns was a serious attempt made to
construct cesspits, which were, it is to be presumed, cleaned out at intervals.[7] But toilets,
with cesspit or sewer, were unknown in humbler homes before the nineteenth century.
In none of the cottages described on pages 121–36 is there any evidence for such a
convenience. In the villages the peasants resorted to the shelter of trees and bushes

6.4. Peasant house in Walachia, Romania. Domestic apartments were on the upper floor. The windowless ground floor served only for storage.

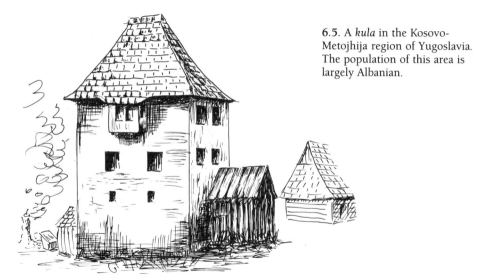

6.5. A *kula* in the Kosovo-Metojhija region of Yugoslavia. The population of this area is largely Albanian.

growing on their tofts. There is, however, some evidence for the use of chamberpots before the nineteenth century.

It is probable that the smells generated by beasts went far toward obscuring those produced by the human animal. Stabling for the plowing oxen, a cowshed, and a pigsty commonly lay close to the house, with between them a heap of dung awaiting transport to the fields. In many types of vernacular building the animals lived under the same roof as the farming family, care usually being taken to insure that the stabling lay at a slightly lower level to prevent drainage into the house. The presence of the animals, it was said, contributed a little warmth to the house, but in summer the flies and stench must have become almost unbearable.[8]

In the long run, however, it was the supply of pure water that presented the most serious problem. In the absence of a piped water supply, the rural community had to rely on springs and wells. Their discharge was sometimes inadequate and always irregular. There were villages, especially in regions of dry subsoil, that owed their location entirely to an abundant spring. In many parts of Europe, place-names incorporate an element meaning fountain or spring, suggesting that these features were far from numerous. There were furthermore "holy" wells, whose miraculous quality probably lay in their reliability.⁹ Large tofts and farms sometimes embraced their own well, but individual wells were impracticable in a large village. The water-bearing rock, or aquifer, would be unlikely to support so many.

Spring water from a mountainous and thinly peopled area may have had certain virtues, but that which came to the surface in the heart of a village community probably had none. Local studies have demonstrated that springs and wells were ill protected against the drainage of stables and manure heaps. Infection must have been spread by contaminated water, not only between animals but also from them to their human neighbors. Major diseases, such as smallpox, typhus, and the bubonic plague, were not spread in this way, but it is impossible not to regard contaminated water as the source of a wide range of diseases of the digestive tract. It is not surprising that dysentery, enteritis, typhoid fever, and, during the nineteenth century, cholera were common.

Quite apart from the quality of water was the amount of it that was available. Almost everywhere there were times when it was desperately short. A summer drought could be disastrous, and in the hilltop villages of southern Europe it was necessary to carry water up from lower ground. People learned to be sparing in their use of water. There was, perhaps, little inducement to perform personal ablutions as frequently as we think necessary today, but shortage of water was at least an excuse. The same goes for the laundering of clothes and the cleansing of cooking vessels and furniture. It is very doubtful indeed whether hot water was regularly used for these purposes, and certain that only cold water was available for personal cleansing.

Pollution extended to the rivers and streams, chiefly because they received the effluent of urban cesspits, slaughterhouses, and tanyards, as well as the seepage from stables and dung heaps along their courses. Flax was retted in the rivers and timber floated along them. In the mid-nineteenth century the river Loire at Nevers, in central France, was described as a virtual sewer. And it was from such rivers that much of the water for domestic use was taken.

"Lighten Our Darkness"

Much of life in preindustrial Europe was lived in darkness, more or less absolute. In village and town, streets were lighted only by the glow that came from the windows of their houses. In the countryside one would not have seen the distant glow of the next town, reflected from low clouds, or the points of light that today mark out each homestead. The night was black, and people rarely left the security of their homes. To be on the streets at night was itself suspicious. There was little need to enforce a curfew; there was so little inducement to break it.

But there was always some form of illumination within homes and cottages, if only the flickering light of the hearth. Firelight is likely to have been supplemented by candle, rushlight, or cresset lamp. The latter derived from the lamps in use in classical times. It was a bowl, often with a tapering or funnel-shaped base for ease of hanging in a metal ring, rather like the sanctuary lamps met with in churches today. The bowl was filled with oil, into which a wick was dipped. Sometimes the bowl was cut in stone and

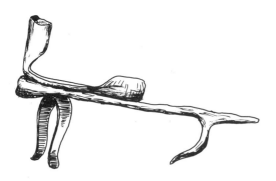

6.6. A medieval candle holder, of wrought iron. (London Museum.)

mounted on a pillar, much in the fashion of a stoop. The alternative was the candle or rushlight, in which the wick or rush was embedded in or impregnated with combustible wax. Oil for the cresset lamp was normally obtained by crushing oil-bearing seeds, such as those of the flax or hemp plant. As a general rule it was easier to obtain beeswax or tallow for making candles or rushlights. In these the combustible material was solid and was melted and drawn up through the wick by the heat of its own combustion. Most candles were made by the "tallow-dip" method, with the wick, usually of flax, being dipped repeatedly in a tub of molten tallow or wax and each dip adding to the thickness of the candle.

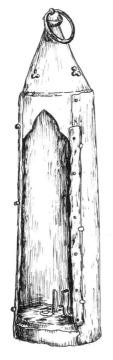

6.7. A medieval lantern. It held a candle and had a "glass" made of horn. (London Museum.)

Candle holders survive from the early Middle Ages (fig. 6.6). They usually had three feet or legs and were of the "pricket" type, with the candle being impaled upon a pointed metal spike. The socket candlestick came in late in the Middle Ages and in time largely supplanted the pricket. In the course of time candlesticks became larger and more decorative. They came to be made of brass and then of silver, and Renaissance paintings sometimes show candlesticks of great size and elaboration. Such candlesticks have continued to be used in churches and to decorate the dining table.

The lantern is a special adaptation of the candlestick.[10] The candle was held, usually by a socket, within a rounded metal container, with horn or glass on one side for the emission of light. Such lanterns (fig. 6.7) came into general use in the thirteenth and subsequent centuries. They could be suspended within the home and could be carried without risk. The late medieval lantern remained little altered, except by the addition of a reflector, until modern times. The alternative illumination for those who had to venture out of doors at night was the torch, usually a piece of wood and twisted fiber that had been soaked in oil or wax. Its unprotected flame was a source of danger, but it was much used, as early paintings sometimes show. Extinguishing a torch was not always simple. Outside some eighteenth-century homes in Bath, there remain today giant cones of iron, into which the flaming head of the torch was thrust to extinguish it.

The nineteenth century saw a fundamental change in modes of illumination. First there was a gradual improvement in the quality of the fats and oils used. In the best candles, tallow gave way to spermaceti, derived from the sperm whale, and this in turn to a variety of distillates of natural oil. At the same time, the mechanism of the lamp itself underwent gradual changes in order to achieve a brighter and clearer flame. But the most important change before the end of the century was the introduction of gas lighting. Gas, distilled from coal or other organic matter, was first used for lighting in the closing years of the eighteenth century. For many years gas lighting was little more than a curiosity. The light was at best of low intensity but was nonetheless used to illuminate some public highways in London and Paris early in the next century. But it was not until the mid-nineteenth century that a public gas supply was established in the more important cities, together with pipelines to carry it both to street lamps and to private homes. Within the cities this provision was, as a general rule, available only in those quarters which could pay for it, and it never made any significant impact on rural areas. Here, oil-burning lamps of increasing efficiency and brilliance continued to be used until electrical illumination arrived. In much of peripheral Europe they continue in use today.

Personal Hygiene

It is a commonplace that before the nineteenth century few gave any serious thought to personal hygiene. Anecdotes about the "great unwashed" abound: people never undressed for weeks at a time; children were literally sewn into their clothes on the approach of winter and not released until spring; for many, a bath was at best an annual ritual. All these conditions, together with the unbrushed teeth and uncombed hair, are matters of common knowledge. Yet there was a strange ambiguity in attitudes toward washing, bathing, and hygiene. Medieval illustrations of people bathing, usually in round tubs, are not infrequent (fig. 6.8), but the practice seems, to judge from the throng of spectators, to have been a social activity. This aspect of it would appear to have derived from the Roman practice of communal bathing. Gone, however, were the bathing establishments and domestic bathhouses of the empire, along with the aqueducts that supplied them. Yet bathing was common in medieval cities, and Lynn Thorndike has commented on the "widespread existence of public baths in medieval towns."[11] At Frankfurt-on-Main, there are said to have been at least fifteen bathing establishments with twenty-nine bath keepers. Separate days were allocated to men and women at some baths, though such a distinction is not seen in Renaissance drawings, which tended to represent the baths as a kind of social center, even as a rather elegant brothel.

It is difficult to tell when private baths became fashionable. In the later twelfth century the king of England's palace at Westminster was furnished with a piped water supply, and a *lavatorium* or wash place was constructed. In the next century the king had a round bowl of "tin," probably a kind of pewter, for his ablutions, and late in the century baths were set up for both the king and his queen. By the mid-fourteenth century both hot and cold water were piped to the royal baths, which were fitted with bronze taps.[12] The records show that money was spent on building and equipping bathhouses at other royal palaces and manors at this time. By the end of the fifteenth century the king had a bathhouse at Windsor Castle. Doubtless some of his nobles followed the royal example, but on this matter the records are silent, and surviving buildings show no evidence. If the king of England had private bathrooms at the houses where he regularly stayed, as early

6.8. Taking a bath. A wood carving of about 1500 in the church of Notre Dame, Villefranche, in the Rouergue of southern France.

as the fourteenth century, one may expect even more adequate provision to have been made in Italy and France, culturally much more developed than England.

A problem in the provision of baths, whether public or private, was the supply of water. In many cities and most homes it was wholly inadequate before the nineteenth century, and the creation of at least two bathrooms in the Palace of Westminster was possible only because a conduit had been constructed leading to it. In the homes of the urban classes there was no suggestion of a bathroom or even of a wooden tub before the nineteenth century, though the gentry were beginning to set aside a small room for the purpose when their great houses were rebuilt or extended. In the homes of the peasant and working classes there was no such provision before the twentieth century. There is no doubt but that some used rivers and lakes for swimming, and in so doing went some way toward cleansing their bodies, but this would have been practicable during only a part of the year, and the quality of the water probably left much to be desired.

It is claimed that public bathing went out of fashion during the Renaissance and was not revived until the eighteenth or nineteenth century. It is more likely that, with the increasing size of houses, bathing tended to become more private among the wealthier classes, who alone could afford the luxury. Public bathing did, however, continue at a number of bathing establishments in western and central Europe, where a constant supply of naturally hot water made it pleasant, and its alleged medicinal qualities, attractive. Such was Bath, in southern England, whose reputation grew in the seventeenth and eighteenth centuries and attracted increasing numbers of the gentry. Such spas must have contributed to a desire for personal cleanliness, but it is noteworthy that in the many drawings and engravings of these establishments the bathers are always shown in the water fully clothed, hatted, and bewigged.

Although the practice of bathing for the purpose of cleansing the whole body remained, until late in the nineteenth century, restricted to a narrow class of the fashionable and well-to-do, far more widespread provision was made for washing the hands. In monastic houses, dipping the hands into water before meals assumed an almost ritual importance, and in the cloister, close to the entrance to the refectory, was normally a *lavatorium,* where a trickle of water made this possible. In the course of the mass, the chalice and paten, as well as the fingers of the priest, were ceremonially washed, and no church in Catholic Europe was without a *piscina,* with its drain for disposing of the water thus used. The desirability of washing was generally recognized, however far the bulk of the population was from doing it in practice. As with so many aspects of material culture, the cult of personal cleanliness diffused slowly from the upper classes toward the lower and also from western Europe toward eastern and northern, and in this the church played a not unimportant role.

Related to the general question of bathing and personal hygiene was that of the availability of soap and the laundering of clothes. Personal cleanliness was difficult to achieve without the detergent qualities of soap. Soap of a kind was known to the ancients. Pliny described it, but it seems to have disappeared from general use in the early Middle Ages and to have been spread again, probably from Italy, several centuries later. It remained, however, an expensive commodity, unknown to the mass of the population. Soap was made by ingesting animal fat, or tallow, with wood ash. This could be done domestically, but by the end of the Middle Ages there were commercial soap-boilers in most of the larger cities. Subsequently, the scale of soap manufacture increased, and with it the range of materials used in its production. Imported vegetable oils tended in the nineteenth century to replace animal fats, and the industry came to be located principally at the ports through which the materials were imported. Nevertheless, before the nineteenth century soap was used almost exclusively by the middle and upper classes. In England, the budgets of working-class families show a very small expenditure on soap in the early nineteenth century, but it was an expensive commodity, more costly, weight for weight, than meat or bacon. Its widespread use came only after the Leblanc process, first used in 1787, cheapened the manufacture of soda, the alkali chiefly used in its manufacture.[13] At the same time fatty oils were being imported from Europe's tropical dependencies and soap making began to establish itself as an important industry in the great ocean ports. At the beginning of the nineteenth century the average consumption of soap in England was only 3.6 pounds a year. By 1861, it had risen to 8 pounds, a development of incalculable importance for health. But this improvement was possible only in the wealthier and more developed countries of Europe. Throughout most of central, eastern, and southeastern Europe, soap remained a luxury known only to the rich.

A change of comparable importance was the growing practice of wearing underclothing made of cotton or fustian, a mixture of cotton and flax. This was made possible by the mechanization and cheapening first of spinning and then of weaving, bringing such light fabrics within the reach of the mass of the population. Garments made from these fabrics could be laundered with relative ease, thus helping to eliminate such vectors of disease as body lice, mites, and fleas.

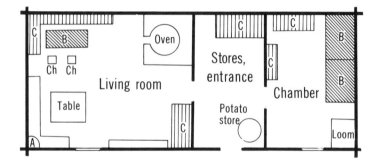

6.9. The organization of the space within a peasant cottage in Hungary, nineteenth century. *A,* cult object; *B,* bed; *C,* closet; *Ch,* chair. (After Béla Gunda, *Deutsches Jahrbuch für Volkskunde* 8 [1962]: 368–91.)

Living Room and Kitchen

The development of the plan of the house has already been traced. The two- and three-roomed house evolved from the single-roomed cottage, and the principal room in the larger structure continued to reflect the varied activities formerly carried on in the smaller. The chief room, known commonly as the "parlor," *Stube,* or *izba,* was as a general rule the largest, and the only one with any form of heating. In its simplest form it was open to the rafters, and its hearth consisted merely of flat stones set in the midst of its floor of beaten earth. Smoke escaped where it could, and it was not uncommon to preserve food by smoking it amid the blackened timbers of its ceiling.

The first significant development was to build a hearth against an outer wall and to enclose it by a stone-built fireplace, with a masonry chimney to carry away the smoke. This change crept in very slowly. Its adoption was a matter more of financial resources than of knowledge or skill, for the fireplace and chimney had to be built of stone, or brick, well laid in lime mortar. The heat of the fire, greatly increased by the draft, could quickly burn through insubstantial masonry, and not a few village fires are known to have originated in this way. It was even the dangerous practice to build rafters and purlins in the chimney stack where it ran through the roof. From the sixteenth century it became common to place a cast-iron fireback against the rear wall and sometimes also the side walls of the hearth. It protected the masonry and at the same time gave scope for decoration. Indeed, some firebacks presented in low relief heraldic and imaginative devices, and even scriptural and rural scenes. The fireback shown in fig. 9.9, made in all probability near Saarbrücken, shows the stages in smelting iron.

The hearth, whether centrally placed or ensconced within a fireplace and against a wall, was the only place where food could be cooked. The range of possibilities open to the cook were limited. The most frequently used method was boiling in a pot—often round bottomed and of earthenware, though increasingly from the later Middle Ages of copper, brass, or iron. It was usually set amid the ashes, but was sometimes placed on a three-legged stand, or trivet or hung from a "gallow" above the fire. Baking was extremely difficult and could be done only by brushing the hot ashes aside and placing the food—most often bread—on the hot stone of the hearth, and covering it with an inverted bowl, over which the ashes could again be heaped. The fireplace built against a wall offered greater scope. In particular, it was easier to raise the cooking vessels above the level of the hearth, and a small oven—usually a cloam or earthenware container with a lid—could be placed in a recess in the wall behind the fire. Above all, the fireplace permitted the installation of spits made of cast iron and turned by a variety of ingenious devices. On the hearth were usually andirons or firedogs, whose purpose was to raise the burning logs above the level of the hearth and thus to improve the draft and produce a better fire (fig. 6.10). As iron became cheaper and more abundant from the sixteenth century, an immense variety of hearth equipment came into use in the homes of the well-to-do, though in the inventories of the poor one rarely finds mention of much more than a pair of andirons, a trivet, and a pothook.[14]

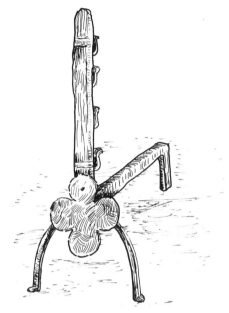

6.10. An andiron, eighteenth century, used to support a log on the hearth. They were in widespread use from the later Middle Ages. The hooks on the rear of the upright were to hold one end of a spit.

The movement of cooking operations from a centrally placed hearth to a fireplace constructed of masonry had an important influence on the foods consumed and the methods of preparing them. It became possible to break with the age-old tradition of consuming almost everything as a kind of gruel or stew. Of course, boiled food remained important, but the advent of light baked bread, made chiefly from wheat or rye, and the introduction of roast rather than boiled meat meant significant improvements in diet. It is difficult to date these changes, because they were first made in the kitchens of the rich and spread slowly to the cottages of the poor.

The appearance of a separate kitchen came even later. It was not normal, even at the end of the Middle Ages, except in great houses and religious institutions, in each of which there was a large number to be fed. Here the kitchen was commonly a freestanding building, often square in plan with a pyramidal roof and louvred ventilation, so that, wrote Alexander Neckam, "passers-by might smell the odour and vapour of the kitchen."[15] Even smells could be a status symbol. Within there was a table for cutting up vegetables and "a cleaning place where the entrails and feathers . . . can be removed and birds cleaned. . . . In the pantry," which Neckam regarded as a separate room, "let there be shaggy towels, table cloth, and an ordinary hand towel which shall hang from a pole to avoid mice."[16] In addition there should be hardware—hooks, mortars, bowls, platters, as well as knives, spoons, a container for cheese, a lantern, and "a garderobe pit for kitchen waste." Many such kitchens survive—though without the equipment listed by Neckam—attached, as a general rule, to the homes of the great.

In humbler homes the change was made when the two-roomed house was expanded to three, and the small room at the lower end of the hall was adapted to the requirements of cooking. This, in fact, became the traditional plan in much of Europe, with the "screens" passage separating the kitchen from the hall. An intermediate stage, dictated perhaps by the risk of fire, was the construction of a separate, freestanding kitchen at a short distance from the main building. This arrangement appears to have been not uncommon in urban houses. It was not until late in the nineteenth century or even in the twentieth that a separate kitchen became the norm in much of eastern Europe.[17] The problem, apart from the cost of constructing a separate room, was that a kitchen separate from the living room necessitated a second fire and thus increased the demand for fuel at a time when it was becoming scarce. On the other hand it solved a problem that had always been present in the design of the principal room of a cottage: how to compromise between comfort and convenience. The separate kitchen meant that the fire, devised and maintained for warmth, ceased to be cluttered with pothooks and spits. It also encouraged the construction of a masonry oven for baking and further diminished the significance of boiled foods. A stone-built oven became increasingly common in the nineteenth century (fig. 6.11).

There were, nevertheless, deep and significant local and regional variations in the design and location of both fire- and cooking places. During the Renaissance, the closed stove became common in Germany. The English traveler Peter Mundy described such a stove, which he called a "cackle oven," at Gdańsk in 1641.[18] It was "made of Cackles, certayne hollow earthen tilles . . . oft greene, blew, etts . . . built in forme off a turrett; a pretty little structure, much adorning the roome. . . . It Casteth a heatt to the Farthest part of the roome. . . ." Mundy took a while to become accustomed to this heating device but eventually found it "commodious and profitable . . . , for by thatt Meanes a little woode will suffice to Make Fire to warme a great Company." A similar stove, Mundy noted, was to be found in the Netherlands, but "made there of Iron for the most part." This was the ancestor of the Franklin stove. In Poland, Mundy found, the stove was being used for cooking as well as heating. In Slovakia both stove and open fire were used, whereas the southern Slavs used only the open fire, baking food under special lids set amid the ashes.[19] In western Europe both the stone-built oven and the hearth with its array of hardware continued in use until they were both gradually displaced in the nineteenth century by a variety of cast-iron ovens. The advent of gas for cooking during the middle years of the century marked the triumph of the latter.

The principal room, call it parlor, hall, or what you will, focused the life of the household. It was, in much of Europe before recent times, the only room in which there was a fire. The family, or at least many of its members, slept in the hall on straw or blankets laid on the floor each evening and cleared away in the morning. By the light of the fire the women spun and all carried on domestic tasks. Here food was prepared, at least until a separate kitchen was built, and here it was eaten at a long table, dragged out into the room at mealtimes and pushed back against the wall at others. It was "commonly the best Furnished room in the house, where the Master thereof, his wiffe and Children (as allsoe strangers) doe sitt, converse, write, passe away their tyme. . . ."[20] Best furnished it may have been, but it was totally lacking in comfort, beyond the warmth shed by the hearth. There were benches or "forms" on which to sit at the table, a rough chair or two, and perhaps a chest and closet. Pegs driven into the wooden walls of the room

6.11. A masonry-built oven in a Hungarian cottage, early nineteenth century. (After J. Paget, *Hungary and Transylvania* [London, 1839].)

served to hang what spare clothing there may have been as well as cooking utensils and other vessels.

The second room is today generally thought of as the bedroom; this is the general connotation of the term "bower." But this was only one of its purposes; it was used for sleeping, but in the colder months only if there was no space in the heated living room. It was used for storage, and this appears in eastern Europe to have been its principal purpose. The weaver kept his loom here, and the spinner her store of thread. The more regular use of the second room as a bedroom followed two significant developments in the sixteenth and following centuries. The first was the installation of hearths or ovens. Peter Mundy noted that "those Cackle ovens are allsoe usuall in Most private Chambers off the house, to bee warmed as occasion shall require, and being once hotte, a small Matter [i.e., fuel] keeps on and continues the heat."[21] Montaigne, who came from southwest France, where the cold of winter was very much less severe than in central Europe, complained bitterly of the conditions that he met with in the upper Rhineland: "there are never any curtains to the beds, and always 3 or 4 beds in a room . . . no fireplaces, and you warm yourselves only . . . in the dining room."[22] He added that the windows even lacked shutters to keep out the cold air. At Baden (Switzerland) he "slept in a room with a stove in it [and] was greatly pleased,"[23] especially when he found that most rooms in this particular hospice had no means of heating.

As Montaigne traveled into south Germany, he found stoves more common in bedrooms, and windows more often glazed. When he descended to the chill of the north Italian plain, he missed the warmth of German bedrooms as much as he did their cleanliness.[24] But Montaigne, and probably also Mundy, were staying at inns or hospices; they probably slept in rooms that we might call dormitories rather than bedrooms, and some form of heating might have been found necessary. Fireplaces or stoves began to appear in the private apartments of the rich in the later Middle Ages. Piers Plowman's lord and lady had "a chambre with a chimneye," but such a luxury did not appear in the cottage before the nineteenth century.

We all spend a third, or even more, of our lives asleep, so that the comfort and convenience of the bed form a significant part of material culture. It is, however, one of the most difficult for the historian to penetrate. How were beds constructed; what bedclothes were used; what, if any, night attire was worn; and, above all, how rapidly and by what stages did the standards adopted by the upper classes spread to the poor? These questions cannot easily be answered, except by means of scanty entries in diaries and the listing of possessions in inventories.

Of course, a few "great" beds have survived, together with legends regarding those who may have slept in them. But humbler beds were too insubstantial to have survived. Beds varied from elaborate structures of wood, with wooden slats or ropes instead of bedsprings (fig. 6.12), to a heap of straw and a blanket. The latter was the kind of bed on which the majority of the population slept before the nineteenth century. It could be placed anywhere within the house or in outhouses or stables. It was customary for farm hands and servants to sleep in this way close to their animals, both to enjoy some of the warmth that they provided and to guard against theft. The bed with frame and mattress presupposed by reason of its size a separate bedroom. The custom developed of fitting high bedposts, between which heavy curtains were stretched at the corners. Their purpose was not to give privacy—that mattered little—but to exclude drafts. The practice ended only when tightly fitted glazed windows and some form of heating were provided in bedrooms.

Andrew Boorde in early sixteenth-century England urged his readers "to have a fyre in your chambre, to wast and consume the evyll vapours within the chambre."[25] He also recommended a red nightcap, a featherbed, a quilt of cotton or wool, and a covering of white fustian. Such comfort was roundly condemned by preachers, no doubt with their eye on the rougher bedding of the humbler members of society.[26] Soft bedding, like frequent washing, was treated as a mark of effeminacy. On cold winter mornings, as also on Sundays, there was a grave temptation to lie on in bed, especially if it was one of the softer and more luxurious kind. Bromyard, a Dominican friar, condemned those who stayed long in "that prison-house of the Devil . . . their own dark chamber, in which they shut themselves up in bed until nine o'clock . . . or until noon. . . . God made the night for rest and the day for working."[27] But no amount of exhortation could reduce the temptation of a warm bed or the pleasure of a scented bath. Such exhortations were aimed at the rich. It was sheer bodily fatigue, not warmth and comfort, that led the poor to lie long on their straw. In modern times denunciations of such forms of luxury disappeared from the rhetoric of the preacher as higher standards of comfort began to pervade all classes of society.

Conditions varied little from one part of Europe to another. The furnishings of a bedroom were a matter of social rather than geographical location. Montaigne expected,

6.12. A medieval bed from Norway

even if he did not always find, the same standards in all the countries he visited. It was not until the nineteenth century that bedroom furnishings began to include more than a bed and a closet. The idea that personal ablutions might be performed in the privacy of the bedroom was a modern refinement, quite unknown to earlier centuries. It is true that a "basin and ewer," often of pewter, sometimes appeared in inventories from the sixteenth century, but they were used for the washing of hands during or after meals. The commode, in which was kept some form of chamber pot, began to appear in bedrooms during the eighteenth century, and Louis XIV had traveled with his *chaise percée*. But the "washhand basin" and water jug were rare as bedroom furnishings at the beginning of the nineteenth century, though common enough in western Europe at its end.

The Measure of Time

Such were the physical conditions amid which most people lived their domestic lives before the middle years of the nineteenth century. Life was, so far as possible, passed out of doors. The home was cramped and dark, and it was better, except in the worst of weather, to be abroad. The daily routine was governed by the sun rather than the clock. Rural people had little sense of time. They arose when it was light, and, except in winter, went to bed soon after dark. The passage of time was marked for them not by the ticking of a clock but by the sounds of nature. One still speaks of "cockcrow" as the time for rising in the morning, and, during the day, the behavior of animals and birds marked the passing hours. In the village the tolling of the Angelus at noon marked a point around which the day's routine could be structured. Towns were filled with the sound of bells.

Public clocks chimed, and church towers and campaniles sent their sounds over the roofs to the surrounding countryside. They rang for births and celebrations and tolled for deaths.

In 1481 the citizens of Lyons "sorely felt the need for a great clock whose strokes could be heard by all citizens in all parts of the town."[28] Peter Mundy commented on the number of clock towers in Dutch cities, and many of them had automatic chiming devices.[29] In Gdańsk and doubtless in many other cities, a watchman was stationed permanently in the high tower of a church so that he could sound a bell whenever a plume of smoke began to rise from any unexpected quarter. The preindustrial world was far from silent, but its sounds, unlike those of today, held meaning and significance. They warned of danger and they marked the passage of time. This was the reason for the strange cacophony of bells. The community needed them. Only later did they become a matter of local pride and emulation.

The need to measure with greater precision the passage of time during day and night came later. Time is a measure of change, and how better to trace its passage than by means of some phenomenon that moved or changed at a steady pace. Only the sun could serve this end, and sundials must have been among the earliest of timekeepers. Quite sophisticated sundials were in use in classical times, and the Tower of the Winds of the first century B.C. in Athens, an octagonal building, had a sundial on each face. Somewhat later the Roman architect Vitruvius expanded on the types of sundial available, and simple dials continued to be used during the Middle Ages and early modern times. Many remain in place today, though for the past century most have been more decorative than useful. There were serious difficulties in relying on the sundial, not least of which was the fact that the sun did not always shine. A secondary problem lay in the fact that the solar hour varied through the year, and most sundials were accurate only in recording noon. Nevertheless, the sundial was much used when, as in the rituals of the church, more or less precise timing was desirable. Scratch dials are often found on the south-facing walls of churches.

Alternative measures of time were the steady drip of water, the burning of a candle or taper, and the fall of sand in an hourglass. All were used, but each had its limitations. They could be used only for short periods, their movement was not always regular, and the candle and taper, at least, consumed relatively scarce commodities, namely, wax, tallow, and oil.

Time to the nearest hour was enough for most people. The coming of the clock—the public clock on church towers and town-hall gables, and the private clock, ticking away noisily in the hall—marked a change in the popular attitude toward time. The clock was a response to the growing need to make the best use of time and to synchronize one person's activities with those of another. And, in its turn, the clock contributed to the greater value that was set on time. People began to count its passage in minutes rather than hours, and with its advent the hour as a measure of time acquired a precision that it had not previously possessed. The Roman day, for example, consisted of twelve hours of daylight and twelve of dark, irrespective of the season. In consequence, daylight hours were short in winter and nighttime hours long, and in summer this arrangement was reversed.[30] It was impossible to reconcile this archaic system of timekeeping with the mechanical clock, and it gradually died out during the Middle Ages. But even in the eighteenth century the traveler in Italy sometimes encountered the use of "Italian" time and had to make the awkward conversion to modern.

The mechanical clock first made its appearance in the thirteenth century.[31] It worked irrespective of the weather. Its motive force was, at first, gravity, and its timing mechanism a pendulum or an oscillating verge and foliot. Timepieces were intimately associated with the church, whose routine demanded the performance of rituals and liturgies at prescribed times. Great churches had mechanical clocks that struck the hours and sometimes even showed the phases of the moon. Humbler churches had a scratch dial on a south-facing wall, which gave a rough indication of the hour but only when the sun was shining (fig. 6.13). Such medieval clocks as have survived, usually in great churches like Wells Cathedral in England and at Basel in Switzerland, are masterpieces both mechanically and in terms of art. This intimate relationship between timekeeping and the church has continued until the present and is represented today by the clock that is so often maintained in the belfry of even the humblest parish church.

6.13. A late medieval scratch dial cut into a south-facing buttress of a church. The gnomon was inserted into the hole and time was read from the position of its shadow in relation to the radiating lines. There appear to have been two dials, one superseding the other.

In the fifteenth century attempts were made to produce a portable clock that could be set up in the home or even carried in the pocket. This idea necessitated replacing gravity as a motive force by the tension present in a coiled spring, which in turn was dependent on producing a steel of suitable quality. This fact alone ensured that "tall" clocks, fitted with weights and a pendulum, remained in widespread use. They were relatively easy to build and maintain, and most domestic clocks operated on this principle until the nineteenth century.

The earliest domestic clocks are of the late fifteenth century. One was set up in Cotehele House, in southwest England, about 1485,[32] but it is of some significance that it was located in the private chapel and that it operated a bell that tolled the hours. About 1535 the Sire de Gouberville, in Normandy, boasted an *horloge* among the furnishings of his manor house.[33] From about this time clocks became more common in the homes of the rich and powerful, and in the larger cities one might even find a clockmaker. By the eighteenth century a clock, usually worked by weights and pendulum, was to be found in most if not all great houses, and before the century's end the number of clockmakers had so increased that a clock was commonly to be found in the homes of petty burgesses and yeoman farmers. But clocks remained relatively expensive until they began to be mass-produced in the nineteenth century. Only then did they begin to penetrate the homes of the masses.

The history of the watch parallels that of the clock. Its mechanism was dependent on the use of a coiled spring, and, for this reason alone, could not have been produced in significant numbers before the sixteenth or seventeenth century. Early watches were bejewelled and highly decorated, more ornamental than useful. Not until the eighteenth century did the carrying of a pocket watch, bulbous and awkward and commonly secured by a chain, become normal among the well-to-do, and not before the later nineteenth did the humbler classes carry on their persons some means of measuring time.

The social implications of timekeeping were immense. The mechanical clock gave a precision to life. One began to estimate the time that a job would take, to make appointments precise to the minute, and to measure "life with coffee spoons." It is significant that clocks became common at the time when the factory crept in as the means of organizing labor, and that they entered almost every home with the coming of the railroad. The factory had to adhere to a fixed schedule, and, once the wheels had begun to turn, the worker had to be in his or her place. The factory clock was the supreme arbiter. The operating rules of a Berlin factory in 1844 contained the following:

> The normal working day begins all seasons at 6am precisely and ends . . . at 7pm, and it shall be strictly observed. The doorkeeper shall lock the door punctually at 6am. . . . Workers arriving 3 minutes late lose half an hour's wages; whoever is more than 2 minutes late may not start work until after the next (meal) break. . . . Any disputes about the correct time shall be settled by the clock mounted above the gatekeeper's lodge. . . . [34] [See p. 380.]

As if to reinforce this schedule, the factory siren would sound at appropriate times, replacing the belfry or town-hall clock. The tyranny of the timepiece could be carried no further.

The railroads claimed to operate with the same precision. Their schedules proclaimed the punctual arrival and departure of trains even though weather and human agency often combined to interrupt their smooth routine. The coming of the railroads ended once and for all one peculiarity of local timekeeping. The sundial and, often enough, local clocks were set to show *local* time. Places to the west would be earlier; to the east, later. But this was no way to operate a railroad. "Railway" or standard time replaced sun's time or even "god's time," though not always without a struggle between the old and the new.

The measure of the passage of time in its broadest sense, of weeks, months, and seasons, was in some ways more important, but at the same time easier. Although crops might themselves have announced the time of harvest, it was less easy in Europe's variable and uncertain weather pattern to know when to prune and plow and sow. Of course, the phases of the moon, the pattern of the stars—so much clearer then than when seen through the polluted atmosphere of today—and the points of sunrise and sunset all gave a rough measure, accurate enough for many of the tasks of the farming year. The church required greater precision, since its festivals had to be celebrated everywhere at the same time. It made use of a calendar derived in part from Jewish practice, in part based on the Roman calendar introduced by Julius Caesar. "He appointed the moon for seasons," wrote the Psalmist, and the date of the Jewish Passover depended on the phases of the moon. The Christian Easter, which at least from the time of the Council of Nicaea in 325, has followed the first full moon after the vernal equinox, is a convenient marriage of the Jewish lunar calendar with the pre-Christian rites of spring.

But neither the lunar month nor the solar year is a precise and unambiguous measure of time, and neither can be divided into a particular number of integral days. The lack of coincidence between them is the reason for the mobility of the feasts of the Passover, of Easter, and of the sequence of Christian festivals that follows it. Throughout the Middle Ages and, indeed, until 1582, the calendar used universally in Christian Europe was that devised by Julius Caesar. The year was divided into twelve months and was said to begin on January 1, though in England an older practice of beginning the year on March 25, regarded notionally as the spring equinox, was perpetuated until 1752. An alternative Roman calendar had also begun in March, thus making the months from September onward the seventh to tenth, as their names still indicate. The problem with the Julian calendar was that its year of 365.25 days was marginally longer than the "tropical" or solar year. In consequence, the festivals of the church drifted very slowly backward in time. After more than fifteen centuries there was a discrepancy of over eleven days. The Council of Trent, in its crusade for uniformity of practice within the Catholic church, set out to remedy this situation. In 1582 Pope Gregory XIII introduced a new, or Gregorian, calendar, which again restored harmony between the movements of the heavenly bodies and the demands of the church.

The Gregorian calendar was adopted almost immediately by the Catholic countries. Protestants showed a similar unanimity in rejecting it until convinced by the impracticability of the old style of the need to adopt it. Great Britain at last fell into line in 1752, by omitting eleven days from the month of September and beginning the next year on January 1, 1753. In southeastern Europe, by and large the areas where the Orthodox church prevailed, the change did not take place until the present century. Even now the Orthodox church continues to adhere to the pre-Gregorian system in its celebration of Easter.

Since very early times the year has been divided into months, ten or twelve in number. The Christian calendar took over the Roman system of twelve months, though their nomenclature derives in part from one of ten. It was used universally for dating correspondence and for indicating the dates of important events. The individual months were associated with events in the rural calendar, with each month having its particular activity. The "labors of the months" formed one of the most popular of these serial illustrations, so beloved of medieval people. They were used in devotional books, church windows, and mural decoration. The duties of each month became stereotyped, and such variations as are found can be related to local climatic and cultural conditions.

A far more important division of the calendar year was the week. It was conceived as a period of time independent of both the month and the year, since these units were not precisely divisible into weeks. The seven-day week became universal in Europe, though other periods have at times been used.[35] The week cannot be related to any celestial phenomenon, but its origin probably lay close to the grass roots of human society. It was a convenient interval between visits to the market, and the names that it has borne are not unrelated to those of periodic gatherings for trading purposes. In the Christian west, however, the first day of the week became identified as a day of rest and religious obligation. It was one on which unnecessary work was forbidden. A mural painting, not uncommon in later medieval churches, showed a suffering figure of Christ surrounded by the tools of the trades. The lesson that the faithful were expected to derive from this image was that whenever they engaged in such activities on the Sabbath, Christ again suffered. At least one such painting included a playing card among the forbidden tools and implements (fig. 6.14).

6.14. A wall painting in the church of St.
Breage, Cornwall, shows the so-called Christ
of the Trades, surrounded by the tools used
by the craftsman, together with a playing
card. This painting is from about 1500. Its
purpose was to warn people to avoid work
on Sundays.

That other weekly function, the market, clearly could not be allowed to take place on a Sunday, even though this schedule has now become the practice in some parts of Europe. Each market had its proper day, prescribed as a general rule by the charter that established it.

The week turned on two fixed points, market day, when the peasant met those from other villages and perhaps gleaned news from the outer world, and the day of enforced rest, welcomed no doubt above all others. The passage of the year was marked by other days of feasting or of celebration. In urban societies these holidays were observed by a cessation of work. In fact, before the end of the Middle Ages there was complaint that their frequency was a serious interruption to other and doubtless more profitable activities. Such enforced holidays became much less frequent after the Reformation, especially in Protestant countries, but they have continued until the present to provide a welcome interruption to the routine of work. Such festivals were always observed less in rural than in urban areas, because work in the fields was less easily interrupted than that at the loom or forge. There was, nonetheless, a sequence of celebrations that culminated at Christmas, the sanctified midwinter feast of the Christian calendar.

An unusually detailed inventory of the nature and hours of work on an English estate has survived from the early eighteenth century.[36] It shows that farm hands were at work from dawn till dusk every day of the year, except on Sundays, when there is no record of any work having been done, and on Christmas day, which was their only holiday.

This schedule was probably exceptional. Even in Protestant Europe there remained folk festivals, most of them associated with the agricultural calendar, which continued to be observed. They broke the monotony of the agricultural routine. They brought the community together for other purposes than work, and they stressed the bond between its members and those who had gone before. They went back to medieval and pagan origins. That was why the Reformers strove so hard to suppress them.

Sundays and other holidays served to articulate the passage of time, breaking it up into short and easily comprehended periods. It is difficult for us to understand how people in a preliterate age viewed time. All days were the same, and it was easy to allow the proper time for plowing or sowing to pass. Hamilton Thompson tells the story of the

6.15. A game of shuttlecock; a late medieval carving in wood. Games such as this occupied the little leisure that people had.

Italian priest in the Middle Ages who forgot that Lent had begun until Palm Sunday was upon him. Then, realizing the dire consequences, he explained to his flock that "Lent this year has been slow and late in coming, because the cold weather and dangerous roads have hindered him from crossing our mountains, and therefore he has come with footsteps so slow and weary, that now he has brought with him no more than a week, and has left the rest behind him on the way."[37] To such people time had little meaning unless punctuated by the recurring festivals of the church or the procession of natural events.

"Our Daily Bread"

Most foodstuffs had to be cooked before they could be digested, and cooking facilities were rudimentary in the extreme except in the homes of the rich and in institutions such as monasteries and hospitals. As noted earlier, the peasant's cottage had no kitchen as such before modern times. Cooking was done on the hearth, which was often centrally placed in the floor of the main room. This setup effectively precluded the use of an oven and thus made it difficult to bake. Not until the hearth came to be built against an outside wall was a niche contrived in which a covered pot made of earthenware could be placed for baking bread. Insofar as oven-baked bread was made, the peasant had to rely on a communal and sometimes outdoor oven, usually a small domed structure heated by burning wood, where the dough was set amid the ashes. Within the cottage, most of the cooking, including the preparation of gruel, was in pots of clay and, after about 1550, increasingly of cast iron. The pots were either supported by a trivet set amid the ashes or suspended by a chain above the fire.

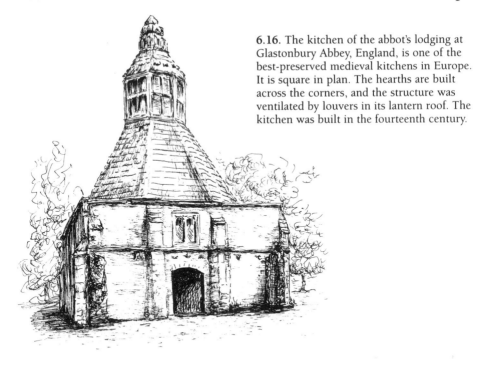

6.16. The kitchen of the abbot's lodging at Glastonbury Abbey, England, is one of the best-preserved medieval kitchens in Europe. It is square in plan. The hearths are built across the corners, and the structure was ventilated by louvers in its lantern roof. The kitchen was built in the fourteenth century.

These humble cooking facilities were contrasted with the elaborate kitchens of the rich. One of the very finest of medieval kitchens is that in which food was prepared for the abbot of Glastonbury and his guests (fig. 6.16). It is a square, masonry-built structure with giant hearths built across each corner. A not dissimilar kitchen was built in the conventual buildings of Durham Cathedral, and yet others in the Bishop's Palace at Chichester and at Dartington Hall in Devon. At the opposite end of Europe a similar but much later kitchen was built in the Rila monastery, high in the Rhodope Mountains of Bulgaria. It is not difficult to visualize what went on in these spacious kitchens. They are illustrated for us in numerous medieval manuscripts (fig. 6.17). Enormous roasts could be turned on spits at any or all of the hearths. Rows of pots could be set among the ashes (fig. 6.18), while at tables in the center of the kitchen servants were preparing vegetables, sauces, and other dishes and carrying them to the hall.

Meals in medieval and modern times were, as a general rule, taken seated at a table. A table and bench were the most common, and sometimes the only, furnishings of the principal room or hall. The classical mode had been to recline on a couch placed against the table, but this practice appears to have been discontinued in the early Middle Ages. Medieval illustrations—and they are numerous—most often show the guests seated along one side of a long, narrow table, while waiters and servants attended them from in front (fig. 6.19). At simpler meals, such as those served in a monastic refectory, the participants sat in two rows, facing one another, a practice that has continued until today. The former mode of seating would appear to have been usual at banquets, where the task of serving the guests was more demanding. It may also have been adopted in the great hall, since it permitted the lord and his family to face down the hall and to be seen by the

6.17. A medieval kitchen. Here only a pot hangs above the fire; the meat being served had evidently been boiled.

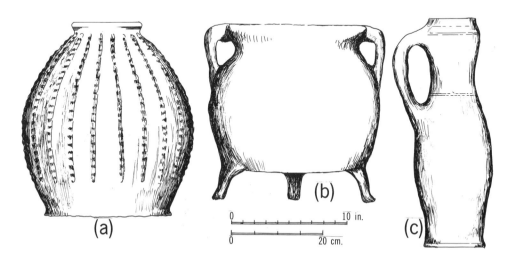

6.18. Medieval pots: (*a*) a large, bulbous pot for storage; (*b*) a pot with three legs to be set amid the ashes of the hearth; (*c*) a tall jug for wine or water at the table.

6.19. A medieval feast. The diners face down the hall and are being served from the front. Note the absence of cutlery and plates.

humbler folk seated there "below the salt." In this respect, Leonardo da Vinci's famous painting of the Last Supper is an accurate portrayal of a Renaissance banquet.

The niceties of eating—tablecloth, napkins, plates, and cutlery—began to appear in the homes of the rich during the Middle Ages. By the period's end they may have been present in houses of petty burgesses and yeoman farmers, but they descended the social scale very slowly and were not universally used even at the end of the nineteenth century. Until well into modern times most people's food was mainly liquid, consisting of a kind of gruel or soup, and was drunk from bowls. When solid food was consumed, like bread, oaten cake, or meat, it was cut with the knife that every diner carried in his belt, and brought to the mouth with the fingers. Tableware thus consisted only of bowls or beakers for drinking and trenchers or plates on which the food was placed. The tendency was for the wide bowl, or mazer, to give place to a plate, and for the drinking horn to be replaced by the beaker, shaped rather like a modern tumbler, and it is this vessel that is represented in most medieval drinking scenes. Only later did the chalice-like cup with stem and the handled tankard come into use. The china cup with handle did not come into general use until the eighteenth century. Such tableware was generally of wood, or "treen," or of coarse pottery. Carved wooden drinking vessels, sometimes highly decorated, have remained in use in southeast Europe until recent years. But most were of earthenware, usually glazed, at least on the inside. For plates, rounded pieces of wood, or trenchers, were used (fig. 6.20).

In the later Middle Ages it became fashionable among those who could afford it to grace their tables with pewter. In the 1460s Margaret Paston, wife of a country squire in eastern England, wrote to her husband asking him to acquire "a garnish or twain of pewter vessels, two basins and two ewers, and twelve candlesticks, for ye have too few of any of these to serve this place."[38] She did not mention plates, though pewter plates were

6.20. Washing wooden platters; a carving in wood from the fifteenth century in Rouen Cathedral.

coming into use at this time. Plates of pottery were not common in Europe before the seventeenth century and did not make their appearance in the humbler homes in the east and north before the nineteenth. Although spoons were known and widely used in the classical civilizations, most people were content to use only the knives that they carried with them. It was customary to reach into the dish and to remove food to the trencher with the fingers. In households of the politer sort, it was usual to provide a ewer of water and a basin for washing the fingers, not, as might be supposed, because they became greasy in the process, but because fellow diners did not like to see dirty hands intruding into the dish. The ewer and bowl remained in use until modern times and survive even today as the finger bowl. At the same time, napkins were commonly provided, both to dry the fingers after this perfunctory ablution at the table and to remove grease from mouth and hands. This almost ritualistic washing of the hands at the table resembles the priestly ablutions during the mass too closely for this to have been entirely accidental.

The use of spoons became increasingly common during the later Middle Ages, and from the sixteenth century their possession by the well-to-do is indicated in countless wills and inventories. The table fork was strangely late in making its appearance. Although it appears to have been used in the later Middle Ages for special purposes, like passing food, it did not come into widespread use before the late sixteenth and seventeenth centuries. The English traveler Thomas Coryat found the table fork in use in Italy, "because," he wrote, "the Italian can not endure by any means to have his dish touched by fingers, seeing that all men's fingers are not alike clean."[39] His contemporary Fynes Moryson, however, rejected such new-fangled ideas and urged the traveler, on returning home, to "lay aside the spoone and forke of Italy, the affected gestures of France, and all strange apparell."[40] Not surprisingly, travelers to England continued to complain of the lack of table forks, and it was not until the eighteenth century that they became as common as spoons in wills and inventories.[41] It was not until about this time that table knives, roughly matching the patterns of forks and spoons, began to be provided at the table, and guests were no longer expected to carry their own.

These observations on the growing practice of providing tableware and cutlery can be said to apply before the nineteenth century only to the upper and middle classes. These niceties spread very slowly among the humbler urban and rural classes, but spread they did. One becomes aware through the literature of the eighteenth century of the slow downward percolation of such standards of behavior. Cutlery and tableware began to appear in inventories, though it is highly improbable that they served, at least in the beginning, for general or everyday use. More likely they were taken from the closet only on special occasions. The table napkin became less common, because less necessary, with the widespread use of forks and spoons, but the bare, stained boards of the table were increasingly likely to be covered with a white linen cloth. The widespread adoption of both table linen and of linen bedsheets during the seventeenth and eighteenth centuries is a measure of the expansion of the domestic weaving industry at this time throughout central and much of western Europe.

The number, timing, and degree of elaboration of meals varied greatly. Andrew Boorde advised early in the sixteenth century that "two meales a daye is suffycyent for a rest [sedentary] man; and a labourer maye eate thre tymes a daye." This seems, indeed, to have been the general practice. Among the greater part of the population, breakfast was a very light meal, and the absence of any reference to it in many treatises on food suggests that many omitted it entirely. If such was the case, the first meal of the day, often called dinner, would have been taken in late morning. For those who did eat breakfast, dinner would in all probability have been postponed until midday or even later. The second important meal, supper, was commonly taken in the early evening. But times were clearly very flexible. During the long days of summer, filled with work in the fields, "supper" may have been postponed until a very late hour. In winter, by contrast, meal times may have been telescoped.

There are many questions we would like to ask of the preindustrial farm worker: did he, for example, trudge back to his cottage for his "dinner" about midday, and how did he know the time? Or was there some semaphore by which the women called their menfolk home? Perhaps it mattered little, because neither dinner nor supper was a meal cooked with care and served when ready. Most ingredients of both meals were boiled in the pot that hung constantly from the pothook above the hearth. It was a gruel made, basically, of cereals and "potherbs" from the garden. Meat, or at least animal fat like lard, may have been added to the stew. It was never a question of *when* the meal was ready; it was always ready. Such a diet was monotonous, unappetizing, and nutritionally barely adequate.

Changes already described in the plan of the home led to better cooking facilities and, in consequence, to a better or, at least, more appetizing diet. The pot continued to simmer on the hearth, but the accumulating hardware made it easier to roast food instead of boiling it, and the appearance of the oven encouraged not only bread making but also the vast range of pastries that characterized nineteenth-century cooking in much of Europe.[42] The diet of the upper classes continued throughout the period to contain a very high proportion of meat, game, and poultry, and this was an important reason for the large kitchens in their homes, with several hearths for roasting.[43] The middle classes had neither the space to prepare such gargantuan meals nor the means to pay for them.

But it is noteworthy that the practice of eating meat on most days was creeping down the social scale, and by the nineteenth century even the humbler classes were taking a modest amount of meat, as distinct from the lard and other fats introduced into their soups, at least once a week.[44] At the same time, the practice was growing of making a meal of two contrasted courses, the first with meat, the second consisting of lighter food with fruit or other sweetening. The adoption of the baking oven was an important step in this direction, and by the end of the nineteenth century the two-course meal was general in western Europe with most classes, and elsewhere had become the custom among all but the poorest.

The Yard

Most homes were set in a garden, toft, or yard. Sometimes the lot was large, an acre or more, and contained farm buildings and a vegetable patch; sometimes, as in cities, it was narrow and constricted, too small to have much economic value. Usually it was fenced, both to contain the animals and poultry that inhabited it and to exclude those of other people. The yard with its buildings can never be excluded from a study of the house itself. The two were closely interconnected. Stables and sheds for the stock might be an integral part of the house and, by contrast, essentially domestic buildings like kitchen, dairy, and brewhouse could be freestanding in the yard. Indeed, Andrew Boorde, master of what was practical, recommended that "the backe-howse [bakery] and brew-howse should be a dystance from the place," presumably because of the danger of fire that they posed. The dairy, by which he probably meant milking shed, "shulde be elongated the space of a quarter of a myle," and "howses of easementes" as far away as practicable, for obvious reasons.[45]

The layout of ancillary buildings depended in part on the size and shape of the plot, in part on physical conditions, and in part on the economy of the farm. These factors were infinitely varied and have combined to produce the endless variety of farm and farm buildings that we see in Europe today. Very broadly, we may divide peasant homes into "unitary" and "mixed," the former consisting only of accommodation for the human members of the farming community, the latter combining human and animal quarters under one roof.[46] The development of the unitary house has already been discussed. It was by far the most common type of dwelling because most of the rural population either did not need or could not afford the more elaborate structures necessitated in the "mixed" house.

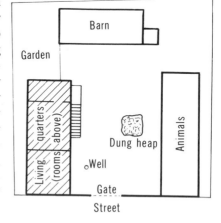

6.21. A farm yard, Bohemia

As a general rule the structures were arranged around a court or yard. Occasionally they butted against the house; more often they were freestanding (fig. 6.21). They might include buildings of a purely domestic nature, like kitchen and brewhouse. But usually they consisted of stable and barn, the one to accommodate the plowing animals, the other to store farm equipment and grain after harvest. Their size and degree of elaboration depended on the holding that they were intended to serve. Most were small, with frame construction and the simplest of truss roofs. The yard might contain more specialized structures, such as the tall, narrow, and well-ventilated cages for storing corn (maize) cobs, found in the Hungarian plain and the Balkans,[47] the ricks supported on stone saddles, the pigsties that became common in central Europe as hogs came in from the forests where they had lived hitherto, and dairies and milking houses. There was often a well, its bucket hoisted by a windlass or, as in the shallow wells of the Hungarian plain, by the long well sweep.

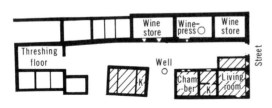

6.22. The yard of a farm built on a narrow lot. Its more southerly latitude is indicated by the presence of a winepress and store.

The mixed house combined most of these functions beneath a single roof. The simplest form of mixed house is the longhouse, already described. It combined living quarters, usually no more than two small rooms, at one end and accommodation for the animals at the other. Sometimes both human and animal occupants used the same entrance.[48] Its advantages were economy of construction, ease of access to the animals whatever the weather, and, in winter, a degree of warmth that was communicated from one species to the other. Such homes were at one time general in Atlantic Europe and have survived in Ireland and Brittany to the present, though they have tended to become obsolete and to be replaced with other types of structure.

In central Europe, however, the mixed house developed during the later Middle Ages on a scale not met with in western. It was a response to the greater importance of animal husbandry and also to the more severe winters, which made it desirable to keep as much farming activity as possible within doors. The internal arrangement of such "byre houses" varied, but, as a general rule, they consisted of three "aisles," like the great barns that they in some ways resembled. In some instances, one aisle was used for human habitation, while the other provided stabling, and the central space, with a large door, was used for storing grain and for threshing. This is the plan shown in figure 4.18 of an East Baltic farm. Alternatively, the central space was used by the human occupants, leaving the aisles for the animals and farm equipment.

The simple mixed house, such as was formerly common in northwest Europe, marked a phase in the development of social and economic conditions. It denoted an increasing importance of animal farming but was abandoned and replaced by discrete buildings as soon as greater wealth made this expansion practicable. Figure 4.21 shows the stages in the growth of the medieval settlement of Gomeldon, in southern England. The long- or mixed houses gave way to a single house, with detached barn and cow byre.

In Sickness and in Death

The specter of illness and death was always present in the family home before the later years of the nineteenth century. People were ill clothed in winter. Their food was often inadequate and always poorly balanced. Their houses were cold, drafty, and damp, and the vectors of disease—rat, flea, and louse—haunted the woodwork and lived in their unwashed clothing. Most of their complaints were ill defined. Piers the Plowman named:

> . . . fevres and fluxes,
> Coughes, and cardiacles   crampes and tothaches,
> Rewmes, and radegoundes   and roynouse scalles,
> Byles and bocches   and brennyng agues;
> Frenesyes, and foule yveles.[49]

—a comprehensive list, even though many of the complaints defy clinical judgment. A few diseases were recognizable, even by the unlettered peasantry. There was no mistaking the plague, and they learned to adopt a rough-and-ready quarantine against it. They could recognize smallpox and also that other pox, syphilis. But such remedies as they tried were, apart from quarantine and the avoidance of contact with the sick, of little or no practical value. Everyone suffered from food that was tainted, and the number who died of food-poisoning must have been immense. The surfeit of lampreys that brought about the death of the English King Henry I "was no doubt dangerously inedible."[50] When we hear how fish from the seacoast was carried great distances inland, we must have grave misgivings regarding its edibility when it reached the consumer.

People displayed a degree of fatalism in the face of illness and death that is quite foreign to beliefs and practices today. The nature of disease and of infection was quite unknown to them. They could neither cure complaints nor take preventive measures. And the horrors of illness and the fear of imminent death were relieved only by the expectation, or at least the hope, that they would be on the side of the angels when they had ceased to breathe. Those wealthy enough took what precautions they could. They commonly isolated themselves from the sick, as the papal court did in its vast castle at Avignon during the Great Plague. They wore nosegays to obscure the smells that were thought to bear infection. And, as a last resort, they endowed chantries and paid in advance for masses to be said for the repose of their souls. This expenditure was doubtless no less effective than payments to quacks and doctors. The poor who could afford none of these things probably fared no worse in illness and death than the rich.

Medical practice, insofar as there was any, derived from the classical writers. Of these the most important was Galen (d. A.D. 200). He was an accomplished anatomist, and his work, summarized and popularized by Avicenna, became the stock in trade of medical teachers in the early universities. Such analytical ideas as he possessed were based on the concept of "humors" with which the human body was endowed in varying proportions. Medical practice consisted in modifying an excess or deficiency in these humors. Doctors trained in the schools of Montpellier or Padua had a not inconsiderable knowledge of anatomy but were quite incapable of understanding the nature of infection. Not until the age of Pasteur, in the second half of the nineteenth century, did the role of pathogens begin to be understood. By the same token doctors were incapable of any form of preventive medicine, except isolation and quarantine, and readily tolerated physical conditions in which germs could multiply without limit.

Their knowledge of anatomy encouraged doctors to perform surgical operations. This they did without either anaesthetic or antiseptic. Their success rate must have been low, but of this there is no statistical information. For ordinary complaints of the kinds listed in *Piers the Plowman*, their remedies consisted of bleedings and purges, intended to rid the body of the offending humors. People were almost unbelievably hardy in this rough age to have survived some of the treatments they received. The techniques were, of course, totally ineffective, and such success as this primitive medicine claimed to have achieved was due entirely to the natural tendency of the body to repair its own scars and to heal itself. Nevertheless, doctors were rewarded generously for their services. Their greed was notorious, a reputation they shared with millers and brewers. "Leches, physicyons, taverners and tollers . . . all suche that by fals soteltees takyn falsely mennus goodes," thundered the preacher, "all suche . . . byn prevey thevys and wyckud in [t]her lyvynge."[51] And Chaucer, who heartily concurred, wrote of the doctor: "For gold in phisick is a cordial; / Therefore he lovede gold in special."[52]

But before the nineteenth century most doctors limited their practices to the cities, where alone they could find a well-to-do clientele. The rich might have a private physician, whose task it was to recommend a diet and to bleed them at intervals. But the poor dispensed with this luxury and were none the worse for it. Andrew Boorde, who had studied medicine at Montpellier, prescribed a diet for men of each of the four humors: the sanguine, the phlegmatic, the choleric, and the melancholic, but gave no rules for determining to which of these categories a person might belong. His prescription reads like a horoscope in the daily press, and was just as valueless. "Rarely is a doctor a good Christian," said the preacher. "Their deeds prove them to be disciples, not of Christ, but of Avicenna and Galen."[53]

Away from the cities and the practice of the doctors, people relied upon simple and perhaps more dangerous remedies. The more educated among them dabbled in medicine, but their skills were little more than a kind of magic. Long practice had taught that certain herbs did good, or at least did little harm, and infusions of wild plants have continued to be used medicinally until very recent times. In a few instances there was a positive ingredient in such remedies, but most, in all probability, were neutral.

William Carnsew, who lived in southwest England in the sixteenth century, was a man of broad education. He read widely and thought of himself as a competent doctor.[54] In this capacity he attended his friends, neighbors, and servants. His favorite remedy was a substance which he called "styby."[55] It was almost certainly antimony sulfide, which occurred in a mine near his home. He prescribed it to all and sundry on any and every occasion. He even gave medicine for toothache. On one occasion his patient, after taking this potion, "hadd 3 vomyttis, on[e] stoole and Ame[n]dyd." It is evident that Carnsew sometimes overreached himself. He gave one of his medicines to the vicar of his parish. Three days later the vicar "was extremly sycke," and five days after this he was dead. Carnsew showed no compunction; his medical interests were uppermost in his mind. He watched "hym openyd" and calmly diagnosed his sickness as "a putrefaction of hys longis [lungs]." When Ralph Josselin's daughter was sick of some indeterminate complaint, he "apprehended it was the spleene, wee applied an oyntment to it, and a plaister of halfe an ounce of oyntment of melibot [a kind of clover] . . . and also 3 spoonefuls of juyce of red fennell clarified with 6 spoonefuls of beare and swetned."[56] The result of this curious medication is not reported.

There must have been thousands of Carnsews, dabbling in medicine with the help of a little medical knowledge gleaned from reading and a blind belief in the efficacy of their "magical" cures. Few communities can have been spared their attentions, but there is no means of knowing the extent of the harm they did. Carnsew was at least a man of intelligence and broad learning. Most of those who prescribed their cures and took their fees were foolish and ignorant and probably made no claim to be anything more than purveyors of a kind of magic. In the early sixteenth century a maidservant "at 16 shillings a year" is reported to have left her employ in order to go into the doubtless more remunerative business of curing sore eyes.[57] For those whose ills did not yield to the potions and incantations of "physicians" of one kind or another there was always the remedy of a pilgrimage. Some saints were identified with the cure of specific ailments, and a visit to their shrines was often the last and most expensive resort for the afflicted. No doubt fresh air and a change of scene had some therapeutic value.

Most medical practitioners were all too ready to assign a name to the diseases that they treated. In a very few instances, like smallpox, plague, and, in the nineteenth century, cholera, the diagnoses were usually correct and the names given to them have been retained today. But in most others both the naming and identification of diseases were based on evidence that would now be rejected. Today disease is attributed to infection, the precise nature of which is, as a general rule, determinable. Earlier diagnoses were based upon a classification of symptoms that had no diagnostic significance. A complaint described as "malignant bilious petechial putrid fever" can mean nothing to a contemporary physician. Its nomenclature belongs to a vanished system of thought, and outside that system it has no value.[58] Diseases were attributed to "vapors" and "influences," an idea that has been perpetuated in our continuing use of the terms "malaria" (bad air) and "influenza." Even the bubonic plague was ascribed to mists that, it was claimed, rose from the damp soil, and the distinguished Dutch physician Boerhaave (d. 1738) developed a whole system of medicine based upon the character and influence of the weather.[59] That is why it is so difficult to determine the real causes of death in earlier times, even when we have medical treatises and "bills of mortality." Little distinction was made between the many complaints of which the most obvious symptom was a high temperature. They were all fevers and were all treated to the same folk remedies.

Lameness, blindness, deafness, tooth decay, and countless other afflictions and disabilities were common and were almost taken for granted. They were the usual accompaniment of old age. The diary that Ralph Josselin kept during much of the seventeenth century is in large part a record of the interminable illnesses of himself and his family. He seems always to have had a cold as well as frequent stomach disorders, "rheums," and "agues," and for years complained of a sore on his navel that would not heal. The cases of stillbirths, miscarriages, and deaths in childbirth that he recounted during his long tenure as rector of Earl's Colne are too numerous to count.

Brueghel's painting of the blind beggars must have portrayed a very common sight. Lameness, again to judge from late medieval and Renaissance painting, was no less common. A misericord from Winchester shows a beggar traveling on all fours, with pads to give some protection to hands and knees. In the late nineteenth century Władisław Reymont described the indeterminate sicknesses that besieged his village in central Poland. It "was afflicted with many sicknesses, as is often the case before spring; for at that time noxious vapours rise up from the thawing ground. Smallpox swooped down first, like a hawk on a brood of goslings, slaying the little ones. . . . Then the grown-ups were assailed by many diseases, and to such an extent that in every other cabin someone lay moaning in expectation of the grave."[60] Nowhere in Reymont's long narrative is there any suggestion that a doctor be summoned, or, in fact, that any significant medical precautions were taken or remedies prescribed. There was, in fact, no doctor nearer than the next large city, and he would have been very unlikely to make the long journey to the village for the sake of a few penniless peasants. Thus has it always been. The Beauce, described in Émile Zola's *Terre,* was no better off, and Balzac's caring doctor in the Alpine valley, described in *Le Médecin de Campagne,* was an exceptional person in his concern, as he was in other respects.

Most of the medicines prescribed by both doctors and quacks were herbal, gathered from the field and woodland. A few may have had some medicinal value, but most at best had the merit of being harmless and at worst were only nauseating or laxative. These qualities may, indeed, have been an advantage when many of the complaints treated arose from eating stale or putrid food. But some of the medications used were themselves extremely dangerous, like the "styby" that Carnsew used on his friends. By the late seventeenth century a number of drugs were prepared and sold by apothecaries. Some merely perpetuated medieval superstitions, but a few had real therapeutic value. Mercury was found to be effective in treating venereal disease. Quinine was brought to Europe in the mid-seventeenth century and proved effective in treating the ague or malaria. Other chemical substances that came into wide if somewhat indiscriminate use were compounds of sulfur and lead or derivatives of plants, such as laudanum, obtained mainly from the opium poppy. There was no restriction on the sale of such medicinal substances before the late nineteenth century, though their price put them beyond the range of all except the well-to-do. Their use was a matter of trial and error. If a drug *appeared* to be successful, its use was continued for every other complaint that showed not dissimilar symptoms.[61]

The fog surrounding the common illnesses and their treatment is lifted a little when it comes to childbirth. At least this occurrence is statistically measurable, and, within limits, we know the number of births and of deaths in childbirth because in much of Europe they began to be recorded in the sixteenth century. The incidence of stillbirths and abortions remains, however, an unknown quantity before the nineteenth century. In rural areas there was before the present century a complete lack of prenatal medical attention. And even in cities a doctor was summoned only if there was imminent danger of miscarriage. The time of birth could be foreseen only approximately, and it was impossible in rural areas to have a doctor in attendance. In most cases only the midwife was present and sometimes there was only an ignorant and unpracticed neighbor. Conditions were primitive. Often only old and soiled bedclothes were used in order to protect others from damage. The midwife herself may have had some experience, and, at least in the cities, some kind of apprenticeship or training. But she had inherited a wealth of folklore and folk remedies that she would under no circumstances renounce.[62] The birth took place inevitably in the cottage, in which there must have lingered infection from every illness that had occurred there, and was "assisted by assorted neighbors who busied themselves by casting horoscopes, muttering incantations, shutting doors, blocking windows and spreading infection."[63] No one had any concept of the need for sterilization or even for common cleanliness. The midwife would have done little more than wash her hands—and possibly not even in hot water—before beginning her work. The description of the birth in Zola's *Terre* is as masterly as it is horrifying.

Danger came from two sources: the purely gynecological problem of the position and movement of the fetus, and that of infection from the physical surroundings. It is difficult to say which was the greater. From the seventeenth century, knowledge of obstetrics and the use of obstetrical instruments increased rapidly, and a competent doctor could guard against some of the difficulties arising from the former source. But the question of infection remained until the late nineteenth and even the twentieth century. The chances of the mother's becoming infected were high, and the risk of death from puerperal fever was not inconsiderable. The midwife, who had herself previously attended other births, was often the carrier of infection, and William Harvey, the seventeenth-century physician who demonstrated the circulation of the blood, was of the opinion, based on his empirical observations, that it was better to dispense with the services of both midwife and doctor. The establishment of maternity or "lying-in" hospitals in the eighteenth century actually increased the danger of infection because they facilitated its spread from one woman to the next through their unsanitized wards. Indeed, they were called "gateways to death."

Infant mortality was high throughout the preindustrial period and remained so during much of the nineteenth century. It was far from unusual for the death rate among children in their first year to approach 40 percent, and there were many instances of levels of mortality much higher than this. The total extinction of whole families was not infrequent. A monument in a parish church in southwest England records the death in the early years of the seventeenth century of Walter Coode (d. 1637) and his wife. Beneath their kneeling figures are skulls representing each of their eight children, all of whom died before their parents. Such happenings were not infrequent, but what makes the extinction of the Coode family noteworthy is that they belonged to the landed gentry and lived in an area that rarely suffered from shortages.

The level of infant mortality—that is, of the death of children in their first year—has been, as Flinn pointed out,[64] one of the most important and least-studied aspects of social history. In England it stood at almost 20 percent before 1750; elsewhere in Europe it was nearer 30. In those countries for which statistics are available the level fell somewhat during the eighteenth century, and more sharply in the nineteenth. Nevertheless the level around 1820 was significantly below 20 percent only in England and Sweden.

Causes of death must remain uncertain, owing to the lack of unambiguous diagnoses and reporting. It is clear, however, that measles, diarrhea, whooping cough, and scarlet fever were very important and remained so throughout the nineteenth century.[65] A significant, though little-known, factor in infant mortality was what, for lack of a more suitable term, may be called infanticide. There were occasions when children were an asset to the family economy, capable of performing simple tasks from an early age. But to many laboring families, they must have been a barely supportable burden. There may be little evidence that they were actually killed, and when cases came before the English courts in the seventeenth century, death was most often attributed to "accident." A common form of accident, readily understandable in the cramped conditions of the simple cottage, was "overlying" by the mother. Who could prove that such a death was not accidental? Who, indeed, could do so even today? Children were allowed to die from neglect or even exposure: "Thou shalt not kill; but need'st not strive / Officiously to keep alive," wrote Arthur Hugh Clough. Not all unwanted children were allowed to die from one cause or another. A large number were delivered to foundling hospitals. In the year 1772, no less than 7672 were admitted to the Parisian *Hôpital des Enfants-Trouvés*.[66] No doubt a high proportion were illegitimate; all were born to parents who had neither the desire nor the means to support them.

The alternative to unwanted pregnancies and births was some form of birth control. That birth control was practiced in the preindustrial age is self-evident. References to it are frequent in the literature, though never explicit.[67] It was denounced by the prophets and the church fathers, and their strictures and exhortations have been repeated until the present. It was, however, practiced in the darkness of the home, surrounded by secrecy and superstition. Various herbal and mineral substances were used, but with what success we cannot possibly know. The most frequent practice, on the evidence of the preachers who denounced it, was that which has come to be known as *coitus interruptus*. It also seems likely that means were used of inducing abortions, chiefly medications and over-great exercise. Birth control appears to have been practiced more regularly and more successfully by the upper classes than among the poor. The reason is likely to have lain in the social conditions of the aspiring members of the bourgeois and noble classes, a point clearly made in a play by G. T. de Valentin of 1706:

> All excesses are fatal to us bourgeoisie.
> We must on occasion from pleasure abstain,
> Having only those children we well can maintain
> 'Tis better to nurture with care just one child
> Than produce half a dozen and let 'em run wild.[68]

It is very uncertain whether the masses of the working people used such practices, at least within marriage, much before the late nineteenth century. In most studies of family patterns, "fertility rates and birth intervals are consistent with normal uncontrolled fertility,"[69] and it is, by and large, this pattern of births on which we must base our examination of population in preindustrial Europe.

Chapter 7

"THE POPULOUSNESS
OF ANCIENT NATIONS"

From plague, pestilence and famine good Lord deliver us.
—Litany of the Anglican Church,
1552 Prayer Book

*B*efore modern times people showed little interest in their own numbers. There was little curiosity, and only in a few instances was there any practical need to know how many lived in this city or that. And if any person or any government should have shown an interest in the matter, there were always the dire consequences to the Israelites of King David's unsuccessful essay in demography to deter them.[1] Direct attempts to "count the heads of the people" were therefore very few before the nineteenth century. But among them were the head counts taken in a number of Italian cities during the Middle Ages. Their purpose was simple. These cities were heavily dependent on imported food, and the city authorities needed to know for good, practical reasons how large their grain stores should be.[2] It is significant that these censuses always recorded the number not of people by sex or age but simply of *bocche,* of mouths waiting to be fed.

Of course, the size of the population was implicit in certain activities of governments, such as collecting taxes and raising armies. Poll taxes and muster rolls provide the historian with an invaluable path into the tangled question of the size of earlier populations, but only in the rarest cases did they contribute to any contemporary estimate. The problem is that such records are far from unambiguous, because all of them excluded certain categories of people. Muster rolls listed only able-bodied men of military age; poll-tax records commonly omitted children below an unspecified age as well as members of religious orders and occasionally those judged too poor to pay.

An alternative was to levy a tax on each household, conveniently termed a "hearth." Hearth taxes were collected and hearth lists have been preserved for parts of western

Europe for the later Middle Ages and the sixteenth century, but as records of population, they are suspect.[3] Doubtless there was initially a more or less careful count of households, but there is good reason to believe that it was rarely updated and that the sum indicated tended to become an arbitrary imposition on each community rather than a measure of its ability to pay. In England hearth taxes were collected in the second half of the seventeenth century. But here the term "hearth" was taken literally, and those homes which boasted two hearths or more were assessed accordingly. A majority of homes were shown each to have had a single hearth, but there were a few large houses with four or five, and in the rare "great" house there might have been a dozen or more.

A change in attitudes toward population and population change became apparent late in the seventeenth century. Population size ceased gradually to be regarded as the result of the inscrutable will of the Almighty and began to be seen as a matter of public concern. Many factors contributed to this. In the first place, the developing spirit of intellectual speculation regarded every field of human endeavor as open to critical enquiry. The nature of sickness and causes of death, the size of population and the direction of change were not exempt. In England, Gregory King formulated an estimate of total population on the basis of the hearth-tax returns, and divided it by social class. At about the same time, Vauban in France published a short monograph on the need for a census, but it is not without significance that he did so anonymously. A few years later, Saugrin manipulated data contained in the reports of the provincial governors, or *Intendants,* to arrive at an estimate of the population of France.[4] Others who in the course of the eighteenth century made similar estimates were Messance and Moheau—both *noms de plume* of persons who did not wish their names to appear—and the abbé Expilly, the only churchman to involve himself in such matters.[5] It is symptomatic of public attitudes that three of the most prominent and perceptive writers on population chose to publish their work anonymously.

In Germany J. P. Süssmilch actually collected data on births, marriages, and deaths and used them to estimate population.[6] Others who used the available data, but less critically than Süssmilch had done, were Karl Büsching[7] and the Comte de Mirabeau.[8] At the same time, interest in population was being stimulated throughout Scandinavia, and in Sweden, which then included Finland, the first modern census was taken in 1749. In Italy, a number of states, including Sardinia-Piedmont, Tuscany, and Parma, made population counts before the end of the century. The revolutionary and Napoleonic period saw a strengthening of the demand for the precise enumeration of the population. Several counts, of varying degrees of reliability, were taken in France. England and Wales held their first census in 1801, anticipated by a year by the first in the United States. Thereafter the practice of counting the population was seen as increasingly necessary, and the last countries to hold a census were the Russian and Ottoman empires at the end of the nineteenth century.

A second factor in the developing interest in population lay in the growing social problems of contemporary Europe. The tightly knit village community was breaking down, society was become more mobile, the vagrant and footloose population was increasing, and the problem of distress, both rural and urban, was greater than ever before. The question began to be asked: was this a sign that population was increasing more rapidly than resources and social institutions could support? These issues had been debated long before Thomas Malthus first formulated his theory of population growth[9] and became increasingly pressing as the nineteenth century wore on.

The outward signs of increasing population were apparent, but opinion was divided between those who welcomed this fulfillment of the biblical injunction to be "fruitful and multiply" and those, more thoughtful and rational, who feared for the additional strain that was being placed on available resources. Among the latter was Thomas Malthus himself. This is not the place to expound or to criticize his theories. Enough to say that, in his view, unrestricted human fertility would lead to an exponential growth in population, which could not possibly be matched by an increase in food and other naturally occurring resources. In brief, he claimed that the human population would increase at a geometrical rate; natural production, only at an arithmetic. The resulting pressure on resources could lead only to the application of "natural checks": famine, disease, war. These had, during the centuries before Malthus, kept population within limits. There had at times been quasi-Malthusian situations, when population pressure, at least locally, led to severe shortages for some sections of society.[10] It has, for example, been shown that between 1248 and 1311 the cropland available per head of population on the Bishop of Winchester's manor of Taunton in southern England fell from 3.3 acres to 2.5, a decline of about 25 percent.[11] One must assume a commensurate decline in food supply, and this, in a population already close to the margin of subsistence, could have spelled disaster.

The Malthusian model has undergone criticism and modification since it was first expounded. The increase in both population and food supply have been far more complex than Malthus had supposed. He assumed a smooth increase in both, though one at a faster rate than the other. At a certain point the lines representing each would intersect, and catastrophe would follow (fig. 7.1). Population growth was, in fact, uneven, interrupted by the accidents of epidemic disease. This process resulted in a changing age structure. A year or two of high mortality, from whatever cause, would be followed a generation later by one of diminished natality, because of the smaller group of potential parents. The graph of population growth was thus marked by a wavelike contour. The wave arising from any particular period of low or high natality would in time die out or be obscured by the waves generated by other crises.

In theory one would expect food production to increase at a diminishing rate because the land factor was constant, and labor inputs would show diminishing returns. This growth was also obscured by the accidents of nature. No two harvest years are the same. Crop yields vary from the abundant to the catastrophic. At intervals of from five to ten years there was a harvest so bad that there was a degree of starvation, increased mortality, and diminished human fertility. Even less frequently there was a run of such years—1315–17 and 1692–94 are conspicuous examples—and then a subsistence crisis of major proportions emerged. A run of good harvests might disguise a Malthusian situation, and a single bad harvest might then bring the Malthusian checks into play when least expected.[12] The reality of the relationship between population and food supply is closer to that shown in figure 7.1b than to the simple Malthusian model in figure 7.1a.

Of all sources available for the study of population and social structure before the first censuses were taken, the most valuable by far are the parish registers of baptisms,

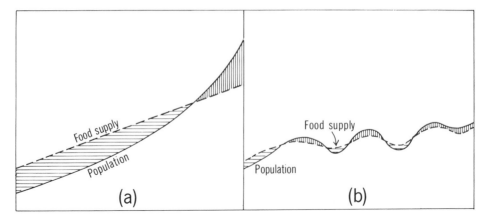

7.1. Graph showing (*a*) the Malthusian expectation of the growth of population and food supply; (*b*) the situation as it may have been in the later Middle Ages.

marriages, and burials. These are rare but far from unknown for the Middle Ages but become increasingly numerous from the middle of the sixteenth century. They permit a continuous record of population to be compiled, month by month and year by year (fig. 7.2). There were months and years, even spans of several years, when total deaths greatly exceeded total births, and one must assume that population declined.

A more refined analysis links the registers of births, marriages, and burials more intimately. It traces successive births in each family and the intervals between them. It follows individuals through marriage and childrearing to death. It allows the family, as it were, to be reconstituted; it shows the age at marriage, the frequency of births, and the age at which children died. It reveals the size of the completed family, when parents were widowed, and whether they married again. The amount of information that can be extracted from parish registers is immense, limited only by breaks in the continuity of the registers themselves and the removal of members of a family to another—and unknown—parish.

The Course of Population Change

It is generally held that population was slowly declining during the closing centuries of the Roman Empire, though for this there is remarkably little hard evidence. It remained low during the early Middle Ages but again began to increase between the tenth and the twelfth centuries. The barbarian invasions and the subsequent inroads of the Norsemen, the Magyars, and the Moors must have had an inhibiting influence, but by the eleventh century population was increasing almost everywhere, and this growth, local, fitful, and uneven no doubt, continued until the early fourteenth century. By this date the population of Europe *may* have been about twice that of five centuries earlier, and *may* have reached a total of between eighty and ninety million. This was probably very considerably in excess of the number even at the peak of prosperity of the Roman Empire.

Population grows when the aggregate number of births, over a more or less pro-

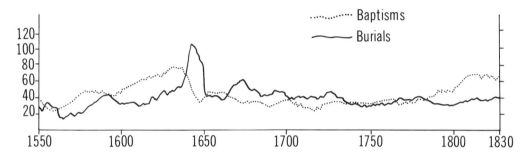

7.2. Graph showing baptisms and burials in an English parish, 1550–1830. Baptisms consistently exceed burials c. 1560–1640 and from c. 1780 onwards. These were periods of rising population. (After E. A. Wrigley, *Population and History* [London, 1969], 82–83.)

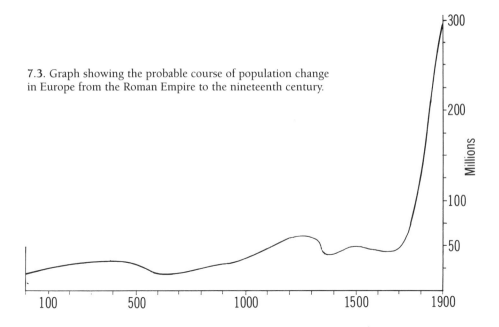

7.3. Graph showing the probable course of population change in Europe from the Roman Empire to the nineteenth century.

longed period, exceeds that of deaths. Complete harmony between natality and mortality should give a stable population, but that has never been achieved. Mortality has always been subject to fluctuations, some of them extreme, and this has in turn influenced the birthrate by reducing the number of parents. The factors in mortality are complex. It has always been influenced by the quality of the harvest, and thus by the weather; by epidemic disease, which might decimate a population in a few weeks or months; and by warfare and civil strife. Of these, harvest failure and epidemic disease must, singly or in combination, be held to have been the chief influences on population growth. Together they account for periods of very high mortality, which have occurred at irregular intervals throughout preindustrial history. But underlying these periods of famine there was a permanent state of under- and malnourishment, and, disguised by periodic outbreaks of epidemic disease, there was the multitude of ills to which flesh is heir. People's helplessness before sickness and lack of food has already been discussed. A high mortality and a low expectation of life at birth were built into the preindustrial population system. Only with better diet, closer environmental control, and a radically different concept of the nature of disease in the later years of the nineteenth century did European man begin to break out of his preindustrial constraints.

The preindustrial demographic system, with its violent incidence of famine and epidemic disasters, had built into it a certain self-correcting mechanism. Heavy mortality was usually followed by a greater availability of land, by earlier marriages, and by larger completed families. And, since these diseases were seldom continental in their scope, they were often accompanied by migration from areas still densely populated to others where land had become more freely available. Recovery from each crisis was immediate and sometimes rapid, and the necessary prelude to the modern increase in population was the elimination or at least the moderation of some of these recurring crises.

The period of population growth, which had begun before the twelfth century, culminated in the first half of the fourteenth. The increase had been encouraged by the availability of land for settlement and cultivation, and this may have led to somewhat earlier marriages. Epidemic disease appears to have been less frequent and disastrous than it later became, and it is even possible that a slight modification in the climate over much of Europe may have led to larger or at least more reliable harvests. It has even been suggested that a state of overpopulation had been reached by the early years of the fourteenth century.[13] If this was indeed the case, much of the population must have been ill nourished and prone to every infection.

Europe was struck during the first half of the fourteenth century by two calamities. The first was the earliest famine crisis of which we have detailed record. For three years, 1315–17, winters were wet and summers both wet and cool. Crops were washed out in the former, and in the latter they failed to ripen. This climatic disaster was not continent-wide, but it was the first of a series of crop failures. The extent to which the resulting malnutrition contributed to the first great epidemic may be debated. The bubonic plague was quite independent of overpopulation and food shortage and would, presumably, have spread even if there had been no subsistence crisis. But whether its depredations would have been so severe may be questioned.

The bubonic plague, whose ravages have generally been called the Black Death, was new to Europe. At least, it had not been known for six centuries.[14] The last outbreak had spead from Egypt to Constantinople in 541, and from here to much of the Mediterranean basin. It had died away by 544 but was followed by a second and apparently less severe outbreak in 558–61. Thereafter it remained endemic for about two hundred years, erupting into major outbreaks every eight or nine years.

The second outbreak of the plague began in 1347 and died away in 1351. Its incidence was erratic. There were communities that were wiped out by the plague, and there were others, insulated by their remoteness, that suffered scarcely at all. As much as a quarter of the population may have perished in the first outbreak of the plague. The disease remained endemic in Europe for almost four centuries and was present in the Balkan peninsula and Ottoman Empire even longer, erupting at intervals into outbreaks of epidemic proportions. Many of the latter were localized, in part because people had

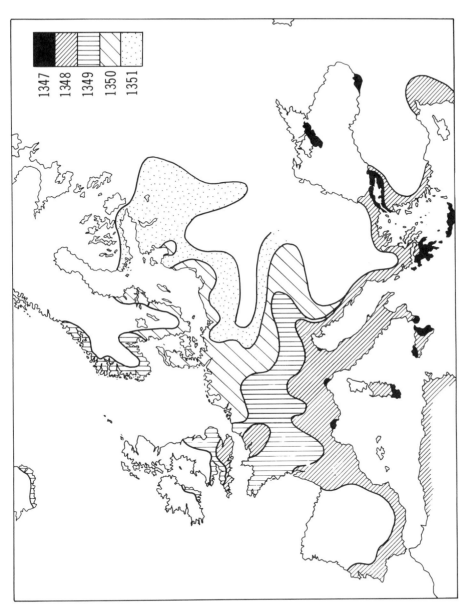

7.4. The spread of the bubonic plague, 1347–51. (After *Sci. Am.*, Feb. 1988, and E. Charpentier, "Autour de la peste noire: famines et épidémies dans l'histoire du XIVᵉ siècle," *Ann. E.S.C.* 17 [1962]: 1062–92.)

learned to quarantine them; in part because steadily improving environmental conditions restricted the spread of disease. But no part of Europe was untouched by the plague at some time.

Data on plague mortality are at best fragmentary, but they confirm both its severity and its capricious nature. A register of burials was kept during these years at Givry, in Burgundy, a place better known today for the quality of its vintage.[15] During the years before the Great Plague about 30 people were buried each year, suggesting a population of 1200 to 1500. But in 1348, in a span of only ten weeks in late summer and fall, no fewer than 615 were buried, almost half the population of the community. The virulence of the plague was probably greatest in the cities. Certainly there is abundant evidence of a sharp drop in the number of "hearths," or inhabited houses, that were the chief unit of local taxation. At Albi in southern France their number fell from 2669 on the eve of the plague to 952 in 1357.[16] At the nearby city of Millau, the decline was similar, from 1541 in 1346 to 918 seven years later. But here, where the run of statistics is unusually complete, the decline had begun at least forty years before the plague struck and continued for many years afterwards. This prolonged drop in population probably reflects the combined effects of famine crises and epidemic disease.[17]

On the other hand, there were places scarcely touched by this outbreak of the plague. For reasons that remain obscure, mortality was low in Flanders, where, with a dense population and closely spaced cities, one would have expected a heavy mortality.[18] There were peaks in 1329, 1333, and 1340, attributable in all probability to famine crises, as well as in 1349, the year of the Great Plague. But plague mortality was here scarcely more serious than the famine crisis of 1333. On the other hand, mortality remained high into the 1370s and was exceptionally severe in 1360 and again in 1367. This increase resulted almost certainly from renewed outbreaks of the plague. The recurrence might have been expected since the primary outbreak of plague in 1349 had been relatively mild and few people would have gained an immunity to it.

The plague remained endemic throughout the rest of the Middle Ages and continued into the sixteenth and seventeenth centuries. There was never again a pandemic comparable with that of 1347–50, but frequent localized outbreaks prevented any general increase in population before the later years of the fifteenth century. This recovery was, however, short-lived. The English population appears to have stagnated.[19] That of the Low Countries showed only a modest upturn. The sixteenth century was one of slow growth almost everywhere, but before its end outbreaks of plague had become more frequent and more severe, and a number of other epidemic diseases, including smallpox, had become prominent and claimed their toll. In Spain the growth that had marked that country's golden age came to an abrupt stop. Central Europe was ravaged by the Thirty Years War; parts of Germany are said to have lost more than half their population, and after the war was over, warfare continued on the borders of France and Germany and in eastern Europe.[20] Even in Great Britain, which underwent no such experiences, population failed to grow significantly during the century. Frequent crop failures added to the miseries of the seventeenth century, which ended with one of the most severe subsistence crises that western Europe had ever experienced.

Early in the eighteenth century conditions changed. The plague ceased its ravages over most of Europe; harvest failures became less frequent and less severe. Food shortages continued to occur, but after 1740 there was no subsistence crisis on the scale of those experienced in the seventeenth century. And over much of the continent population began that slow but steady increase which was to continue through the nineteenth and into the twentieth century. There were, before the early nineteenth century, no censuses to measure this growth, but its dynamics become apparent from the analysis of parish registers. The evidence points to the middle third of the eighteenth century as the period when this change in demographic behavior first became apparent. In Italy it appears to have begun earlier, and in Scandinavia and eastern Europe, several decades later. But by the later years of the century the movement was common to the whole of Europe.

The population of Europe, excluding eastern Europe and the Balkans, stood at about 75 million in 1700. By 1800 it had increased to almost 110 million, an increase of over 45 percent. This rate of increase was common to most of the continent. Only the Netherlands, where growth had shown little interruption during the previous century, was an exception. After the Napoleonic Wars and the food crisis that followed almost immediately, the upward trend in population was resumed and intensified. By 1850 the total, without eastern Europe and the Balkans, had risen to 150 million, and a half century later to 220 million. If Austria-Hungary, the Balkans, and Russia are included, the totals were respectively about 285 and 445 million. The population increase during the latter half of the century alone was of the order of 60 percent, and over the century as a whole it approximately doubled. Such a rate of increase was completely without precedent either in Europe or in the rest of the world at this date, though faster growth has been experienced in some Third World Countries in the middle years of the present century. Beside it the growth that so alarmed Thomas Malthus and others in the eighteenth century seems utterly trifling.

Yet the rates of growth in fact varied greatly between countries. Overall growth was greatest in Great Britain—about 250 percent—and least in Ireland, where there was a net decline of 35 percent between 1821 and 1900. The growth in Germany—about 180 percent—was more than four times that in France, which was only about 39 percent.

So momentous an increase is difficult to understand and to explain. The fundamental question is whether it can be attributed to an increase in human fertility, or to a decline in the death rate, or to a combination of these two factors. It has been demonstrated that human fertility fluctuated very little and overall showed remarkably small changes before the middle years of the twentieth century. It is no less apparent that the death rate has fallen, especially among the young, and that the expectation of life at birth has increased from, on average, forty years in the eighteenth century to seventy or more at present.

The Pattern of Births

The size of a completed family has always depended upon a number of factors, of which the age of the parents at marriage is one of the most important. Others are the duration of breast-feeding, since conception is unlikely while the mother is nursing a previous child; the adequacy of diet; the amount of strenuous labor on the part of the mother; and, of

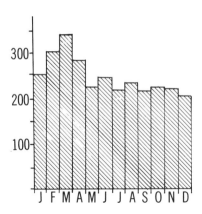

7.5. Aggregate births, c. 1600–c. 1800, in an English parish. Note the very high level of natality, February to April, and the low level in the fall.

course, the prevention of conception by artificial means. Of these factors, only age at marriage is comparatively easy to determine, and the practice of birth control the most difficult. We have already noted that the latter was common in preindustrial times, especially among members of the middle and upper classes. Until the eighteenth century birth control was not *socially* necessary or even desirable; Europe was able to support the increases that occurred. Thereafter, with a more rapid rate of increase, fears were expressed—and not only by Thomas Malthus—that population might become too large for resources currently available to support it. There can be no question that, for a variety of reasons, birth control came to be practiced. The most important factor was the simple fact that, with a declining death rate, it was no longer necessary to have large families. But this consideration was probably hidden to most people before the recent past and certainly did not influence their behavior. More important to them were the compulsion to see that their farm holding passed intact to an only son, the reluctance to bear the cost of rearing more children than they thought necessary to preserve their families, and the desire to emulate the behavior of classes above them in the social scale.

Age at marriage was as a general rule somewhat higher in preindustrial societies than at present. In all western countries where families have been "reconstituted" from baptismal records, women rarely married before the age of twenty-five, and the age of their partners was often greater. On average they bore their last child at about forty, so that the typical childbearing period, unless interrupted by accident or death, was about fifteen years. This might seem long enough to produce a sizable family. In fact, however, births were not as frequent as is sometimes supposed. The number of births outside marriage was relatively small, but premarital conceptions were numerous. Up to a fifth of first births were conceived in this way, and the "shotgun marriage" must have been very familiar to rural communities in preindustrial and even later Europe. Thereafter births were fairly widely spaced, at intervals, it is often said, of thirty months. In fact, this intergenesic period tended to increase with the age of the mother, so that it was not often that a completed family could have many more than six children, though exceptional instances of ten or a dozen are well known. The reasons for the infrequency of births are many, quite apart from any voluntary restrictions there may have been on the part of the parents. Temporary sterility, known as amenorrhea, is probably the most important. Against the voluntary restriction of births must be set the almost universal desire for children, if only for practical reasons. They were for most people the only available insurance against illness and old age. On the land and in the workshop the labor of children was a cheap and necessary adjunct to that of their parents, and the income from child labor in the early factories was a necessary, even if socially undesirable, supplement to the family income.

A distinction has been made in these respects between society in western and northern Europe on the one hand and that in eastern and southeastern on the other.[21] In western Europe not only was age at marriage relatively high, but a significant proportion of the population within the childbearing age—up to one-half—was at any one time unmarried. By contrast, in eastern and southeastern Europe—not to mention the Third World—a very high proportion of the population married, and at a very much earlier age. One looks for an explanation for this contrast in the differing material conditions of the two kinds of society. In western society, it had become normal for the partners in a marriage to wait until they had accumulated sufficient money and material goods to be able to set up home. For the woman a dowry or a well-filled "bottom drawer" was regarded as essential; for a man, a farm holding or a trade. He had therefore to wait until he had inherited the one or had served his apprenticeship for the other. In eastern Europe the situation was different. Expectations were lower. The system of large house-holds and extended families, culminating in the Balkan institution of the *zadruga,* made it easier for the penniless couple to marry at an earlier date, and, lastly, land was more abundant and there was never any great difficulty in either acquiring a holding or finding employment on an estate. The "child-rich Slav" was not altogether a figment of the western imagination.

The western pattern of marriage, together with the relatively high level of child mortality, was calculated to keep the size of the family *relatively* small and to raise those fears, which have been mentioned above, for its survival. There were no such fears in eastern and southeastern Europe.

The level of mortality was high in preindustrial societies, and remained so until late in the nineteenth century. It was, furthermore, highly unstable, with short periods of very high mortality resulting from food crises and epidemic disease. The effect of such periods of high mortality was to allow those who survived to inherit land or to acquire a business at an earlier age than would otherwise have been possible. This state of affairs in turn encouraged earlier marriage for a period, and, presumably, a larger family than would otherwise have been the case. A mortality crisis was to this small extent self-correcting. It could also be self-perpetuating, and a period of low birthrate might be reflected in a smaller number of births a generation later.

The high level of child mortality was normal until comparatively recent times. In preindustrial Europe, from a quarter to a third of all children died during their first year. In France, in the parishes where families have been reconstituted from baptismal registers, little more than half survived to the age of ten, and even fewer to fifteen.[22] Conditions improved somewhat in the later eighteenth century, but even so the survival rate to the age of fifteen was only 54 percent. Not until the early nineteenth century did it even approach two-thirds. In a family with six live births, it could not be assumed that more than three children would grow to adulthood, and, if allowance is made for those who did not marry, or were sterile, or died during their childbearing age, only two might be expected to have completed families of their own. Such a calculation is only the roughest approximation. Conditions varied greatly with social class and convention. Those in England were different from those in France, or Switzerland, or the Balkan peninsula. They differed as between countryside and town. Indeed, one wonders how it was possible that population was able to increase as it did in the later eighteenth and nineteenth centuries. Birthrates varied, but there was little scope apart from earlier marriage, for which there is little evidence in western Europe, for any significant increase. The explanation must lie in changes in the pattern of death.

The Pattern of Death

At least until the middle years of the nineteenth century the pattern of death was characterized by dramatic short-term fluctuations, attributable essentially to famine and epidemic disease. Their spacing was irregular in time, and they were often local in occurrence. There were continentwide epidemics, as of the bubonic plague in the Middle Ages and of cholera in the nineteenth century; harvest failure might span several countries, as it did in 1315–17 or in 1816. But there were times when epidemics were contained so that only a few communities suffered and when abnormal weather conditions affected only restricted areas. We have, in consequence, a picture of almost random blows delivered at the body of Europe's population. In the end, few areas escaped, but, chance being what it is, some places suffered abnormally and others escaped almost unscathed. Roger Schofield has defined "crisis mortality" as a year in which mortality was more than double the normal, and on this basis found that in a sample of fifty-four English parishes, seven experienced such crises more than ten times between the sixteenth century and the early nineteenth; twenty suffered five times or more; and only four had no such crisis at all.[23]

Other countries fared less well than England. This was due, in part, to the marginal nature of their environments or to the destruction of crops and property in the course of military campaigns. Finland and the rest of Scandinavia, for example, appear to have suffered very severely indeed, but the phenomenon of crisis mortality was common to the whole of Europe, from Norway to Greece and from Spain to Russia.

The two factors in crisis mortality, shortage of food and epidemic disease, are closely interlinked, but for purposes of this discussion must be taken separately. Nor can the question of the *volume* of food be separated from that of its nutritional value. Many diets that seemed adequate to those who consumed them were in fact lacking in some essential respect. Nor can high mortality be ascribed only to epidemic disease. There was a "normal" mortality attributable to diseases that were in general not communicable or, at least, not epidemic, such as those of the respiratory and digestive systems, the heart, liver, or kidneys. Many of these were not recognized for what they were until recent times. These nonepidemic diseases fluctuated, and it is impossible statistically to separate them from true epidemics.

We have already seen how precarious was the food supply of people before the industrial age. Crop yields were low, and there were times when the amount of grain harvested was scarcely greater than that which had been sown. This left little for the support of the community. If one assumes that for most crops a fourfold return was normal, then a quarter of the harvest had to be set aside for the next year's crop. A threefold yield meant that only two-thirds was available as food, and anything less than twofold was disastrous. Crops failed not infrequently. There was, on average, a disastrous crop failure about every five years. Bad weather assumed many forms. It might take the shape of prolonged drought in summer, when the grain withered in the ear, or of deep frost in winter, when the plow would not penetrate the soil and fall-sown crops were killed, or of frequent and heavy rains in late fall, winter, and spring, making the ground too wet to plow and sow, or of cool and wet summers when the crops ripened late or not at all. All these contingencies were familiar to the peasant. They are recorded in the accounts of bailiffs and stewards, explaining why the harvest was so thin and rents were not paid. They are reflected in the high price of cereals and in the parish registers that record the greater mortality that followed.

There is no adequate record of all the subsistence crises that afflicted European people in the preindustrial age, nor the means to measure their intensity and the suffering which they caused. They struck in different ways, for in no two years was the pattern of weather quite the same. Sometimes it was the fall-sown crops that failed. The peasant had then to resow in spring with whatever seed he could get. Sometimes heavy rain in later winter delayed spring plowing, so that oats and barley had too little time to grow and mature. Sometimes both fall- and spring-sown crops failed. Any crop failure led not only to a smaller amount of food being made available for human consumption, but to a lowering of the quality of the diet. Lack of the fall-sown breadgrains resulted in greater reliance on the spring-sown coarse grains, and if these also failed the peasant had recourse to the bitter buckwheat or chestnuts, pulverized and cooked, or even to the bark of trees and wild herbaceous plants.

Yet not everyone suffered in times of scarcity and want. On such occasions the price of foodstuffs rose. Indeed, the graph of grain prices is itself a fair measure of subsistence crises (fig. 7.6). The rich dipped deeper into their pockets, the grain dealers grew rich, and the poor starved. Other crises that beset people in this preindustrial age, like epidemic disease, came unheralded. There was no escaping them. But the approach of famine could be

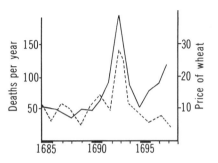

7.6. Mortality (solid line) and price of grain in *livres* per *setier* (dotted line) at Pontoise, near Paris, during the famine crisis of the 1690s.

recognized months ahead of the event. It was often known in spring whether the harvest in the following summer would be disastrous. The grain jobbers sensed the market and acted accordingly, buying and storing what surplus was still available and forcing up the price for those who had to buy. The following winter would be disastrous for all except the rich, who could pay the inflated prices demanded by the merchants. The meager harvest was soon exhausted, and the poor—and that was the majority—were forced to live on anything that their stomachs could digest. Demand was switched to coarser and less appetizing foods, and the price of these also joined in the upward spiral. Late winter and spring following a bad harvest was a terrible time for almost everyone. But the peasant knew what to expect. "That diseases prevailed; that some died of starvation; that quarrels and fighting were rife among them; and that death was now taking a heavier toll than in preceding years. To such things the people were accustomed, and bowed to them as to the inevitable. . . ." These words could have been written at almost any time and of any place in preindustrial Europe. In fact they were written near the end of the nineteenth century and related to events within their author's memory. They come from that epic of the peasant world, Reymont's *Chłopi*. In even bleaker terms, Archbishop Eudes of Rouen in the thirteenth century recorded, as he made his visitation of religious houses in his diocese, how in spring their store of grain was nearing exhaustion: "only two measures of wheat to last until August," and wheat that "will not last beyond the feast of St John [June 24]."[24] It was not only the poor and the peasant who suffered from poor harvests.

Three Subsistence Crises

Among all the subsistence crises that struck at some part or other of Europe before the modern age, three stand out by reason either of their severity or of the fullness with which they were documented: those of 1315–17, of 1692–94, and of 1816–17. In the severity of the famine and the depth of human and animal suffering, they may in fact have been no worse than others that have not been recorded in such intimate detail.

The summer of 1314 had been wet, but not abnormally so, over much of northern Europe. The following winter was cold, but it was not until the spring of 1315 that the weather really deteriorated.[25] The rains began and, over much of western and central Europe, they continued through the summer and into the fall. Many areas were flooded and crops rotted in the ground. The disaster in the Low Countries was compared with Noah's flood. The heavy rainfall was accompanied by unusual cold during the summer months, so that crops that had escaped the deluge failed to ripen. Available grain was quickly exhausted, and by the spring of 1316 famine conditions prevailed over large areas. It was reported that people were reduced to cannibalism. As always happened under such conditions, disease stalked in the wake of famine. Ergotism and dysentery followed the eating of contaminated foods. Resistance to epidemic disease was reduced, and skin complaints, resulting from vitamin deficiency, became common.

To make matters worse, the winter of 1315–16 was long and very severe, and in Germany crops were destroyed by the frost. The following summer was again wet, though less so than the previous summer had been. Harvest was small in most areas but sufficient to moderate the extremes of famine—and there were, furthermore, far fewer mouths to be fed. In 1317 the crisis continued in eastern Europe and the Danube valley, but in the west the worst was over. Survivors could eat more adequately for a few years, before the next famine crisis hit. It is impossible to estimate the mortality from the great food crisis of 1315–17. That its consequences were exacerbated by the dealers who raised the prices of breadgrains above the reach of the poor is clear from the chroniclers. They wrote of the appalling mortality that resulted directly from the famine and of its indirect consequences in robbery and violence. What they could not know were its long-term effects: the diminished birthrates of the famine years, the greater exposure to epidemic disease, the lives blighted by rickets, other deficiency diseases, and malnutrition.

The famine years came near the end of a very long period of sustained population growth, when the margin of cultivation was expanding, when soil of ever-diminishing quality was brought under the plow, and the average peasant holding became smaller and more and more divided. The consequences of this Malthusian situation were disguised by a run of good years. Then bad weather struck, with the results that have been described. The long period of rising population ended. It is not without significance that many born during and soon after the famine crisis of 1315–17 were among those struck down by the Great Plague a generation later. It was many years before famine on the scale of 1315–17 again stalked the land, but there was always scarcity and want, and, as always, the poor bore the suffering of the whole of society. The art of the later Middle Ages and Renaissance, despite the luxury and the bounding vitality that it portrays, is nonetheless filled with cripples and beggars.

The second example of a famine crisis—that of 1692–94—came at the end of a century filled with catastrophe. There were short periods marked by very cold winters and cool, wet summers. The 1680s were somewhat milder, but then came the barren years of the 1690s.[26] They were, almost without exception, cool and wet. Superficially the weather during these years bore a similarity to that of 1315–17. It was not the cold that caused the damage but heavy and persistent rain. Conditions in France were described in graphic detail in the reports submitted by the regional governors, or *Intendants,* to their Controller General in Paris. The *Intendant* of Provence reported that the rains had swept away the fall-sown grain, and when the land was resown in late winter, the new seed was also carried off in the continuing deluge.[27] In Languedoc both grain and that other support of the poor, chestnuts, failed, and the peasants were obliged to eat wild nuts and grass that the human stomach could scarcely digest. The suffering appears to have been greatest in the hills of central France, where physical conditions were in any case least encouraging for agriculture. The *Intendant* of Limoges declared that by the end of the winter, 70,000 people within his jurisdiction had been reduced to a diet of putrid chestnuts, and that even these were almost exhausted. The next harvest was ruined by the rain, and even the hardy buckwheat failed. The weather was so bad that peasants did not dare—so the *Intendant* reported—sow their fields; it is more than likely that they had eaten the seed. Buckwheat became the basic food of the well-off; the poor ate the roots of wild plants and the bran discarded by the miller. Little did they know that this latter was a better source of vitamins than the foods they normally consumed. The *Intendant* of Montauban reported in 1694 that, as a result of the bad harvests of the last two years, from a half to two-thirds of the population in some parishes had perished, so that not enough people remained to till the fields. Coastal towns received some breadgrain imported from the Baltic, but means of transport were lacking to carry it far inland. Through their reports the *Intendants* appealed to the central government for supplies of food, but there was little that it was able or willing to do. The famine, more localized than in 1315–17, took its course, and within a year or two, better harvests sufficed for the reduced population.

The third subsistence crisis was that of 1816–17. It differed in important respects from those which had gone before. These had been due to essentially meterological conditions that defied both explanation and anticipation. But in 1815, Mount Tamboro, a volcano in the East Indies, had erupted with great violence, passing into the atmosphere more dust than any other eruption of modern times. The effect was to spread a blanket through the atmosphere, reducing the effectiveness of the sun's insolation and lowering the temperatures worldwide. It was several years before this atmospheric dust sank to earth, but 1816 and 1817 were the worst, with cold winters, very late springs, and cool summers. The severe weather was felt everywhere; in New England, 1816 was "the year without a summer."[28] "Grain harvest," wrote Post, "failed in 1816 from the Mississippi River in the west to the borders of the Russian Empire in the east, from

Scotland in the north to the kingdom of the Two Sicilies in the south."[29] Grain prices on average doubled during the following winter, and in severely affected areas like Switzerland and south Germany they increased more than fourfold. There was scarcity everywhere, and in central Europe this situation reached famine proportions.

The death rate increased in 1817, the year following the first bad harvest, and its rise was greatest in south Germany, Switzerland, and northern Italy, where its increase above the level of 1815 was of the order of 40 to 50 percent. By 1818 conditions both of food supply and of mortality had returned almost to normal, and the crisis was effectively over. Its course had been different in several respects from that of any earlier food crisis. Although death rates increased, there is little evidence of any real epidemic, though malnutrition unquestionably led to increased mortality from pulmonary and digestive complaints. The incidence of typhus and smallpox was greater, but the death rate itself was consistently lower than would have been the case from a crop failure of this magnitude a century earlier.

One reason lay undoubtedly in the greater efficiency and effectiveness of governments in bringing food to the most affected areas. Compared with the 1690s, relief efforts were highly successful. At the same time, improved means of transportation and communication allowed grain to be brought from areas that still had a surplus to those which suffered most. But there was yet another factor. It has always been assumed that epidemic disease followed in the wake of famine, preying upon a debilitated and susceptible population. This time there was no real epidemic, thus raising the question whether there was in fact a simple and direct causal connection between famine and epidemics. The causes of the latter are undoubtedly far more complex than this. They relate not only to the volume but also to the quality of food available, as well as to social conditions including the degree of overcrowding and the state of housing, water supply, hygiene, and sanitation. All these factors could operate to bring about epidemics without any contributory harvest failure, and they had all, by and large, improved during the previous century.

The food crisis of 1816–17 was not the last experienced. There were many poor harvests during the century, and in 1846–47 disaster again struck in northwestern Europe. It was cold and wet, but another factor was the potato blight, which may not have been wholly attributable to the weather. The potato had become a very important part of the diet in the Low Countries, northwest Germany, and, above all, Ireland, where the crop failed almost completely. Mortality was high and there was a massive migration. The population of Ireland has still not regained the level of the years before the Potato Famine. There was again a widespread crop failure in the mid-1850s, but by this time governments could turn to overseas sources of breadgrain, and there was neither widespread famine nor heavy mortality.

The relationship between diet and disease, famine and epidemics is probably close but is nonetheless difficult to trace. Some diseases, such as dysentery and ergotism, can be attributed in part to the consumption of putrescent food. Those due to vitamin deficiencies are more clearly related to unbalanced diet, but there is no clear-cut link between inadequate diet, on the one hand, and plague, smallpox, typhus, and cholera. All that can be said is that inadequate or unbalanced diet may have weakened human resistance to infection. It is unlikely that anyone actually died of famine. The cause of death was always an infection or a failure of one or more of the bodily organs.

Disease and Its Vectors

In developed societies today the expectation of life at birth is seventy or more years, and there is a probability that when death comes it will be through heart failure or cancer, and a near certainty that plague, smallpox, tuberculosis, typhus, and a number of other infectious diseases will play no role. This pattern of death is new and is a consequence of the virtual elimination of these latter diseases in all advanced countries. But long before antibiotics and other modern drugs became available, the pattern of mortality was changing. Predominant causes of death were different in the eighteenth and nineteenth century from those which had been most important in the Middle Ages. Leaving aside accident and warfare, causes of death were of two kinds: epidemic diseases and, second, the ever-present ailments to which flesh is heir: pulmonary, respiratory, and digestive complaints, rickets and other deficiency diseases, and the rest. In most instances it is impossible to know what was the cause of death in earlier times. A few diseases, of course, had their telltale signs, which all could understand. There was no mistaking smallpox, or the plague, or syphilis after it had appeared in Europe about 1500. But fever, vomiting, and diarrhea did not indicate a specific ailment, and contemporary diagnoses of the causal complaint could sometimes be very wide of the mark. Indeed, it was not until the present century that correct diagnoses of some complaints became possible. In seventeenth- and eighteenth-century England an attempt was made to distinguish between plague deaths and those from other complaints—the so-called bills of mortality. Physicians were probably fairly accurate in diagnosing the bubonic plague but in other respects were totally unreliable.

Many diseases showed a seasonal rhythm. The highest mortality came under *normal* conditions in late winter and early spring. This was a time when food shortages were most acute and bronchial complaints most common. Parish registers show a relatively low death rate in late summer and fall. It rises in the winter months and peaks in late winter and spring, before declining again through the summer. Figure 7.7, which is based on a number of parish registers in the southwest of England, shows the *aggregate* number of deaths in each month during the seventeenth and eighteenth centuries. This graph could have been repeated endlessly in those parts of Europe for which mortality data are available.

This was the "normal" pattern of death, revealed when data first became available in parish registers, and it continued little changed through the nineteenth century. The only difference is that the level of the death rate, that is, its relationship to the total population, tended to fall from the later eighteenth century.

Superimposed upon the normal pattern of mortality was that induced by epidemic diseases. These were the greatest killers of preindustrial Europe, decimating the population in a few weeks or months. Their

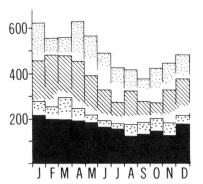

7.7. Aggregate deaths in four separate parishes. c. 1600–c. 1800, superimposed. Note the consistent pattern of high mortality in winter and early spring, and the low level in summer.

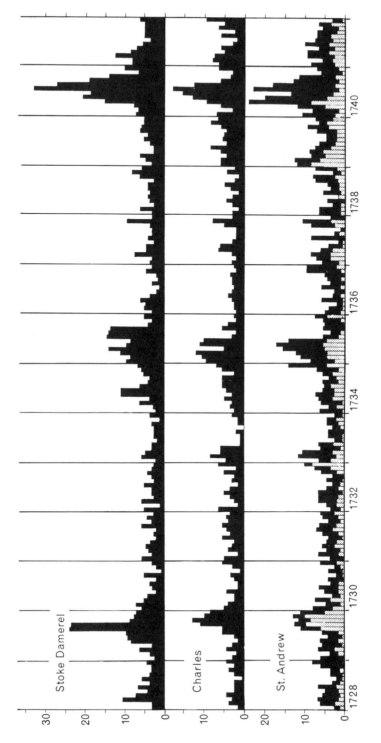

7.8. Graph of mortality, by month, within the three parishes that made up Plymouth, England, 1728–41. Note (1) the extreme irregularity of the totals; (2) the peaks in total mortality. These were due, as a local doctor's diary makes clear, to smallpox and, in the case of children, measles. The stippled area in St. Andrew indicates child mortality. (After N. J. G. Pounds, "John Huxham's Medical Diary," *L.P.S.*, no. 12 [1974]: 34–37.)

incidence was almost random. An outbreak could not be anticipated, and it was difficult to take precautions against it. In a sense, epidemic disease is a product of civilization. Each disease is spread by a bacterium or virus that is adopted, albeit unconsciously, by a human host. In many, perhaps most, instances, it fails to multiply and dies. Alternatively, it multiplies, infects and perhaps kills its human host, and is transmitted to others. In most instances the organism is conveyed by a vector, such as an insect or contaminated food or water. In a few instances, of which smallpox and the common cold are the most important, it can be passed directly from person to person without an intermediary. It is clear that the transmission of a disease is dependent on the frequency of contacts between people and the vectors that ferry the germ organisms between them. During much of prehistory, it is held, human groups were small, and contact between them was infrequent. If a pathogen appeared in such a group, events might follow any one of three possible courses. The organism might not find a receptive human host and would then die; it might multiply in its host, spread to the rest of the group, and infect and kill the whole; or, lastly, it might kill some but allow the rest to build up an immunity to the particular disease and thus to survive. Such an immunity might in some instances be inherited by the next generation, but in time it would wear off and a "normal" vulnerability would be restored. The infrequency of contacts between human groups would greatly reduce the possibility of the wider transmission of a disease, and for this reason epidemic disease was probably of only minor significance among prehistoric societies. Even in modern times truly isolated communities were able to escape the spread of epidemics that overwhelmed neighboring areas. One cannot, however, discount the passage of pathogens from animal populations, since many diseases are common to humans and wild life. Rabies, brucellosis, and certain forms of tuberculosis are unpleasantly familiar examples. Nevertheless, it is probably true to say that primitive man was relatively free from infectious diseases, and that these became really significant only when the human population had become more numerous and more settled, and contacts between groups had become more frequent.

These factors would help to explain the spread of smallpox and syphilis, both of them essentially person-to-person diseases, in early modern times. Typhus, which also became a significant cause of death at this time, was spread in crowded and congested conditions, in which its vector, the body louse, could move easily from person to person. The multiplication of pathogens was inhibited in much of Europe by cool temperatures generally and cold winters in particular. Tropical Africa and south and southeast Asia, by contrast, constituted vast "disease pools" from which pathogens might be diffused by human and animal carriers. If there was little or no contact and communication between these regions and the rest of the world, the spread of their diseases would be, at most, exceptional. Faster and more frequent travel brought them within easier reach of Europe. Even so, if travel was very slow, the pathogen would either have killed its host or would itself have died before the end of the journey. Time and distance provided the best form of quarantine. But such conditions changed in historical times. Contacts between different societies became more frequent, and disease spread more readily within them. The great plague of Athens of 431 B.C., perhaps the first great European epidemic to be recorded, is a case in point. The precise nature of the pathogen and how it was carried to Athens are not known, but, once established in the city, it spread rapidly through the dense population of refugees from the Spartan invasion of Attica. It lasted more than two years, at the end of which the population had either died or gained immunity.

A not dissimilar disease erupted in the Byzantine Empire in A.D. 541 and lasted for half a century before it finally died away. It was almost certainly the bubonic plague, and its spread from Egypt was traced by Procopius. He implies that it was carried by ship and "always took its start from the coast, and from there went up to the interior." It seems to have been largely restricted to the coastal regions of the Mediterranean and never to have been transmitted to northern Europe.

Eight centuries elapsed before its next documented outbreak. In 1347 plague reached the Black Sea ports by way of the caravan routes that led to China. In modern times cholera came by the same route. From the Crimea the plague was carried in the holds of Genoese ships first to southern Italy, then to southern France, from which it spread across most of Europe. It was the greatest killer that Europe had ever known, and it spread gloom and fear over the continent for more than three centuries. It spread across the land like an advancing wave. It moved faster than the great Byzantine plague and covered a greater area, probably because people and their goods were far more mobile than they had been eight centuries earlier. It cast its long shadow before it, and those who could fled to the security of the forests and mountains. Here it was that Boccaccio's companions, refugees from the plague in Florence, whiled away their time telling the stories of the *Decameron* until they could return. For the plague was short-lived. It was like the tide that rose and fell, and as it retreated it left a decimated population, the dead unburied and the fields untilled. The papal court barricaded itself within the vast *Châteauneuf* at Avignon and remained secure only because all contact with the outside world was cut off. Mortality was immense. Whole communities were wiped out. Overall, Europe may have lost as much as a quarter of its population. But there were communities that appear to have escaped because, by chance, the vectors of the plague never reached them. Others, chiefly small and closed, were almost wiped out. The Great Plague has come to be regarded as a turning point in European history, separating a period of growth from one of decline. This is undoubtedly an exaggeration, but the impact of the plague cast a shadow across European society until the eighteenth century. It inspired a larger literature and aroused a deeper fear than any other disease before recent times. Many perceptive observations were made about the plague and the ways in which it spread, but its true nature and cause were not elucidated before the present century. It was variously ascribed to exhalations from the ground, the influence of the stars, and, with greater reason, to unburied bodies, filth, and overcrowding. A sixteenth-century writer on the plague noted that "for the most part it doth come by receauing into our custody some clothes, or such like things that have been used about some infected body, wherein the infection may be hidden a long time."[30] It became the practice to burn the clothes, beds, and bedding of those who had died of plague. In their empirical way, those who decided to take this measure were right. The culprit, the common flea, was most often to be found in dirty clothing and soiled bedding, but the crime was not pinned on the real offender.

In fact, the plague came in several strains. The bubonic plague was the most common, the pneumonic the most deadly, but there were others, each with its particular etiology. The transmission of the plague was, as a general rule, through an association of the rat and the flea. The pathogen developed and multiplied in the bloodstream of the rat, which had itself developed an immunity to it. It was carried from rat to rat and from rat to people by the flea (*xenopsylla cheopis*). Rats infested ships, and fleas were a fact of life. Infected rats took passage from the Black Sea ports and came ashore at Messina, Genoa, and elsewhere. At once the parasitical fleas took their leave and moved to human clothing and bedding, where they remained, able to transmit the pathogen for a very long time.

It is apparent that conditions that favored rats and fleas—dirt, squalor, congestion, crumbling wooden construction—were also conducive to the spread of plague; and no less clear that the best antidote was a combination of personal hygiene and masonry construction, neither of which was frequent or widespread before the eighteenth century. There may have been other factors in the gradual disappearance of plague from Europe, but foremost must have been the gradual improvement in the material conditions of life. "It cannot be too often stressed," wrote Shrewsbury, "that the density of the house-rat population in a given area governed absolutely the intensity of the disease in that area."[31] The flea tended to be inactive in cold weather, and a severe winter stopped absolutely its marauding raids. An outbreak of plague almost always occurred during the heat of summer, continued during the months of high temperature, but slowly disappeared during the fall.[32] Wherever the data are available, a similar pattern of incidence can be demonstrated. The total death toll in Exeter, in southwestern England, in the years 1591–92 is shown in figure 7.9. The plague began late. Not until August did the level of mortality rise much above the normal, and the worst months were September and October, but in this instance the plague lingered through the following winter, which appears to have been exceptionally mild, and erupted again with extreme virulence in August of 1592.[33]

This was the pattern of plague: a severe epidemic, which tapered away as the susceptible were infected and died and the rest acquired some degree of immunity. A few years of freedom from infection followed, before the plague again struck a new and vulnerable population. The Great Plague of 1348–51 was followed by a second epidemic in 1360–61 and by a third from 1365 to 1371. Thereafter the plague became more sporadic in its occurrence. It remained endemic in the cities, which provided more abundant and more secure shelter for its hosts the rat and flea. And so it continued through the fifteenth and sixteenth

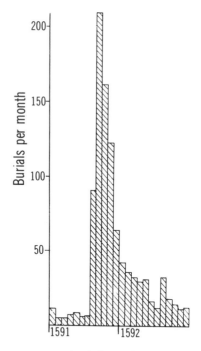

7.9. Graph of plague deaths, by month, at Exeter, England, 1591–92. (Based on Ransom Pickard, *The Population and Epidemics of Exeter* [Exeter, 1947].)

centuries. No part of Europe, except the Arctic, was spared. Marching armies carried infection with them. It was spread throughout central Europe during the Thirty Years War and gave rise to a far greater mortality than the fighting itself (fig. 7.10). In 1665

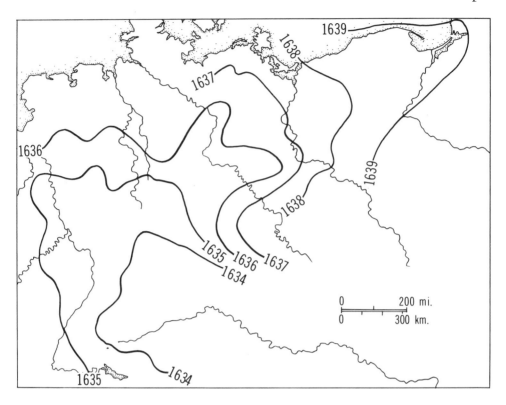

7.10. The spread of plague in central Europe during the Thirty Years War. (After E. Keyser, "Die Pest in Deutschland und ihre Erforschung," *Actes du Colloque International de Démographie Historique* [Liège, 1965], 369–77.)

there occurred one of the last great outbreaks in the west. The plague reached London in the summer and reached its peak in September. Before the end of the year, about 70,000, or some 16 percent of the city's population, had died. Before the plague had ended the Great Fire swept through much of the area, destroying both bacterium and vector. The plague spread to the counties bordering London, but, with one significant exception, did not reach the rest of the country. The exception was the village of Eyam, amid the hills of Derbyshire. If any place could have been thought secure from the plague it was Eyam. But infection reached it, so it is thought, by way of a bundle of clothing sent there from London. The plague at Eyam was contained, largely through the voluntary quarantine that its small population imposed upon itself, though in thus sacrificing itself the community was almost wiped out.

The plague spread to the Low Countries and wrought great damage in Brussels (fig. 7.11) and other cities, but henceforward Britain was free of it.[34] The last epidemic in western Europe was in Provence, especially in the city of Marseilles, in 1720. There were cases in Spain after this, and the plague remained endemic in the Balkan peninsula into the nineteenth century and was reinforced by the movement of Turkish troops. But it never penetrated central Europe, largely because, until 1871, the Austro-Hungarian monarchy maintained a highly successful quarantine against the Ottoman Empire.[35]

The significance of the plague in restricting population growth has long been discussed. There is no simple answer. The diagnosis of plague was generally fairly sure, but few statistics are available for the earlier outbreaks. Cases of very high mortality are well known. They passed into local folklore and are often cited as typical of Europe as a whole. What is less readily apparent is the number of villages that remained isolated from the plague, insulated by distance from their neighbors. The practice of quarantining infected areas became general, usually with considerable success, and postmedieval outbreaks rarely spread far. We can, for example, assume that in thinly populated eastern Europe, the incidence of plague was only sporadic, and the overall death rate relatively low. It would be wrong to

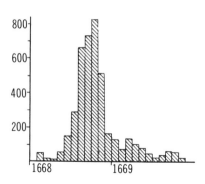

7.11. Plague deaths at Brussels, 1668–69. This outbreak was a continuation of that in London and was the last significant outbreak in northwest Europe.

extrapolate from known areas of high mortality to the rest of the population, and estimates of 50 percent mortality are grossly misleading. On the other hand, Shrewsbury's claim that in Britain "the national death-toll from the Great Pestilence did not exceed a twentieth of the population" may be somewhat conservative.[36]

No less important than the gross totals of fatalities were the age groups most at risk. A high death rate among the aged would have produced an immediate drop in population but would have had little long-term effect, but among the young it would have gravely reduced the size of the next generation. The plague, we are told, struck at young and old, and the French chronicler Jean de Venette even claimed that the young suffered the most severely.[37] On the other hand, the high mortality left many tenements vacant in every community that was stricken, and this, in turn, permitted the young to inherit and to set up home at an earlier age than they might otherwise have done. It was the repeated hammer blows of the plague throughout the fifteenth and sixteenth centuries that prevented the population from recovering in any significant fashion. The steady rise in population in western Europe *after* the last epidemic is not proof that it was the plague that had held it down, but it suggests that the pestilence was a significant factor (fig. 7.3).

The plague was far from being the only source of epidemic disease, but it was the most important. Leprosy, a disorder of the nerve centers leading to lesions and deformities, was feared almost as much as the plague itself. It was probably spread by direct contact, and medieval people were probably correct in founding leper houses and isolating lepers from the rest of the community, even though they were likely to diagnose any skin infection, even acne, as leprosy.[38] In England, no leper houses survived the Middle Ages, and in France those that remained were closed by Louis XIV—evidence, if any were needed, that leprosy as popularly conceived had disappeared.

Typhus was probably a more significant disease from the demographic point of view, and its association with famine conditions is more clearly demonstrable. Its vector was the body louse, and the most important preventives were soap, water, and clean clothing. Famine conditions may have weakened human resistance to its microorganism, but its spread was more likely to have been hastened by the tendency under such conditions for people to huddle together for warmth and shelter.[39] It was particularly likely to infect soldiers, who had little opportunity to wash or change their clothing, and also the population of prisons; hence its alternative names, trench and gaol fever. It became progressively a disease of the poorer classes and survived until recently in the slum quarters of the great cities.

The greater mobility and more frequent contacts that characterized Europeans from the sixteenth century brought with them a train of new diseases. One of the first to appear was syphilis. There was no indisputable case of the disease before Columbus's return from the New World, and the first known epidemic was that which decimated the army of the French King Charles VIII before Naples in 1494. It was then spread across Europe, chiefly by soldiers who had served in the Italian Wars. It acted like a new disease attacking a virgin population, which lends some support to the ancient view that it came to Europe from the Americas in the ships of Columbus, a suggestion that has been strongly criticized. It soon lost its epidemic character, and, though causing much distress, has had little demographic impact.

The same could not be said of smallpox. The earliest indisputable references to it occurred in the first decades of the sixteenth century, when the name "small" pox was given to it to distinguish it from the "great" pox, or syphilis. By the end of the sixteenth century it was second only to plague as an epidemic disease, and it remained one of the most lethal of all human illnesses into the nineteenth century. Smallpox was often mentioned in diaries and other records, and in Josselin's diary of 1616–83 it appears in sheer malignancy to share the honors with bubonic plague.[40] Epidemics were frequent throughout the seventeenth and eighteenth centuries, until in the closing years of the latter a remedy was found. It was a person-to-person disease—there was no vector other than an infected human being—and it had no seasonal rhythm like typhus and the plague. Only lack of human contact was a certain preventative. The more frequently people met, the more likely was it to be transmitted. On the other hand, anyone who had had it and had recovered thereby acquired a lasting immunity. This characteristic of smallpox proved ultimately to be the means of halting its progress.

In 1717, that intrepid Englishwoman Lady Mary Wortley Montagu wrote from Constantinople, where her husband was British ambassador to the Porte, that smallpox, "so fatal and so general amongst us" in England, "is here entirely harmless." This, she explained, was due to the practice of "engrafting," a process of infecting a person with pus drawn from someone suffering from the smallpox. The mild dose of the disease that resulted gave immunity from the real thing. Lady Mary was convinced of the efficacy of the procedure, and through her influence, inoculation became common in England. The overseers of the poor recorded small payments for inoculating paupers, but in many cases expenditure on their subsequent burial showed that inoculation was not always as safe as Lady Mary had supposed. Indeed, an entry in a parish register in the late eighteenth century claimed that a victim of the disease had died of smallpox "in the ordinary way, not as a result of inoculation."

The horrors of smallpox provoked a vast literature and not a little active research. Among those who studied the disease was Edward Jenner, a physician living in Gloucestershire, England. He noted that those whose daily business it was to deal with cattle never developed smallpox, and he linked this with the fact that cattle themselves were liable to a poxlike disease, which came to be known as "cowpox." He experimented with inoculating a boy with matter from the postules of an infected cow on the assumption that the mild infection that resulted would give immunity to smallpox itself. He was proved correct. The new process of vaccination—the name itself derives from *vacca,* a cow—was adopted quickly and within a generation displaced the older and less satisfactory method of inoculation. The relative importance of both inoculation and vaccination in reducing mortality has been a matter of controversy.[41] On the one hand, inoculation has been claimed as the most important single factor in the eighteenth-century population increase in the west; on the other, it has been argued that the successful practice of vaccination accounted for only a minute part of the total reduction in mortality in the century that followed.[42] It seems that both arguments are probably exaggerated. Whatever may be said of the success of inoculation—and it was far from complete—Edward Jenner's discovery marked a significant improvement and greatly reduced the sum total of human suffering. The Scandinavian governments made vaccination compulsory, and though it is impossible to separate the effects of vaccination from those resulting from other medical and environmental changes, it does seem that it played a very positive role.

If the prevailing epidemic disease of the sixteenth and seventeenth centuries was the bubonic plague, and that of the eighteenth, smallpox, "the classic epidemic disease of the nineteenth" was cholera. Its impact was frightening; its consequences, profound. It had long been endemic in southern Asia, and there were numerous instances of its appearance in Europe before the nineteenth century, brought usually by ships from India or the Middle East, but it failed each time to gain a firm grip. It was spread through human excreta and acquired through drinking contaminated water. The proper conditions for its spread just happened not to have been achieved on a sufficient scale before the 1830s for the disease to reach epidemic proportions. But in the 1820s it reached Russia and was distributed by the soldiery during the Polish War of 1830–31.[43] Mortality was very high, especially in the crowded quarters of east European cities, where ghettoes are said to have suffered particularly severely. It was carried by sea from Russian ports to western Europe, and overland into central Europe and the Balkans. In 1831 it appeared in England, by 1832 in the Low Countries, in 1834 in Spain and Portugal, in 1835 in northern Italy, by the next year in Rome, and in 1837 it reached Palermo in Sicily. It was most severe in the cities. In Paris mortality doubled during the cholera epidemic. By 1838 the first epidemic was over, but others, more localized in their occurrence, were to follow until the end of the century. The behavior of cholera was thus broadly similar to that of plague in 1348–51.

Cholera was vaguely associated in people's minds with dirt and congested housing, and it was observed that serious outbreaks were almost always urban. The disease was spread along the rivers, for the simple reason that they received the discharge from sewers and cesspits. In France, it was said, the washerwomen who did their laundry along the river's banks were most affected by it. The mounting evidence clearly pointed to contaminated water as the chief vector of the disease. Nevertheless, it was not until September 1854 that Dr. John Snow plotted on a map the location of cases of the disease during the short-lived Soho (London) epidemic. They formed a cluster centering on a pump in Broad Street, from which the district was supplied with water (fig. 7.12). This was the culprit. An infected person had brought the pathogen to the area and had proceeded to infect others by way of a cesspit and a pump that supplied drinking water. The Broad Street pump was closed and this particular outbreak ended. But the situation

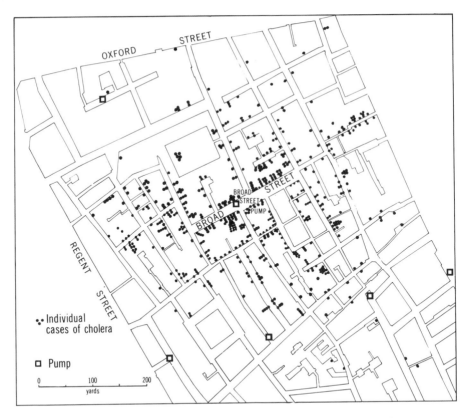

7.12. The Broad Street pump and its relation to the cholera epidemic of the mid-nineteenth century in London. (After J. Snow, *Snow on Cholera* [New York, 1936].)

was not—indeed, could not be—remedied, until a piped water supply was made available from an area safe from contamination. This was the lesson for all European cities, though some were remarkably slow to learn it: that a piped water supply very greatly reduced the incidence of cholera, dysentery, typhoid, and a number of other communicable diseases.

By the end of the nineteenth century, most epidemic diseases had been conquered in Europe, if not also in the rest of the world, and the death rate had dropped from twenty-five to forty per thousand of population to levels closer to fifteen or twenty. Of course there were diseases that were not significantly reduced: diseases of the heart and lungs, kidneys, and other organs, but these were not epidemic diseases. They had accounted for a level of deaths that may have varied between winter and summer but probably did not change greatly from one year to another. If one could calculate the probability of dying from plague, or smallpox, or cholera, the odds would probably have been high in the later Middle Ages and early modern times. But they would have gradually diminished until by 1900 the chances were almost nil in western Europe and low in eastern and southern. The probability of dying from heart disease, or of diseases of the respiratory and digestive tract, or of cancer increased proportionately, and tuberculosis became one of the more significant causes of death during the nineteenth century.[44] It was spread from person to person, but its development was encouraged by damp, congested, and unventilated conditions. The slums of the growing industrial cities of the nineteenth century were ideal for its propagation. Tuberculosis came to be feared almost as much as plague and smallpox had been, and during the nineteenth century it may have accounted for a higher proportion of deaths than any other disease. It was a wasting disease, "Where youth grows pale, and spectre-thin, and dies," and must have left millions too enfeebled to work. Late in the nineteenth century the incidence of tuberculosis began to decline, owing in large measure to the improvement of the environment. During the same period pneumonia, measles, diphtheria, and scarlet fever, which had taken the place of epidemic diseases as the great killers, themselves began to decline in importance. By the mid-twentieth century, heart disease, stroke, and cancer were left as the most important causes of death.

This radical change in the pattern of death can have resulted only from improved medicine or from environmental change, and the relative importance of these factors has been the subject of vigorous controversy. Medical research could have had little impact on disease until the nature of infection had been discovered, and this did not occur until the last quarter of the nineteenth century. Of course, progress had been made empirically. First inoculation against smallpox and then Jenner's discovery of vaccination in 1796 were of immense importance in lowering mortality, but they sprang from empirical observation, and even after his discovery had been widely adopted, Jenner was no nearer an understanding of the nature of infection and of the antibodies that fought it. Snow's identification of the Broad Street pump as the source of the Soho cholera epidemic of 1851 was again empirical, and the fact that it came to be recognized that a supply of pure water was a precondition of better health told nothing of the nature of disease.

Not until Pasteur and Koch, in the 1880s, succeeded in isolating certain bacteria, particularly those of tuberculosis and hydrophobia, was the nature of infection made clear. This discovery at once led to the search—highly successful in most instances—for the means of fighting the disease in question. The result was a sharp drop in mortality from a broad range of infectious diseases. This change marks the transition from an age of medical empiricism to one of science. The empiricism of Jenner and Snow had been important in reducing the incidence of disease and its resulting mortality. But the reduction in mortality, as also in morbidity, or sickness, during the first half or two-thirds of the nineteenth century must be ascribed by and large to environmental change.

Before, however, we turn to these changes in the physical environment in which people lived, we must look briefly at three other factors in mortality. It is known, as a result of modern studies of infection, that if a disease has been overcome, a period of immunity from reinfection follows. This phenomenon was, of course, the scientific basis of both inoculation and vaccination against smallpox. It was this acquired immunity which prevented some epidemics from being even more disastrous than in fact they were, and provided a short respite from them during which the population could recover. A person could, in fact, be reinfected only after this acquired immunity had worn off, and in some instances it lasted for life.

A second consideration is the fact that the pathogens themselves may undergo mutations and thus assume new forms against which acquired immunity is of no avail.

The influenza virus, for example, appears to be one that is particularly susceptible to such mutations. Lastly, new infections against which there can be no immunity have spread from the disease pools of Africa and Asia. Syphilis may have been among them. The plague and cholera certainly were, and also lasa and marburg fevers and a number of tropical diseases. Most recently, we have seen the spread of AIDS, perhaps the most significant of all because it attacks the immune system. In the past such "invaders" struck at a virgin population that had no protection against them. In recent times medical research has at once set about the task of identifying the pathogen, and then of finding the means to destroy it.

Health and the Material Environment

The conquest of epidemic disease before the late eighteenth century, when the practice of vaccination was first adopted, thus seems to have been largely, if not entirely, the consequence of environmental improvement. And, though medical developments played an increasingly significant role in the nineteenth century, the continued improvement of diet, housing, sanitation, and water-supply remained of great importance. For the purposes of this discussion, environmental factors are grouped under the four heads housing, water supply and sanitation, personal hygiene, and diet.

The development of housing has been examined in chapters 4 and 6. The extent of the improvement is apparent. Homes became more spacious; the number of rooms increased, allowing for greater privacy and family life. Separate kitchens began to be built, thus removing the preparation of meals from the living room, and the construction of ovens facilitated the baking of bread and freed people from the eternal diet of thin gruel. These developments improved the comforts and conveniences of life. They did not necessarily contribute to a reduction in mortality or to halting the spread of disease. At the same time, however, methods of construction improved. Wooden or framed buildings were placed on stone footings, which served in some measure as a damp course. The floors of the cottage ceased to be of beaten earth and began to be covered with slabs of cut stone. Windows were made larger and were closed not with wooden shutters, which never succeeded in excluding the draft, but with small panes of glass leaded together.

These changes in their totality revolutionized domestic housing, but they came slowly and by small increments. Furthermore, they were initiated in the most advanced areas of the continent and were first adopted only by the rich, who could afford to pay for them. The progression of new standards of comfort to other classes was very slow. Long before the end of the Middle Ages these improvements had all been adopted in the homes of the gentry and in the town houses of merchants and well-to-do craftsmen in western and southern Europe. They were slower in spreading to eastern and northern. From the later Middle Ages these classes began to live in considerable comfort. The wealthiest of them had the living rooms of their homes paneled with oak or wainscot and hung with tapestries. Floors were paved with stone flags or "planched" with wood. The elimination of wattle and daub and of timber framing set directly in the earth meant that there were fewer places for rats and mice to hide and for insects to breed. The progress of flooring in stone or wood was an important factor in eliminating sources of infection. The "terriers," or surveys of church possessions, that were compiled in Britain in the seventeenth and eighteenth centuries, show how these new fashions were slowly creeping downward from the great house to the rectory or parson's house. In the latter, earthen floors, damp and vermin infested, were only slowly giving way to wood and stone. Often the parsonage had but one ground-floor room planched; the rest were of earth. But the cartoons of Rowlandson and Hogarth of a somewhat later date invariably show the floors decently boarded or flagged. The interiors shown in Dutch and Italian paintings of the sixteenth and later centuries—most of them of middle-class homes—seem always to have been of wood or stone. But such refinements were not adopted in the cottages of the rural proletariat before the nineteenth century and in parts of eastern and southeastern Europe not before the twentieth.

Closely related to the quality of housing was the provision of toilets and the means of sanitation, for it was through human excreta that a number of diseases were propagated. Little provision was made in rural areas before the twentieth century, and, from the strictly medical point of view, little may have been needed. The wide spaces of the countryside made it relatively easy to keep the water supply free from contamination. The situation was far more difficult and dangerous in urban areas, and the more congested a city was, the more difficult it was to avoid the spread of disease.

A toilet with a sealed drain leading either to a public sewer or a private cesspit is a necessity in a modern house. Yet this urgent demand for sanitation is of recent origin. Until late in the nineteenth century that most essential of sanitary refinements, the water closet, was known only in the houses of the rich. In the towns there were public toilets—batteries of them, as there had been in Roman cities—built out over rivers or cesspits. In London, in the later Middle Ages, there were at least sixteen such public toilets. But those who had the space and could afford it dug private cesspits, as deep as practicable and lined with masonry where possible. A rough wooden seat was fitted above them, and there are instances of those using them being drowned when the rotting seat and floor collapsed into the pit below. As a general rule, however, cesspits were cleansed at intervals, and their contents, as in both Paris and London, were taken to fertilize the surrounding fields.[45] The use of cesspits continued in some European cities, in Paris for example, till late in the nineteenth century. They remained a source of infection; flies and other insects bred in them, and on a hot summer's day the stench became unbearable.

Closely related to the question of sanitation was that of water supply and personal hygiene. Water for drinking, cooking, and every other purpose had at first been taken from springs, wells, or the nearest river. Much was contaminated, and the degree of pollution of the more readily available sources increased steadily through the Middle Ages. Those who admired the sparkle of well water could not have known that the minute air bubbles derived from the bacteriological decay of organic matter. Rivers were the universal repository of rural and urban waste, so that only mountain streams remained wholly uncontaminated. Cities were the most serious sources of contamination. Whatever might have been required by city ordinances—and they were often both particular and precise in this respect—it was quite impossible to restrain the tanner and the butcher from disposing of their noisome and offensive waste in the easiest way possible. It was enacted in some instances that water be drawn from a river upstream of a city, and that waste be deposited downstream, without, of course, any thought for the health and well-being of the next settlement. Whether or not cesspits were used, human excreta ultimately reached the river.[46] Figure 7.13 shows how cholera was spread along

7.13. The spread of cholera in England, 1831–32. (After M. Howe, *Man, Environment and Disease in Britain* [Harmondsworth, 1976].)

the more important rivers of Great Britain because their water was used for domestic purposes. Cholera was conquered when a piped supply of water from a secure source was made available. Statistics are not available to show what other diseases were reduced or eliminated by the improved water supply, but it requires no great perspicacity to know that dysentery, typhoid, scarlet fever, and many others must have been greatly reduced.

The role of diet—the adequacy and the composition of food—in the population increase of modern times has been fiercely debated. To Malthus its importance was clear. Food shortages, arising from overpopulation, were a positive check on further growth. In the final analysis, he must be proved correct: without food there could be no life. But, on the other hand, it cannot be disputed that the "high death rates of the past were due primarily to disease rather than to starvation alone."[47] The question at issue is, then, whether and to what extent the inadequacies and insufficiencies of diet were a predisposing condition; whether they made morbidity and mortality more likely. " . . . the slow growth of the human population before the eighteenth century," wrote Thomas McKeown, "was due mainly to lack of food, and the rapid increase from that time resulted largely from improved nutrition. The influence of food on population size in the historical period was determined essentially by the relation between nutritional state and response to infectious disease."[48] This is, indeed, a strong statement. We are invited to believe, to revert to a question raised earlier, that the severity of the plague of 1349 was in some way due to the shortages that had arisen during the previous generation, or that the cholera epidemic of the 1830s can be ascribed in part to the malnutrition of the urban poor.

The study of the role of mal- and undernutrition in the past is bedeviled by the lack not of mortality statistics but of data on the causes of death. An important reason for the emphasis given to plague and smallpox in studies of morbidity and mortality is that they are diseases that could be readily diagnosed in a prescientific age. It is unlikely that, in this respect, many mistakes were made. But it has already been shown that one must suspect most other diagnoses, or, at least, one should assume that familiar medical terms held different meanings to those who used them in the past.

Food shortage is itself a somewhat elastic term. One must distinguish between belt-tightening and famine conditions, difficult though this might be. In a self-sufficing rural community there are no standards against which to measure the adequacy or inadequacy of food supply. In cities, where most people have to buy their food, price is a measure of scarcity and has been used by Appleby to relate shortage of food to disease. "We can find," he wrote, "little correlation between high bread prices and plague epidemics in London."[49] There were grave food shortages without succeeding epidemics, and, conversely, epidemics without shortages as measured by the price of breadgrains. The incidence of smallpox also shows no correlation with the price of bread. Appleby's conclusion is that "it was possible for disease to have been extremely virulent . . . despite relatively low population density and relatively good diet." "The finest August that anyone could remember," wrote the anonymous Parisian diarist, "both grain and vegetable harvests were very good, but the death-rate from plague and from epidemics was dreadful," the worst "since the great mortality of 1348."[50]

But one must beware of regarding disease as a wholly autonomous factor in mortality and population growth. It is now known that some of the diseases that were not susceptible to easy diagnosis in the past were strongly influenced by diet. Tuberculosis, which, as has been seen, was a very significant cause of death in the nineteenth century, was highly sensitive to food intake, and there is good reason to think that nutrition contributed significantly to bronchitis, emphysema, and other pulmonary complaints. It is important also to distinguish between mortality and morbidity. For the latter there are no statistics before the recent past, and even for the present they are far from satisfactory. But it is part of our received wisdom that a person who is adequately fed is less prone to infection than one who is not. An adequate intake of vitamins and trace elements was more a matter of luck than of judgment, and their lack must in all places and at all times have been a source of ill health if not of disease. The importance of carbohydrates, the chief source of calories, and of protein, on the other hand, has always been more apparent, and when we speak of shortages, it is these foods that we usually have in mind. A case in point is amenorrhea. This is the diminished fertility of women suffering from an acute shortage of food, which may in fact fall far short of famine. There is said to be abundant evidence that amenorrhea is an important factor in the drop in the number of conceptions following food crises.[51] Though it may be difficult to prove statistically, there appears to be a significant relationship between the improvement of human diet and the general level of health. Higher levels of nutrition were, it is claimed, the most important factor in the general decline in mortality and increase in longevity in the nineteenth century.

A difficulty in such general discussions of health, mortality, and food supply is that we tend to generalize for a broad area, to conflate urban with rural conditions, when there may have been, especially in the nineteenth century, sharp differences between them. To some extent the available statistics leave little alternative. It is reasonable to suppose that food supply was likely to be both more adequate and better balanced in rural areas than in urban, and, as a general rule, the worst of material living conditions were to be found in the growing cities. It is to these conditions that our attention must now be turned.

Chapter 8

THE URBAN WAY OF LIFE

The city-community is a multitude of men united by a bond of association, so called from the citizens . . . the actual inhabitants of
the city.

—Isidore of Seville

Classical civilization was founded upon the city. Each city was the focal
point, the central place of its local area, where people could meet and
conduct their business and where they were entertained with spectacles and plays. There
was no real barrier—political, administrative, social, or psychological—between town
and country. Together they made up the *civitas*, the city region. The city was not
primarily a place where manufacturing and commerce were carried on, though industry
was demonstrably important in many cities such as Pompeii. Cities were the administrative, cultural, and social centers of their regions, and city regions were the building
blocks of which the Roman Empire was made. These regions were administratively
dependent on their central cities, and with their taxes they contributed to its maintenance and beautification. The city was supported financially by its region, for most had
little by way of basic activity of their own, just as Rome itself was supported by all the
civitates of the empire. Urbanism in this sense never spread far beyond the boundaries of
the empire and decayed during its later centuries. The evidence points to a decline in the
urban population and to an unwillingness to invest in public buildings in the central
place. Local landowners and farmers abandoned their town residences and retreated to
their rural estates and farms, which they developed where possible into self-contained
and self-sufficing entities. This retreat to the countryside was never complete. Cities
around the Mediterranean litoral, those of Italy in particular, remained populous, but in
these areas the roots of urbanism went much deeper than in the more northerly
provinces of the empire. But even in the latter, few cities were ever completely abandoned. All declined, but most appear to have retained a small and perhaps mainly

agricultural population. Their public buildings crumbled, their water supply systems silted, and the amenities that distinguished city life from that of a village were gradually eroded. And with the decay of the city, political control passed to the rural areas.

The Classical Heritage

The walls hastily thrown around cities in the later years of the empire gave them no protection from internal decay and but little from barbarian invaders. An Anglo-Saxon poem described a ruined and abandoned city, probably Bath:

> the work of giants moldereth away.
> Its roofs are breaking and falling; its towers crumble in
> ruin. Plundered those walls with grated doors—their walls
> white with frost. Its battered ramparts are shorn
> ruined, all undermined by eating age.[1]

In the fifth century, Sidonius Apollinaris wrote to a friend from, as he put it, "within the narrow enclosure of half-burned and ruined walls, with terror of war at the gates." Evidently the city of Clermont, of which he was bishop, was not wholly abandoned, but urban life, as classical people conceived it, had ended. Most Roman cities outside Italy may have been reduced to the size and functions of a village, but life continued. There were few Roman cities that did not revive and again become centers of population and of civilized life, but the function of the medieval and modern city differed significantly from that of the urban central place of Greek and Roman times. Only in its site and occasionally its street plan was the medieval and modern city heir to the Roman.

The barbarian kingdoms that succeeded to the provinces of the Roman Empire had no need for cities. Their kings and chieftains were mobile, moving from one estate to another, with their retinue of soldiers and servants. Outside Italy and the Byzantine Empire the seat of authority no longer lay within the walls of a city. It was in the countryside, in the rural palaces of petty kings. Even Charlemagne spent much of his time moving from one estate to another. He had his favorite palaces—at Ingelheim, Nijmegen, Aachen—but he had no capital in the later sense of the word. The leaders in this warlike and barbaric society acquired land, either by seizure or by grant from their ruler. This was the only form of wealth, apart from booty gained in war, that they could appreciate, and in general they lived on their rural estates. They owed loyalty and some form of service to their leaders, who were generally conceived as having given them their land, and they in turn demanded service and loyalty from those who inhabited and cultivated it. Such was the feudal pyramid that evolved during the earlier centuries of the Middle Ages, with the king at the summit and the broad mass of unfree peasants at its base, all held together by bonds of loyalty and mutual obligation. There was no room for the city in this feudal world-view. It could not be fitted into its self-contained system, nor was there much need for the services that it could furnish. Yet cities continued throughout the feudal centuries to be inhabited, even to grow in size and number, until Europe became again a continent of cities. But it was a different kind of urbanism that grew and prospered during the Middle Ages.

The physical remains of the classical cities were still present during the feudal centuries. People could admire them or build their superstitions around them. They used their ruins as quarries, and if early medieval people built in brick, as some of them did, they tore it from the structure of demolished Roman buildings. The one thing they did not do was to understand them.

Two threads linked medieval urban development with that of the Roman Empire: the church and the merchant class. The Christian church was from its earliest days an urban institution. Its first cells were in cities, and when, in A.D. 323 under Constantine, it became the official religion of the empire, its churches were built beside the forum and its bishops rivaled in power and prestige the civilian officials. The latter ceased to function, at least in the Western Empire, during the fifth century, but the bishop remained the local representative of the eternal church. And as barbarian kingdoms one by one adopted Christianity, so the bishop's authority was extended and confirmed throughout the city region, which became, in fact, his diocese. This continuity from the Roman civil jurisdiction to the medieval religious can be demonstrated in most parts of the empire, but nowhere more clearly than in Rome itself. Here the popes were heirs to the emperors, in part because they had tampered with the latter's last will and testament; in part because they had remained when others had fled. "The Papacy," wrote Thomas Hobbes, "is not other than the Ghost of the deceased Roman Empire, sitting crowned upon the grave thereof."[2] The bishop's church, his *cathedra* or seat, was established near the city center, where, indeed, it remains today. Pilgrims came to pray there, especially if the place could establish a link with the apostles or had managed to acquire a holy and miracle-working relic. And traders came to satisfy the needs of the church and its servants and to make what profit they could from the business of pilgrimage.

Urban Rebirth

The walls that the Romans had cast around most of their cities continued to provide some protection for those living within. Others such as merchants, who had goods to protect, might seek the security of the town, and doubtless some peasants who cultivated the surrounding fields chose to live within its walls. It was the merchant who formed the second thread in the continuity of urban life. No community could be entirely self-sufficing. There was always something—salt, weapons, metal goods, garments—that was wanted from beyond its boundaries. There were people like Priscus the Jew, who served as a kind of agent for King Chilperic of the Franks, "whom he helped . . . in the purchase of precious things."[3] Slaves seized in frontier wars against the "Slavs" and booty looted by Norse raiders all passed into the hands of traders and nourished the channels of a small but growing commerce.

Places that had never felt the hand of Rome developed into trading settlements, roughly fortified with palisade and ditch. Small, protected merchants' towns were established near the Rhine mouth, along the coasts of northern Europe, and on the eastern frontier of Germany against the Slavs. Some disappeared, but others became the nuclei of important medieval and modern cities.

There were other reasons for the continued use of urbanlike settlements during the Dark Ages. The period of barbarian invasions was followed by one of great insecurity. Warfare within Europe and the continuing danger of invasion from without were a threat to life and property. Even those who had no need to live in cities nevertheless felt the need for protection, and there is good reason to think that over much of Europe, Roman towns and even earthwork enclosures of the Iron Age served as places of refuge. The twelfth-century chronicler Helmold described how in Holstein the "people came out of the stronghold in which they were keeping themselves shut up for fear of the wars. And they returned each one to his own village or holding, and they rebuilt houses and churches long in ruins because of the storms of the wars."[4] Over much of east central Europe, such fortifications were being erected, the *grody* and *hrady* of the Slavs and *Burgwalle* of the Germans. Most were only a few acres in extent—large enough to hold the rural population of the surrounding districts, yet small enough to be defended. They seem to have had permanent structures for the storage of weapons, as well as space for farm animals driven there for safety. In Anglo-Saxon England this practice was more highly organized. A document of the early tenth century, known to posterity as the *Burghal Hidage,* lists more than thirty of these refuges—several of them sites of Roman towns—together with an indication of the area for which each was to serve as a place of safety. Many of the *burhs* listed here, together with those which are known from other sources, had been hastily created on naturally defended sites to serve as places of refuge. A few were more carefully planned and constructed. There were four in southern Britain—Wallingford, Oxford, Cricklade, and Wareham—which had been laid out with a pattern of straight streets, intersecting at right angles. Do we have here a conscious imitation of a Roman city?

These places were not towns, but they had the potential of developing into towns. The towns of the later Middle Ages were the result of the convergence of many lines of development: the survival of Roman towns, the formation of merchants' settlements, and the creation of places of refuge in troubled times. None of these functions would have seemed important to the Romans. These places lacked that intimacy between central place and city region which was the chief characteristic of both Roman *civitas* and Greek *polis,* and it is difficult to see how, in an age of increasing feudal control of the land, this relationship could have been revived or perpetuated. The separation of town from country was of the essence of feudalism.

To all this the cities of Italy, of Provence, and of some other parts of the Mediterranean basin formed a partial exception. They declined in size. Some decayed to the point of becoming villages; a very few even disappeared. But in most there was a continuity of urban life from the Roman period to the high Middle Ages. Their old relationship to their surrounding territories either was preserved or reasserted itself. City regions never passed wholly under feudal control, as they did north of the Alps. Castles were built in the open country, but the landowning classes or feudal aristocracy tended to live in the cities. This pattern, on the one hand, developed in the nobility a very different attitude toward trade, commerce, and the crafts from that shown in the north. In Mediterranean Europe the aristocracy engaged in trade. In the north they treated it with disdain, tolerating it only because it could be useful or profitable to them. In the former, the presence of the nobility tended to introduce to the city the feuding that characterized the feudal aristocracy everywhere. Medieval cities in southern Europe bristled with tall towers that were the strong points in this internal strife. These *turri* survive at Bologna and San Gimignano, and they were once numerous in many other cities. The kind of warfare waged through the streets between their occupants is immortalized in the feud of Montagues and Capulets.

The social consequences of this difference in the relationship of town and country north and south of the Alps is aptly illustrated by the remark made by Fra Salimbene as he watched the progress of the French king Louis IX through the town of Sens. The women of the town who turned out to see him pass seemed, he wrote, "for the most part like handmaids: yet, if the king had passed through Pisa or Bologna [in Italy], the whole flower of the ladies of those cities would have gone out to meet him. Then I remembered that this is indeed the custom of the French; for in France it is the burgesses *only* who dwell in the cities, whereas the knights and noble ladies dwell in the villages and on their estates." And not only in France; throughout northern Europe the landowning aristocracy lived in castles and palaces on the land that they controlled.

Not until the seventeenth century did this situation begin to change, with the building of urban palaces for the richer and more powerful of the nobility. By this time governmental functions had become concentrated in the capital. There the king or prince established his principal residence, and around it the nobles gathered to bask in the sunshine of royal favor or to vie for royal patronage. London, Paris, Vienna, Warsaw each witnessed the building of these aristocratic homes. This development marked a profound change in their behavioral pattern. The great landed families of Poland, the Potockis, the Branickis, and others, forsook their estates in the Ukraine, White Russia, and Lithuania and rivaled one another in the splendor and luxury of their living in the great palaces that they built in Warsaw. The same happened in almost every European capital city. On a humbler scale the squirearchy began to acquire town houses, smaller and less sumptuous than the palaces of the nobility, in whatever town lay nearest to them. They were attracted by the developing social life of the towns, by opportunities for trade, and by the prospect of participating in political life. In these ways the city began to reassert itself as a cultural and social center, which indeed it has since remained.

The town or city is extraordinarily difficult to define, however clear may be most people's concept of it. This is because it has always served a number of functions, whose relative importance has changed from age to age and from one place to another. Most, however, would agree that it is a relatively large and closely built settlement; that it is larger than a village, with a population that runs to thousands rather than hundreds; and that, although it may carry on small-scale agriculture, its basic functions lie in commerce, the crafts, and the whole range of tertiary activities, from education to transportation and public administration. But the town, as it struggled into existence in the early Middle Ages, was more than this. It was a legal entity. It had rights and privileges solemnly conferred on it by a grant or charter. It needed such protection, for it had been born into a hostile feudal world that had little understanding of or appreciation for what it stood for. There are three criteria by which we are accustomed to judge a city or town: its size, its function, and its legal status, and of these the last was by far the most important in the early stages of growth. The guarantee that it provided was a necessary condition of the others. Even the city that had survived from the Roman period found it desirable to obtain a charter, a written guarantee that its privileges were legally held and could not be extinguished by the harsh realities of this rough, feudal world. Even so, the grant of a charter and the creation of a *legal* borough was no guarantee that it would grow and flourish and become a town in any other sense. Europe is strewn with towns that were in this sense stillborn.

What, then, were the privileges that a city thus acquired and that distinguished it from a village? It was excepted from the customs and practices of feudal landholding. Its citizens became free to go and come as they wished, to practice trade, to carry on their crafts, to marry and build a home. They did not thereby cease to owe obligations to the lord who enfranchised them, but these debts were precise and limited, consisting commonly of an annual payment that could not be increased. City residents ceased, in most respects, to be subject to their lord's court; a token appearance and a small payment were all that was expected of them. Instead, they had a court of their own in which they could settle the disputes that arose among them. They could regulate their own affairs, and the craftsmen and traders among them were encouraged to form a gild to supervise their activities and to maintain standards. An essential privilege of the incipient town was that of holding a weekly market and commonly a yearly or even twice- or thrice-yearly fair. The market was where the community conducted much of its business; it bought agricultural produce from the rural folk and in return sold them the products of local crafts. The fairs, which were held less frequently, attracted traders from greater distances. They brought goods unobtainable locally—quality cloth, decorative and luxury goods of all kinds. Trade was one of the most vulnerable activities in a feudal society, and was difficult, almost impossible, to carry on without some kind of guarantee of protection.

It must not be assumed that the lord or king who made such far-reaching concessions expected nothing in return. He looked for a steady revenue from the rents that his town provided and from tolls levied on market and fair. He may also have seen in his proprietary town a means of acquiring both the products of the local craftsmen and exotic goods brought by traders from afar. One thing did not enter his head. He never conceived of himself as leading or furthering a revolution that would in time create a middle class, increase the volume of production and trade, raise material standards, and destroy the feudal order.

Urban Living

The urban revolution—if we can describe as revolutionary a process as slow as the creation of a system of cities and towns—has been a fact of incalculable importance for human welfare. On the one hand, the city is an efficient mode of settlement because it reduces "the friction of space." It allows people to live close to their market and to their place of work. It encourages specialization and, because of the size of its market, it makes large-scale production economic. On the other hand, urban living created problems unknown in the countryside, problems of water supply, of sanitation and street cleaning, of traffic, fire, and tall, unstable buildings. Feeding an urban population could not altogether be left to market forces operating for a day each week. A food supply had to be organized; distant sources had to be tapped, and a class of food merchants, *blattiers* or corn jobbers, had to be developed.[5] The crowding of people into a confined space increased the frequency of human contact and the speed with which epidemic disease was spread. Disease might disappear in the loneliness of the countryside for lack of human contacts, but in the city it was more likely to become endemic. It was not that the rural cottage was cleaner and more sanitary than the urban home; only that it enjoyed the insulation, the quarantine, provided by space.

The problems of urban living sometimes brought their own solutions. Rural dwellers might never have introduced a piped water supply and a satisfactory mode of disposing of sewage, because these problems rarely seemed important enough to challenge them.

In cities, however, the significance of water supply and sewage disposal was incalculable. Their influence on health could not be disguised even though the processes by which they operated were not known. Thus it was that innovations came first to the cities and only subsequently were they adopted in rural areas, where their advantages were perhaps more marginal. Until late in the nineteenth century, death rates remained higher, often significantly higher, in cities than in rural areas, and the larger the city, the higher the death rate was likely to be. A consequence of this was that it was rare for an urban population to be able to reproduce itself. Without a steady movement from the countryside, urban population in almost every instance would have declined; without a massive immigration, cities could not have grown. Cities were the source of innovation; they were also the centers where disease pools survived longest and from which at intervals the pathogens spread to infect the surrounding countryside.

Much as the feudal classes might distrust the urban bourgeoisie, the usefulness of the latter was without question, and territorial lords and princes vied with one another to found cities. There was already a thin scatter of urban foundations. But to them was added another category, the "planted" town. The feudal lords encouraged the foundation of towns, laid out their street plan, endowed them with a church, sometimes also with a monastery, and collected the rents and tolls that arose. It was a tacit admission that free men in pursuit of their own profit would do more for their lords than all the resentful serfs bound to the soil.

A Flemish chronicler reconstructed the foundation of the city of Bruges. Its nucleus was the castle, now vanished, of the Counts of Flanders:

> In order to satisfy the needs of the castle folk, there began to throng before (the count's) gate near the castle bridge traders and merchants selling costly goods, then inn-keepers to feed and house those doing business with the prince . . . ; they built houses and set up inns where those who could not be put up at the castle were accommodated. . . . The houses increased to such an extent that there soon grew up a large town which in the common speech of the lower classes is still called "Bridge," for Bruges means "bridge" in their patois.[6]

This description was written in the fourteenth century, but it related to events some three centuries earlier. It was the kind of thing that the chronicler had seen happening over all of Europe, except in parts of the Mediterranean basin, where there was little scope for further urban foundation. But not every incipient town, clustered before the gate of a castle or of a monastery—for the monks were no less eager to profit from urban life than the lay lords—was to grow into a city of the size and importance of Bruges. That city was unusually favored with opportunities for trade, and it expanded to become the largest commercial emporium in northwestern Europe. Many grew to be towns of only a few hundred people, retaining close links with the agriculture of the surrounding fields. Others were stillborn. The lord granted a charter of liberties and allocated space for a town to be planted and to grow. Doubtless he advertised the fact, appealing for settlers to come and take up burgage lots within the town at the customary rent and to establish a weekly market. But very few came, and the borough never took off. Nothing fails like failure. In the absence of market and craft industries, the settlement reverted to its agricultural origins. Its charter became a meaningless curiosity and was forgotten.

One cannot say how many such *villes manquées* there may have been—hundreds in all probability—but successful towns were numbered in their thousands. The earliest in western Europe dated from the tenth or eleventh century. A wave of urban foundation spread eastwards across the continent until it reached the forest and steppe of Russia. The ideals and the practices of urbanism spread outward, so that there was a broad similarity between the customs and institutions of towns in Britain and Poland, Switzerland and Sweden.[7] The small and none too successful town of Breteuil in Normandy grew up below the castle of Duke William and received a charter about 1060. Soon after the Norman conquest of England in 1066, the "laws" of Breteuil were granted to Hereford, and the customs of Hereford afterwards became a model for those of some thirty boroughs in Wales and the Welsh Border.[8] Similarly in continental Europe, the "laws" of Magdeburg, a town of Carolingian origin, and those of Jihlava (Iglau), in Bohemia, were diffused through much of eastern Europe. It was not that these towns— Breteuil, Magdeburg, Jihlava—were important at this time; only that their charters and the recital of rights and privileges that they contained were familiar to or struck a chord with those who were engaged in founding new towns.

Wherever the density of population was thought sufficient to justify it, a town was created, and often enough in places too poor to support one. For hope sprang eternal in the minds of lords who strove to capitalize on their broad acres. By 1200 western Germany had been broadly urbanized, though there remained scope for the foundation of yet more towns in the later Middle Ages. By 1250 the wave of urban foundations was approaching the Oder. The next century saw the planting of numerous towns in Silesia and Bohemia. By 1400 the wave had spread across Poland and into the Carpathian mountains and the Hungarian plain, and at the dawn of the modern era towns were springing up in Russia and the plains of the lower Danube.

The number of towns that had been founded by the sixteenth century was immense. In German central Europe there must have been from three to four thousand. In Poland and western Russia they must have numbered up to a thousand, and in England and Wales some three hundred. Add at least two thousand for France and the Alpine countries, and we have a total of eight thousand or more, all of them places that whatever their size and functions, possessed the legal status of towns. Then the rush to establish new towns faded. Few were founded in the west after the Black Death and the abrupt drop in population that followed. There was neither a need for them nor the people to inhabit them. Europe was already over-urbanized. The amount of business to be transacted was too small for those which already existed, and many of them slipped back unnoticed to the status of village. Apart from the creation of a small number of towns for very special purposes, usually military, mining, or commercial, no new towns were founded before the nineteenth century. Europe's urban map was effectively complete by the fifteenth century. Expansion after that date was mainly in eastern Europe, Scandinavia, and Russia.

During the next six hundred years, by a kind of selective process, some towns grew, a few decayed, and the rest survived, little altered, into modern times. The map of European cities in 1800 differed little from that of the later Middle Ages.

Urban Size

The majority of cities and towns in preindustrial Europe had no more than a thousand or fifteen hundred inhabitants, and the smallest had fewer than a good-sized village. It would have been difficult on purely functional or economic grounds to distinguish between a large village and a very small town, and this makes any attempt to enumerate towns or to estimate the total size of urban population a somewhat artificial exercise. Only the possession of a charter of incorporation, with the privileges that it conferred, distinguished the one from the other. At the lower end of the scale were those lapsed towns where the "citizens" went about their business in the fields and maintained their barns along the High Street. But above the level of the humblest towns were a vast number of small towns, still in part rural, but embracing both craftsmen and traders, and alive once a week with the clatter and traffic of the market.

Higher on the urban scale were towns of three or four thousand people. Rural functions did not disappear as towns became larger, but they employed a progressively smaller proportion of the total population. Commerce and the crafts became more important, both relatively and absolutely, until the level was reached of the truly large cities, with fifty thousand or more inhabitants. They embraced a heterogeneous population. The urban peasant still journeyed to the fields each morning but was in every other respect submerged by the mass of craftsmen, traders, and entrepreneurs of all kinds, as well as by members of the professions, by ministers of the church, and by those who lived on income from rural lands or just by their wits.

Figure 8.1 shows the distribution of the larger cities in preindustrial Europe in the fifteenth century. They are seen to be most numerous and also largest in northwest Europe and in Italy, the one the scene of a not inconsiderable medieval industrial development; the latter inheriting an urban structure from the classical world.

No city was able to grow by the natural increase of its own population. The balance of births and deaths was always such that a continuing immigration from rural areas was necessary even to maintain a constant level of population. The reasons were well known. Cities contained, as we have seen, a pool of pathogens that circulated through a densely packed population. They were spread by infected food and contaminated water-supply, by vermin and insect pests and, in certain restricted cases directly from person to person.

A second factor restricting the growth of urban population lay in the relatively high average age at marriage and, in consequence, the smaller size of the completed family. If it can be assumed that most urban immigrants were in their teens or early twenties, it might be several years before they could establish themselves and be able to create a home. It appears, furthermore, that a relatively high proportion of urban population did not marry; they remained for the whole of their lives household servants of some kind.

The source of urban immigrants is difficult to determine. The British census of 1851 gave, in the enumerators' books, the parish of birth of each person counted. In such cases the proportion of migrants in the total population and the average distance they had traveled can be calculated without difficulty, but this kind of evidence is highly unusual, and nothing of this kind exists for earlier periods. Migrants to the city sometimes carried with them the name of their home village, which became their patronymic. Such surnames allow one to trace the source of at least a small part of the migrants to the city.[9] It is difficult to generalize from such scanty evidence, but it does seem that most growing cities derived their immigrant population from relatively short distances. Indeed, it is probable that most migrants would have visited the city, perhaps many times on market days, before making the decision to migrate. Not until the nineteenth century, when urban growth was very rapid and railroad transport was available, did people migrate

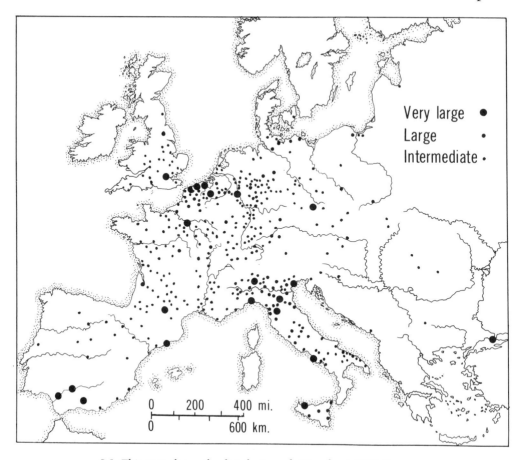

8.1. This map shows the distribution of cities about 1500. It demonstrates the concentration of urban population in northern Italy and the Low Countries. It is difficult to give a precise size scale, but "very large" cities may be taken to have over 30,000; "large," 10–30,000; and "intermediate," 5–10,000. It is impossible to represent the thousands of small and very small towns.

over really large distances. Even so, much of the permanent migration of modern times was preceded by temporary or seasonal movement. In many growing cities, like Paris and Lyons, the demand for labor arose mainly in the summer. That was when much of the building construction was done. There was little employment or accommodation for casual workers during the winter months, so they returned home. Many of the construction workers in Paris in the early nineteenth century came from the Central Massif, no less than two hundred miles away. But as urban conditions improved later in the century, more and more stayed over rather than return to the primitive conditions of their villages in the Auvergne. Migrants from southern Italy to the mill towns and industrial centers of the north, and from eastern Germany to the Rhineland covered even greater distances. Here the migrants had no familiarity with the cities and regions to which they were bound. They faced difficulties and problems unknown to the short-distance migrants who walked to their nearest city during the Middle Ages and early modern times. They were moving into an unfamiliar environment. Their patois may not have been understood. They might have belonged to a different church from that of their new neighbors. They faced almost invariably a housing shortage and, in many cases, the undisguised hostility of the local people.

Most migrants from the countryside to the city were poor. They did not hold land— or they would not have left it. They had little chance of inheriting a holding, and the choice before them was to compete with other landless laborers and cottagers for casual employment on the land of others, to take up a domestic craft, which most likely would have been weaving, or to migrate to the uncertain life of the city and join the growing urban proletariat of unskilled and half-employed. All the evidence points to the abundance and cheapness of labor in most cities: the large numbers who paid no taxes, the swarms of underpaid household servants, and the mutterings of discontent that periodically broke into outbursts of violence.[10]

The City Plan

The origin and early history of the city were betrayed in the pattern of its streets and the disposition of markets, churches, and other public buildings. The city in most of Europe was walled (fig. 8.2). Only in England and Scandinavia did one find cities without walls, but even here there were often gates across the streets where one entered the town, and sometimes a ditch or bank to mark its limits. Walls were both symbolic and practical. They separated two different jurisdictions and two kinds of society. They divided the free, urban burgess from the peasant, who long retained the marks of his former servility. The armorial bearings that they displayed on their gates, no less than the walls and towers themselves, were a measure of the corporate pride and arrogance of city folk. At the same time, walls served a practical purpose. They gave protection to the city in an age when warfare was endemic and armies had learned to live off the land they wasted. Few cities had walls strong enough to withstand a regular siege, but most fortifications protected their citizens from the casual bands of looters that made life miserable in the open country. Most citizens slept more comfortably in their beds in the knowledge that the gates were closed and barred, even if a watchman did not always walk the ramparts.

The effect of walls was to constrict the growth of the town, to bring about a degree of congestion, and to lead to the building of houses of three and even more floors. Only where towns were unwalled were wide streets and a spacious layout normal features of the urban scene. As cities grew in size, new lines of walls were sometimes built to enclose them. At Cologne, for example, one can trace no fewer than four sequential lines of walls (fig. 8.3), and the evidence for expansion is no less apparent in Paris and Prague, Basel and Bruges, and, indeed, in countless other cities in preindustrial Europe. On the other hand, there were cities in which the area enclosed by the walls was never fully built up. As a general rule, these cities had inherited their defensive walls from the Roman Empire, and the medieval and early modern city occupied only the central parts of its classical predecessor. In these instances part of the enclosed area was occupied by gardens and orchards. In most others the line of the walls was, for reasons of economy, kept as short as was practicable and enclosed a minimum of open space. A circle encloses the greatest possible area in relation to its perimeter, and there were many cities—prominent among them Bruges and Nördlingen—whose walls formed an almost perfect circle.

Cities retained their walls throughout the Middle Ages. In the sixteenth century a

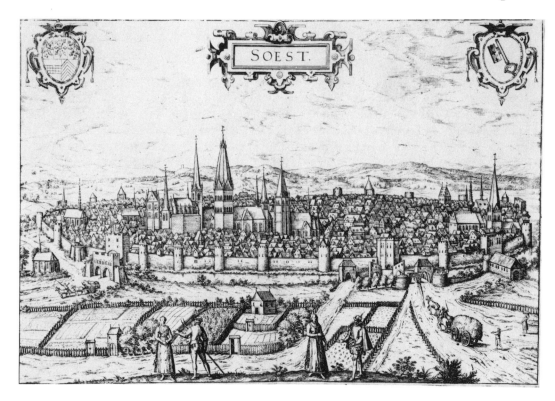

8.2. A view of Soest, Westphalia, in the seventeenth century. (Engraving by Caspar Merian.)

very small number—those of great military or strategic importance—were modified in order to be defended by and against artillery. But in most, the walls ceased in modern times to be useful or even decorative. They gradually fell to ruin. The cost of repairing them was too great and the benefits too small, until, in the eighteenth or nineteenth century, the walls were demolished and their site cleared. Today a few fragments of the ancient walls may survive, perhaps because they marked property lines or had been incorporated into houses built against them. But the number of cities in which the ancient walls still constitute a large or impressive monument are very few indeed. Paradoxically, walls are most likely to have survived around small towns, where, in the absence of urban growth, there was little incentive to destroy them. The small Bavarian town of Mainbernheim is a case in point. It can never have had more than a few hundred inhabitants, and its population today is perhaps smaller than that during the later Middle Ages. Walls with tall, round towers still encircle it, one still enters by the medieval gate, and there are still farm buildings within. The ditch that once surrounded it now grows produce. Yet this very small town was once capable by its passive strength of holding off any band of peasants or marauders that might assail it.

In any city, the pattern of streets was of fundamental importance both to its inhabitants and to posterity. The streets may today have an air of permanence, now that property lines have been established and mapped. But this was not the case in an age of

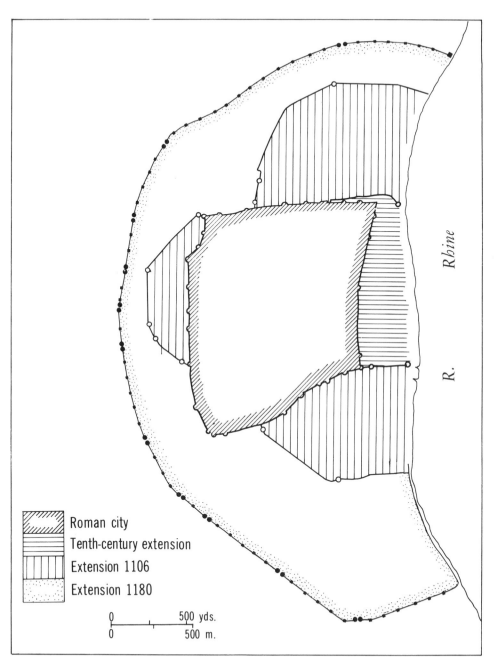

8.3. The growth of the city of Cologne, as shown by successive lines of the city walls.

Roman city
Tenth-century extension
Extension 1106
Extension 1180

0   500 yds.
0   500 m.

Rhine

R.

uncertain public control. Private building was allowed to encroach onto the streets, and whenever buildings were destroyed and roads obliterated beneath their rubble, streets and buildings were frequently realigned. No Roman city ever retained unaltered its original street pattern, though in a few cities of northern Italy the distortion of the Roman plan has been slight.[11] Elsewhere, however, the medieval and modern street plans have diverged fundamentally from the Roman. If, as at Winchester, a regular grid pattern appears to have survived,[12] this is likely to have been because the continued use of the city's gates imposed certain constraints on the roads that lay between them. Winchester's town plan, despite its classical appearance, is, in fact, Anglo-Saxon.

Cities of more recent origin show every possible variety of plan. In their layout some cities were but villages writ large, with curving streets and narrow alleys and courts. Rome itself had been like this, and many a city in the Mediterranean basin has inherited such an unplanned, almost chaotic pattern. But many—perhaps most—of the cities that grew up during the period of medieval urban expansion had about them some element of planning and design. Many of those which had been "planted" and incorporated by their lords had a nucleus around which they had, as it were, crystallized. This nucleus was in many cases a castle or a royal palace, as indeed was the case at Bruges, which has already been cited. It might alternatively have been a monastery or minster church. Many towns in western and central Europe owed their origin to the physical needs of a community of monks. Examples range from Glastonbury and Ely in England to Corvey and St. Riquier in France and Fulda and St. Gallen in central Europe.

The castle town was usually established below the castle itself, which commonly occupied some local eminence. The castle served to protect the town, and the town's walls were often linked with those of the castle. This pattern of city and castle merely reproduced the relationship, though under radically different social conditions, that had once existed between the Greek city and the acropolis beneath whose shadow it had grown. The castle town was likely to have a broad main street, which widened into a marketplace, for it was from the town's commercial functions that its founder hoped to profit. The monastery town was likely to be broadly similar in its plan, with its main street sweeping away from the abbey gate.

Alternatively, the new town might be laid out, often on a virgin site, as a pattern of straight streets, intersecting more or less at right angles. In such cases there was no question of slow, organic growth. The town sprang from a decision of the lord who held the land and was planned by his "surveyor," who marked out the streets with a measuring rod, dividing their frontages into plots for the future settlers. Of course, there were instances where not all the plots were taken up. New Winchelsea is an example. Old Winchelsea had been a royal town and an important port on the south coast of England. In the later years of the thirteenth century it was battered by storms and encroached upon by the sea. In 1287 its citizens abandoned it, and the king set about creating a new town a mile or two away, on a low hill, secure from storm and flood. The king's surveyor—his name was Thomas Alard—laid out the streets, straight and as nearly parallel as he could make them with his line. They may not have intersected exactly at right angles, but the resulting city blocks were more or less rectangular. Some blocks were left for building churches and establishing a marketplace. The rest were divided into plots, as many as twenty in the most densely settled of them, and the whole was protected by gates and the steepness of the hill on which it stood.

But the king and his surveyor judged badly. The town was greater than the demand for plots. Not all the blocks within the town were taken, the river silted, the port decayed, and the city gradually became depopulated. By the eighteenth century it was "rather the skeleton of an ancient city than a real town,"[13] and such it has remained. There were many Winchelseas in medieval Europe, cities planned with high hopes but little foresight.

Several urban patterns might indeed be fused. The original settlement might have been laid out according to one plan and its suburbs extended according to another. Take, for example, the city of Kraków in Poland (fig. 8.4). Its nucleus was the Wawel, the castle set on a crag above the Vistula, which became the seat of the Polish kings. Below it there grew up in the eleventh and twelfth centuries the Slavic city, with narrow and twisting streets. To this was added in the next century a planned or "German" town, established by newcomers from the west, who may indeed have been largely of German origin. Their city was laid out according to a pattern of regular blocks, with a large, rectangular central area being left free as the *Rynek* or marketplace. Or take the English town of Ludlow, in origin a castle town with a broad main street, which served as a marketplace, running from the castle gate to the church. To this core was added in stages a town planned as a series of nearly rectangular blocks, and the whole was eventually surrounded by a wall. There were cities with a building history even more complex than these examples. Some German cities evolved from a number of discrete but closely placed cells—a cathedral, a monastic church, a village, a "planted" and planned settlement—until, sometime in the late Middle Ages, these elements merged to form the later city. Magdeburg (fig. 8.5) and Hildesheim (fig. 8.6) developed in this way, but in most parts of Europe there are many other cities whose complex pattern of growth remains frozen in the layout of their streets and the placement of their churches and public buildings.

Even in the Middle Ages most of the streets and alleys of a city bore names. Some names were merely descriptive: wide, long, narrow, dark. Others bore the name of a public building, most often a church, that lay against them. Yet others were named for the people who lived there—Lombards or Jews—or for a craft carried on or the goods sold there. And some bore personal names, either of landowner or resident. Different sections of a single street might bear different names, and the names themselves might change with the people or the buildings that gave rise to them. Houses were not numbered in the medieval town. The earliest instance of street numbering is said to have been in fifteenth-century Paris, but it does not seem that house numbers were used in smaller cities until, in the nineteenth century, the development of the postal system made it desirable.

But the city plan was not only made up of streets. It embraced open spaces: markets, squares, the cemeteries that surrounded the churches, and, in odd corners of the city that had not been built up, tracts of garden and orchard. Town markets were of all sizes and shapes, from the vast open spaces met with at Arras (fig. 8.7) or Kraków, to streets that were merely wider than usual, like the Długi Targ (Long Market) at Gdańsk. Larger cities usually had more than one market. To some extent these served the needs of particular quarters of the city, but, as a general rule, they became specialized centers of trade: the hay market, corn market, butter market. In some instances these commodity markets have remained active, though today they tend to be used mainly by wholesalers and specialized merchants who distribute their goods to local shops.

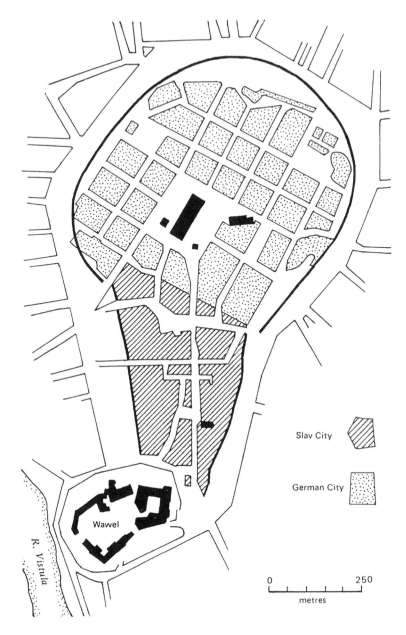

8.4. The city of Kraków, Poland. The old, or Slav, city grew up
beneath the Wawel, or castle of the kings of Poland. The planned, or
"German," city was added in the thirteenth century and contained the
chief centers of medieval commerce.

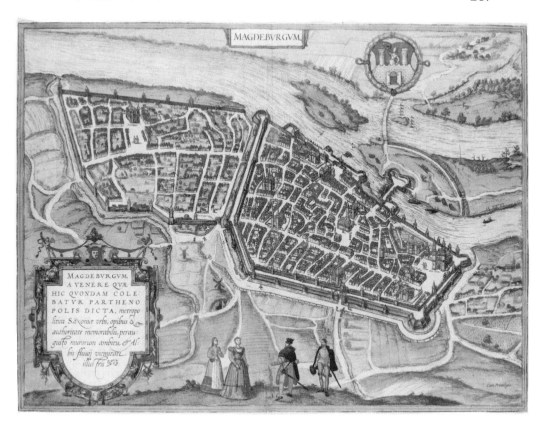

8.5. The city of Magdeburg, east Germany, as shown by Braun and
Hogenberg, late sixteenth century. The old city is to the right; the less
densely settled later medieval city to the left. North is to the left of
the picture, and the River Elbe flows from right to left.

In most cities of small or medium size it was a general market that came alive for one
day in each week. Stalls were set up in the streets, and countryfolk brought their
vegetables and livestock, foodstuffs that in general had only a short life but were in
regular demand in the cities. Peasants traveled varying distances to market, with their
goods carried on horses or donkeys, in horse-drawn carts, or even on their own backs.
The local craftsmen offered their own wares for sale: cloth and leather and metal goods.
There were beads and trinkets to tempt the peasant who had just disposed of a pig or a
pair of chickens, and, as if this were not enough, there were taverns, expecting to do
business as soon as a peasant had a few coins in his pocket.

The weekly market, with its coarse fun and crude exploitation of those who knew too
little about the value of their wares, was a focal point in the lives of both town and
countryfolk. It continued active into the nineteenth century, and in some areas, particularly of eastern and southeastern Europe, into the twentieth. Here, despite the
collectivization of agriculture and the role assumed by government in the wholesale
trade, the small town market remains active and unchanging. An unforgettable picture of

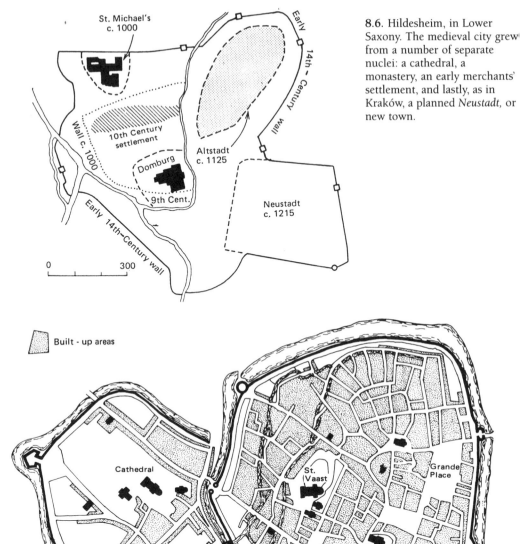

8.6. Hildesheim, in Lower Saxony. The medieval city grew from a number of separate nuclei: a cathedral, a monastery, an early merchants' settlement, and lastly, as in Kraków, a planned *Neustadt,* or new town.

8.7. The city of Arras, northern France. The old city, known as *la cité,* lies to the left, around the cathedral, and occupies a Roman site, while the later merchants' town (*la ville*) lies to the right, around the ancient abbey of Saint-Vaast. (Based on J. Lestocquoy, *Les Dynasties bourgeoises d'Arras.*)

8.8. The marketplace at Pirna, in Saxony, as painted by Canaletto Bellotto when court painter to the king of Saxony in the eighteenth century.

a market is painted by Reymont in *Chłopi*: the petty haggling of peasant and trader and the undercurrent of intrigue, suspicion, and jealousy that marked everyone's dealings with everyone else, culminating in near inebriation in the taverns at the end of the day. The medieval market scene would have been little different.

The Church in the City

The topographers and engravers of the sixteenth and seventeenth centuries delighted in portraying views of the cities. They showed the walls and gates, just a little exaggerated to suit the pride of the burgesses, the roofs of the urban houses, and, rising above them, the massive bulk of the city churches with their towers and spires. They must have enjoyed their "skyline" as much as any American in the present century, for their cities were dotted with churches that appeared to compete for public notice. The preindustrial city might well seem to have been overendowed with churches. There were parish churches, each serving the spiritual needs of a small segment of the city. There was never any accepted ratio of parishes to population. There were cities divided between dozens of parishes: Norwich, in England, had at the end of the Middle Ages almost fifty parishes for a population of about five thousand, and most of their churches still stand today, offering a capacity grossly in excess of the city's needs. There were well over a hundred in London before the Great Fire of 1666. On the other hand, there were cities that could boast no more than two or three parish churches, and some that had none, since they belonged to a rural parish whose church lay beyond their walls and across the fields. Citizens were baptized in the church of their particular parish and were buried in its cemetery, and between these terminal rites of passage the church served as a social as well as a religious center. The gilds, of which many parishioners were members, maintained chapels within the church, and the parish as a whole contributed to its fabric. Urban churches received little income from tithe, and the direct burden of their construction and maintenance devolved directly on their parishioners. Urban parishes varied in wealth and resource even more than rural parishes, and in consequence urban churches embraced not only some of the humblest structures but also many of the largest and most magnificent. These are a lasting monument to the rich merchants of the city— for medieval urban wealth came largely from trade—who built them to the honor of God, no doubt, but also to their own glorification.

In addition to a considerable number of parish churches, there were usually non-parochial chapels with more restricted rights and privileges. Then there were houses of the mendicants or orders of friars, and, most often in a suburb of the city, a monastery of monks or canons. Monastic foundations came relatively early to the urban scene; some, indeed, were the nuclei around which the town grew. The friars came in the thirteenth century. They were the social workers of their age. They rarely established their houses in rural areas. Instead, they made for the cities, where there was greater opportunity for their missionary work, and the larger the city, the greater was the opportunity open to them. Indeed, it has been suggested that the number of houses of friars was a measure of a city's social deprivation and need.[14] Friars' churches were not parochial; they were not the foci of secular activities, and they had no baptismal font and no cemetery, except for the friars themselves. Instead, these churches, with large, barnlike naves, were for preaching, and it was through their preaching that the friars made their greatest impact on the urban populace.

Beside its numerous churches and religious foundations, the city would have a number of public buildings, centrally placed and often fronting the principal square or marketplace. They had been built for the convenience of trade or of city government: a gild or town hall, where the city's elite could meet either for the conduct of the city's business or for feasting and celebration; sometimes a market hall, where market records could be kept and tolls collected, and in the shelter of which at least some of the traders could set up their stalls. There might also be a "hospital" for the aged and infirm, not a place dedicated to healing the sick, but one allowing them to live out their days in at least relative comfort. There were hundreds, even thousands, of such foundations, each endowed by the pious or generous of an earlier age. The hospital was essentially a church, with the sick lying on their beds in the nave, from which they could observe and profit from the rituals of the church as they were performed in the chancel.

Some hospitals were reserved for certain categories of people, for gild members and those of reputedly unblemished life. The provision for men seems always to have been greater than that for women, despite the greater longevity of the latter. Another group that often received separate provision were the lepers. Here charity was tinged by the desire to isolate those infected, and leper hospitals were commonly sited near the town gate or beyond its walls, so that the need would not arise for the leper to intrude into the crowded streets.

A small number of cities, both medieval and modern, were the seats of bishops. They possessed cathedral churches, episcopal palaces, chapels, and the administrative machinery of their dioceses. The great majority of cathedral cities in western and southern Europe were of Roman origin—the administration of the church, as it were, taking over from the imperial officials as the empire came to an end. In most instances the cathedral was a very public building, centrally placed and often dominating the principal square with its massive presence. Only rarely, and usually when it also served as a monastery, was it shut away in a corner of the city. An episcopal presence meant much to a city. It was supported by the income from the lands possessed by both bishop and chapter. The cathedral and diocesan staffs lived in some degree of luxury. Their palaces and guest houses were frequented by kings and nobles and served by a horde of retainers and servants. The construction and maintenance of the churches—for they were, almost by definition, large—called for an army of masons of all degrees. The church was a great employer, and any cathedral city, from Rome itself to the poorest and humblest in northern Europe or the mountains of southern Italy, had a very large tertiary sector in its economy.

Conditions of Life in the Preindustrial City

The city has been, at least since classical times, the "promised land" of the dispossessed and indigent. There was, it was supposed, greater opportunity in the city than in the countryside for both legitimate employment and illicit gain. The landless peasant and the refugee from the law sought asylum in its anonymity. This social problem has been worldwide and manifests itself today in the frightening increase of a Mexico City or of a Calcutta, as well as in the less spectacular growth of countless smaller places. In preindustrial Europe the social consequences of a large-scale influx into the cities were much less severe than they are to-day. Cities were smaller and the numbers of migrants fewer. Nevertheless, immigration from the countryside intensified the problems inherent in any large and closely concentrated society in an age that was scientifically undeveloped and technologically backward. Disease spread more quickly through urban space and mortality was always higher. The population of Verona was twice abruptly reduced by a half within two centuries (fig. 8.9).

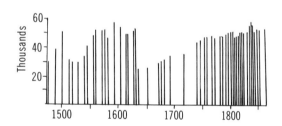

8.9. Graph showing the population of the Italian city of Verona from the late fifteenth century to the early nineteenth. The abrupt drop about 1630 was due to an outbreak of plague that approximately halved the population.

But here a distinction must be drawn between the large city and the local market center. The latter answered only to the needs of the local area; it was itself occupied with agriculture and as likely to develop a class of landless unemployed as any village. It offered no anonymity to escaping countryfolk and was more likely to have been a source of migrants than their haven. In fact, the small town was often, as the evidence makes clear, a stopping point for the peasant on his way from his village to the distant city. It was where he gained information about the opportunities that might be available and got his bearings before heading for his "promised land."

At the opposite extreme were the larger cities, those of, let us say, more than five or ten thousand inhabitants. This was no longer a face-to-face society; the newcomer could merge into it almost unnoticed, and no truly reliable estimate could be made of its size. Such a city was large enough for a stratification, both social and spatial, to become apparent. There were classes and quarters, and few citizens, in all probability, were familiar with every twist and turn in their own city. It was only in the large city that material conditions began to diverge significantly from those of the countryside.

Urban housing was in the first instance very similar to rural, subject to the same constraints set by the physical environment and serving the same basic human needs. But a further limitation applied in most cities: shortage of space. The urban building plot became, by successive division and subdivision, significantly smaller than the rural toft. Although housing in many small towns continued to conform with rural patterns, with hall and bower and perhaps a service annex, set parallel with the street, in medium-sized and large cities, the design of the house was adapted increasingly to the restrictions of urban space. This objective was accomplished, broadly speaking, in four ways. In the first place, town houses became contiguous; the space between them was eliminated, except for occasional passageways to gain access to the yard at the back of the house, and streets came to be lined with *rows* of houses.

This step was, of course, only a return to Roman tradition, as illustrated at Pompeii or Ostia. This tradition had survived in Italy and in many cities of the Mediterranean basin. It spread to France and the Rhineland, perhaps in the twelfth and thirteenth centuries, and then to the larger cities in the rest of Europe. Panoramic views of cities made in the sixteenth century, particularly those associated with Sebastian Münster and Braun and Hogenberg, show serried rows of houses near the centers of their cities, passing outward toward the periphery into a zone of detached homes of almost rural appearance. This picture is supported by the little archeological evidence that is available. Although change may have been minimal in many small towns, all the larger have suffered drastic rebuilding in modern times, with the almost complete destruction of earlier buildings in and near their centers. Nevertheless, the excavation of sites, usually in preparation for modern redevelopment, shows how widely and how early the practice developed of building conjoined houses into a street.

At the same time the orientation of the house on the plot or burgage tended to change. It began to present its narrow end to the street and to extend farther into the yard or garden that lay behind. By the sixteenth century such deep, narrow-fronted houses had become normal around the town squares and near the city centers of the larger cities. This arrangement of the house cut down drastically on the amount of light available in its rooms. Although, with the increasing availability of glass, windows were made larger, the interiors of most urban homes were prevailingly dark. Various devices were employed to improve the lighting, including the building of a narrow spur from the house, occupying only part of the width of the plot. And there were, of course, homes— usually of the well-to-do citizens—in which no need was experienced to conform with the trend. Here the house was built, sometimes on a double lot, parallel with the streets, its hall lighted with large windows and only the ends of the house without significant illumination. All these types and gradations of urban housing are still apparent in many of the smaller towns in which the urge to destroy and rebuild has been felt less deeply.

The third way of coping with the growth of urban population was to add upper floors. The rural cottage often had an upper story or a loft above the bower; sometimes a second floor was built throughout the house. But in the more closely built areas of towns, upper floors—not only a second but even a third and a fourth—were constructed. And the whole was even raised over a stone-lined basement. This type of construction was assisted by a growing use of masonry, at least in the lower floors. It was also made possible by the increasing sophistication of timber construction, with more elaborate and reliable methods of jointing timber with mortise and tenon. As a general rule, the upper floors were jettied over the lower. Windows were sometimes bowed or constructed on an oriel plan in order to maximize the amount of light entering the room. The roof was usually gabled toward the street and often highly decorated. The jettied upper floors reduced yet more the width of already narrow streets, until they were little more than tunnels into which the sunshine rarely penetrated. Such housing could never have been endured into modern times on anything more than a small and local scale, and it is impossible to point today to a street that wholly retains its sixteenth- or seventeenth-century gloom, congestion, and confusion. The best of such architecture is to be found in those small towns of central Germany which escaped destruction in the Second World War. Quedlinburg, Einbeck, and Goslar may serve as examples, but even here much of the more congested urban building has been destroyed.

The fourth way of accommodating a large and growing population was to be found mainly in the large cities, and then only in the later eighteenth and nineteenth centuries. It consisted of filling in the spaces that lay between and behind the rows of houses. This area had previously consisted mainly of gardens, and there was room only for short rows and small clusters of houses. They were ranged along narrow alleys and around diminutive courts. Sometimes they were built back-to-back, with a common roof. Recognition of the need for sanitation and water supply was perfunctory in the extreme. Such houses often rose several stories high, cutting off the light from buildings already there. Trees and grass disappeared beneath masonry and the rough paving and cobbles of streets and courts.

This development is commonly regarded as a consequence of the Industrial Revolution, of the forced concentration of large numbers of workers in close proximity to the factories in which they worked. In fact, it antedated the factory age and was apt to occur wherever and whenever there was rapid urban growth. It was found in Mediterranean cities like Naples, Palermo, and Barcelona, long before these cities began to develop modern industry. And in the great cities of northern Europe, notably Paris and London, such courts were built that long antedated modern factories. It was both an attempt to increase the stock of housing where it was most needed and a means of maximizing profit from the possession of burgage lots. It implied as well a complete lack of regulation by public authority both of building standards and of the location of new buildings.

The choice of building material had an important influence on the health and well-being of citizens. Wood was at first the universal building material. It was cheaper and more easily obtainable than stone, unless there was a convenient Roman site to rob. A particular objection to masonry building was that it required lime, which was costly and far from universally available. Only in Mediterranean Europe was masonry generally used. Until the eleventh century the use of stone was, at least north of the Alps, by and large reserved for church architecture. Change came very slowly. Wooden buildings decayed readily and were particularly susceptible to fire. Roofs were at first of thatch, which was even more flammable than timber framing. Wooden shingles were better and were, in fact, commonly used, but tiles, the most expensive roofing of all, did not become common until modern times. The London building assize of 1189 clearly envisaged a growing use of stone in domestic architecture, and, in particular, for the party walls between houses. Nevertheless, even in the early nineteenth century most urban building was in wood, and stone was commonly used only in basements and ground floors.

With growth in the size of settlements, those two necessities of human existence—water supply and sanitation—assumed an increasing importance. But they presented serious technical problems and their financial cost was high. The consequences of failure to provide for them were not at first apparent, and so they tended to be neglected until disaster struck. The two were closely—too closely—interlinked. Most of the water was drawn from soil into which the sewage was allowed to discharge. The result was that pathogens, when present, were able to pass from the one to the other, with disastrous consequences for urban health.

The Romans, blessed with a lower population and with cities of smaller size, had developed ingenious and successful means of water supply. At the end of the Roman period most of these works were neglected and fell into decay. No doubt urban demand for water and for the bathing establishments that it supplied had sunk to so low a level that repairing them did not seem worthwhile. There is evidence that Pope Adrian I, in the eighth century, caused repairs to be made on the Roman aqueducts, and Roman-style water supply systems were also established about this time elsewhere in the Mediterranean basin.[15] But this was rare. Medieval towns and cities were thrown back on the use of wells and of such springs as arose within their limits. The well became the most common urban source of water. It was usually lined with masonry, and some even made use of animal power to lift the water to the surface. As a general rule, there was no need for deep wells, since most cities lay on relatively low ground and the water table came close to the surface. Where, as was often the case, a city had been founded on a gravel terrace, there was usually an abundant supply of well-filtered water. But the rapid development of cities, especially in modern times, stretched the resources of the best aquifer and greatly impaired the quality of the water.

The chief problem was the unrestricted creation of cesspits and soakaways. There was no conceivable way of separating contaminants from the water that made its way into the wells, and all human diseases that could be spread through a combination of human excreta and groundwater—foremost among them cholera, dysentery, and enteritis—were carried in this way. There can be no question but that most of the severe outbreaks of cholera in nineteenth-century Europe were spread through polluted well water.[16]

The foremost of alternative sources of water was the river. Most cities outside Mediterranean Europe lay on the banks of a river, and many of them were subject to winter flooding. The river offered an abundant source of water of varying degrees of impurity. In fact, every river throughout the more populous parts of Europe was polluted from the Middle Ages onward, and the situation cannot be said to have improved markedly in modern times. The river was the ultimate receptacle into which the waste of society was thrown. Urban cesspits drained into them; the waste of tanyards, often deliberately sited on their banks, was swept into them, and butchers dumped into them such offal as was not consumed by dogs. At Valladolid, in Spain, the river Pisuerga had in

1577 to be cleared of such waste to enable it to flow freely, and similar conditions must frequently have arisen.[17] The coming of modern industry brought no change in the conditions of rivers, only different pollutants. To sewage was added the waste of chemical and dyeworks.[18] In 1846, T. C. Banfield noted that the dyers and calico printers along the river Wupper in the Rhineland "dye its waters a different colour every hour of the day."[19]

Such were the conditions under which all too many people obtained much of their water supply. The balance between wells and the river doubtless varied from place to place and was dependent on the local topography and geology. Lister warned visitors to Paris in 1698 that the river water was "very pernicious to all Strangers."[20] A century later, according to Mercier, much of the city's water was taken from the Seine, a business that employed, he said, with some exaggeration, 20,000 water carriers from morning to night.[21]

Attempts to remedy the situation were stultified by the failure to realize that it was dangerous and wrong. When water-supply systems were built, it was more for convenience and to obtain a regular supply than for reasons of health. Indeed, it was not until the mid-nineteenth century that the association of certain diseases with a contaminated water supply was made. Even then, as we have seen, the *nature* of infection was not known.

Apart from a very few attempts made in the Mediterranean basin to resuscitate or imitate the Roman hydraulic engineering works, the earliest water-supply systems of the Middle Ages were developed by the church. Monasteries possessed the necessary wealth, and their close links with Rome may have made them more familiar than the laity with the waterworks of the later empire. Even in cities that, it might have been thought, would have had an adequate system of wells, religious communities acquired wayleaves and built conduits to their houses. In England, the earliest systems of which we have record were constructed in the twelfth century. The cathedral of Canterbury had a highly sophisticated system of conduits that brought water from the hills to the east, passing it through settling tanks and under the city wall before it reached the monastery, where pipes took it to the cloister, the infirmary, and the kitchen.

Another early conduit was that cut in the next century to supply St. Nicholas Priory, Exeter, as well as Exeter Cathedral. In this case the conduit consisted in large measure of tunnels cut through the hard rock on which the city was built. At Cambridge the Greyfriars built a conduit from a spring two miles to the west and carried it beneath the river Cam. In its long, unguarded course it was tapped into by the scholars of one of Cambridge's colleges, who thus obtained an illicit supply of their own.

In the later Middle Ages the technique of building conduits of stone, wood, or lead was developed, and even the use of the siphon was revived. The superiority of water from rural springs to that of a polluted river must have seemed obvious, and in the later Middle Ages towns turned increasingly to such sources. In the twelfth century William Fitzstephen wrote of the springs in the vicinity of London that their waters were "sweet, wholesome and clear," and it was these springs which the religious institutions tapped with conduits that they constructed to the city. In some instances it was possible to engineer a leat, an open channel through which water flowed slowly from the spring to the city. A conduit was, however, superior. It was sealed; water passed through it under pressure and, at its destination, could be made to rise in a fountain. Sometimes a cistern was constructed in order to produce a head of water. A disadvantage was that it was impossible to control the flow through the conduit, and for much of the time the water ran to waste. Conduits and fountains began to assume great importance in the life of some cities where for geological reasons springs offered little scope. The fountain was built in the main square of the town and was, as a general rule, elaborately decorated. At Bern (Switzerland), fountains lined the principal streets (fig. 8.10).[22] The decision to construct the conduit is said to have arisen from the very hot, dry summer of 1393, but it was not until 1420 that wooden pipes delivered the first water to a street fountain. The stone-built fountains that are today so decorative a feature of the city were mostly constructed in the sixteenth and seventeenth centuries. At this time fountains, supplied by conduits, began to spread through the cities and towns wherever it was practicable to construct them.

The first half of the nineteenth century witnessed a revolution in urban water supply, made possible by improving technology and necessitated by the growing size and congestion of cities. The crucial step was the introduction about 1825 of the use of cast-iron pipes. These permitted wells to be sunk to far greater depths than had previously been possible. In 1841 a well near Paris was taken down to 1,800 feet, far below the reach of contaminated surface water. At the same time, iron pipes replaced the unsanitary wood- and stone-built conduits. In the middle years of the century the larger cities began to reach farther into the countryside in their search for an abundant and uncontaminated source. Paris continued until the 1860s to derive most of its water from the Seine, but then Haussmann, the architect who was rebuilding much of the city, constructed a pipeline to bring water from the chalk beds of Champagne. In many of the larger cities of Germany, a piped water supply was obtained from distant sources, to the benefit of both the convenience and the health of the citizens.[23] The time, however, had not yet come when the supply system could be linked with a faucet in each house. That had to await the twentieth century. Nor were standpipes installed in every part of the city. They came first to the well-to-do sectors and spread only slowly through the humbler quarters.

The financial advantages of a piped water supply were not at first apparent. It is noteworthy that in Germany the city of Essen established an advanced type of water-works as early as 1865, but only because the iron and steel mills of the city required it. A pipeline network was established throughout the Ruhr industrial region during the following years. Ordinary people benefited greatly, but the needs of the ironmasters were paramount in the construction. Some cities, among them Hamburg in Germany and Toulouse in France, delayed the construction of modern water-supply systems, with disastrous consequences, which included Hamburg's cholera epidemic of 1892.

The collection and removal of sewage is the reverse problem to that of water supply. The Romans had constructed sewers—the *Cloaca Maxima* in Rome, begun at least as early as the third century B.C., is an example—but never on the scale of their water-supply systems. They built toilets but, generally speaking, did not construct any system of flushing them. In this respect, monastic houses showed a marked improvement over conditions in Roman cities. But they had advantages denied to earlier peoples—abundant space, usually a flowing stream, and complete freedom to plan their buildings. In the typical monastic plan, as it evolved in the eleventh century, the toilet, or *reredorter*, was built at the end of the dormitory and projected over a river or at least over a small

8.10. A decorative fountain of 1543, one of many lining the principal streets of Bern, Switzerland, and constituting until modern times the chief source of water for the city. (Courtesy of Swiss National Tourist Office.)

canal that diverged from it and joined it lower down. Both in sanitation and water-supply, monasteries were a model for their age, with beneficial consequences, which unhappily we cannot measure, for the health of their inmates.

The ordinary urban population enjoyed no such advantages. The larger cities had communal toilets sometimes projecting over a bridge or a river bank, more often built above a cesspit. In medieval London there are known to have been sixteen public latrines, but this, in a population of twenty-five or thirty thousand, was totally inadequate.[24] In consequence there were private cesspits almost everywhere. They were dug in the yards behind the houses, sometimes even beneath the floorboards of a house. Sometimes they were masonry lined, sometimes enclosed by wickerwork (fig. 8.11). At intervals they were cleared and their contents either deposited in the river or spread on the fields of vegetables beyond the walls. The stench must have been appalling. In summer the cesspits were a breeding place for flies and other pests, and at all times a source of infection. The river Fleet was "so obstructed by dung from privies built thereon and other filth" that it no longer provided sufficient security to the Fleet prison, built against it.[25] The London building assize of 1189 attempted to regulate the construction of private cesspits, enacting that they should be at least 2½ feet from adjoining property,

8.11. A cesspit in medieval London. It was lined with wickerwork,
which has been carbonized and preserved in the damp soil.

unless lined with stone, when they might be nearer.[26] Evidently those who drafted the
assize were primarily concerned about seepage from the pits.

Conditions varied from one city to another. They were clearly least objectionable in
lightly built-up cities where toilets could be built in gardens, remote from the house, and
worst among the alleys and courts of the densely concentrated industrial cities. In some
cities a network of large, masonry-lined sewers was built early in the nineteenth century,
taking both domestic sewage and storm water. London was one of them. Edinburgh,
Brussels, Berlin, and several other large cities had such sewers at a relatively early date.
But they all discharged into the river, and the efficiency with which they worked merely
served to increase the level of pollution downstream. In Paris, Haussmann built a partial
sewer system beneath the quarters that he was rebuilding, but late in the century there
were said to be still seventy thousand *fosses* or sewage pits.[27] Typhoid was ever present,
and in 1884 there was a severe cholera outbreak. And yet the resistance to constructing
sewers was for many years insurmountable. The landlords objected to paying for the
work, and the *vidangeurs,* whose unsavory task it was to cleanse the pits, to their loss of
earnings.[28] And so it was that in the poorer quarters of the city the cesspit remained in
use well into the present century.

Related to the disposal of sewage were the construction, maintenance, and cleansing
of the city streets. The frequency of traffic made it necessary to lay some kind of paving
on their surface. The Romans had made extensive use of stone slabs, but, unless stone lay
to hand in ruined buildings, medieval people resorted to simpler and less satisfactory
materials. Commonly pebbles were merely set in sand and were easily dislodged by
passing traffic. The use of paving slabs became more common in the later Middle Ages,
but stone "sets" and bricks as well as any unconsolidated stone rubble were also used.

8.12. Latrine outlets on the wall of a medieval castle, Orford, Suffolk. Excreta were allowed to accumulate against the wall until disposed of.

Paris was said, in 1698, to be largely paved with "square Stone, of about eight or ten Inches thick."[29] But at Toulouse, even at the beginning of the present century, most streets were still of cobbles set in sand.[30]

There was little improvement in streets until late in the nineteenth century. Their rough and uneven surface allowed mud to accumulate and made cleaning difficult. The absence of house-to-house collection of refuse meant that much of it was merely deposited in the street. Add to this the droppings of horses and even night soil and the contents of cesspits, and one has an accumulation so obnoxious that city authorities were obliged to take action.[31] They tried, not always successfully, to limit the number of animals that roamed the streets. In 1481 Frankfurt banned pigs, because "their stench in the alleys and squares was unbecoming a city."[32] Valladolid attempted to do the same, but with little effect.[33]

Most streets were constructed with a shallow depression along them, so that water was deflected from the houses on each side. The effect more often was to turn the middle of the street into a watercourse in bad weather. A convex profile was already in use on country roads when, in the 1840s, this mode of construction was adopted in Paris. It necessitated a sidewalk along each side both for the convenience of pedestrians and to protect buildings. Water and refuse then tended to accumulate in the gutters, from which they could more easily be removed. This type of street became general by the end of the century, except in eastern and southeastern Europe, where even today the central gutter can still be met with.[34]

Street cleaning was, as a general rule, perfunctory and irregular before the late nineteenth century. In Paris in 1417 the condition of the streets had become so bad that everyone, including even priests, was required to assist in cleansing them. Lister described how it was done in Paris with "a heavy Drag with a horse, which makes a quick riddance."[35] In medieval London the cleaning seems to have been more carefully organized and more effective than in many cities. The accumulated waste was gathered into heaps by "rakers" and transported by tumbrils or small carts.[36] Such appears to have been the normal mode of street clearing, executed with varying degrees of care and efficiency. But the amount of dirt on the roads was such as to employ armies of "crossing sweepers" in Dickensian London and to require, far into the present century, the services of water carts to spray the dust on a summer's day.

In London and elsewhere there was a gild of "paviors" charged with maintaining the road surface. It is to be feared, however, that their idea of "paving" consisted of little more than adding more sand and pebbles whenever the surface became worn and potholed. The result was to raise the level of the street until it stood several feet above that of the houses on each side. This situation must have been the origin of many of the domestic basements that are known to have been present in medieval houses.

Within every city and town, except the smallest, there were "quarters," areas distinguished by a social class or even an ethnic group that inhabited them. The powerful and rich lived near the center. Their opulent homes, jettied over the street, with elaborately carved gables, fronted the main square or market, well placed for their owners to participate in the city's business. As one moved away from the center there was a steep gradient in personal wealth and domestic comfort, from the homes of craftsmen and petty shopkeepers to those of the humblest and poorest, which often lay near the periphery. But this is only a generalized picture. There were infinite variations on this theme, and every city was in most respects unique. In many, the homes of the rich burgesses have been destroyed and rebuilt, in some instances many times. Some remained until the destruction of the Second World War. In a few instances they have survived intact until today, as in the *Grande Place* at Brussels, around the old markets at Prague and Kraków, and in a number of other central European cities. In many of the larger cities there was a ghetto, inhabited by the generally small Jewish community. It is often supposed that the Jews were forced to live segregated from their fellow gentiles. This, indeed, became the case in parts of Russia and eastern Europe, but in the first instance they chose to live together for mutual help and protection.[37] In fact, as surviving documents show, they took steps to prevent gentiles from settling among them.

Architecture is not the only measure of social status within the city. To contemporaries it would have been apparent in dress and diet, but if these factors can no longer be evaluated, it is nevertheless sometimes possible to measure the taxable income of the citizens. A tax register for the city of Paris of 1438 shows not only an immense range in personal wealth but also its concentration in specific quarters. The areas of greatest wealth per head lay on the right bank of the Seine, near the city center, where, in fact, the most fashionable shops are found today.[38] Figure 8.13, based on the work of Pierre Deyon, shows the average household tax levied in each street in the city of Amiens. Apart from a relatively high level of wealth along the north-south axis of the city and a similar area in the cathedral precinct to the southeast, Amiens conforms with the model described above, where income diminishes with increasing distance from the center. Similar data for fifteenth-century Genoa show a not dissimilar pattern, notwithstanding the fact that the city area is bounded by the coast and port. The richest area, as measured

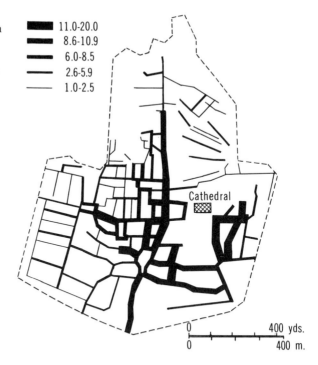

8.13. Map of Amiens, northern France, showing the tax (in *livres tournois*) paid by each house. Note the concentration of wealth near the city center and around the cathedral. (After Pierre Deyon, *Amiens capitale provinciale* [Paris, 1967], 543.)

11.0-20.0
8.6-10.9
6.0-8.5
2.6-5.9
1.0-2.5

Cathedral

0   400 yds.
0   400 m.

by the amount realized by the tax on personal property, lay near the center and close to the docks. A comparison of figures 8.14 (a) and (b) shows that the richest quarters were among the least densely populated.[39]

By the nineteenth century this simple urban pattern had disappeared from most of the larger cities. They had turned themselves inside out. The urban elite had left, or were in the process of abandoning, the city center and were building more spacious homes in the suburbs. There were several reasons for this shift; the greater wealth of the patrician families, their demand for more domestic space and greater comfort, and, later in the century, the improving transportation facilities between the suburbs and the central city. But underlying these changes was a revolution in the way people lived. The place of work was becoming separated physically from the home. In earlier centuries the merchant had, quite literally, lived above his shop, and the craftsman had carried on his business within his cottage. This was changing. The workman was very slowly being absorbed into some form of factory employment, and the merchant was content to turn his home into a combination of countinghouse and warehouse, while he and his family moved elsewhere.

The effect of such changes, which were spread, according to location and degree of economic development, over the eighteenth and nineteenth centuries, was to strengthen yet more the compartmentalization of the city. The social zonation ceased to be more or less concentric. Instead, well-to-do and working-class quarters crystallized, lying as a general rule at opposite ends of the city. This segmentation was especially marked in the largest cities. In Paris the elite moved from the heart of the old city to the north of the *Ile de la Cité,* into the northwest quadrant.[40] At the same time, the eastern quarters became

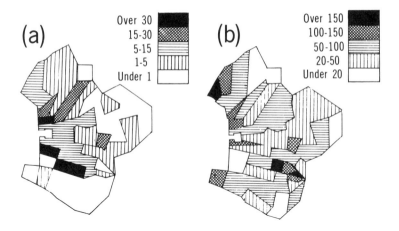

8.14. Genoa in the late Middle Ages. (*a*) Average income per family;
(*b*) number of houses per hectare (about 2.4 acres). The greatest
congestion was to be found, as might be expected, in the poorest
quarters. (After J. Heers.)

the principal areas of industrial development and working-class housing. A not dissimilar pattern emerged in both London and Berlin, with upper-class housing very broadly to
the west and the industrial and working-class areas to the east and northeast. In Vienna
the elite moved out beyond the Kärntner Tor toward Grinzing and into the hills that rose
westward toward the Wienerwald.[41] Similar patterns emerged in Brussels, Rome, and
indeed, in almost every large and growing city.

The ways in which social quarters crystallized within the preindustrial city have
often been attributed to urban meteorological conditions. The more desirable locations
lay on rising ground, above the fog and damp of the river plain, or upwind from the
industrial quarters. In regions where westerly winds prevailed—and this was most of
Europe—the western suburbs were undoubtedly more congenial. But there were other
factors. Manufacturing was attracted to the means of transportation—in London toward
the docks, in Berlin to the canals that transected the Spree valley. The quality of housing
and the provision of utilities differed fundamentally between these extremes in urban
settlement. The dense building, the tenement blocks, the courts and alleys continued to
occupy parts of the central city but occurred principally in these developing industrial
quarters.[42] In social terms, two cultures were emerging, physically separated so that each
could, if it wished, turn its back on the other. Nor was this development limited to the
growing and industrializing cities. It was to be found in cities of intermediate and even of
small size. Social segregation was the keynote of urban growth in the nineteenth century.

There were other factors in the material welfare of the urban population than water
supply, sanitation, and the density of housing. How did people cook their food and keep
themselves warm in winter? What fuel did they use and how far back can we push the
problem of atmospheric pollution? What were the hazards of fire and flood, or even of
venturing alone into the darkened alleys of the city, whether preindustrial or modern?
The growing density of housing, built in large measure of wood, increased the danger of
fire, and this must have constituted for many city dwellers their greatest fear.[43] There was

scarcely a city in Europe that did not at some time experience a disastrous conflagration. In some they were frequent. In Constantinople there are said to have been no fewer than twenty-two major fires between 1633 and 1701.[44] Some urban fires were utterly devastating. A burgess of Mons recorded in his diary of 1518 that in nearby Armentières fire destroyed thirteen hundred houses, leaving only three standing.[45] Shortly afterward, both Valenciennes and Reulx were similarly devastated. The town of Jülich in the lower Rhineland was so completely destroyed by fire in 1547 that an Italian architect, Pasqualini by name, was brought in to repair the city.[46] The best known of great urban fires was that of London in 1666, when about four-fifths of the city was destroyed. Fires appear to have been less frequent in Mediterranean Europe, probably because the need for domestic heating was felt less keenly, but also because a far greater use was made of masonry construction. To the countless accidental fires must be added the many occasions when cities were deliberately burned in the course of military campaigns. Urban destruction was especially frequent in the Thirty Years War, culminating in the destruction of Magdeburg by the imperialists under Tilly in 1631. Perhaps the most momentous instance of the burning of a city was that of Moscow in the fall of 1812, forcing Napoleon into retreat. If such incendiarism can be said to have had any benefits, these would include the purging of the city of endemic diseases, and the city ordinances that sometimes resulted, ordering a greater use of masonry in buildings.

The cause of urban fires lay most often in the arrangements made for heating and cooking. These necessarily involved a hearth or an oven, and the fuel most commonly used was wood, which often burned irregularly and scattered sparks into the room. A chimney carried smoke from the house, and as the buildings became taller, so the chimneys grew longer and more tortuous. Chimneys were particularly dangerous in two ways. Soot accumulated in their bends and junctions and was likely to ignite into a fire that was extremely difficult to put out. At the same time the unwise practice developed of building the ends of floor joists into the chimney stack without at the same time protecting them from the heat and flames. Many an urban fire originated and spread unseen beneath the floorboards. There were even instances of chimneys built largely of wood. In earlier centuries it had sometimes been the practice to erect the kitchen as a detached building in the yard behind the house. This arrangment was no longer possible in the more congested conditions of modern times, and the risk of kitchen fires was greatly increased.

Related to countless hearths in the more congested quarters were the prevailing smoke and dirt. Mercier wrote of eighteenth-century Paris that "la fumée éternelle . . . s'élève de ces cheminées."[47] Chimneys were probably not tall enough, and most of the smoke remained near the ground. Moisture condensed on the smoke particles, and some cities became notorious for their fogs. Fog swirls perpetually through the London of Charles Dickens. In the seventeenth century the problem began to be intensified by the use of coal instead of wood. There had always been a prejudice against the use of coal, which, in the words of a proclamation of 1307, produced "an intolerable smell . . . and the air is greatly infected to the annoyance of [those] there dwelling and to the injury of their bodily health."[48] In the sixteenth century the burning of coal in Paris was totally forbidden. In London it proved impossible to enforce a similar ban, and the pollution that resulted prompted John Evelyn to write one of the most violent diatribes against its use.[49] In the German states attempts were made to restrict the use of coal, but all such efforts failed in the end for the simple reason that sufficient wood was not available for all the uses to which the fuel was put. After about 1835 the smoke of railroad locomotives was added to that of the factory and domestic hearth. And all the while smoke and fog added to the discomforts of urban living.

Of the problems of life in cities, the lack of street illumination must have been, until late in the nineteenth century, one of the most serious. Streets were always dark at night; even the windows of nearby houses were usually shuttered. Those who could afford it walked the streets accompanied by a servant carrying a torch. In Paris in 1405 lanterns were ordered to be placed in the streets, but, since the order was repeated a year or two later, it was probably not fully observed. Street lighting on a regular basis was impossible before the use of coal gas was introduced. The first city to have any measure of gas illumination was London in 1813. By the mid-century gas lighting had been adopted in most of the larger cities of western and central Europe, but, largely on account of the cost and complexity of installing a gasworks and pipeline, it was adopted very much later by the smaller towns. But by the twentieth century street lighting was general in western and central Europe, though rare in eastern.

It is impossible to exaggerate the social consequences of the installation of street lamps. Urban roads ceased to be deserted after dark, and, if lighting failed to make them totally safe, it at least encouraged more people to venture out singly and in groups. Social life benefited, at least among those with the leisure to pursue it. But street lights merely prolonged the hours of work for others. Shops were kept open till late at night, and the hours worked by shop assistants, which had previously terminated when darkness fell, were now extended as long as there were potential customers in the streets.

The development of the internal pattern of the city was shaped by the means of transport available. Public transportation systems—bus, tramway, and railroad—did not become important before the middle years of the nineteenth century. Previously horses and horse-drawn wagons and coaches were used, but for journeys within the city and its environs most people walked. The absence of public transport was of little importance when people lived at or very close to their place of work. This began to change in the nineteenth century, when the rich began to move to the suburbs, and the poor went to work in factories. This trend has continued, and with it, the need for internal urban transportation has increased. Until the nineteenth century most cities were small enough for a person to be able to walk across them. The only difficulty the pedestrian would encounter was the depth of mud and filth that lay about the streets. Indeed, in one English city at the end of the Middle Ages the walls were said to have been kept in repair only because their rampart walk provided a dry path from one side of the city to the other.

Before the coming of the bus and tram the horse-drawn coach provided the chief means of transit. Long-distance coaches were driven to inns near the city center, and the richer citizens had their own carriages and horses. These were commonly kept in stables and coach houses, often known in England as "mews." Passage through the narrow streets was fraught with difficulty if not danger, especially in the larger cities. Mercier catalogued the accidents that had resulted from *voitures* traversing the streets of Paris.[50] At the very least, the pedestrian risked being spattered with mud. Added to this traffic was the press of peasant carts and wagons that were driven into the marketplaces. The resulting congestion can be imagined; indeed, it can still be witnessed in the small towns of eastern Europe, where the streets are rendered impassable by the throng of slow-moving, horse-drawn vehicles.

In some cities riverboats were used to facilitate movement. Ferries across the river supplemented the bridges, and small boats, known in Germany as *Märktschiffer,* plied up and down the river. But this adjunct was not practicable in most cities.

The first urban transit systems derived from the coaches or *voitures.* They used horse-drawn buses, which offered a service "for all"—hence their name of *omnibus.*[51] The first operated in Nantes (France) in 1826. The next was established in Paris, where the need was far greater. But the roughly paved streets exerted a heavy drag on the vehicles, which was not reduced until they were fitted with flanged wheels and made to run on rails laid along the streets. The system lost in flexibility but became mechanically more efficient. The horse tram, with or without rails, spread through most of the larger cities of Europe and went far toward solving the problem of internal transit. At the end of the century electric power began to replace horsepower, and early in the present century the motor bus restored a degree of flexibility to the transportation system. Berlin had a rudimentary system of motor buses by 1902.

In the meantime, the bicycle had evolved almost to its modern form, providing a cheap, convenient, and individual mode of transport. The importance of the bicycle to the urban classes in the late nineteenth and twentieth centuries was incalculable. Although the earliest models were too highly priced and inefficient to have had much social significance, the so-called safety bicycle, which came onto the market in the 1880s, commanded a mass market. For an increasing number of people, especially in the larger cities, it solved the problem of the journey to work and at the same time provided a means of recreation. Journeys into the countryside began to play a role in the lives of increasing numbers. The significance of the bicycle in improving the material conditions of a large sector of the urban population has never been fully appreciated. But the bicycle remained too expensive for the really poor well into the present century. It was the vehicle of the urban lower middle class, and such it remained until displaced by the automobile. The bicycle, furthermore, was almost restricted to western and central Europe. It made little headway in Mediterranean Europe, and even less among the prevailingly rural population of eastern, where most people were generally speaking too poor and the roads too muddy and rutted for the bicycle to have had any practical use.

The Urban Population

How many people and what proportion of the total population lived at any one time in cities? Some rough indication of city size has been given above, but it is very difficult to say how many cities belonged to each size category at any particular date. Not until late in the nineteenth century did census data become generally available, and even so the information was totally unreliable for Russia and the Balkans. Urban statistics furthermore are bedeviled by the uncertainty surrounding the definition of city. That used in this chapter is a functional one, but the census defines a city in terms of its size. It is a nucleated settlement of more than two thousand or five thousand or wherever the cutoff is fixed. Such a definition inevitably excludes many towns with indisputably urban functions but embraces the huge villages that were to be found in southern Italy and the Hungarian plain.

Although it is not difficult to formulate estimates of the number of cities and of the total urban population for particular areas during the later Middle Ages, any such study which purports to cover the whole of Europe is fraught with immense difficulty. The evidence is too uncertain and discontinuous. That the level of urban development varied greatly from one area to another is apparent. In highly urbanized regions, such as northern Italy and the southern Low Countries, the urban population may have risen as high as 25 or 30 percent of the total. In Scandinavia and the plains of eastern Europe it may have been as low as 5 percent. Late in the seventeenth century the French provincial administrators, or *Intendants,* were called upon to formulate estimates of the size of towns under their jurisdiction, and these figured largely in the work of the eighteenth-century demographers. Numerous estimates were made in Germany, the Low Countries, and France of the population in at least the larger cities. Büsching, Mirabeau, and Saugrin published figures, but these were only estimates, and no great reliance can be placed on them. Not until the nineteenth century does an acceptable picture emerge of urban population. Despite the many difficulties, Paul Bairoch has compiled estimates of both total urban population and the number of cities with over 20,000 inhabitants (Table 2).[52]

Table 2. Development of Urban Population

Year	Total Population in Millions	Urban Population in Millions	Percentage of Total	Number of Cities with over 20,000 Inhabitants
1500	(100)*	9.3	9.3	89
1600	(130)	12.6	9.7	——
1700	(145)	15.2	10.5	126
1800	205.5	25.2	12.3	194
1900	414.4	137.8	33.2	1009

*Figures in parentheses are approximations.

The urban pattern in Europe was at no time even or uniform. In large areas such as Scandinavia, eastern Europe, and the Balkan peninsula, there was no great demand before the late nineteenth century for the kinds of service that cities could offer. Elsewhere, notably in England, the southern Low Countries, and southwest Germany, there was a net of closely spaced towns, most of them small, but with a scatter of medium-sized and large cities. In the later Middle Ages cities were largest and most numerous in two areas: the Low Countries and neighboring parts of France, and in the plain of northern Italy.

The urban pattern that emerged during the Middle Ages changed little before the late eighteenth century. The urban population approximately doubled in this period, but much of this growth took place in a small number of great cities. These included London, Paris, Amsterdam, Naples, and Constantinople, as well as some of the political capitals of central Europe. In the late sixteenth century, the Italian Giovanni Botero wrote a treatise on *The Causes of the Magnificency and Greatness of Cities.*[53] In it he elaborated what he considered to be the reasons for urban growth. Among them he listed "the commodity of the site" and "the fruitfulness of the country." But he realized that these elements did not provide a complete explanation and added the institutions of the church and the universities as factors in urban growth. "Some good store of vendible merchandise," or, in other words, the possession of a basic industry, was also important, but "the greatest means to make a city populous and great is to have supreme authority and power; for that draweth dependency with it, and dependency concourse, and concourse greatness." He was right; urban growth before the industrial age was largely in the capital cities, and was, in modern terms, a spin-off effect of the functions of government.

From late in the eighteenth century the ranks of the rapidly growing cities were joined by the new centers of industrial growth. In Botero's words, "the commodity of the site" and "some good store of vendible merchandise" took over as the driving forces in urban growth. Although it is impossible to make a classification of nineteenth-century cities on the basis of their functions, it is nevertheless apparent that a class of industrial or manufacturing cities was emerging and was growing rapidly (see chap. 11).

There was always a great variation in wealth *within* the city. This range was inevitable since at any one time there were those newly arrived penniless folk from the countryside as well as established burgesses. In most cities there were too many of the former, competing for the unskilled jobs that were open to them and depressing the level of wages. They commonly outnumbered all other social groups. Precise figures are unobtainable, simply because the poor paid no tax, and their very existence was forgotten in the public records. Among those sufficiently affluent to pay the Parisian tax of 1421, the richest were up to thirty times better off than the poorest, and this does not take into account many of the humbler craftsmen as well as the army of unskilled and poor who were excluded from the tax roll. The graph in figure 8.15 shows how the taxpayers in seventeenth-century Amiens and eighteenth-century Paris were apportioned among the several income groups.[54]

In 1789 a survey of the city of Orléans showed the population structure detailed in Table 3.[55] There is no indication of the level of wealth or income of each of these groups, but there was probably a very rough correspondence between the "workers" at Orléans and those below the tax threshold in Paris. Both were miserably poor, and their housing and living conditions totally inadequate. Without a statistical basis, it is impossible to say what proportion of the total population was made up of the very poor. The Orléans evidence suggests that they constituted over a half, with a further quarter, made up of petty craftsmen and traders,

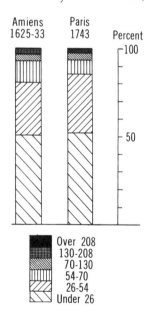

8.15. The structure of the population of Amiens and Paris. The great range in wealth (given in *livres*) and the vast numbers of the very poor are apparent. The richest category was not present in Amiens.

living close to the margin of subsistence. This is confirmed by other sources. At Bayeux, in Normandy, in the later eighteenth century, "over half of those rated on the tax lists hovered dangerously on the fringe of destitution." There were, in a city of no more than 10,000, 3,000 "on the brink of destitution and 1,800 who had crossed that boundary."[56]

Wage levels were extremely low, providing no more in many instances than was necessary to purchase five or six pounds of bread when prices were normal. It is difficult to visualize the material conditions under which such people lived. The ordinary worker's income, even when he was fully employed, was barely enough to feed himself, least of all a family, and this left nothing for clothing and accommodation, which were of the most primitive order.

Table 3. Social Structure of Orléans, 1789

	Total	With families and dependents
The Church	160	5–600
The Nobility	160	5–600
Upper Bourgeoisie	500	1,500
Middle Bourgeoisie	500	1,500
Lower Bourgeoisie	4,300	13,000
Workers	8,000	24,000
	13,620	41,000–41,200

A large part of the population in all large and medium-sized cities was close to destitution, living in abject poverty and in the worst possible physical conditions. But the smallest towns were in some measure protected from this. Theirs was a face-to-face society, in which everyone knew everyone else and the stranger was at once recognized and made unwelcome.[57] The burgesses formed a tight oligarchy that controlled settlement and employment. There was no half-employed and destitute population, because there was no unrestricted immigration. This situation began to change in the early nineteenth century. Factory production and improved transportation struck at the basis of the small towns' exclusiveness, and they either developed industry, grew larger, and became like the rest, or stagnated, merged with the rural background, and ceased to attract immigrants.

Conclusion

The medieval city had begun as a kind of intruder into a feudally ordered society, tolerated because of the benefits that it could confer. Although it could exercise no control over its surrounding rural areas, it was nonetheless dependent on them for the supply of food, for the sale of its products, and, most important of all, for the population with which to sustain its growth. This symbiotic relationship between town and country has continued to exist and to develop in ways that medieval people could never have envisaged. The city has spread into the countryside, absorbing and transforming rural settlements, and in its search for water, for industrial power, and for the means of disposing of industrial and domestic waste, it has sent its tentacles far into its surrounding region.

Chapter 9

TOWARD A CONSUMING SOCIETY

A large consumption among the poor [was] of more consequence
than among the rich.

--—Arthur Young

*B*ehind the expansion in agriculture, the improvement in diet, the increase
in population, and advances in the material conditions of life, which have
been discussed in the last five chapters, there lie the changes in technology that made
these developments possible. The history of material culture is, in its final analysis, that
of tools and techniques, of innovation, and of the diffusion of changes in the ways of
making and doing things. The role of technological advance has been in the main to
speed up productive processes and to increase the effectiveness of human labor. Each
successful innovation allowed an individual to produce more goods with a similar
investment of effort. It increased the speed of traditional processes, like spinning and
weaving; it produced substitute materials, such as steel alloys and synthetic fibers; and it
introduced new motive forces—water, wind, and the expansive power of steam—which
increased manyfold the energy available and, in consequence, the scale and speed of
production.

Development and improvement in one field was followed by advances in others.
Progress in ironworking led to the manufacture of more effective equipment for agriculture, better tools for the craftsman, nails for timber construction, horseshoes, metal
springs for carriages, and iron tires for wheels of carts. And each of these advances had as
its consequence an increase in food production, a wider market, and greater comfort and
amenities. The ramifications of any particular advance in technology or management
had no limit. Its consequences spread ever wider as, by a kind of multiplier effect, it
influenced other aspects of human activity. Inevitably, material progress tended to
accelerate, as small advances in individual fields were reflected in progress in others.

Growth became exponential, culminating in the developments that have become known collectively as the Industrial Revolution. The history of this movement tends to be expressed in terms of inventions in iron and steel production, the cotton-textile industry, and the steam engine. It was, however, a movement on a very broad front, and it resulted from the interaction of an immense number of innovations, some of them in themselves of only marginal importance. It did not erupt suddenly onto the European scene. In this sense it was not a revolution; its roots lie not with innovators in the later eighteenth century but with countless inventions and improvements, many of which originated in the later Middle Ages and slowly worked their way through the industrial system. The graph of progress in these respects is characterized not by a series of giant steps or quantum jumps from one stage to another, but rather by a smooth but slowly accelerating progression.

The consequences of an innovation were not often immediately apparent. It commonly took many years for it to become known and accepted. Of course there have been instances of innovations that satisfied an obvious and widely felt need and were accepted relatively quickly. The introduction of the basic process of steelmaking in 1879 is one. The need for a process for handling phosphoric iron-ores had long been felt. Chemists and metallurgists were actively seeking a way of making steel from them, and steelmakers were ready to accept any successful innovation immediately. There are, of course, other instances of the conscious search for a solution to a widely experienced technical problem. But most innovations crept in slowly and almost unobserved. It is a mistake to assume that the innovator or inventor was always welcomed. All too often he upset a social balance and interfered with a set of related activities. Though some might profit from an invention, far too many lost for it to have been accepted with any kind of rapture. It has taken almost two centuries for the factory to displace the domestic worker, and a century after the application of steampower to industrial processes, there were still factories operated by the waterwheel.

For successful innovation, four sets of conditions have to be satisfied. In the first place, the essential resources or raw materials must be present, or at least obtainable. These might include, in addition to labor, stone and clay, metalliferous ores and other materials, timber and fuel. Second, an innovating society must have access to knowledge of the new process or method. In modern societies this requirement may present little difficulty. They are, by and large, literate, and the the press and trade and commercial journals are generally adequate to make the potential market familiar with any innovation. Not so, however, in the past. Innovation was diffused very slowly, and, if it proved successful, was more likely to have been kept secret for as long as possible. There was never any question of instant acceptance; only of the slow spread of an idea and its implementation. Such diffusion can, as a general rule, be traced only in the most general way. The spread of the water and windmill, of the spinning wheel and the pottery and brick kiln, can be roughly traced; that of the "steeling" of tools, the scarfing of timber joints, the horizontal loom, and the lathe can be followed only in the broadest outline.

Not unrelated to the acquisition of new tools and techniques is the ability to pay for them. Skilled craftsmen have, generally speaking, proved costly. They have to be attracted to a developing area and paid relatively highly for the knowledge and skill that they could impart. In the past a veil of secrecy tended to envelop innovations. More recently the patent laws have served to protect inventors and their work. In either case, knowledge or expertise had to be bought.

There must finally be some perceived advantage in adopting a new process or technology. To us, with the benefit of the long view of historical development, the advantages may seem obvious, and we may be tempted to condemn the obstinacy and blindness that hindered the adoption of innovations in the past. But this vision was always hidden to contemporaries. In the late eighteenth century Arthur Young was vigorous in his denunciation of the foolishness of open-field farming, but to those who practiced it, it was a means of smoothing out the inequalities in village society, of fertilizing the land, and of maintaining sheep and other farm stock. It was but one element in a complex system of interlocking structures. To interfere with it would be to jeopardize the whole. The same might be said of the linked small holding and domestic craft industries, which continued to exist, if not also to flourish, unlike late in the nineteenth century, despite the competition of the cheaper and more effective factory industry.

Readiness even to perceive the advantages of innovation varied greatly. Stuart Piggott's contrast between conserving and innovating societies has already been noted. Resistance to change may spring from several sources. In all of us there is an inbuilt reluctance to change our pattern of life. Change involves risk, demands mental effort, and raises problems of adapting to a new set of circumstances. When these circumstances are underpinned by law and custom, change is rendered all the more difficult. The writer must have read hundreds of agricultural leases of the seventeenth and eighteenth centuries that required for the period of their applicability the continued practice of a farming system that was already obsolete when the leases were drawn. Law can in time be revised, but manorial and village custom can prove remarkably durable and intractable. In the field of agriculture, in which custom has always been most deeply entrenched, it required legislation in much of Europe to override the customary local practices of open-field farming and fallow grazing.

The model that has been proposed is that of progress, continuous but slow, achieved by the accumulation of small increments in each of many branches of human activity. Advance in one leads to advance in all others that can in some way be related to it, so that progress is seen to accelerate. Yet there was not, indeed there could not be, a steady and continuous expansion in the supply of consumer goods of all kinds. This condition would have depended on continuing availability of the resources from which they were made. Resources are finite and some are very restricted. Exhaustion or depletion of a resource is accompanied by a rise in its price and a shift to alternate materials. Shortages showed themselves during the preindustrial age in many commodities, but one example must serve. There was in some parts of Europe during the later Middle Ages and early modern times a growing shortage of large timber for structural purposes. Cottages surviving from this period show an increasing use of smaller timbers, and it is reasonable to suppose that the shortage was a factor in the growing use of alternate or substitute materials. At the same time the depletion of the forests affected the supply of charcoal for the smith, of fuel for the home, and of potash for the glassmaker and soap-boiler. In time, of course, substitutes—chiefly from overseas sources of supply—were found. But the expansion of any productive activity that used expendable resources could not, from the nature of things, be ever upward.

To speak of rising standards in diet and in material comforts is to generalize. Such improvements were not common to all segments and classes of society. Nor was this picture true of all parts of Europe. Indeed, it is probably correct to say that the humblest classes everywhere lived as close to starvation and destitution in the early nineteenth century as they did a millennium earlier.[1] The depictions of poverty presented during the first half of the last century by people varying in their outlooks as much as Edwin Chadwick, Friedrich Engels, and John Hollingshead are not fundamentally different from those offered by La Bruyère in the seventeenth century and the *Vision of Piers Plowman* in the fourteenth. The difference between these periods lies in the increase in the numbers who lived above this level, and the increasing disparity between rich and poor. The *average* consumption both of food and of consumer goods increased very considerably, but this increase was very largely to be found among the better off.[2]

This raises the further question: how numerous were the more affluent classes and where were they to be found? Throughout this long period, both rich and poor lived side by side; only their relative numbers varied. Attempts have been made on the basis of taxation returns to compute the sizes of income groups. This can be done for some cities, especially the city republics of Italy, but on any kind of national basis it is not possible before the late nineteenth century. Nevertheless, it can be inferred that the more well-to-do classes, made up of yeoman farmers and substantial peasants, of middle-class townsfolk and of *rentiers* and landowners everywhere, were relatively most numerous in Great Britain and northwest Europe, and in parts of France, the Rhineland, and northern Italy. Only in these areas was there a significant and growing market for consumer goods before the nineteenth century. It must be assumed that this market was small throughout eastern and southeastern Europe and that it was poorly developed in Spain and much of France, Germany, and Scandinavia. Arthur Young was shocked by the abysmally low purchasing power of the rural population of France. It must have been even smaller in eastern Europe and Russia, where much of the agricultural population still possessed a servile status.

The pattern of craft industries mirrored the purchasing power of the market that they served. Both urban and rural crafts emerged during the Middle Ages in northern Italy and throughout northwestern Europe and retained their importance, despite local fluctuations, into the nineteenth century. This was fertile ground for innovation, and it is difficult to find a single technological innovation from the Middle Ages to the nineteenth century that did not have its origin in this region. Elsewhere, craft industries remained small-scale, primitive, and unprogressive, and their market restricted to their local areas. Such regions proved remarkably unreceptive to innovation, and, apart from a few industrial centers, where large-scale technology had been imposed by western entrepreneurs, the technical and material levels were no higher at the beginning of the present century than they had been in the west two hundred years earlier.

Production and Power

Consumer goods, at least before the present century, can for convenience be grouped under five heads. They consisted, in the first place, of clothing and footwear, as necessary in a cold climate as food itself. This group of industries made up, both in the numbers employed and in the total value of its output, the most important of the five categories. Next came the products of miners and metalworkers, ranging from the work of the smiths, who forged agricultural tools and tempered weapons, to the delicate creations of jewelers and goldsmiths. Pottery, bricks, tiles, and glass constitute a third group of manufactured products, and one of steadily increasing relative importance. Fourth were the products of workers in wood: rough furniture for the home, doors and shutters for unglazed windows, and more sophisticated panels and screens for churches. From the seventeenth century woodworkers made the grand furnishings of great homes. Closely related to carpentry and joinery, and often enough practiced by the same craftsmen, was, lastly, building construction. Until the nineteenth century timber construction remained important everywhere, except in southern Europe, though in the larger cities stone and brick were replacing wood. There was always a need for men skilled in erecting roofs and jointing timber, and masons were increasingly important even in the peasant regions of Europe's northern and eastern periphery.

Craft industries grew in complexity, in the scale of their production, and in their degree of specialization in the thousand years that elapsed between the Dark Ages and the Industrial Revolution. The Romans had used to the full the technologies that they had inherited from Iron Age Europe, but they added little to them. Mechanical power, rotary motion, the use of gears and screws and of high temperatures for smelting and working metals by and large escaped them, as did also the horizontal loom, the spinning wheel, and vegetable dyestuffs.[3] It was the Middle Ages that were inventive in these respects, and it was on a foundation of medieval innovation that modern industrialized society was built.

Development in manufacturing technology during the preindustrial period took place mainly in three fields: the use of mechanical power; the improvement in machines, including machine tools; and the general area of chemicals and chemical engineering. Most significant of these was the use of mechanical power. The Romans had used waterpower to operate mills for grinding, but the paucity of suitable rivers in the Mediterranean region must have deterred innovation in this field. The Roman water-wheel was undershot, merely dipping into the water and turning slowly with the flow of the current. In the course of the Middle Ages larger and more efficient wheels were devised, and overshot wheels of increasing size and power were built. Their uses multiplied, as they were adapted to fulling cloth, crushing ore, pumping water and operating the bellows of a blast furnace. In the eighteenth century, harnessed to shafts and belt drives, they provided power for the first modern factories.

The waterwheel came to be supplemented from the later Middle Ages by the windmill. It had certain advantages. Its arms would continue to turn after the rivers that powered the watermills had dried up or turned to ice. The journal of an anonymous Parisian described how, during an abnormally severe winter in the early fifteenth century the citizens were obliged to rely on windmills.[4] Engraved city views of the sixteenth and seventeenth centuries often represented windmills mounted upon the walls and towers. But there was a limit to the size and capacity of a windmill. Large units of power could not be developed, and, apart from its use in restricted areas for pumping water, the windmill served only to grind cereals and oil seeds.

The role of mechanical power was to multiply many times the output of a worker. It ended the ordeal of grinding grain in a hand quern and increased greatly the output of the textile and metal industries. In the long run, it cheapened production and made more goods available to a larger proportion of the population. But a limit was set to the size and efficiency of the waterwheel both by the strength of the materials—mainly wood—of which it was made, and by the size of the streams that were employed to turn it. The demand for ever larger units of power could only be satisfied by the adoption of the steam engine. The first operable steam engine was patented in England, in 1698, by Thomas Savery. Shortly afterward Thomas Newcomen built a more efficient machine, which came to be widely used during the eighteenth century. Both machines worked on the "atmospheric" principle, by which movement was created by the condensation of steam and creation of a vacuum within the cylinder. From the first, the Newcomen-type engine was used for pumping water from mines, for which its slow reciprocating movement was especially suited. Indeed, the further development of the mining indus-try at this time would have been inconceivable without it.

Many improvements were made in the action of the atmospheric engine before, in 1769, James Watt was granted a patent for a steam engine with separate condenser. In this machine the piston was moved by the *pressure* of steam, which was drawn out and condensed separately. It proved to be a faster-acting and very much more efficient engine, and became in time the principle source of power in the newly developing factories. The conversion of reciprocating into rotary motion had long been a problem for engineers. Newcomen's engine had merely been coupled by means of a rocking beam with pump rods that descended into the earth. Watt developed a more sophisticated system whereby the connecting rods that descended from the beam turned a horizontal shaft. Such a machine could be used relatively easily to drive separate machines, as in a textile factory, by means of belt drives. It could be made to turn the rolls of an ironworks and to generate the blast for a smelting furnace, and early in the next century it was mounted on a carriage that it propelled along the road or over tracks laid down for it.

The invention, development, and diffusion of the steam engine was probably the most important and far-reaching technical innovation since the discovery of smelting itself. It became the basis of nineteenth-century factory development and transportation, with all the social and economic consequences that these entailed. Yet the steam engine displaced older and simpler sources of energy very slowly. Most eighteenth-century factories, in both Great Britain and continental Europe, were located and built to use waterpower, which seemed cheap, universal, and inexhaustible. The steam engine, by contrast, required mineral fuel in immense quantities, for its thermal efficiency was low. But coal was highly localized in its occurrence, and, until the development of railroads and, to a more limited degree, canals and navigable rivers, it was not everywhere available. The logic of the situation was that, before the railway age, factories designed to use steam power had to be established close to the coalfields, some of which became highly industrialized and urbanized.

There were, however, many regions that developed factory industry without resort to steam power, at least in their early stages of growth. Among them were the textile regions of Catalonia in Spain, of northern Italy, and of Łódź in Poland. In some such instances there was never a period when coal and steam provided the chief motive force. Water-power continued to be used until it was replaced by electricity late in the nineteenth century.

At the same time, the waterwheel, which could, mainly for structural reasons, generate only small units of power, gave way to the turbine generator. This device made use of the vast potential inherent in mountain streams and in all water bodies that descended from a considerable altitude. Such hydroelectric stations normally required a large expenditure on dam and pipeline construction, but as sources of energy they were immense. Above all, they could supply power, if necessary, in very small amounts over a vast area.

The increasing use of mechanical power from the later Middles Ages onward was a powerful factor in changing the material conditions of life. Its role in increasing the volume of production both absolutely and relative to the labor consumed has already been noted. In this respect, its consequences were wholly beneficial. But mechanical power was, at least in its earlier phases, available only in relatively large units. Some of these were, indeed, too large, and thus called for a far-reaching reorganization of production. A waterpowered flour mill, if large enough to be efficient, could serve a large area but called for a considerable investment and needed to be kept fully employed. Hence the social pressures to abandon the hand quern and to grind at the lord's mill. The coming of the steam engine posed the same problem, but on an immensely larger scale. Within the sphere of textile production, the alternatives ultimately came to be the domestic spinner and handloom weaver on the one hand, and the factory with an employment of many hundreds on the other. And in the competition between the old and the new, between small-scale production and large, it was always the latter that eventually won.

Closely related to the use of mechanical power was the development of devices whereby this power could be transmitted and used. The early watermills had used gears, with wheels and teeth of wood. The earliest clockmakers in the thirteenth century used metal wheels in the mechanism of their clocks. At the same time, trip-hammers, of metal and wood, were developed for fulling mills and for bellows and hammers in metal works. But there was little advance in mechanical engineering in the strict sense before the eighteenth century. This was due in part to the high price and uneven quality of steel. A partial remedy was found in the mid-eighteenth century in Huntsman's process for making crucible steel. Huntsman was by profession a clockmaker. He needed metal of a high and uniform quality for the springs of his watches and clocks and felt compelled to make his own steel.

Another factor in the slow development of mechanical engineering was the lack of precision resulting from the primitive character of the lathes and drills available. Watt was, for example, gravely hindered in building his steam engines because cylinders were imperfectly bored and were incapable of maintaining a high pressure. Improvements came very slowly in all these respects. It was not until the seventeenth century that the lathe came into general use for turning articles of metal or wood. It was used by cabinetmakers, but, being itself largely built of wood, it was an imprecise instrument and did not until the early nineteenth century acquire its modern character. Only then did the lathe become a precision instrument.

Most of these early developments in engineering took place in England. The techniques of mechanical spinning, of the power loom, of puddling iron, and of steelmaking were relatively simple and were easily acquired in continental Europe. An obstacle to their spread was, as a British parliamentary commission demonstrated in 1825, the lack of machine tools with which to build the equipment.

Advance in the chemical aspects of technology was more difficult to achieve, because it was not until late in the eighteenth century that the nature of chemical reactions began to be known. Nevertheless, significant developments did occur before this date, though most were made empirically. As the basis of chemical change began to be understood, so it became possible to experiment in a meaningful fashion. Solutions began to be sought for clearly recognized problems. Foremost among these, at least in the early days of the chemical industry, was a means of producing on a large scale the common acids and alkalies and thus of obtaining soda. It is beyond the scope of this book to examine the processes that were actually developed in the late eighteenth century; sufficient to stress their social importance.

The use of the common alkalies for making glass and soap had been known since ancient times, but the processes were limited by the prevailing shortage of materials, primarily of woodash. Not until the late eighteenth century was the Leblanc method of making soda from common salt introduced. Woodash, much of it imported from North America and the Baltic, continued to be used, despite its high cost. But the Leblanc process gained in importance until it was replaced during the middle years of the nineteenth century by the somewhat simpler Solvay process. The net result of these processes was an immense increase in the production of soda ash and the cheapening of the products that were chiefly derived from it. Soda, either sodium carbonate or caustic soda, became the basis of two of the most socially important developments of modern times: soap and glass, the one essential for cleanliness and health, the other for the construction of light and habitable homes. Both contributed immeasurably to the higher standards of material well-being that were achieved in the nineteenth century.

The Organization of Production

Changing technical and commerical conditions brought about fundamental changes in the organization of production. During the Middle Ages and early modern times, most production was on a domestic or craft basis. The craftsman produced to satisfy the needs of his family and in some measure his neighbors. He may, indeed, have been engaged only part-time in his craft, working for the rest on his small holding. Members of his household and family in all probability contributed. It was the women—the "spinsters"—who supplied the male weavers with thread, and, often enough, the carding of the fibers preparatory to spinning was the work of children. The local community, if not the family, was able, as a general rule, to produce most of the manufactured goods that it needed, as well as the raw materials from which they were made: wool and flax, clay for pots, timber for woodworking, and perhaps even a low-grade iron ore, from which the local smith produced the simplest pieces of hardware.

In much of Europe this domestic system of production, in which the craftsman was but semi-specialized, prevailed until late in the nineteenth century. This was especially the case with cloth production and simple woodworking. Metal fabrication was, however, generally left to the specialized smith from a relatively early date, and the tailor, sometimes itinerant, tended to take over the manufacture of rough homespun cloth into garments. By and large, the craftsman was becoming a specialist, buying his raw materials and devoting himself exclusively to his craft. He usually sold directly to the consumer, with the consequence that his place of work became his shop. With increasing specialization, the craftsman became dependent on an ever-broadening market. The village community ceased to suffice, and he looked for the greater opportunities offered by the city. But not all crafts were drawn in this way to the towns. Mining and smelting were carried on where their basic materials, ore and fuel, were to be found. Mills were attracted to sources of waterpower, and the fulling process, which began to be mechanized during the later Middle Ages, also left the cities for the countryside.

The rural community, in general, produced most of the manufactured goods that it needed. Urban crafts were for townsfolk. The countryman, from the earliest times for which we have records until the late nineteenth century, had little use for the products of the urban cordwainer, or tailor, or armorer. These goods were for the middle and upper classes. Even the urban weavers tended to produce a cloth of higher quality and better finish than the rough woolens and linen worn by the peasant. In dress, as in other patterns of consumption, there was a world of difference between the peasant and the townsman.

One thinks of urban medieval manufactures as organized into and controlled by gilds, one gild to each craft, its elected officers maintaining discipline and order among its members and ensuring the proper training of apprentices and the quality of workmanship. It is doubtful whether this idealized world of Hans Sachs ever existed. Gilds were, in fact, exclusive, autocratic, and a brake on technical progress, and their overregulation contributed to a new diffusion of craft industries from the towns to the countryside. Most affected by this dispersion of craft industries was clothworking in all its branches. This enterprise had, in fact, never abandoned the rural cottages where cloth had always been woven. The balance, at least in western Europe, had merely tipped in favor of the city. There were many reasons why in the late Middle Ages this balance again tipped toward the rural industry. The rigidity of the gild system and its unwillingness to innovate or experiment was one. Another was the growing use of waterpower to full the cloth, and a third was the introduction of lighter and more loosely woven fabrics—the so-called new draperies—the manufacture of which was often excluded from the town by urban regulations.

Underlying the change, however, was the emergence of the "putting-out" system. The rural craftsman worked in relative isolation. There was no clientele on his doorstep, waiting to buy his product, and the restrictiveness of urban gilds prevented him from selling directly in the nearest town. This impasse was resolved by the merchant. By origin he was likely to have been a successful urban craftsman himself. Instead of expanding urban production, which was commonly prohibited by gild regulation, he extended his help and protection to the unorganized rural workers, supplying them with raw materials and collecting and marketing their products. This system emerged in western Europe during the later Middle Ages, first and foremost in the clothing industry but also in leather-, metal-, and even woodworking. It lasted into the nineteenth century and in some restricted areas into the twentieth. This putting-out system was especially suited to those industries which embraced a series of sequential stages. The clothing industry is an obvious example, consisting as it does of at least five stages: carding or combing, spinning, weaving, dyeing and fulling, and finishing. The merchant customarily obtained raw wool and put it out in turn to the appropriate craftsmen, until a marketable piece of cloth was at last delivered by the finisher.

The merchant had become increasingly involved in other branches of industrial production besides textiles. Pottery had come to be confined, as it had been under the Roman Empire, to a relatively small number of sites, where the materials, primarily clay and fuel, were most readily available. This concentration necessitated the intervention of middlemen between producer and consumer, though there was no question of their supplying materials, which could, as a general rule, be obtained locally. The same goes for the materials required by glassmakers, miners, and all primary metalworkers. Secondary metalworkers, among whom we must number the smiths, lorimers, armorers, locksmiths, and those engaged in an almost infinite number of specialized metalworking crafts, dealt directly with the public but had, as a general rule, to obtain their raw materials through the merchants who dealt in bar iron, brass, leather, and other materials.

Much has been written in recent years about the phase of industrialism that preceded the fully fledged factory system. It has come to be called "proto-industrial." It differed from simple craft production in the breadth of its market and the intervention of the middleman between producer and consumer. It was distinguished from factory industry by the small scale of each unit and, in most cases, its independence of mechanical power. That the system lent itself to abuse is apparent. Organization was almost impossible among the scattered domestic workers, and they rarely had any alternative to accepting the payment offered by the merchant.[5] There can be no question but that conditions among domestic workers deteriorated, and that in the nineteenth century they were sometimes even worse than in factories. Yet one must not be too sweeping. There were prosperous domestic workers, from among whom the middlemen were recruited, as well as those who struggled on the edge of destitution.

In many parts of Europe domestic industry was practiced only part-time, serving merely as an adjunct to agriculture, supplementing the income from a holding that had become too small to support a family or providing work during the dark days of winter when there was little to do in the fields. But the domestic system was more than this. It contributed to the fragmentation of farmholdings, to early marriage, and thus to larger families, just because it constituted an alternative source of income. It was related to the system of land tenure. It was not generally practiced where primogeniture was the rule, and the eldest son waited expectantly for the demise of his father and the inheritance that would follow. A full holding left little time for industrial pursuits. It was most common where partible inheritance was the rule, and holdings became gradually smaller as they were divided and subdivided between heirs. Here a craft became essential for the support of a family, and when times were bad the craftsman merely worked longer, produced more, and further depressed the market. This was the lesson of the crisis among domestic weavers in the 1840s.

Some parts of Europe became notorious for their minute holdings and the corresponding importance to the rural population of the uncertain market for craft products. Flanders was such an area. Linen weaving was practiced by the peasants who had grown the flax, and the cloth was sold in local markets, the best of it, we are told, in winter, when the peasants worked longest at their looms.[6] Conditions in Flemish cottages, where the artisan strained over his loom by candle or rushlight, can readily be imagined. The Flemish linen weavers suffered disastrously during the depression of the 1840s, when the collapse of the market for their fabrics coincided with the failure of the crops that had been their alternative source of support.[7] The domestic craftsman, working at home in the bosom of his family, might seem to have been more happily placed than the factory worker subjected to the noise and dirt and rigid regime of machines. This is doubtful. Audiganne in the 1840s found conditions worse and hours of work longer among domestic workers than in the factory.

The domestic industry was in the end extinguished by the competition of factory production, but not without a long and painful struggle. Domestic spinning ended in much of Europe during the first half of the nineteenth century, though it survived in parts of eastern Europe until the mid-twentieth. The handloom slowly succumbed to the factory-operated power loom. But stocking weaving, lace making, and straw plaiting declined more with changes in fashion and popular demand than through the competition of factory production. In the end, domestic crafts were practiced only by aging men and women who had been obliged progressively to trim their profit margins until both they and their craft succumbed.

In the end it was the factory that triumphed. Its essential feature was its use of mechanical power, derived from either flowing water or steam. And, since these units of power were generally large, factories also had to be large. A kind of bridge between the domestic workshop and the factory had been provided by a large workshop in which workers plied their craft manually but under supervision. There were such "factories" in classical times. In the fifth century B.C. Cephalus employed 120 slaves in his Athenian shield factory. There were other instances before, about 1540, William Stumpe, a clothier, used the buildings of the dissolved Malmesbury Abbey for his handloom weavers. In more recent times the woolen industry of Verviers, in southern Belgium, was organized on a manual basis but in workshops. It was but a short step to mechanize such factories, using first water and later steam power.

The Textile Crafts

The textile crafts were the domestic industries *par excellence*. Clothing was a necessity, and, though skins and furs might be important, there was everywhere a demand for fabrics of wool, flax, or cotton, and, for the few who could afford them, of silk. A nineteenth-century traveler in Bulgaria found "a loom in nearly every other house," and "still more numerous were the spinstresses—all the widows and quite a few of the married women too, earning their living by the spinning wheel. All day long until late in the evenings, the village was filled with the continuous sound of spinning wheels whirring, looms banging, cogs rattling and mallets tapping."[8] So it was throughout much of preindustrial Europe. Until late in the Middle Ages—the date varied from one part to another—the family, or at least the local community, produced its own cloth of wool or flax, dyed and finished it, and made it up into clothing.

But some areas acquired a more than local reputation for the quality of their cloth. This fame they owed to the excellence of the wool, the superiority of the local craftsmanship, or perhaps to better marketing. Some English cloths appear to have enjoyed a high reputation from quite early in the Middle Ages, and Flanders and France achieved a similar renown. Northern and central Italy began to produce cloth of the highest quality, which was marketed in much of Europe and the Mediterranean basin. But the situation was always fluid. Some places that produced fine cloth lost their markets, while other producing centers came to the fore. Politics and warfare played a role in the fluctuating fortunes of the manufacture and trade in fine cloth. Changes in the supply of good-quality wool, like the decline of the English export to the Low Countries, were important, but a continuing influence was the capriciousness of fashion. As long as dress remained the most conspicuous outward symbol of class, there were always those who had the wealth and desire to lead the way. Silks and cotton prints came into and out of fashion. Broadcloth declined in favor as worsteds and serges came in. The growing use of underclothing increased the demand first for linen and then for cottons. As noted earlier, even the papal curia was not immune to fashion, and readily adopted the latest scarlet silk for its regalia in the fifteenth century when the dyers had perfected their craft.

The industry, at least before the last century, adapted slowly or not at all to these changes, and many were the weavers from the later Middle Ages to the recent past who were left underemployed because demand had shifted elsewhere. But these changes in fashion and supply concerned only a minority of craftsmen and consumers. The bulk of the rural population and, indeed, much of the urban, could take no part in the competition of conspicuous consumption. In weave, color, and design, their clothing differed scarcely at all between the thirteenth and the nineteenth centuries. They wore it until it fell from their backs, torn, soiled, and rotted with sweat. And when it was replaced, it was with more of the same kind, woven at home or in the community and cobbled together by the local tailor.

Most cloth in the preindustrial age was of wool. The wool shorn from the sheep was first washed in a detergent—commonly lye—to rid it of its grease and dirt. It was then

carded or combed, according to the length of the fibers (fig. 9.1). Short wool was carded, using cards, flat pieces of wood fitted with protruding hooks that tore through the knots and removed burrs and other foreign matter, leaving a soft and rather spongy mass of wool, ready for the spinner. Combing was reserved for the longer wools. Its purpose was to remove the short threads and leave only a smooth skein of long threads. Although combing had been known in classical times, it appears not to have been practiced again until the later Middle Ages, perhaps because there was little demand for cloth woven from the smooth, combed wool. Carding and combing, which called for no great strength or dexterity, were often regarded as children's work.

Spinning was universally by means of distaff and spindle. The bundle of carded or combed wool was placed for convenience on the end of the distaff. The thread was then drawn out by the fingers of the spinner, given a twist, and wound

9.1. A woman carding wool; after a drawing in the Holkham Bible.

onto the spindle. The latter, made of wood or bone, was fitted with a round bob or weight, the spindle whorl, which served as a flywheel and gave an impetus to the turning spindle. The tools of hand spinning have scarcely changed from prehistoric times to the present. The writer once watched a peasant woman in the mountains of eastern Slovakia, distaff tucked under her arm, her right hand drawing out the thread and her left giving at intervals an impulse to the turning spindle, while all the time she watched her geese as they pecked at the roadside vegetation. The picture could be mirrored in almost every detail in painted Attic vases of twenty-five centuries earlier or in drawings in medieval manuscripts. In principle the spinning wheel differed in no way from the distaff and spindle; only the turning spindle was operated mechanically by means of a large flywheel. The spinner still had to draw out the thread from the bundle placed on the distaff. The act of spinning became almost automatic. It was repetitious and boring, a suitable accompaniment to the chatter of women gathered in the gloom of a cottage during the dark evenings of winter.

The loom in use in the early Middle Ages was probably similar to that employed in classical times. It was a narrow, vertical loom. The warp was wound onto an upper roller and was held taut by weights while a heddle separated the threads for the weaver to pass the shuttle. The vertical loom was a piece of furniture that could be fitted into a small peasant cottage, and it remained in use in such circumstances into modern times. A bottom roller came to replace the warp weights, allowing a longer piece of cloth to be woven. The professional weaver, however, learned to use a horizontal loom (fig. 9.2). This version was more strongly constructed; it was wider and stood upon legs. The heddles, for there were several to allow different kinds of weave to be executed, were

9.2. A weaver at his loom; an engraving of the fifteenth century by Jost Amman. This scene shows the horizontal loom, which replaced the vertical loom (fig. 3.22).

worked by pedals. The whole process was faster than that on the vertical loom and allowed a piece of cloth up to twenty to thirty feet long and five to six feet wide to be made. The wide, horizontal loom was a response to the growing demand for cloth of superior quality.

There was little change in the design of the loom before the eighteenth century. The weaver sat on his bench, threw or passed his shuttle through the shed, or space opened by the movement of the heddle, caught it and passed it back, pausing only to use his comb to press the threads of the weft tightly together or to refill his bobbin. Sometimes, to produce a piece of cloth of exceptional width, a very wide loom was used, with two men seated before it, passing the shuttle to and fro between them.

The wool was commonly, though not always, dyed before being used. This permitted patterns of contrasted colors to be woven. Where there was any variation in the strength or toughness of the wool, the stronger was used for the warp threads, since they took the greatest strain and were subjected to the roughest handling. There was, for example, a prejudice against thread spun on the spinning wheel for this purpose, and a preference for hand-spun thread. When mixed fibers, such as wool and flax or wool and cotton, were used, the weaker was always used for weft.

The advent of the horizontal loom, fitted with pedals, allowed more complex patterns to be developed. They were produced by linking the heddles not with alternating warp threads, but by skipping groups of threads. Such refinements were not needed in cloth intended for domestic or even local use, but they were an essential ingredient of the more refined cloth that in the later Middle Ages began to command a national or even continental market. Fragments of cloth recovered from early medieval graves sometimes show relatively complex weaves.[9]

The cloth taken from the loom was far from ready for use. As Piers Plowman wrote:

Cloth that cometh fro the wevying is noght comly to were
Tyl it is fulled under fote, or in fullying Stokkes.
Wasshen wel with water and with tastes cracched,
Y-touked and y-teynted, and under tailloures hande.[10]

First the cloth had to be cleaned; sometimes it also had to be dyed. It almost always needed to be thickened, felted, or fulled. The intensity of this process varied both with the kind of cloth desired and the variety of wool used. The cloth was placed in a vat with water and a detergent and then trampled by the bare feet of the fuller until the fibers had meshed together, obscuring the weave. A variety of substances were used as fulling medium. Most often the medium was fuller's earth, a very fine clay with detergent qualities, but naturally occurring salts and organic materials, and even urine, were used. The process came, at least in northwestern Europe, to be mechanized, with a waterwheel lifting and letting fall wooden beaters, which served instead of the feet of the fuller. The cloth commonly shrank in the course of fulling and was usually stretched on tenterhooks. In one former clothworking region of England, where no weaver has worked for almost two centuries, an alley still bears the suggestive name of "Tenter Lane."

9.3. Teasels mounted on a wooden frame for raising the nap on cloth; from the shield of a Bohemian clothworkers' gild, c. 1520.

A softer finish was given to the cloth by raising the fiber ends, or nap. Traditionally this result was achieved by means of the sharp spines that covered the seed head of the teasel plant (fig. 9.3). The nap was then cropped with large shears to give an even finish (fig. 9.4). Some types of cloth, notably the high-quality broadcloth produced in Florence, were napped and sheared many times before they were ready for the market. Cloth finishing was a lengthy and laborious process, and the craftsmen were important members of society. Although the weaving industry was as much rural as urban, cloth finishing was most often carried on in the towns and was supervised by the merchants who were best able to judge both its quality and the demands of the market. There was no limit to the combinations of color, weave, and finish that became available for those who could afford them before the end of the Middle Ages. Cloth was embroidered and

9.4. A shearer using large shears to crop the nap on a piece of cloth to produce a smooth surface. (Jost Amman.)

9.5. A dyer at work by a vat of steaming dye. (Jost Amman.)

gold and silver threads were used to decorate it. But these refinements were denied to the majority, who wore coarse brown or gray homespun, woven in the cottage, dyed, if dyed at all, with such vegetable materials as were locally available, and fulled and finished only in the most rudimentary fashion. This situation did not change before the nineteenth century, when cloth from the factory began slowly to displace the coarse domestic product.

Although woolen cloth was worn in much of Europe, there were parts where linen was no less important. The flax plant was grown widely, both for the thread that derived from the stalks of the unripe plant and for the oil extracted from its ripened seeds. The peasants grew it throughout northern Europe. When grown for flax, the stalks were pulled rather than cut. They were retted by soaking them in water to loosen the woody tissues and then scutched to break them up. This was done either by beating them with a wooden mallet or by drawing them between the wooden beams of a "flax breaker." Lastly, the threads were cleaned of remaining tissue and split by being dragged across a board fitted with metal spikes. It was an arduous and time-consuming business, but fitted into the peasants' calendar because much of this work could be done in winter. The spinning and weaving of flax were closely similar to those of wool. Indeed, the same equipment was used, and in central Europe a mixed wool-flax fabric was produced, known as barchent.

The finishing of linen was a good deal simpler than that of cloth. Its essential feature was bleaching. This process usually consisted of boiling the linen in a bath of lye and then spreading it in the sun for weeks, even months, at the end of which it had acquired the white color for which it was noted. The panoramic views of cities in the seventeenth century sometimes showed pieces of linen stretched on the ground or spread over racks, slowly bleaching in the sun. It was in the main a peasant industry because the processes were arduous rather than difficult, and the peasantry could themselves grow their own raw materials. It became the mainstay of rural life across northern Europe from Brittany to Silesia, and garments were made as much of linen as of woolen cloth. In the Low Countries the manufacture of linen *toiles* came to the fore as the traditional cloth industry declined. It tended to remain a domestic or craft industry, in part because the spinning of flax proved more difficult to mechanize than that of other fibers; in part because in the nineteenth century cottons cut into the market and entrepreneurs were reluctant to invest in linen manufacture.

9.6. The seal of a clothworkers' gild in fifteenth-century Bohemia. It shows shears, teasels, and other tools used in finishing cloth.

Cotton was grown in Europe only to a very limited extent. It was unsuited to European climates, and cotton weaving became important only when Europeans were able to exploit the cotton fields of North Africa, Asia, and lastly, North America. The cotton available in the Middle Ages was short stapled and weak. It was used in Italy to make an all-cotton fabric but north of the Alps was usually used mixed with wool.[11] In fact the warp of the cloth called fustian was made of wool, and the weft of the more fragile cotton.

The processes of spinning, weaving, and finishing cotton cloth were very similar to those in the manufacture of linen. In fact, when, in the eighteenth century, the pattern of demand had changed, it proved quite easy for the peasants who had worked with flax to pick up the skills necessary to handle cotton. But the fashion of wearing cotton was inspired not by the product of peasant looms in northwestern Europe but by a cloth from India. Cotton cloth was brought to Europe in the ships of the East India Company. Even its name, calico, derived from the Indian port of Calicut. The finishing of cotton cloth rarely consisted of more than washing and bleaching. But the smoothness of good cottons lent itself to the printing of patterns on them, at first with wooden blocks, later with rollers. This practice had begun in India, and calico prints were at first sold under the name of *indiennes*. The development of a mass demand for cottons was hindered by both the high price of the imported fabric and the resistance offered by the traditional industries to its manufacture in Europe.[12] In the traditional gild-ridden centers of the woolen industry, cotton spinning had little chance of developing. It was principally where the older textiles were not securely entrenched that the cotton industry developed: in Lancashire, England; Chemnitz in Saxony; the Vosges mountains of Alsace; Catalonia; and Łódź, Poland.

Cottons were at first an up-market material but rapidly progressed downward as they became cheaper and more widely available. The demand for cottons led in the early eighteenth century to a search for methods of speeding up the processes of their manufacture, especially spinning. Twenty spinners are said to have been necessary to keep one weaver fully employed, and in the eighteenth century an acute shortage of thread developed. A number of mechanical spinning devices achieved some success before, in 1769, Richard Arkwright patented his water-powered spinning machine. This invention, made in England, quickly spread to western Europe and was of the greatest importance in the development of the factory production of cloth of all kinds.

It is impossible to measure with any precision the increase in textile production that resulted from the diffusion of these innovations. The import of raw cotton into Great Britain—a rough measure, of the growth of the manufacture of cotton textiles—increased slowly between the late seventeenth century and the second half of the eighteenth. Between 1750 and 1800 it increased twenty-five times, and during the next half century the growth in consumption was tenfold. There are no comparable figures for continental Europe, where, in any case, the period of rapid expansion came a half century or more later.

Growth in the woolen industry was very much slower and appears overall to have done little more, except in Great Britain, than keep pace with the growth in population. Linen production actually declined, as a direct result of the rapid expansion of cotton. One must, however, beware of translating into social terms the overall increase of cotton production. Demand for prints was first mainly up-market, and consumption may have been very wasteful. In Great Britain average consumption of cotton cloth could not have been more than five pounds a year, little more than the equivalent of a set of new underclothing for each person. By 1850, without allowing for exports, the figure would have been about twenty pounds. Even when allowance is made for the large export of cotton cloth, the amount available for domestic consumption still remained not inconsiderable. Clearly there was a marked improvement in material welfare in this respect during the nineteenth century. The contribution thus made to public health is not readily measurable, but possession of a larger wardrobe and the greater facility with which cottons could be laundered must have increased personal cleanliness and reduced the liability to such diseases as typhus. However, we must not assume too readily that the bulk of the population washed their bodies or their clothing frequently. They did not. Eugen Weber cites evidence from nineteenth-century France for a laundering that took place only once a year.

The only other textile product to command a market in Europe, at least before the present century, was silk. The silk fabric known to the Romans had been imported from Asia. It was not until the sixth century that the silkworm was itself introduced from China into the Byzantine Empire. Sericulture spread first in southern Italy and later in northern and in France. The rearing of the worms became, and has since remained, a peasant activity. It demanded a short period of intense activity each year. After the worms had hatched, their voracious appetites had to be satisfied with immense quantities of mulberry leaves. Then, as they passed into the chrysalis stage, they enveloped themselves in a cocoon of very fine silk formed from a secretion from their own bodies. The silk had then to be reeled and thrown. Reeling consisted of winding the thin threads onto reels; throwing, of twisting several such threads together to make thread strong and thick enough for weaving. Reeling and throwing took the place of spinning in other textile industries. The preparation of the thrown thread was arduous and time-consuming. It dominated the lives of the peasantry in silk-producing regions for several weeks each year, when the trays of worms filled their narrow cottages and the peasants themselves lived and slept out of doors.

Silk weaving was never an occupation of the peasantry. It called for delicate hands and a finesse found only among professional silk weavers. A small number of silk-weaving centers, foremost among them Lucca and Venice in Italy and Lyons in France, had emerged before the end of the Middle Ages. These were joined by a few others, including Krefeld in western Germany and the London suburb of Spittlefields, but there were rarely more than half a dozen producing centers of significance at any one time. Silk was extremely costly to produce, and demand was small and elastic. Most silk workers enjoyed royal or at least aristocratic patronage. In an age when status was demonstrated in dress, there was a premium on highly skilled silk weavers and dyers. They were rewarded and protected. The French kings had their silk weavers at Amboise, and even Frederick the Great attempted—unsuccessfully—to grow mulberry trees and rear silkworms in the savage climate of Brandenburg.

But the possession and wearing of silk also became the ambition of the successful and aspiring middle classes, and, as surviving wills and inventories often show, a piece of silk ribbon was likely to become a treasured possession even of the humblest. In the seventeenth and eighteenth centuries demand for silk increased among the middle classes. The cultivation of the mulberry and the rearing of silkworms spread as a peasant activity in Italy and southern France and was introduced into Spain. The volume of raw silk available increased. Simpler and cheaper forms of silk fabric became available and their sales moved increasingly down-market. Most important of these were ribbons. They called for only a very small loom, and ribbon weaving became a domestic craft in several of the silk-producing areas, notably in the Lyons region and in Switzerland. The Revolutionary and Napoleonic wars brought an end to many of the silk manufactures that had depended on aristocratic patronage, but the weaving of simpler silk goods continued and even expanded to satisfy the growing middle-class market.

Silk was not the only luxury fabric of the preindustrial age. It became customary during the Renaissance to cover the rough interior walls of great houses with tapestries. Their very high cost of manufacture put them beyond the reach of all but the rich, though humbler people would use light, painted cloth in the same way. Tapestries began to be woven in the Low Countries in the fifteenth century, and from here Flemish craftsmen carried the art of tapestry weaving to Paris and a few other centers of conspicuous consumption. Demand for tapestries continued until the advent of plastered walls covered with wallpaper relegated them to museums and collections.

Tanning and Leatherworking

The making and fashioning of leather is almost as old a craft as clothworking itself. Indeed, the wearing of skins was older than that of woven cloth. But, with the adoption of clothing, leather was relegated to the making of footwear and such articles as purses, belts, shields, and even bottles and buckets. The basic processes in the preservation of skins and hides have already been discussed. They were susceptible to an immense variation, according to the tanning agents used and the ways in which the hides were scraped and manipulated. The village tanner continued until recent times to produce a coarse leather by tanning oxhides with oak bark. The leather produced was used to make footwear and domestic utensils such as blackjacks (tankards) and pots. But in eighteenth-century Spain the practice developed of shaving away and treating the leather until a soft, thin, and pliable material was left (fig. 9.7). This could in turn be dyed, embossed, and decorated. It was used for slippers, purses, and decorative work, and, like silk, it was very expensive and called for a wealthy clientele. In consequence, true Cordovan leather, or cordwain as it came to be called, was never a product of the local craftsman. It was made by the urban specialist, and then only in the larger cities. The term "cordwainer," however, traveled down-market and became in early modern times a euphemism for cobbler or shoemaker.

9.7. A leatherworker shaving away a hide to produce a thin, soft leather for shoes, purses, and belts. (Jost Amman.)

"Aelfric's Colloquy" of about A.D. 1000 has the shoemaker proclaim that "I buy hides and skins and prepare them by my art and make of them various kinds of footwear— slippers, shoes and gaiters; bottles, reins and trappings; flasks and leathern vessels; spurstraps and halters; purses and bags. None of you could pass a winter without the aid of my craft."[13] Here we have the unspecialized leatherworker. Within a century or two his craft had split into as many specialist activities as the woolen industries. There were in every large city curriers, tawyers, cordwainers, and other specialized leatherworkers as well as simple tanners, each with his own craft organization. And so the industry remained until the nineteenth century, carried on in small workshops, almost incapable of mechanization, with tanning commonly in rural areas, where the hides and skins were most readily available, and the fabrication of leather goods in cities and towns, where craftsmen and customer came face to face. Not until late in the nineteenth century did the cobbler or cordwainer give way to a faceless factory worker who made footwear to prescribed size and styles for a distant and unseen market.

The Metal Crafts

The crafting of metal for tools and weapons, building construction, and decorative purposes was second in importance only to the clothing industries, and was incomparably more varied. It ranged from goldsmithing to the forging of simple iron goods. All these branches had in common only the fact that they used ore taken from the ground, smelted and refined it by some form of heat process, and fabricated it for the market. The metals known and in regular use before the industrial age were the precious metals, gold and silver; the nonferrous metals, copper, lead, and tin, to which should be added zinc,

9.8. A smith working at his forge

though it was not known in its metallic state before the eighteenth century; and, above all, iron in its several forms. Most people in preindustrial Europe made little use of any of these metals, with the exception of iron, which entered into their daily lives at almost every point. Their agricultural tools were tipped or shod with iron, and their carts and wagons had iron tires. They used knives and other cutting tools of steel. Locks and hinges were of soft iron, and within the house were iron trivets, andirons, rushlight holders, and cauldrons. Iron nails were used in wooden construction, swords and armor were of steel, and lances and arrows were tipped with iron.

Yet ironworking before the eighteenth century was a slow, laborious, and sometimes even primitive occupation. Its ores were varied in their chemical composition and called for a variety of smelting techniques. They yielded metals that ranged from soft to cast iron, each with its appropriate method of refining. The ores of iron were abundant and easily mined, and, though the volume of metal produced undoubtedly declined, the techniques employed during the Roman Empire continued into the early Middle Ages. Even during the period of the invasions, swords and other weapons, as well as armor and tools continued to be made. The chief centers of production were much the same as they had been in classical times: Spain, eastern France, and the lower Rhineland, Styria, Carinthia, and the Alps, but others were established, like the Pyrenees, Savoy, Sweden, and, in southern England, the Weald and Forest of Dean. But there were few among the more populous areas of Europe where simple low-shaft furnaces were not used to smelt some kind of ore and produce a poor-quality iron for agricultural and domestic purposes. Toward the end of the Middle Ages the sides of the hearth began to be built higher and thicker, and, with more efficient waterwheels, a stronger "blast" was obtained. In the end the temperatures reached within the furnace were high enough (about 1500 degrees centrigrade) for the metal to melt and absorb sufficient carbon from the fuel to become cast iron.

Until this development occurred, however, the simpler smelting devices had yielded only a bloom of soft iron. It was hammered repeatedly to expel as much slag as possible and then forged into the bars and billets that became the raw material of the smith. Soft or wrought iron could be welded but would not hold a cutting edge unless it had been "steeled." In the later Middle Ages techniques were developed for making wire by drawing thin strips of soft iron through holes of progressively smaller diameter. This in turn permitted the manufacture by the smith of objects as diverse as needles, nails, and chain mail.

The blast furnace that has, in modern times, come to dominate the industry evolved slowly from the low-shaft furnace. This crucial development appears to have taken place in the Rhineland or eastern France. It spread to England early in the sixteenth century and was adopted in the Wealden iron industry. It was used in France and central Europe. But it was not seen as the solution to the ever-present problem of the shortage and high price of iron. The metal that it produced had at first only a limited usefulness. The high temperatures at which it operated resulted from the greater height of its shaft, its stronger blast, and the good insulation of its massive walls. These allowed the iron to absorb a relatively large amount of carbon, and this in turn made the metal more fluid so that it could be poured into a mold. At the same time, however, it made the metal hard, intractable, and brittle when cold. Cast or high-carbon iron could be used in only one way—for making castings, which became increasingly numerous and important from the early sixteenth century. But for all other uses to which iron was customarily put, the metal had to be refined. The level of carbon that it contained had to be reduced or eliminated, and this could be done only in the oxidizing flame of the refiner's hearth.

For this reason the direct or "bloomery" method long continued in use, though it was of diminishing importance. Gradually it was replaced by the indirect method, in which the ore was first smelted in a blast or "high" furnace and then refined on the hearth. The indirect method increased the scale of production, but it made far heavier demands on fuel. So extravagant was it that forests were in some areas depleted and the industry obliged to move in search of forests new. Shortage of charcoal, not shortage of ore, was always the limiting factor. It became necessary, for example, to separate refining from smelting, since the local forests were rarely able to support both. The iron industry was drawn to the virgin forests of Poland and Russia, attracted not so much by the available ore as by the unlimited reserves of timber.

The problem of fuel supply for the industry was ultimately solved by the use of coal or coke in the blast furnace. But charcoal smelting continued to be practiced in many areas like Scandinavia and southeast Europe well into the twentieth century. Here a combination of conservatism and lack of commercial contact with the rest of the world kept the small-scale craft industry in being long after it had disappeared from the rest of the continent.

Until the eighteenth century, iron of whatever kind was a valuable commodity. Its cost, relative to that other essential, woolen or linen clothing, was high indeed and did not begin to fall until well after the appearance of the blast furnace and puddling process.

One is frequently surprised by the high value put upon iron tongs, andirons, and other domestic ironware in inventories. Iron was costly to make, and the volume of production remained very small. Most bloomeries worked only in summer, rarely employed more than three or four men, and produced no more than a few hundredweight of iron in a season. Early in the seventeenth century, when the blast furnace was in regular use, only about twenty-five thousand tons of cast iron were produced in England and Wales. About 1400 the total output of soft iron in the whole of Europe could not have been much more than thirty thousand tons, and in 1500, only forty thousand. If Russia and the Ottoman Empire are excluded, these figures give an annual consumption of little more than one pound for each head of the population.[14] The armor of a knight might weigh up to a hundred pounds, and, if we add the metal used in making weapons—a sword might contain up to ten pounds of steel—and arrow heads, which were turned out in their thousands, one can see that little was left for building construction, and almost none for ordinary civilian and domestic needs. Most iron goods, such as hinges and locks, the craftsman's simple tools, the knife that every man and most women carried in their belts, and the decorative grills met with in churches, were made to last. There was never any question of frequent replacement. This was not a "throw-away" society. On the contrary, tools of iron and steel were mentioned in wills as among their owner's prized possessions, and their value was put very high in inventories. Even a small "piece of iron" of no particular shape or use was valued; some day a smith might make something of it.

The scarcity and high price of iron were matters of great social importance. Nails were used sparingly, and timbers were generally jointed and made fast with wooden dowels. Simple agricultural tools, like spade and fork, were made of wood tipped with iron (fig. 5.3). The teeth of the harrow were wooden pegs, and the plow was built of wood with at most a colter of steel and an iron tip to the plowshare. Nor was domestic ironwear more abundant. An iron trivet, a pothook, a rushholder, and perhaps door fastenings were the most that even the homes of the gentry could boast.

Unless refined to bar or soft iron, the high-carbon metal that was in the sixteenth century beginning to flow from the blast furnaces had only one use. It could be poured into molds to make iron castings. Castings of all kinds came into widespread use. Cast iron was used increasingly to replace bronze and welded iron in the manufacture of guns, but it was in domestic ironware that most people encountered it. The practice was growing, and spreading from the great house downward to the cottage, of building the domestic hearth against a side of the hall. To protect the wall from the heat, firebacks were fitted. Thousands have survived in western and central Europe, most of them with heraldic, religious, or other designs in relief (fig. 9.9). They continued to be fitted until the nineteenth century, when they began to be replaced with firebricks made of refractory clay. In many homes cast-iron firebacks of the eighteenth century remain *in situ*. Iron cooking pots were made, and in the eighteenth century cast-iron wood-burning stoves, sometimes known as Franklin stoves, came into use. In the mid-nineteenth century their use spread to eastern Europe, and the Polish peasant Josef Słomka described in his memoirs how in his youth they were spreading among the cottages of the peasantry.[15] At the same time cast-iron water pipes began to be made, at first by casting them in molds, then by spinning the hot metal within a revolving tube. Iron pipes assumed great importance when cities began to construct water-supply systems and to lay gas mains

9.9. A cast-iron fireback of the seventeenth century. It shows, bottom right, a blast furnace and, to the left, a refinery. In the distance ore is being mined and a cart brings either ore or charcoal to the furnace. (Historical Museum, Saarbrücken.)

beneath their streets. Indeed, many such utilities would have been impossible without them. Cast iron was heavy, it could not be welded, its brittleness required a wide safety margin in all castings, but its contribution to material welfare cannot be questioned. One has only to note the items of cast iron that appeared in probate inventories to be aware of its growing importance. Not until the late nineteenth century did steel begin to replace it.

Steel continued to be made in very small quantities, either by the direct process, in which the blast of air was manipulated on the hearth to make the metal take up the requisite amount of carbon, or by recarburizing soft iron. The latter was probably the more important, but whichever method was used, the resulting steel was uneven in quality and often contained particles of slag that repeated hammering by the smith had failed to expel. Steel weapons and tools left much to be desired. The readiness with which swords broke when struck only added to the reputation of the few sources of good quality steel. Building accounts show a quite extraordinary expenditure on sharpening adzes and chisels, which had probably been made from a very impure metal.

This state of affairs changed only slowly. The volume of steel made increased during the eighteenth century; it became cheaper in relation to other commodities, but there was little improvement in its quality. Many of its shortcomings could be eradicated if the metal were melted, thus evening out the carbon content and permitting the slag to float to the surface. But such a process was also likely to bring about other changes within the metal unless it was carefully controlled. About 1750 Benjamin Huntsman devised a method of sealing bar iron, together with carbon and a flux, into a crucible and heating it in a furnace especially built for the purpose. When the crucible was opened, a steel of more even quality was poured into a mold, hence its name of cast steel. The process remained a secret for many years and was not significant in continental Europe until after 1815. But it was relatively cheap and easy and led to a great increase in the use of steel for machines as well as for weapons, tools, and all forms of domestic hardware. Table cutlery, for example, became common once it was found that it could be stamped from sheets of rolled steel.

Bar, soft, or wrought iron had, however, still to be made laboriously on the hearth, with an immense consumption of charcoal. Many experiments had been made with refining cast iron by eliminating its carbon, before, in 1784, Henry Cort patented his method of "puddling" high-carbon iron in a reverberatory furnace. The method was quick and relatively economical, except in human labor. Puddling was perhaps the most arduous occupation generated by the Industrial Revolution. Nevertheless, the production of soft iron increased sharply. More metal became available, and at a lower price, for the crucible furnaces, just at a time when demand for steel from every type of consumer was increasing.

These technical advances were achieved in Great Britain. They had gained little acceptance in continental Europe before the French Revolution. But after the peace of 1815, the relative backwardness of continental Europe compared with England was revealed, and there was a rush to adopt the new technologies. The new methods, adapted to local conditions, swept across the continent, cheapening and increasing immeasurably the output of iron and steel. Without Huntsman and Cort there could have been no machine age, and the railways would not have spread their web over the continent.

The Nonferrous Metals

The nonferrous metals were of much less importance in the lives of most people. Gold and silver were minted into coins, and the circulation of money was a necessary accompaniment of developing trade. These metals were a physical embodiment of wealth to a far greater degree than they are today and were used in vessels and ornaments in both churches and the homes of the laity. Gold and silver were not as a general rule wasted or lost. There was some attrition through use, but the production of new metal only increased the total stock. Europe produced little gold, and most new metal was obtained, at least before the sixteenth century, from West Africa by way of the trans-Saharan caravan routes. Thereafter new stock came from Asia and the New World. Europe, on the other hand, was a significant producer of silver, much of it associated with lead. To a rising output within Europe was added from the 1530s a growing influx of silver from the Americas. European production, chiefly from central Europe, then declined, but the increased availability of silver coin was a contributory factor in the price inflation of the sixteenth century, the worst that ever afflicted western man before the twentieth century.

Most people before the nineteenth century never saw a vessel of gold or silver or handled a coin of precious metal. Lead was of far greater importance in their daily lives. Its ore was found widely in Great Britain and central Europe. It was easily smelted, and the metal could be cast, hammered, or rolled into sheets. It was used for roofing large buildings, for fixing small pieces of glass into windows, and for holding the dowels that fastened blocks of masonry. Lead sheeting was used, as the Romans had used it, to make water pipes. The fountains that began to adorn cities at the end of the Middle Ages made use of lead piping, and from the seventeenth century lead downspouts began to be fitted to the roofs of great houses to carry away rainwater. Lead cisterns were used to store water, and, alloyed with 5 to 10 percent of tin, lead yielded pewter, which came increasingly into vogue in the late Middle Ages for making plates, dishes, and drinking vessels.

Copper occurred less widely than lead and was until modern times of less importance. It was easily smelted, but by itself was too soft for regular use. It was chiefly used, alloyed with tin or zinc, to make, respectively, bronze and brass. These were relatively expensive metals but were used to make bowls and cooking and drinking vessels. They rivaled pewter in the closets of the rich and were used in a variety of decorative metalwork. The craftsmen who worked in brass and bronze were likely to be found only in the larger and more important centers. There was little call for their wares in small towns, and none in the countryside. Nonetheless a few centers of this branch of manufacture emerged, notably Cologne, Liège, and the town of Dinant, on the Meuse, which gave its name to *dinanderie*—brassware.

Pottery and Brickmaking

The crafts of making pottery, bricks, and tiles are better known than most others, if only because their products are almost indestructible and survive in their millions. The Roman traditions of throwing pottery on a wheel and decorating it in relief with molds or dies were lost in much of the empire after the barbarian invasions, and the use of bricks survived only in the Mediterranean basin. Throughout barbarian Europe pots were hand built, that is, shaped by the unaided fingers from a lump of clay. The clay itself was coarse and ill prepared, and the vessel that resulted was irregular and thick sided. The older traditions had been preserved in the south, and, reinforced by the example of the Byzantines and the Arabs, gradually returned to central and northwestern Europe. Wheel-turned pottery was again made in England before the end of the Anglo-Saxon period, and the use of the potter's wheel gradually spread throughout much of Europe. Early wheels were probably turned slowly by hand. Then the kick wheel was introduced, operated by the potter's feet, thus leaving both hands free to manipulate the clay (figs. 9.10, 9.11). Georg Agricola's *De Re Metallica* of 1556 showed a potter's workshop, with the potter himself seated at a kick wheel. Later engravings show the wheel being operated by a kind of belt drive. But whatever the mechanism, throwing a pot called for skill and artistry, and a not inconsiderable amount of time. Pottery did not come cheap.

The making of pots, as also of bricks and tiles, was practiced in most parts of Europe; everywhere, in fact, that clay was found. Yet the quality of the clay from the potter's point of view varied greatly. It was dug from shallow pits and first washed and strained—the term used is levigated—and reduced to a smooth, even paste. After shaping, it was heated in a furnace to convert the soft clay into a hard, brittle material. It was then

9.10. A terra-cotta bas-relief showing a potter using a kick wheel; central European, sixteenth century.

finished with the addition of decoration and glaze. The nature of the clay, the construction of the furnace, and the temperatures reached, all influenced the quality of the pottery. Glaze was added to make the vessel watertight and to prevent it from discoloring. It might consist of nothing more than a "slip," or thin clay painted over the surface, or, especially from the later Middle Ages, it might be a lead glaze, which, when heated, bonded with the clay of the pot. The refinements that could be introduced were almost infinite. In Italy the practice developed of putting enamel decoration and finish on a pot of coarse ware, thus producing *faience* or *majolica*. In the Netherlands, the use of a fine white clay and a high furnace temperature produced the smooth china known in the seventeenth century as "delft." In the next century came the manufacture of porcelain, using a fine white clay, commonly kaolin, and a fused igneous rock. In purely aesthetic terms, eighteenth-century porcelain, whether from Meissen, Sèvres, Copenhagen, or Limoges, was the highest point reached in the history of European ceramics. A good porcelain was soft white in color, translucent and even in texture, and was said to ring with a pure, bell-like note when struck. It is not surprising that the industry, like silk and tapestry weaving, enjoyed noble and royal patronage—indeed, it could not have existed without it—or that porcelain began to displace silver plate from the tables of the rich. Great houses throughout Europe were graced with sets of porcelain, some of which have survived the hazards of bankruptcy, spoliation, and careless servants to become museum pieces today.

   At its simplest, the pottery kiln consisted of little more than a hole in the ground in which the unburned pots were placed, together with fuel, and heated until they were hard. They were often deformed in the process, in addition to picking up soot from the fuel. The result was at best rough, peasant ware. In the course of time, and strongly influenced by Arab craftsmanship from Spain, the kilns became more elaborate. They were built of masonry with chambers, separate from the fire, in which the pots were placed. Numerous such kilns have been excavated, and their general shape is well known. By the sixteenth century the larger pottery kilns had achieved a size and style that remained little changed before recent times. Potteries shown by Agricola or by his Italian contemporary Piccolpasso were large, employing several craftsmen. They mass-produced dishes, bowls, and jugs, which they sold mainly to the gentry and urban middle classes. But simpler kilns continued in use in areas uninfluenced either by Arab craftsmanship or by strong urban demand, and that shown in figure 9.12 was in fact used in recent times in Poland.

9.11. A potter using a kick wheel; Poland, nineteenth century. (After K. Moszyński.)

The products of medieval pottery kilns appear to have consisted overwhelmingly of jugs. Many were tall, slender, and sometimes elaborately decorated, but some were broad based and bulbous. Some, indeed, were shaped like a human face, a tradition that appears to have been of great antiquity and was continued in the "toby" jugs of the nineteenth century. But earthenware storage jars and cooking pots were also of great importance. The former were often of great size, bulbous, with a relatively narrow neck. Their decoration was usually simple, and their function the preservation of grain from rodents. Until late in the Middle Ages, and in some areas far longer, cooking pots were of pottery, large, plain, and often with convex bases, which could be set amid the ashes on the hearth. Not until the fifteenth century did earthenware cooking pots begin to give way to more durable articles of metal. Small bowls and drinking pots were made, but one looks in vain for anything resembling a modern plate or cup among the products of the medieval potter. The place of the former was taken by wooden trenchers, and the small china cup did not come into use until the seventeenth or eighteenth century.

This period saw fundamental changes in pottery manufacture. Attempts to imitate the true Chinese porcelain, which became a highly valued import from the Far East, led to experiments with crushed bone, glass, and flint, with ball and china clay, and with such minerals as steatite. From these experiments there arose a great number of highly refined types of china, collectively known as "soft-paste" ware. At the same time the range of china goods increased. Plates were introduced in the sixteenth century and rapidly displaced both pewter and the wooden platters that had been most widely used hitherto. Production of many forms of chinaware was quickened and cheapened by the use of metal or plaster molds in which the clay was pressed. This method was par-

9.12. A pottery kiln. (After K. Moszyński.)

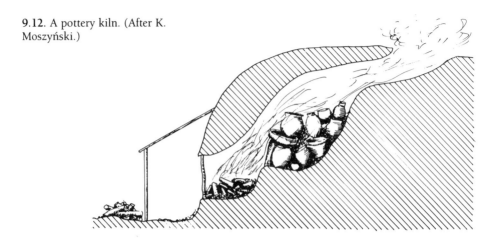

ticularly effective in making plates, which by the later eighteenth century were being produced in immense numbers and to a uniform shape and size in the principal potteries of western Europe. The best china continued to be hand painted, but designs, even pictorial scenes, began to be affixed to the body of the china by means of transfers, and decorative pieces shaped by wooden stamps were added by hand and fused onto the pot or plate.

A lead was taken in many of these advances by Josiah Wedgwood, a potter working near Stoke-upon-Trent in the English midlands. But his innovations were quickly adopted by other potters and spread to western and central Europe. The use of china at the table and for ornaments and decoration was quickly adopted by the upper and wealthier classes. The well-to-do soon had a sideboard filled with bone or soft-paste china, and the fashion of eating off plates and drinking from china cups spread downward to the lower levels of society, though it was not until late in the nineteenth century that their use could be termed universal.

Clay was also used for making bricks as well as tiles of all kinds: roofing and ridge tiles, floor tiles, inlaid or embossed tiles, and even glazed tiles for walls. There was no limit to the sizes and patterns that were made or the uses to which they could be put. Brick and tile techniques were widely used under the Roman Empire. It cannot be said that they were completely forgotten during the centuries that followed, but they ceased to be widely practiced. Brick and tile were used only where they could be retrieved from abandoned Roman buildings. Brickmaking was revived during the Middle Ages. The burning of bricks in England appears to have begun as early as the late twelfth century, and it was certainly practiced earlier in the Low Countries. Areas where clay prevailed were, by that fact alone, deprived of good building stone, and, whenever timber was scarce or undesirable, it was natural to turn to brick. Brick construction spread across northern Europe. From Flanders to Gdańsk it became the dominant building material, and such cities as Lübeck and Amsterdam give the impression even today of having been built largely of brick. Brick was of small importance in France and of none in Mediterranean Europe. Its use spread in eastern England but never achieved its north European importance, largely because good, free-cutting stone was readily available.

In the later Middle Ages brick became important in domestic architecture. Some great houses were built entirely of brick, especially in the Low Countries and eastern England. Brick was used between the studding of timber-framed buildings, and in chimney, hearth, and foundation it entered into the construction of the humblest cottage. Brickmaking was relatively cheap. The clay was dug from shallow pits and allowed to weather, often through the winter. Then it was well puddled or trodden by the bare feet of the workmen and cast in rough wooden molds (fig. 9.13). The bricks were first air-dried for a period and then fired in a kiln. Kilns were large: those in Hull (Yorkshire) were capable of taking ten thousand bricks at a time. Brick-

9.13. The brickmaker. Bricks are being shaped by hand in a wooden mold. In the middle distance is a brick kiln. (Jost Amman.)

making was a foremost medieval instance of mass production. The scale of production increased in modern times, but the method of production underwent little change before the present century.

An important reason for the growing popularity of brick was its fire-resistant quality. The use of roofing tile spread for the same reason. Roofs had previously been of thatch or wooden shingles, even more flammable than timber framing. In 1212 the city of London ruled that roofs had to be of tile, and other cities, both in England and continental Europe, followed. Tiles were made in much the same way as bricks, but their thinness made them more difficult to handle until they had been burned. Ridge tiles, sometimes called "cresting" in the records, were also made. In northern Europe tiles were mostly flat and were expected to be of uniform size, though the great number of complaints shows that they often failed in this respect. In southern Europe, as well as in parts of France, the Roman tradition of using curved pantiles has continued until today.

From the thirteenth century, tiles, more carefully made and with a smoother finish than roofing tiles, began to be used for flooring. Of necessity they were uniform in size. They were burned to shades of red, brown, and yellow, and were used to make a pattern. They were then embossed with heraldic or other decorative devices. A final stage in the development of flooring tile was to fill the shallow impression with clay of a different color. Such tiles were adapted to vertical as well as horizontal faces, but their use, at least before the end of the Middle Ages, was restricted to churches and the homes of the wealthy. In early modern times, tiles, often of white clay, fancifully decorated and glazed, came into wider use in the home, and it was not uncommon, especially in the Low Countries, for walls to be completely tiled.

A feature of the brick-and-tile industry was the continuity of its technology. Neither methods of production nor designs have greatly changed from the Middle Ages until the recent past. One can only say that sizes, especially of bricks, have become standardized, and the volume of output has increased immeasurably. The use of brick and tile has contributed significantly to human welfare. The resulting reduction in the fire hazard has itself been of great importance. But the added cleanliness and durability of buildings was a major contribution to health and well-being.

Building Construction

It is natural to turn from tile and brickmaking to the construction industry. Construction was, and indeed still is, carried on at two different and contrasted levels. Most widespread is what may be termed vernacular construction, the erection of buildings of local materials, by local craftsman, who may or may not have been professionals, and according to methods and designs traditional in the area. Vernacular building is contrasted with "polite" or "grand" architecture.[16] This type of construction was executed by professional masons and carpenters, using materials that were likely to have been brought, at some expense, from considerable distances. In style and design it belonged to a much broader tradition. The cutoff between the two may be difficult to determine, but most buildings can be assigned to one category or the other. Churches can be assigned without question to the polite or grand classification, but some parish-church architecture, particularly in its detail, may verge on the vernacular. It is impossible, before modern times, to draw a clear distinction between church and domestic architecture. They employed the same master masons and craftsmen and made use of similar materials and even styles. The fenestration and roofing of a great hall were often identical with those of a church, and the wooden churches of eastern Europe belong, together with cottage and manor house, to a peasant tradition. But we are concerned here not with the aesthetic appeal of architecture but with the degree to which buildings served human needs and administered to people's comfort and convenience. In buildings, it might be said, is written much of the social history of western man. In their totality they mirrored more accurately the level of human welfare than any other aspect of human achievement. That is why the builder, whether mason or only rough carpenter, is so important in western society.

Vernacular architecture clearly drew upon the services and skills of the professional carpenter-joiner and mason, but it made great use of the unspecialized skills of local people. Many are the traditions surrounding the mutuality and self-help of the local community. Manorial bylaws commonly preserved the right of the peasant to take not only *firbote,* or domestic fuel, but also *husbote,* or building timber, from the domanial wood. The peasant often built his own cottage, calling on his neighbors for assistance only in such crucial operations as roof-raising. The styles and materials used in vernacular architecture, summarized in chapter 4, always betrayed a powerful influence of both the local environment and local traditions.

Building above the vernacular threshold required professional craftsmen and more refined methods and materials. Furthermore, buildings of this level are more abundantly represented today because they have survived in far greater numbers. Grand architecture was far more likely to have been in masonry than was vernacular architecture, and church building, with exceptions only in Scandinavia and Eastern Europe, was almost exclusively in stone. Such building called for a hierarchy of control. At its summit was the person—bishop, abbot, landed aristocrat, or lord of the manor—who commissioned the building and prescribed certain guidelines: size, style, materials. He usually commissioned a master mason—*magister cementarius,* as he was called in the records—who in turn worked out the detail of the plan and recruited the workmen who were to be employed on the project (fig. 9.14). From the later Middle Ages there was likely to have been a written contract between the commissioning person and the master mason. The master mason *may* have lent a hand in the actual work of building; more likely he prepared plans and supervised the work. In medieval drawings he is sometimes represented as wearing a cloak and gloves and holding a wand of office.

9.14. Funeral slab of a master mason, bearing square and compasses. (After Pierre du Colombier, *Les Chantiers des cathédrales* [Paris, 1973], 103.)

The master mason was the nearest approximation that we find in the Middle Ages to an architect. It was not until the sixteenth century that the true architect came into his own. Henceforward he was identified with the building, and one does not think of the great churches and houses of the Renaissance apart from the architects who designed them. From this time, the role of the true architect broadened until in the nineteenth century he was designing urban homes for the working class. The architect thus took over part of the role formerly played by the master mason but normally handed over to a contractor supervision of day-to-day operations on the building site.

On any building site of more than modest size there was usually an army of workers, for building was highly labor intensive. Building construction began in the quarry, where the stone was rough hewn and sometimes partially dressed to reduce its weight in transportation. Wherever a good-quality stone came to the surface there were likely to be quarries, most of them small and all of them shallow, for the early mason lacked the means both of keeping the quarry clear of water and of lifting large pieces of stone to the surface. The transportation of building stone was a serious problem. Whenever possible it was moved by raft or barge along the waterways. Quarries found near the coast, like those at Caen in northern France, Purbeck and Bere in southern England, and Carrara in Italy, owed their wide importance to the fact that the stone could be transported by sea. In areas where good stone was abundant, it was used in vernacular architecture at an early date. Elsewhere, the peasant used pieces, often recognizable in cottage architecture, retrieved from grander buildings that had been demolished or altered.

At any important building site there was a body of masons. At their head there were those who in Great Britain were called "freemasons," because they carved and in other ways prepared free-cutting stone, or ashlar. They worked on the building site, usually

9.15. A medieval building scene. This illustration depicted the
building of the Tower of Babel; hence the collapsing ladders. (After P.
du Colombier, fig. 13.)

within the shelter of their "lodges," temporary structures in which they kept their tools
and even slept. The "rough" masons spread the mortar and laid the stone that had been
cut by the freemason. Much of the building made use of rubble stone, such as occurred
close to the surface. It was easy to quarry and lay but demanded larger quantities of
mortar, which in some measure offset its cheapness. Many a building, both lay and
ecclesiastical, was largely of rubble masonry, with freestone used in the coins, moldings,
and tracery. In the grander building of the eighteenth century the same often happened,

with the façade of freestone often covering a rubble core, and the back quarters, domestic offices, and stables largely rubble built.

At the base of the constructional labor force were the unskilled and semiskilled, who carried and lifted the stone, burned the lime, and mixed the mortar. Though the body of building workers might appear to have been stratified, there was in fact a considerable social mobility within it. The reason lay in the fact that building workers were of necessity itinerant, moving from one building site to another, incapable of any kind of gild organization, and dependent, when work at one site was finished, on rumor and report for the location of the next job. This mobility helps to account for the recurrent motifs in architecture in all parts of Europe. It does not appear to have been difficult for the worker to rise to the status of freemason, and a freemason on an important site might graduate to become a master mason on a lesser project and so rise to the summit of his profession.

The mason worked with simple tools that changed little before the advent of power tools in recent times. Stone was split with wedges and was shaped with axe or adze; the markings on the stone today often show which tool had been used. Carving was with hammer and chisel, the latter requiring frequent sharpening and retempering. Mortar was laid by means of a trowel of recognizably modern shape, and the stone tapped into place by means of a mallet.

On an important building site there were other craftsmen no less mobile than the masons themselves. There were smiths, who forged hinges and locks; glaziers, who leaded the glass into window openings; carpenters, who fitted doors and constructed the roof; roofers skilled at fitting slate and tile; and, at a later date, plasterers, decorators, and artists. The balance of importance between the crafts changed with changing fashions and aspirations. Glaziers, plasterers, and joiners became more important with growing demands for luxury.

The Food and Drink Industries

Most foodstuffs called for some form of preparation before they could be eaten and digested. The human species had lost the animal's capacity to consume grain, foliage, and roots, as well as meat, in their raw or natural state. Furthermore, since many foodstuffs were produced seasonally, some form of food preservation became desirable. Many of the activities associated with the preservation and preparation of food have from prehistoric times to the present been carried on within the home. The small quantities involved and the need to prepare and cook them immediately before eating left little alternative. But there were other activities that could be carried on more economically on a larger scale than was possible within the home, and some that called for professional skills.

Grinding or milling of grain was practiced universally, since the breadgrains provided the bulk of human food intake before the recent past. Only in arctic regions and in some mountainous areas were cereals and milling of little importance. Although the domestic, or hand, quern survived until the recent past in many areas of Europe, and is still used in eastern Europe and the Balkans, the tendency has been, at least during the last thousand years, for milling to pass to the professional miller who operated a water or windmill. As discussed in chapter 5, the mill became a dominant institution in rural society and was also to be found in most cities. The miller was normally paid for his services by a small share of the grain that passed through his mill. Cereals could, with care, be preserved for a considerable period, but, once ground, could readily develop fungi or become infested with insects or vermin. For this reason the general tendency was to grind cereals only when they were needed.

Next to the miller came the baker. Baking was a common, if not completely normal, domestic function. A kind of flatbread could be baked on the hot stones of the hearth, but few homes before modern times had an oven. For this reason resort was had to communal ovens in some villages and towns. The solution to the problem was to employ the services of a professional baker (fig. 9.16), who either made bread and sold it or baked other people's bread for a commission. The honesty of the baker was no less suspect than that of the miller, and in England the Assize of Bread aimed to protect the customer from his machinations.

Two other practitioners of the food industries were distrusted fully as much as the miller and baker—these were the brewers and butchers:

> Brewesters and bakesters, bocheres and cokes,
> For thise aren men on this molde that moste harm worcheth
> To the pore people that parcel-mele buggen.[17]

> (Brewers and bakers, butchers and cooks: for they are the kind who most harm poor people who can only buy in pennyworths.)

Brewing, like baking, was a domestic pursuit that gradually became professionalized during the Middle Ages. The industry was difficult to accommodate within the narrow confines of the cottage, and its product was in universal demand. Chaucer's Pardoner, we may remember, would not begin his tale until he had fortified himself at a local alehouse.

A fermented drink, prepared usually from malted cereals, was made in most of Europe except the south. Although barley came to be the preferred cereal, most others were used on occasion. Before recent times the quality of beer varied greatly; it deteriorated readily and was susceptible to adulteration. Brewers and alewives always operated under the watchful eye of authority. Beer of whatever origin was the most important drink until modern times. "Ale for an Englysshe man is a naturall drynke," wrote Andrew Borde,[18] and the reason was that its low alcohol content was sufficient to neutralize the bacteriological content of water. In rural areas the peasant usually brewed his ale, free from the supervision of public authority, and in manor houses and communities like hospitals there was usually a brewhouse separate from the kitchen. In the cities people were more likely to rely on brewers, who produced beer or ale for sale. They were a numerous profession; in sixteenth-century Coventry there were no fewer than sixty in a population of little more than six thousand, and the same might have been found throughout western and central Europe.

The ale brewed during the Middle Ages was, whatever the grain used, a thick and, to us, unpalatable drink. Its alcohol content was low, and it could not be kept for more than a short period. The use of hops, both as a flavoring and as a preservative, was introduced in western Europe in the later Middle Ages and spread to central and eventually to eastern Europe. Henceforward, the term beer was commonly used for a fermented liquor in which hops had been used. Both ale and beer were more than drinks. They were ways

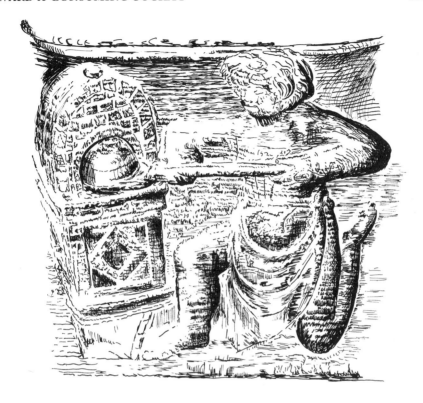

9.16. A baker using a shovel to take bread from an oven; a French woodcarving of the sixteenth century.

of consuming cereals and their caloric value was high. When discussing the nutritional value of diet, one must not forget the very considerable consumption of ale and beer.

Wherever the grapevine could be grown, ale and beer were of little importance, and where the climate was too harsh for the vine, wine was nevertheless imported for those who could afford it. There was a considerable long-distance trade in wine under the Roman Empire. It lapsed during the ensuing period of invasions but was then slowly rebuilt. We can distinguish those areas where the vine was a normal crop and supplied the principal drink of the populace (fig. 9.17) from those where wine, usually of a superior quality, was produced for export. Beyond the latter were restricted areas where wine of indifferent or poor quality was made for religious and sacramental purposes. Among these were southern England, the Low Countries, Brandenburg, and parts of Poland. Considerable changes took place in the geography of viticulture between the early Middle Ages and the nineteenth century. They were a response both to developing trade, increasing specialization, and considerations of national policy. England, for example, abandoned its own vineyards in favor of wine from Gascony, which was under its political control. Later the import of the rich, dark "port" wine from Oporto reflected Britain's political alliance with Portugal. In southeastern Europe, viticulture disappeared with the triumph of Islamic fanaticism, only to revive in Hungary and the Balkans with the end of Ottoman rule.

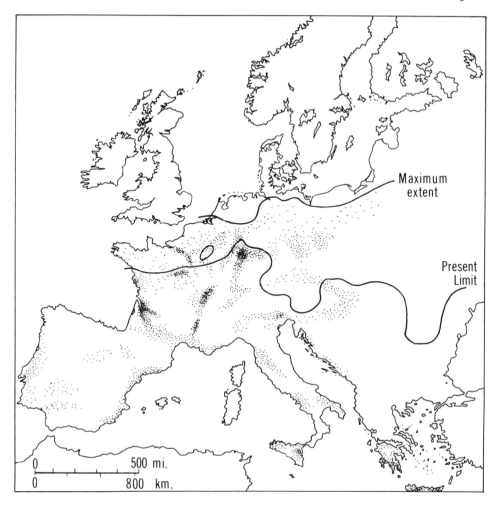

9.17. A map of wine production, showing the retreat of the vine. The prevailing drink beyond the area of viticulture was ale or beer.

The distillation of fermented liquor to produce "schnapps" or *aqua vitae* first developed in the later Middle Ages.[19] Distilling was known to the ancients but had to be perfected before it could be adapted to fermented liquor. This step was accomplished by the medieval alchemists. By the fourteenth century it was a common practice to distill any liquor fermented from grain or fruit. Monasteries began to produce such liquor, flavored with herbs from their own herb gardens, and some, including the austere Carthusian order, have continued to do so until today. Such fragrant liqueurs became popular as a remedy for the plague. They doubtless induced a sense of well-being but were otherwise totally ineffective. Wine was distilled to produce brandy, or *brantwein,* in the fourteenth century, and gin (from *geneva,* meaning juniper) was distilled and flavored with the berries of the juniper bush. It was more difficult to produce a distillate from a malt liquor, because the low sugar content had to be supplemented with yeast. For this reason whisky and vodka entered into the human diet relatively late. Not until the sixteenth century were malt liquors distilled on a significant scale. Distilling tended throughout northern Europe to be a manorial prerogative, perhaps because few could afford the necessary equipment. In Scotland every laird came to have his still, and in eastern Europe each member of the *szlachta* produced and sold his own vodka, often through a Jewish tavern keeper who held a local monopoly. The quality of the drink varied from manor to manor, according to the materials and methods used. The quality of the water was important, and various minor and often secret processes contributed to the subtlety of the product. It was not until the early nineteenth century that certain producers in northwest Europe began to capitalize on their natural advantages to produce whisky for the market. At about the same time, in central and eastern Europe, potatoes sometimes replaced rye or barley malt in the production of vodka.

Chapter 10

THE MEASURE OF PROGRESS

Such a run of wet seasons as we have had in the last ten or twelve
years would have produced a famine a century or more ago.

—Gilbert White,
The Natural History of Selborne

The last six chapters have surveyed the long period of intermittent growth
between the collapse of the Western Empire in the fifth century A.D. and
the eve of the Industrial Revolution. Both agricultural output and total population
increased, cities multiplied, and people's view of the world and of their own relationship
to it underwent fundamental changes. Above all, there was a significant improvement in
the level of material welfare throughout Europe. *On average* people lived better in the
eighteenth century than they had done in earlier centuries. This higher standard of living
is implicit in the expanded volume and variety of foodstuffs and consumer goods. It is
more difficult to say *who* lived better, for it cannot be demonstrated with any degree of
assurance that the benefits of this growth were spread across all classes and degrees of
wealth. Indeed, it can be claimed that the rise in standards for the poorest between the
early Middle Ages and the eighteenth century was negligible. Furthermore, the range of
difference between the level of welfare of the rich and the well-to-do on the one hand and
that of the rural and urban masses on the other was itself continuously changing. In
times of crisis and scarcity the rich suffered in relative terms much less than the poor.
There were, on the other hand, times when labor was scarce and the workman was able
to extract a high price for his services, and, by contrast, others when political and
economic pressures forced down the general level of the working class. If it can be said
that the standards of all classes improved overall during the period, their levels did not
rise at parallel rates.

A historian finds it difficult to comprehend the vast perspective of material history,
because standards are not susceptible of objective measurement. They are subjective.

What was desirable or enjoyable in one age might be discarded in another. The preferred food at one time might be rejected a century or two later. Fashion and taste change for no apparent reason. Each age has its own standards, its own scale of values, and its own objectives. It is impossible to say that one society was in material terms better or less well off than another, when their expectations may have differed radically. The revolution of rising expectations is a modern phenomenon. There was no such beacon to guide and focus the efforts of past generations. Stability was the most they could hope for, and stability was something that they rarely achieved. Their levels of welfare were always at risk, threatened from two directions: from the natural hazards of the physical world, and from the social structures and economic systems that controlled their lives.

Crisis and Catastrophe

Catastrophe was always imminent in preindustrial Europe. Its consequences are minimized today, if not entirely eliminated, by scientific measures to monitor and control the physical environment, by systems of rapid communication and transportation, and by networks of mutual assistance. In the past, catastrophe in Europe was more frequent and more profound, and in its scale came close to conditions experienced today in some Third World countries. Crises came in many forms. Most frequent were severe weather, crop failure, and famine. The warning in *Piers Plowman* that within five years, "through floods and through foul weather crops shall fail," had the ring of truth. This disaster is what happened at some such intervals of time in most of Europe. On each occasion physical well-being received a blow, and the process of rebuilding had to begin again.

Europe was, by and large, free from those other natural catastrophes—earthquakes, tidal waves, volcanic eruptions—which afflict many other parts of the world. But this immunity has been far from absolute, as the debate over the end of the Minoan culture has shown. In more recent times the disastrous harvest of 1816 was due to volcanic activity as far away as the East Indies, and the random incidence of such events of nature cannot be said to have become less frequent.

Crisis came also in the form of epidemic disease. Harvest failure and famine could be anticipated. They cast a long shadow before them, and those who had the means speculated on the future price of grain. But epidemic disease struck unseen and without warning. It might in some respects have been prevented by a more careful management of resources and greater attention to water supply and sewage disposal. But the etiology of disease was a mystery before the late nineteenth century. There was no preventive medicine and no remedy. Population was weakened and decimated repeatedly in the course of history and was saved from virtual extinction only by the fact that enough were preserved through their acquired immunity to create the next generation. After each such crisis it took decades, even generations, to rebuild the damaged stock of people.

Other catastrophes were due more directly to human agency. The hazard of fire was always present in a society that built largely with wood. Villages, even cities, might be destroyed by fire, and their rebuilding might take years of intensive work. Warfare added an even more destructive dimension. War was endemic in medieval and early modern Europe, and attempts, especially by the church, to limit its depredations met with only limited success. Until the eighteenth century little effort was made to provision an army in any regular way. It lived off the country, looting and destroying wherever it moved.

Indeed, there were times, notably during the Hundred Years War in western Europe and the Thirty Years War in central, when its movements were determined as much by the availability of food as by the location of the enemy.

That armies were undisciplined goes without saying. But they also spawned bands that did little other than live off the countryside that they ravaged. The taxrolls of fifteenth-century Burgundy reported repeatedly that villages had been destroyed by the *écorcheurs* and thus could pay no tax. The great city of Antwerp was reduced to ruins by the unruly Spanish soldiery in 1576, and when Tilly and the Catholic armies took Magdeburg in 1631, they left scarcely a person alive or a building standing. Mansfeld's campaign across south Germany, from Bohemia to the Rhineland, left a trail of destruction and helped to inspire the gruesome drawings of Callot and the bitter denunciations of Grimmelshausen. In 1637 the Rhineland was described as "a country where many thousands of men have died of hunger and not a living soul can be seen for many miles along the way."[1] It has been estimated that more than half the land in Germany was wasted in the course of the Thirty Years War, and that mortality reached 40 percent over large areas.[2] Even this level of destruction was exceeded in Turenne's devastation of the Rhenish Palatinate in 1674—"the most thorough application within the limits of the historical consciousness of western Europe of what is now call a 'scorched-earth' policy."[3] To these examples of savagery should be added that period in Polish history which historians call *Potop*—"the Deluge"—when eastern Europe was overrun by Brandenburgers, Swedes, Cossacks, and Ottomans.

Military campaigns have often been described from the point of view of the soldiers who took part in them, from Froissart to Sassoon, but very rarely from that of the population who lived in the path of the armies or on the fields of battle. Grimmelshausen and Callot were among the few who have in their different ways recorded the horrors experienced by the civilian population. Nor were these depredations restricted to physical destruction. Armies were probably the most important agents in the spread of disease. There were few epidemics to which military operations did not contribute. Plague accompanied the armies in the Thirty Years War. Typhus, otherwise known as trench fever, traveled with the soldiers, and the great cholera epidemic of 1831 began with the movements of Russian soldiers sent to suppress the Polish rising of the previous year.

Catastrophe, whether its causation was natural or human, has been of incalculable importance in human history, leading to destruction, suffering, and mortality. Crisis expressed itself most often in famine. Whether the crops were burned by marching armies or washed out by incessant summer rain, the result was the same: poor harvest, high prices, and famine. And each crisis left as its legacy a generation weakened by malnourishment and exposed to every infection. On the other hand, there were times, as in the fourteenth century, when heavy mortality had the effect of relieving a state of overpopulation. Manorial records show how the premature death of parents allowed their children to inherit, to set up homes, and to establish families at an earlier age than might otherwise have been possible. The evidence is overwhelming that after the Black Death had taken its toll, the pressure of population was relieved. Marginal land was abandoned, and *average* crop yields improved.

One can compile a catalogue of crises of major or minor importance, localized or widespread in their occurrence. Always disease followed in the wake of famine. The year

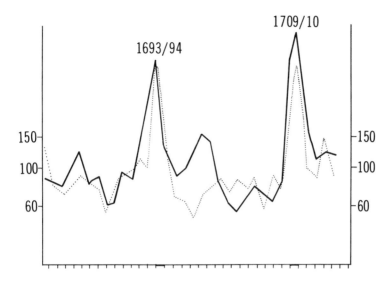

10.1. Mortality and grain prices at Gien, Burgundy. Mortality is
represented by the solid line; grain prices by the dotted. The two lines
almost coincide. The graph shows departures from the average (=
100). (After J. Meuvret, "Crises de subsistence et la démographie de la
France d'Ancien Régime," *Pop.* 1 [1946]: 643–50.)

1257, wrote Matthew Paris, "was barren and meager; for whatever had been sown in
winter, had budded in spring, and grown ripe in summer, was stifled and destroyed by
the autumnal inundations. . . . This pestiferous year . . . gave rise to mortal fevers."[4]
Every time a poor harvest threatened, prices rose. The citizens of London, to quote
Matthew Paris again, were forbidden to buy "corn for store, with a view to selling it at a
dearer price . . . as they made a general practice of doing." The regrator was a continual
menace in early societies. Van Werveke has shown how the consequences of the very bad
harvests of 1315–17 were made worse for all except the rich by the operations of the
grain dealers.[5]

Social Structures

A second variable that affected the well-being of the mass of the population was the
social structure that encompassed it. Society throughout the centuries being considered
was highly structured. It was dominated by a system of classes between which there was,
as a general rule, very little mobility. Not even the barbarian peoples who invaded
Europe and the empire in the early Middle Ages were entirely without social classes. The
importance of class structure in the context of this book lies in the fact that the
interdependence of classes was expressed in the exploitation of one by another and that
the level of exploitation was continuously changing with economic and political conditions. This structured society culminated in the emergence of the system of landholding,
economic relations, and social organization generally known as feudalism. The whole

period from the decay of the Roman Empire to the nineteenth century was marked by the slow growth and even more gradual disintegration of this system.

Feudalism, in brief, was a system whereby land was occupied in return for service. Land, the supreme form of wealth in a self-sufficing society, was held to be owned by the king, prince, or chief. Tracts of land were allocated to those who served him in return for the service that they owed. This service might be personal, administrative, or, most often, military. The nobles and barons held courts and dispensed justice in the name of their ruler; they spent time at his court and in his company; they advised and supported him; and, above all, they protected him from his enemies, a euphemism for following him in his feuds and wars. But this feudal nobility had itself to be supported. It required its own retainers and fighting men both to protect itself and to fulfill its own obligations to its lord and ruler. These subordinates in turn had to be given land by the nobles, so that they could support themselves and perform the duties required of them. At the base of the feudal pyramid was the mass of the peasantry, who tilled the land and produced the surplus that was consumed by those who occupied the social strata above them.

This is a highly simplified picture of feudal society. Reality was immeasurably more complicated; its stratification much less clear. The subtenant of a lord in one place might be his feudal superior in another. And the gradations of status among the peasant masses almost defy generalization. Service was tied to land, and landholding involved service, often commuted for a money payment, which in turn became a simple rent. But services that were not thus commuted tended to become "lost." The obligation to serve a lord in battle for a certain number of days in each year might be divided with the partition of the land with which it was linked. Some holdings came to owe only a minute fraction of a fighting man. In time this ceased to be "collected," and the obligation was conveniently forgotten. The seventeenth-century surveyors of one English barony noted with some chagrin that "we cannott find whoe are the present tennants in fee of the foresaid lands." In other words, the obligation to serve the lord with sword and lance was in total abeyance. In this way did some of the obligations of feudalism disappear. But not all. If the lord ceased gradually to honor his obligations to *his* lord or his king, he continued nonetheless to exact service, or money in lieu of it, from those who held land of him. The latter continued to labor on the lord's demesne or to pay a rent instead. The lord's land tended to become a freehold, held freely and without obligation, but those lower in the social scale remained tenants, subject to a variety of constraints on their right to lease or alienate their land or to pass it on to their heirs. As often as not they had no security of tenure and were even restricted in the crops they might grow.

Much land in all parts of Europe was held by the church. Cathedral chapters and monasteries held manors, each parish priest possessed his glebe, and the church possessed a limited right—that of collecting tithe—over all land. The church had a longer memory, or kept better records, than lay lords, and the obligations that were owed to it continued to be exacted to the full.

What we are concerned with here is the unstable relationship between landowner and land user, between lord and tenant, the one having shed most of his obligations regarding his land, the other obliged to pay whatever his lord thought that he could exact. It is easy to interpret the resulting social history in terms of competition between the two broad classes, the landowner and the peasant. No doubt the one did attempt to exploit the other, but it would be wrong to ignore the built-in safeguards that peasant societies possessed. Most formed village communities, each with their "customs," which almost assumed the status of law. Instances are numerous of the lord being obliged to withdraw from an extreme position when it was demonstrated that his actions conflicted with custom. The strength of custom was very powerful indeed, and if it could be demonstrated that things had been done in a certain way "since the time whereof memory is not to the contrary," it would be a very bold—or rash — lord, who attempted to do otherwise. This is not to say that there were not peasant risings in all parts of Europe from England to the east Baltic. They have been catalogued, mapped, and teased to death by Marxist historians for what little light they can be made to shed on the class struggle and the emergence of capitalism.

Wages and Prices

There were, however, economic trends that benefited now one sector of society, now another. These were caused, on the one hand, by fluctuations, long-term or short, in climate and agricultural production, and, on the other, by movements in population and demand. It is almost beyond the ingenuity of the historian to measure fluctuations in welfare. There is, however, one surrogate that can be used—prices. These must be handled with care and have little significance unless compared with wages.

To use prices and wages as a measure of welfare implies that people were paid for their labor in coin and that they used the money they received to purchase the necessities of life. In fact, most people throughout the preindustrial period neither received wages nor bought the essentials of daily living. Their labor was owed in return for the holdings they cultivated. They produced themselves most of the foodstuffs and commodities they needed, and, for the rest, they relied upon the mutuality of the village community. Price series and wage series can record only the material conditions of those sectors of society which relied upon a money or exchange economy. They tell us nothing of the peasant who rarely handled a coin. Those who used money as a measure of value and medium of exchange were, by and large, members of a few restricted crafts such as masons and carpenters. Nevertheless, even the peasant had at times to venture into the market, because his degree of self-sufficiency was never absolute. Indeed there were times, as, for example, after a very bad harvest, when he was obliged to buy grain for consumption and for seed. How he managed it, we do not clearly know. The evidence from wills, inventories, and other records suggests that he borrowed. There were always well-to-do peasants, not to mention the professional moneylender, ready to profit from others misfortunes. A large proportion of the peasantry, even in the nineteenth century, were in debt much of the time.

The price series compiled by Phelps-Brown and Hopkins (fig. 10.2) is based on sources from southern England and relates only to craftsmen in the building trades.[6] It expresses the ability of these relatively privileged wage earners to buy a composite unit of consumables, made up of breadgrains, meat, fish, butter, cheese, and drink, as well as clothing, fuel, and lighting. Throughout the thirteenth and fourteenth centuries, the price of commodities remained high relative to wages, despite an improvement in the latter after about 1300. The effect of the Black Death and the ensuing labor shortage was to bring about a rise in wage levels. On the other hand, the price of commodities tended to drop after about 1370 and continued to do so intermittently until the end of the next

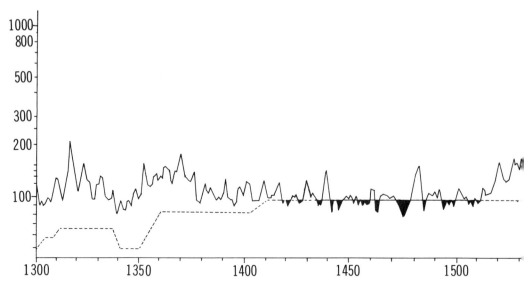

10.2. The true measure of progress: the correlation between real wages and food prices. In this graph the dotted line represents the wages received by building workers; the solid line, the price of a composite basket of food. (After E. H. Phelps-Brown and Sheila V. Hopkins.)

century. For a period of almost a hundred years, prices remained low relative to wages, and building craftsmen and, the evidence suggests, most other wage earners enjoyed a level of prosperity that they had never previously known. This happy period came to a close between 1510 and 1520. Wages increased between 1530 and 1560, but prices rose much more sharply and continued to do so until the middle of the seventeenth century.

Many reasons have been offered for the unfavorable movement of prices at this time. Most often cited has been the price inflation induced by the import into Europe of bullion from the New World. But the price increase became conspicuous even before American silver began to flood the European markets. Alternatively, silver from the mines of central Europe, pouring onto the European markets through the marts of the Low Countries, has been blamed. Both factors operated, but it is likely that the increase in population significantly above its postplague levels had, on the one hand, increased demand for consumer goods and, on the other, depressed the market for labor.

For a period of some three hundred years, the cost of living, relative to wages, remained high, and not until the second half of the nineteenth century was the building worker again able to buy with his wage packet as much as he had done about 1500. But since the mid-nineteenth century there has been a continuous increase in the volume and variety of goods that a workman has been able to purchase. This discussion and the graph in figure 10.2 represent only the level of welfare of building workers. This group was relatively privileged, but there was nevertheless a considerable range in income between the well paid freemason and those who only carried stone and mixed mortar, and there must have been many, even within these trades, whose welfare was little above

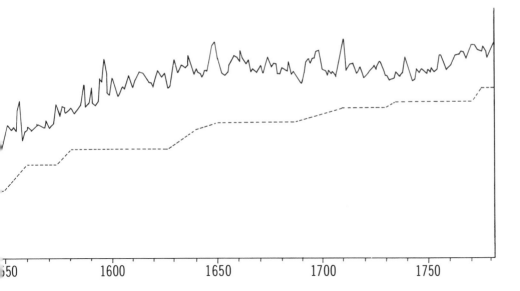

the subsistence level. Nor can it be assumed that all wage earners fared similarly. Demand for their skills fluctuated, and there must have been times when many were underemployed, if not wholly unemployed. It is, lastly, quite impossible to extend this graph to the peasantry, who until the nineteenth century made up a large part of the total population. They were dependent only marginally on the market, and their level of welfare depended primarily on the success of their own crops. It might be argued that they fared less well than the building workers during the later Middle Ages because they received a smaller payment for that part of their product which they sold. It is by no means clear that the decline in food prices was matched by a similar drop in those of other consumer goods.

A further complication is that, during times of high prices, the consumer would tend to substitute cheaper goods for more expensive. More breadgrains and less meat would enter into the diet, and coarse grains would tend to be substituted for wheat. All such considerations might have the effect of modifying the general level of well-being suggested by figure 10.2, but they would not alter its general applicability. The same trends can be assumed, with perhaps greater reservation, for the rest of Europe. But the farther one moves from southern England, where the Phelps-Brown and Hopkins data were collected, the less applicable their model might become. This would be the case especially for the nineteenth century in eastern and southeastern Europe. Here the level of industrial growth was appreciably lower than in the rest of Europe. Demand for labor off the land was smaller and wage levels reflected the scarcity or abundance of labor. The evidence suggests that for much of the time there was an abundance of labor, and that its "price" was accordingly low. This reacted in turn on purchasing power and thus on both the demand for manufactured goods and employment in manufacturing industries. The income in real terms of the peasant, and, indeed, of most of the population in eastern and southeastern Europe, improved much less rapidly than in western.

Servitude and Status

There was no necessary connection between personal status and level of income. The villein who was only half-free was not *necessarily* worse off than the freeman with a minute holding, and examples are too numerous to cite of the gentry whose total income was less than half that of a comfortable peasant leaseholder. Nevertheless, status was a factor influencing welfare, if only because those of inferior status owed obligations and services that deprived them of the freedom to manage their own affairs. Most obvious of such constraints were the obligations to remain on the lord's land and to supply labor services on his demesne. Such requirements arose very early in the Middle Ages. The duties of the *gebur* (villein) were defined in an Anglo-Saxon source of about 1000 as "two days at week-work at such work as is bidden him every week throughout the year, and in harvest three days . . . , and from Candlemas to Easter three," but these services, it was recognized, varied and were "in some places heavy, in others moderate." The peasant was not his own man, and even on his own plowlands he had to follow the custom of his community.[7]

During the following centuries the peasant in most of western Europe succeeded in freeing himself from the worst of these seigneurial constraints. Status became less important and a man's economic position, which, by and large, meant the size of his holding, began to matter more. Even before the Black Death, the peasant had made considerable progress in France, England, and the Low Countries. Thereafter labor shortage and the relative abundance of land greatly enhanced his bargaining power. When the lord had ceased to farm his demesne himself there was indeed little point in continuing to exact services that had ceased to be necessary. Dues were then commuted for a money payment and the peasant became a tenant. Conditions of tenancy might vary greatly. The peasant might have a lease for years, or for lives; he might be at the mercy of his lord, who could turn him out at little notice, or, on the other hand, his tenancy might approximate to a freehold, with absolute security of tenure. The distinction between free and unfree disappeared in the west, but fundamental differences in personal standing continued and may, indeed, have increased in many areas elsewhere.

The peasant in eastern Europe as well as in a few other areas of the continent did not share in the general amelioration of status that occurred in the west. Beginning in the fifteenth century, his status was depressed; he became bound to the soil and his labor obligations to his lord were intensified. The east European peasant was passing into a "second serfdom" at the very time that his western counterpart was succeeding in throwing off all servile constraints. "By the end of the fifteenth century, . . . from the Elbe to the Volga," wrote Blum, "most of the peasantry were well on their way to becoming serfs."[8] This process seems first to have gained momentum in the plains of eastern Germany and Poland and to have spread southward to Hungary, Romania, and the Balkans and eastward into Russia. Conditions for the peasantry were at their worst in the sixteenth and seventeenth centuries in the northern part of this broad region, but deteriorated somewhat later in the south. Conditions began to improve during the later eighteenth and early nineteenth centuries. Servile constraints were ended in Prussia in 1807, and in 1848 throughout the Hapsburg lands, but not until 1861 in Russia and even later in Romania. They ended in the Balkans only when the Slavic peoples revolted successfully against the Ottoman Empire.

One tends to regard the "freeing of the serfs" as a grand gesture by which a number of people were suddenly made to enjoy the delights of freedom. As a general rule it did not happen like that. The few constraints that remained at the time of the French Revolution were, it is true, swept away. But in most instances the lords who thus lost the *corvée,* or unpaid labor, of their peasants, demanded—and got—compensation for the loss of *their* rights. The servile peasantry, in fact, bought its freedom, and if, as was generally the case, the peasants could not pay in cash (which, of course, they would have had to borrow), they gave up some part of their holding. Many were the peasant farms thus made too small to support a family, and the peasants themselves reduced to penury. Faced with this choice, the romantic would choose Freedom, but there is good reason to think that many a peasant in eastern Germany had second thoughts.

The phenomenon of the second serfdom was clearly of great significance. It was the source of immense hardship and was an important cause of the slow development of eastern compared with western Europe. It has given rise to a very large literature, especially as it lends itself to a Marxist interpretation. A prominent factor in its develop-ment was the market, which was developing not only in western Europe but also in the urbanized regions of the Ottoman Empire, for breadgrains. The territorial lords, it is claimed, exploited their lands and their peasantry in order to profit from these oppor-tunities. The second serfdom was thus seen as a phase in the struggle between feudalism and the developing capitalist system. But why, it may be asked, did this not also happen in western Europe, where the urban market was most developed? Two factors distin-guished eastern from western Europe during the later Middle Ages and the centuries that followed. In the first place, central authority in the east was weak, unable to exercise effective control over the provinces, at the same time that in the west royal and princely power was being strengthened. The administration of justice and control over the courts passed largely into the hands of the landed nobility, which used them in their own interests. Second, the urban structure in the east was weak, and the urban middle class small and politically powerless. The cities tended to be by-passed by the nobles, as they sold their wheat and rye to the merchants, who shipped it to the west. In western Europe a peasant with grievances could flee to the city and be lost. Such recourse was not, by and large, available in the east before the industrial growth of the nineteenth century. And even then, there were landowners in both Poland and Russia who used the serfs whom they owned to work in their own factories and mines.

The example of the Ottoman Empire throws some light on events in the rest of eastern Europe.[9] The Turkish conquest was followed by the confiscation of peasant land and the creation of estates—*čifliks*—held by the military service of *sipahi* cavalry. The system bore an uncanny similarity to the baronial system and knight service in the west, and it underwent a similar course of disintegration and change. The power of the Ottoman sultans weakened and became more arbitrary. Military duties ceased to be performed or even demanded, and the *čiflik* became a *timar,* an estate held almost unconditionally by a Turkish owner. Cvijič has given us a description of the *timar* as it existed in late nineteenth-century Macedonia. The peasant, usually an orthodox Chris-tian, was more tightly regimented even than on the great, feudally held estates of eastern Germany. He lived with his family in a compound and was fed, clothed, and watched over by his master, on whose lands he grew cereals, corn, and tobacco for the market. The *timar* closely resembled a Southern plantation and, like both the latter and the east

European estate, was infused with a powerful commercial motive, namely, the profits to be had from selling grain to Constantinople and the few other large cities of the Ottoman Empire.

This retrograde movement was not restricted to eastern and southeastern Europe. It was to be met with in other areas where central authority was weak and the urban middle class had made little progress. Among such areas were southern Italy, Sicily, and much of southern Spain. In all these regions the process of creating large estates, or *latifundia* as they are often called, went ahead in the closing centuries of the Middle Ages and in early modern times, always at the expense primarily of the peasant classes.[10]

The well-being of the rural masses was thus determined both by their personal status and tenurial relations with their lord and by the size of the holding that they could cultivate to satisfy their own needs. The latter varied greatly. There may indeed never have been a time when every peasant family held a complete "mansus" or "hide," the notional unit of land thought necessary for its support. In the course of time such equality as there may have been disappeared. It had to do so. With increasing population, land became scarce and holdings were divided and subdivided between heirs. Families died out and their strips and parcels were acquired by others, who added them to their own. And there were always the improvident and the unfortunate, forced to part with land to pay debts or to satisfy social and other obligations.

It is by no means easy to arrive at a picture of land occupation even in modern times. The chief difficulty is the confusion between ownership and occupation. Many a large holding, not to mention an estate, was in part leased to tenant farmers on a rental or sharecropping basis. It is the size of these latter units, together with the obligations that they carried, that we need to know about in order to form some estimate of the level of welfare of the rural population. The pattern of land occupance was, furthermore, continuously changing with the purchase and sale, partition and consolidation of parcels of land. On balance the tendency in much of Europe, probably during the eighteenth century, certainly during the nineteenth, was for holdings to fragment and for their average size to become smaller.

France, for example, became a land of peasant proprietors during the Revolution, and, though the estates were in some measure reconstituted after 1815, much of the land continued to be cultivated in small, freehold units of peasant families. In 1862, more than a half of farm holdings were of less than 5 hectares (12.4 acres), and 85 percent had each less than 20 hectares (49 acres).[11] The proportion of very small holdings actually increased during the next two decades. The situation in Belgium was yet more extreme. In 1910, after a long period during which holdings were increasingly partitioned and fragmented, almost 80 percent were of less than 5 acres, and only 2.4 percent had more than 50 acres.[12]

In Germany there was a very great variation both in the size of tenements and in tenurial conditions between one part of the country and another. The west and, in particular, the southwest were characterized by holdings of excessively small size. There were areas, especially Franconia, where more than a quarter of the parcels were of less than one hectare (2.47 acres).[13] Eastern Germany was notorious for its great estates. Part of this area was in fact cultivated as peasant holdings, but even after the freeing of the serfs, much continued to be worked in large units by hired workers. The tendency was for peasant holdings in the German east to become smaller, leading to the very considerable migration of the peasantry to the developing industrial regions of northwestern Germany.

The Monetary System

Most of Europe's rural population—and that group, before the nineteenth century, made up more than three-quarters of the total—practiced in some degree a self-sufficing economy. But their self-sufficiency, even in the early Middle Ages, was far from absolute. They had to buy salt, such metal goods and pottery as they used, and perhaps occasionally a piece of cloth. There were also times when they had to purchase the seed that they sowed, and sometimes, when harvests had been poor, they may have been obliged to obtain breadgrains. They may have commuted their obligations to their lord for a money payment, and when arraigned before the manorial court they faced the possibility of having to pay a fine in coin. Those among them who possessed only a minute holding commonly worked for a wage on the lands of those better off than themselves. And most who tilled the soil had at some time a small surplus that they sold into the market. Money entered into all these transactions, and when chroniclers and others quote with alarm or surprise the price of grain during a famine crisis, we may be sure that they were writing with the experience of the local marketplace in mind.

Prices fluctuated, probably more widely in reality than the records indicate, for our price series are based only on what was paid by households and communities that kept records. The peasant and the petty merchant made no record of their transactions, and local circumstances may have forced prices well above their recorded levels.

Coins were first minted on a significant scale in classical Greece. None date from before the eighth century B.C. Almost from the first they assumed the form that time has consecrated and made almost universal. They were small, rounded disks of metal, impressed with a symbol of the authority that issued them. The "owls" of Athens became known and used throughout the Greek world. Aegina displayed a tortoise, and Corinth, a winged horse. Rome was late in adopting a metallic currency, but when it did so, it followed closely the Greek example. A long succession of imperial coins showed the emperor on the obverse and an inscription or geometrical design on the reverse. Roman coins were imitated first by the Celtic rulers of pre-imperial Europe and later by the barbarian rulers of the states that succeeded to the empire. Coins were stamped from silver, bronze, and, very much less frequently, from gold or electrum, a gold-silver alloy. Their value in exchange transactions was exactly that represented by the intrinsic value of the coin itself, and the symbols of authority that they bore on their obverse, and sometimes reverse as well, were intended to serve as guarantee of their integrity.

The coin was made sometimes by casting it in a mold but usually by striking thin disks of metal between dies (fig. 10.3). The coin that resulted bore a clear impression on its face, but its edge might be quite irregularly rounded, an open invitation to the dishonest to "clip" the coin by cutting away thin slivers of metal. Despite the fiercest penalties, this practice never quite disappeared until perfectly rounded coins with milled edges appeared in the nineteenth century. Clipping was important because the coin was not so much a symbol of money, like a torn or damaged bank note, but was intrinsically valuable. To trim metal from its edge was to diminish its value as a means of exchange, without reducing its "face" value. It was a mode of deception that could be countered

10.3. A moneyer striking coins from disks
of metal; central Europe. (After a sixteenth-
century painting.)

only by weighing the coins. Hence the common association of value with weight. The exchange value of a silver coin—for bronze coins were scarcely worth the trouble of mutilating—was thus a somewhat variable quantity.

At the same time, the silver or gold content of a coin could be diminished by incorporating in it a quantity of base metal. Debasement of coinage was a device employed by governments in grave financial difficulties. It was self-defeating, because the degree of adulteration of the noble metal was quickly and easily determined by the assayer, and the coinage was, in terms of commodities or other monetary systems, devalued. The use of two or even three metals simultaneously implied a constant relationship between them. Gold, for example, was commonly assumed to have been, weight for weight, twelve times that of silver. But gold and silver varied both in the volume available and in the demand for each. The earlier equivalent of dealers would buy the one or the other, and in doing so would bring about even greater deviation from what was regarded as the "natural" relationship between the coinage systems. Early merchants and money changers always found their transactions complicated by the problems of bimetallism.

The complications of currencies and exchange rates before the nineteenth century make those of today seem simple. One has only to look at one of the treatises, such as Pegolotti's *Trattura della Mercatura* of the fourteenth century, that set out to clarify these matters for the merchant, to realize the complexities and ramifications of earlier mone- tary systems. If the value of coinages was so fluctuating and uncertain, how did a merchant keep his books or quote his prices? The answer is that he used a "money of account," a monetary system that had no independent existence but to which all other currencies could be converted by an arithmetical calculation. Such a fictional system was that of "pounds, shillings, and pence," or, in its French form, *livres, sous,* and *deniers,* or, in Latin, *libri, solidi* and *denarii.* The *solidus* and *denarius* had, indeed, been coins, but their relationship in accounting—twelve *denarii* to the *solidus*—was entirely arbitrary. The "pound" was in origin a measure of *weight* but, in terms of value, came to be thought of as the equivalent of twenty "shillings." The idea of a money of account has not wholly disappeared from the modern world, but it ceased to be significant when money became tokens, of little intrinsic value.

In the later Roman Empire, gold, silver, and copper were all used for minting coins. Gold was little used, but there was a multitude of small copper coins of low value. They reflected the need among ordinary people for coins of small denomination to carry on their daily business in shops and markets. We must think of the average Roman carrying a handful of small change in his pocket or purse, with the odd silver coin of higher denomination. Roman currency declined in importance as the barbarian kingdoms took over from the empire. Gold coins ceased to be minted, and the small copper coins passed gradually out of use. There ceased to be a need for small change as society became increasingly self-sufficing. Silver coins continued to be minted, but they were not used for petty transactions. Their intrinsic value was too high. The silver penny became the standard coin throughout western and central Europe, but its intrinsic value varied from country to country. England maintained a currency of high quality. It was reminted at frequent intervals, so overcoming the problem of debasement. In continental Europe, on the other hand, government's control of the coinage was lax. The feudal baronage issued coins in which the metal was increasingly debased, and periodic "reforms" of the coinage became necessary in order to upgrade the quality of the metal.

In the later Middle Ages, with the increase in the volume of trade, demand increased for coins of larger denomination than the penny. The fact that a hoard of more than 150,000 pennies was found in the Low Countries is indicative of the problem faced by merchants. The Italians found the answer when they minted a larger silver coin, known as the "grosso," "ducat," or "matapan." Their example was followed by the French "gros" and the English "groat." All these names emphasize the largeness of both the coin and its value. The English groat was consistently four times the value of the silver penny.

At the other end of the scale, the breakdown of local self-sufficiency and the emergence of a market economy brought with it a demand for coins of very small denomination. When Chaucer's Pardoner paused to fortify himself at a roadside ale-house, what coin did he use, or did he pay for a round of drinks for the whole company? We do not know, but coins of lesser value than a penny, which represented almost a day's wage for a laborer, began to be minted to satisfy this everyday need. In England the half-penny and the quarter-penny, or farthing, began to be struck. They were of silver but much smaller in size. In much of continental Europe, however, the silver was debased by alloying it with increasing quantities of base metal, usually copper. This so-called black money was essentially token money. No one bothered to insure that the intrinsic value of such small change answered to its face value. But the minting of such coins raised another problem: the cost of striking them was so high in relation to their face value that few moneyers wanted to be bothered with them.

The gradual emergence during the Middle Ages of a money economy raised yet another problem, the supply of money itself. The money supply was restricted by that of the metals from which it was struck. Very little gold has ever been mined in Europe, and the supply of silver was extremely limited. Much of the gold was used for plate and decorative purposes and had probably been brought from West Africa by way of the trans-Saharan caravan routes. Supply was small, and this alone would have limited the use of gold currency. Only the Byzantine Empire made any considerable use of the precious metal in its "bezants." Silver was universally used for currency. It was mined in several parts of Europe, notably in the Harz Mountains of Germany and in Bohemia. It served many uses. A large amount was absorbed by the decorative arts, some was used chemically and in crafts such as glass painting, and the rest was minted. There was always a drain of precious metals to the Middle East and the rest of Asia to redress the balance of payments on trade. It is likely that the amount of silver available in Europe for circulating currency was too small, and this contributed to the long-term stability of prices. There was no inflationary situation before the sixteenth century, when conditions of monetary supply underwent a profound change. In times of scarcity, when grain prices rose sharply, the volume of currency available to pay the inflated prices was quite inadequate. No doubt the frequent complaints referred primarily to the lack of small coins, but this was a reflection of a general shortage.

Ordinary people went about their business without a purse full of small change. The slender evidence suggests that they secreted the little coined money they possessed somewhere in their cottages. The tradition of the peasant keeping his money in a sock under the bed has endured until modern times. Inventories of the movable goods left at death usually recorded the sums of money in hand. They were always very small; bullion was more often kept in the form of silverware. Nor did the merchant take with him a purse full of silver pennies or groats to carry on his business. Clearly he needed cash for his journey, but his transactions were by credit notes, or bills of exchange. These were contractual obligations to pay so much to such and such a person "at usance," the customary term for payment at a later date. At intervals accounts were balanced and debts paid, and the amount of coin that changed hands was often quite small. In such ways problems arising from the shortage of cash and the difficulty and danger of transporting it were minimized. The practice bore a certain resemblance to the checking system today.

In the sixteenth century this situation changed. From being relatively scarce, bullion became abundant. First, the silver mines of Bohemia were expanded. Joachimstal (Jachymov) in 1519 began minting silver *thäler* (dollars), which became almost the symbol of a sound currency. Then mining spread to the mountains of Slovakia, where the Fuggers and Welsers, prominent banking houses in south Germany, accumulated their wealth. Silver was shipped down the northern rivers to the Baltic and thence to western Europe. The peak of central European silver mining was reached about 1529.[14] Much of the silver passed into hoards and was used in making the now-fashionable silverware, but enough entered into circulation to influence the general level of prices. Within a generation or two bullion began to arrive in Europe from a very different source and on a far greater scale. By the mid-sixteenth century the Spaniards had reached and overrun both Mexico and the Andean regions of South America. These lands were not familiar with iron, but they had accumulated hoards of bullion. This commodity was, from about 1520, shipped back to Europe on an increasing scale. Most of it arrived in the Spanish port of Seville, where it passed into the charge of the state trading organization, the *Casa de la Contratación.* The Spanish state was in urgent need of money. Apart from paying for its own extravagance and inefficiency, it had to finance its foreign wars. Much of the New World silver, minted into coins, paid the wages of the Spanish and imperial armies in the Low Countries, Germany, and Italy, and was spent wherever they happened to be serving. Thus the bullion of the New World passed rapidly into circulation in the Old, without any commensurate increase in the Old World's productivity. As every monetarist knows, this combination was the ideal prescription for inflation, and it is customary to blame the rise in prices of the sixteenth century mainly on the inflow of silver from the New World.

But there were other factors at work. It is significant that the price rise was greater with foodstuffs than with most other goods. Inflation was clearly not uniform, suggesting that changes in consumer demand also influenced the price level. Population was increasing, harvests continued to be uncertain, and some increase in the price of breadgrains was to be expected.[15] This rise influenced the general level of welfare, especially of the growing body of those who were dependent, partly or wholly, on a wage income. At the same time there was in many parts of Europe a boom in building construction, which drew money into the economy and fueled the inflationary trend.[16] The price rise continued through the early decades of the next century, then stabilized, and thereafter showed only the normal fluctuations that could be expected between good years and bad. In the seventeenth century prices even fell slightly before beginning a very slow increase, which continued through the period of the Industrial Revolution.

The price inflation of the sixteenth and early years of the seventeenth century was only the second of major importance within the historical experience of western man. The first had been in the third and fourth centuries A.D. The consequences of the sixteenth-century inflation varied from region to region and from class to class. It was clearly of no great importance in areas where a "natural" economy continued to prevail. The price rise was experienced, generally rather modestly, in Scandinavia, and more conspicuously in eastern Europe, where the increased demand for cereals in the west communicated itself by way of merchants to the grain growers of Poland and the Ukraine. Here, also, prices continued to rise through the seventeenth century, probably on account of shortages induced by the almost continuous warfare. But the price rise was greatest and most serious throughout western Europe.

A. P. Usher has emphasized that, with a poorly developed and very expensive transport system, grain prices might vary sharply between one region and another.[17] This continued to be the case until the mid-nineteenth century, when the means of cheap transportation reduced the friction of distance and allowed prices to find their level. There were times when whole regions or countries suffered from a subsistence crisis, which the best of transportation systems could have done little to alleviate. There were others when shortages were local and could have been remedied with better means of transporting grain. Average prices have little significance, and it is dangerous to extrapolate from one market center to complete a run of figures for another. The price series compiled by Monique Mestayer and reproduced in figure 10.4 relates only to the grain market at Douai in northern France.[18] Of course, the peaks in this price series would be reproduced in similar series, if they were available, in other parts of western Europe. But it must not be assumed that every rise and fall in the price of wheat and oats in the Douai market was replicated in every other. All would have had certain features in common:

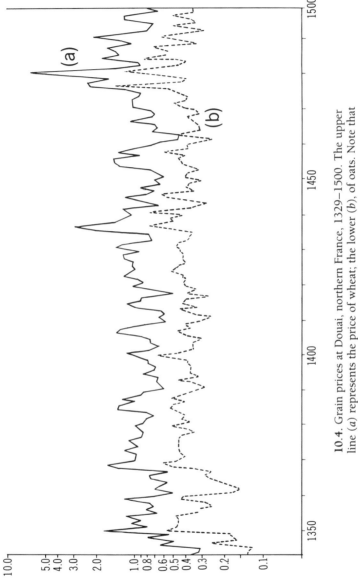

10.4. Grain prices at Douai, northern France, 1329–1500. The upper line (*a*) represents the price of wheat; the lower (*b*), of oats. Note that in times of scarcity the price of oats approaches that of wheat. (After Monique Mestayer.)

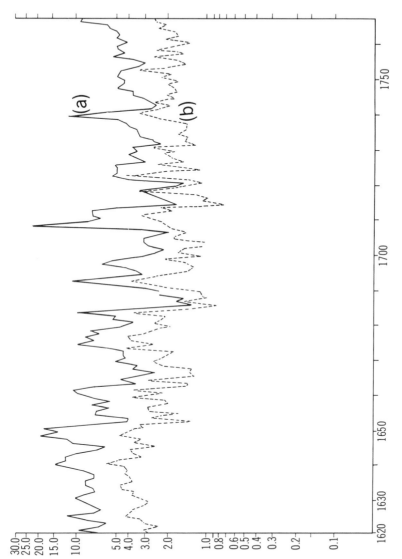

10.4 (cont'd). Grain prices at Douai, 1620–1770. Note (1) the tendency for the graph to flatten after c. 1700, indicating a relative absence of crises; (2) the way in which the price of oats approximates that of wheat.

the extreme year-to-year fluctuations and the similar, but not identical, trends in the prices of bread- and coarse grains. There were years when one failed but not the other, but as a general rule the high price of breadgrains led people to turn to coarse grains, driving their price up as well.

The prices shown in figure 10.4 are averages for the year. But there were also fluctuations within the year. As a general rule, prices were low after harvest, especially if the harvest had been a good one. They rose during the winter and spring. Grain that had been bought and held by the corn bodgers was brought onto the market when it seemed most profitable to do so. But prices generally continued to rise during the late spring and early summer, as stocks held by the peasant dwindled and became exhausted, and were at their highest on the eve of the next year's harvest.

If we return to figure 10.4, we can see how every five or six years shortages of grain forced prices up to levels several times greater than their normal or average. Occasionally, no more than two or three times a century, a combination of weather, warfare, and other adversities drove prices even higher. These were the catastrophes from which it took society decades to recover. Such conditions prevailed in 1438, 1482, and 1526. After about 1580 such exceptional years became more frequent.[19] The second half of the seventeenth century, by all available criteria, was one of the most adverse in the recorded history of Europe. Conditions culminated in 1709–10, when bad harvests and the Duke of Marlborough's wars in the Low Countries forced prices, at least in the Douai market, higher than had ever been known.

The price of grain has been emphasized because breadgrains formed the basic foodstuff; demand was constant and inelastic. For this reason records of food prices have been kept more fully and carefully than for other commodities. When series are available for goods other than basic foodstuffs, they are seen always to fluctuate less violently and, in times of inflation, to rise less steeply. Presumably, whenever times were hard, so large a share of disposable income went to foodstuffs that demand actually declined for other commodities.

After 1709–10 conditions improved, and from 1740 there was a period of relative stability. Prices were rising but very slowly. There were, of course, poor harvests, and one hears of food riots in the cities, but this may have been in part because the mechanism of supply had not fully adjusted to the increasing population. Severe winters and wet summers do not seem to have influenced the supply and price of breadgrains as severely as in previous years.

The causes of this greater stability in agricultural prices are obscure. Doubtless many factors contributed to it; fewer occurrences of severe weather, some improvement in agricultural techniques, less destruction in the course of military campaigns and, as seems not improbable, more prolonged labor on the land, at least in Protestant Europe. Whatever its cause, this relative stability in prices had very significant consequences. The disposable income of all who did not practice a near-subsistence agriculture was increased, and this circumstance can, in turn, have led only to a greater demand for durable goods as well as for consumables other than the basic foods. This expanded market appears to be reflected in the greater activity of cottage industries and of the merchants who supplied the raw materials and sold the products. Most of the innovations of the eighteenth century, including the spinning jenny and Huntsman's process for making steel, aimed in the first instance only to supply better and more abundant materials for the domestic producers of durable consumer goods. Arthur Young was emphatic that what was needed was an increased production of such goods for a mass market. If the proto-industrial phase in the development of the European economy was based upon an increasingly effective consumer demand, this can only have been made possible by the greater real income that resulted from a more assured harvest.

Progress was, inevitably, far from consistent over the whole of Europe. It was most marked in the west, northwest, and in Scandinavia, where the social system allowed the peasant to enjoy more fully the profits that resulted from improved environmental conditions. Elsewhere the profits were, in varying degrees, drained off in rents and servile obligations. They passed into the hands of the landowning classes and the merchants, paying not only for their graceful living but also for their building programs, which have bequeathed to posterity, among thousands of other buildings, Palladian Warsaw and baroque Vienna. But almost everywhere the benefits of a more rewarding agriculture percolated downward during the latter half of the eighteenth and early nineteenth centuries. It was late before they became conspicuous in eastern Europe and the Balkans, where a servile status survived in some areas until the 1860s. That Polish peasant Jan Słomka, whose reminiscences throw so much light on material conditions in late nineteenth-century Poland, noted how by small increments the material standards of his people were improved. The 1870s, he noted, were the time when the iron stove became common in the cottages, and other goods that served the comfort or convenience of the peasantry made their appearance. In western Europe, the poorer classes, both urban and rural, began to have the money to purchase pieces of furniture, china for the table and for decorative sideboards, as well as an extra suit of clothes for Sundays.

The Growth of an Exchange Economy

During the years that followed the collapse of the Roman Empire in the west, the volume of trade, whether long-distance or local, was small. There may never have been, in the words of the Belgian historian Henri Pirenne, "an economy of no markets," but markets were indeed few, and the goods traded, restricted in both their volume and variety. Trade in articles of everyday use virtually disappeared. The more refined types of pottery, bronzes, statuary, and cloth vanished from much of Europe, and such trade as continued to be carried on, at least outside Mediterranean Europe, was in goods of small bulk and relatively high value. Glass for church windows, lead for masonry construction, fine cloth, and Byzantine silks made up most of it. Everywhere the local community made do with whatever goods it produced. If it lacked the raw materials to make this article or the skills to fabricate that, it made do with whatever was available.

The next thousand years and more were marked by increasing specialization in the manufacture of goods of everyday use. Specialization has been of fundamental importance in human history. It contributed to a greater expertise, increased the efficiency of the processes, and led to a greater volume of output at a lower price. Furthermore, the specialist, with his greater familiarity with materials and processes, was in a far better position to innovate than those who followed a craft only intermittently and to satisfy the need of their family. Neolithic men who dug and knapped flints at Spiennes or Grimes' Graves were specialists. So also were the metalworkers who set up their furnaces and forges within some of the great Celtic *oppida*. The classical world was notable for the range of specializations that were pursued—in potting, weaving, metalworking, as well as in the arts of building and decoration. Few such specializations were continued through the early Middle Ages. Only in a few Italian cities, in Constantinople, and, after the eighth century, in Moorish Spain, does one find clear evidence for the regular pursuit of manufacturing or for any form of organization of craftsmen.

In the slow revival of manufacturing and trade during the early Middle Ages, the demands of the church and of the emerging feudal aristocracy played an important role. These two orders of society produced little if any of the goods they required; they were overwhelmingly dependent on trade for the satisfaction of material needs. Only in the supply of foodstuffs could they rely, as a general rule, on the production of their own demesnes. Even the obligations owed to them by their tenants were as a general rule discharged in kind. But no estate, however broad its acres and intensive its cultivation, could provide all that was needed by its lords and owners. The production of wine, salt, and olive oil were all more localized than the growing of breadgrains. Most people, of course, had to dispense with such luxuries. The feudal and religious orders obtained them either by trade or by acquiring distant estates that could produce them. A series of ninth-century surveys of monastic land shows not so much an evolving pattern of trade as the acquisition of distant parcels of land that were capable of yielding such necessities as could not be grown or made nearer to home. Monasteries in northwest Europe acquired vineyards in climatically more favorable areas, and each year, after the grape harvest, sent their servants to bring home the wine. The lay aristocracy was more mobile than a community of monks. It could, and almost invariably did, travel from one part of its estates to another, eating its way through the accumulated store of food.

But measures of this kind could not remedy all the shortages that were experienced. Merchants were needed who could bring more esoteric goods—glass for windows, cloth of better quality than local homespun, metalware, jewelry, and luxuries of all kinds. Kings sometimes sent such items as gifts to one another. Offa of Mercia, in England, sent a cloak to Charlemagne. Such scraps of evidence show how small was the volume of goods traversing the roads of early medieval Europe. Two contrasted patterns of trade gradually emerged from the hypothetical "economy of no markets." The one was the small-scale demand for sophisticated goods such as entered into long-distance trade. It was strongly up-market and was satisfied by a few merchants who covered immense distances with their wares. Many of these traders were "Syrians," who not only bridged the gap between Italy, Byzantium, and the Levant, but also traveled freely between the Christian and Moslem worlds. At the same time there was a local trade, part of the mutuality that characterized rural communities: exchange of crops, seeds, and the tools of agriculture. Often enough this was barter; no money changed hands. Frequently there was no suitable coin to circulate. The emergence of nonagricultural communities served only to increase demand of this kind. There was, in the economist's terms, a predisposition to trade at the local level, awaiting only the creation of favorable conditions. These would have included not only a convenient currency but also a prearranged place and time to do business and an assurance that some kind of law and order would prevail.

There was no need to reestablish markets in much of southern Europe, where there had been contraction in the volume of trade but no prolonged interruption. In Europe north of the Alps, on the other hand, such business had to be built up anew. Grants of market privileges were made in their thousands. The earliest were in western and northwestern Europe, but a wave of such grants spread eastward, until its energies were dissipated in the plains of eastern Poland and Russia. The great period of market foundation in western Europe was the eleventh and twelfth centuries; in central, the twelfth and thirteenth. The process continued through the last centuries of the Middle Ages in eastern Europe, but in the Balkans had to wait until after the Ottoman conquests.

Not all markets prospered. Some were stillborn. Few traders came, and profits to their lords were minimal. Other markets blossomed into instruments of both local and long-distance trade. Some continue to be held in the present century, while others, though legally still in existence, have in more recent times lost their business to shops permanently established in the cities. A factor in the success or failure of a market was its location—its position not only in relation to roads, bridges, and fords, but also relative to other and competing markets. Modern theory holds that on a land surface of uniform quality, there should be a regular spacing of markets, each with its own market area. Many are the instances of one lord establishing a market to rival or outbid that of another; in the end one of them was bound to fail. English law developed a common-sense way of dealing with this situation. When the establishment of a new market was proposed, an enquiry was instituted: would it be to the injury of established markets? This depended on how near they were, and so the rule was devised that a market should serve an area delimited in terms of a market journey. A day's journey was reckoned to be twenty miles. A man might be expected to pass a third of the day at the market, leaving two-thirds for travel, which would allow a maximum distance of $6\frac{2}{3}$ miles each way.[20]

It was unusual for the density of the market network to be greater than this, and in much of Europe markets were scattered much more sparsely over the land. This was primarily because the density of the population was low, and the demand for market services, small. In such areas, which included much of northern, eastern, and south-eastern Europe, there was inevitably a relatively high degree of local self-sufficiency because the local mechanism for sale and exchange was imperfectly developed.

On a prescribed day of the week—for it was of the essence of a market that it should be regular—wooden stalls, pictured in countless medieval manuscripts, were set up in the marketplace, the open space set aside for them, and sometimes overflowed into neighboring streets. In the larger cities there came to be two or more markets, usually held on different days and specializing in different commodities: grain, hay (for there were countless horses in every city), butter, wine. Of course, those who sold in the town market paid various tolls and stallage charges for the privilege of setting up shop in the middle of the street. Those of them who already had shops in the city streets, especially if they were well known, preferred to do their business across their own counters, rather than on makeshift stalls, and it might require a city ordinance for them to close their shops when the market was in session.

The activities of the market were sometimes supplemented by those of a fair. The fair was a regular but less frequent gathering of merchants. Trade in local agricultural produce was of negligible importance at fairs. Instead merchants from greater distances met and exchanged their wares. It was at the fairs that one could buy silk and valuable cloth, jewelry, glass, and metalware. Fairs were commonly associated with markets, though there was broad distinction in both the commodities they handled and the kinds of person frequenting them. But a network of fairs ceased gradually to be necessary. Many fairs decayed early or failed entirely to develop. Some, including the most famous,

the cloth fairs of Champagne, were relatively short-lived. They met the needs of merchants in the twelfth and thirteenth centuries and were then overtaken by the expanding
functions of the cities.

Not all markets gave rise to towns, but all towns had markets. In many instances,
charters created towns *as* market centers, and trade, much of it local and short-distance,
was their primary function. But towns quickly developed another and different function:
manufacturing. Crafts had always been carried on, however small their scale, in rural
areas. Spinning was an occupation of every cottage; a loom was to be found in most
homes; the smith, one of the earliest of specialist craftsmen, made spades, plowshares
and colters, and simple ironware. Such craftsmen may have worked at their trade only
part-time; they sold their goods to their neighbors and may have been paid in kind. The
rise of the city changed this. Crafts, or at least many of them, moved to the towns. The
urban craftsman, as a general rule, had a larger clientele. He could increase the scale of
his business; he could even specialize within his craft. In the larger cities the crafts of
smithing, clothworking, and cloth finishing proliferated into an immense number of
very highly specialized trades. In Paris, about 1300, there were almost 450 separate
crafts, each with some kind of gild organization.[21] No doubt Paris carried the organization of these specialties to an extreme, but in London in 1422 there were 111 separate
"mysteries." Smaller cities than Paris or London had fewer gilds, but it cannot be
assumed that the number of specializations was any lower; each gild was more broadly
based. Nevertheless, as we turn to the smallest cities and towns, we find that narrow
specializations have, as a general rule, disappeared, and that, as in Aristotle's small *polis,*
each craftsman practiced a broad range of related crafts. Evidence is scanty for the
numbers of crafts, their organization, and their membership. It is probable that by the
later centuries of the Middle Ages a degree of specialization was achieved in at least the
larger cities that was not exceeded before the nineteenth century.

The role of the market tended to decline. More and more business was done by
craftsmen and traders from their own shops, which could be kept open from daylight to
dusk on every day except Sundays and festivals of the church. In the end the open
market became, by and large, a gathering of countryfolk who had no other *pied à terre*
within the city from which to sell their produce, their poultry, and their other animals.
Much of the commercial business of the city was thus gradually transferred from the
market to the shop and became a permanent rather than an intermittent activity.

There was no distinction between residential areas and those devoted to crafts and
commerce, though certain less salubrious trades, like tanning, tended to be concentrated. In those trades where it was possible—cobbling, leatherworking, making clothes
and small metal goods—shop and workshop were one, and the master and his appren-
tice commonly lived above the shop. Only in southeastern Europe and areas strongly
influenced by a Middle Eastern or Islamic tradition was the separation of place of work
and residence rigorously maintained.[22] There the market was extended through the
week; it became permanent and was sometimes roofed to protect it from the weather. In
it were all the goods that in other cities were to be found only in shops. The great market
at Istanbul perpetuates today a long tradition of trading in the Islamic world.

As the function of the market in western and central Europe narrowed, the shop
gradually came into its own. This development was, in fact, a reversion to a classical
tradition that had never been abandoned in Italy and other parts of southern Europe.

The arched openings of the *tabernae* in Trajan's market survive along the Via Biberatica today and are replicated in places as far apart as Ostia and Dubrovnik. The medieval shop was broadly similar, a small room opening directly onto the street, with shuttered windows and some form of counter for the display of goods. In modern times the windows were glazed, window displays became the vogue, and gas lighting allowed shops to stay open longer, especially in winter.

The triumph of the urban shop over the market, partial though it was, made the services of the middleman all the more important. Whereas the peasant, the producer, brought his agricultural produce to the weekly market and sold it fresh to the consumer, the shopkeeper could not himself, as a general rule, go out into the field to obtain the materials that he processed and sold. He was dependent on the merchant or middleman who brought the bar iron for the smith, grain for the baker, wood for the joiner, wool for the weaver, leather for the shoemaker. There were exceptions. The potter, often located out on the edge of the city, sometimes dug and prepared his own clay, and the butcher may have obtained his live animals in the local market, as indeed in many places he still does. Thus, by the end of the Middle Ages, the shopkeeper was well on the way to becoming a retailer, drawing his wares through complex and devious channels from their rural producers.

The role of the middleman in European society and economy has been immense, and in the changing conditions of the Industrial Revolution his presence was probably critical. The term is taken to include "the series of traders through whose hands commodities pass on their way from the maker or producer to the consumer."[23] Sometimes the role of the middleman consisted merely in buying, transporting, and reselling. These were the functions of the agents of the Italian merchant houses that bought up the wool produced on the lands of English monasteries and arranged for it to be shipped to Flanders or to Italy. We have seen the somewhat more complex and more sinister activities of the grain bodgers or *blattiers,* who bought up grain from the landowner and peasant, often in advance of the harvest, and held it, as occasion offered, until its price had risen sufficiently to offer a handsome profit. The extreme fluctuations in harvest played into the hands of the grain dealers, who always had their store of wheat or rye awaiting the arrival of conditions of famine or destitution. Forestalling became one of the mortal sins of medieval commerce, but all the injunctions and denunciations of the church were ineffective in checking it. Right down until the nineteenth century, especially in eastern Europe, the middleman continued not only to supply breadgrain to the city in normal times but to exacerbate the suffering of all except the rich in times of hardship and shortage.

It was in the textile industry, with its considerable number of sequential processes, that the middleman acquired his greatest importance. No doubt the peasant who wore his own cloth cared nothing for dyeing and finishing, but there was a market in the cities and among the well-to-do for fabrics that had passed through all the traditional stages of production. The urban dyer, fuller, and finisher probably worked for a middleman and never came face to face with the customer who bought the products of their craftsmanship. It was the merchant, or clothier, who made this contact. His operations usually extended over a broad area but centered in his chief town. Here he stored his wool; here, in all probability, he had it washed, combed, and dyed; and here he kept his finished cloth before marketing it. Such cities as Amiens, Ypres, Bruges, and Ghent in northwest

Europe; Kraków in eastern; Brunswick and Nuremberg in central; and Florence and Prato in southern became centers of the cloth trade and sites of markets like the Cloth Hall at Ypres and the Sukiennice (which means the same) in Kraków. At each of these focal points of the clothing industry, the merchants formed a close-knit and wealthy society, bound together by ties of both consanguinity and greed. Theirs was a monopolistic position within the region they served. They agreed on prices among themselves and used whatever pretext they could to reduce what they paid to the domestic spinners and weavers who formed the greater part of their labor force.

The domestic industry increased in modern times both in the numbers employed and in the volume of cloth of all kinds produced. The system had a built-in mechanism for its own increase. It encouraged early marriage and larger families and thus fed ever-increasing manpower into the industry. In the commune of Avesnes-les-Aubert, in northern France—to take only one of many examples—the proportion of the population, itself growing steadily, which was engaged in weaving of linen increased from about 45 percent in 1757–69 to 68 percent only twenty years later. Rates of growth were probably not dissimilar throughout northern France, the southern Low Countries, and the northern Rhineland. This overwhelming dependence of the rural population on weaving linen and woolens was less marked in central and eastern Europe only because population density was lower and holdings were larger. Nevertheless, linen weaving was of considerable importance as a supplement to agriculture throughout the northern plain of Europe, as well as in the hill country of southern Germany and Bohemia.

The domestic industry probably reached its greatest extent in the last decades of the eighteenth century. Statistics are hard to come by, but a few examples will show its importance. In the *généralité* of Amiens, there were about 170,000 textile workers in 1785, almost a third of the total population. This concentration on spinning and weaving gave hostages to fortune.[24] The continued income of the workers was dependent on a steadily high demand and an absence of competition. Of the linen woven in the Saint-Quentin district, more than a third was sold elsewhere in France and in French colonies, and a fifth to Spain and its overseas possessions. These markets were very uncertain, and, by and large, overseas markets were lost early in the next century. This situation, combined with the slow growth of factory production, first of thread, then of cloth and linen, undermined the rural industry throughout northern Europe.[25] Domestic weavers from Flanders to Silesia saw demand for their products slipping away. Their misery was compounded, at least in northwest Europe, when the other mainstay of the peasant, the potato, was killed off in the blight of the 1840s.

The Friction of Distance

Underlying the diffusion of innovation and the growth of an exchange economy were human attitudes toward distance and travel. It is a commonplace that in preindustrial Europe roads were bad and travel difficult and slow, and that few people ever left the parish or commune in which they had been born. This was, indeed, the case during much of the period. Most people knew little about their neighbors beyond the limits of their own community, and nothing of foreign peoples. Even their rulers in many instances had no clear comprehension of the extent and nature of the lands they possessed, despite their continuous movement from one royal home to another. The story is related of Emperor Charles V that he was traveling with his retinue close to the boundary between the German Empire and France, when he saw a town on the opposite bank of the river Meuse. "Whose is it," he asked, "does it belong to me or to the King of France?" None of those around him could answer, so messengers were sent to ask of the citizens whose they were, to which kingdom they owed loyalty. They were able to show that their city was part of France, and the emperor continued on his way, his curiosity satisfied.

At about the same time, in England, John Leland was commissioned by Henry VIII to tour the country and to make a catalogue of the relics of antiquity. Leland went beyond his brief, and, as he himself wrote, traveled for six years, "boothe by the Se Costes and the midle Partes, sparing nother labor nor Costes." The result was the first extended description of a country, so written that the reader could learn what it was like, what were its cities and the regions of which it was composed. This was a compendium of useful information of service to the government. But it was also something more. In his address to the king, Leland wrote that he was "totally enflamed with a love to see thoroughly al those partes of this your opulente and ample Realme."[26] His motives were a compound of curiosity and patriotism, of a desire to see and to understand and of a deep-seated feeling that he and this land belonged together. He had become the citizen of a country, not merely a member of a small and local community.

This feeling was not limited to England. It was felt from France to Poland, where Jan Długoszcz wrote a strongly patriotic history at this time. But the most deeply felt utterances of this newly found patriotism came from Machiavelli and Guicciardini in Italy and from Conrad Celtis, Johannes Stumpf, and Ulrich Mutius in Germany.

These writings betray a new attitude toward space and distance. The one was there to be explored; the other to be overcome. It was no accident that this trend occurred at the same time as the great discoveries, when European peoples found a new world in the Americas, in Asia, and in Africa. Those who cared to know and to understand had their mental horizon extended and their world so broadened that it would have been incomprehensible to people even of the later Middle Ages. Before these revolutionary changes of the sixteenth century people had traveled only if they had to. If one excludes the journeys made by pilgrims to the religious shrines scattered about Europe, there was no travel merely for the sake of seeing and learning about new places. The necessary curiosity was not there, and the medieval imagination greatly exaggerated the horrors of travel. Bernard of Clairvaux is said to have crossed the Alps with his eyes blindfolded so that he would not see the wildness of the scene, led by a servant whose sensitivities were perhaps less developed. Contrast this with the attitude that assumed literary form in the eighteenth century. "I love all wild and solitary places," wrote Wordsworth, and subsequent generations have tended to echo the romantic poet rather than the medieval monk.

Between these extremes we find a realistic presentation of landscape in many of the Italian painters of the Renaissance and, much more powerfully, in the work of Pieter Brueghel (d. 1569). Many of his pictures, even of the flat Flemish landscape, show in one corner an alpine scene, lovingly remembered from the time of his youthful Italian journey.

The cult of travel for its own sake, which was initiated in the sixteenth century, continued to spread and to strengthen. By the end of that century there was a host of people, from the courtly Montaigne to the humble Thomas Platter and Peter Mundy, who faced the perils of the road, satisfied their curiosity, and recorded, often with clinical precision, what they had observed. A century later such a tour had become part of the education of a gentleman. But by this time the infrastructure of travel—inns, roads, bridges—had been greatly expanded, and those who took the Grand Tour in the eighteenth century faced fewer hazards than those who had followed a similar route two centuries earlier. But by this time their curiosity had become stereotyped. They had a list of cities, galleries, curiosities, and sights that they *had* to visit, guided by the same herd instinct that guides American tourists around Europe today.

The world view of most people before the intellectual revolution of the sixteenth century was simpler and more limited. Most writing was in some sense theological; it was by churchmen, and, though it might record the happenings in the lay world of kings and princes, the attitudes of the church were constantly intruding. This world was considered to be but a preparation for the next; it was fundamentally evil, and its study could not be allowed to become an end in itself. Yet there were exceptions, even in this theologically dominated world. Petrarch climbed a mountain near Avignon to enjoy the view, and when William Langland wrote *The Vision of Piers the Plowman,* he pictured himself lying on the flanks of the Malvern Hills and gazing eastward across the valley of the Severn. The beauty of that scene must have moved him as deeply as it does some of the motorists who pause on that narrow road today and enjoy the view across to Bredon and the Cotswolds. It was, as it still is, "a fair field full of folk." The man who carved the wooden bench ends of about 1500 in Altarnon church in Cornwall pictured the moors nearby with sheep grazing amid the granite boulders. His world view was not wholly obscured by theological dogma. He could portray what he saw in nature and clearly derived satisfaction and joy from doing so. From the sixteenth century onward, the creation of such scenes became commonplace. Though expressed in terms of differing schools of art and according to varying conventions, the portrayals reflect this new attitude toward space and distance, which were seen as phenomena to be overcome, used, and even admired for their own sakes.

The Modes of Travel

From the earliest times till the nineteenth century there were only two ways to travel— by foot, horse, or vehicle along poorly constructed roads, and by boat on the rivers and around the coasts of Europe. Both were used, though their relative importance varied with personal resources and local circumstances. Movement by water was, as a general rule, cheaper and less uncomfortable than that by land, but waterways were narrowly circumscribed and were often not usable in areas where the need for them was greatest.

The Romans left to western and southern Europe a legacy of carefully engineered and well-built roads that became the envy of posterity. But comparatively few of them were much used after the Western Empire had ended. They were conceived for military purposes, and even under the empire they appear to have been little used by civilian and merchant. A few segments of Roman road were incorporated into later road systems, but, by and large, they came to serve only local needs or passed completely out of use.

Roman roads represented a heavy investment of labor and capital. They were built to last, as, indeed, some of them have done. The roads created during subsequent centuries were, by contrast, haphazard in their planning and crude in their construction. Yet they have, for the most part, remained in use till today. According to G. K. Chesterton, "the rolling English drunkard made the rolling English road." This may not have been precisely the case, but there was nevertheless a certain randomness in the layout of both English and continental roads that would have astonished the Romans. The Roman road system had been imposed upon the land by an authority possessing both absolute control and a vision of the needs that it had to satisfy. Medieval roads, by contrast, were created piecemeal by local people to satisfy local needs. Of course they incorporated segments of Roman road, even of prehistoric routeways that suited their purpose. But of a wider view of the needs of long-distance traffic or of a regional or national network they showed not a trace. A national road net is something more than a summation of all the local road systems.

The idea that roads were primarily, almost exclusively, for the local communities that they served died very slowly. The reason was not that governments altogether lacked the vision necessary to conceive of countrywide road nets. They had no means of imposing this vision on the land, and left road building, or rather road mending, for there was scarcely any new construction, to local initiative, unwillingly paid for by locally imposed taxes. Nevertheless, out of these local patterns of roads attempts were made, not without some success, to fashion systems of main or trunk roads. Segments of local road were threaded together, and the result gained publicity as the main route between this city and that. Such a system was that represented, albeit crudely, in the Gough map of England of the fourteenth century. Later in the century a "road book" was completed of the major roads radiating from the Flemish city of Bruges. It was a list of places along each of the roads, and since the roads were represented as running to the limits of the continent, and even beyond, it conveyed an immense amount of travel information. It is doubtful whether the Bruges Itinerary was compiled for the use of the city's merchants; it included too many places with which they could have done little business. As it outlined the routes not only to Rome, but also to Santiago de Campostela in northwest Spain and to Jerusalem, it is most likely to have been consulted by the pilgrims who sought to follow these routes. The itinerary told the traveler nothing about the conditions he would be likely to find along the roads. His disillusion, as he mounted the alpine passes or threaded the defiles of the Balkans, is left to our imagination.

Toward the end of the sixteenth century, Charles Estienne produced a more detailed and more informative road book for France. Thereafter travel narratives, guides, maps, and itineraries followed one another from the presses of western Europe, and by the eighteenth century it was not difficult to discover, before setting out, the best way to get to almost any place within the continent or even beyond.

The increasing volume of travel was matched by a continuing improvement in the infrastructure of travel. Inns were established where the traveler could rest overnight. Posting stations were set up where relays of horses were available. Bishop Burnet, inveterate traveler and acute observer, described the large Swiss village of Splügen, supported almost wholly by the traffic across the Alps between south Germany and Italy. Its inhabitants were carriers, and, in addition to an inn, there were "above five hundred Carriage-Horses that belong to the Town."[27] Bridges were built, and where they did not exist, ferries were established. Frontier posts controlled the flow of traffic with, as it seems, a minimum of interference and interruption. This infrastructure sprang from the growing demand for the facilities of travel, but it also imposed a kind of straightjacket on movement. Travelers tended to go only where the roads were known, hostelries established, and a change of horses available. In the past, a vast number of routes had been used across the Alps by those intrepid travelers who were prepared to grope their way along faintly marked tracks. Travel then narrowed to the few routes that, like the Great St. Bernard and the Simplon, had reputable hostelries where the traveler could rest and obtain food. The effect of the growing concentration of traffic along a small number of well-advertised routes was to deepen the isolation of those intervening areas left untouched by the newly developing traffic. The phenomenon is no less familiar today, when motorways and interstates remove the flow of traffic from countless small places that had once profited from it.

But what of the roads travelers used and the vehicles in which they rode? Here change was less conspicuous. Nowhere in Europe, before the nineteenth century, was there a public authority charged with the building and maintenance of roads. These tasks, if they were discharged at all, were delegated to local bodies that rarely felt any inclination to assist long-distance travelers who only passed through their territory. Change came first in France, where Jean Baptiste Colbert in the later seventeenth century attempted to improve the quality of the roads. He acted through the provincial *Intendants* and conscripted local labor for the purpose. His plans, however, did little more than arouse intense opposition. In fact, the administration had little expertise and no capital to invest. It was not until 1747, with the creation of the *École des Ponts et Chaussées,* that the actual construction of roads received much attention, and not before the Napoleonic period was much progress made with constructing bridges and highways.[28]

In Britain a system of roads was built in Scotland after the suppression of the Rising of 1745. The roads were well engineered and well built, but their purpose was wholly military, and they did little to improve welfare or encourage economic development. Not until the act of 1835 was control of some highways taken out of the hands of local or parochial authorities and made subject to an overall plan. In the rest of Europe even this modest degree of progress was prevented by the political fragmentation of the continent and the shortsightedness and incompetence of governments. It is indicative of conditions of travel in central Europe that the construction of a road through Meiningen was a condition of adhesion to the German customs union.

The actual quality of road surfaces varied greatly throughout medieval and modern times with the nature of the bedrock and the kind of use, or misuse, it had received. As a general rule the roads that traversed lowland areas, floored with clay, and the alluvial plains of the great rivers were the worst. Their surfaces, even during a summer drought, were covered with deep ruts over which carts bumped their uneasy way and which horsemen avoided. At other times the hollows filled with water and wagons sank to their axles in the mud. Repair of such roads consisted of little more than pouring fresh clay into the depressions because little else was available. Clay-land villages were almost cut off to wheeled traffic for much of the year, and horsemen and pedestrians were able to get through only because they could abandon the roads and travel through woodland and across fields. It was the clay-land villages that, until late in the nineteenth century, had the least contact with the world beyond and preserved longest their primitive autarchy and ancient practices. The bands of clay that encircled Paris and lay in diagonal strips across England each constituted a barrier to movement, and throughout northern

Europe routes avoided wherever practicable the alluvial lowlands that bordered the great rivers.

By contrast, movement was relatively easy in regions where hard rock formed the surface. Wherever practicable roads followed ridges rather than valleys, because steep inclines and rough, stony road surfaces were preferable to the deep mire of the clay lands. The readiness with which travelers in a preindustrial age took to the hills may seem surprising to us, accustomed as we are to roads that take the topographically easy route along the valleys. The Ardennes plateau, for example, was traversed by roads that were regularly used, and even the Alps presented less difficulty in this respect than many a lowland area in northwest Europe. Nevertheless, road travel remained slow, uncomfortable, and very expensive into the nineteenth century. Shakespeare's words must have aroused a sympathetic echo in many minds: "These high wild hills and rough uneven ways / Draws out our miles and makes them wearisome."

Roads in medieval and early modern Europe were less a narrow ribbon, flanked by woodland and cultivated fields, than a broad strip within which a traveler picked his way between the furrows and potholes. Generally speaking, an attempt was made to prevent woodland or any growth that might afford shelter to robbers from invading the road. Nor was there in many instances a single route between neighboring cities. The traveler might usually be able to choose between two or more, according to which villages he wished to pass through or to avoid. The route actually followed was likely to be dictated by the weather and the condition of the bridges. One route asserted its primacy over others only when an attempt was made to improve it for long-distance traffic. In England, a turnpike trust was created for this purpose; in France, the administration handled the efforts to mend road surfaces.

In all road systems, bridges played a crucial role. Many small streams could be forded except in times of high water, but bridges or ferries were essential wherever major routes came to a river. No public authority had the obligation to build, repair, or maintain them. These tasks were left to private enterprise, which discharged the obligation in at best a random and perfunctory manner. Bridges were built sometimes by private benefactors, sometimes by city authorities, sometimes by speculators who hoped to receive a toll from every traveler who used them. Sometimes their repair and maintenance was a matter of chance; sometimes an endowment was set aside for the purpose. Some bridges were fortified and formed part of a city's defenses. Others had a chapel built on them, where masses were said for the pious builder, who thus combined public good with his own spiritual welfare. In any case, caring for a bridge was a haphazard arrangement, and many were the travelers who must have completed their crossing with feelings of relief.

Who used the roads of preindustrial Europe, and how did they transport themselves and their goods? Travelers formed a very mixed group. Kings and members of the aristocracy, whose domains often spanned a very wide area, were in almost constant movement. They traveled with their retinue on horseback, while their women and children, as well as their baggage, accompanied them on four-wheeled wagons, each drawn by a team of horses or oxen.[29] These wagons, as illustrated in, for example, the Luttrell Psalter, resembled the peasant vehicles that had long been used around the villages. They were large vehicles with fixed axles, so that turning them was difficult, and their wheels were often shod with iron to get a better grip on the soft ground. They had no springs, and travel in them over rough roads must have been a bitter experience.

10.5. Travelers setting out to cross the Alps with a train of pack animals. After a cartoon for a painted glass window, early seventeenth century. (Historical Museum of Bern.)

Merchants more often traveled on horseback, with their wares balanced on pack animals. Many a bridge was built just wide enough to accommodate a file of horses or mules. Safety usually required the merchant to travel in convoy. Only the penniless individual traveled the roads on foot and alone, his poverty serving as his only protection.

Much of the movement, at least on medieval roads, was accounted for by the business of the church. The western church had a hierarchical and centralized administration; diocesan administration called for frequent consultation between bishop, archdeacon, and parochial clergy; and between the bishops' seats and Rome there was a constant flow of correspondence and movement of priests and messengers. Add to this the intercourse between monastic houses, especially those within a single order, the movements of the friars, and the procession of pilgrims to the countless shrines of Catholic Europe, and we have a body of travelers that in the aggregate may have exceeded all other groups.

The speed of travel was slow. For those who traveled on foot, twenty miles a day was the maximum that could be expected. A horseman could cover much greater distances; fifty miles and more in a day were not uncommon, provided that relays of horses were available.[30] It was in this way that politically important news was carried about Europe. The slightest acquaintance with the great medieval chronicles will show how rapidly and, in general, how accurately news of the major events in the affairs of state and church was brought to monasteries, where it was recorded. On 4 November 1576, the Spanish soldiery pillaged and burned the city of Antwerp. On 4 December an obscure Cornish squire in the far southwest of England, living removed from the well-traveled highways, entered the fact in his diary.[31] The spread of news became even more rapid in the centuries that followed but at no time could it exceed the speed of a galloping horse.

10.6. The great bridge at Dresden, as painted by Canaletto Bellotto.

At the end of December 1253, Archbishop Eudes Rigaud of Rouen set out for Rome. He crossed the Alps by the Simplon Pass on 7–9 February and reached Rome on 11 March, having rested for only fourteen days. In all, he covered 1185 miles in sixty-one days, an average of almost 20 miles a day. His return was made in July, August, and September. This time he crossed the Alps by the Mont Cenis and accomplished his journey of 1102 miles in fifty-two days of travel, an average of over 21 miles a day. The record does not tell us how he traveled, and we must assume that it was by horse.

In the next century Barthélemy Bonis traveled on a kind of private pilgrimage from Avignon to Rome. Despite the fact that, as his journal shows, he took a prolonged "dinner" break each day, he covered the 705 miles in twenty-two days, at an average speed of 32 miles a day.[32] It is remarkable that the Alpine crossing caused little appreciable reduction in his speed of travel. These speeds must be regarded as typical for the later Middle Ages, the merchant traveling somewhat faster than the churchman and his retinue. In the mid-fifteenth century Isabella of Portugal covered very considerable distances in a day in the course of her travels in the Low Countries, but she appears to have traveled in a "chariot," probably a two-wheeled vehicle, lighter and easier to manipulate than the four-wheeled wagon in which noble families customarily journeyed.[33]

10.7. The transport of merchandise in the seventeenth century. A
four-wheeled wagon with basketwork sides is used. Central Europe.

Until the coming of the railways in the 1830s, the fastest mode of travel was by horse.
But for those who could not or did not travel on horseback, there were improvements in
the seventeenth and eighteenth centuries. The wagon evolved into the coach or diligence, with the provision of a cover and windows against the weather, springs for
improved comfort, and a lighter construction for greater speed. The term "coach" came
into use in the seventeenth century for this vehicle and derived ultimately from the
Hungarian town of Kocs, where it was first made or used. The coach was for a long
period used only by the elite, and among the oldest surviving examples are the "state"
coaches still used on ceremonial occasions in England.

During the eighteenth century the use of the coach became more popular. Its
construction was simplified, it became more compact, and, in addition to the protected
accommodation within, it was fitted with seats on its roof. In this form it was capable of
carrying a considerable number of passengers—up to a dozen in the case of the largest.
Coaches began to assume a variety of forms and to take on the wide range of names by
which they have since been known: hackney, fiacre, diligence, cab, and other familiar
terms.

This development was in response to a growing demand for travel facilities. Like all
other means of public travel, a coach service was profitable only if it was well used, and
for this it had to be both regular and as punctual as road and weather allowed. These
demands led to the organization of relays of horses, which in turn increased the speed
and broadened the appeal of coach travel. The eighteenth century saw the development

of a coach service from short and irregular journeys to one that spanned most of western, central, and southern Europe, and allowed the traveler to journey at a moderate speed and with little interruption from England to Italy and Portugal to Poland.

The gradual emergence, first in France, the Low Countries, and England, later in central and southern Europe, of a public transport system constituted a social revolution of not inconsiderable importance. It allowed people of moderate means to travel more or less where they wished. It allowed a postal system to operate with considerable success in much of Europe. It broadened people's mental horizons and facilitated the flow of ideas and innovations. The first railway carriages of the 1830s were little more than stagecoaches mounted on flanged wheels and made to fit onto iron rails, and the railway concept was only an extension of coach travel.

Waterborne Transport

The role of navigable waterways in internal transport and communications has often been stressed. Movement by water, it is said, was cheap, but slow, and thus tended to be used for the bulk transport of goods in regular demand. Waterborne transport was, however, greatly restricted, not only by natural impediments—shallows, floods, ice—but also by man-made obstacles such as mills and fishweirs. Rivers, furthermore, rarely seemed to flow where the need for transportation was greatest. Nevertheless, despite these handicaps, great use was made of rivers—so great, in fact, that it became profitable for neighboring landowners to burden them with tolls. In a few instances—the river Rhine is one—the tolls became greater than the traffic could bear, and riverborne trade virtually ceased.[34]

Very small rivers, which might now seem unnavigable, were used, and in some instances, where the speed of the current was great, only downstream traffic was normal, with the roughly constructed ships being broken up at their destination and used for building or fuel. Many were the cities that throughout the preindustrial period were supplied with food and fuel by riverboats. Grain from Artois was carried down the Scheldt and its tributaries to Ghent and other cities in Flanders. A vast number of boats supplied Paris with timber, coal, and foodstuffs from most parts of the Seine river system. London, Lyons, the Rhineland cities, and many in central Europe were similarly served. At Paris quays bordered the river, and a vast army of porters distributed the food and other goods from them to almost thirty city markets. In some cities—Frankfurt and Mainz were conspicuous examples—there was also a service of small vessels for passengers. These were the *Märktschiffer,* or "market boats," which carried the peasants and their produce to the urban markets. Even today, produce is brought to Helsinki by boat and offered for sale on the quays.

Riverboats were of many kinds, adapted to navigational conditions of different rivers. Most were either propelled by oars or pulled, by means of a towrope, by men or animals on the bank. Every river in regular use had its towpath, and many were the complaints that it had been washed away by floods or that its surface was so deep in mud that its usefulness was limited. Sails were sometimes used, but sailboats were difficult to operate on a twisting river. They were, however, used on the Rhine, where the waterway was broad enough for a vessel to tack, and also on the Loire, where the prevailing westerly winds were said to assist vessels on their upstream voyage.[35]

Although riverboats varied greatly in size and were adjusted to the capacity of the rivers that they served, the majority were very small indeed. Most were little more than open rowboats. Those actually designed to carry freight rarely had a capacity of more than 50 *tonneaux,* or about 200 cubic meters (or 260 cubic yards). This was about the size of the vessels that supplied Paris with grain and other foodstuffs.[36] On the Vistula, where the grain traffic was of exceptional importance, rather larger, shallow-draft boats were used, with a capacity that increased from about 12 lasts (24 metric tonnes) in the sixteenth century to 25 lasts (50 metric tonnes) in the eighteenth.[37] But only on the major rivers, like the Rhine, Elbe, and lower Seine, where there was a steady movement of bulky commodities such as cereals, salt, fuel, and ores, were vessels of this size in regular use. The peasant who took his produce to market by boat probably found that his maximum cargo was less than a ton, and he would, in fact, have rarely needed anything larger.

Only in the Netherlands was boat traffic developed on a more intensive scale. In the seventeenth century the English traveler William Bromley found the road from northwest Germany into the northern Netherlands "only passable in Summer, for most of the Winter it is under water." But once he was in the Netherlands, conditions of travel improved greatly. Bromley moved "in large cover'd Boats drawn by Horses. . . . The Hour of the Boats coming in, and going out, is so punctually observed, that upon the Ringing of a bell it goes off, without staying for any Person whatsoever."[38] A few years earlier Sir William Temple had noted that canals "do not only lead to every great town, but almost to every Village, and every Farm-House in the country," and he commented on "the infinity of sails that are seen everywhere coursing up and down upon them."[39] Such a regular boat traffic had begun in some parts of the Netherlands as early as the first half of the sixteenth century. The network of boat services was gradually extended until "there were very few population centers of any importance which it did not touch."[40]

The smaller riverboats appear to have been owned by the men who operated them. On the larger rivers the boatmen were commonly united in gilds in order to preserve their rights of navigation against all the pretensions of riverine landlords. On some rivers they had an uphill struggle to keep the channel clear of mills and weirs and to secure their rights to use a towpath.

The idea that rivers were more intensively used than roads in the preindustrial age dies hard. In fact, travelers rarely went by boat, and only the coarsest freight regularly used water transportation. River craft were poorly constructed and leaked so badly that freight was often damaged. Salt, which formed the most important upstream freight on the river Loire, regularly lost a large part of its volume by solution in the water that leaked into the boat. On the other hand, building materials, especially timber and stone, traveled by water wherever practicable. One can, for example, trace the movement of important building stones in England and northwest Europe along the rivers and around the coast to the construction sites. Very rarely is such stone to be met with more than a mile or two from a navigable river or coastal port.

The chief problem with the use of rivers for travel and transportation was that they did not always flow where the need for them was greatest. From the seventeenth century attempts were made to supplement rivers with artificial waterways that would not have this disadvantage. In 1642 the Canal de Briare was completed from the Loire to the Seine in order to bring provisions from the Central Massif to Paris. Later in the same century the Languedoc Canal was built from the Garonne to the Mediterranean. This was unquestionably for its time a great feat of engineering. The Briare and Languedoc canals were successful both technically and economically and led to a great number of canal projects, many of which were ill conceived, poorly managed, and contributed little to the wealth of their promoters or the well-being of the population. Not until the eve of the Industrial Revolution did canals begin to contribute significantly to the economic life of western and central Europe. In southern Europe neither rivers nor canals played any important role in the development of transportation and travel.

Islands of Isolation

By the eighteenth century a system of roads had come to permeate most of Europe. It is impossible to exaggerate the importance of the road, that clearly marked if not always easily traversed strip of land which wound its way from one settlement to the next. No city ever grew up without a preexisting network of roads that converged on its site. Wherever an important road crossed a river, a town is likely to have developed to serve the needs of the traffic and to profit from the break-of-bulk that so often occurred at such points. Along the roads there were inns, which themselves in many instances became the foci of settlements.

Not only people and freight moved along the roads. Ideas were also passed from one community to another in this way. Europe is full of instances of how architectural styles, folkways, and even political ideas were carried along the roads, influencing places that they touched, but ignored by areas that they passed by. The trackless forest or mountain range where there were no paths was a barrier, perceived by those who lived nearby as even less penetrable than in fact it may have been. The Gothic style of architecture spread along the pilgrim route that ran from the Pyrenean crossings to Santiago de Campostela. The "breath of freedom," it has been said, blew along the St. Gotthard road soon after it had been opened up, from the Italian cities to the rebellious Swiss cantons. Ideas of urban independence spread along the roads that ran eastward from the Rhine to the plains of Poland. Everywhere we find evidence that material life was shaped by the traffic in goods and ideas that followed the roads.

Yet the road net that had evolved by the eighteenth century was a loose and open one. Between the major roads there were still vast areas reached only by tracks through the forests, their primitive self-sufficiency little touched by the great world outside, awaiting the construction of roads and the arrival of wheeled traffic. Balzac has described the impact on a remote community in the Alps of Savoy of the opening of a road from the world beyond.[41] But not every community was opened up even by the end of that century. Throughout Europe there were villages that not even a ripple from the great events in the outer world had been able to reach. There was, for example, a community in the Argonne in eastern France that did not know whether it belonged to France or to the German empire and had always thought itself independent of both, as in all probability it had effectively been. And more than a century later, the village of Minot, in the heart of northern Burgundy, was almost self-sufficing, distrustful of outsiders and regarding marriage beyond its limits as peculiar, if not morally wrong. Of course, it sold a few goods into the wider market—timber, charcoal, surplus grain—as it had to do in order to discharge its obligations to the state, but little money circulated in this small community of about 500 because the mutuality of a primitive society served instead of payment. Such communities endured into the present century in western and central Europe, and even longer in eastern Europe and the Balkans, where forest and mountain provided a more effective insulation from the outside world. In the latter regions travel and communication have, since prehistoric times, tended to follow a few well-marked valley routes, leaving the intervening mountain masses in almost complete isolation. Even today the remoteness of some of these regions, like the Bihar, Rhodope, Montenegro, and North Albanian Alps, is extreme, and here are still to be found structures and practices of the greatest possible antiquity.[42] Agriculture has continued until recently to be carried on with tools identical with those shown on painted Greek vases, the narrow vertical loom remains in use, and the houses of the villagers today appear to replicate those shown in the carvings on Trajan's Column in the Roman Forum.[43]

The isolation of rural communities, their suspicion of all outsiders, and their unwillingness to have regular intercourse with their neighbors did not prevent certain regionalisms from developing. For no community was complete isolation possible. From the earliest times in human history there were shortages that could be remedied only by trade, barter, or raiding. Even within closed regions, neighboring villages had to suppress their natural inclinations toward hostility in favor of cooperation and what can at best be described as unfriendly rivalry.

How were such cultural regions created? What factors limited their extension in space, and what separated one such region from another? To some extent the underlying factors were environmental. Similarity of resource in soil, woodland, grazing, and minerals might lead to cooperation and mutual assistance. These factors might be expected to produce similar societies, so that no one would appear "foreign" to the others. Alternatively, minor contrasts in resource might lead to cooperation and complementarity, as between the mountain people who bordered the Great Plain of Hungary or the Lombardy plain in northern Italy and the agricultural people who inhabited the lowlands.[44]

At the same time the spread of ideas and of innovations within a restricted area might lead to local rivalry and imitation and to the evolution of common styles and methods of doing ordinary things. The spirit of emulation has been an important factor in the emergence of localisms. In 1449 the tower of the small Devon borough of Totnes fell down. Church towers were a matter of pride in this part of England, for it was from its tower that the parish gave an audible symbol of its presence. The collapsed tower had to be rebuilt, so the city fathers nominated some of their number to make a tour of neighboring church towers—four were specified by name—and to build as good a tower as these. Today one can readily detect the family resemblance between the church towers of this part of England. On a different scale, one can detect the architectural similarities between buildings in Bavaria and Bohemia, in the Hanseatic ports of the Baltic, and in the Gothic churches of the Paris basin. In all parts of Europe, one finds these localisms, most obvious in architecture, for buildings are by their nature conspicuous and durable, but also in the tools of agriculture, in the construction of carts and wagons, in diet, and in dress.

Distance and physical obstacles set limits to these localisms. To us, the distances in question might seem short and the obstacles far from insurmountable. But it all depends on how one perceives one's environment, and in this, logic rarely enters. The people of the Burgundian village of Minot refused to have dealings with those of their neighbor to the northeast. "For marriages," said one of the local population, "we don't go any further than Moitron," about halfway there. "From the direction of Moitron came neither good winds (the cold northeasters of winter) nor good people." This village maintained contact only with "those communities that show the same physical features, the same lay of the land, the same balance between field and forest. Whatever lies beyond, Minot neither wants to know nor to marry."[45]

Localisms form a patchwork quilt that gives to every part of Europe its color and character. Most have no simple origin or explanation. They arise from the ways in which people have perceived their environment and their neighbors. They are the stuff of which local history is made because they give personality to an area. Sometimes administrative areas are made to coincide more or less with such localisms and may thus help to preserve their identity. Even today changes in such administrative structures, accompanied by the fashioning of new, artificial, and usually foolish names, is apt to run into strenuous opposition from powerful forces of tradition. In the past such localisms were even more real because they were an essential part of people's world view; they delimited a mental horizon. The gradual attrition of localism in the course of the last two centuries has been brought about in the main by the opening up of communications—the building of roads and the establishment of a postal service. Only in very recent years, and still not in some remote areas, has the force of the media been brought to bear on local cultures, with their immense power to unify and to reduce all to a common level. A popular culture is in the process of overtaking and obliterating these localisms.

PART THREE

The Period of

Rapid Growth

INTRODUCTION

The Past is Never Dead. It's not even Past.
                    —William Faulkner

Material life devours novelty and reproduces it as domesticated
commonality.
                    —Robert Blair St. George

A period of intermittent and at best slow growth came to an end in much of Europe in the late eighteenth and early nineteenth centuries. In the words of one analysis of the events of this period, the European economy then "took off into sustained growth." The beginnings of regular and uninterrupted economic expansion varied greatly within Europe. Growth became conspicuous and measurable first in northwest Europe, specifically in Great Britain and the southern Low Countries, then in the Rhineland, Switzerland, and parts of France. It came much later to Scandinavia, Spain, and Italy but by the end of the nineteenth century had not really appeared in much of eastern Europe and the Balkans. Even in the early twentieth century there remained areas quite untouched by the revolution in industrial production and living standards.

The Industrial Revolution, if we may stay with a term that has become hallowed by a century of use, was characterized by an acceleration in the slow rate of growth that had prevailed for the past thousand years. If the term "revolution" denotes a sudden or dramatic change, then the expression is a misnomer. Advances were made now in this branch of production, now in that. Innovation here facilitated development there. It was the cumulative effect of invention and discovery, as each influenced growth in every other branch of activity, that seemed to deserve the epithet of "revolution." The Industrial Revolution, marked a change in the factors of production. The input of capital increased, that of labor, at least in relative terms, diminished, and the production per unit of labor became significantly greater. It thus became possible for the individual consumption of clothing, metal goods, and other items of daily use to increase significantly. Agriculture, and thus food supply, improved through the increasing use of better tools and equipment, from the steel plow to field tile and chemical fertilizer. It must not, however, be assumed that these advances were due entirely to mechanical invention or innovation. Many arose from better management or organization, from the speedier flow of information, from the increased size of the market and the economies of scale, and from superior work discipline.

One cannot say that the wave of innovation that appears to have characterized the later eighteenth and the nineteenth centuries had any clear-cut origin and date. One may point to crucial developments such as the adoption of coke fuel in the blast furnace, the puddling of iron, the production of crucible steel, and the many technical inventions in the textile industry. But none of these innovations took place in isolation. Each was preceded by a long period of experimentation and development, each sprang from progress in a number of fields of activity, and each impinged on every other. It has been argued whether or not the Industrial Revolution was *necessarily* preceded by radical change in agriculture. That it was accompanied by development in agricultural technique is apparent. It is no less clear that developments in manufacturing contributed to the success of agriculture. But it is pointless to argue which came first. They grew together, each influenced by and influencing the other.

The Industrial Revolution can be seen as a series of innovations and adaptations intended to circumvent or overcome bottlenecks and shortages in an industrial structure that had already developed almost as far as it could along traditional lines. The weaver was short of thread; the metalworker, of charcoal; the smith, of iron. The alternative was to use mechanical power and substitute materials. The expansive power of steam at first supplemented and then replaced the energy inherent in flowing water. And this step in turn was made possible by the mining of solid fuel and the processing of metallic minerals. At the same time, the steam engine permitted mines to reach new depths in the search for coal and metallic minerals. Although the earliest use of steam engines was in mines, steam power was quickly adapted to the factory, and by the middle years of the nineteenth century, industrial production had come to be dominated by the steam engine.

It is difficult to give a date to this sequence of technological inventions. Not only did they have small and sometimes obscure beginnings, but they also had their origins at varying times in different countries. Innovations, now in one branch of production, now in another, were carried by entrepreneurs from one country, one industrial center, to another. There was a degree of industrial espionage, as producers attempted—always in the end unsuccessfully—to safeguard their "secrets." In a few instances—mechanical spinning of cotton and puddling iron, for example—one can trace the diffusion of the new technology, but others are more difficult to follow.

What, then, were the long-term consequences for material standards of life of this long-drawn-out sequence of interrelated inventions and innovations? By and large, these were, before the end of the nineteenth century, fourfold. In the first place, they brought about a fundamental change in the pattern and nature of human settlement. The new industrial enterprises were in general and of necessity large, and they required a commensurate labor force. Workers were drawn to their places of work, giving rise to large industrial villages and manufacturing cities. At the same time, this precise location of industrial enterprise called into being an infrastructure of commerce and transportation, as well as, in many instances, a range of finishing and ancillary industries. The consequence was an explosion in urban population in the industrializing countries, paralleled, as a general rule, by a contraction in rural. For a period, congestion and squalor without parallel characterized most rapidly growing cities, as utilities and amenities failed to keep pace with the expanding population. Not until the end of the nineteenth century or even the twentieth were urban slums removed and replaced on any significant scale.

A second consequence was the sharp increase in manufactured goods. Apart from textiles, these were at first mainly capital goods: machines, buildings—especially factories—railroads, docks, and ships. But gradually manufacturers turned to the production of goods that can be classed as consumer oriented. Many would now be termed "durables": furniture, kitchenware, clothing, and footware. It is in the slow expansion in the volume and variety of such goods among most classes that one can appreciate most easily the general improvement in material well-being.

In the third place, public health was greatly improved during the period of industrial growth, despite a deterioration of conditions during rapid urban expansion. The revolutionary advances in medical knowledge that accompanied and followed the discovery of the nature of infection came in the closing years of the century. They were preceded by a number of significant changes of a more practical kind, including a greatly increased use of masonry construction instead of timber; deeper wells for water; the building of cisterns and water-supply systems; the increased availability of soap and of clean linen; and, perhaps most important of all, developments in sewage disposal. None would have been possible without advances in the textile, metal, and chemical industries.

Lastly, the factory system made possible an increase in production far beyond the needs of any local society. Output became dependent on export both to maintain full production and to obtain imported raw materials. The marginal decline in prices was itself in some degree a consequence of broader and especially overseas markets. For European peoples a growing import of foodstuffs became possible, spelling the end of the sequence of subsistence crises that had characterized earlier centuries. At the same time, the export of European products, technologies, and industrial expertise allowed those countries that we loosely call the Third World to build up their own manufactures on a scale that, in some instances, came to rival that of Europe. During prehistoric times, Europe had been the recipient of the technological innovations made in the non-European world of the Middle East. Now, from the middle years of the nineteenth century, Europe began to repay its debt and to supply its more advanced technologies to the rest of the world.

It should not be assumed that all parts of Europe benefited in equal measure from these developments. There remained "islands of backwardness," areas where traditional crafts had never been developed beyond the level of local self-sufficiency, where resources were inadequate to attract modern industry, and where agriculture remained backward, even primitive. Here it was difficult to generate the surplus necessary to acquire even the simplest consumer goods, and local self-help was restricted by ignorance of what was practicable and of ways of achieving it. Such regions of social deprivation covered much of eastern and southeastern Europe and were to be met with in pockets, more or less extensive, elsewhere, even in the present century.

Chapter 11

THE NINETEENTH CENTURY

Not until about 1870 did the peasants begin to build proper brick
chimneys, when the iron cooking stoves came in, which are now
used everywhere in the kitchens.

—Jan Słomka

Hitherto, it is questionable if all the mechanical inventions yet
made have lightened the day's toil of any human being. They have
enabled a greater proportion to live the same life of drudgery and
imprisonment and an increased number of manufacturers and
others to make fortunes.

—John Stuart Mill,
Principles of Political Economy, 1848

The factory, powered mechanically, became the essential institution of the
new industrial age. In 1835 Andrew Ure defined a factory as "the combined operation of many orders of work people . . . tending with assiduous skill a system
of productive machines continuously impelled by a central power."[1] Large-scale, complex organization and the employment of mechanical power were its characteristics. The
nineteenth century had been preceded by many large-scale means of organizing labor.
There were *ergastula*, or large workshops, in classical times, and William Stumpe the
clothier turned Malmesbury Abbey into a vast workshop in which Leland found rows of
happy weavers, singing as they sped their shuttles. But no use was made of mechanical
power. Traditional craftsmen employed their accustomed methods under the watchful
eye of their master. The earliest mills at Verviers were similar. On the other hand, the
flour mill and fulling mill were operated mechanically by waterwheels, and in the field of
metallurgy, waterpower was used to operate slitting and rolling mills and to generate a
blast for the furnace. Yet these operations are not generally reckoned to have been
factories because their scale was too small.

Although the factory is indissolubly linked with the steam engine, the earliest true
factories were in fact powered by water. For this reason they were more rural than urban
and were often located within the hills, where the potential power was greatest.[2] There
were even mills in the flat country of northern France, where instead of water the horse
whim served to turn the shafts and operate the spinning machines. Factories such as
these were more often than not located in sparsely populated areas, and their success was
dependent on attracting a labor force and providing some kind of housing for it.

Many reasons could be advanced for the spread of the modern factory. In the first place demand for the commodity in question had outstripped supply. This situation was due in some measure to a rising population; in some degree also to the fact that its material standards were improving. Then there was a growing export of consumer goods to Europe's overseas colonies and dependencies. Not a few textile mills based their prosperity on sales to Spanish America or the West Indies, and the decline in these trades spelled ruin to industries in southern France and Catalonia. This growing demand could be satisfied most easily by the mechanization of at least certain stages in the productive process.

Mechanization, second, called for large units of power. The largest waterwheels could develop almost as much energy as a steam engine, and those which operated some of the early textile mills were very large indeed. There were economies in building even larger power units, and, unless energy was to go to waste, the factory had to be proportionately big. In this respect there was no change when the steam engine began to replace the waterwheel. Large engines called for large factories. Not until the advent of the electric motor and the internal combustion engine late in the century did it become both practicable and economic to equip a small workshop with mechanical power.

Supply of materials was easier to a factory than to dozens of separate craft shops. Roads and spurs from railroad or canal could be constructed, and the same means could be adapted to transmit the products. Last, the factory permitted the employer to exercise a tighter control over the work force than would otherwise have been possible. A higher degree of work discipline could be maintained, time wasting and incipient unrest could be checked, and, as a last resort, management in many instances owned the housing in which its workers lived and could evict them at will.

No branch of manufacturing had ever stood entirely alone. It was part of a web of industrial activity, a stage in a complex process. Nowhere were the interrelationships more apparent than in the metal and textile industries. But during the Industrial Revolution, these linkages became more numerous and complex. Additional stages— cotton printing, for example—were added to the textile industry. The products of the metal industries began, in one way or another, to be used in most others, and the all-pervasive role of the chemical industries spread through every branch of production. It might almost be said that every branch of industrial production became either a supplier of materials to almost every other or a consumer of its products. These close interrelationships came to be reflected in the location of manufacturing. One successful branch of industry attracted others, if only to economize on the costs of transportation between them. Specialized centers of production, of iron, steel, or textiles, became gradually less specialized as other and, superficially regarded, unrelated branches of production joined them in the scramble for space.

In this book we are concerned neither with evolving industrial technologies nor with the economics of industrial location, but with the human consequences of both. These ramifications can, for convenience, be considered under seven far from exclusive heads. First must come a discussion of the types of housing that developed in the new centers of industry. Nineteenth-century rural housing differed in no fundamental respect from that of the eighteenth. The changes, for both good and ill, took place mainly in the cities and other centers of industry. Conditions of work, second, underwent no significant change on the land. It was in manufacturing that they were altered—at first for the worse, until improvements were gradually made later in the century.

Improvements in housing were paralleled within the house in better and more

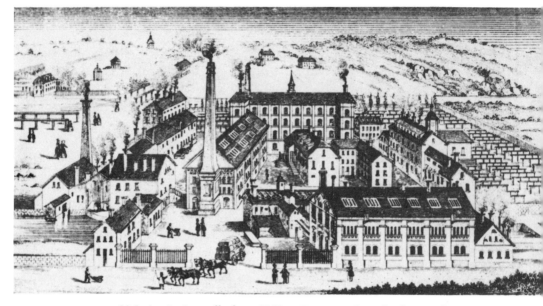

11.1. A spinning mill, about 1850, at Hagen, in the Ruhr district of Germany.

abundant furnishings, in equipment and decoration, so that the house became, in fact, a home. At the same time, the provision of utilities, especially for lighting, heating, and cooking, for water supply and the disposal of sewage, were improved and extended.

Scarcely less important than these changes in the physical conditions of life were the greater variety of foodstuffs available and the increased regularity of supply. The improvement in diet was due not only to a slow increase in real incomes, but also to developments in shops, shopping practices, and the mechanics of food distribution. And this, finally, was a consequence of the revolution in transportation. The friction of distance was eroded. Supplies were maintained to the cities, whatever the harvest conditions may have been. People were encouraged to venture beyond their local communities and thus to gain some experience of a wider world. Local cultures began gradually to yield before a spreading popular culture, broadly uniform over large areas.

These many and varied improvements in the level of human welfare were but the response to greater productivity and the resulting fall in the cost of consumer goods relative to earnings. Figure 11.2 shows, from early in the nineteenth century, how the gap between earnings and expenditure gradually closed until, from about 1875, wages exceeded expenditure.

Urban and Working-Class Housing

The concentration of the working population around factories and in rapidly growing industrial cities was the most conspicuous social consequence of industrialization. The fundamental reason for this condition was the lack of public transportation, which would have allowed people to live at a greater distance from their place of work.

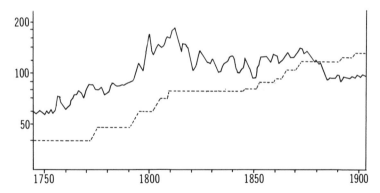

11.2. Graph showing the price of a composite unit of consumables (solid line), and average wages (dotted line). Not until about 1875 does the wage index rise above the cost of living index. See fig. 10.2.

Instances are known of men walking as much as ten miles from the cottages where they lived to their work, but this was rare. There was a premium on sites close to the factories, and these were closely built up without regard to health or convenience. In some parts of Europe people were attracted in their thousands from an over-populated countryside to the "promised land" of the rapidly growing cities. For their part, industrialists and factory owners encouraged this migration, confident that greater numbers spelled in the long run a cheaper and more tractable labor force. In many instances factory owners themselves acquired land close to their works and put up workers' housing. Houses were often packed together as closely as practicable, without regard to either ventilation or sanitation. In much of central Europe, housing assumed the form of tenement blocks. In some cities of northern England, the airless "back-to-back" houses, without any possibility of a through breeze, became the rule. In older towns, the "lots" behind the houses were transformed into courts, often entered only by a tunnel through the surrounding structures. A second floor was normal, a third frequent, and sometimes even a fourth or fifth, all supported on foundations that were intended for much less substantial buildings.

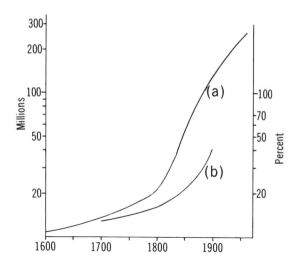

11.3. Graph showing (a) the growth of urban population and (b) urban population as a proportion of total population.

In the early 1840s Friedrich Engels was sent to England by his father, a cotton manufacturer in the Rhineland, to study the industry as it was carried on in Lancashire. He traveled widely and wrote one of the most damning accounts of the social consequences of industrialization. The pattern was everywhere the same: courts and alleys built on every available piece of land near the city centers. Of Glasgow he wrote: "The Wynds . . . contain a fluctuating population of fifteen to thirty thousand human beings. This quarter consists wholly of narrow alleys and square courts, in the middle of every one of which there lies a dung heap. Revolting as was the outward appearance of these courts, I was not yet prepared for the filth and wretchedness within. . . ."[3] But it was Manchester that he came to know most intimately and that figured most prominently in his study:

> First of all, there is the Old Town . . . , which lies between the northern boundary of the commercial district and the [river] Irk. Here the streets, even the better ones, are narrow and winding . . . , the houses dirty, old and tumbledown, and the construction of the side streets utterly horrible. Going from the Old Church to Long Millgate, the stroller has at once a row of old fashioned houses at the right, of which not one has kept its original level; there are remnants of the old pre-manufacturing Manchester, whose former inhabitants have removed with their descendants into better-built districts. . . . Here one is in an almost undisguised working-men's quarter, for even the shops and beerhouses hardly take the trouble to exhibit a trifling degree of cleanliness. But all this is nothing in comparison with the courts and lanes which lie behind, to which access can be gained only through covered passages, in which no two human beings can pass at the same time. Of the irregular cramming together of dwellings in ways which defy all rational plan, of the tangle in which they are crowded literally one upon the other, it is impossible to convey an idea.[4]

Engels' account of industrial Britain may have been overdrawn, and recent research has shown that much of his description was taken at second hand and introduced for polemical purposes. Nevertheless, his descriptions are in some respects confirmed by other observers. Foremost among these was Edwin Chadwick, who, in 1842, wrote his *Report on the Sanitary Conditions of the Labouring Population of Great Britain.*[5] His style was more clinical, but the conclusions were the same. He described filth, squalor, and overcrowding without parallel, and to this state he related, as Engels had failed to do, the incidence of disease. Furthermore, Chadwick found the sanitary conditions in many small towns in no way better than in the largest, even though the degree of overcrowding was generally less.

These developments in British industrial cities can be paralleled a half century later by those in the Polish textile center of Łódź. Figure 11.4 shows the stages by which a block of land was infilled with miscellaneous factory and domestic buildings. In all growing cities, an increased density of housing rather than a wider spread was used to accommodate the immigrant workers, and the resulting problem was not overcome until the development, late in the century, of tramways and buses—not to mention the bicycle.

In the second half of the nineteenth century, the last phase was reached in the development of high-density urban housing—the tenement block. It was the apotheosis of the court and alley described by Engels, streamlined, mass-produced, and equipped with a bare minimum of those common necessities which had so often been absent from courts and alleys earlier in the century. The tenement was a peculiarly German invention. It was multistoried and built of masonry. Apartments, almost identical in plan within each block, consisted at most of two rooms. There was rarely any provision for heating and but little for cooking. Indeed, it would have been impossible to contrive chimneys in the thickness of their walls. Water was usually available at a standpipe in the court, where there were also sewers, or at least a cesspit, and common toilet facilities.

A number of reports, compiled for the British Board of Trade at the beginning of the present century, described these tenements, together with numerous plans and sections. "In some of the larger towns," wrote a surveyor, "these erections often resemble large barracks built round small, paved courtyards. . . . Nothing could be more depressing. . . . Merely a builder's device for exploiting costly sites." Such housing was to be found in every large city in nineteenth-century Germany. At the growing industrial town of Königshütte (Królewska Huta) in Upper Silesia, it was reported, "practically the whole working-class population . . . may . . . be said to live in tenements of one or two rooms."[6] There were even places within this industrial region

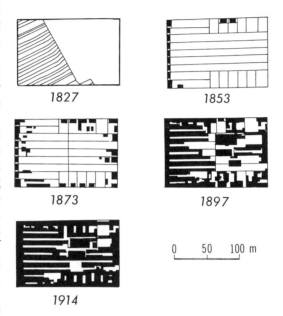

11.4. Łódź, Poland; the development of a single block within the city. (After A. Ginsbert, *Łódź* [Łódź, 1961].)

where these tenements degenerated into *Schlaffhäuser,* crude, unheated, and unfurnished dormitories in which unmarried workers slept. They cannot have been a great deal better than that which the visitor sees today at the nearby concentration camp of Oświęcim (Auschwitz).

Tenements were rare in Belgium, where there was a tradition of living on and cultivating small garden plots, but Paris was described, not without some exaggeration, as a "city of large houses. . . . the tenement system prevails universally." But outside Paris and a very few large cities like Lyons and Marseilles, urban growth was slow; there was no need for such dense housing, and France was spared the worst excesses of central European high-rise, high-density housing.

Some of the physical consequences of such congestion have already been described: the cramped quarters, the fetid air, the stench of sewage, the polluted water-supply, and the all-pervading smoke from factory chimneys. This has become the material of social novelists from Dickens and Hugo to Zola and Reymont, as well as of the reports of governments and other bodies. The human degradation that resulted is well known, and conditions were remedied only slowly during the century. Yet one should not generalize. The number of cities that exhibited these worst aspects of modern industrialization were relatively few. They included many in northern Britain and in the industrialized belt that was developing in northwest Europe from northern France to the Ruhr. Such conditions were also to be found in several of the great capital cities, including Paris, Berlin, and London, and they were at their worst in Upper Silesia. But there were, on the other hand, factory owners, even early in the nineteenth century, who, like Robert Owen at the New Lanark Mills in Scotland, erected what was for its time almost ideal workers' housing. Owen's *Report to the County of Lanark* of 1821 roundly condemned the "courts, alleys, lanes" of contemporary industrial cities and argued for "free space for air and light and easy communication."[7] This may have been practicable at Owen's New Lanark Mills because their scale was small and their location rural. It was more difficult in the rapidly growing industrial cities, where factories crowded upon one another in order to share the local site advantages. Nevertheless, as the century wore on, such improved homes became more common, especially in Germany and, in particular, in the Ruhr. Here the Krupps, belying their popular image, put up some of the best workers' housing to be found in Europe.

Nor did all industrial developments contribute to the growth of large, congested cities. Some, in Catalonia, for example, and in parts of France and northern Italy, continued to rely mainly on waterpower, and this dependence in turn restricted their size and commonly led to a preference for a rural location. Some types of industry were carried on in units that, if not necessarily small, were at least scattered and led to a more dispersed pattern of settlement. Among these were most branches of the mining industry. Some coal mines did indeed attract the manufacturing industries which consumed the fuel they produced, so that all were together swallowed into a vast urban sprawl. But it is probable that most coal mines and almost all metalliferous mines gave rise at most to mining villages and small towns, which never exhibited the worst aspects of nineteenth-century congestion.

Of course, a row of miners' cottages in a village was not necessarily more spacious or salubrious than one of back-to-back houses in a dense, urban sprawl, but the wind blew more freely about it. There was no pall of smoke hanging permanently over it, and, in northern France, Belgium, and in many other coalfields there might be a small garden patch, which, if managed with care, provided both recreation and profit. But in neither urban nor rural workers' housing was there running water, toilet, or any form of internal sewage disposal before the end of the century at the earliest. At most a standpipe provided water; more often there was a communal well or pump. An external privy, often serving the needs of several families and regularly cleaned by none, discharged into a cesspit.

Such conditions improved only slowly and erratically, as public authorities gradually and in some instances reluctantly implemented health regulations. The sequence of cholera epidemics, beginning in 1832, served to remind governments that disease sprang in large measure from squalid living conditions. Improvements came first in northwest Europe and spread slowly toward the east. One can look at rows of working-class housing in western Europe and, even without the aid of date stones and historical maps, estimate the approximate year of their construction. The quality of their workmanship, their plan and floor space, fireplaces and chimneys, size and number of windows and external doors, and the placement of the toilets, sewers, and water supply all underwent slow change, which can be dated and, in the aggregate, present a measure of rising material standards.

It is difficult to measure this slow advance and to show how far central Europe lagged behind western, and eastern Europe and Russia behind the rest. It is not recorded how far people had to go on a cold wet night to find the nearest available toilet. Nor can we tell how many each toilet served and how long was the line waiting before it each morning. Improvements were by very small and unrecorded increments.

Middle-class housing differed mainly in being better built and more spacious. Usually there were servants whose task it was to give the residence an air of superficial cleanliness. The middle classes were, however, able to afford the little extra that it took to secure a relatively safe water supply, to site the cesspit at a distance from other utilities, to "hook on" to the sewer when this became possible, and to light their homes with gas. This advantage is reflected in the highly localized nature of urban epidemics, notably cholera, typhus, and dysentery, which always afflicted the poorer areas more severely than those better off. It was the relatively well-to-do who first learned to wash regularly and to take baths, because only they could afford the necessary facilities.

Conditions of Work

It is generally held that the process of industrialization entailed a worsening of conditions of work as well as of living conditions. Factories exposed the worker to hazards unknown to the older domestic crafts. Machines themselves posed a danger from their unguarded flywheels and moving parts. Wherever hot metal was handled, there was a risk. All miners were in varying degrees exposed to danger from dust, and lung complaints were almost normal among older workers. Tool grinders inhaled silica dust as well as fine particles of steel. Conditions were little better in some smelting and metal-fabricating works. Zinc smelting, for example, led to the production of fumes in which lead, zinc, and cadmium were prominent, as well as sulfur dioxide. The result was to produce at the smelting works in Vieille Montagne in Belgium and in Upper Silesia conditions of work that were among the worst encountered anywhere in the whole period of the Industrial Revolution. Factories were always noisy and dirty, cold in winter and exceedingly hot in summer, and everywhere there was dust and smoke that blackened the skin and choked the lungs.

Physical conditions of work improved only very slowly. It was easy to legislate for the provision of toilets or to limit the hours of work, more difficult to prescribe how dust was to be controlled and ventilation secured, and quite impossible to eliminate human carelessness as a factor in accidents. Indeed, it might almost be said that the growing complexity of machines increased the dangers and risks to the factory workers. It was impossible to guard against all the contingencies that arose in factory or mine; the only alternative was to insure against them. To some extent, insurance was provided by the mutuality of working communities, by their tendency to come to the help of one another in time of emergency. But this irregular and unsystematized relief was totally inadequate in an industrial society.

The view that society owed something to those who had served it or had been injured and maimed by its own instruments took hold very slowly. In England so-called Friendly Societies increased rapidly both in number and in the scope of their activities during the middle years of the century, and they contributed significantly to the security of those sufficiently well off to make regular contributions to their funds.[8] In some parts of continental Europe, miners also formed friendly societies. Ultimately, however, these obligations were assumed by the state, at least in western countries. The German government instituted a system of sickness insurance in 1883, of accident insurance a year later, and of old-age insurance shortly after that. Great Britain followed slowly in the wake of Germany, and France, despite its veneer of socialism, was one of the last countries in western Europe to adopt such measures. It is probably true to say that until the end of the nineteenth century the majority of workers had no security against the consequences of accident and illness, other than that provided by such associations as they formed among themselves.

The number of hours that the worker spent at his labor in the course of the day, week, or year was a significant factor in his general welfare. Yet, unless maximum hours were prescribed by legislation, the length of the workday is extraordinarily difficult to evaluate, and even then there is no assurance that the law was obeyed. It is necessary, in the first place, to distinguish between the factory worker and miner, on the one hand, and the far greater numbers who worked, perhaps irregularly, in the privacy of their homes. Second, the extent of the observance of "holy days" is almost wholly unknown before modern times. And when hours of work were, at last, prescribed by law or gild ordinance, it is almost impossible to discover with what vigor they were enforced. As early as 1495, in England, Parliament defined working hours because workers "waste much part of the day . . . sometimes in late coming into their work, early departing therefrom, long sitting at their [meals] and long time sleeping after none [noon]." How little things have changed. Most subsequent legislation aimed however, to restrict excessive hours rather than to encourage punctuality and application.

It was the medieval practice, long continued in Catholic countries, to observe the important feast days of the church by ceasing work. The number of holidays varied. They always included Sundays and the major festivals, as well as the name days of local saints and of the patrons of particular crafts. In the fifteenth century the number of feast days observed by masons amounted, in addition to Sundays, to almost fifty. It might be said that the number of working days rarely exceeded 280 in a year and often fell considerably short of this. In addition to this not inconsiderable total of nonworking days, Saturdays and the days before important feasts were not always treated as full workdays.

The Protestant Reformation brought about a significant change. Many of the feast days disappeared from the calendar. One cannot ascribe this wholly to a combination of religious bigotry and the Protestant work ethic. There is, it has been said, "an inverse relationship between the number of hours spent at work and the real-wage level of the working man."[9] The sixteenth century was a period of falling real-income levels, of which longer hours were merely a symptom. The "erosion of working man's leisure" culminated in the total abolition of all "holy days" except the austere Protestant Sabbath. The record of labor inputs on a western England estate farm in the middle years of the eighteenth century showed a full day's work on every day of the year, except Sundays and Christmas Day, and even this day was lost when Christmas itself occurred on a Sunday.

The length of the working day was governed by a number of factors, of which the duration of daylight and the need to maintain the continuous operation of machines and equipment were the most important. A blast furnace, for example, could not be extinguished overnight, and it appears to have been customary for glassblowing, for somewhat similar reasons, to have been a continuous process. Such examples aside, it appears to have become normal in traditional industries for the worker to be employed effectively for ten hours a day. This time was commonly expressed as from 6:00 A.M. to 6:00 P.M., with two hours off for meals. The working day seems previously to have been somewhat longer. The shorter hours of the eighteenth century correspond to rising real-wage rates.

The trend toward a shorter working day continued throughout the nineteenth century, but this improvement was interrupted in the case of the new factory industries, especially those engaged in the manufacture of cottons. "Hours were more likely to be lengthened in an industry where a traditional labor force was nonexistent or where it was replaced by a new labor force, often composed largely of women and children." This trend is best documented in the cotton mills of Lancashire but seems to have been present in all developing factory-based textile industries. In the Alsatian industry, which centered in the city of Mulhouse, "the shift is from 15 to 15½ hours, out of which there are 13 to 13½ hours of effective work."[10] The reason is not far to seek. The work force consisted in large part of women and children, who were more amenable to this kind of discipline than men. The proprietors sometimes excused themselves by claiming that the work of tending spinning machines and mechanical looms was far from arduous. But the fundamental reason was that the factory and its spinning and weaving equipment represented a very large capital investment, which its owner felt obliged to operate for as long a period each day as practicable.

Hours of work were gradually reduced in many industries in the course of the century. The reasons were twofold. Labor was becoming more efficient, so that the need for long hours was less apparent, and, second, governments legislated, usually on grounds of health, in favor of a shorter working day. First to come under scrutiny was the length of the day for children. In Great Britain the first limitation on child labor was imposed as early as 1819. Restrictions on women's work followed, and then the hours worked by men in the factories were brought into line with those in the more traditional industries. Progress was slower in continental Europe. In Germany the government seemed reluctant to legislate on the actual conduct of factories, and in France most units of production were so small that regulation might have seemed impracticable. In eastern and southeastern Europe, no attempt was made to regulate working conditions, but, on the other hand, factories were too few for their regulation to have been a significant matter. In Great Britain by the end of the century the working week was as a general rule fifty-five hours or even less, but up to an hour a day was added in the rest of western Europe.

In Catholic Europe certain festivals of the church continued to be observed by absence from work, even though factories always tried to impose their own discipline. In Protestant Europe, where the tedium and exhaustion of work were not relieved in this way, the question of holidays is more obscure. In some areas and in some factories it was usual to work a short day on Saturdays, even though this may have meant nothing more than quitting an hour or two earlier. Nevertheless, the practice spread in western Europe, and before the end of the century it was somewhat unusual to work much more than half a day. The working week of fifty-five hours thus came to be made up of five days at ten hours and a half day on Saturday.

In factories, work was strictly governed by the clock. This was inevitable where machines were centrally operated, as in textile mills. And the practice spread to other places of work. The factory clock supplemented or replaced that in the town hall or church tower, just as its "hooter" or siren took over the role of the church bell. Together they marked the time when factory gates were opened and closed, admitting workers and holding them fast until their shift was over. The regulations governing labor in a Berlin foundry in 1844 included the following:

> The working day begins in all seasons at 6 A.M. precisely and ends . . . at 7 P.M.; and it shall be strictly observed.
>
> Five minutes before the beginning of the stated hours . . . until their actual commencement, a bell shall ring and indicate that every worker . . . has to proceed to his place of work, in order to start as soon as the bell stops.
>
> Workers arriving two minutes late shall lose half an hour's wages; whoever is more than two minutes late may not start work until after the next break, or at least shall lose his wages until then. Any disputes about the correct time shall be settled by the clock mounted above the gatekeeper's lodge.[11]

The tyranny of the clock had fully asserted itself and was to remain a feature of the industrial scene. The counterpart to the factory clock was the domestic timepiece, necessary if the worker was to reach the factory gate before the bell ceased to sound, and from the middle years of the century the alarm clock came into widespread use.

The worker had, of course, to allow time to *walk* to his place of work for the appointed hour. For many this presented no problem. Their rows of tightly packed homes lay almost within the shadow of the factory, and the journey to work could have occupied no more than a few minutes. But a high price had to be paid for this convenience. Land values and rents became inflated in the close vicinity of the factory, and for many there was no alternative but cheaper accommodation at a greater distance, and thus a longer walk to work. Villermé recorded that at Mulhouse, "the poorest, who could not afford the current high rents, have been forced to live a league, a league and a half or even further outside the town, and consequently to make journeys daily in the morning and the evening to and from work."[12] A return journey of up to ten miles, over and above a working day of twelve to fourteen hours, was not uncommon, and how people were physically able to sustain this pace over the years is incomprehensible to us.

It might be supposed that the domestic worker, plying his loom, lathe, or wheel in the security of his home, was in a happier position, able to determine his hours of work and to achieve better working conditions. He was, as a general rule, a free agent in these respects, but he was at the mercy of market forces, fully as much as the factory worker. Except for the craftsman who continued to produce for direct sale to the consumer, the domestic worker was in the hands of a middleman, who supplied his working materials, sometimes owned the equipment he used, and always collected and sold the product of his labor. If times were bad the merchant took less of his product, and in prosperous times he paid him no more. Above all, in many branches of production the domestic worker was in competition with the machine-made products of the factory. The latter were, as a general rule, cheaper, their quality was often more uniform, and they came gradually to dominate the market. In the face of such competition, the domestic worker had to content himself with a smaller payment for each item, and thus to work even longer hours. Armand Audiganne, in 1848, wrote of "the absolute destitution, the deepest misery" of the domestic worker and added that hours of work in a factory were often fewer than for "those who work freely at home in their families."[13]

In time the domestic industry succumbed to this competition. That of Flanders was gravely weakened during the recession of the later 1840s, coinciding as it did with the potato blight, which ravaged the small holdings of the weavers. Other domestic manufactures gradually decayed during the second half of the century, as young men turned to the factory for employment and others grew old on the job. By the end of the century, domestic workers were a rapidly disappearing race. Such was the fate of the handloom weavers, of those who operated stocking frames and ribbon looms, as well as of many who worked in metals, like the nailers, screw makers, grinders, and gunsmiths. But there was an elite even among domestic workers, craftsmen who throughout the century faced little competition from factory-based industry.[14] They included the cutlers of Sheffield and of the German Sauerland, toolmakers and gunsmiths, pottery decorators and cabinetmakers. By and large, the tasks of these trades could not easily be mechanized, and they remained throughout the century in the hands of craftsmen. Watch- and clockmaking continued to be largely a domestic industry even longer. Even gunmaking at Liège and in Thuringia was largely in the hands of craftsmen who worked at home. In general, they possessed skills above the average and enjoyed conditions of work and levels of remuneration that were correspondingly higher.

In the 1840s Frédéric Le Play conducted a survey of the material conditions of life of a widely varied sample of workers. He dealt with miners and ironworkers but did not include factory workers. Most of those who appeared in his study were craftsmen whose work occupied a room within their homes or a shed erected in the yard. Perhaps for this reason Le Play rarely indicates their hours of work, which were probably too elastic. He does, however, describe their housing and its furnishings, their diet, dress, and recreations. Most had avoided the horrors of the "courts" of the industrial cities, but their accommodation was nonetheless mean and constricted, and their furnishings consisted of little more than the bare necessities of table, chairs, and bed. Gradations within the working class are reflected most prominently in their diet. It is not easy to calculate from Le Play's statistics the comparative expenditure on different items of food, when allowance has to be made for children of varying and unspecified ages. It is apparent, however, that the breadgrains made up much of the diet of all classes and that potatoes came second in most instances. Most variable was the consumption of meat and of other animal fats, such as lard. These were negligible in the diet of the poorest but formed a significant, if not large, component of the diets of the more highly skilled and better rewarded craftsmen.

The Home and Its Furnishings

The third quarter of the nineteenth century was a period of rapid change in most parts of Europe. The first phase of the Industrial Revolution had been characterized by the expansion of the textile and capital-goods industries. Only when the railroads had very largely been laid down, factories built and equipped with steam engines, and the bulk of the population adequately clothed, did manufacturers discover the need for other markets to develop and conquer. The real income of the average person was slowly increasing. The bare necessities of life were consuming a slightly smaller slice of the weekly wage, and the very small surplus was giving a degree of elasticity to this marginal demand. Diet improved, though not always in ways that were nutritionally or socially desirable. The quality and variety of clothing increased. Above all, there was an increasing demand for what can only be termed durable consumer goods.

This phenomenon was, by and large, only the downward diffusion of patterns of demand from the upper to the middle classes, and from the middle to the lower and working classes. But demand underwent significant changes in the process. Whereas the items thus popularized had previously been delicately and skillfully crafted, they now began to be mass-produced. The cabinetmaking and marquetry produced by a Chippendale or a Hepplewhite were imitated by the humbler joiner and ultimately by the village carpenter. Shape and function were throughout more or less the same, but the artistry displayed in their manufacture underwent a radical transformation. It was not that the humbler classes were incapable of appreciating superior workmanship; merely that the latter could not be produced in quantity and, in any case, cost too much. The same broadening of the pattern of demand, accompanied by a deterioration in quality, is apparent in almost every aspect of domestic life—in the provision of chinaware and table cutlery, of storage pots and cooking vessels, of pictures and mural decoration, beds and bedding, stoves, hearths, and cooking utensils.

It is impossible to establish a chronology for such changes. One can say only that they were first apparent in the homes of the rural gentry and rich burgesses, and that they passed by a kind of imitation to the richer peasants and more successful artisans, and from them to the humbler members of society. In most respects higher standards were first established in western and southern Europe, in particular in the Low Countries, France, and Italy. From here they were diffused very slowly and in an almost random fashion. Both Montaigne and Thomas Coryat began to use a fork at table in Italy, and since they appeared to approve of the practice, it is not unlikely that they continued it after they had returned home. In a somewhat similar vein, a Polish gentleman, visiting Rome in the sixteenth century, was much taken by the cloth, with its broad, brightly colored stripes, from which the uniforms of the Papal Guard were made. In consequence the folk costume of the women of the Łowicz district has today a broadly similar pattern.

But as a general rule, the popularization of the possessions and practices of the elite was dependent on mass-production. Spoons and forks began to be stamped from sheets of mild steel and protected from rust not by silver but by a coating of tin or enamel. Coarse pottery was thrown on wheels turned by machine, was shaped with templates, and decorated, if decorated at all, with transfers. Developments in the art of iron founding gave rise to a wider range of cooking pots, and the greater availability of cast iron contributed not only to the decorative, efficient, and economical fireplaces that were spreading among the homes of those who could afford them, but also to the freestanding stoves of the kind associated with Benjamin Franklin, which Jan Słomka observed in the cottages. At the same time, the textile industries had the capacity to encourage and then satisfy a growing demand for tablecloths of cotton or linen, sheets and other forms of bedding, and brightly colored prints for dresses and curtains.

The increasing level of comfort encouraged most people to spend a longer period within their home, and this trend, in turn, contributed to the desire for more and better furniture and for surroundings that were less drab than bare wood. A lime plaster had long been used on the outside walls of some buildings, daubed over wattle or lathes. Sometimes patterns, known as pargetting, were impressed into the wet plaster either with the trowel or with wooden molds. In the seventeenth century, wooden paneling gave way to plastered interior walls and ceilings, sometimes tricked out with moldings and representations of still life. Plastered walls had at one time been painted, sometimes with floral designs, sometimes with secular or even religious subjects. The idea of attaching patterned paper to plastered walls arose in Europe probably as early as the sixteenth century, but wallpaper as it is known and used today was an invention of the eighteenth.[15] Diderot's *Encyclopédie* contained an article on wallpaper (*papier peint*), and among the drawings prepared for it, but not in fact used, was one depicting the stages in papering the walls of a room. Among these eighteenth-century papers was the so-called flock paper, to which a velvety surface in patterned relief, made usually of particles of wool, had been added. It served to reinforce the idea that wallpaper derived in both origin and function from the use of tapestry and drapes.

The history of the manufacture of wallpaper took a course similar to that of cotton prints. The designs and patterns were first imprinted with wooden blocks, then with rollers. Indeed, the same figures were sometimes used for both calico and paper prints, and the practice of matching wallpaper with draperies and upholstery, which arose in this way, has since remained with us. In addition to patterns that repeated themselves at regular intervals, representations of physical scenes were used. In 1814, for example, a wallpaper was produced with realistic representations of the buildings of Paris. Such mural decorations were, and remained, extremely expensive. In relative terms they were almost as costly as tapestries had been, and, like tapestries, they adorned only the homes of the rich.

By the mid-nineteenth century, however, the cheaper, machine-printed paper was becoming available, just at the time when the middle classes were acquiring the wealth to buy and use it. Papers of an ever-widening range and variety poured from the presses. Their tasteless designs were spread over the walls of middle-class homes and, later in the century, of those of the working classes. Embossed papers and washable papers were introduced, adding to the cleanliness of kitchens and toilets. By the end of the century the use of wallpaper was general in urban homes in western and central Europe. Only in rural areas, where cottage walls offered too rough a surface for paper, was it not generally to be found.

This roughness in no way prevented decorating with pictures, religious objects, and embroidery. In the homes of the rich, the walls were often painted with geometrical or real-life designs. Sometimes they were hung with tapestries to hide their roughness and diminish the draft. From the time of the Renaissance, pictures painted onto canvas or wood were hung on the walls. The motifs changed with changing fashion, but always portraits made up a significant proportion of them. The art of engraving was developed in the later Middle Ages. In the seventeenth century, it was adapted to portraiture and became an important "reproductive medium." In the late eighteenth and early nineteenth centuries the scope of engraving, as a general rule on mild steel, was greatly extended. It was used to reproduce well-known paintings, to illustrate books, and, significant in the present context, to produce pictures that could serve for decoration or instruction. Most were religious, or at least moral, in tone, and many were pictorially in deplorable taste. They differed in subject matter, as might be expected, between Catholic and Protestant countries. Some such prints were hand colored, but from about the 1840s colored prints began to be made by a variety of processes and, mounted in garish frames, became the poor man's answer to the great art of the rich. At the same time samplers and pieces of embroidery were added to the growing collection of folk art that was beginning to adorn the walls of even the humblest home.

Mural decoration had been made possible by the development of printing. Printed books, however, were slower in making their appearance in the home. By the end of the sixteenth century, book production was a large and expanding industry in most parts of Europe, but the "consumption" of books was reduced by the slow growth in literacy. A further problem was that most books were printed in Latin or the recognized language of each country or region, whereas much of the rural population knew only a local *patois*. Books, ostensibly in their own language, had not only to be read to these people, but also translated. Nevertheless, as Natalie Davis has shown, a literate member of the community would sometimes read to a group of villagers on winter evenings. The books most favored were traditional tales, rustic calendars, and religious and devotional books, peddled around the countryside by colporteurs or chapmen. From the late fifteenth century, small books of only a few pages, known today as chapbooks, were printed and sold, especially in France. Some were devotional or practical, but most contained popular romances. They circulated in their hundreds in the seventeenth and eighteenth centuries. They provided some entertainment and instruction and were the nearest most people ever came to true literature. Most of the rural population until late in the nineteenth century possessed no books, and the inventories of the wealthiest and best educated among them showed very few.

Only the rich could afford to build up a library, and only the educated felt any need for one. Books remained very expensive until at least the middle years of the nineteenth century. Editions were small and their circulation very limited. Private libraries were accumulated by those who had the means or the inclination. Indeed, the possession of a collection of books became a mark of culture among the well-off. Some private libraries, including those administered by the universities, were large, though not public in the sense that they were open to all. In the course of the eighteenth century, "national" libraries were established, their nucleus in most instances being a private collection bequeathed to or otherwise acquired by the state. Local public libraries were, by and large, the creation of the second half and, most often, the last quarter of the nineteenth century. Not until then was the level of literacy sufficient to demand general access to books by large numbers of the population.

The provision of some means of both heating and cooking might have been regarded as essential in a house, if it were not for the fact that it was sometimes lacking. The English Hearth Tax of 1664 showed the occasional cottage that had no hearth and thus paid no tax. But it was in the congested housing of early nineteenth-century industrial workers that the hearth was most likely to be found wanting. Little attempt was made to provide for heating in the earliest tenement houses, and the only protection against the cold of winter was to crowd together in the smallest space possible. Even cooking was often by means of a communal oven or stove located in a stairway. But this was a consequence of the overhasty building of cheap workers' housing. It was remedied in the course of time, though conditions in this respect remained primitive even at the end of the century in many industrialized areas in central and eastern Europe.

In other respects, modes of heating and cooking were improving through the middle years of the century. The dominant feature of the changes taking place at this time was the separation of the functions of heating and cooking. The removal of the latter to a separate kitchen facilitated the process. The hearth located in the main living room or parlor was gradually restricted to its primary purpose of providing warmth. This step was accomplished by building a raised fireplace against a wall in whose thickness a chimney was constructed. The fire was usually contained within an iron basket. It might serve to heat a pot or kettle but was not designed for cooking. Broadly speaking, the small, raised fire basket became common in parts of northwest Europe, where the fuel used was mainly coal. By contrast, in central Europe and beyond, where wood was more widely used, a larger stove of masonry or cast iron was more common. It was usually freestanding but had an external flue and was sometimes covered with decorative tiles. It was a remarkably efficient space heater, but was ill suited to preparing food.

The necessary corollary was a separate cooking place, normally located in a kitchen built for the purpose. Before the advent of gas and electricity, solid fuel had to be burned, and the cooking setup consisted essentially of a fireplace and an oven above it. A separate flat area above the fire allowed pots to be boiled, but there was no room in the nineteenth-century kitchen for the apparatus of spits and trivets that had once graced the hearth. A revolution was effected in the kitchen, as in the living room, by the introduction of fireplaces, ovens, and stoves of cast iron. These began to appear in northwest Europe in the mid-nineteenth century, but their diffusion was slow before the widespread use of gas for cooking and heating. The gas cooker made its appearance in the second half of the century and was quickly adopted wherever a gas supply made this possible. And this was, by and large, only in the cities. It was usually difficult to adapt older housing to newer modes of heating and cooking, which were introduced, as a general rule, mainly in newly built homes. In peasants' cottages, particularly in central and eastern Europe, the older modes of heating and cooking have survived into the present century.

Central heating of large buildings became practical at the end of the eighteenth century. Steam or hot water was conducted from a central furnace through iron pipes to the rooms to be heated. It was adopted in many great houses in western Europe in the early years of the nineteenth century and was widely used by the middle years. It was a very long time before such comforts were adopted even in the larger homes of the middle class. They were dependent on the manufacture, at a relatively low price, of suitable furnaces, as well as of cast-iron pipes and radiators. Very few homes, even in the most affluent and developed parts of Europe, were so equipped by the end of the century, and, it is almost superfluous to add, such innovations were quite unknown in the homes of the working classes and of the rural poor.

The furnishings of all homes, except those of the wealthy, underwent a slow improvement during the century. The great houses changed little in this respect. Indeed, many of them still proudly exhibit even today their eighteenth-century carpeting, furniture, and decoration. But they served to set a standard for the emulation of the middle classes. Hence the multiplication of furniture in the style of the eighteenth-century masters. Printing had made drawings of such furnishings widely available, commerce was making superior timber abundant, and the varied output of factories and workshops included the tools and templates that the craftsman needed. Not that nineteenth-century craftsmanship consisted only of pale imitations of that of an earlier age. It originated the robust tables, chairs, and chests, somewhat tasteless in their decoration but strongly built and durable, that we sometimes call Victorian. The quality of this furniture is attested by the vast quantities of it still in use in all parts of Europe.

The furniture that crept slowly down the social scale in the course of the nineteenth century included not only simple tables and chairs, which replaced the "forms" or benches of an earlier age, but also pieces in which metal played an increasingly important role. The greater availability of steel wire encouraged sprung upholstery. Cast iron, often with an excess of brass embellishment, replaced the wooden boxes that had previously been used, and the ropes and wooden slats on which the sleeper had lain gave way to a variety of iron beds and steel sprung mattresses. Everything combined to make sleeping more restful and more comfortable. Advertising, which became widespread in newspapers and journals in the middle years of the century, presented what to contemporaries must have been alluring pictures of these luxuries, and it is evident that many people were persuaded to invest their discretionary income in these new delights. At the same time living rooms and bedrooms became less sparsely furnished. The greater volume of personal possessions, like clothing and decorative china, called for chests and closets in which to store them, and for "dressers" for the display of china, brass, and pewter.

These developments were a token of the greater pride that was being taken in the home and its furnishings. The house was no longer merely a shelter from the elements; it was becoming a home in which people took pleasure in spending a significant part of their lives. This transformation could not have been accomplished without a significant shortening of the working day and a reduction in the amount of women's work in factory and field. The wife was gradually ceasing, at least in parts of western Europe, to be a supplement to the family income and was becoming, in the American expression, a homemaker.

These changes were accompanied by a greater attention to cleanliness. Plastered walls and floors covered with boards or flagstones were an improvement on the earth, sand, and rushes that had done service in the eighteenth century and were still found very widely in the early years of the nineteenth. Such simple adjuncts of domestic cleanliness as bristle brushes, metal scrapers for soiled boots, galvanized buckets, and enameled pails became more common, and, above all, soap was made cheaper and more abundantly available by recent advances in chemistry.[16] There was in Britain a tenfold expansion in soap production between 1830 and 1875, and increase was no less marked in France and other parts of western Europe. This growth was assisted by the import of vegetable oils of tropical origin, which had the further advantage of permitting a wider variety of soaps to be made. Soap became more easily attainable at the same time that people's discretionary expenditure was increasing. Budgets of working-class families show on average a very slow increase in the consumption of soap, though of this tendency there are no comprehensive statistics.

The more widespread use of soap had broad ramifications. Its contribution to personal cleanliness is too obvious to mention. But the importance of washing clothing and bedding required more careful demonstration. In 1752 Johan Zacharius Platner published his *Tractat von der Reinlichkeit,* in which he stressed the importance of regular ablutions "for all those whose work brings them into contact with dirt and grime, and, indeed, for everyone," and he pointed out that clothing had also to be regularly cleansed.[17] The chemical basis of the latter was not demonstrated until early in the present century, but the empirical demonstration of the advantages of cleanliness were becoming apparent. The laundering of clothes had been practiced since classical times, though certainly not on a regular basis, and scarcely at all by the laboring classes, who would have soiled their clothes more readily than any others. In parts of France, even late in the nineteenth century, the family laundered its clothes only once a year, and early in the present century it was unusual even in relatively advanced areas to have a "wash" more than four times a year. Laundering usually consisted of little more than beating the clothes with a beater in a solution of lye. The process often took place—and indeed still does in some areas—along the banks of a river. It was the practice in some areas merely to stack the soiled clothing and to pour lye over it, leaving the latter to infiltrate the cloth. In the better-appointed kitchens hot water was used, but it was not until the mid-nineteenth century, when it had become cheap and abundant, that soap was to be much used in the laundry. A consequence of the separation of kitchen and living room was the construction, as a permanent feature, of a boiler for the laundering of clothes. It consisted generally of a metal vessel built over a fireplace, in which the clothes were boiled.

It is impossible to measure the consequences of the use of soap and of the frequent laundering of clothes, not only for personal comfort but also for health. At the very least, the extermination of mites and lice that followed can only have had a beneficial effect on human well-being. The disappearance of typhus is one of its more obvious results.

Public Utilities

The Industrial Revolution was important in extending the range and variety of comforts within the home. It was even more so in its contribution to conveniences outside the household: the supply of water, the disposal of sewage, the supply of gas for street and domestic lighting. All were dependent in some measure on the technological developments of the Industrial Revolution, in particular on the manufacture of cast and welded iron pipes. The most revolutionary of these innovations was the manufacture and distribution of coal gas. The existence of "flammable airs" had long been known, and experiments were sometimes performed with them. The *Philosophical Transactions* of 1739 had described such a process. Before the end of the century successful attempts had been made to use gas, derived from the destructive distillation of wood or coal, for lighting, and in 1799 Philippe Lebon, in Paris, took out a patent for the manufacture and use of gas from wood. But already William Murdock had used gas, generated by heating coal in a retort, for lighting his home in Redruth, Cornwall. Shortly afterward Murdock moved to Birmingham, where, in association with Matthew Boulton and James Watt, he was able to produce the cast-iron equipment necessary to make, transport, and burn coal gas. Watt's Soho works were illuminated with gas, and Murdock adapted his apparatus to the lighting of mills, thus making possible longer hours of uninterrupted work. In 1807 gas lighting was first used for the illumination of a London street, and in 1812 a company, subsequently known as the Gas Light and Coke Company of London, was formed.[18] This is not the place to trace the vicissitudes of this and its rival companies, which were numerous, each serving some part of the metropolis and its growing suburbs, each with its battery of retorts, its supply of coal, and network of pipes to serve its area. The absurdities of overlapping systems of gas supply led late in the century to their amalgamation into a smaller number of companies, each serving a larger area and a vast number of consumers. The example of London was quickly followed by other large British cities and by Paris, Berlin, and others in central Europe. By 1850, 50 German cities had some form of gas illumination; by 1860 the total had increased to about 250. This rapid growth in the use of gas was paralleled elsewhere in western and central Europe. The reason was the completion of the primary railroad network, without which most cities could not have secured a supply of coal.

The links between the supply of gas and the iron industry were close. The gas companies were heavy consumers of iron. Cast-iron pipes underlay the streets, and pipes of smaller bore, usually welded from soft iron, were used to supply individual homes. Lamp standards of cast iron arose along the streets, illuminating them with their glass-enclosed jets, and the lamplighter, with his ladder and torch, became a familiar figure. Until the last quarter of the century, gas was used almost exclusively for illumination. Then, in the 1880s, it was first used for heating and cooking. Foundries began to turn out gas stoves, gas ovens, and gas fires in ever-increasing numbers. For a generation, dependence on gas was absolute except in those rural areas where gas had not yet been made available.

The social importance of gas was incalculable. In many places entertainment and socializing became more common, primarily because a row of gas lamps, lighted at dusk and extinguished by a peripatetic lamplighter sometime in the early hours, made the streets safer and cut down on crime. Shops, lighted with a flickering gas jet, no longer had to close at sundown. The domestic weaver could work in greater comfort, and the factory could be operated during the dark days of winter. It is gaslight that sheds its wan glow over the streets and offices of Dickensian London and the Paris of Hugo and Balzac. The invention later in the century of the incandescent gas mantle served to improve the illumination provided by the gas jet. To what extent people's sight was improved by better-lighted homes and their health by the superior cooking facilities that gas made possible is something that we cannot measure. But it cannot be doubted that it was considerable. The coming of gas also had an adverse side. It marked the beginning of long hours for those who worked in shops. It was the source of not inconsiderable pollution, "stinking drains due to gasworks effluent and the discharge from . . . syphons in the sewers . . . [as well as] broken road surfaces,"[19] and everywhere near a gasworks the nauseating smell of coal gas itself.

Gas supply was economically practicable only where population was dense and hundreds of households could draw from a single pipeline. If a gas supply penetrated the countryside, it was only in anticipation of urban expansion. Here domestic lighting continued to be mainly by candle and oil lamp until the coming of electricity. The oil lamp itself underwent considerable improvement during the century. Devices for hold-ing the wick and separating the flame from the oil intensified the light that it shed and made its management very much safer. Nevertheless, the upsetting of an oil lamp remained one of the most frequent causes of domestic fires.

The construction of electricity generators and of a supply network came almost a century later than the gas system. It called for a different range of industrial products, which began to be made only late in the process of industrialization: cable made from copper, insulators of porcelain, and insulation of rubber and lead, as well as steam and water turbines and generators, which called for highly developed engineering skills. The earliest generators, like the gasworks themselves, were dependent on coal and were located in the larger cities. Electricity was publicly available in Paris from 1875 and in Berlin after 1884. But it proved difficult for electricity to cut into the market already held by the gas companies, especially as the latter devoted considerable efforts to improving the burners, stoves, and fires that used their product. Electricity met with less competition in rural areas, where gas was little used, but the high cost of laying cables in a sparsely populated region restricted rural electrification until the twentieth century.

The iron pipes that carried gas beneath the streets of the great cities could have served no less well for the supply of water. Many cities did, indeed, possess a piped water supply, even before the Industrial Revolution, but the "pipes" were often no more than wooden conduits, even more infected than the water that passed through them. It was long before urban dwellers realized that the laying down of iron water pipes was of even greater importance for health and welfare than were iron gas mains. Even by the mid-nineteenth century there were few cities that drew their water from uncontaminated sources by means of sealed pipes, and not until the end of the century, by which time it had been demonstrated irrefutably that many common diseases were waterborne, was water piped to individual homes.

Sewage disposal was of greater fundamental importance in the nineteenth century than either a piped water supply or street lighting, because its impact on public health was far more profound. Yet it received less attention than either before the end of the century, largely because of the general ignorance of the nature of infection. Of course, stinking drains were unpleasant, but pollution that poured into the local river was merely carried downstream and, it was hoped, neutralized before it reached the next city. So cavalier an attitude to one of the most urgent problems of modern urban congestion was changed only slowly. In many cities sewer systems were constructed only after the population had been decimated by cholera. Yet it is a curious fact that their construction was less dependent on the products of modern industry than was either gas or water supply. Most sewers—certainly all the early sewers laid under the great cities of western Europe—were built of masonry, and the pipes that fed into them from separate houses were of glazed earthenware. A modern sewage system is a complex piece of engineering, but those laid down before the end of the nineteenth century were technically simple and could have been built a hundred years earlier if the will had been present to do so. It was all a matter of perception and priorities.

Food and Diet

The last aspect of material life to be considered is food supply and diet. The impact of industrialization is here less obvious and less direct. Broadly speaking, the supply of food was increased and made more reliable in three ways. In the first place, industrial developments made it possible to supply better tools to the farmer. The all-steel plow and harrow; haymaking, harvesting, and threshing machines; and seed drills and cutters for preparing animal feed all underwent improvements in design and construction. They ceased, in general, to be the joint products of the local carpenter and smith, and were turned out from foundries and engineering works. Their effect was to make agricultural work faster and more effective, but their adoption represented a large capital investment and was practicable only for the richer farmers and on large estates. It was, as indeed it remains, the practice to hire the more elaborate pieces of equipment as and when they were needed, but the steel plow succeeded in displacing its clumsy predecessors over much of Europe in the course of the century.

No less important was the availability of fertilizer and other soil additives. Lime and marl, not strictly fertilizers, had long been used but were difficult to transport. From the middle years of the century, with the expanding railroad net, they became more widely available, with a consequent extension of the cultivated area and improvements in yields.

A second factor in the improvement in food supply was the greater degree of local specialization. This was also made possible by improved transportation. Butter, cheese, and even liquid milk began to be transported to the centers of population from very considerable distances. Near most large cities, "market gardening" and the production of vegetables and fruit became a highly intensive business. Such specialization led both to an improvement in quality and to a great increase in the volume of such commodities available in urban markets and shops. The chief beneficiary of these developments was the urban population, which from the middle years of the century began, overall, to eat relatively well. Change was less conspicuous among the rural population, which clung more tenaciously to traditional foods and was, in any case, less well placed to benefit from the new specializations.

A third reason for the improvement in diet during the century lay in the growing supply of foodstuffs from what has come to be called the European "periphery." This broad entity included not only Russia and the eastern provinces of Europe but also overseas sources of supply in both the New World and the Old. Cereals made up the greater part of this import. They came from Poland, Russia, and Romania and from North Africa and the Levant. In the nineteenth century the flow of grain began from the prairies of North America and the plains of Argentina and Australia. Much of Europe came ultimately to benefit from this import, but the countries in greatest need were those in which industrialization and urban growth had been pursued most vigorously, and these were Great Britain, the Low Countries, and western Germany. Eastern Europe also supplied live animals, driven on the hoof from the plains of Hungary and the Ukraine. The New World supplied sugar, coffee, and cocoa, and from China and, later, Ceylon and India came tea and rice.

Imported foodstuffs competed in varying degrees with those which were produced within Europe, and the attitudes of European governments toward trade reflected internal politics and pressures. In Great Britain the desire of the industrialist for cheaper food led to abolition of duties on imported grain in 1846. The Low Countries and Switzerland, by and large, encouraged imports. France continued to protect its farmers, and in Germany the landed interests in the east succeeded in keeping duties on imported foodstuffs fairly high. Nevertheless, despite these variations in tariff policy, essential foodstuffs became more abundant and, in relative terms, cheaper. A new world had been brought into being to redress the food balance of the old.

In any direct sense this greater availability of food owed little to the Industrial Revolution, yet without imports on this scale its fulfillment would have been impossible. Specialization and export were central to industrial development. Exported cloth, railroad equipment, and engineering products not only kept European factories in full production but also paid for the growing import of food. When the European artisan breakfasted on coffee and wheat bread, as he was beginning to do in the middle years of the century, he might, had he known, have thanked the industrialists who shipped railroad equipment and other manufactured goods to Asia and the New World.

That there was a great improvement in the diet of all classes between 1800 and 1900 is apparent, but it is extraordinarily difficult to measure this change. The wealthy classes had fed abundantly if not always well, and it is possible to study their diet through the account books and diaries that they have left. The middle classes tended to follow the example of their social superiors, reducing their consumption of breadgrains and increasing that of vegetables, fruit, meat, fish, and animal fats as occasion offered. It is the diet of the humbler classes, who must have made up three-quarters of the population, about which there is the greatest uncertainty. Some concern was felt as early as the first half of the century for the diet of the working classes. Its inadequacy must have been apparent both to employers and to the public at large. This sentiment gained expression in the 1840s in the survey that Frédéric Le Play conducted into the material conditions of life of a broad sample of workers from Russia to Spain and northern England. But the study of working-class diets is beset with difficulties, in part because there must have been very considerable differences between periods of relative prosperity and times of depression. Such cyclic fluctuations were, by and large, absent from the life of the peasant classes, and were not of great significance to the artisan who worked for a local clientele within his own community. But as soon as the craftsman began to work for a merchant who distributed his goods more widely at home and abroad, the mutuality of the old system disappeared. Periods of full employment alternated with times when factories reduced their activity and the merchant no longer required the product of domestic workers.

A further problem in evaluating diets is how to allow for children. A teenager might eat as much as an adult, whereas a child might require a smaller volume of more particular food. Nor is it altogether clear how much food value was contained in the not inconsiderable consumption of alcohol. The amounts of food eaten are, lastly, expressed in the weight of the several items, in their price, or in their caloric value, all of which can be converted only with difficulty and the probability of error into a common denomination.

It is, however, apparent that undernourishment and malnourishment were widespread among both urban and rural populations. But conditions varied greatly. Although cereals constituted the foundation of the diet, milk, butter, and cheese were relatively important in the Alps and other mountainous areas. Vegetables were significant among the rural population, especially where the peasant toft was large enough for the cultivation of greens and roots. Meat entered into the diet in extremely variable amounts. Very rarely was it entirely lacking, though Le Play cited a Carinthian charcoal burner whose diet included almost no milk, meat, or animal fat.[20] On the other hand, the ironworkers at Dannemora, Sweden, and in the mountains of Slovakia consumed, in terms of weight, far more milk, meat, and eggs than they did breadgrains. Urban workers appear to have fared a great deal less well than rural. This plight was due in part to their low incomes but probably in far greater measure to the difficulty in supplying urban areas with liquid milk and green vegetables. Very broadly, it can be said, the lower the real income of the worker, the more heavily was his and his family's diet made up of breadgrains. The caloric intake of the least favored is said to have derived to the extent of 80 percent from cereals, whereas the moderately well-to-do obtained no more than half from this source. In certain poverty spots, such as the Auvergne and the Morvan in France, a soup made from oats, buckwheat, and potatoes constituted most of the diet even at the end of the century.[21]

Food everywhere consumed a large but variable part of the real income of the family. In general, the lower the total income, the higher was the proportion expended on food, and the smaller the discretionary expenditure left for the worker's family. In the cases examined by Le Play, the cost of food accounted for 32 percent of the total budget in the case of a well-to-do clockmaker in Geneva, and 83 percent in that of the charcoal burner already mentioned. Very broadly speaking, the poorer craftsman spent more than 50 percent on food; those in better circumstances, somewhat less. The cutler at Solingen and the Sheffield joiner both spent about 45 percent; the Rhineland handloom weaver— whose profession was depressed at this time—66 percent.

During these same years an intensive study was made of incomes and expenditures in Manchester and its industrial suburb of Dukinfield.[22] In all, nineteen families were studied. For all of them flour was the "major staple," and on average each person consumed about five pounds a week, either as bread or in the form of gruel. A similar amount of potatoes was eaten, and these two foodstuffs together provided at least 70 percent of the caloric intake. The greatest variation was in the consumption of meat, which ranged from 2.2 pounds per head down to 0.6 pounds per head per week. In addition, very small quantities of milk, eggs, butter, cheese, and sugar were bought. The survey made no mention of fruit and vegetables. It is difficult to believe that these foods did not enter into the diet, though supplies in so urbanized an area are likely to have been small and irregular, and it is most unlikely that the families surveyed possessed any kind of garden.

An attempt has been made to assess the nutritional value of the diets recorded. On average, members of the families studied consumed 2300 calories a day, rather more in Manchester; considerably less in Dukinfield. A recommended daily allowance would have been between 2500 and 3000. Almost half the population surveyed consumed less than the recommended daily allowance of protein, though most took sufficient iron and, thanks to the considerable potato consumption, a more than adequate amount of vitamin C. It has been concluded that more than a third of the families studied were receiving a diet sufficiently deficient in calories and protein to be seriously inadequate. It is very likely that this diet would have some immediate effect upon health and the ability to resist disease. The sample studied was, it is to be presumed, fully employed; one can only guess what would have been their diet during periods of sickness or unemployment. These figures, it must be remembered, relate to the Manchester described in the more lurid pages of Friedrich Engels.

To what extent, one may ask, was the Manchester of 1841 typical in this respect of other rapidly growing industrial cities? Unhappily, there is every reason to suppose that conditions in most large British cities were closely similar, and that they were no better, and probably worse, in continental cities that were growing rapidly at this time. People fed no better in the working-class quarters of Paris, Lille, and Lyons, of Essen, Berlin, and Łódź. Indeed, the slender evidence suggests that in many instances they were even worse off.

It cannot be doubted that the quality of diet improved almost everywhere during the second half of the century, but conditions between the late eighteenth and the middle years of the nineteenth have been the subject of a "most interesting and most inconclusive debate." Broadly speaking, the "optimists" are pitted against the "pessimists."[23] Their debate has elicited much useful information, but no statistical series that could be used to show whether average consumption of the basic necessities of life actually increased or declined during the period and as a result of industrialization. Supplies increased, but so also did the number of consumers. One may fairly question both the use of average figures of consumption per head and the citing of literary descriptions, as in Dickens, of gargantuan meals. The bald statement that "the consumption of *basic* foods in 1850 London was not widely inferior to that of modern England" may be accepted only if one remembers that, in the households of the well-to-do, there was a large and growing consumption of *nonbasic* foods, and that the range of difference between the moderately rich and the poor may have been increasing.

The quality of diet of the laboring population appears overall to have declined, as one might have expected it to do. Industrializing cities had, by definition, a high proportion of workers, recent immigrants from the countryside. Their numbers depressed wages, so that factory workers, especially those in the textile industries, were among the most poorly paid. But, in the present context, a critical factor was the failure of shopping, market, and distributional facilities to keep pace with the expanding population. In most cities the established shops handled mainly the luxury goods of the grocer's trade. The grocer was, even in England, a purveyor of "luxuries to the rich" as late as the middle of the century.[24] The basic foods were still largely handled in the weekly or twice-weekly market, which served as an outlet for the products of the local region. Increasing demand "strained to a breaking point the facilities of the market square." What was wanted was a "local, easily accessible grocery and general provisions store," but it was not until the later years of the century that, in much of Europe, the inadequate mechanism of the market and its gathering of peasant wagons was replaced by shops regularly supplied by a wholesaler. One tends to forget that during the early phases of industrialization the housewife had to spend long periods literally searching for food and waiting in line for her turn to purchase it. How women who were employed all day in the mill managed to get to the shops is far from clear.

Much of the better-quality foodstuffs, such as fruit, green vegetables, fish, and meat had only a short shelf life. This factor militated against the poor, who could shop only at irregular intervals. Their tendency was inevitably to rely on foods that would keep well, and this meant, apart from considerations of cost, breadgrains, root crops, cheese, and meat that had been smoked or salted. Sugar consumption increased sharply in Great Britain and probably in the rest of Europe throughout the century, not because of any food value, for it had little, but because it would keep.[25]

A further constraint on the improvement in diet was a lack of facilities to cook and prepare foods of better quality. Crudely built tenements, which housed a large part of the working population, often lacked kitchens and, indeed, any private cooking facilities. In this respect peasant housing was incomparably superior, with its hearth and stove of masonry or cast iron. Little provision of this kind was made in most industrial workers' housing until late in the century. The predominance of boiled and fried foods in working-class diets sprang in part from the lack of facilities for cooking of any other kind. Not until the widespread adoption of the gas stove in the closing decades of the century did the means become widely available for the more refined and palatable preparation of food. Inadequacies of diet might have been due primarily to low real income, but they remained significant longer than was necessary because of the poor systems of distribution and indifferent means of preparation. In the long run, however, it was the further expansion of factory industries that provided the remedy. The building of railroads and roads, the construction of warehouses and refrigeration plants, the laying down of gas lines and the installation of cast-iron stoves were all part of a revolution that in the latter half of the nineteenth century went far toward transforming the diet of the urban proletariat.

The Mechanics of Distribution

Preindustrial societies relied chiefly on the urban market for the supply of the daily necessities of life. There had, of course, been shops, but these tended to be associated with the sale of restricted categories of goods: the products of craft industries; foodstuffs that had to be imported from distant regions, such as wine, salt, and spices; and those, such as meat, bread, and ale, which required some form of processing. Other goods, including most forms of food, were sold and bought at the stalls set up in the markets. "The shop sold exotic products, the market sold local produce."[26] The shop had been slowly gaining in importance for a century or more before the Industrial Revolution. Some merely sold the products, footwear or clothing, for example, of the craftsman who worked within and who made goods to fit particular customers. A few such shops have remained active, especially in small towns, into the present century, but most other shops were dependent on the wholesaler, who supplied exotic goods that, like the articles of the grocer's trade, accounted for much of their business.

The rise of the middleman was an essential precondition of an increase in the number and business of urban shops. Wholesalers were, as a general rule, specialized and dealt mainly in goods that were light and easily transported. They distributed groceries, which at the time consisted mainly of coffee, tea, cocoa and chocolate, sugar, spices, and salt, all of them relatively expensive and capable of being stored for long periods. As cities increased in size, they outgrew the food resources of their local region. The first sign of this imbalance was the growing importance of the dealer in cereals, the corn bodger or *blattier,* who combed the countryside for grain, which he bought, stored, and released onto the urban markets as need arose or prices increased. The peasant continued to drive his wagon to the town market once a week, as, in many parts of Europe, he continues to do even today. But an increasing proportion, even of agricultural produce, was being handled by middlemen and retailed through shops. The face-to-face character of the old system was very slowly being eroded. The number and nature of the shops underwent a gradual change. The grocer, who had once sold mainly exotic goods like tea, coffee, and spices, now broadened his stock. He carried oatmeal, flour, cheese, and most foodstuffs that made up a normal diet. The mercer, who had formerly specialized in buttons, thread, and all the accessories of clothing, began to handle cloth of all kinds, and the disappearance of the smith meant that "ironmongery"—nails, screws, and small items of cast or welded iron, now in increasing demand—was obtained from a factory by way of a wholesaler and sold over the counter.

There were immense advantages for the customer in the new system of trading. Unlike the market, the shop was open every day except Sunday, and the introduction of gas lighting lengthened shopping hours in winter. The advantage must have been incalculable for those who worked long in factory and workshop and were quite unable to get to the market during the relatively short period when the peasant had produce to sell. Most shops were owned, or at least rented, by those who kept them. Most sales were for cash, but it is evident that credit was often given either to favored customers or to those who were temporarily embarrassed.

At the same time that shops were becoming more numerous and more specialized in the cities, they were beginning to invade the villages. Countryfolk had previously been obliged to obtain whatever goods they could not produce for themselves from the nearest town or from the peddler or colporteur. These lonely people traveled the countryside with their cart or pack animal, or even a load piled high on their backs. They retailed small items, intrinsically of low value, but much appreciated in the villages. Some carried religious tracts and popular calendars; others dealt in ribbons and trinkets such as would in the cities have been sold by the mercers and haberdashers. In western Europe their importance was at its peak in the eighteenth century, when, it is said, some 2000 licenses to peddle goods were granted each year in England alone. At the other end of Europe they continued active till the end of the nineteenth century. Reymont described with what rapture the peddler's coming was anticipated in his Polish village. But in the west the peddlers succumbed when "their old enemies the shopkeepers had usurped their function even in the remotest places. The shadowy figure of the peddler still persisted . . . and still persists, but only as a curiosity on the fringe of retail trade and no longer an integral part of it."[27]

A final step in the development of shopping, at least in the nineteenth century, was the emergence of the store, the very large shop with a wide range of goods, sold usually at relatively low prices. The earliest of such stores was established in Paris in the 1850s.[28] It compensated for its low profit margin by its massive turnover. Only the largest cities were able to support such stores, and their spread during the later decades of the century was slow. In fact, Woolworth, Bon Marché, and other such stores belonged rather to the early twentieth century than to the nineteenth. The spread of stores, many of them local branches of a centrally managed concern, into cities of ever smaller size provides clear evidence of improving standards and of the growth in mass demand.

The Revolution in Transportation

The social and economic developments of the nineteenth century would have been inconceivable without a revolution in the means of transportation. In the eighteenth century most people who were obliged to make long journeys traveled by coach. Freight was carried in horse-drawn wagons, unless a waterway lay conveniently to hand. Roads remained bad until the middle years of the nineteenth century in western Europe, and even longer in eastern. Dangers were great—from robbery, from the breakdown of vehicles, from floods and damaged bridges, and from the conditions met with in the inns along the routes. Yet people did manage to travel, and in growing numbers, and there was even a kind of regularity in the coach services provided in much of Europe. Coaches, furthermore, became more comfortable as the use of steel springs spread more widely.

Glass windows, first installed in the late seventeenth century, protected at least the "inside" travelers against the weather, and, despite the quality of the roads, travel became faster. In 1754, for example, it took the regular coach four and a half days to cover the two hundred miles from London to Manchester. By 1770, the scheduled time was two days in summer and three in winter. A half century later this time was reduced to less than thirty hours, and when the first railroad trains made the run, the coaches were doing it in about eighteen hours.[29] An average speed of from eight to ten miles an hour was normal in England before the coming of railroads, and this was the best that could be expected in most of continental Europe.

From about 1840, the railroads began to compete with coaches and within a short time had driven them from the roads of much of Europe. Railroad trains were faster—in general up to four or five times faster; they were less vulnerable to the hazards of weather, more comfortable, and, above all, a great deal cheaper, especially when one remembers the cost of overnight accommodation for coach travelers and the extraordinarily high level of tipping that was expected of them.

Throughout this period the wagon was used on the same roads to transport freight. It carried heavier loads than the coach and was much slower. The wagon was used not only for the intermittent transport of such things as building stone but also for the more regular movement of wool, cloth, ironware, salt, and exotic foods. Raw cotton was transported by wagon from the port of Rouen to manufacturing centers in Alsace—a distance of over three hundred miles—until railroads took over the task. The journey was very slow, especially in winter, when the roads were deep in mud, and proportionately expensive. An industry had to be very efficient indeed in order to survive under such conditions. This example may have been an extreme one; most commodities were transported over much shorter distances.

Goods were, as a general rule, handled by carters, who plied their business between the more important cities in most parts of Europe. Sometimes they were required to be licensed by a public authority. Usually they kept to a more or less regular schedule, so that the merchant and the traveler could rely on their services. On the roads of Spain, Richard Ford found "few travellers save the migration caravans which bring corn down from Salamanca and take back salt from Cadiz."[30] Normally the merchants traveled in caravans for security, and at night bivouacked beside the road. France, England, the Low Countries, and much of central Europe were overspread by a network of carriers' routes. A shopkeeper in the small English town of Kirkby Stephen, in Westmorland, obtained his stock-in-trade—much of it haberdashery, writing paper, books, and small ironware—through the common carrier from many parts of the country.[31] The carrier also conveyed money and financial documents, a measure of the relative safety of the roads at this time. Before the railroad age, London was linked by the carrier with almost all parts of the country, and without his services the shops would not have been able to obtain their stock of "grocery," mercer's goods and other semiluxuries that could not be produced locally.[32] The services of the carter were supplemented by the packhorse, which carried a lighter load but was able to negotiate roads and narrow bridges that were impassable to the wagon.

The carter did not lose his importance with the coming of the railway. There were very extensive areas, especially in Europe's eastern and northern periphery, that the railroad never reached. But it did come within a measurable distance of them, and their

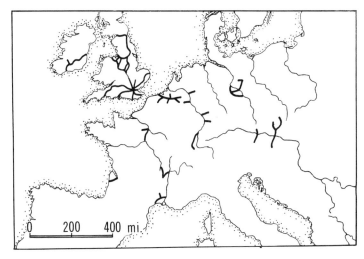

11.5. The European railroad net, 1840.

presence served to stimulate trade. In such areas the carters became more, not less, important. "Traffic . . . on roads serving as feeders to the railways increased with general levels of economic activity. . . . The existence of the railway stimulated the development of roads leading to its stations [depots]."[33] The carter continued to link most villages with the outside world, bringing supplies for their general store and carrying the occasional villager to the distant city, until the motor bus, the truck, and the private car took his place in the present century. But there was a change in the nature of the traffic using the roads. The carriers had formerly conveyed goods from one end of the country to another. This service was gradually usurped by the railroads.[34] The traffic of the common carrier became strictly local, between village and market town and railroad depot.

Important as road traffic remained throughout the century, it was the railroad that took almost all the long-distance travel and transport. The total mileage of track increased rapidly between the 1840s and 1880 (figs. 11.5–11.7). In 1835 there were only 442 miles (711 km) of public railroad in operation, three-quarters of it in Great Britain. By 1850 the total had risen to 14,298 miles (23,042 km), and by 1880 to 97,541 miles (157,071 km), including Russia. The network was dense in England and through-out western and central Europe. It still formed only an open pattern in southern and eastern Europe, as well as in southern Sweden, and was almost completely lacking in northern Scandinavia and the Balkan peninsula.

The construction of railroads was not wholly determined by economic consider-ations. Some lines, especially in Russia and the Balkans, had primarily a military or strategic importance. But, by and large, they went far toward satisfying the public need for travel and transportation. At the same time, however, they stimulated a demand for travel that had scarcely existed when people traveled by coach and sent their goods by common carrier. In 1845 about fifty million passenger journeys were made by rail. Thirty years later this total had risen to more than a billion, an increase of about twentyfold, and before the end of the century by a further 50 percent. On average every

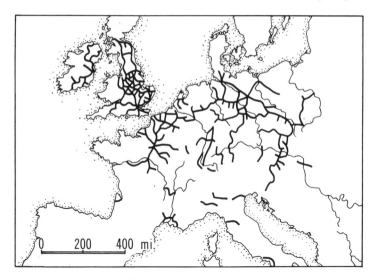

11.6. The European railroad net, 1850.

person living in 1900 could have made at least five journeys by rail. Of course, there were many in the peasant regions of the east and south to whom the railroad locomotive was still a dangerous monster. But even they were not immune in their daily lives to the consequences of the development of a railroad system. Thanks to its speed and the volume of freight that it could transport, local shortages had at last disappeared. Famine, at least in time of peace, was no longer thinkable. The supply of goods to shops and other retail outlets had become regular and predictable, so that storekeepers no longer felt obliged to accumulate an inventory against bad weather and infrequent deliveries. They could order goods from a catalogue in the certainty that they would be delivered within a few days, so much did the railroad companies pride themselves on their punctuality and reliability. Coal became in much of Europe one of the most considerable items of freight. In almost every city there came to be a dealer who was able to sell coal in small quantities to individual households. The savage specter of winter cold and the danger of hypothermia did not vanish overnight. There remained the large body of those who could not afford the cost of a bag of coal, but for most, winter had lost its sting.

The railroads not only distributed food, fuel, and consumer goods; they also carried mail and newspapers. Indeed, the newfound speed and intensity of communication was one of the most powerful factors in breaking down localisms of every kind. The middle years of the century saw the development, at least in western and central Europe, of a national press. The daily newspaper, brought by fast train from the capital, or at least from the chief regional center, began to appear on the breakfast table. And at about the same time the mail carrier might deliver letters that had been mailed in a distant part of the country as recently as the previous day. The speed with which news began to travel was a fact of immense private, as it was also of public, importance. It affected everyone, whether at the level of public affairs, of private business, or just of social communication. For good or ill, today's events in one corner of the land became tomorrow's news throughout the country. Of course, this revolutionary change was tied to two others: the spread of literacy and the cheapening of the medium by which the message was carried.

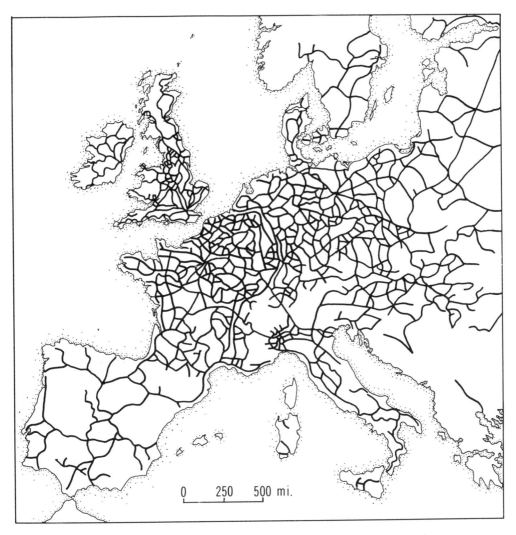

11.7. The European railroad net, 1880. By this date the basic network
was complete.

In most communities there had always been a few literate members, even though both
their reading skills and the volume of literature available to them were strictly limited. A
small literate class emerged first in the cities, where there existed both a need for literacy
in the conduct of business, and the schools where such a skill could be gained. From
towns in western and central Europe, literacy spread to rural areas and thence to the
peripheral regions of Europe. But at the end of the nineteenth century, the rural
population in much of eastern and southeastern Europe was still, by and large, illiterate,
their mental horizon restricted to their community and neighboring areas that they
could know at first hand.

Literacy is extraordinarily difficult to measure because it exists at widely differing
levels. The ability to read fluently and the possession of a wide vocabulary are very far

from widespread even today. A high proportion of the population, especially in much of eastern and southern Europe, still read slowly and possess only a limited vocabulary. The chapbooks, which provided much of the reading matter in the eighteenth and early nineteenth centuries, were very undemanding, and those who read them to an admiring group of friends and neighbors would have been unable to cope with literature in any more refined sense. At the bottom of the scale of literacy were those who signed their names in a shaky but legible hand. This ability can by no means be taken to imply that they could read even the simple text of a chapbook. The early newspapers, it should be added, were published for those who were literate at a relatively high level and would probably have been understood by relatively few of those who absorbed the "literature" of the chapbook and shepherd's calendar.

The cost of communication was relatively high. That of mailing a letter in the early days of the postal system could have meant almost an hour's work for many people. And the cost of a daily newspaper, without the heavy subsidy provided today by advertising, was considerably higher. Most people, until late in the century, could not afford the luxury of literacy.

No less important in broadening people's mental horizons and increasing their awareness of other lands and marginally different cultures was the expansion of the means of personal travel. Coach travel had been both expensive and uncomfortable. Railway travel was cheap, and, whatever might be said of the smoke and soot belched from the inefficient locomotives, it was swifter and more comfortable. Among the merits claimed for the railroads that began to radiate from the greater European cities was their ability to take urban dwellers for a day's excursion into the peace and quiet of the countryside. But, such excursions aside, travel for pleasure was long restricted to the well-to-do. The mass of the population had neither the leisure nor the money for such extravagances. Nevertheless, the cult of the sea began to attract those who could afford the luxury of a holiday beside it. From the 1830s the French Riviera began to attract visitors, and Biarritz and the warm shores of Italy followed. At the same time inland resorts began to develop or to expand. The town of Spa in southern Belgium was their archetype. Baden Baden, Bad Ischl, Karlsbad, and Marienbad followed. The *bad* in their names suggested that bathing or taking the waters was an important element in their attraction. In fact, this feature was sometimes little more than a disguise for gambling and intrigue, which came to be their primary functions.

At the same time the increasing body of the middle class was in the later years of the century turning to its own less glamorous resorts. These were, by and large, coastal, and most lay within a few hours' journey of the populous and industrialized centers of northwest Europe. A week or two beside the cool, windy beaches of Le Touquet or Deauville, Brighton or Eastbourne or Sopot, waiting for the sun, which all too rarely shone, became the ambition of countless middle-class families. As a holiday week became institutionalized among the working classes during the present century, they too came to regard a week at the sea first as a luxury, then as a necessity. And with this new demand came the rows of hotels and boarding houses, from the sophisticated to the seamy, which arose to satisfy the varied tastes and demands of their new patrons. This cult of the summer holiday, restricted though it was to northwestern Europe, must be looked upon as a very significant improvement in material standards and probably also as a contribution of no small importance to public health and general well-being.

Chapter 12

CONCLUSION

Empiricism can culminate in a Ming vase; it can never culminate in a plastic cup.
> —A. Rupert Hall, *The Changing Technical Act*

. . . the most important discoveries and inventions . . . did not arise . . . out of some mystical inner drive of the Faustian soul: they were wind-blown seeds from other cultures.
> —Lewis Mumford, *Technics and Civilization*

Some eight thousand years separate us from those first European farmers who tilled the coastal plains of Greece, and it has been almost six thousand since agriculture began to be practiced along the Atlantic shores of Europe. A span of eight millennia from the time when sedentary agriculturalists first scratched the soil to this present age of great cities, intensive agriculture, and high technology surely demonstrates no mean rate of progress. That progress was at first very slow is obvious. It is no less clear that the rate of development was exponential, accelerating with the coming of metals and their spreading use in almost every branch of human activity. Today the rate of technological progress is almost frightening in its speed and complexity.[1]

There has been continuous growth in man's manipulative skills and in his ability to experiment and innovate. Discoveries and innovations, once made, have never been wholly lost. They may for a time have ceased to be practiced on any significant scale, as happened, for example, with the building crafts after the end of the Roman Empire in the west. But they were never forgotten and always they provided the foundations on which future advance rested.

The initial discoveries and innovations were brought into Europe from without. In the main they came from the eastern Mediterranean and the broad, indefinite region of the Middle East. They were the practices of cultivating the soil, of smelting and fabricating metals, and of living in large settled communities, which we call, for lack of a better name, "cities." Such innovations *could* have come from other hearths that had developed them before they appeared in Europe itself. The Indian subcontinent and China both developed in step with the Middle East and ahead of Europe. We can, however, be reasonably sure that little inspiration came from beyond the great barrier of the Sahara Desert in Africa and none from the unknown and inaccessible continents of Australasia and the New World.

It was the Middle East that continued for several millennia to inspire development and material progress in Europe. This was the fountain from which a stream of invention flowed toward the west. Even in the period of the Roman Empire it would be difficult to deny that in material terms the Levant was ahead of much of Europe, and that when that empire was partitioned under Diocletian, it was the Eastern Empire that seemed the richer, the more prosperous, and the more secure. How long, we may ask, did the east retain this material advantage? It was still rich enough in the twelfth century to attract the marauding Crusaders and to reward them with cultural ideas and artifacts to take back to the west. "Recent studies have shown," in the words of William Woodruff, "that between the third and the fifteenth centuries Chinese and Indian science and technology were more advanced than those of Europe."[2] Yet there was no further innovation and advance in this general region. Material conditions were not significantly different in the nine-teenth century, when Europeans first began to visit and to describe the region, from those encountered by the Crusaders seven centuries earlier. In the meantime, Europe had forged ahead. Material conditions had improved beyond all recognition. It was now Europe that gave its innovations to the Middle East.

Stuart Piggott drew a distinction of fundamental importance between what he called innovating and conserving societies, the former prepared to experiment and to adopt technological advances; the latter, once they had established a stable relationship with their environment, feeling no need for change.[3] Middle Eastern societies, at least within the historical period, must be said to belong to the latter. Their religion, which they adopted from the seventh century, was not one to encourage innovation. Indeed, with its insistence that this world was but a preparation for another, it might be said to have positively discouraged progress. Muslim societies were among those in which, in Ruth Benedict's words, "technology is unbelievably slighted even in those aspects of life which seem necessary to ensure survival."[4] Attitudes toward innovation and change can be greatly influenced by religious conviction. Both Islam, with its belief that material progress in this world was irrelevant to a more important life in the future, and Confucianism, which emphasized respect and obedience within a hierarchically orga-nized society, did nothing to encourage material advance. A social structure in which each individual was locked into a particular role in society, as in most forms of feudalism, also offered no scope for social mobility and did nothing to encourage innovation.

But such attitudes and structures are not permanent or immutable. They can decay within and be influenced from without. Western feudalism was itself a hierarchical structure, but even before it had fully evolved, it began to adapt to new, commercially oriented orders of society. And Christianity, for all its reverence for asceticism and its stress on this world as merely a prelude to the next, never showed itself to be particularly hostile to material advance in the former. The supreme example of an abrupt change from a static to a dynamic society was demonstrated in Japan after the Meiji Restoration in 1868. A submissive and structured society, such as that of Japan, may be resistant to innovation, but its inbuilt tendency to conform and to obey authority makes it easier for it to change when ordered or encouraged to do so from above. The revolution effected by

Kemal Atatürk in Turkey after the end of the caliphate in 1924 shows how attitudes can change fundamentally, even in Islam, over a short period of time, when the government wills that they should.

This, however, brings us no closer to an understanding of why in Europe, from the beginning of the age of metals, innovations followed one upon the other with, at times, an almost bewildering exuberance. Piggott's contrast between innovating and conserving societies was not conceived in the context presented above. He was referring to differences between cultures *within* Europe, where innovation was a highly localized phenomenon. The early farmers and metalworkers, the later textile industries, and the subsequent developments in engineering and chemistry each occupied only a very small area of the continent, and as late as the nineteenth century there were areas as little touched by modern innovation as the Middle East was at the same time.

In both the Middle East and in some degree also in China and India, a period of innovation came to an end more or less at a time when localized advance began in Europe. Piggott stressed that a conserving society had established "a satisfactory *modus vivendi* . . . within its natural surroundings [and] no urgent need [was] felt to alter the situation." But what if the natural surroundings themselves changed? Can it be argued that natural, environmental change shook people out of that lethargy which has been dignified as "conserving"? The extent of environmental change throughout the historical period is too apparent to need further emphasis here. The nature of late and postglacial changes is now beginning to be understood, and, with it, their significance for human development. The desert areas began to intensify, the great river valleys to develop their vast, alluvial floodplains, and their rivers to irrigate and fertilize them. These changes created opportunities as well as difficulties. A slight fluctuation in rainfall or in the moisture content of the soil could have profound implications in a marginal environment—and much of the Middle East and North Africa was marginal.[5] Adaptation in settlement, economy, and the material aspects of life was essential for the continued existence of society. This adjustment and readjustment to a changing physical environment could be achieved only by innovation, especially the adoption of agriculture and the practice of irrigation. An innovating society came into being and remained inventive until it had established a new and stable relationship with its environment.

It cannot be emphasized too strongly that material development of necessity took place later in Europe than in the Middle East, South Asia, and other hearths of human development. The reason was, of course, the glaciation that made much of the continent uninhabitable at a time when agriculture and the use of metals were being developed in the Middle East. Environmental changes parallel with those which elsewhere were driving people from the margins of expanding deserts into the river valleys could here have had little significance. But as the climate ameliorated and the ice retreated, population in Europe grew and spread and was receptive to the new technologies that had been devised in the Middle East. By and large, European societies were in varying degrees innovative. A stable relationship with the environment seems not to have been established, at least for prolonged periods, and out of this lack of adjustment, from the stimuli and the shortages that arose from it, sprang those technological innovations which collectively we call progress.

It would be a grave mistake to regard such progress as something that had to happen. It has already been emphasized that the very idea of progress is a modern one, and the thought that it has been in some way inevitable must be regarded as a conceit of the Victorians, notably Herbert Spencer. It has been suggested earlier that material progress is in some sense an accident, either a simple and unplanned happening, recognized as of value and repeated, or, more generally, a way out of a dilemma, itself the result of contingencies that were unexpected. The discovery of metals may exemplify the former; the development of animal rearing and cultivation, the latter. What, then, could have been the contingencies that from prehistoric times to the recent past have shaken western man out of his comfortable groove and have interrupted the stability of his relationship with his physical and social environment? On this we can only speculate. One thing, however, is certain: such contingencies must have been either external to man, part of his physical environment, or internal to human society, an aspect of his mental processes or social organization.

One factor making for instability must have been population growth and its relationship to the space that it could command. It is difficult to deny the significance of population increase in earlier times and its continued importance even today. Population pressure as an agent of change has never been restricted to the simple statistic of the number of people per unit of cultivable land. It has been reflected in shortages of timber for construction and fuel, of fibers for weaving, of fabric for clothing, of tools for cutting. And always the solution of one problem, as by a kind of dialectic, created others and led to scarcities in other fields. Material progress bred on itself and, beyond a certain point, acquired a kind of inevitability. Only in this restricted sense did there *have* to be material progress.

Related to the question of population pressure is that of secular change in the environment. The existence of such change cannot be disputed, but its influence is extremely difficult to assess, largely because the extent of these changes, except in the recent past, is not susceptible of measurement. Climatic fluctuations during the prehistoric period were of such amplitude that they must have influenced human ecology. Movements during the historic period have been of a much smaller magnitude, and their influence more questionable. Of course, year-to-year fluctuations occurred and affected the level of welfare at the time. But short-term crises passed, and a kind of normalcy always returned. What is questioned here are the possible consequences of long-term, cyclical change. Le Roy Ladurie, while admitting that such changes are, within limits, measurable, doubts whether they were of sufficient magnitude to have had any significant effect on ecological relationships.[6] Others have attributed major historical changes to climatic fluctuation.[7] There is no conclusion to this debate, but it may be doubted whether, in the *historical* period, climatic fluctuation can be dragged into the discussion as a *deus ex machina* to interpret the inexplicable.

On the other hand, changes that may be of marginal or even of no significance in the well-developed areas of western, central, and southern Europe, could have great importance on the geographical borders of European civilization. A drop of one degree Centigrade in the average temperature, or the shortening of the growing season by a few days, might, in Scandinavia, mean the difference between the success and failure of a crop. Again, a society might be so intimately adjusted to its environment—as, for example, among certain peoples who practiced a highly specialized form of irrigated agriculture—that a slight physical change might force them to innovate and modify their material culture or, alternatively, might bring about the disintegration of their society.

If we assume that the natural human inclination is to seek some form of stability, of equilibrium with the physical world, it seems that population growth and consequent shortages and scarcities have been the most likely sources of cultural change. Innovation is not a natural human pursuit; it is one to which mankind has resorted only with reluctance. Much has been written about the human tendency to speculate on the nature of things and on man's role in nature. But this is metaphysics and has nothing to do with innovation in material things. It may be that such speculation was most active when there was a degree of adjustment to the physical world and pressures from this direction were least.

If we discount changes in the physical environment, we are left with human fertility as the factor most likely to disrupt the precarious balance between the human species and its environment. Every major innovation had as its result, if not also its purpose, an increase in human control over physical things. The ironical fact is that this slowly tightening control extended not only to the soil, water supply, and metals but also to pathogens and their spread. As one disease after another came to be controlled by eliminating its vectors, a powerful restraint on population growth was removed. This situation led to an increasingly rapid expansion of population and increasing pressure on scarce resources, which in turn led to the need for further innovation and experiment. Thus the spiral of invention and discovery, chasing an ever-growing population, became a fact of life in nineteenth-century Europe and has since spread to the ends of the earth. Europe's ever-broadening search for markets and materials spelled an end to any stable relationship between the human species and its physical and biological environment.

Before we turn to the reception of European skills, technology, and material standards in the rest of the world, it would be well to look into that other set of factors influencing the equilibrium between the human species and its environment: the structure of human society itself.

The human species, apparently like most other members of the animal kingdom, does not welcome change. As a general rule it prefers a stable relationship with both its physical surroundings and with the society of which it is a part. If there must be change, then it is preferable that it should be part of a slow and continuous process, never abrupt or far-reaching. Folklore and history are filled with stories of the individual who intruded into a static social and economic system, sometimes tolerated, occasionally expelled, on rare occasions welcomed. A. J. Toynbee has made great play with the myth of the "revolutionary," the Promethean figure who brought a new fire to kindle the lagging spirits of mankind. Such people were imbued with what Toynbee, adapting a Chinese expression, called the spirit of *Yang*, the drive to experiment, innovate, and change, in the face of that of *Yin* which constrained people to make as little mental and physical effort as possible.[8]

This urge to innovate, to change, and to progress has been restrained in varying degrees by social structures and social pressures. The existence of an innovator calls for some degree of social mobility. Great wealth, power, or prestige is the reward for successful innovation, and there have been societies in which such upward pressures could not be tolerated. There have been others, more loosely structured, in which the individual endowed with energy, ability, and good fortune could progress. A loose social structure that permitted, even if it did not actually encourage, social mobility has been a precondition for innovation and material progress.

Among cultures that have generally been regarded as unprogressive and antipathetic to innovation are the feudal society of the West and those Oriental societies which found their cultural expression in Confucianism. The former contained the seeds of its own destruction. An intrusive commercial and urban class was present from the start and derived from the cultures of the classical world. Attempts to assimilate it to feudal society were, by and large, unsuccessful, and feudalism, with its hierarchical structure of social orders, slowly disintegrated. The other example of a stable society, that of China, proved more enduring, because its ideal of stability and harmony was enshrined in a social structure that emphasized status, respect, and discipline, and in the ethics of Confucianism.

At the opposite pole from the conserving society of China must be set the innovating society that emerged in the West from the breakdown of feudalism. The Marxist interprets this tableau in terms of Hegelian dialectics. The conflict between feudal and commercial society, abundantly exemplified in the problems faced by merchants in obtaining and then protecting their rights to do business, gave rise to a capitalist system. Capitalism fed upon experiment and innovation because these contributed to the productive process and thus to profitability. However strenuously resisted by some segments of society—the Luddite for example—innovation and material progress became a fact of life in western society.

The Periphery

A factor in the general improvement of the living standards of most Europeans in recent centuries has been their commercial relationship with the rest of the world. One of the themes developed in this book has been that fundamental innovations, which originated outside Europe, were elaborated and developed within Europe by societies that felt the need to overcome scarcities and constraints. In doing so, they evolved a highly technical material culture, capable, if properly managed, of supporting a very high standard of living. In the meantime, the rest of the world, in a multitude of different ways, had achieved some kind of equilibrium with its environment and felt little compulsion to innovate and "progress." There is no particular merit in "development," except insofar as it makes the human condition happier and more agreeable. Development, as understood in Europe, became a necessity because it was a means of coping with scarcity.

Europeans cannot be said to have impinged on the non-European world in any significant fashion before the age of the great discoveries in the sixteenth and seventeenth centuries.[9] They established no settlements, and commercial exchange was restricted to bullion and a few luxury commodities. Climbers may today ascend a mountain "because it is there," but this was not the reason why Columbus crossed the Atlantic or Vasco da Gama rounded the Cape and reached India. Both were in search of scarce commodities for which European peoples were experiencing a need, and they hoped, by going to the sources, to obtain them more cheaply and in greater abundance.

The great discoveries and the settlement and commerce that followed wrought a profound change. European peoples began to exploit their expanding periphery. Not only did they import commodities that they found to be useful or profitable. They stimulated their production. They created plantations and opened mines. They built the infrastructure—roads, railroads, docks, and shipping services—that was necessary for the development of trade. They moved people about in order to satisfy their need for labor, and they imposed taxes that could be discharged only by earning money from service to European enterprises. They used their newly acquired lands as a frontier, where part of their population, whether unwanted at home or not, could be settled. The expansionist policy of each country was shaped by the environment of the lands that it occupied and the needs and constraints of the home country. No two countries pursued identical or even similar policies, but they were unanimous in their pursuit of profit and security for themselves.

Overall, the periphery was exploited in order to remedy scarcities that had arisen, largely as a result of increasing population and the developing scale of manufacturing, in Europe itself. Industrial raw materials like cotton, wool, and jute, rubber and softwood timber; luxuries like coffee and tea; and necessities like the breadgrains, sugar, and meat were all produced for the European market, and their relative cheapness allowed them to be consumed in relative abundance. In this the Americas assumed a particular importance. The long separation of the New World from the Old meant that some quite different species had evolved in the former from those known in the latter. Some of these were of great food or industrial value and were furthermore capable of translation to Europe. The social consequences of the introduction of corn (maize) and of the potato have already been stressed. Tobacco, cacao, and rubber were also among New World imports to Europe.

The number of imperial powers that thus controlled the development and trade of the European periphery was small. In the first instance, there were only five: Portugal, Spain, France, Great Britain, and the Netherlands. To these were added late in the nineteenth century Germany, Italy, and Belgium, but by the time they arrived on the colonial scene the pickings had become somewhat lean. Other imperialists, like Denmark and Sweden, had no real significance, but Russia must be regarded as a colonial power in view of its occupation of Siberia, even though its leaders crossed no ocean in the process. The independence first of the United States and then of most of Latin America in no way diminished the role these countries were playing in the supply of foodstuffs and raw materials. Indeed, left to themselves, they exploited their resources more fully and poured ever-increasing volumes into the European market.

These imports from the periphery did not go unrequited. They were paid for by the export of commodities, almost exclusively manufactured, and the peripheral market came to be of immense importance as a marginal consumer of the products of European industry. Many a European manufacturer was kept in business in the nineteenth century only because a significant part of his product was taken by the colonies.[10] To some extent this was a managed trade, controlled by the imperial power in its own interests. Insofar as it was able, it eliminated competition for its exports within its dependent territories.[11] Independent countries, first and foremost the United States and China, were not susceptible to this kind of influence, but were nonetheless important trading partners. The first break in this system of monopolization by colonial powers did not come until 1885, when, by the Congo Act, the trade of the Belgian Congo was opened to the commerce of nations without discrimination. Gradually the favored relationship between imperial power and colony was reduced. It ceased to exist as soon as dependent territories gained independence: the United States from 1783, Canada from 1867, Australia from 1901, and so on, until today the dependent empires have almost vanished.

Investment and Welfare

In these ways the European peoples paid for their imports from the non-European world. In fact, many of them shipped out far more goods than were necessary to pay for current imports, and the difference was invested in the overseas territories. The scale and range of this investment were immense.[12] It ranged from railroad and dock construction to the building of schools and the laying of water-supply and sewage systems. The greater part went, without question, into large-scale, capital-intensive projects related to the economic development of the territories in question. During the later nineteenth century, the most demanding of these undertakings was the construction of a network of communication and transportation: roads, bridges, railroads, and docks. This system aided the export of goods and had the further advantage that it consumed the products of European industry and provided work for its laboring masses. In fact, the building of overseas railroads began at about the time when the European net was nearing completion.

Yet the export of European capital and expertise was restricted both in its sources within Europe and in the countries in which it was invested. It came from a very limited area of the continent. No more than six countries supplied together more than 90 percent of the total foreign investments of European nations.[13] Part of this total was, of course, invested in other countries within Europe, but a significant part went overseas. There is no record of Europe's outflow of capital. In 1914 known investments amounted to almost forty billion dollars, and the total may have been greatly in excess of this. Nor is it possible to say how this immense sum was divided among the infrastructures of commerce, manufacturing, and such projects as water supply and education. But there can have been few countries that did not themselves benefit directly from this investment. At the least, western expenditure on medicine, public health, and education must have had a profoundly beneficial effect on the indigenous population.

Apart from Russia's modest investment in Siberia and Central Asia before 1914, eastern and southeastern Europe made no contribution to extra-European trade and received little from the rest of the continent. Investment was least in Australasia but was for the rest divided not unequally among the continents.

In any consideration of the export of European material culture, it is important to recognize the fact that almost the whole of the land surface of the globe has for some period in its recent past been tributary to one European country or another. Some territories broke free from this tutelage before others were occupied, but if we can regard Central Asia and Siberia as "colonies" of Russia, and if we disregard Antarctica, we are left with only China, Korea, Japan, Thailand, Iran, and Liberia which have never in any formal sense been colonies. And even these countries in varying degrees received investments of European capital and expertise.

It is convenient to divide this non-European world into those territories in which European peoples settled in significant numbers and made permanent homes, and those in which they were merely birds of passage, coming to develop resources, to carry on trade, to bring some form of education, religious belief, or medical services, and then, in most instances, to return whence they came. The French, with their fine feeling for *le mot juste,* have termed these two categories *colonies de peuplement* and *colonies d'exploitation.* As a general rule, the former territories had no dense native population. There was little or no resistance to European settlement, and by and large a material culture evolved that owed almost everything to its European origins and example. The United States and Canada, Australia and New Zealand belong without question to this category. In all of them European styles of building, methods of cultivating crops, and modes of laying out cities prevailed from the first, modified only by the physical conditions and materials found locally. The log construction of North America derives directly from European example, and in most other respects the material equipment of life remains, with little modification, that of Europe.

These territories of European settlement had a very great physical advantage over other regions that Europeans came to dominate. Their climates were not wholly European, but they were not so different that they were difficult or unacceptable. "In most cases," Carl Sauer wrote of North America, "the colonists were at no loss to identify the native plants and animals which they found. . . . It would be impossible, indeed, to cross an ocean anywhere else and find so little that is unfamiliar in nature on the opposite side. In all the lands of earliest colonization . . . flora and fauna were closely related to those in the European homeland and indicated to the settlers that they were still under familiar skies and seasons." In only one respect was the physical contrast more strongly marked: in its climate. "This [North America] was indeed a lustier land to which the settlers had come, a land of hotter summers and colder winters, of brighter and hotter sun and more tempestuous rain, a land suited to and provided with a greater variety of vegetation than the homelands of Europe."[14]

But there were areas of the world where the climates were a great deal less friendly to Europeans than those of North America. Much of Africa and of South and Southeast Asia, and parts of Central and South America were hostile to European man in more ways than one. There were areas too dry for human settlement, and others so hot and humid that a profuse flora and fauna almost crowded mankind from the scene. Such lands held abundant resources in their rocks and soils, but, by and large, Europeans excused themselves from the hardships of developing them. Furthermore, *some* of these areas, notably South and Southeast Asia and parts of intertropical Africa, were already densely populated by peoples who had become in some degree climatically acculturated and had acquired a degree of immunity to their indigenous diseases. Europeans could settle among them and carry on fieldwork only with considerable difficulty. The fierce climates harbored pathogens that by and large were unknown in the cooler and more equable climate of Europe. McNeill has spoken of the "disease pool" of Africa, from which in recent times many tropical diseases have been spread.[15] India was no less prolific in this respect, so that it might be said that large-scale European settlement in the tropics was prohibited to Europeans who had not acquired an immunity to their diseases.

Such were the *colonies d'exploitation,* where a European elite directed and supervised the labor of the local peoples—laid out plantations, opened mines, and developed the infrastructure of commerce. The colonial policies of the European powers were immensely varied. There was a world of difference between "indirect rule" in British Nigeria and the "culture system" in the Dutch East Indies. But, however implemented, these policies had in common the desire to maximize the production of scarce commodities and to transmit them in increasing quantities to European markets.

It is not possible, however, to differentiate sharply between the two types of overseas dependency. There were parts of the tropical world where altitude reduced the temperature and humidity, producing physical conditions as conducive to European living as they were to agricultural production. Among them were the plateau that makes up much of southern Africa and the belt of highlands that lies across the equator in East Africa. In Central and South America, there were comparable upland regions in Mexico, Brazil, and throughout the Andean region. In each of these areas there was, when Europeans first came, a native population of some size, already cultivating the soil and living in villages and even urban settlements. The European newcomers here imposed themselves as a landowning and ruling elite on the local populace. A plural society evolved, with two or even more social and economic strata, polarized by racial origins. Europeans' policies toward the indigenous peoples were susceptible of immense variation, from one of rigid separation in South Africa to that of merging the two cultures to produce a *mestizo* population in Mexico and Peru.

The modes of European occupation and settlement in non-European territories influenced greatly the latter's receptivity to European culture, both material and spiritual. In those areas in which Europeans made their homes in significant numbers, there was never any question that material culture was going to be European, modified in only a minor degree to suit the local environment. By and large, such territories kept pace with developments in Europe. In some respects they were even in advance of them, since the greater space available removed some of the restraints on urban development that had been present in Europe. Europe, for example, never really exported the tenement block or the urban courts of western industrial cities on any significant scale. Nor were water supply and sewage disposal problems of quite such moment as in the more crowded lands of Europe.

Of course, such regions of European settlement were, at least before the present century, the recipients of massive European investment. The earliest railroad systems were fabricated in Europe, many of the early factories were equipped from Europe, and even agricultural tools were imported. But in the course of time—in some instances a very short period of time—these dependent territories acquired the skills to manufacture their basic necessities themselves. But the new countries were of vaster extent than any European country. It was possible for communities to become "lost," hidden amid their mountains and forests, and immune to subsequent developments in culture, until "discovered" in more recent times.[16] There are commonly more cultural anachronisms to be found in the "new" countries than in the "old," and their cultural spectrum is broader than in Europe.

In those territories where Europeans made no permanent settlements, where they came to do a job, to earn a pension, and retire to more congenial climes, the acceptance of "Western" material standards was less general and predictable. The indigenous peoples had over several millennia built up a material culture of their own and had established a more or less stable relationship to their environment. The supreme example of such stability was China, where the "farmers of forty centuries"[17] had created so intimate a relationship that no change was desirable or even possible without perhaps disastrous consequences for the precarious balance of the environment.

China is, indeed, a special case, an instance of population growth without development, at least before recent times. It appears to have lacked the pressures and scarcities that would have prompted innovation. The Chinese population is said to have increased about sixfold between the fourteenth and the nineteenth centuries, a far greater rate of growth than was to be found in the West at this time. And yet technology throughout this period has been described as stagnant. "When changes took place at all, they occurred over such a long period that even a sensitive contemporary observer might fail to notice them."[18] Increased demand for food was not matched by any improvement in the tools and methods of agriculture; "on the North China Plain, most tools used in the twentieth century were well known as early as the Northern Wei Dynasty [fifth century A.D.] and perhaps the Han [ended in third century A.D.]. What is perhaps somewhat more surprising is that there is little evidence of change in the implements used anywhere in China, at least after the fourteenth century."[19] The paradox is difficult to resolve. Granted that society was ultraconservative and innovation was contrary to the prevailing Confucian ethic, but how could it have survived? Perkins has claimed that existing technologies were pressed to their extreme, so that no advance was possible beyond the level reached in the nineteenth century "without a major technological breakthrough."[20] And that would have been inconceivable without the import of Western science.

China had two advantages that together allowed it to coast along for two thousand years of increasing population without any significant innovation. The first was space. From its hearth in southeast China, population migrated westward to Yunnan and Szechwan and northward into the upper Hwang Ho basin and Manchuria. The other was genetic change in the character of rice and, to a less significant degree, of other cereal crops. It was noted above that the mere fact of choosing seed for planting is an unconscious method of genetic selection. This happened in China, and the improved strains must have been cultivated increasingly and over an ever-widening area. The most important genetic change was the mutation that produced a quicker-ripening rice. The result was similar to the production of fast-growing, drought-resistant strains of wheat in North America, except that the latter arose from the deliberate and conscious efforts of plant breeders. The use of a quick-maturing rice permitted double cropping in the south and the advance of rice growing along its northern frontiers of cultivation. Add to these two factors a more intensive but still traditional use of labor and the careful husbanding of human and animal waste to serve as fertilizer, and we have the circumstances that permitted Chinese society the luxury of its technological conservatism supported by its Confucian philosophy.

Nevertheless, a point was reached, even in China, at which an ever-increasing population could not be supported without technological change. China has, during the present century, accepted—to all appearances unwittingly—the science and technology of the West. At the same time the Chinese have tried—by and large successfully—to restrict the further growth in population. This latter step was unquestionably facilitated by the hierarchical and authoritarian structure of Chinese society, in which obedience was almost a way of life.

Japan faced similar problems to those of China in the nineteenth century: a growing population and a traditional and, compared with the West, backward technology. Added to this was an awareness of the aims of western imperialism and a fear that this might destroy the indigenous culture of Japan. The result was the Meiji Restoration (1868) and the opening up of Japan to Western technology. The Japanese became the most successful of non-European peoples in adopting the science, technology, and material standards that had been developed in the West. Their success appears to have been due to the fact that this social and economic revolution was made to look like a return to ancestral values. The abolition of the Shogunate and the restoration to power of the Japanese emperor symbolized the new and at the same time traditional leadership, while the discipline of this highly structured society ensured that it would follow wherever its new leaders took it.

Nowhere else among non-Western societies was Western culture, even extending to Western music, accepted so readily and so successfully. Elsewhere, elements of Western technology, notably its transportation and communication systems, have been adopted, and, more slowly, Western manufacturing systems and standards of medicine and hygiene.

It has been emphasized that the development of modern material and technical standards was accompanied in the Western world by a decline in the death rate. This was followed within a relatively short period of time by a fall in the birthrate. The total increase in population in the whole Western world was of the order of 100 percent during the period of rapid industrial growth, at the end of which a kind of stability was again achieved. In the non-Western world the adoption of Western standards of health and hygiene, halting and incomplete though it was, cut the death rate drastically. The extent of the drop in mortality (and also in morbidity) varied greatly from one country to another. In some, mortality was cut from about thirty per thousand of population in a year to less than twenty.

This decline in the death rate was achieved over a period of a decade or two, much too rapidly for there to have been any social adaptation or response to it. In Europe and in those countries which derived their population and material standards from Europe, the corresponding change had been very slow. Society was innovative and fluid, and social attitudes were able to adapt to the threat of increasing population by a lowered human fertility. Not so in the non-Western world. Here the rapidity of the change and the relative inflexibility of social structures and attitudes have prevented any comparable adaptation. The result has been that in much of the non-Western world, population growth threatens to outstrip the production of food and consumer goods. Of course, the latter has increased with the introduction of Western agricultural techniques and methods of manufacture, but not everywhere on a scale sufficient to keep abreast of the rapidly growing population.

The lesson of this history is that the introduction and slow diffusion of Western methods of production, of hygiene, and of medicine is not enough. It has to be accompanied by a change in social attitudes, by the encouragement of innovation, and by the abandonment of the biblical injunction, common to most of the non-Western world, to "be fruitful and multiply." It is to their immense credit that Japan and then China have accepted this condition of material progress. In India a similar injunction by the government has, by and large, gone unheeded, and in black Africa the spectacle of population growth with no commensurate advance in technology, is frightening in its scale. Unless the rest of the developing world adopts policies broadly similar to those of China and Japan, the spiral of population growth and lagging food production will be on a scale that would have dismayed Thomas Malthus.

ABBREVIATIONS

A.A.A.G.	*Annals of the Association of American Geographers* (Washington, D.C.)
A.A.G. Bij.	Afdeling Agrarische Geschiedenis Bijdragen (Wageningen, Netherlands)
Acad. Roy. Belg.	Académie Royale de Belgique (Brussels)
Accts. & Pap.	Accounts and Papers, HMSO (London)
Ag. Hist. Rv.	*Agricultural History Review* (Reading)
Am. Hist. Rv.	*American Historical Review* (Bloomington, Ind.)
Ann. Dem. Hist.	*Annales de Démographie Historique* (Paris)
Ann. E.S.C.	*Annales: Economies—Societies—Civilisations* (Paris)
Ann. Midi	*Annales du Midi* (Toulouse)
Ant.	*Antiquity* (Newbury)
Ant. Class.	*L'Antiquité Classique* (Louvain)
Arch.	*Archaeologia* (London)
B.A.R. Suppl. Ser.	British Archaeological Reports, Supplementary Series (Oxford)
Bibl. Ec. Ch.	Bibliothèque de l'Ecole des Chartes (Paris)
Bibl. Rev.	*Bibliothèque de la Revolution de 1848* (Paris)
Bull. Phil. Hist.	*Bulletin Philologique et Historique de la Comité des Travaux Historiques et Scientifiques* (Paris)
Bus. Hist.	*Business History* (Liverpool)
Cah. Hist. Mond.	*Cahiers d'Histoire Mondiale* (Paris)
Cal. Cl. R.	Calendar of Close Rolls, HMSO (London)
Cal. Pat. R.	Calendar of Patent Rolls, HMSO (London)
C.B.A. Res. Repts.	Council for British Archaeology, Research Reports (London)
Chât. Gaill.	Château Gaillard (Caen)
Ec. H.R.	*Economic History Review* (Cambridge)
Econ.	*Economica* (London)
E.E.T.S.	Early English Text Society (London)
E.H.E.S.S.	Ecole des Hautes Etudes en Sciences Sociales (Paris)
E.H.R.	*English Historical Review* (London)
Eth. Slav.	*Ethnologia Slavica* (Bratislava)
Geog.	*Geography* (London)
G.J.	*Geographical Journal* (London)
G.R.	*Greece and Rome* (Oxford)
H.M.S.O.	Her [His] Majesty's Stationery Office (London)
Inst. Urb. Arch.	Instytut Urbanistyki i Architectury (Warsaw)
Jb. Ges. Volksw.	*Jahrbuch für Gesetzgebung, Verwaltung und Volkswirtschaft im deutschen Reich* (Leipzig)
Jl. Bus. Hist.	*Journal of Business History*
Jl. Hist. Med. All. Sci.	*Journal of the History of Medicine and Allied Sciences* (Minneapolis)
Jl. Intdis. Hist.	*Journal of Interdisciplinary History* (Cambridge, Mass.)
Jl. Pol. Econ.	*Journal of Political Economy* (Chicago)
Jl. Roy. Inst. Cornw.	*Journal of the Royal Institute of Cornwall* (Truro)
Jl. Transp. Hist.	*Journal of Transport History* (Leicester)
K.H.K.M.	*Kwartalnik Historii Kultury Materialnej* (Warsaw)

Linc. Rec. Soc.	Lincolnshire Record Society (Lincoln)
L.P.S.	*Local Population Studies* (Nottingham)
L.R.S.	London Record Society (London)
Med. Arch.	*Medieval Archaeology* (London)
Mid. Hist.	*Midland History* (Birmingham)
P. & P.	*Past and Present* (London)
Pat. Lat.	Patrologia Latina, ed. Migne
P.P.S.	*Proceedings of the Prehistoric Society* (London)
Proc. Am. Phil. Soc.	*Proceedings of the American Philosophical Society* (Philadelphia)
Prof. Geog.	*Professional Geographer* (Washington, D.C.)
Quell. Forsch. Aggesch.	Quellen und Forschungen zur Agrargeschichte (Stuttgart)
Rec. Hist.	Recueil des Historiens des Gaules et de la France (Paris)
Rv. Hist. Mod. Cont.	*Revue d'Histoire Moderne et Contemporaine* (Paris)
Rv. Midi	*Revue du Midi* (Toulouse)
Rv. Nord	*Revue du Nord* (Lille)
Sc. Ec. Hist. Rv.	*Scandinavian Economic History Review* (Stockholm)
Schr. Ver. Sozp.	*Schriften des Vereins für Sozialpolitik* (Berlin)
Sci. Am.	*Scientific American* (New York)
Spec.	*Speculum* (Boston)
Tid. Kon. Ned. Aards.	*Tijdschrift van het Koninklijk Nederlandsch Aardrijkskundig Genootschap* (Amsterdam)
Tr. I.B.G.	*Transactions, Institute of British Geography*
Tr. Lancs. Ches. Ant. Soc.	*Transactions of the Lancanshire and Cheshire Antiquarian Society*
Tr. Roy. Soc. Trop. Med.	*Transactions of the Royal Society for Tropical Medicine* (London)
V.S.W.	*Vierteljahrschrift für Sozial- und Wirtschaftsgeschichte* (Leipzig)
Zt. Ges. Staatsw.	*Zeitschrift für die Gesamte Staatswissenschaft* (Tübingen)
Zt. Stadtgesch.	*Zeitschrift für Stadtgeschichte, Stadtsoziologie und Denkmalpflege* (Stuttgart)

NOTES

1. PROLEGOMENON

1. Robert Muchembled, *Culture populaire et culture des élites dans la France moderne (XVe–XVIIIe siècles)* (Paris, 1978).

2. *Vision of Piers Plowman*, C Text, IX, 347–50.

3. E. Le Roy Ladurie, *Montaillou: Cathars and Catholics in a French Village* (London, 1978).

4. Joseph W. Goering, "The Changing Face of the Village Parish," in *Pathways to Medieval Peasants*, ed. J. A. Raftis (Toronto, 1981), 323–33.

5. Muchembled, *Culture populaire,* 117.

6. Ibid., 124; Carolly Erickson, *The Medieval Vision: Essays in History and Perception* (New York, 1976).

7. Mikhail Baktin, *Rabelais and His World,* trans. H. Iswolsky (Cambridge, Mass., 1968); Natalie Zemon Davis, "The Reason of Misrule," in *Society and Culture in Early Modern France* (London, 1975), 97–123; Peter Burke, *Popular Culture in Early Modern Europe* (London, 1978); Heinz Biehn, *Feste und Feiern in alten Europa* (Munich, 1964).

8. W. M. McGovern, *From Luther to Hitler* (London, 1946), 31.

9. A. C. Swinburne, *Hymn to Proserpine.*

10. John Bossy, "The Counter-Reformation and the People of Catholic Europe," *P. & P.* 47 (1970): 51–70; James Obelkevich, ed., *Religion and the People, 800–1700* (Chapel Hill, 1979).

11. H. R. Trevor-Roper, "The European Witch-craze of the Sixteenth and Seventeenth Centuries," in id., *Religion, the Reformation and Social Change* (London, 1967), 90–192; R. Muchembled, "The Witches of the Cambresis," in Obelkevich, *Religion and the People,* 221–76.

12. Elizabeth L. Eisenstein, *The Printing Press as an Agent of Change* (Cambridge, 1979); id., *The Printing Revolution in Early Modern Europe* (Cambridge, 1983); N. Z. Davis, "Printing and the People," in *Society and Culture in Early Modern France,* 189–226.

13. P. Chaunu, "Sur la fin des sorciers au XVIIe siècle," *Ann. E. S. C.* 24 (1969): 895–911.

14. For a conscious revival of folk customs, see R. W. Ambler, "The Transformation of Harvest Celebrations in Nineteenth Century Lincolnshire," *Mid. Hist.* 3 (1976): 298–306.

2. REVOLUTION AND DIFFUSION IN PREHISTORIC EUROPE

1. Henry de Lumley, "A Paleolithic Camp at Nice," *Sci. Am.,* May 1967.

2. Jaquetta and Christopher Hawkes, *Prehistoric Britain* (Harmondsworth, 1943), 117–18.

3. J. B. Bury, *The Idea of Progress* (London, 1932), 1–36.

4. J. G. D. Clark, *Prehistoric Europe* (London, 1952), 16.

5. Mark N. Cohen, *The Food Crisis in Prehistory* (New Haven, 1977); Karl W. Butzer, *Environment and Archaeology: An Ecological Approach to Prehistory* (London, 1972).

6. Frederick E. Zeuner, *A History of Domesticated Animals* (London, 1963).

7. E. S. Higgs and M. R. Jarman, "The Origins of Agriculture: A Reconstruction," *Ant.* 43 (1969): 31–41.

8. Barbara Bender, *Farming in Prehistory* (London, 1975); *The Domestication and Exploitation of Plants and Animals,* ed. P. J. Ucko and G. W. Dimbleby (London, 1969), esp. 47–66; *Early European Agriculture: Its Foundations and Development,* ed. M. R. Jarman, G. N. Bailey, and N. N. Jarman (Cambridge, 1982).

9. J. Wilke, R. Bettinger, T. F. King and J. F. O'Connell, "Harvest Selection and Domestication in Seed Plants," *Ant.* 46 (1972): 203–209.

10. Jarman, Bailey, and Jarman, *Early European Agriculture*, 18.

11. Ibid., 19.

12. Robert J. Braidwood, "The Agricultural Revolution," *Sci. Am.*, Sept. 1960.

13. H. T. Waterbolk, "Food Production in Prehistoric Europe," *Science* 162 (1968): 1093–1102.

14. Colin Renfrew, "The Social Archaeology of Megalithic Monuments," *Sci. Am.*, Nov. 1983.

15. Graham Clark, "Farmers and Forests in Neolithic Europe," *Ant.* 19 (1945): 57–71.

16. Stuart Piggott, *Ancient Europe* (Edinburgh, 1965), 40.

17. Sir Lindsay Scott, "Pottery," in *A History of Technology*, ed. Charles Singer et al., 1:376–412 (Oxford, 1954).

18. Piggott, *Ancient Europe*, 53–55.

19. Patricia Phillips, *The Prehistory of Europe* (Bloomington, Ind., 1980), 228–64.

20. R. J. Forbes, *Studies in Ancient Technology* (Leiden, 1963), 7:115.

21. R. Maddin, J. D. Muhly, and T. S. Wheeler, "How the Iron Age Began," *Sci. Am.*, Oct. 1977.

22. T. A. Rickard, *Man and Metals* (New York, 1932), 2:832.

23. *An Essay Upon Various Arts by Theophilus*, trans. Robert Hendrie (London, 1847), Bk. 3, 223.

24. *Odyssey*, trans. E. V. Rieu (Harmondsworth, 1946).

25. V. Gordon Childe, *Ancient Dwellings at Skara Brae, Orkney* (London, H.M.S.O., 1950).

26. R. R. Schmidt, *Jungsteinzeit-Siedlungen in Federseemoor* (Stuttgart, 1930).

27. Konrad Jazdzewski, *Poland* (London, 1965), 122–23.

28. P. K. Baillie Reynolds, *Chysauster* (London, H.M.S.O., 1960).

29. G. Bersu, "Excavations at Little Woodbury, Wiltshire," *P.P.S.* 5, part 2 (1940): 30–111.

30. Clark, *Prehistoric Europe*, 146–49.

31. John Collis, *Oppida: Earliest Towns North of the Alps* (Sheffield, 1984).

32. Stuart Piggott, "Early Towns in Europe?" in *The Origins of Civilization: Wolfson College Lectures, 1978* (Oxford, 1979), 34–53.

33. H. Schutz, *The Prehistory of Germanic Europe* (New Haven, 1983), 250ff.

34. Barry Cunliffe, "Hill-forts and Oppida in Britain," in *Problems in Economic and Social Archaeology*, ed. G. de G. Sieveking, I. H. Longworth, and K. E. Wilson, 343–58 (London, 1976); id., "The Origins of Urbanisation in Britain," in *The Beginnings of Urbanisation in Barbarian Europe*, B.A.R. Suppl. Ser., 11 (Oxford, 1976), 135–61.

35. Eva Pretres, "The Late Pre-Roman Age in Hungary with Special Reference to Oppida," in *The Beginnings of Urbanisation*, B.A.R. Suppl. Ser., 11 (Oxford, 1976), 51–80.

36. Barry Cunliffe, "Aspects of Urbanisation in Northern Europe," in *Roman Urban Topography in Britain and the Western Empire*, ed. F. Grew and B. Hobley, 1–5, C.B.A. Res. Repts., 59 (London, 1985).

3. THE CLASSICAL FOUNDATIONS OF WESTERN CULTURE

1. *The Letters of Cassiodorus*, ed. Thomas Hodgkin (London, 1886), nos. 8, 31.

2. Aristotle, *Politics*, I, ii.

3. Strabo, *Geography*, III, 2, 15.

4. C. Müller, *Geographi Graeci Minores* (Paris, 1882), I, cap. 23.

5. J. G. Frazer, *Pausanias' Description of Greece* (London, 1898).

6. G. Downey, "Libanius' Oration in Praise of Antioch (Oration XI)," *Proc. Am. Phil. Soc.* 103 (1959): 652–86.

7. Aristotle, *Politics*, I, ii.

8. N. J. G. Pounds, "The First Megalopolis," *Prof. Geog.* 17 (1965): 1–5.

9. Strabo, *Geography*, VIII, 8, 1.

10. Pausanias, VIII, 23, 1.

11. Xenophon, *Cyropaedia*, VIII, ii, 5.

12. A. W. Gomme, *The Population of Ancient Athens* (Oxford, 1933), 47.

13. Demosthenes, *Olynthiac,* III, 25.

14. Pseudo-Dicaearchus, caps. 2–4.

15. Xenophon, *Hellenica,* V, iii, 16.

16. Ramsay MacMullen, "Barbarian Enclaves in the Northern Roman Empire," *Ant. Class.* 32 (1963): 552–61; id., *Enemies of the Roman Order* (Cambridge, Mass., 1966).

17. St. Jerome, *Pat. Lat.,* XXXVI, col. 382.

18. O. G. S. Crawford, "Our Debt to Rome," *Ant.* 2 (1928): 173–88.

19. H. J. Eggers, *Der Romische Import im freien Germanien* (Hamburg, 1951); Sir Mortimer Wheeler, *Rome beyond the Imperial Territories* (London, 1954), 63–90.

20. A. Boethius, "Roman and Greek Town Architecture," *Göteborgs Hogskolas Arsskrift* 14, no. 3 (1948).

21. Juvenal, *Satires,* I, 3, ll. 190–98.

22. Cicero, *Ad Atticum,* XIV, ix, 1.

23. Giantilippo Carettoni, Antonio M. Colini, Lucos Cozza, and Guglielmo Gatti, *La Pianta Marmorea di Roma Antica: Forma Urbis Romae* (Rome, 1960).

24. Sir Mortimer Wheeler, *Roman Art and Architecture* (Oxford, 1964), 12.

25. Amedeo Maiuri, *Herculaneum* (Rome, 1962).

26. G. Calza and G. Becatti, *Ostia* (Rome, 1965), 16–20.

27. G. C. Boon, *Roman Silchester* (London, 1957).

28. Frontinus, *De Aquis urbis Romanae,* I, xi, 16.

29. Aristophanes, *Acharnians,* ll. 33–36.

30. A. H. M. Jones, *The Later Roman Empire, 284–602* (Oxford, 1964), 2:712.

31. A. J. Toynbee, *Hannibal's Legacy* (London, 1965), 2:247–52.

32. Vergil, *Eclogues,* II, 66; *Georgics,* I, 169–75.

33. Pliny, *Natural History,* XVIII, xlviii, 171–73.

34. Jane M. Renfrew, *Paleoethnobotany* (New York, 1973), 81.

35. Pliny, *Natural History,* XVIII, xiv, 74.

36. Hans Helbaek, "Early Crops in Southern England," *P.P.S.* 18 (1952): 194–233; S. Applebaum, "Roman Britain," in *The Agrarian History of England and Wales,* vol. 1, Part 2 (Cambridge, 1972).

37. Menander, *The Arbitrants,* ll. 25–30.

38. Silius Italicus, *Punica,* VII, 364–66.

39. Aristophanes, *Acharnians,* ll. 994–98.

40. Tacitus, *Germania,* cap. 28.

41. Ibid., XLVI.

42. Oliver Davies, *Roman Mines* (Oxford, 1935); E. Ardaillon, *Les mines de Laurion* (Paris, 1897).

43. Varro, *Rerum rusticarum libri III,* I, xvi, 4.

44. Pausanias, III, xii, 10.

45. R. J. Forbes, *Studies in Ancient Technology* (Leiden, 1964), 8:94ff.

46. Ibid., 96.

47. Cyril Aldred, "Furniture: To the End of the Roman Empire," in *A History of Technology* (Oxford, 1956), 2:221–58.

48. Giselda M. A. Richter, *Ancient Furniture* (Oxford, 1926).

4. THE COMMUNITY OF THE VILLAGE

1. H. J. Keuning, "L'habitat rural aux Pays Bas," *Tid. Kon. Ned. Aards* 55:644–45.

2. Jean Brunhes, *Human Geography* (London, 1952), 186–94.

3. August Meitzen, *Siedlung und Agrarwesen des Westgermanen und Ostgermanen, der Kelten, Romer, Finnen und Slaven* (Berlin, 1895).

4. Harry Thorpe, "The Influence of Enclosure on the Form and Pattern of Rural Settlement in Denmark," *Tr. I.B.G.* 17 (1951): 111–29.

5. J. Ward Perkins, "Etruscan Towns, Roman Roads and Medieval Villages: The Historical Geography of Southern Etruria," *G.J.* 128 (1962): 389–405.

6. Procopius, *Histories,* IV, iii, 27–29.

7. *The Chronicle of the Slavs,* ed. F. J. Tschan (New York, 1935).

8. Gheorghe Anghel, "Typologie des églises fortifiées de Roumanie," *Chât. Gaill.* 9–10 (1982): 13–33; E. G. Sebastian, "German Fortified Churches in Transylvania," *Ant.* 6 (1932): 301–306.

9. *The Chronicle of Jean de Venette,* trans. J. Birdsall (New York, 1953), 85; also *Annales Gandenses,* ed. H. Johnstone (London, 1951), 5, 55.

10. J. Emerson Tennent, *Belgium* (London, 1842), 1:129.

11. Catherine E. Boyd, *Tithes and Parishes in Medieval Italy* (Ithaca, N.Y., 1952).

12. Philip E. Mosely, "The Distribution of the Zadruga within Southeastern Europe," *The Joshua Starr Memorial Volume, Jewish Social Studies* 5 (1953): 219–30; also Georg Tschemschiroff, "Die bulgarische Hauskommunion," *Jb. Ges. Volksw.* 61, pt. 1 (1937): 181–220; E. A. Hammel, "The Zadruga as Process," in *Household and Family in Past Time,* ed. P. Laslett, 335–73 (Cambridge 1972).

13. S. E. West, "The Anglo-Saxon Village of West Stow: an Interim Report of the Excavations 1965–8," *Med. Arch.* 13 (1969): 1–20.

14. J. M. Houston, *A Social Geography of Europe* (London, 1953), 80–107.

15. *Cambridge Economic History of Europe,* 2d ed. (Cambridge, 1966), 1:462–63.

16. Paul Teleki, *The Evolution of Hungary and Its Place in History* (New York, 1923), 54–87.

17. J. M. Houston, *The Western Mediterranean World* (London, 1964), 240–50.

18. Jovan Cvijič, *La Péninsule Balkanique* (Paris, 1918), 215–24.

19. Bruce McGowan *Economic Life in Ottoman Europe* (Cambridge, 1981), 121–70.

20. Gerald Brennan, *Spanish Labyrinth* (Cambridge, 1943).

21. A. N. J. den Hollander, *Nederzettingsvormen en -problemen in de Groote Hongarsche Laag-vlakke* (Amsterdam, 1947).

22. Jerome Blum, *The End of the Old Order in Rural Europe* (Princeton, 1978).

23. W. O. Ault, "Open-field husbandry and the village community: a study in agrarian by-laws in medieval England," *Proc. Am. Phil. Soc.,* n.s., 55 (1965), part 7.

24. Cecil Stewart, *Serbian Legacy* (London, 1959).

25. Jean Chapelot and Robert Fossier, *The Village and House in the Middle Ages* (London 1985).

26. *Ze Studiów nad Budownictwa wiejskim,* Inst. Urb. Arch. (Warsaw, 1957).

27. Kazimierz Moszyński, *Kultura Ludowa Slowiań* (Kraków, 1929), 1:459–564.

28. Stanislaw Serafin, *Architectura i Krajobraz Wsi* (Warsaw, 1958).

29. I. O. Peate, *The Welsh House: A Study in Folk Culture* (London, 1940).

5. FIELDS, FARMS, AND FOOD SUPPLY

1. Galbert of Bruges, *The Murder of Charles the Good, Count of Flanders,* ed. J. B. Ross (New York, 1960).

2. *Vita Sancti Brioci,* as quoted in G. H. Doble, *Saint Brioc* (Exeter, 1928).

3. Marginal drawing in medieval manuscript, after Oskar Jäger, *Geschichte des Mittelalters* (Bielefeld, 1903).

4. Suger, *De rebus in administratione sua gestis,* X, *Oeuvres complètes de Suger* (Paris, 1867), 164–65.

5. W. G. Hoskins, "Three Studies in Family History," *Devonshire Studies* (London), 1952, 78–119.

6. Pol de Limbourg, *Les Très Riches Heures du Duc de Berry,* ed. J. Longnon and R. Cazelles (London, 1969).

7. *Chronicle of the Slavs,* 1, 57.

8. Pliny, *Natural History,* XVIII, 18.

9. "The Husbandry of Walter of Henley," cap. 51, in Dorothea Oschinsky, *Walter of Henley and Other Treatises on Estate Management and Accounting* (Oxford, 1971).

10. W. H. McNeill, *Europe's Steppe Frontier* (Chicago, 1964), 5.

11. Frederic Seebohm, *The English Village Community,* ed. of 1926 (Cambridge), 15–16.

12. Thomas Tusser, *Five Hundred Pointes of Good Husbandrie,* ed. W. Payne and S. J. Herrtage (London, 1878).

13. Arthur Young, *Travels in France during the Years 1787, 1788 and 1789,* ed. J. Kaplow (New York, 1969), 299.

14. F. W. Maitland, *Domesday Book and Beyond* (Cambridge, 1897), 337.

15. Donald N. McCloskey in *Research in Economic History,* ed. P. Uselding, 1 (1976).

16. H. S. A. Fox, "The Alleged Transformation from Two-field to Three-field Systems in Medieval England," *E.H.R.* 39 (1986): 526–48.

17. Charles Higounet, *La Grange de Veulerent* (Paris, 1965).

18. *Die Urbäre von S. Pantaleon in Köln,* ed. Benno Helliger (Bonn, 1920), 256.

19. Jane M. Renfrew, *Paleoethnobotany* (New York, 1973), 104–15.

20. Roger Grand and Raymond Delatouche, *L'Agriculture au Moyen Age* (Paris, 1950).

21. Capitulare de villis, *Monumenta Germaniae Historica, Legum Sectio,* I (Hannover, 1883), 82–91.

22. R. N. Salaman, *The History and Social Influence of the Potato* (Cambridge, 1949).

23. Roger Dion, *Histoire de la vigne et du vin en France des origines au XIXe siècle* (Paris, 1959).

24. J. C. Webster, "The Labors of the Months in Antique and Medieval Art," *Northwestern University Studies in the Humanities* 4 (Evanston, Ill., 1938); James Fowler, "On Mediaeval Representations of the Months and Seasons," *Arch.* 44, pt. i (1873): 137–224; K. Jasinski, "Illustracje Kalendarzowe w Polsce rekopisie wroclawskim z okolo 1300," *K.H.K.M.* 7 (1959): 203–28.

25. Pol de Limbourg, *Les Très Riches Heures.*

26. Jean Lederer, "Les mendiants de Bruegel, un document pour l'histoire de Flandres sous l'occupation espagnole," *Scrinium Lovaniense* 24 (1961): 452–65.

27. Gösta Berg, "Sledges and Wheeled Vehicles," *Nordiska Museets Handlingar* 4 (1935).

28. *Egil's Saga,* trans. E. R. Eddison (Cambridge, 1930), 57.

29. Alfons Dopsch, "Die landesfurstlichen Urbare Nieder- und Oberosterreichs aus dem 13. und 14. Jahrhundert," *Osterreichische Urbare,* i (Vienna, 1904).

30. Cornwall Record Office, Truro, *The Spoore Book.*

31. E. Estyn Evans, "Transhumance in Europe," *Geog.* 25 (1940): 172–80; Elwyn Davies, "The Patterns of Transhumance in Europe," *Geog.* 26 (1941): 155–68.

32. Julius Klein, *The Mesta* (Cambridge, Mass., 1920).

33. A. J. B. Wace and M. S. Thompson, *The Nomads of the Balkans* (London, 1914), 73–96.

34. B. H. Slicher van Bath, *The Agrarian History of Western Europe A.D. 500–1850* (London, 1963).

35. *The Register of Eudes of Rouen,* trans. S. M. Brown (New York, 1964).

36. *Two Fifteenth Century Cookbooks,* ed. Thomas Austin, E.E.T.S., 91 (1888).

37. A. R. Bridbury, *England and the Salt Trade in the Later Middle Ages* (Oxford, 1955).

38. Andrzej Wyczański, *Studia nad Konsumpcja Żywnosci w Polsce w XVI i pierwszej połowie XVII w* (Warsaw, 1969).

39. John Storck and W. D. Teague, *Flour and Man's Bread: A History of Milling* (Minneapolis, 1952).

40. E. C. Curwen, "Querns," *Ant.* 11 (1937): 133–51; id., "More about Querns," *Ant.* 15 (1941): 15–32.

41. V. G. Childe, "Rotary Querns on the Continent," *Ant.* 17 (1943): 19–26.

42. L. A. Moritz, *Grain Mills and Flour in Classical Antiquity* (Oxford, 1958).

43. M. T. Hodgen, "Domesday Water Mills," *Ant.* 13 (1939): 261–79; Zofia Podwińska, "Rosmieszczenie wodnych młynow zbożowych w Małopolsce w XV wieku," *K.H.K.M.* 18 (1979): 373–402.

44. Richard Bennett and John Elton, *History of Corn Milling,* 4 vols. (London, 1898–1904).

45. Storck and Teague, *Flour and Man's Bread,* 160–61.

46. Quoted in J. C. Drummond and Anne Wilbraham, *The Englishman's Food* (London, 1939).

47. *The Travel Diaries of Thomas Robert Malthus,* ed. Patricia James (Cambridge, 1966), 60.

48. Quoted in Drummond and Wilbraham, *The Englishman's Food,* 19.

49. Sir William Ashley, *The Bread of our Forefathers* (Oxford, 1928), 7.

50. William Harrison, *The Description of England,* ed. G. Edelen (Ithaca, N.Y., 1968), 133.
51. Wyczański, *Studia nad Konsumpcja.*
52. *Locke's Travels in France,* ed. J. Lough (Cambridge, 1953), 236.
53. H. L. Duhamel de Monceau, *Practical Treatise of Husbandry* (London, 1759), 283–86.
54. Émile de Laveleye, *The Balkan Peninsula* (London, 1887), 86.
55. R. N. Salaman, *History of the Potato.*
56. K. H. Connell, "The Potato in Ireland," *P. & P.,* no. 23 (Nov. 1962): 57–71.
57. *Two Fifteenth Century Cookbooks.*
58. *Piers Plowman,* B Text, X, 94.

6. THE PRIVACY OF THE HOME

1. B. Hanawalt, *Crime and Conflict in English Communities 1300–1348* (Cambridge, Mass., 1979), 76–83.
2. *Cal. Pat. R.,* Richard II, 1385–89, 42.
3. *Meier Helmbrecht,* ll. 1203–1209, in *Peasant Life in Old German Epics,* ed. C. H. Bell, 69 (New York, 1931).
4. A. H. L. Pitt-Rivers, *King John's House, Tollard Royal, Witts* (printed privately, 1890); id., *On the Development and Distribution of Primitive Locks and Keys* (London, 1883).
5. *Odyssey,* XXI, 46–50.
6. *Medieval Catalogue,* London Museum (London, 1967), 133–50.
7. E. L. Sabine, "Latrines and Cesspools of Medieval London," *Spec.* 9 (1934): 303–21; *London Assize of Nuissance 1301–1431,* ed. H. M. Chew and William Kellaway, L.R.S., 10 (1973); *Public Works in Medieval Law,* ed. C. T. Flower, 2 vols. (Selden Soc., 1915–23).
8. Guy Thuillier, *Pour une histoire du quotidien au XIXe siècle en Nivernais,* E.H.E.S.S. (Paris, 1977).
9. N. J. G. Pounds, "Holy Wells and Climatic Change," *Folklore* 54 (1943): 262–64.
10. F. W. Robins, *The Story of the Lamp* (Oxford, 1939); *Medieval Catalogue,* 184.
11. Lynn Thorndike, *A Short History of Civilization* (London, 1927), 323; id., "Sanitation, Baths and Street-cleaning in the Middle Ages and Renaissance," *Spec.* 3 (1928): 192–203.
12. *The History of the King's Works, The Middle Ages* (London, H.M.S.O., 1963), 1:549–50.
13. C. E. Wilson, *A History of Unilever* (1954), 1:9–20.
14. L. A. Shuffrey, *The English Fireplace* (London, 1912); J. Seymour Lindsay, *Iron and Brass Implements of the English House* (London, 1964).
15. U. T. Holmes, *Daily Living in the Twelfth Century: Based on the Observations of Alexander Neckam* (Madison, Wisc., 1952).
16. Ibid., 100–101.
17. Jan Botik, "Slavonic Parallels of the Dwelling Forms of the Enlarged Families," *Ethn. Slav.* 12–13 (1980–81): 11–39.
18. *The Travels of Peter Mundy in Europe and Asia 1608–1667,* ed. Sir Richard C. Temple, Hakluyt Soc., 4:110.
19. J. Botik, "Slavonic Parallels."
20. *Travels of Peter Mundy,* 4:110.
21. Ibid., 111.
22. *The Diary of Montaigne's Journey to Italy in 1580 and 1581,* ed. E. J. Trechmann (London, 1929), 21.
23. Ibid., 31–32.
24. Ibid., 81.
25. Andrew Boorde, *A Dyetary of Helth,* ed. F. J. Furnivall, E.E.T.S. (London, 1870), 246–47.
26. G. R. Owst, *Literature and the Pulpit in Medieval England* (Oxford, 1961), 411.
27. Quoted in ibid., 112.
28. Quoted in C. M. Cipolla, *Clocks and Culture, 1300–1700* (London, 1967), 42.
29. *Travels of Peter Mundy,* 4:184.
30. J. P. V. D. Balsdon, *Life and Leisure in Ancient Rome* (London, 1969), 17.
31. C. F. C. Beeson, *English Church Clocks* (London, 1971).
32. *Cotehele House,* London, National Trust.

33. *Un Sieur de Gouberville,* ed. Abbé A. Tollemer; Introduction by E. Le Roy Ladurie (Paris, 1972).

34. S. Pollard and G. Holmes, *Documents of European Economic History,* vol. 1, 1750–1870 (London, 1968), 534.

35. M. S. Broughall, "The Pattern of the Days in Ancient Rome," *G.R.* 5 (1935–36): 160–76.

36. N. J. G. Pounds, "Barton Farming in Eighteenth Century Cornwall," *Jl. Roy. Inst. Cornw.,* n.s., 7 (1973): 55–75.

37. *Visitations in the Diocese of Lincoln 1517–1531,* ed. A. Hamilton Thompson, Linc. Rec. Soc., 33 (Lincoln, 1940), xl.

38. *Paston Letters,* Everyman ed., 1:26–27.

39. Thomas Coryat, *Coryat's Crudities* (Glasgow, 1905), 1:236.

40. Fynes Moryson, *An Itinerary* (Glasgow, 1907), 1:98.

41. Charles Oman, *English Domestic Silver* (London, 1968).

42. T. C. Barker, J. C. McKenzie, and J. Yudkin, eds., *Our Changing Fare: Two Hundred Years of British Food Habits* (London, 1966), 24.

43. R. N. K. Rees and C. Fenby, "Meals and Meal-times," in *Englishmen at Rest and Play,* ed. R. Lennard, 205–34 (Oxford, 1931).

44. Frédéric Le Play, *Les Ouvriers européens* (Paris, 1855).

45. Boorde, *Dyetary of Helth,* 239.

46. Jean Chapelot and Robert Fossier, *The Village and House in the Middle Ages* (London, 1985).

47. Ivan Balassa, "Die südslawisch-ungarischen Beziehungen im Maisbau," *Ethn. Slav.* 7 (1975): 85–104.

48. Linda Dumpe, "Baltisch-slawische Elemente in der Anlage der Stallbauten Ostlettlands (Latgale)," *Ethn. Slav.* 8–9 (1976–77): 45–60.

49. *Piers Plowman,* B Text, X, 94.

50. T. S. R. Boase, *Death in the Middle Ages* (London, 1972).

51. Quoted in Owst, *Literature and the Pulpit,* 351.

52. G. Chaucer, *Canterbury Tales,* "Prologue," ll. 443–44.

53. Quoted in Owst, *Literature and the Pulpit,* 351.

54. N. J. G. Pounds, "William Carnsew of Bokelly and his Diary, 1576–7," *Jl. Roy. Inst. Cornw.* 8, part 1 (1978): 14–60.

55. Also in *The Diary of Ralph Josselin 1616–1683,* ed. Alan Macfarlane (Oxford, 1976), 165.

56. Ibid., 281.

57. A. Abram, *English Life and Manners in the Later Middle Ages* (London, 1913), 193.

58. Jean-Pierre Peter, "Disease and the Sick at the End of the Eighteenth Century," in *Biology of Man in History,* ed. R. Forster and O. Ranum, 81–124 (Baltimore, 1975).

59. Lester S. King, *The Medical World of the Eighteenth Century* (Chicago, 1958).

60. W. Reymont, "Winter," in *Chłopi,* 253.

61. Thuillier, *Histoire du quotidien,* 99–109.

62. Merry E. Wiesner, "Early Modern Midwifery: A Case Study," in *Women and Work in Preindustrial Europe,* ed. Barbara A. Hanawalt, 94–113 (Bloomington, Ind., 1986).

63. L. Clarkson, *Death, Disease and Famine in Pre-Industrial England* (London, 1975), 6.

64. Michael W. Flinn, *The European Demographic System, 1500–1820* (Baltimore, 1981), 91–92.

65. G. Melvyn Howe, *Man, Environment and Disease in Britain* (Newton Abbot, 1972).

66. Flinn, *European Demographic System,* 41.

67. P. P. A. Biller, "Birth-Control in the West in the Thirteenth and Early Fourteenth Centuries," *P. & P.* 94 (1982): 3–26; Jean-Louis Flandrin, "Contraception, Marriage and Sexual Relations in the Christian West," in *Biology of Man in History,* 23–47.

68. Quoted in *Population Studies* 11 (1957–58): 46–63.

69. Flinn, *European Demographic System,* 40.

7. "THE POPULOUSNESS OF ANCIENT NATIONS"

1. 1 Chron. 21:1–17; 2 Sam. 24:1–15.

2. Julius Beloch, *Bevolkerungsgeschichte Italiens,* 3 vols. (Berlin, 1937–61).

3. N. J. G. Pounds, "Overpopulation in France and the Low Countries in the Later Middle Ages," *Jl. Soc. Hist.* 3 (1970): 225–48; id. and C. C. Roome, "Population Density in Fifteenth Century France and the Low Countries," *A.A.A.G.* 61 (1971): 116–30.

4. Saugrain, *Dénombrement du royaume de France* (Paris, 1709); id., *Nouveau dénombrement* (Paris, 1720).

5. L'abbé Expilly, *Dictionnaire géographique, historique et politique des Gaules et de la France*, 6 vols. (Paris, 1762–70); M. Moheau, *Recherches et considérations sur la population de la France* (Paris 1778).

6. J. P. Süssmilch, *Die göttliche Ordnung in den Veränderungen des menschlichen Geschlechts*, 2 vols. (Berlin, 1762).

7. Karl Büsching, *A New System of Geography* (London, 1762).

8. Comte de Mirabeau, *De la Monarchie Prussienne*, 4 vols. (London, 1788).

9. T. R. Malthus, *An Essay on the Principle of Population* (London, 1798).

10. M. M. Postan and J. Hatcher, "Population and Class Relations in Feudal Society," *P. & P.*, no. 78 (Feb. 1978): 24–36.

11. J. Z. Titow, "Some Differences between Manors and their Effects on the Condition of the Peasant in the Thirteenth Century," *Ag. Hist. Rv.* 10 (1962): 1–13.

12. Jean Meuvret, "Crises de subsistence et la démographie de la France d'Ancien Régime," *Pop.* 1 (1946): 643–50; for popular reaction, see George Rudé, *The Crowd in History* (New York, 1964).

13. Pounds, "Overpopulation in France."

14. J.-N. Biraben and J. Le Goff, "La peste dans le Haut Moyen Age," *Ann. E.S.C.* 24 (1969): 1484–1510.

15. P. Gras, "Le régistre paroissial de Givry (1334–1357)," *Bibl. Éc. Ch.* 100 (1939): 295–308.

16. Geneviève Prat, "Albi et la Peste Noire," *Ann. Midi* 64 (1952): 15–25.

17. Philippe Wolff, "Trois études de démographie médievale en France méridionale," in *Studi in onore Armando Sapori* (Milan, 1957), 1: 493–503.

18. M. Aubry, "Les mortalités lilloises (1328–42)," *Rv. Nord* 65 (1983): 327–42.

19. J. Hatcher, *Plague, Population and the English Economy 1348–1530* (London, 1977).

20. Gunther Franz, *Der dreissigjährige Krieg und das deutsche Volk* (Stuttgart, 1961); R. J. G. Concannon, "The Third Enemy: The Role of Epidemics in the Thirty Years' War," *Cah. Hist. Mond* 10 (1966): 500–11; C. M. Cipolla, *Cristofano and the Plague* (London, 1973).

21. J. Hajnal, "European Marriage Patterns in Perspective," in *Population in History*, ed. D. V. Glass and D. E. C. Eversley (London, 1965), 101–43.

22. M. W. Flinn, *The European Demographic System, 1500–1820* (Baltimore, 1981), 130–31.

23. R. S. Schofield, " 'Crisis' Mortality," *L.P.S.* 9 (1972): 10–22.

24. *"Polyptychum Rotomagensis Diocesis,"* *Rec. Hist.* 23 (1894): 228–329.

25. H. S. Lucas, "The Great European Famine of 1315, 1316 and 1317," *Spec.* 5 (1930): 343–77; H. van Werveke, "La famine de l'an 1316 en Flandre et les régions voisines," *Rv. Nord* 41 (1959): 5–14; C. Weikinn, *Quellenkunde zur Witterungsgeschichte Europas von der Zeitwende bis zum Jahre 1850* (Berlin, 1958), vol. 1.

26. E. Le Roy Ladurie, *Times of Feast, Times of Famine* (New York, 1971), 59.

27. *Memoires des Intendants sur l'état des Généralités*, ed. A. M. de Boislisle (Paris, 1881).

28. H. Stommel and E. Stommel, "The Year without a Summer," *Sci. Am.*, June 1979.

29. J. D. Post, "Famine, Mortality and Epidemic Disease in the Process of Modernization," *Ec. H. R.* 29 (1976): 14–37.

30. S. Kellwaye, *A defensative against the plague* (London, 1593).

31. J. F. D. Shrewsbury, *A History of the Bubonic Plague in the British Isles* (Cambridge, 1971).

32. Charles Creighton, *A History of Epidemics in Britain* (Cambridge, 1891), 1:187.

33. C. Easton, *Les hivers dan L'Europe occidentale* (Leyden, 1928).

34. Bartolomé Bennassar, "Organisation municipale et communautés d'habitants en temps de Peste," in *Villes de l'Europe Méditerranéenne* (Nice, 1969), 139–43.

35. G. E. Rothenberg, "The Austrian Sanitary Cordon and the Control of the Bubonic Plague: 1710–1871," *Jl. Hist. Med. All. Sci.* 28 (1973): 15–23.

36. Shrewsbury, *History of the Bubonic Plague*, 52.

37. *The Chronicle of Jean de Venette,* trans. and ed. J. Birdsall and R. A. Newhall (New York, 1953), 48–51.

38. Creighton, *History of Epidemics,* 1:69.

39. MacArthur, "Old-time Typhus in Britain," *Tr. Roy. Soc. Trop. Med.* 20 (1926–27): 487–503.

40. *The Diary of the Rev. Ralph Josselin 1616–1683,* ed. Alan Macfarlane (Oxford, 1976).

41. P. E. Razzell, "Population Change in Eighteenth Century England," *Ec. H. R.* 18 (1965): 312–32.

42. T. McKeown, *The Modern Rise of Population* (London, 1976), 108.

43. R. E. McGrew, *Russia and the Cholera, 1823–1832* (Madison, Wisc., 1965); L. Chevalier, "Le Choléra: la première épidémie du XIXᵉ siècle," *Bibl. Rev.* 20 (1958).

44. G. Melvyn Howe, *Man, Environment and Disease in Britain* (Harmondsworth, 1976), 198.

45. L. Chevalier, *Labouring Classes and Dangerous Classes* (London, 1973), 202.

46. A. H. Petermann, *Cholera Map of the British Isles, Showing the Districts attacked in 1831, 1832 and 1833* (London, 1852).

47. S. C. Watkins and E. van de Walle, "Nutrition, Mortality, and Population Size: Malthus' Court of Last Resort," *Jl. Intdis. Hist.* 14 (1983–84): 205–26.

48. T. McKeown, "Food, Infection and Population," *Jl. Intdis. Hist.* 14 (1983–84): 227–47.

49. A. B. Appleby, "Nutrition and Disease: The Case of London, 1550–1750," *Jl. Intdis. Hist.* 6 (1975–76): 1–22.

50. *A Parisian Journal 1405–1449,* ed. J. Shirley (Oxford, 1968), 286.

51. E. Le Roy Ladurie, "Famine Amenorrhoea (Seventeenth–Twentieth Centuries)," in *Biology of Man in History,* ed. R. Forster and O. Ranum, 163–78 (Baltimore, 1975).

8. THE URBAN WAY OF LIFE

1. *Select Translations from Old English Poetry,* ed. A. S. Cook and C. B. Tinker.

2. T. Hobbes, *Leviathan,* iv, 47.

3. Gregory of Tours, VI, 5.

4. *The Chronicle of the Slavs,* ed. F. J. Tschan (New York, 1935), 123.

5. A. P. Usher, *The History of the Grain Trade in France 1400–1700* (Cambridge, Mass., 1913), 12–44.

6. G. Fagniez, *Documents rélatifs à l'histoire de l'industrie et du commerce en France,* Collection de Textes, 1 (1898), 54–55.

7. Maurice Beresford, *New Towns of the Middle Ages* (London, 1967), 199.

8. Mary Bateson, "The Laws of Breteuil," *E.H.R.* 15 (1900): 73–78, 302–18, 496–523, 754–57; 16 (1901): 92–110, 332–45.

9. M.-T. Morlet, "Les noms de personne à Beauvais au XIVᵉ siècle," *Bull. Phil. Hist.* (Paris, 1955–57): 295–309; id., "L'origine des habitants de Provins aux XIIᵉ et XIVᵉ siècle d'après les noms de personne," ibid. (1961): 95–114.

10. M. Mollat and P. Wolff, *The Popular Revolutions of the Late Middle Ages* (London, 1973).

11. J. S. P. Bradford, *Ancient Landscapes: Studies in Field Archaeology* (Bath, 1974).

12. Martin Biddle, "The Evolution of Towns: Planned Towns before 1066," in *The Plans and Topography of Medieval Towns in England and Wales,* ed. M. W. Barley, 19–32, C.B.A. Res. Rept., 14 (London, 1976).

13. Daniel Defoe, *A Tour through England and Wales,* Everyman ed., 1:130.

14. J. Legoff, "Apostolat mendiant et fait urbain," *Ann. E.S.C.* 23 (1968): 335–48.

15. F. W. Robins, *The Story of Water Supply* (Oxford, 1946), 91.

16. G. Melvyn Howe, *Man, Environment and Disease in Britain* (Harmondsworth, 1976), 187–88.

17. B. Bennassar, *Valladolid au Siècle d'or: une ville de Castille et sa Campagne au XVIᵉ siècle* (Paris, 1967), 154.

18. John Simson, "Die Flussvereireinigungsfrage im 19 J.," *V.S.W.* 65 (1978): 370–90.

19. T. C. Banfield, *Industry of the Rhine* (London, 1846–48), 2:231.

20. Martin Lister, *A Journey to Paris in the Year 1698,* ed. R. P. Stearns, (Champaign-Urbana, 1967), 172.

21. L. S. Mercier, *Tableau de Paris* (Amsterdam, 1782), 1:154.

22. Paul Schenk, *Berner Brunnen-Chronik* (Bern, 1945).

23. A series of studies of German *Gemeindebetrieben* (local utilities) was published in *Schr. Ver. Sozp.*

24. E. L. Sabine, "Latrines and Cesspools of Medieval London," *Spec.* 9 (1934): 303–21.

25. *Public Works in Medieval Law*, ed. C. T. Flower (Selden Soc., 1923), 2:32ff.

26. *De antiquis legibus liber: Cronica maiorum et vicecomitum Londoniarum*, ed. Thomas Stapleton (Camden Soc., 1846), vol. 34.

27. G. Jacquemet, "Urbanisme parisien: la bataille du tout-à-l'égout à la fin du XIXᵉ siècle," *Rv. Hist. Mod. Cont.* 26 (1979): 505–48.

28. Louis Chevalier, "Le Choléra: la première épidémie du XIXᵉ siècle," *Bibl. Rev.* 20 (1958).

29. Lister, *Journey to Paris*, 8.

30. A. Armengaud, "Quelques aspects de l'hygiène publique à Toulouse au début du XXᵉ siècle," *Ann. Dem. His.* (1975): 131–38.

31. *A Parisian Journal, 1405–1449*, ed. Janet Shirley (Oxford, 1968), 103.

32. F. Bothe, "Frankfurts Wirtschaftsleben im Mittelalter," *Zt. Ges. Staatsw.* 93 (1932): 193–219.

33. Bennassar, *Valladolid*, 154.

34. O. Birkner, "Die Bedeutung der Bauordnung im Städtebau des 19. Jahrhunderts," *Zt. Stadtgesch.* 3 (1976): 26–37.

35. Lister, *Journey to Paris*, 26.

36. E. L. Sabine, "City Cleaning in Mediaeval London," *Spec.* 12 (1937): 19–43.

37. Irving A. Agus, *Urban Civilization in Pre-Crusade Europe* (London, 1965), Document 42.

38. Jean Favier, *Les Contribuables Parisiens à la Fin de la Guerre de Cent Ans*, Hautes Études Médiévales et Modernes, 11 (1970).

39. J. Heers, "Urbanisme et structure sociale à Gênes au moyen-âge," in *Studi in Onore di Amintore Fanfani* (Milan, 1962), 1:369–412.

40. Adeline Daumard, *La Bourgeoisie Parisienne de 1815 à 1848*, Centre de Recherches Historiques (Paris, 1963).

41. M. L. Langer, "The Pattern of Urban Revolution in 1848," in *French Society and Culture since the Old Regime*, ed. E. M. Acomb and M. L. Brown, 90–118 (New York, 1966).

42. A series of reports was published by the British Board of Trade at the beginning of the present century on "Working Class Rents, Housing and Retail Prices." These appeared in Parliamentary Papers.

43. *A Paris Journal*, 48, 51.

44. Robert Montran, *Istanbul dans la seconde moitié du XVIIᵉ siècle*, Bibliothèque Archéologique et Historique de l'Institut Français d'Archéologie d'Istanbul, 12 (1962), 30.

45. *Le Journal d'un bourgeois de Mons (1505–1536)*, ed. A Louant (Paris, 1969), 132.

46. *Quellen zur Rechts-und Wirtschaftsgeschichte der rheinischen Städte: Jülische Städte*, Bd. 2, ed. F. Lau, *Gesellschaft für Rheinische Geschichtskunde*, 1932.

47. Mercier, *Tableau de Paris*, 2:303.

48. *Cal. Cl. R.*, Edw. I, 1302–1307, 537.

49. John Evelyn, *Fumifugium: or the Inconvenience of the Aer, and Smoake of London* (London, 1661).

50. Mercier, *Tableau de Paris*, 1:117.

51. John P. McKay, *Tramways and Trolleys: The Rise of Urban Mass Transport in Europe* (Princeton, 1976), 10–11.

52. Paul Bairoch, *Taille des Villes, Conditions de Vie et développement économique*, E.H.E.S.S. (Paris, 1977).

53. Giovanni Botero, "A Treatise Concerning the Causes of the Magnificence and Greatness of Cities," in *The Reason of State*, ed. P. J. and D. P. Waley, 225–80 (New Haven, 1956).

54. Favier, *Les Contribuables Parisiens*, 33.

55. Georges Lefebvre, *Études Orléanais*, vol. 1, Commission d'Histoire Économique et Sociale de la Révolution, Mémoires et Documents, 15 (Paris, 1962).

56. Olwen H. Hufton, *Bayeux in the Late Eighteenth Century: A Social Study* (Oxford, 1967), 58.

57. Mack Walker, *German Home Towns: Community, State and General Estate* (Ithaca, N.Y., 1971), 140, 217–47.

9. TOWARD A CONSUMING SOCIETY

1. M. M. Postan and J. Hatcher, "Population and Class Relations in Feudal Society," *P. & P.,* no. 78 (Feb. 1978): 24–36.
2. Olwen H. Hufton, *The Poor of Eighteenth-Century France 1750–1789* (Oxford, 1974).
3. Jean Gimpel, *The Medieval Machine* (London, 1977).
4. *The Goodman of Paris,* ed. Eileen Power (London, 1928).
5. Gerhard Hauptmann, *Die Weber: Schauspiel aus vierziger Jahren,* first published 1892; many editions and translations.
6. J. Emerson Tennent, *Belgium* (London, 1842), 1:129.
7. G. Jacquemyns, *Histoire de la crise économique des Flandres (1845–1850),* Acad. Roy. Belg., Mémoires, 2ᵉ ser., 26 (1929), 15ff.
8. T. G. Vlaykov, quoted in *Contrasts in Emerging Societies,* ed. Doreen Warriner (Bloomington, Ind., 1965), 241.
9. Agnes Geijer, "The Textile Finds from Birka," in *Cloth and Clothing in Medieval Europe,* ed. N. B. Harte and K. G. Ponting, Pasold Studies in Textile History, 2 (London, 1983), 80–99.
10. *Piers Plowman,* B Text, XV, 444–47.
11. M. F. Mazzaoui, "L'organizzazione delle industrie tessili nei secoli XIII e XIV: I cotonieri Veronesi," *Studi Storici Veronesi Luigi Simeoni* 18–19 (1968–69), not paged.
12. "Textile Printing in 18th Century France," *Ciba Rv.* 31 (March 1940).
13. *English Literature from Widsith to the Death of Chaucer,* ed. Allen R. Benham (New Haven, 1916), 26–33.
14. R. Sprandel, "La production du fer au moyen âge," *Ann. E.S.C.* 24 (1969): 305–21.
15. J. Słomka, *From Serfdom to Selfgovernment: Memoirs of a Polish Village Mayor* (London, 1941), 18.
16. This is the terminology adopted by R. W. Brunskill in *Vernacular Architecture* (London, 1971), 29.
17. *Piers Plowman,* C Text, IV, 80–81.
18. Andrew Boorde, *A Dyetary of Helth,* ed. F. J. Furnivall, E.E.T.S. (London, 1870), 256.
19. R. J. Forbes, *Short History of the Art of Distillation* (Leiden, 1948), 89ff.

10. THE MEASURE OF PROGRESS

1. Quoted in Henry Kamen, *The Iron Century* (London, 1971), 42.
2. Gunther Franz, *Der Dreissigjahre Krieg und das deutsche Volk,* Quell. Forsch. Aggesch., 7 (1961).
3. Sir George Clark, *War and Society in the Seventeenth Century* (Cambridge, 1958), 78.
4. *Matthew Paris's English History,* ed. J. A. Giles (London, 1852–54), 3:255.
5. H. van Werveke, "La famine de l'an 1316 en Flandre et les régions voisines," *Rv. Nord* 41 (1959): 5–14.
6. E. H. Phelps-Brown and Sheila V. Hopkins, "Seven Centuries of Building Wages," *Econ.* (1955): 195–206; id., "Seven Centuries of the Prices of Consumables, Compared with Builders' Wages," *Econ.* (1956): 296–314.
7. *English Economic History: Select Documents,* ed. A. E. Bland, P. A. Brown, and R. H. Tawney (London, 1914), 6.
8. Jerome Blum, "The Rise of Serfdom in Eastern Europe," *Am. Hist. Rv.* 62 (1956–57): 807–36.
9. Bruce McGowan, *Economic Life in Ottoman Europe* (Cambridge, 1981), 71–79.
10. J. Vicens Vives, *An Economic History of Spain* (Princeton, 1969), 299.
11. Michel Augé-Laribé, *L'Évolution de la France Agricole* (Paris, 1912); George W. Graham, "Scale and Organization in French Farming, 1840–1880," in *European Peasants and their Markets:*

Essays in Agrarian Economic History, ed. W. N. Parker and E. L. Jones, 293–326 (Princeton, 1975); Roger Price, *The Economic Modernisation of France* (London, 1975), 45–79.

12. Émile de Laveleye, "The Land System of Belgium and Holland," in *Systems of Land Tenure in Various Countries,* ed. J. W. Probyn, 443–95 (London, 1881); B. Seebohm Rowntree, *Land and Labour: Lessons from Belgium* (London, 1911), 43.

13. K. T. Eheberg, "Die Landwirtschaft in Bayern," *Jb. Ges. Volksw.* 14 (1890): 1121–41.

14. J. U. Nef, "Silver Production in Central Europe, 1450–1618," *Jl. Pol. Econ.* 49 (1941): 575–91.

15. Carlo M. Cipolla, *Money, Prices and Civilization in the Mediterranean World* (Princeton, 1956).

16. Ingrid Hammerstrom, "The Price Revolution in the Sixteenth Century: Some Swedish Evidence," *Sc. Ec. Hist. Rv.* 5 (1957): 118–54.

17. A. P. Usher, *The History of the Grain Trade in France 1400–1710* (Cambridge, Mass., 1913), 20–118.

18. Monique Mestayer, "Les prix du blé et de l'avoine de 1329 à 1793," *Ann. E.S.C.* 45 (1963): 157–76.

19. Andrew B. Appleby, *Famine in Tudor and Stuart England* (Liverpool, 1978).

20. F. Pollock and F. W. Maitland, *The History of English Law* (Cambridge, 1898), I:634–88.

21. *Réglemens sur les arts et métiers de Paris rédigés au XIIIe siècle, et connus sous le nom du Livre d'Étienne Boileau,* ed. G. B. Depping (Paris, 1837).

22. Xavier de Planhol, *The World of Islam* (Ithaca, N.Y., 1959), 9–28.

23. R. B. Westerfield, *Middlemen in English Business, 1660–1760* (New Haven, 1915).

24. P. Guinet, "Adaptations, mutations et survivances proto-industrielles dans le textile du Cambrésis et du Valenciennois du XVIIIe au début du XXe siècle," *Rv. Nord* 61 (1979): 19–69.

25. G. Jacquemyns, *Histoire de la crise économique des Flandres (1845–1850),* Acad. Roy. Belg., Mémoires, 2e ser., 26 (1929), 44–45.

26. *The Itinerary of John Leland,* ed. L. T. Smith (London, 1907), 1:xli.

27. *Bishop Burnet's Travels through France, Italy, Germany and Switzerland,* ed. of 1750 (London), 88.

28. Henri Cavaillès, *La Route Française: son Histoire, sa Fonction* (Paris, 1946).

29. M. W. Labarge, *Mediaeval Travellers: the Rich and the Restless* (Toronto, 1982).

30. C. A. J. Armitage, "Some Examples of the Distribution and Speed of News in England at the Time of the Wars of the Roses," in *Studies in Medieval History* (Oxford, 1948), 429–54.

31. N. J. G. Pounds, "William Carnsew of Bokelly and his Diary, 1576–7," *Jl. Roy. Inst. Cornw.* 8, pt. 1 (1978): 14–60.

32. E. Forestié, *Les Livres de Comptes des Frères Bonis,* Archives de la Gascogne, 20, 1890.

33. Monique Somme, "Les déplacements d'Isabelle de Portugal et la Circulation dans les Pays-Bas Bourgignons au milieu du XVe siècle," *Rv. Nord* 52 (1970): 183–97.

34. N. J. G. Pounds, "Patterns of Trade in the Rhineland," in *Science, Medicine and History,* ed. E. A. Underwood, 2:419–34 (Oxford, 1953).

35. Roger Dion, *Le Val de Loire: étude de géographie régionale* (Tours, 1934).

36. Gustave Guilmoto, *Étude sur les Droits de Navigation de la Seine de Paris à Roche-Guyon du XIe au XVIIIe siècle* (Paris, 1889).

37. H. Obuchowska-Pysiowa, "Warunki naturalne, technika i organizacja spławu wiślanego w XVII wieku," *K.H.K.M.* 13 (1965): 281–97.

38. W. Bromley, *Several Years' Travels, Performed by a Gentleman* (London, 1702), 271, 280.

39. Sir William Temple, *Observations on the United Provinces of the Netherlands,* ed. G. N. Clark (Oxford, 1932), 93.

40. Jan de Vries, "Barges and Capitalism: Passenger Transportation in the Dutch Economy, 1632–1839," *A.A.G. Bij.* 21 (1978): 33–398.

41. Honoré de Balzac, *Le Médicin de Campagne.*

42. C. S. Coon, *The Mountains of Giants* (Cambridge, Mass., 1950).

43. Émile de Laveleye, *The Balkan Peninsula* (London, 1887), 71–72.

44. H. G. Wanklyn, *The Eastern Marchlands of Europe* (London, 1941), 248ff.; C. A. Macartney, *Hungary and Her Successors* (Oxford, 1937), 79ff.

45. Eugen Weber, *Peasants into Frenchmen* (London, 1979).

11. THE NINETEENTH CENTURY

1. A. Ure, *The Philosophy of Manufactures* (London, 1935), 13.

2. J. Tann, *The Development of the Factory* (London, 1970), 3.

3. Friedrich Engels, *The Condition of the Working Class,* ed. W. O. Henderson and W. H. Chaloner (Oxford, 1958). The editors demonstrate the inaccuracy of much of Engels' account.

4. Ibid., 81.

5. Edwin Chadwick, *The Sanitary Condition of the Labouring Population of Great Britain,* ed. M. W. Flinn (Edinburgh, 1965).

6. *Report of an Enquiry by the Board of Trade into Working Class Rents, Housing and Retail Prices . . . in the Principal Industrial Towns of the German Empire,* Accts. & Pap. (1908), 108:14, 85.

7. Robert Owen, *A New View of Society and Report to the County of Lanark,* ed. V. A. C. Gatrell (Harmondsworth, 1970).

8. Margaret Fuller, *West Country Friendly Societies* (Reading, 1964).

9. M. A. Bienefeld, *Working Hours in British Industry* (London, 1972), 8.

10. L. R. Villermé, quoted in S. Pollard and C. Holmes, *Documents in European Economic History,* vol. 1, *The Process of Industrialization 1750–1870* (London, 1968), 492.

11. Schroter and Becker, *Die deutsche Maschinenbau-industrie,* quoted in Pollard and Holmes, *Documents,* 534.

12. L. R. Villermé, in *Documents,* 490.

13. A. Audiganne, *De l'Organisation du Travail* (Paris, 1848), 66–67.

14. Frédéric Le Play, *Les Ouvriers européens* (Paris, 1855).

15. "Wall-coverings," *Ciba Rev.,* no. 3 (1937).

16. C. Singer et al., *A History of Technology,* vol. 4 (Oxford, 1958), 254; vol. 5 (Oxford, 1958), 823–35.

17. Quoted in "Soap," *Ciba Rev.,* no. 56 (1947): 2019.

18. Stirling Everard, *The History of the Gas Light and Coke Company* (London, 1915).

19. Ibid., 148.

20. Le Play, *Ouvriers européens,* 95.

21. Abel Poitrineau, "L'alimentation populaire en Auvergne au XVIIIᵉ siècle," in *Pour l'Histoire de l'Alimentation,* ed. J.-J. Hemardinquer, *Cahiers des Annales* 18 (1970): 146–53; Guy Thuillier, "L'alimentation en Nivernais au XIXᵉ siècle," ibid., 154–73; Frank Spooner, "Régimes alimentaires d'autrefois: proportions et calculs en calories," ibid., 35–42.

22. J. C. McKenzie, "The Composition and Nutritional Value of Diets in Manchester and Dukinfield 1841," *Tr. Lancs. Chesh. Ant. Soc.* 72 (1962): 123–40.

23. E. J. Hobsbawm, "The British Standard of Living, 1790–1850," *Ec. H. R.* 10 (1956–57): 46–68; R. M. Hartwell, "The Rising Standard of Living in England, 1800–1850," ibid. 8 (1960–61): 397–416.

24. Janet Blackman, "The Development of the Retail Grocery Trade in the Nineteenth Century," *Bus. Hist.* 9 (1967): 110–17.

25. G. N. Johnstone, "The Growth of the Sugar Trade and Refining Industry," in *The Making of the Modern British Diet,* ed. Derek Oddy and Derek Miller, 58–64 (London, 1976).

26. T. S. Willan, *An Eighteenth Century Shopkeeper: Abraham Dent of Kirkby Stephen* (Manchester, 1970), 12.

27. D. Davis, *A History of Shopping* (London, 1966), 246–47.

28. Pierre Léon, "L'épanouissement d'un marché national," in *Histoire économique et sociale de la France* (Paris, 1975), vol. 3, pt. 1, 275–304.

29. H. W. Hart, "Notes on Coach Travel," *Jl. Transp. Hist.* 4 (1959): 146–50.

30. Richard Ford, *A Hand-book for Travellers in Spain, and Readers at Home,* ed. of 1966 (Arundel [England]).

31. Willan, *Eighteenth Century Shopkeeper,* 15–18.

32. Alan Everitt, "Town and Country in Victorian Leicestershire: The Role of the Village Carrier," in *Perspectives in English Urban History,* (London, 1973), 213–40.

33. Roger Price, *The Economic Modernisation of France* (London, 1975), 11.

34. Dominique Renouard, *Les Transports de Marchandises par Fer, Route et Eau depuis 1850,* Recherches sur l'économie française, vol. 2 (Paris 1960), 37.

12. CONCLUSION

1. H. Finer, *Europe the World's Banker,* Council on Foreign Relations (New Haven, 1930).

2. William Woodruff, *The Impact of Western Man* (New York, 1966), 165.

3. Stuart Piggott, *Ancient Europe* (Edinburgh, 1965), 17–18.

4. Ruth Benedict, *Patterns of Culture* (New York, 1959), chap. 2.

5. K. W. Butzer, "Physical Conditions in Eastern Europe, Western Asia and Egypt before the Period of Agricultural and Urban Settlement," *Cambridge Ancient History,* vol. 1, part 1 (Cambridge, 1970), 35–69.

6. Emmanuel Le Roy Ladurie, "Pour une histoire de l'environnement: la part du climat," *Ann. E.S.C.* 25 (1970): 1459–70; also id., *Times of Feast, Times of Famine* (New York, 1971).

7. Notably Ellsworth Huntington, H. T. Buckle, and A. J. Toynbee.

8. A. J. Toynbee, *A Study of History,* vol. 3 (Oxford, 1934), 112–27.

9. I. M. Wallerstein, *The Modern World System* (New York, 1974).

10. Eric Hobsbawm, *Industry and Empire* (Harmondsworth, 1969).

11. J. Furnivall, *Netherlands India* (Cambridge, 1939).

12. Finer, *Europe the World's Banker.*

13. These were the United Kingdom, France, Germany, Belgium, the Netherlands, and Switzerland.

14. Carl O. Sauer, "The Settlement of the Humid East," in *Climate and Man,* Yearbook of Agriculture, U. S. Dept of Agriculture (Washington, D.C., 1941).

15. William H. McNeill, *Plagues and Peoples* (New York, 1976).

16. Harry M. Caudill, *Night Comes to the Cumberlands* (Boston, 1963).

17. F. H. King, *Farmers of Forty Centuries* (London, 1927).

18. D. H. Perkins, *Agricultural Development in China 1368–1968* (Chicago, 1969), 7.

19. Ibid., 56.

20. Ibid., 58; also Ping-ti Ho, *Studies in the Population of China, 1368–1953* (Cambridge, Mass., 1959), 169.

SELECT BIBLIOGRAPHY

The following periodicals are of value for material culture:

Ethnologia Slavica (Bratislava)
Folk-Life (Cardiff, England)
Journal of Interdisciplinary History (Cambridge, Mass.)
Kwartalnik Historii Kultury Materialny (Warsaw)
Technology and Culture (Detroit)

PART I: ORIGINS AND DISPERSALS

M. Bakhtin, *Rabelais and His World*. Bloomington, Ind., 1984.

J. P. V. D. Balsdon. *Life and Leisure in Ancient Rome*. London, 1969.

B. Bender. *Farming in Prehistory*. London, 1975.

R. and C. Brooke. *Popular Religion in the Middle Ages*. London, 1984.

P. Burke. *Popular Culture in Early Modern Europe*. London, 1978.

K. W. Butzer. *Environment and Archaeology: An Ecological Approach to Prehistory*. London, 1972.

J. G. D. Clark, *Prehistoric Europe: The Economic Base*. London, 1952.

M. N. Cohen. *The Food Crisis in Prehistory*. New Haven, Conn., 1977.

J. Collis. *Oppida: Earliest Towns North of the Alps*. Sheffield, 1984.

N. Z. Davis, "The Reasons of Misrule." In *Society and Culture in Early Modern France*, 97–123. London, 1975.

R. J. Forbes. *Studies in Ancient Technology*. Leiden, 1964–   .

K. Greene. *The Archaeology of the Roman Economy*. London, 1986.

M. R. Jarman, G. N. Bailey, and H. N. Jarman. *Early European Agriculture: Its Foundations and Development*. Cambridge, England, 1982.

E. Le Roy Ladurie. *Montaillou*. London, 1978.

J. Liversidge. *Britain in the Roman Empire*. London, 1968.

R. MacMullen. *Enemies of the Roman Order*. Cambridge, Mass., 1966.

R. W. Malcolmson. *Popular Recreations in English Society 1700–1850*. Cambridge, England.

R. Muchembled. *Culture Populaire et culture des élites dans la France moderne*. Paris, 1978.

J. Obelkevich, ed. *Religion and the People 800–1700*. Chapel Hill, N.C., 1979.

J. Percival. *The Roman Villa*. London, 1976.

S. Piggott. *Ancient Europe*. Edinburgh, 1965.

J. M. Renfrew. *Paleoethnobotany*. New York, 1973.

P. J. Reynolds. *Iron-Age Farm: The Butser Experiment*. London, 1979.

C. Singer et al. *A History of Technology*. 5 vols. Oxford, 1954–58.

P. J. Ucko and G. W. Dimbleby. *The Domestication and Exploitation of Plants and Animals*. London, 1969.

A. van Gennep. *Manuel de Folklore Française Contemporain*. 7 vols. Paris, 1937–58.

F. E. Zeuner. *A History of Domesticated Animals*. London, 1963.

PART II: PREINDUSTRIAL EUROPE

C. T. P. Bailey. *Knives and Forks*. London, 1927.

R. Bennett and J. Elton. *History of Corn Milling*. 4 vols. London, 1898–1904.

T. S. R. Boase. *Death in the Middle Ages*. London, 1972.

F. Braudel. *Capitalism and Material Life*. London, 1973.

——. *The Structures of Everyday Life*. New York, 1981.

J. Brunhes. *Géographie Humaine*. Paris, 1925.

F. F. Cartwright. *Disease and History*. London, 1972.

J. Chapelot and R. Fossier. *The Village and the House in the Middle Ages*. London, 1985.

C. M. Cipolla. *Clocks and Culture 1300–1700*. London, 1967.

E. L. Eisenstein. *The Printing Revolution in Early Modern Europe*. Cambridge, England, 1983.

——. *The Printing Press as an Agent of Change*. 2 vols. Cambridge, England, 1979.

J-L. Flandrin. *Families in Former Times*. Cambridge, England, 1979.

M. W. Flinn. *The European Demographic System, 1500–1820*. Baltimore, 1981.

R. J. Forbes. *Short History of the Art of Distillation*. Leiden, 1948.

R. Forster and O. Ranum, eds. *Biology of Man in History*. Baltimore, 1975.

B. Geremek. *Truands et Misérables dans l'Europe Moderne*. Paris, 1980.

J. Gimpel. *The Medieval Machine*. London, 1977.

B. A. Hanawalt. *The Ties that Bind*. Oxford, 1986.

J.-J. Hémardinquer. *Pour une Histoire de l'Alimentation*. Paris, 1970.

B. A. Henisch. *Fast and Feast*. University Park, Pa., 1976.

A. A. Hopkins. *The Lure of the Lock*. New York, 1928.

J. Hornell. *Water Transport: Origins and Early Evolution*. Cambridge, England, 1946.

N. Iorga. *L'Art Populaire en Roumanie*. Paris, 1923.

D. S. Landes. *Revolution in Time: Clocks and the Making of the Modern World*. Cambridge, Mass., 1983.

P. Laslett. *The World We Have Lost*. New York, 1965.

P. Leser. *Entstehung und Verbreitung des Pfluges*. Münster, Westphalia, 1931.

London Museum. *Medieval Catalogue*. London, 1954.

A. Macfarlane. *The Origins of English Individualism*. Oxford, 1978.

B. McGowan. *Economic Life in Ottoman Europe*. Cambridge, England, 1981.

T. McKeown. *The Modern Rise of Population*. London, 1976.

W. H. McNeill. *Plagues and Peoples*. New York, 1976.

——. *Europe's Steppe Frontier*. Chicago, 1964.

M. Mollat, ed. *Études sur l'Histoire de la Pauvreté*. Paris, 1974.

K. Moszynski. *Kultura Ludowa Słowiań*. 2 vols. Krakow, 1929.

L. Niederle. *Manuel de l'Antiquité Slave*. 2 vols. Paris, 1926.

J. Obrebski. *The Changing Peasantry of Eastern Europe*. Edited by B. and J. Halpern. Cambridge, Mass., 1976.

A. F. Pitt-Rivers. *On the Development and Distribution of Primitive Locks and Keys*. London, 1883.

A. Quiney. *House and Home*. London, 1986.

J. A. Raftis, ed. *Pathways to Medieval Peasants*. Toronto, 1981.

E. T. Renbourn and W. H. Rees. *Materials and Clothing in Health and Disease*. London, 1972.

F. W. Robins. *The Story of the Lamp*. Oxford, 1939.

——. *The Story of Water Supply*. Oxford, 1940.

G. Rudé. *The Crowd in History*. New York, 1964.

J. Storck and W. D. Teague. *Flour for Man's Bread: A History of Milling*. Minneapolis, 1952.

R. Straus. *Carriages and Coaches: Their History and Evolution*. London, 1912.

G. A. Thrupp. *The History of Coaches*. London, 1877.

P. J. Ucko, R. Tringham, and G. W. Dimbleby. *Man, Settlement and Urbanism*. London, 1969.

R. W. Unger. *The Ship in the Medieval Economy 600–1600*. London, 1980.

A. P. Usher. *The History of the Grain Trade in France 1400–1700*. Cambridge, Mass., 1913.

A. J. B. Wace and M. S. Thompson. *The Nomads of the Balkans*. London, 1914.

M. Walker. *German Home Towns: Community, State and General Estate*. Ithaca, N.Y., 1971.

D. Warriner. *Contrasts in Emerging Societies*. Bloomington, Ind., 1965.

B. K. Wheaton. *Savouring the Past: The French Kitchen and Table from 1300 to 1789*. London, 1983.

L. White. *Medieval Technology and Social Change*. Oxford, 1962.

PART III: THE PERIOD OF RAPID GROWTH

J. Blum. *The End of the Old Order in Rural Europe.* Princeton, N.J., 1978.

J. Burnett. *A Social History of Housing 1815–1970.* Newton Abbot, England, 1978.

D. Davis. *A History of Shopping.* London, 1966.

H. Feis. *Europe, the World's Banker, 1870–1914.* New Haven, Conn., 1940.

E. and A. Forster, eds. *European Diet from Pre-Industrial to Modern Times.* New York, 1975.

P. Léon. *L'Épanouissement d'un marché national, Histoire Économique et sociale de la France.* Vol. III. Paris, 1970.

F. Le Play. *Les Ouvriers Européens.* Paris, 1855.

J. P. McKay. *Tramways and Trolleys: The Rise of Urban Mass Transport in Europe.* Princeton, N.J., 1976.

W. W. Rostow. *The Stages of Economic Growth.* Cambridge, England, 1960.

J. Tann. *The Development of the Factory.* London, 1970.

J. Vial. *L'avènement de la civilisation industrielle de 1815 à nos jours.* Paris, 1973.

E. Weber. *Peasants into Frenchmen.* London, 1977.

W. Woodruff. *The Impact of Western Man.* New York, 1966.

INDEX

Editor:	Risë Williamson
Book & Jacket designer:	Matthew Williamson
Production coordinator:	Harriet Curry
Typeface:	Berkeley with Galliard display
Typesetter:	Keystone Typesetting, Inc.
Printer and binder:	Maple-Vail Book Mfg. Group

NORMAN J. G. POUNDS, the distinguished scholar, is author of a number of major studies of the geography and history of Europe. Professor Pounds is president of the Royal Archaeological Institute and a fellow of the Society of Antiquaries of London.